American Lives

Wisconsin Studies in American Autobiography

WILLIAM L. ANDREWS
General Editor

American Lives

An Anthology of Autobiographical Writing

Edited by Robert F. Sayre

THE UNIVERSITY OF WISCONSIN PRESS

The University of Wisconsin Press
114 North Murray Street
Madison, Wisconsin 53715

3 Henrietta Street
London WC2E 8LU, England

2   4   6   8   10   9   7   5   3   1

Printed in the United States of America

Library of Congress Cataloging-in-Publication Data
American lives : an anthology of autobiographical writing /
edited by Robert F. Sayre.
746 p.   cm. — (Wisconsin studies in American autobiography)
Includes bibliographical references and index.
ISBN 0-299-14240-X   ISBN 0-299-14244-2 (pbk.)
1. Autobiographies—United States. 2. United States—Biography.
I. Sayre, Robert F.   II. Series.
CT211.A48   1994
920.02—dc20   94-11251

CONTENTS

Contents

Contents

Many people have helped in putting together this anthology.

The title, American Lives, comes from a course which Wayne Prophet and I established in the University of Iowa Undergraduate Core Curriculum in the 1970s—a pioneering effort in both the study of autobiography and the expanding of the American literary canon. Soon after, Albert Stone came to the University of Iowa from Emory University, already working on his important book, *Autobiographical Occasions and Original Acts: Versions of American Identity from Henry Adams to Nate Shaw,* and one of the results was a conference to which we invited Francis Russell Hart, Michael Cooke, Clark Blaise, Barrati Mukerjee, and other writers and critics of autobiography. In 1978 and 1979, the National Endowment for the Humanities, through its innovative Program for the Professions, made me the director of two summer seminars for people who were not professors of literature but would be interested in how the reading of autobiography might contribute to their personal and professional development. This rare opportunity to try out study of autobiographies with superior groups of "students" whose interests were as diverse as the subject matter itself was a wonderful experience.

Beginning in the 1970s, I was also fortunate to have graduate students who worked on different kinds of autobiographical writing: David Newquist, who made a careful study of *Black Hawk's Autobiography;* Eric Sandeen, who did a complete edition of the letters of Randolph Bourne; Joanne Jacobson, who did a critical study of the letters of Henry Adams; Kathleen Welch, working on the literary autobiographies of Mary McCarthy and others; Hertha Wong, examining the early origins of American Indian autobiography and so challenging the assumption that the genre was only Euro-American and Christian; and, most recently, Donald Scheese, who has demonstrated autobiography's importance to American nature writing.

Throughout this period I have read and sometimes reviewed the ever-expanding critical and theoretical books on autobiography, ingesting them over such a long period that some of their ideas (or my understandings of them) have become a part of my own conceptions of American autobiography. Careful readers of the introductions and headnotes to this book will spot these borrowings, and I have tried to acknowledge them wherever I was aware of them. But let me also list their names here: James Cox, James Olney, Elizabeth Bruss, G. Thomas Couser, Thomas Cooley, Paul John Eakin, Janet Varner Gunn, Sacvan Berkovitch, Lawrence Buell, Phillipe Lejeune, Roy Pascal, Steve Shapiro, Herbert Leibowitz, Ruth Banes, Sidonie Smith, Karl Weintraub. I also want to acknowledge the direct and indirect help of Sherman Paul and Wayne Franklin, two colleagues whose exciting reports on their venturesome, diligent reading led me to some of the writers included here. Sandra Gustafson from the University of California, Berkeley, suggested a very revealing writer whom I had overlooked, Nathan Cole.

Once the assembly and writing of this anthology actually began, the University of Iowa graduate college became very helpful by paying for my Research Assistants, starting with Nina Metzner, who had been a student in one of my courses in American autobiography. Konan Amani took over from her in the summer of 1991; Dallas Liddle took over in 1991–92, tracking down biographical information on little-known contributors, drafting several headnotes, and pursuing all kinds of additional facts, titles, and critical articles; and Bill Dix and Michael Tavel came to my aid in the fall of 1992 and spring of 1993. A project of this kind, which is an engineering and administrative task as well as literary, critical, and historical one, would have been utterly impossible without their curiosity, insights, legwork, and computer skills.

I also want to thank Jay Semel and Lorna Olsen at the University of Iowa Center for Advanced Study, where for several semesters I read and wrote about the autobiographies of little-known or forgotten groups of Americans, like war prisoners and conscientious objectors. Thinking one's way into such writers and their books required the support and interest of many friends and good conversationalists, particularly Fred Will.

As portions of my introductions were finished, I had very helpful advice and encouragement from Nina Metzner, Paul Baender, Tom Lutz, and Carol de St. Victor. The invited readers for the University of Wisconsin Press, Timothy Dow Adams and Eric Sundquist, also had many helpful suggestions, as did another reader, at an earlier time, who preferred not to reveal his/her name.

But finally, I want to express my deepest thanks to William L. Andrews, the general editor and founder of the Wisconsin Studies in American Autobiography, who has recognized the promise of this book ever since I first proposed it to him in 1987, when he asked to republish my study of the autobiographies of Franklin, Adams, and Henry James, *The Examined Self.* As the months and years went by, he advised on proposals for the book and gave good suggestions of works to be included, drawing on his long familiarity with Afro-American autobiography and the history of all American autobiography. Later, he read all of my introductions and headnotes and advised me on the critical bibliography.

A matter which some readers may want to have explained is the policy I have adopted towards the inclusion and exclusion of the well-known longer works of American autobiography—Franklin's *Autobiography*, Frederick Douglass's *Narrative*, *The Education of Henry Adams*, Jane Addams's *Twenty Years at Hull House*, Richard Wright's *Black Boy*, Mary McCarthy's *Memories of a Catholic Girlhood*, among others. Space obviously prohibits including even a chapter of all such works. Moreover, one chapter frequently fails to stand alone, or it gives a distorted sense of the whole book. Most serious students of autobiography would, in any case, prefer to read all of such a book and not try to puzzle out just a part of it. Thus, the general policy in *American Lives* is not to take excerpts from classic longer works. Those works will already be familiar to some readers, and, in the classroom, they can be assigned in addition to the readings given here. I am not, therefore, expecting a reader of this anthology to skip a work like Franklin's *Autobiography;* on the contrary, such a work is repeatedly referred to, and I would expect someone to read it or refer to it again while reading the pieces printed here. For it "belongs" in many places—with Jonathan Edwards and the writers included in the "Great Awakenings, New Individuals" section of the book (Part Two), with the works in "National Identities" (Part Three), and, for its connection to any number of later figures, with writers from P. T. Barnum to Andrew Carnegie.

The excerpts that are given here are generally from less familiar works or from very long ones few people wish to read in their entirety. Lydia Sigourney's *Letters of Life* is historically very important, because it is both the first autobiography in America by a professional writer and a landmark in women's autobiography, but it is virtually unknown. Grant's *Memoirs* are too long for most readers, but the Appomattox chapter is famous and is also quite characteristic of Grant's understated authority. The chapters from *The Living of Charlotte Perkins Gilman* are not nearly so famous as "The Yellow Wallpaper" and are a very interesting contrast to it. Passages such as Douglass's account of his escape, which was not given until his *Life and Times* (1881), and Gertrude Stein's "The Gradual Making of *The Making of Americans*" have been chosen especially because they make such useful supplements to these writers' well-known longer works (*The Narrative* . . . and . . . *Alice B. Toklas*). These passages also stand well by themselves, especially when provided with headnotes to locate them within the longer texts and to provide additional context.

But one of the other goals in this book has been to highlight many shorter works of autobiography, such as letters, essays, poems, and speeches. Initially, I saw a need for an anthology because in courses on American autobiography I wanted to assign famous short works like Edwards's "Personal Narrative" and various modern essays which were otherwise available only in big general anthologies or in expensive separate volumes. As I examined the subject further, I discovered many more short pieces—captivity narratives, shorter journals, war memoirs, political autobiographies, newspaper columns, brief apologias of different kinds—which all clearly belonged to the history of autobiographical writing in America but which were often neglected merely because they were short, occasional, or fugitive. Examples are the pension applications of Sarah Osborne and Nathan Jennings, *The Life and Religious Experiences of Jarena Lee,* Lincoln's "To Jesse W. Fell, Enclosing Autobiography," Carnegie's "How I Served My Apprenticeship," Fitzgerald's "Crack-Up" essays, Roderick Seidenberg's celebration of the World War I conscientious objectors, and Jeanne Wakatsuki Houston's "Beyond Manzanar." What variety and what rich and telling stuff! Clearly there was material for a practical anthology of American autobiography which would not just depend on chapters from longer works or on merely repackaging some items from American literature texts. These works belonged to the record, as poems and short stories and essays belong to the literary canon, and to think that American autobiography was only full-length books was as misguided, perhaps, as thinking that American fiction was only novels. *American Lives: An Anthology of Autobiographical Writing* is the revealing result.

As regards editorial practices, the goal has been to use accurate copies of first editions and not alter them. Thus seventeenth- and eighteenth-century spelling, capitalization, and punctuation are not modernized. Obvious typographical errors have been corrected, however. Explanatory footnotes are used only with words, names, and places that cannot be found in standard desk dictionaries, *Webster's New Biographical Dictionary* (Merriam-Webster, 1983), and good atlases.

American Lives

On Reading and Writing Autobiography

"Autobiography is easy like it or not it is easy for anyone can write it." So wrote Gertrude Stein in 1937 in *Everybody's Autobiography,* provocatively mimicking a common opinion about autobiography. The author by then of *The Autobiography of Alice B. Toklas* and various other experiments in autobiography, she was clearly being ironic, and her omission of punctuation makes us read the sentence in different ways. Autobiography is and is not easy, whether you like it (or that) or not; anyone/not anyone/and maybe no one can write it. Yet many a one, almost everyone, has at one time or another tried.

It is also easy, or not easy, to define autobiography. How long must it be? How many years of a person's life must it cover? How much fictionalizing is permitted, and is an autobiographical novel really an autobiography or not? These and other questions have vexed many past and present readers and writers of autobiography and will no doubt continue to, for the answers are not easy. Another reason for confusion is that the word *autobiography* is only about two hundred years old,[1] although we now apply it to works written long before the word was coined, works with older names like "confession," "apology," "memoir," "diary," "letters," "journal," or "narrative." Still, in ordinary speech and writing we use the word with reasonable confidence that we and others know what it means: a kind of writing in which the author tells something about his or her own life. Not "biographical writing," which is written about some one else, but "autobiographical writing"—written by one's self.

Moreover, confused or not, modern American readers increasingly turn to autobiographies and autobiographical writing with many interests and expectations, hopeful that it will reveal things to them that they might not

1. Thomas Cooley, *Educated Lives: The Rise of Modern Autobiography in America* (Columbus: Ohio State Univ. Press, 1976), p. 3, locates the first appearance of the word *autobiography* in the British *Monthly Review* in 1797. This is earlier than the first usage given in the *Oxford English Dictionary,* which is 1809. Cooley also notes that the first use of the word in the title of an American book was *The Autobiography of Thomas Shepard, The Celebrated Minister of Cambridge, N.E.* (Boston, 1832)—a title not used by Shepard himself when he wrote the short piece in the 1640s.

find elsewhere. We can find autobiographies by everyone from anthropologists to zoologists, by the young and the elderly, by the rich and poor, and by people from nearly every ethnic and religious group, political position, sexual preference, and part of the United States. This kind of writing, which many readers and writers once scorned because they thought it was "easy"— or dull or egotistical or too historical and not imaginative, or vice-versa—has included some of the best and most varied and exciting literature of the last twenty-five years: books like *The Autobiography of Malcolm X, The Armies of the Night, The Woman Warrior,* and *Speak, Memory.* We also can see (if we had not seen before) that many of the American classics are autobiographies: *The Autobiography of Benjamin Franklin, Walden, Song of Myself,* and *The Education of Henry Adams.* Additional classics of autobiography have recently been rediscovered, like *Incidents in the Life of a Slave Girl, Personal Memoirs of Ulysses S. Grant,* and *Black Elk Speaks.*

Therefore, rather than try right off to define autobiography or further pursue Stein's questions about whether it is easy and who can write it, we might be wiser to think some more about what autobiographies *reveal*— what they tell us that other kinds of literature may not. Of course, they do not reveal the same things to all people. Readers read for different reasons, and what they expect to find revealed is not always what is revealed. Likewise, writers often reveal more or less than they promise or intend. Writers write and readers read for pleasure, too, not only to inform and be informed. Nevertheless, autobiographies are a very revealing kind of writing in many different ways, including the following.

1. Many people's first answer to what autobiographies reveal is that they reveal secrets: they tell things that the author has never told before, at least in print or to a wide, general audience. "Now! For the First Time!" "Hitler's Mistress tells all!" These are the advertising headlines and jacket blurbs that address (and engender) this expectation about autobiographies and what they "reveal." The *National Enquirer* and other magazines assault us weekly with stories of celebrities or victims or criminals supposedly confessing secrets of all kinds.

The classics of confessional autobiography also depend on this basic situation of the writer's having exclusive knowledge of his or her own experience. Thus the first confession in literary history, St. Augustine's (345–430), tells the story of his conversion to Christianity, a story which had to be told from the inside. Rousseau's promise in his *Confessions* (published after his death in 1778) that he is going to reveal what has never been revealed before, "man in all the truth of nature," can be fulfilled only by him because, he alleges, no one else has yet tried to live so strictly according to nature as he has and still dared to tell the truth.

Writers of confessions can further reveal how their lives now appear, after the changes and conversions they recount. Indeed, it is the conversion that gives them a new perspective on their lives. It helps them to organize their stories. It has made life meaningful—and made it over into something they wish to tell other people.

But even where autobiographers do not confess in the sensational or religious senses, their books may be read simply for what they reveal about their authors's lives and experience. "Although every one cannot be a Gargantua-Napoleon-Bismarck and walk off with the great bells of Notre Dame," Henry Adams said, referring to the interest we have in the lives of the great, "every one must bear his own universe, and most persons are moderately interested in learning how their neighbors have managed to carry theirs."[2] We are not only interested in "neighbors"—people presumably like ourselves—we are also interested in people unlike ourselves. We want to read stories of adventure, hardship, and travel; and we want to read stories by people of different race, religion, wealth, and class. In America, where there are so many differences, this is all the more important. One of the greatest reasons for the growth of interest in autobiography in the last twenty-five years may be the need to learn about other Americans of different cultures, by finding autobiographers both like and unlike ourselves.

2. Not all revelation comes from confession, however. Nor is confession the only kind of autobiography, even though it is one of the most important. Another kind of autobiography reveals the author's defenses and justifications. It gives "my side of the story." It is a carefully considered explanation and defense. If the author is a general who has lost a battle, then this autobiography explains what went wrong, answers the accusations of his critics, and reassures the readers that he is still wise and loyal. If the author has been an unpopular radical or reformer, an anarchist like Alexander Berkman or an anarchist and feminist like Emma Goldman, it reveals the misunderstood motives. Berkman's *Prison Memoirs of an Anarchist* (1912) are his account of why he attempted to kill Henry Clay Frick and his story of his behavior in prison, including how he has changed. Goldman's *Living My Life* (1931) seeks to defend her sexual experiments and political dissent.

The archetype of this kind of autobiography is the apology, or *apologia*. The Latin word is sometimes preferred because it suggests something other than an "apology" in the more common sense, an "I'm sorry." Indeed, it can be the very opposite. The self-apologist may have some regrets and may admit to some mistakes, but his or her ultimate message is "I was right." The

2. Henry Adams, *The Education of Henry Adams*, ed. Ernest Samuels (Boston: Houghton Mifflin, 1973), pp. 4–5.

apology, therefore, usually tries to reveal those deeper motives or lines of argument that have not been known to the public or to the writer's accusers.

3. In both confessions and apologies there may also be kinds of revelation of which the authors were unaware. Autobiographers, like everybody else, sometimes lie. Sometimes these lies may be only exaggeration, irony, or understatement. Sometimes they are conscious, sometimes unconscious. Memory itself is a very tricky faculty. We know that it often erases or blocks out unpleasant experiences; but we also know that in the form of a sense of shame or a guilty conscience, it may dwell on and magnify the unpleasant. Vindictively, we may also magnify our unpleasant memories of other people. We brood. Or we can, by means of conscious and concerted mind control, work and talk and write our way free of obsessions, just as we sometimes undermine our pleasures.

The critical reader of autobiography has many ways of seeking out these further kinds of revelation. Facts can be checked. The reader can go to biographies of the famous autobiographers like Franklin or Whitman and see what the biographer's version is. With less famous writers, this is not so easy, but there are still many other records—newspapers, city directories, high school yearbooks, other people's diaries and memories and letters—that enable the serious or skeptical reader to do what Albert Stone (echoing Sigmund Freud) called "reality testing."[3] In these ways, the reader can look for forms of self-deception and inconsistency that the writer was unaware of and that even make up patterns of the writer's character.

All writing, as all speech and discourse, it can be argued, reveals more than the writer or speaker knows. The choice of words, the attitudes towards the audience, the tones—all the components of style can tell as much about the speaker-writer as the actual substance. And the unique feature of autobiography is that its writers are exposing or displaying their styles about themselves. "Style is crucial interpretive evidence about any autobiography. [It magnifies] character so that we can study it close up."[4]

To put this another way, anyone can write a person's biography; only one person can write that person's autobiography. (The matter of dictated, ghost-written, and re-written autobiographies we will take up later.) Only one person has the unique knowledge and unique access to it; only one person can also distort it in such revealing and mis-revealing ways. And only one person can speak about herself or himself in her or his own words, whether the words be kind or cruel, accurate or inaccurate, insightful or deceived.

4. But what autobiography reveals about the author is only the beginning of

3. Albert E. Stone, *Autobiographical Occasions and Original Acts* (Philadelphia: Univ. of Pennsylvania Press, 1982), p. 12 and passim.
4. Herbert Leibowitz, *Fabricating Lives* (New York: Knopf, 1989), p. xxiv.

its interest, and to become too absorbed in the life and character of the auto-biographer can be a limitation. "Man knows himself only in history, never through introspection," said Wilhelm Dilthey, the nineteenth-century German historian who saw autobiography as the primary historical document.[5] Dilthey may have exaggerated. He was an historian, not a psychiatrist. But his emphases on autobiographies as elemental historical writing, as written in the flow of time, and as the means by which the writer developed relations to the rest of human life, are all instructive. The autobiographer writes history; the reader of autobiography finds history revealed.

But there are many kinds of history. Therefore, we need to reflect on the particular kinds revealed in autobiographies.

The first is what we might call scrapbook history, since autobiography is, in a way, a kind of scrapbook, someone's personal scrapbook, and the possibilities for its contents are just as rich and heterogeneous. Lucy Larcom's *New England Girlhood* tells of her experiences working in the Lowell, Massachusetts, mills from 1835 to 1845, an experience shared by hundreds of other young New England women. Her descriptions of that time and place illustrate a vital episode in American industrial and social history. The report she gives of her excitement in meeting girls from other towns and farms, of the lectures and classes they attended, and the magazines they wrote for and edited also shows that Lowell was not then the grim, satanic mill-town we might have thought. Walt Whitman's *Specimen Days* (a title that virtually announces that the book is a scrapbook) records the sights and sounds and sufferings, the amputations, diseases, and deaths, in Civil War hospitals better than any official history. Similarly, the hundreds of American slave narratives contain facts about slavery that, until the last thirty years, were not told in textbooks. Nor do magazines and television programs, focused as they are on the lives of celebrities, reveal the experiences of working people and ordinary members of the middle class. American autobiography as a whole, then, is a kind of vast national scrapbook preserving people's pain and joy and perhaps otherwise-forgotten experiences.

To some historians, of course, scrapbooks are not history. They are too random, accidental, and disorganized. They are more like the junk in an attic or in the bottom of a purse. They are also not continuous narratives, which many people would further argue is a necessary feature of respectable history—and autobiography. But respectable autobiography, like respectable history, omits a lot of the things only scrapbooks seem able to preserve. It is only in thumbing through a scrapbook that we come across the other things that someone, fortunately, saved. Then, in some way or another, these un-assimilated or ignored bits of information may fit in for us, contradicting

5. Wilhelm Dilthey, *Pattern and Meaning in History*, ed. H. P. Rickman (New York: Harper Torchbooks, 1961), p. 138.

some orthodoxy or stereotype, making a time and place more vivid, telling us something we never knew and could not have learned anywhere else.

Of course, what may have been an accidental discovery for one reader may have long been familiar to another. Similarly, what seems scrapbook history to the reader may not have been thought of in that way by the autobiographer who wrote it down. Roderick Seidenberg, the World War I conscientious objector who wrote of the great Leavenworth strike of 1919, was writing about an event which had been headlined at the time and was still remembered in 1932. It was personally important to Seidenberg. In a history of the development of nonviolent protest in America, it might also be important. Since such histories are not very common, or widely known, the event of the strike might seem isolated; at some point, however, the interested reader might learn enough to overcome that isolation (which is not just the event's but the reader's, too) and re-integrate the event with American history. At that point, the scrapbook will have performed a service. It will have recalled something from near oblivion and awakened someone to a new perception of American history. It may also no longer be a scrapbook.

What seems a scrapbook to one person was once someone else's treasure, their keepsake, and this takes us to a second level of historical revelation in autobiography: what it reveals about the cultural values of the person who wrote it and the audience it was written for.

What people choose to preserve in an autobiography is not accidental. It is chosen over other experiences and then written down in a particular way. These choices of content, form, and style, therefore, reveal a great deal about the values of the autobiographers and their cultures. *A True History of the Captivity and Restoration of Mrs. Mary Rowlandson* was published in 1682, about an experience that began in February, 1675/76. Before the great Puritan-Indian war of 1675–76, King Philip's War, there had been few if any Puritans captured by the Indians. Afterwards, narratives of such experiences became a common kind of literature. They told a story which people wanted to read or to hear told first-hand by the captive, or second- or third-hand by ministers in sermons or by neighbors gathered around the fire. The story had suspense, violence, and a dangerous, exotic setting. For the Puritan, it could be made an allegory of trial and redemption, as it was also a medium of anti-Indian propaganda, at a time when Indians, French, and British were contending for control of North America. Stories of Indian captivity were written and preserved, making this form of autobiography a convention that expressed the terror and faith within the Puritan community.

For this reason, the kind of autobiography which different generations of Americans have chosen to write, to publish, and to read can tell us a great deal about the peculiar experiences, the hopes and fears, and the values and ideals of those generations. To write an autobiography about Indian captivity, the author needed, obviously, to have been captured, held, and then released (or to have escaped). But what made this a story someone *would* write arose from the culture's having recognized and sanctioned it as a significant story, while also establishing how the story was to be told and interpreted. John Smith treated his capture by Powhattan's people as just a short incident. Daniel Boone's brief account of his captivity, as given to/retold by John Filson, is also markedly different from Mary Rowlandson's. By Boone's time, captivities were still exciting material, but the Puritan readers were gone, and with them the Puritan kinds of sanction for the story: the idea of the captivity as a test of faith, the sense that God ordained it, and thus the whole drama of earthly trial and redemption. These themes may have remained latent in Boone's story, but they were no longer primary. With the Revolution, new captivity stories were available, such as Ethan Allen's, where the focus was the prisoner's brash and resourceful American patriotism. This was the new "religion" that was tested and that sustained him against the new enemy, the cruel and haughty British.

What this brief history of captivity stories is meant to illustrate is that over time autobiographies change in more than just content. They also change in form, emphasis, and sense of audience. They change with the changing values and concepts of character and society. Formulae and conventions change, reflecting changes in society and the society's most basic goals and standards. With these changes come changes in what autobiography is thought to be, which is a very good reason for approaching definitions of autobiography very cautiously. They, too, are historically determined. A rigid definition from one time may not fit another. A reader who expected that autobiography must tell a long story of religious conversion, such as St. Augustine's, would entirely miss the intense, foreshortened test of religious faith that is given in Mary Rowlandson's story. Yet certain other features or functions of autobiography may remain the same. A reader who saw that from the very beginnings of American autobiography, with John Smith and Mary Rowlandson, stories of captivity were stories of a trial of someone's faith would more easily grasp the underlying religious significance of Ethan Allen's and Daniel Boone's stories—or of the stories of American hostages in Iran and Lebanon.

5. In appealing to the hopes and fears, goals, and common experiences of their time and culture, autobiographers also develop and reveal their concepts of self, that particular revelation of autobiography that philosopher-historian Karl Weintraub[6] has called its most interesting and significant.

Today, as Weintraub and many other people have observed, Americans like to think of themselves as having great respect for the uniqueness of the individual. Each individual has special gifts, a personality of his or her own,

6. Karl J. Weintraub, "Autobiography and Historical Consciousness," *Critical Inquiry* 1 (1975): 821–48. Also see *The Value of the Individual* (Chicago: Univ. of Chicago Press, 1978).

and thus something peculiarly his or her own to offer to the wider society. So we believe that education, from earliest childhood to colleges and graduate schools, should nurture and develop each individual, allowing him or her to reach a greater self-fulfillment. In marriage, work, recreation, and the other institutions of our society we further encourage everyone to make their own contributions and be as independent and free as they can. At least, this is our ideal, and, in truth, we often judge our institutions by how much freedom they give us for creativity and self-development. A good job is one that allows a person to be creative. A bad marriage is one that is oppressive and confining. To some degree, we realize that these goals are utopian: not all jobs are challenging and creative all the time to all people. We also realize that there are dangers in saying to everyone, "do your own thing," and that total individual freedom can lead to "rampant individualism," gross selfishness, and social and economic anarchy. But on the whole, Americans would rather risk the disappointments of falling short of their utopian goals than limit the rights and potential of the individual.

What autobiography can teach us is that this conception of the self as totally unique, as ineffable and wonderful, and as therefore deserving the greatest possible freedom, is one which has developed historically. It has not always existed. It has grown up out of many earlier conceptions of self which were related to their historical and cultural contexts.

It is interesting to note how the very word "individual," which is so important to modern Americans (and indirectly to the history of autobiography), has changed its meanings over the course of the last five hundred years or so. According to Raymond Williams in *Keywords*,[7] the word was first an adjective describing something indivisible, as in "the hye and indyvyduall Trynyte" (1425) or "the individuall Catholicke Church" (John Milton, 1641). Until the late seventeenth century, this was its most common meaning. But in the eighteenth century, logic and biology began to speak of "an individual" that was separate from others, while still representative of others like it. Plants and animals could be classified in different categories such as class, genus, and species, with the "individual" as a particular representative of a species. Not until the late eighteenth and early nineteenth centuries did usage of "the individual" become common (and favorable) to denote a person uniquely different from all others. The "individual" of these periods was also more readily understood to be a man, normally a white man of some education, wealth, and talent. It was property-holding white men who could vote and participate in politics and whose *individual interests* therefore had to be recognized by leaders and reconciled with other men's interests.

Concepts of self have changed, too. The self to the Puritans was "'the

7. Raymond Williams, *Keywords: A Vocabulary of Culture and Society* (New York: Oxford Univ. Press, 1976), pp. 133–36.

great snare,' 'the false Christ,' a spider's 'webbe [spun] out of our bowels,' the very 'figure or type of Hell.'"[8] It was the origin of vanity, greed, and disregard for others. Thus John Calvin wrote that we must "rid our selves of all selfe-trust." Trusting the self would not give Christians adequate guidance on earth or gain them salvation. But opposed to such a wicked, sinful self was the *soul,* which was the spirit of God within each person. "The way of the soul . . . starts 'with a holy despair in ourselves' and proceeds 'with a holy kind of violence' back to Christ; it means acknowledging the primacy of that which is Another's and *receiving* the ability to respond."[9] The presence of such opposites within each person led to the intense inner conflict which is to be seen in Puritan autobiography. Indeed, Puritan conversion narratives, of which there are hundreds, were the chosen medium of Puritan culture for expressing and attempting to resolve this conflict.

To Ralph Waldo Emerson and his fellow Transcendentalists, "self-trust" was the antithesis of what it had been to John Calvin. "Trust thyself: every heart vibrates to that iron string," is the theme of Emerson's essay "Self-Reliance," and the contrast between Calvin's words and Emerson's epitomizes the changes between seventeenth- and early eighteenth-century American Puritanism and nineteenth-century American romanticism. Yet Emerson was also appropriating to the *self* some of the divine spirituality which Puritans identified with the *soul,* and he was not expecting expressions of the self to be highly particular, eccentric, or unique. On the contrary, he and his contemporaries in general, not just other Transcendentalists, expected autobiography to express universals and to be uplifting, refined, and almost impersonal. They could still recognize, like their Puritan ancestors, that an impure self could be vain, divisive, greedy, and undeserving of celebration. Even Whitman, celebrate the self though he did, still tried to distinguish between the trivial particulars of his life ("My dinner, dress, associates, looks, compliments, dues . . .") and the essence, "the Me myself" that "Stands amused, complacent, compassionate, idle, unitary" ("Song of Myself," section 4). Ironically, early reviewers of *Leaves of Grass* thought that it contained too much of Whitman the man and was too autobiographical, when, as some modern critics have observed, the first edition of 1855 was almost an anonymous poem.[10] Whitman's name did not appear on the title page, and the famous engraving opposite it was of a sort of American "everyman." Whitman and his early critics may have been in greater agreement on their concepts of self than we have realized.

8. Sacvan Bercovitch, *The Puritan Origins of the American Self* (New Haven: Yale Univ. Press, 1975), p. 18.
9. Bercovitch, *Origins,* pp. 17–18.
10. Leslie Fiedler, "Images of Walt Whitman," in *Collected Essays of Leslie Fiedler,* vol. 1 (New York: Stein and Day, 1971), p. 152. Also see Malcolm Cowley's introduction to *Walt Whitman's Leaves of Grass: The First (1855) Edition* (New York: Viking, 1959), p. vii.

Further commentary on how autobiographies reveal the author's and a culture's concepts of self will be found in the introductions to the eight general periods of American autobiography into which this book is divided. Those periods cover roughly thirty to ninety years each, and within each there is always a variety of people and stories, of *lives*. No reader should expect to find all the lives within each period illustrating one specific concept of self. Some periods also overlap, because a person who lived in one period some-times did not write his or her autobiography until well into the next period, and because generations do overlap. At any given point in time, there are three to five generations alive at once—children, youths, the early middle-aged, the older middle-aged, and elders. Each experiences any given event, like a war, for example, in very different ways. Thus each also develops its sense of the nation and of other people in different ways. In the 1930s, for example, the elder generation of autobiographers, containing people such as Lincoln Steffens and Charlotte Perkins Gilman, were writing about their childhood and careers in the late nineteenth century and early twentieth century. They had been relatively unaffected by the Great War of 1914–18, and still thought of themselves as progressives, holding, in some way, to a sense of progress and believing in the feasibility of a rationally organized society. Simultaneously, however, younger writers like Gertrude Stein and F. Scott Fitzgerald, whose generation felt both devasted and liberated by the Great War, were living without those progressive values, living "experimental lives" in which they faced their despair and sought new values.

6. Given these variations between generations, as well as differences between individuals, we have to refine the broad idea, concepts of self, into more subtle and specific parts. An autobiography not only reveals an author's broad concepts of the self as, say, a Transcendental universal or as a participant in the progress of American civilization; it also reveals those quirkier or more specific modes of behavior, styles, tastes, educations, and vocations which might be called "forms of identity." Thoreau, Whitman, and Emerson, as lit-erary historians have long noted, held similar concepts of self. Their forms of identity, however, were very different, with Thoreau liking (and writing about) solitude and walks in the fields around the village of Concord, Emer-son liking to putter in his orchard and have the company of other members of the Boston and Concord gentry, and Whitman writing about his walks in busy Manhattan and Brooklyn and his ferryboat rides. Their favorite literary forms are different as well: Thoreau preferred the essay and the extended per-sonal journal; Emerson also wrote essays and journals, but without Thoreau's kind of topographic details; and Whitman worked from random notes and jottings, which he built up into poems or newspaper articles.

Concepts of self seem more historically determined than forms of identity. The concept of progress, as we have suggested, affected several generations of

Americans, giving them a faith that their lives might acquire meaning within a culture or civilization that was expanding in power, growing in refinement and education, and able to accommodate ever larger numbers of other people. To stand outside that late Victorian and early modern concept of self took the heroic independence and ironic skepticism of a rare individual, such as Henry Adams. With respect to forms of identity, however, people may be more psychologically than historically determined, exercising their freedom to respond to the needs of their own character. Dorothy Day, in *The Long Loneliness,* chooses to become a Catholic and also chooses to have her baby and raise it herself. Catholicism and single motherhood were radical choices for a woman of her background, but she was able to justify them to herself and to use her autobiography as a way of justifying them to her readers, beginning with the already large circle of readers of her newspaper, *The Catholic Worker.*

Are forms of identity determined or chosen? The question is answered differently, of course, by each autobiographer, and the student of narrative theory might add that this is a question which *generates* autobiographical narrative. Why did I do what I did? How did I become what I became? Narratives are written to give people and institutions legitimacy, and autobiographies are written to give their authors their legitimacy, their author-ity. Some authors, therefore, stress their freedom, others the necessities which drove them to the course of life and form of identity they took. Both can be convincing accounts, depending on the circumstances of the writer and the reader.

7. Autobiographies, therefore, may reveal as much about the author's assumed audience as they do about him or her, and this is a further reason why they need to be read as *cultural documents,* not just as personal ones.

An instructive way of realizing how an autobiography is a revealing cultural document is to undertake the experiment of writing a brief chapter of one's own history.

What shall it be? From the start, with the question, "What shall I write about?" the autobiographer is implicitly asking, "What are people interested in? What has happened to me that I can tell them, that I want them to know, and that they want to know? Will it make them respect me or hate me? What have I done that is different . . . or that is similar to what others have done?"

The reason we have so many familiar species and sub-species of autobiography—the high school student's story of "what I did last summer"; the stories of the big game, the big date, and the big trip; the stories of the first day at college; stories of joining a church, stories of jobs, of arguments, arrests, sickness, accidents, and so on—is that all of these are implicitly recognized autobiographical conventions. We have heard or read them before, from friends and family, or watched them played out in movies and on television. In this respect, they are not peculiar to autobiography, but when we select stories from our experience which fit into these forms, we demonstrably make them autobiography. And the same goes for many other kinds of stories which are the stuff of longer, published autobiographies: rags-to-riches stories, stories of athletes and their careers, movie stars' memoirs, the trials of immigrants, discoveries of one's new identity, prisoners' stories, or protest stories. The person who casts his or her life history into one of these forms is acknowledging the power of these literary-cultural conventions.

Sometimes we say, derogatorily, that these conventions are clichés and that fitting our stories into one or another of them turns us from individuals into types, even stereotypes; that the full variety and complexity of a life is lost, even killed, when it is simplified into just one conventional kind of story; and that such stories, in a way, write themselves, needing no creative or original author. The so-called "death of the author," which theorists of the novel wrote about a few years ago, happened to autobiographers long ago. But there is another sense in which all autobiography is a form of suicide (and biography a homicide), as Henry Adams said when he referred to the writing of his *Education* as a way of "taking" his life.[11] For most writers, once the story is written down, it is *finished*. It is over; it has been told that way, to the exclusion of other ways; it has been polished and improved; and it would be hard to deconstruct and put together another way.

Nevertheless, there are also great advantages, great powers, to having a story that is formed and defined. In being "simplified," it is clarified—made more recognizable to others and so more convincing and efficient. Invisibly, without everyone quite knowing this, it takes on the authority of all the previous tellings of similar stories. The latest rags-to-riches story, like Lee Iacocca's, is quickly accepted, because the type is familiar and already widely acknowledged. The latest story confirms all the earlier ones, and they sanction it, imparting to it their collective momentum. The new heroes of such stories are readily acclaimed. They are cultural types, leaders, symbols of their times. For this reason, a great deal of recent study of American autobiography has been directed at this process of identity formation, self-advertisement, and self-mythologizing.[12]

11. Adams, *Education*, pp. 512–13.
12. See, for example, Mutlu Konuk Blasing, *The Art of Life: Studies in American Autobiographical Literature* (Austin: Univ. of Texas Press, 1977); G. Thomas Couser, *American Autobiography: The Prophetic Mode* (Amherst: Univ. of Massachusetts Press, 1979); Albert E. Stone, *Autobiographical Occasions and Original Acts* (Philadelphia: Univ. of Pennsylvania Press, 1982); Gordon O. Taylor, *Chapters of Experience* (New York: St. Martin's Press, 1983); William L. Andrews, *To Tell a Free Story: The First Century of Afro-American Autobiography, 1760–1865* (Urbana: Univ. of Illinois Press, 1986); Sidonie Smith, *A Poetics of Women's Autobiography: Marginality and the Fictions of Self-Representation* (Bloomington: Indiana Univ. Press, 1987); Ormond Seavey, *Becoming Benjamin Franklin: The Autobiography and the Life* (University Park: Pennsylvania State Univ. Press, 1988); Joseph Fichtelberg, *The Complex Image: Faith and Method in American Autobiography* (Philadelphia: Univ. of Pennsylvania Press, 1989); Timothy Dow Adams, *Telling Lies in Modern American Autobiography* (Chapel Hill: Univ. of North Carolina Press, 1990).

As the autobiographer writes, whether writing just a short essay or a whole book, she or he also turns to kinds of rhetoric—arguments, images, tones, references, and allusions—which further strengthen and justify the story. Should persons be writing an apologia, especially one written in response to a conflict with someone, such rhetorical development is all the more inevitable. They try to express sentiments or positions that will gain the most sympathy. They appeal to the audience's standards of justice, propriety, and morality, in so doing trying to represent themselves as adhering to these values and their opponents as having infringed on them. Even in other kinds of autobiography, these same tendencies are present. Confessional autobiographers convert *from* a kind of life that is unsatisfactory *to* a kind of life which is ultimately more acceptable not only to the writer but to some present or future audience. Or, if they do not make it acceptable to all, they at least show readers why it is the right choice for them. Once again, therefore, the autobiographer is not writing just his or her own story, but a story that derives from and refers back to the materials, traditions, and values of a culture.

Of course, not everyone can easily find the narrative forms and rhetorical strategies which are most appropriate to them and which make the strongest appeal to their audience. This is most obviously true in the case of people who need translators, editors, and ghost-writers. In America, historically, these people have most often been Indians, escaped slaves, and new immigrants. Some did not know English, or could not write. Others still did not know the customs and conventions of other Americans and the kinds of stories which people did and did not want to read. Thus, beginning with Black Hawk's *Autobiography* (1833), if not before, Indian autobiographies have been "bicultural, composite composition[s], the product of a collaboration between the Native American subjects of the autobiography, who provide its 'content,' and its Euro-American editor, who ultimately provides its 'form' by fixing the text in writing."[13] This kind of bicultural, composite, immigrant autobiography in America is harder to date exactly. But one beginning of it, surely, was the study *The Polish Peasant,* done by Thomas and Znaniecki in Chicago between 1918 and 1920. The dominant English-speaking population of Chicago felt anxious about the presence of large numbers of immigrants and wanted to know more about their political opinions, education, and character. Thomas and Znaniecki collected dictated autobiographies as sociological data. These underlying interests in social control illustrate how in dictated autobiography motives of the editor can be very different from the motives of the subject. In colonial New England, it was very common for ministers to publish the confessions they received from condemned prisoners

13. Arnold Krupat, "Native American Autobiography," in *American Autobiography: Retrospect and Prospect,* ed. Paul John Eakin (Madison: Univ. of Wisconsin Press, 1991), p. 179. Krupat distinguishes between these "Indian autobiographies" and "autobiographies by Indians," which "are indeed self-written lives," though also with an "element of biculturalism."

as lessons to other men and women.[14] Even without motives such as these, editors still shape stories to conform to *their* concepts of self and identity rather than the subjects' concepts. Therefore, some readers prefer to call such stories "life histories" rather than true autobiographies.

To see how different autobiographies and "life histories" can be, follow the writing of a chapter of autobiography by narrating some events of your life to someone else and having him or her "ghost write" them. For variety, the ghost can pretend to be an anthropologist, journalist, gossip writer, or social worker. Other ground rules should specify the audience addressed and whether the story is to be made sympathetic or unsympathetic. The results will invariably be very instructive. To the "subject," it will be like having someone redo your wardrobe. To the "ghost writer," it will be like trying to wear someone else's clothes. The greater the differences between the styles of the writer and the subject, the more one learns. Yet however much this exercise may reveal the faults and distortions of dictated autobiography, it does not necessarily prove that dictated autobiographies should not be done. They still help to tell and defend the life stories of people who might never have told their own—people like Black Elk or Malcolm X—and the more interested we are in getting other people's stories, the more these will be written. Moreover, the situation of editor to subject is simply the extreme of the normal autobiographical situation of writer to subject. For the person who writes is never exactly the same as the person who lived. Every autobiographer is, in a way, a "ghost."

Thus both reading and writing autobiographies can be very revealing experiences. One learns more about other people, about the cultures they lived in, and about the relationships between cultures and concepts of self. But one also learns about autobiography itself—about the kinds of autobiography which have been written and about the power and authority which they have had at different times and in different parts of American society.

Perhaps one should also be prepared to realize that "American autobiography" is not independent from other kinds of writing, such as novels, histories, and biographies, or independent from other autobiographical traditions in other cultures. Indeed, "concepts of self" show up in all forms of writing and in other arts, from painting to architecture. In this anthology, therefore, we will sometimes refer to other arts and even include excerpts from biographies and other writings. We will also continue to refer to other, non-American autobiographers, because their influence has been significant. Sophisticated writers like Henry Adams and Gertrude Stein may have been

14. See Ronald A. Bosco, "Early American Gallows Literature: An Annotated Checklist," *Resources for American Literary Study* 8 (1978): 81–107, and Daniel E. Williams, "'Behold a Tragic Scene Strangely Changed into a Theater of Mercy': The Structure and Significance of Criminal Conversion Narratives in Early New England," *American Quarterly* 38 (Winter 1986): 827–47.

more consciously aware of their predecessors, but unsophisticated writers were also influenced by them. How one speaks or writes about one's self is almost constantly affected, positively or negatively, by how other people have spoken and written about themselves. We, as Americans, may value the individual, but we are still not so individual as we think!

A sense of how pervasive and subtle and complex these relationships among all kinds of autobiographies are should be sufficient justification for this anthology's combining of well-recognized "literary" writers like Emerson, Fitzgerald, and James Agee with unknowns like Stephen Burroughs and Warren Goss, with political and historical figures like John and Abigail Adams and Frederick Douglass, and with naturalists, businessmen, agitators, and so on. They may not normally "talk" to each other, but they are more or less aware of each other and aware of each other's ways of living and writing. This is to say, people write as they do not only to sound like someone they admire; they also wish to avoid sounding like someone they do not admire—who is "old-fashioned" or of an alien class, race, or political stance. Perhaps a similar phenomenon affects other genres, as when high-brow male novelists of the late nineteenth century both imitated and avoided the female sentimentalists and local colorists. But in autobiography this seems especially true. "The true history of American autobiography and the culture in which it is produced and consumed," Paul John Eakin has speculated, "may turn out to be the history of identifiable groups within the culture and of the network of relations among them." [15]

This anthology is not a history. But it is historically organized, for the reasons given above, and it does try to suggest how intricate and fascinating the "network" of autobiographical writers has been.

---

15. Paul John Eakin, "Introduction," in *American Autobiography: Retrospect and Prospect,* ed. Eakin, p. 12.

PART ONE

Explorers, Governors, Pilgrims, and Captives, 1607–1700

Although it is becoming clear that native Americans had long possessed various traditions for oral and pictorial stories about themselves,[1] what is called autobiographical writing begins in America with the journals and histories of the explorers, who recorded their experiences for themselves and their supporters and critics back in Europe. The first extensive description of what is now the United States is *Adventures in the Unknown Interior of America* by Cabeza de Vaca, one of four survivors of a disastrous expedition to Florida in 1527. His ten-year journey of exploration and flight took him along what is now the Gulf Coast, through Texas, New Mexico, and Arizona, and down to Mexico City. Between the lines, his narrative also tells and implies so much about him that it can well be considered autobiography.

Beginning in the 1580s, many narratives of exploration were edited and published by the great Elizabethan geographer Richard Hakluyt (c. 1552–1616), who wished to promote more English exploration and settlement in the new world. The emphasis in these is, naturally, on the places visited and things seen. The explorers had been sent to look for gold and precious gems, to seek a new route to the Indies, to convert the natives to Christianity, so to advance English power, which was in competition with the French, Spanish, and other European nations. These were the subjects the backers of the expeditions wanted to hear about—not the life histories of the writers. By the same rule, the water-color paintings of Virginia which were done by John White to accompany Thomas Hariot's *Briefe and True Report of the New-Found Land of Virginia* (1588, 1590) were of the birds and fish, the animals and plants, and the native people and their dwellings, dress, and customs. The purpose of these expeditions was exploration of the "new-foundland," not self-exploration. "Autobiography" did not exist.

Yet in a larger sense these early writers and artists were expressing them-

---

1. See Hertha Wong, *Sending My Heart Back Across the Years: Tradition and Innovation in Native American Autobiography* (New York: Oxford Univ. Press, 1992), pp. 25–56.

selves and even exploring themselves. In their enthusiasm and curiosity about new places and people, they were expressing a new, expansive, outward-looking spirit. Simultaneously, they were learning more about their capacities for suffering, endurance, and leadership.

Explorers began to write still more directly about themselves when it became necessary for them to defend their actions against rivals or to explain why they had not done some of the things their backers had directed them to do. No one demonstrates this more vividly than John Smith, member of the Jamestown Colony of 1607, and its eventual, then deposed, leader. Smith first wrote *A True Relation of Occurrences and Accidents in Virginia* (1608), a very short account (only forty pages in all) of the sea voyage and first year of the Jamestown settlement. That Smith, rather than someone else, reported on these "occurrences and accidents," was because other men died, became sick, or proved incompetent. The party originally contained 105 men, who sailed from England on New Year's Day, 1607, and arrived at the mouth of Chesapeake Bay at the end of April. By the time their ship started back to England in June, 1607, some had already been killed by Indians, and most of the original leaders were sick or dying or discredited, Smith says. By the end of December, only 30 men were left.[2] Smith began to take command because he was successful in trading with the Indians for food. Without him, he implies, the whole settlement would have starved. Once in command, he insisted on building stronger defenses and on sterner discipline. He punished Indians who stole English tools and weapons, and he put down the quarrels among the English. He also discouraged the pursuit of gold and easy riches, which some colonists had expected, and instead made the men cut down trees and plant corn. In these ways he began to demonstrate—and advertise—the kind of character he thought was essential to building a new, permanent, self-sustaining colony. "Captain John Smith," as one recent admirer has written, noting his archetypal stature as a Euro-American male, is "Father of Us All."[3]

Returning to England and then making later journeys to New England, Smith published three more books about America: *A Map of Virginia, with a Description of its Commodities, People, Government, and Religion,* in 1612; *A Description of New England,* in 1616; and *The General Historie of Virginia, New England, and the Summer Isles,* in 1624. Of these, *The General History* is the longest and the one that has had the greatest impact on later writing, if only because it includes the story of Smith's rescue by Pocahontas. But the Pocahontas story also has led to questions about Smith's reliability, because he never mentioned the rescue in *A True Relation,* even though it supposedly happened during the first year, the period of that narrative. More doubt has

2. *Travels and Works of Captain John Smith,* ed. Edward Arber, intro. by A. G. Bradley, 2 vols. (Edinburgh: John Grant, 1910), p. xii.
3. John Seelye, *Prophetic Waters: The River in Early American Life and Literature* (New York: Oxford Univ. Press, 1977), p. 57.

been cast on *The General History* because it is written in the third person singular and includes various testimonies by other men. The likeliest explanation is that Smith was using the *General History* not only to elaborate on his earlier accounts but also to further advertise his own exploits. The third person means of narration made such self-advertisement more rather than less feasible—as other autobiographers have also realized.

The last book Smith wrote, *The True Travels, Adventures, and Observations of Captain John Smith*, 1630, was also in the third person singular. It briefly describes his family background—he was the son of a Lincolnshire yeoman—and then narrates his almost unbelievable adventures in Italy, Turkey, and Austria in the years before he set out for America. He had fought in great battles and sieges, been taken into slavery, acted as diplomat, and become a bold, swaggering soldier of fortune. It was these experiences which prepared him for the dangers and uncertainties of colonization in America. The telling of them was yet another way of continuing to promote himself and gain favor from his aristocratic patrons.

What Smith's *True Relation* and *General History* also did was to establish an American tradition of the governor's narrative as a combination of personal history and history of the colony. The needs for such narratives were, as in Smith's case, for records, for justification, and for promotion of further colonies. Governors were the logical persons to write them because they knew the colonies' affairs, dealt with all the members and the European backers, and were often the best educated, most literate people in the communities. They directed their community's destiny, and that destiny was finally discerned and inscribed in the narrative.

Two of the most important later governor's narratives are William Bradford's *Of Plymouth Plantation, 1620–1647*, about the Separatists from the Church of England who founded the Plymouth Colony, and John Winthrop's *Journal*, the record of his leadership of the Massachusetts Bay Colony. They were very different men, and their books are equally different. Bradford, the more modest and self-effacing of the two, wrote *Of Plymouth Plantation*, a kind of meditative history which he began in 1630 and resumed in 1644. Winthrop, on the other hand, was a wealthy attorney, and he wrote the *Journal* in the form of daily entries. But both had a Christian-classical ideal of continuous dedication of the governor to the welfare of the community. The tribute which Bradford paid to John Robinson, an earlier leader of the Separatists, expresses this ideal well. Robinson led the people, "So . . . they grew in knowledge and other gifts and graces of the Spirit of God, and lived together in peace and love and holiness . . . And if at any time any differences arose, or offenses broke out (as it cannot be but some time there will, even amongst the best of men) they were ever so met with and nipped in the head betimes, or otherwise so well composed, as still love, peace, and communion was continued. Or else the church purged off those that were incurable and incorrigible, when, after much patience used, no other means would serve, which seldom came to pass. Yea, such was the mutual love and reciprocal respect that this worthy man had to his flock, and his flock to him, that it might be said of them as it once was of that famous Emperor Marcus Aurelius, and the people of Rome, that it was hard to judge whether he delighted more in having such a people, or they in having such a pastor." Such men were also expected "to give directions in civil affairs and to foresee dangers and inconveniences, by which he was very helpful to their outward estates and so was every ways as a common father unto them."[4]

The Puritans viewed history as the working out of God's design. This made their venture in the New World a holy project, and all the more important to record and study. Leaders like Winthrop or Bradford were further revered as new embodiments of Biblical leaders. Thus Cotton Mather later wrote a short biography of John Winthrop which he entitled *Nehemias Americanus,* or the American Nehemiah. Winthrop was like the leader of the Israelites who came after Moses and led them into Canaan.[5]

The governor's narrative was no place for highly personal reflection. Nor was it for the ordinary person to write. However, several other tenets of Puritan belief also made autobiographical writing extremely important to commoner people.

One such tenet was its radical Protestant emphasis on individual salvation and the need of the individual to experience divine blessing for himself or herself, without the intercession of priests or a church hierarchy. The greatest certainty of this salvation was the experience of conversion, coming after the recognition of sin and a sense of God's favor. It could come to any man or woman, and writing down the stages of the experience was both beneficial to the individual and instructive to friends, children, and other church members. *The Autobiography of Thomas Shepard* is one of the most famous illustrations of such a text. Shepard was an important early minister and therefore not a typical Puritan, and yet as a minister his influence was great, and he often served "as stenographer of his congregation's confessions."[6]

Anne Bradstreet's poems and her prose letter "To my Dear Children" illustrate the Puritan practice of careful self-scrutiny. Everything that happens is a potential sign of God's favor or disfavor—a spiritual message. The fire that destroyed her house was the occasion for grief and also for meditation on the superiority of a heavenly "house on high erect, / Framed by that

---

4. William Bradford, *Of Plymouth Plantation, 1620–1647,* ed. Francis Murphy (New York: Random House, 1981), p. 18.
5. For a brilliant, extended study of this biography, and the Puritan idea of typology, see Sacvan Bercovitch, *The Puritan Origins of the American Self* (New Haven: Yale Univ. Press, 1975).
6. Daniel B. Shea, "The Prehistory of American Autobiography," in *American Autobiography: Retrospect and Prospect,* ed. Paul John Eakin (Madison: Univ. of Wisconsin Press, 1991), p. 32.

mighty Architect," as she wrote in "Some Verses upon the Burning of our House, July 10th, 1666." The works of God in the visible world are emblems of the invisible world. Sickness or despair or doubt were occasions for self-examination, during which she found some sin she had not repented or duty she had neglected, and after such afflictions she had "abundance of sweetnes and refreshment." Such experiences and the lessons learned from them were what she wished to pass on to her children.

The writers of Puritan diaries had roughly similar motives. The young Samuel Sewall could not even feed his chickens without being "convinced what need I stood in of spiritual food, and that I should not nauseat daily duties of Prayer, &c." (January 13, 1677). The diary was a place to preserve such reflections, meditate further on them, and observe in what directions his soul was tending. He kept notes on sermons he had heard. And he kept an account of deaths and disasters in his family and community which might have divine meaning. A modern reader might just say that Sewall was superstitious, and he did, in fact, believe in witches—that, for instance, demons could possess people's souls. But after a series of accidents and deaths which he took as signs of God's disfavor, he performed the extraordinary act of publicly asking the pardon of the people and of God for his decisions in the Salem witch trials, in which he had been a judge. He then duly copied the text of this formal request for pardon into his diary.

Sewall's lengthy diary also has some of the qualities of the governor's narrative. He was an important leader. His acts affected the life and well-being of the community, even when he was just called out at night to quiet rowdy drinkers in a tavern. Yet there is also a crusty, status-conscious streak in Sewall that makes a reader suspect that another reason he kept his diary was simple vanity. He liked writing down the names of all the Puritan dignitaries with whom he dined. He was sensitive to the ups and downs of his popularity. Late in life he became comically self-conscious in his attempt to marry a wealthy widow, Madam Winthrop. Spanning so many years, his diary documents the changes in Puritan society, from a harsh and dramatic sense of divine presence to a more relaxed and comfortable worldliness. Distress with this worldliness would help engender the so-called "Great Awakening" of the 1730s and '40s, when Jonathan Edwards revived the practice of recording conversion narratives and writing intense examinations of the state of the soul.

In the 1680s, meanwhile, another kind of story had been published which was the beginning point of what would become the most egalitarian and popular form of early American autobiography, the narrative of Indian captivity. *The Soveraignty and Goodness of God, . . . a Narrative of the Captivity and Restauration of Mrs. Mary Rowlandson* was published in Boston in 1682, with a second edition coming the same year from a press in Cambridge, "on authority of the General Court." No complete copy of the first edition has survived (good evidence of how widely the book was read[7]), and another edition was printed in London, also in 1682. Since then, over thirty more editions have been printed. Mary Rowlandson's story of her eleven-week captivity with Indians in the late winter and spring of 1676 was the first great American autobiographical best-seller.

The basis for her interpretation of her experience was the same sense of providential design that empowered other Puritan and personal historians. Mary Rowlandson saw her captivity as God's will and as a lesson, therefore, to her and her readers. However, the story of a woman and her child being captured in a surprise attack during an all-out war, and then of the child's dying while the woman almost starves and is forced to walk, though injured, for miles in the snow and to sleep on the ground, living among "savages," and of the woman finally being ransomed and rejoining her family was a lot more than just a pious lesson. It was a thriller—a scary, gruesome thriller, that still had a pious coating and a happy ending. Americans, or the Americans-to-be, had discovered their first original literary genre, and in the centuries to come they would develop it not only in autobiography but in fiction, drama, film, biography, and journalism.

Besides being thrillers—and many later ones were much more sensational than Mary Rowlandson's—why were captivity narratives so popular? One reason, it has been suggested, was that Euro-Americans needed them to counter the demonstrable superiority of Indian life. As Benjamin Franklin, among others, pointed out, more captives stayed among the Indians than returned. When whites were raised among Indians, they preferred to stay; whereas when Indians were raised among whites, they preferred to go back to the forest.[8] A story which emphasized the cruelty and barbarism of Indians had a necessary propaganda value. Such a story also fitted into a basic ritualistic pattern of a person's "Separation, Transformation, and Return."[9] The captive was separated from the group, underwent a trial of faith while also being changed by contact with an alien society which was regarded as the opposite of one's own, and then was reunited with the group, reaffirming its way of life. Such an experience, therefore, helped Americans to define themselves and their new, insecure society—or collection of little, heterogeneous, insecure societies, as they were in the seventeenth and eighteenth centuries. Whatever American "civilization" was, it was the opposite of "savagery." An encounter with Indians therefore made an "American." The captive had encountered her or his "other," the creature who had preceded the Euro-

7. Richard VanDerBeets, ed., *Held Captive by Indians: Selected Narratives, 1642–1836* (Knoxville: Univ. of Tennessee Press, 1973), pp. xxv–xxvi, 42.
8. See letter from Benjamin Franklin to Peter Collinson, May 9, 1753, in *The Papers of Benjamin Franklin,* vol. 4, ed. Leonard W. Labaree et al. (New Haven: Yale Univ. Press, 1961), pp. 481–82.
9. Richard VanDerBeets, "The Indian Captivity Narrative as Ritual," *American Literature* 43 (January 1972): 548–62.

peans and was the "original," the "primitive," the "barbaric," and come back. In coming back, the former captive endorsed his or her "old," new American society. This strengthened the Euro-American society's confidence in its superiority, and re-integrated the former captive, who might otherwise be suspected of being not really loyal, of having become a conjurer or witch.

For all these reasons, captivity narratives signified to Euro-Americans a new concept of self *as* both European and American: European in values, origin, and ultimate loyalty, American in experience and skills of survival. At the same time, they have perhaps contributed to a kind of enduring American paranoia—fear of the wilderness, fear of Indians and people of other races, and the sense of being endangered and embattled.

Mary Rowlandson's *The Sovereignty and Goodness of God* affirmed that Americans were God's chosen people . . . but that they were also constantly at risk. It, and other early autobiographical writing, helped to make, to unite, and to frighten a people.

John Smith (1580–1631)

from *A True Relation* and
The General Historie of Virginia

A True Relation (1608) is a brief account of the Jamestown colony's first year, written from Smith's point of view and emphasizing and justifying his own actions. He bargains with different Indian nations and their leaders, describes their towns and houses, and disciplines other expedition members. Yet, simple as this seems, it is not an easy document for modern readers. Place names are strange, and the times and durations of different events are often unclear. It is also often unclear why these events are selected for description and how they fit together.

The names of the places, tribes, and chiefs were strange to Smith, too, however. In the first year he and the English had barely learned them. Smith also lacked a more comprehensive view of events because he was just becoming established as leader. Indeed, when the little party of 105 men arrived in Virginia, he was excluded from the governing council because he had led a mutiny during the ship's stop in the Caribbean (though he does not tell us this here). The *True Relation* therefore emphasizes his activities because they are what he knew best and because by making them into the settlement's history, he consolidated his power. He impressed his character on the settlement and on the "true" relation. He also needed to defend his actions, sometimes against criticisms the reader is scarcely aware of.

In the passage below he describes conditions in June, 1607, as he begins to take charge, describes his negotiations with the Indians for food, defends the execution of Captain Kendall, and then narrates his visit to and imprisonment by Powhatan. Later he narrates more diplomacy with Powhatan and other chiefs, justifies his sternness in dealing with them and their followers, and tells a little about an expedition to look for precious stones.

The passage from *The General Historie* (1624) describes Pocahontas's saving him from execution. The pages before it give a much longer account of his capture, the way he was led to Powhatan's town, and how he was treated. Comparing the two accounts, one can see many differences, the most important being that in the latter Smith was not just defending his actions, he was mythologizing them, turning himself from leader into legend.

The selection below is from *A True Relation of Such Occurrences and Accidents* of Noate as Hath Hapned in Virginia and from *The General Historie of Virginia, New England, and the Summer Isles,* both of which are included in *Travels and Works of Captain John Smith,* ed. Edward Arber (Edinburgh: John Grant, 1910). The information in brackets is from this same edition. The standard biography of Smith is Philip Barbour's *The Three Worlds of Captain John Smith* (Boston: Houghton Mifflin, 1964).

from A True Relation

. . . The day before the Ships departure, the King of *Pamaunke* [*i.e., Opechancanough*] sent the Indian that had met vs before in our discouerie, to assure vs peace; our fort being then palisadoed round, and all our men in good health and comfort, albeit, that thro[u]gh some discontented humors, it did not so long continue. For the President and Captaine *Gosnold,* with the rest of the Counsell, being for the moste part discontented with one another, in so much, that things were neither carried with that discretion nor any busines effected in such good sort as wisdome would, nor our owne good and safetie required, whereby, and through the hard dealing of our President, the rest of the counsell beeing diuerslie affected through his audacious commaund; and for Captaine *Martin,* albeit verie honest, and wishing the best good, yet so sicke and weake; and my selfe so disgrac'd through others mallice: through which disorder God (being angrie with vs) plagued vs with such famin and sicknes, that the liuing were scarce able to bury the dead: our want of sufficient and good victualls, with continuall watching, foure or fiue each night at three Bulwarkes, being the chiefe cause: onely of Sturgion wee had great store, whereon our men would so greedily surfet, as it cost manye their liues: the Sack, Aquauitie, and other preseruatiues for our health, being kept onely in the Presidents hands, for his owne diet, and his few associates.

Shortly after Captaine *Gosnold* fell sicke, and within three weekes died. Captaine *Ratcliffe* being then also verie sicke and weake, and my selfe hauing also tasted of the extremitie therof, but by Gods assistance being well recouered. *Kendall* about this time, for diuers reasons deposed from being of the Councell: and shortly after it pleased God (in our extremity) to moue the Indians to bring vs Corne, ere it was halfe ripe, to refresh vs, when we rather expected when they would destroy vs:

About the tenth of September there was about 46. of our men dead, at which time Captaine *Wingfield* hauing ordred the affaires in such sort that he was generally hated of all, in which respect with one consent he was deposed from his presidencie, and Captaine *Ratcliffe* according to his course was elected.

Our prouision being now within twentie dayes spent, the Indians brought vs great store both of Corne and bread ready made: and also there came such aboundance of Fowles into the Riuers, as greatly refreshed our weake estates, wherevppon many of our weake men were presently able to goe abroad.

As yet we had no houses to couer vs, our Tents were rotten, and our Cabbins worse then nought: our best commoditie was Yron which we made into little chissels.

The president['s], and Captaine *Martins* sicknes, constrayned me to be Cape Marchant, and yet to spare no paines in making houses for the company; who notwithstanding our misery, little ceased their mallice, grudging, and muttering.

As at this time were most of our chiefest men either sicke or discontented, the rest being in such dispaire, as they would rather starue and rot with idlenes, then be perswaded to do any thing for their owne reliefe without constraint: our victualles being now within eighteene dayes spent, and the Indians trade decreasing, I was sent to the mouth of the riuer, to *Kegquouhtan* an Indian Towne, to trade for Corne, and try the riuer for Fish, but our fishing we could not effect by reason of the stormy weather. The Indians thinking vs neare famished, with carelesse kindnes, offred vs little pieces of bread and small handfulls of beanes or wheat, for a hatchet or a piece of copper: In like man[n]er I entertained their kindnes, and in like scorne offered them like commodities, but the Children, or any that shewed extraordinary kindnes, I liberally contented with free gifte [of] such trifles as wel contented them.

Finding this colde comfort, I anchored before the Towne, and the next day returned to trade, but God (the absolute disposer of all heartes) altered their conceits, for now they were no lesse desirous of our commodities then we of their Corne: vnder colour to fetch fresh water, I sent a man to discouer the Towne, their Corne, and force, to trie their intent, in that they desired me vp to their houses: which well vnderstanding, with foure shot I visited them. With fish, oysters, bread, and deere, they kindly traded with me and my men, beeing no lesse in doubt of my intent, then I of theirs; for well I might with twentie men haue fraighted a Shippe with Corne: The Towne conteineth eighteene houses, pleasantly seated vpon three acres of ground, vppon a plaine, halfe inuironed with a great Bay of the great Riuer, the other parte with a Baye of the other Riuer falling into the great Baye, with a little Ile fit for a Castle in the mouth thereof, the Towne adioyning to the maine by a necke of Land of sixtie yardes.

With sixteene bushells of Corne I returned towards our Forte: by the way I encountred with two Canowes of Indians, who came aboord me, being the inhabitants of *waroskoyack,* a kingdome on the south side of the riuer, which is in breadth 5. miles and 20 mile or neare from the mouth: With these I traded, who hauing but their hunting prouision, requested me to returne to their Towne, where I should load my boat with corne: and with near thirtie bushells I returned to the fort, the very name wherof gaue great comfort to our despa[i]ring company:

· · ·

Hauing thus by Gods assistance gotten good store of corne, notwithstanding some bad spirits not content with Gods prouidence, still grew mutinous; in so much, that our president hauing occasion to chide the smith [*James Read, the Blacksmith*] for his misdeamenour, he not only gaue him bad language, but also offred to strike him with some of his tooles. For which rebellious act, the smith was by a Iury condemned to be hanged, but being vppon the ladder, continuing very obstinate as hoping vpon a rescue, when he saw no other way but death with him, he became penitent, and declared a dangerous conspiracy: for which, Captaine *Kendall,* as principal, was by a Iury condemned, and shot to death.

This conspiracy appeased, I set forward for the discouery of the Riuer [of] *Checka Hamania.* This third time I discouered the Townes of *Matapamient, Morinogh, Ascacap, moysenock, Righkahauck, Nechanichock, Mattalunt, Attamuspincke,* and diuers others: their plenty of corne I found decreased, yet lading the barge, I returned to our fort.

Our store being now indifferently wel prouided with corne, there was much adoe for to haue the pinace goe for England, against which Captain *Martin* and my selfe stood chiefly against it: and in fine after many debatings *pro et contra,* it was resolued to stay a further resolution:

This matter also quieted, I set forward to finish this discouery, which as yet I had neglected in regard of the necessitie we had to take in prouision whilst it was to be had. 40. miles I passed vp the riuer, which for the most part is a quarter of a mile broad, and 3. fatham and a half deep, exceedy o[o]sey, many great low marshes, and many high lands, especially about the midst at a place called *Moysonicke,* a *Peninsule* of 4. miles ci[r]cuit, betwixt two riuers ioyned to the main by a neck of 40. or 50. yards, and 40. or 50 yards from the high water marke: On both sides in the very necke of the maine, are high hills and dales, yet much inhabited, the Ile declining in a plaine fertile corne field, the lower end a low marsh. More plentie of swannes, cranes, geese, duckes, and mallards, and diuers sorts of fowles, none would desire: more plaine fertile planted ground, in such great proportions as there, I had not seene; of a light blacke sandy mould, the cliffes commonly red, white, and yellowe coloured sand, and vnder, red and white clay; fish [in] great plenty, and people [in] aboundance: the most of their inhabitants, in view of the neck of Land, where a better seat for a towne cannot be desired:

At the end of forty miles, this riuer inuironeth many low Ilands at each high water drowned, for a mile, where it vniteth it selfe at a place called *Apokant,* the highest Towne inhabited.

10. miles higher, I discouered with the barge: in the mid way, a greate tree hindered my passage, which I cut in two. Heere the riuer became narrower, 8. 9 or 10. foote at a high water, and 6. or 7. at a lowe: the streame exceeding swift, and the bottom hard channell: the ground, most part a low plaine, sandy soyle. This occasioned me to suppose it might issue from some lake or some broad ford, for it could not be far to the head, but rather then I would endanger the barge [*i.e., by going up with it further*]. Yet to haue beene able to resolue this doubt, and to discharge the imputation[s] of malicious tung[e]s, that halfe suspected I durst not, for so long delaying: some of the company as desirous as my self, we resolued to hier a Canow, and returne with the barge to *Apocant,* there to leaue the barge secure, and put our selues upon the aduenture: the country onely a vast and wilde wildernes, and but onely that Towne:

Within three or foure mile, we hired a Canow, and 2. Indians to row vs the next day a fowling. Hauing made such prouision for the barge as was needfull, I left her there [*at Apocant*] to ride, with expresse charge not any [one] to go ashore til my returne.

Though some wise men may condemn this too bould attempt of too much indiscretion, yet if they well consider the friendship of the Indians in conducting me, the desolateness of the country, the probabilitie of some lacke [*i.e., lake*], and the malicious iudges of my actions at home [*i.e., James Town*], as also to haue some matters of worth to incourage our aduenturers in england, [these] might well haue caused any honest minde to haue done the like, as well for his own discharge as for the publike good:

Hauing 2 Indians for my guide and 2 of our own company, I set forward, leauing 7 in the barge:

Hauing discouered 20 miles further in this desart, the riuer stil kept his depth and bredth, but [was] much more combred with trees:

Here we went ashore (being some 12 miles higher then the barge had bene) to refresh our selues, during the boyling of our vi[c]tuals: One of the Indians I tooke with me, to see the nature of the soile, and to crosse the boughts [*windings*] of the riuer: the other Indian I left with Maister *Robbinson* and *Thomas Emry,* with their matches light[ed], and order to discharge a peece, for my retreat, at the first sight of any Indian.

But within a quarter of an houre I heard a loud cry, and a hollowing of Indians, but no warning peece. Supposing them surprised, and that the Indians had betrai[e]d vs, presently I seazed him and bound his arme fast to my hand in a garter, with my pistoll ready bent to be reuenged on him: he aduised me to fly, and seemed ignorant of what was done.

But as we went discoursing, I was struck with an arrow on the right thigh, but without harme: vpon this occasion I espied 2. Indians drawing their bowes, which I preuented in discharging a french pistoll:

By that I had charged againe, 3 or 4 more did the like: for the first fell downe and fled: At my discharge, they did the like. My hinde [*Indian*] I made my barricado, who offered not to striue. 20. or 30. arrowes were shot at me but short. 3 or 4 times I had discharged my pistoll ere the king of *Pamaunck* called *Opeckankenough* with 200 men, inuironed me, eache drawing their bowe: which done they laid them [*themselves*] vpon the ground, yet without shot [*shooting*]:

My hinde treated betwixt them and me of conditions of peace; he discouered me to be the Captaine: my request was to retire to the boate: they demaunded my armes, the rest they saide were slaine, onely me they would reserue:

The Indian importuned me not to shoot. In retiring being in the midst of a low quagmire, and minding them more then my steps, I stept fast into the quagmire, and also the Indian in drawing me forth:

Thus surprised, I resolued to trie their mercies: my armes I caste from me, till which none durst approch me.

Being ceazed on me, they drew me out and led me to the King. I presented him with a compasse diall, describing by my best meanes the vse therof: whereat he so amazedly admired, as he suffered me to proceed in a discourse of the roundnes of the earth, the course of the sunne, moone, starres and plannets.

With kinde speeches and bread he requited me, conducting me where the Canow lay and *Iohn Robbinson* slaine, with 20 or 30. arrowes in him. *Emry* I saw not.

I perceiued by the aboundance of fires all ouer the woods [*the sense requires here,* that they were a party hunting deer]. At each place I expected when they would execute me, yet they vsed me with what kindnes they could:

Approaching their Towne [*Rasawrack*], which was within 6 miles where I was taken, onely made as arbors and couered with mats, which they remoue as occasion requires: all the women and children, being aduertised of this accident, came foorth to meet them, the King [*Opechancanough*] well guarded with 20 bowmen 5 flanck and rear, and each flanck before him a sword and a peece, and after him the like, then a bowman, then I on each hand a boweman, the rest in file in the reare, which reare led foorth amongst the trees in a bishion, eache his bowe and a handfull of arrowes, a quiuer at his back grimly painted: on eache flanck a sargeant, the one running alwaies towards the front, the other towards the reare, each a true pace and in exceeding good order.

This being a good time continued, they caste themselues in a ring with a daunce, and so eache man departed to his lodging.

The Captain conducting me to his lodging, a quarter of Venison and some ten pound of bread I had for supper: what I left was reserued for me, and sent with me to my lodging:

Each morning 3. women presented me three great platters of fine bread, more venison then ten men could deuour I had: my gowne, points and garters, my compas and my tablet they gaue me again. Though 8 ordinarily guarded me, I wanted not what they could deuise to content me: and still our longer acquaintance increased our better affection:

Much they threatned to assault our forte, as they were solicited by the King of *Paspahegh* [*then present*] who shewed at our fort great signes of sorrow for this mischance [*i.e., Smith's capture*]. The King [*Opechancanough*] tooke great delight in vnderstanding the manner of our ships, and sayling the seas, the earth and skies, and of our God: what he knew of the dominions he spared not to acquaint me with, as of certaine men cloathed at a place called *Ocanahonan*, cloathed like me: the course of our riuer, and that within 4 or 5 daies iourney of the falles, was a great turning of salt water:

I desired he would send a messenger to *Paspahegh* [*the district in which James Town was situated*], with a letter I would write, by which they shold vnderstand how kindly they vsed me, and that I was well, least they should reuenge my death. This he granted and sent three men, in such weather as in reason were vnpossible by any naked to be indured. Their cruell mindes towards the fort I had deuerted, in describing the ordinance and the mines in the fields, as also the reuenge Captain *Newport* would take of them at his re-turne. Their intent, I incerted the fort, [as also of] the people of *Ocanahonum* and the back sea: this report they after found diuers Indians that confirmed:

The next day after my letter, came a saluage to my lodging [*still at Rasa-wrack*], with his sword, to haue slaine me: but being by my guard intercepted, with a bowe and arrow he offred to haue effected his purpose: the cause I knew not, till the King vnderstanding thereof came and told me of a man a dying, wounded with my pistoll: he tould me also of another I had slayne, yet the most concealed they had any hurte: This was the father of him I had slayne, whose fury to preuent, the King presently conducted me to another Kingdome, vpon the top of the next northerly riuer, called *Youghtanan*.

Hauing feasted me, he further led me to another branch of the riuer, called *Mattapament*; to two other hunting townes they led me: and to each of these Countries, a house of the great Emperour of *Pewhakan*, whom as yet I supposed to bee at the *Fal*[*l*]*s*; to him I tolde him I must goe, and so returne to *Paspahegh*.

After this foure or fiue dayes marsh [*march*], we returned to *Rasawrack*, the first towne they brought me too: where binding the Mats in bundels, they marched two dayes iourney, and crossed the Riuer of *Youghtanan*, where it was as broad as *Thames:* so conducting me to a place called *Menapacute* in *Pamaunke*, where the King inhabited.

The next day another King of that nation called *Kekataugh,* hauing receiued some kindnes of me at the Fort, kindly inuited me to feast at his house,
the people from all places flocked to see me, each shewing to content me.

By this, the great King hath foure or fiue houses, each containing fourescore or an hundred foote in length, pleasantly seated vpon an high sandy
hill, from whence you may see westerly a goodly low Country, the riuer before the which his crooked course causeth many great Marshes of exceeding
good ground. An hundred houses, and many large plaines are here togither
inhabited. More abundance of fish and fowle, and a pleasanter seat cannot
be imagined. The King with fortie Bowmen to guard me, intreated me to
discharge my Pistoll, which they there presented me, with a mark at six score
[yards] to strike therwith: but to spoil the practise, I broke the cocke, whereat
they were much discontented, though a chaunce supposed.

From hence, this kind King conducted mee to a place called *Topahanocke,*
a kingdome vpon another Riuer northward: The cause of this was, that the
yeare before, a shippe had beene in the Riuer of *Pamaunke,* who hauing beene
kindly entertained by *Powhatan* their Emperour, they returned thence, and
discouered the Riuer of *Topahanocke:* where being receiued with like kind-
nesse, yet he slue the King, and tooke of his people, and they supposed I were
hee. But the people reported him [to be] a great [*tall*] man that was [the]
Captaine, and vsing mee kindly, the next day we departed.

This Riuer of *Topahanock* seemeth in breadth not much lesse then that we
dwell vpon. At the mouth of the Riuer is a Countrey called *Cuttata women:*
vpwards is *Marraugh tacum, Tapohanock, Appamatuck,* and *Nantaugs tacum:* at
Topmanahocks, the head issuing from many Mountaines.

The next night I lodged at a hunting town of *Powhatams,* and the next day
arriued at *Waranacomoco* vpon the riuer of *Pamauncke,* where the great king
is resident. By the way we passed by the top of another little riuer, which is
betwixt the two, called *Payankatank.* The most of this Country [is] th[r]ough
Desert, yet exceeding fertil; good timber, most[ly] hils and dales, in each
valley a cristall spring.

Arriuing at *Weramocomoco* [*on or about 5 January 1608?*], their Emperour
proudly lying vppon a Bedstead a foote high, vpon tenne or twelue Mattes,
richly hung with manie Chaynes of great Pearles about his necke, and couered
with a great Couering of *Rahaughcums.* At [his] heade sat a woman, at his
feete another; on each side sitting vppon a Matte vppon the ground, were
raunged his chiefe men on each side the fire, tenne in a ranke, and behinde
them as many yong women, each [with] a great Chaine of white Beades ouer
their shoulders, their heades painted in redde: and [*Powhatan*] with such a
graue and Maiesticall countenance, as draue me into admiration to see such
state in a naked Saluage.

Hee kindly welcomed me with good wordes, and great Platters of sun-
drie Victuals, assuring mee his friendship, and my libertie within foure days.

Hee much delighted in *Opechan Comoughs* relation of what I had described to him, and oft examined me vpon the same.

Hee asked mee the cause of our comming.

I tolde him being in fight with the Spaniards our enemie, beeing ouer-pow[e]red, neare put to retreat, and by extreame weather put to this shore: where landing at *Chesipiack*, the people shot [at] vs, but at *Kequoughtan* they kindly vsed vs: we by signes demaunded fresh water, they described vs vp the Riuer was all fresh water: at *Paspahegh* also they kindly vsed vs: our Pinn[a]sse being leak[i]e, we were inforced to stay to mend her, till Captaine *Newport* my father came to conduct vs away.

He demaunded why we went further with our Boate. I tolde him, in that I would haue occasion to talke of the backe Sea, that on the other side the maine, where was salt water. My father [*i.e.*, *Newport*] had a childe slaine, whiche wee supposed *Monocan* his enemie [had done]: whose death we intended to reuenge.

After good deliberation, hee began to describe [to] mee the Countreys beyonde the Falles, with many of the rest; confirming what not onely *Opechan-canoyes*, and an *Indian* which had beene prisoner to *Pewhatan* had before tolde mee: but some called it fiue dayes, some sixe, some eight, where the sayde water dashed amongest many stones and rockes, each storm; which caused oft tymes the heade of the Riuer to bee brackish:

Anchanachuck he described to bee the people that had slaine my brother: whose death hee would reuenge. Hee described also vpon the same Sea, a mighty Nation called *Pocoughtronack*, a fierce Nation that did eate men, and warred with the people of *Moyaoncer* and *Pataromerke*, Nations vpon the toppe of the heade of the Bay, vnder his territories: where the yeare before they had slain an hundred. He signified their crownes were shauen, long haire in the necke, tied on a knot, Swords like Pollaxes.

Beyond them, he described people with short Coates, and Sleeues to the Elbowes, that passed that way in Shippes like ours. Many Kingdomes hee described [to] mee, to the heade of the Bay, which seemed to bee a mightie Riuer issuing from mightie Mountaines betwixt the two Seas: The people cloathed at *Ocamahowan*, he also confirmed; and the Southerly Countries also, as the rest that reported vs to be within a day and a halfe of *Mangoge*, two dayes of *Chawwonock*, 6. from *Roonock*, to the south part of the backe sea: He described a countrie called *Anone*, where they haue abundance of Brasse, and houses walled as ours.

I requited his discourse (seeing what pride hee had in his great and spa-cious Dominions, seeing that all hee knewe were vnder his Territories) in describing to him, the territories of *Europe*, which was subiect to our great King whose subject I was, the innumerable multitude of his ships, I gaue him to vnderstand the noyse of Trumpets, and terrible manner of fighting [that] were vnder captain *Newport* my father: whom I intituled the *Mewora-*

mes, which they call the King of all the waters. At his greatnesse, he admired: and not a little feared. He desired mee [*i.e., the English*] to forsake *Paspahegh* [*i.e., James Town*], and to liue with him vpon his Riuer, a Countrie called *Capa Howasicke.* Hee promised to giue me Corne, Venison, or what I wanted to feede vs: Hatchets and Copper wee should make him, and none should disturbe vs.

This request I promised to performe: and thus, hauing with all the kindnes hee could deuise, sought to content me, hee sent me home, with 4. men: one that vsually carried my Gowne and Knapsacke after me, two other loded with bread, and one to accompanie me.

This Riuer of *Pamaunke* is not past twelue mile from that we dwell on, his course northwest and westerly as the other. *Weraocomoco* is vpon salt water in bredth two myles, and so [the river] keepeth his course without any tarry-ing some twenty miles; where at the parting of the fresh water and the salt, it diuideth it selfe into two partes, the one part to *Goughland,* as broad as *Thames,* and nauigable with a Boate threescore or fourescore miles, and with a Shippe fiftie: exceeding[ly] crooked, and manie low grounds and marishes, but inhabited with aboundance of warlike and tall people. The Countrey of *Youghtomam,* of no lesse worth, onely it is lower; but all the soyle, a fatte, fertill, sandie ground. Aboue *Manapacumter,* many high sandie mountaines. By the Riuer is many Rockes, seeming, if not, of seuerall Mines.

The other branch a little lesse in breadth, yet extendeth not neare so farre, nor so well inhabited, somewhat lower, and a white sandie, and a white clay soyle: here is their best *Terra Sigillata.* The mouth of the Riuer, as I see [*saw?*] in the discouerie therof with *captain Newport,* is halfe a mile broad, and within foure miles not aboue a Musket shot: the channell exceeding good and deepe, the Riuer straight to the deuisions. *Kiskirk* [is] the nearest Nation to the entrances.

from The General Historie of Virginia

. . . Not long after, early in a morning a great fire was made in a long house, and a mat spread on the one side, as on the other; on the one they caused him to sit, and all the guard went out of the house, and presently came skipping in a great grim fellow, all painted over with coale, mingled with oyle; and many Snakes and Wesels skins stuffed with mosse, and all their tayles tyed together, so as they met on the crowne of his head in a tassell; and round about the tassell was as a Coronet of feathers, the skins hanging round about his head, backe, and shoulders, and in a manner covered his face; with a hellish voyce, and a rattle in his hand. With most strange gestures and passions he began his invocation, and environed the fire with a circle of meale; which done, three more such like devils came rushing in with the like antique tricks, painted halfe blacke, halfe red: but all their eyes were painted white, and some red stroakes like Mutchato's, along their cheekes: round about him those fiends daunced a pretty while, and then came in three more as vgly as the rest; with red eyes, and white stroakes over their blacke faces, at last they all sat downe right against him; three of them on the one hand of the chiefe Priest, and three on the other. Then all with their rattles began a song, which ended, the chiefe Priest layd downe fiue wheat cornes: then strayning his armes and hands with such violence that he sweat, and his veynes swelled, he began a short Oration: at the conclusion they all gaue a short groane; and then layd down three graines more. After that, began their song againe, and then another Oration, ever laying downe so many cornes as before, till they had twice incirculed the fire; that done, they tooke a bunch of little stickes prepared for that purpose, continuing still their devotion, and at the end of every song and Oration, they layd downe a sticke betwixt the divisions of Corne. Till night, neither he nor they did either eate or drinke; and then they feasted merrily, with the best provisions they could make. Three dayes they vsed this Ceremony; the meaning whereof they told him, was to know if he intended them well or no. The circle of meale signified their Country, the circles of corne the bounds of Sea, and the stickes his Country. They imagined the world to be flat and round, like a trencher; and they in the middest.

After this they brought him a bagge of gunpowder, which they carefully preserved till the next spring, to plant as they did their corne; because they would be acquainted with the nature of that seede.

Opitchapam the Kings brother invited him to his house, where, with as many platters of bread, foule, and wild beasts, as did environ him, he bid him wellcome; but not any of them would eate a bit with him, but put vp all the remainder in Baskets.

At his returne to *Opechancanoughs,* all the Kings women, and their children, flocked about him for their parts; as a due by Custome, to be merry with such fragments.

> But his waking mind in hydeous dreames did oft see wondrous shapes,
> Of bodies strange, and huge in growth, and of stupendious makes.

At last they brought him to *Meronocomoco* [5 *Jan.* 1608], where was *Powhatan* their Emperor. Here more than two hundred of those grim Courtiers stood wondering at him, as he had beene a monster; till *Powhatan* and his trayne had put themselues in their greatest braveries. Before a fire vpon a seat like a bedsted, he sat covered with a great robe, made of *Rarowcun* skinnes, and all the tayles hanging by. On either hand did sit a young wench of 16 or 18 yeares, and along on each side the house, two rowes of men, and behind them as many women, with all their heads and shoulders painted red: many of their heads bedecked with the white downe of Birds; but every one with something: and a great chayne of white beads about their necks.

At his entrance before the King, all the people gaue a great shout. The

Queene of *Appamatuck* was appointed to bring him water to wash his hands, and another brought him a bunch of feathers, in stead of a Towell to dry them: having feasted him after their best barbarous manner they could, a long consultation was held, but the conclusion was, two great stones were brought before *Powhatan:* then as many as could layd hands on him, dragged him to them, and thereon laid his head, and being ready with their clubs, to beate out his braines, *Pocahontas* the Kings dearest daughter, when no intreaty could prevaile, got his head in her armes, and laid her owne vpon his to saue him from death: whereat the Emperour was contented he should liue to make him hatchets, and her bells, beads, and copper; for they thought him as well of all occupations as themselues. For the King himselfe will make his owne robes, shooes, bowes, arrowes, pots; plant, hunt, or doe any thing so well as the rest.

> They say he bore a pleasant shew,
> But sure his heart was sad.
> For who can pleasant be, and rest,
> That liues in feare and dread:
> And having life suspected, doth
> It still suspected lead.

Two dayes after [7 *Jan.* 1608], *Powhatan* having disguised himselfe in the most fearefullest manner he could, caused Captain *Smith* to be brought forth to a great house in the woods, and there vpon a mat by the fire to be left alone. Not long after from behinde a mat that divided the house, was made the most dolefullest noyse he ever heard; then *Powhatan* more like a devill then a man, with some two hundred more as blacke as himselfe, came vnto him and told him now they were friends, and presently he should goe to *Iames* towne, to send him two great gunnes, and a gryndstone, for which he would giue him the Country of *Capahowosick*, and for ever esteeme him as his sonne *Nantaquoud*.

2

Anne Bradstreet (c. 1612–1672)

To my Dear Children and
In reference to her Children

Anne Bradstreet arrived in Massachusetts with her parents and husband in 1630, alarmed to find, as she says below, "a new world and new manners, at which my heart rose. But after I was convinced it was the way of God, I submitted to it." She had enjoyed a privileged life and good education. Her father, Thomas Dudley, had been steward to the Earl of Lincoln, and he became deputy governor of the Massachusetts Bay Company. Her husband Simon later was governor.

Wealth and education did not fully protect her from the hazards of pioneer life: in particular, a harsh climate, illness, the birth of eight children, and the loss of a house in a fire. Out of these experiences she drew occasions for some of her best poetry, the first collection of which was published at the instigation of her family, without her knowledge or consent, in 1650. The Tenth Muse, as this collection was entitled, vividly evokes the feelings of a Puritan woman, especially the satisfactions she got from her children and family life, yet, in its ironies and exaggerated humility, it often protests against the restrictions of the woman's role.

These two autobiographical letters to her children are not ironic in this way, but they do reveal her gentle mixtures of play and seriousness and her strict adherence to the Puritan world view. Every event, and especially every affliction, must be examined for its divine message. Sickness is an occasion for reviewing one's spiritual life and can become a blessing. Thus, despite misery and dependence, the individual life is also exalted. It is the site of cosmic contest between good and evil. God makes himself manifest to each and every soul.

These two pieces allow for interesting comparison and contrast: both are addressed to her children, but in different forms and different moods. Further, one can ask whether the primary audience is really the children or herself.

The best reader's edition of Bradstreet, which has an excellent foreword by Adrienne Rich, is The Works of Anne Bradstreet, ed. Jeannine Hensley (Cambridge: Harvard Univ. Press, 1967). "To my Dear Children" was written in 1656. The actual date for "In reference to her Children . . ." is not 1656, as stated in its title, but 1659.

To my Dear Children

This Book by Any yet unread,
I leave for you when I am dead,
That, being gone, here you may find
What was your liveing mother's mind.
Make use of what I leave in Love
And God shall blesse you from above.
A.B.

My Dear Children

I, knowing by experience that the exhortations of parents take most effect when the speakers leave to speak, and those especially sink deepest which are spoke latest—and being ignorant whether on my death bed I shall have opportunity to speak to any of you, much lesse to All—thought it be best, whilst I was able to compose some short matters, (for what else to call them I know not) and bequeath to you, that when I am no more with you, yet I may bee dayly in your remembrance, (Although that is the least in my aim in what I now doe) but that you may gain some spiritual Advantage by my experience. I have not studyed in this you read to show my skill, but to declare the Truth—not to sett forth myself, but the Glory of God. If I had minded the former, it had been perhaps better pleasing to you,—but seing the last is the best, let it bee best pleasing to you.

The method I will observe shall bee this—I will begin with God's dealing with me from my childhood to this Day. In my young years, about 6 or 7 as I take it, I began to make conscience of my wayes, and what I knew was sinfull, as lying, disobedience to Parents, &c. I avoided it. If at any time I was overtaken with the like evills, it was a great Trouble. I could not be at rest till by prayer I had confest it unto God. I was also troubled at the neglect of Private Dutyes, tho: too often tardy that way. I also found much comfort in reading the Scriptures, especially those places I thought most concerned my Condition, and as I grew to have more understanding, so the more solace I took in them.

In a long fitt of sicknes which I had on my bed I often communed with my heart, and made my supplication to the most High who sett me free from that affliction.

But as I grew up to bee about 14 or 15 I found my heart more carnall, and sitting loose from God, vanity and the follyes of youth take hold of me.

About 16, the Lord layd his hand sore upon me and smott mee with the small pox. When I was in my affliction, I besought the Lord, and confessed my Pride and Vanity and he was entreated of me, and again restored me. But I rendered not to him according to the benefitt received.

After a short time I changed my condition and was marryed, and came

40

into this Country, where I found a new world and new manners, at which my heart rose. But after I was convinced it was the way of God, I submitted to it and joined to the church at Boston.

After some time I fell into a lingering sickness like a consumption, together with a lamenesse, which correction I saw the Lord sent to humble and try me and doe mee Good: and it was not altogether ineffectuall.

It pleased God to keep me a long time without a child, which was a great grief to me, and cost mee many prayers and tears before I obtaind one, and after him gave mee many more, of whom I now take the care, that as I have brought you into the world, and with great paines, weaknes, cares, and feares brought you to this, I now travail in birth again of you till Christ bee formed in you.

Among all my experiences of God's gratious Dealings with me I have constantly observed this, that he hath never suffered me long to sitt loose from him, but by one affliction or other hath made me look home, and search what was amisse—so usually thus it hath been with me that I have no sooner felt my heart out of order, but I have expected correction for it, which most commonly hath been upon my own person, in sicknesse, weaknes, paines, sometimes on my soul, in Doubts and feares of God's displeasure, and my sincerity towards him, sometimes he hath smott a child with sicknes, sometimes chasstened by losses in estate,—and these Times (thro: his great mercy) have been the times of my greatest Getting and Advantage, yea I have found them the Times when the Lord hath manifested the most Love to me. Then have I gone to searching, and have said with David, Lord search me and try me, see what wayes of wickednes are in me, and lead me in the way everlasting: and seldome or never but I have found either some sin I lay under which God would have reformed, or some duty neglected which he would have performed. And by his help I have layd Vowes and Bonds upon my Soul to perform his righteous commands.

If at any time you are chastened of God, take it as thankfully and Joyfully as in greatest mercyes, for if yee bee his yee shall reap the greatest benefitt by it. It hath been no small support to me in times of Darkness when the Almighty hath hid his face from me, that yet I have had abundance of sweetnes and refreshment after affliction, and more circumspection in my walking after I have been afflicted. I have been with God like an untoward child, that no longer then the rod has been on my back (or at least in sight) but I have been apt to forgett him and myself too. Before I was afflicted I went astray, but now I keep thy statutes.

I have had great experience of God's hearing my Prayers, and returning comfortable Answers to me, either in granting the Thing I prayed for, or else in satisfying my mind without it; and I have been confident it hath been from him, because I have found my heart through his goodnes enlarged in Thankfullnes to him.

I have often been perplexed that I have not found that constant Joy in my Pilgrimage and refreshing which I supposed most of the servants of God have; although he hath not left me altogether without the wittnes of his holy spirit, who hath oft given mee his word and sett to his Seal that it shall bee well with me. I have sometimes tasted of that hidden Manna that the world knowes not, and have sett up my Ebenezer, and have resolved with myself that against such a promis, such tasts of sweetnes, the Gates of Hell shall never prevail. Yet have I many Times sinkings and droopings, and not enjoyed that felicity that sometimes I have done. But when I have been in darkness and seen no light, yet have I desired to stay my self upon the Lord.

And, when I have been in sicknes and pain, I have thought if the Lord would but lift up the light of his Countenance upon me, altho: he ground me to powder, it would bee but light to me; yea, oft have I thought were it hell itself, and could there find the Love of God toward me, it would bee a Heaven. And, could I have been in Heaven without the Love of God, it would have been a Hell to me; for, in Truth, it is the absence and presence of God that makes Heaven or Hell.

Many times hath Satan troubled me concerning the verity of the scriptures, many times by Atheisme how I could know whether there was a God; I never saw any miracles to confirm me, and those which I read of how did I know but they were feigned. That there is a God my Reason would soon tell me by the wondrous workes that I see, the vast frame of the Heaven and the Earth, the order of all things, night and day, Summer and Winter, Spring and Autumne, the dayly providing for this great houshold upon the Earth, the preserving and directing to All to its proper end. The consideration of these things would with amazement certainly resolve me that there is an Eternall Being.

But how should I know he is such a God as I worship in Trinity, and such a Saviour as I rely upon? tho: this hath thousands of Times been suggested to mee, yet God hath helped me over. I have argued thus with myself. That there is a God I see. If ever this God hath revealed himself, it must bee in his word, and this must bee it or none. Have I not found that operation by it that no humane Invention can work upon the Soul? hath not Judgments befallen Diverse who have scorned and contemd it? hath it not been preserved thro: All Ages maugre all the heathen Tyrants and all of the enemyes who have opposed it? Is there any story but that which showes the beginnings of Times, and how the world came to bee as wee see? Doe wee not know the prophecyes in it fullfilled which could not have been so long foretold by any but God himself?

When I have gott over this Block, then have I another putt in my way, That admitt this bee the true God whom wee worship, and that bee his word, yet why may not the Popish Religion bee the right? They have the same God, the same Christ, the same word: they only enterprett it one way, wee another.

This hath sometimes stuck with me, and more it would, but the vain fooleries that are in their Religion, together with their lying miracles and cruell persecutions of the Saints, which admitt were they as they terme them, yet not so to bee dealt withall.

The consideration of these things and many the like would soon turn me to my own Religion again.

But some new Troubles I have had since the world has been filled with Blasphemy, and Sectaries, and some who have been accounted sincere Christians have been carryed away with them, that somtimes I have said, Is there faith upon the earth? and I have not known what to think. But then I have remembred the words of Christ that so it must bee, and that, if it were possible, the very elect should bee deceived. Behold, saith our Saviour, I have told you before. That hath stayed my heart, and I can now say, Return, O my Soul, to thy Rest, upon this Rock Christ Jesus will I build my faith; and, if I perish, I perish. But I know all the Powers of Hell shall never prevail against it. I know whom I have trusted, and whom I have beleived, and that he is able to keep that I have committed to his charge.

Now to the King, Immortall, Eternall, and invisible, the only wise God, bee Honoure and Glory for ever and ever! Amen.

This was written in much sicknesse and weaknes, and is very weakly and imperfectly done; but, if you can pick any Benefitt out of it, it is the marke which I aimed at.

In reference to her Children, 23. June, 1656

> I had eight birds hatcht in one nest,
> Four Cocks there were, and Hens the rest,
> I nurst them up with pain and care,
> Nor cost, nor labour did I spare,
> Till at the last they felt their wing.
> Mounted the Trees, and learn'd to sing;
> Chief of the Brood then took his flight,
> To Regions far, and left me quite:
> My mournful chirps I after send,
> Till he return, or I do end,
> Leave not thy nest, thy Dam and Sire,
> Fly back and sing amidst this Quire.
> My second bird did take her flight,
> And with her mate flew out of sight;
> *Southward* they both their course did bend,
> And Seasons twain they there did spend.
> Till after blown by *Southern* gales,
> They Norward steer'd with filléd sayles.

43

A prettier bird was no where seen,
Along the Beach among the treen.
I have a third of colour white,
On whom I plac'd no small delight;
Coupled with mate loving and true,
Hath also bid her Dam adieu:
And where *Aurora* first appears,
She now hath percht, to spend her years;
One to the Academy flew
To chat among that learned crew:
Ambition moves still in his breast
That he might chant above the rest,
Striving for more then to do well,
That nightingales he might excell.
My fifth, whose down is yet scarce gone
Is 'mongst the shrubs and bushes flown,
And as his wings increase in strength,
On higher boughs he'l pearch at length.
My other three, still with me nest,
Untill they'r grown, then as the rest,
Or here or there, they'l take their flight,
As is ordain'd, so shall they light.
If birds could weep, then would my tears
Let others know what are my fears
Lest this my brood some harm should catch,
And be surpriz'd for want of watch,
Whilst pecking corn, and void of care
They fall un'wares in Fowlers snare:
Or whilst on trees they sit and sing,
Some untoward boy at them do sling:
Or whilst allur'd with bell and glass,
The net be spread, and caught, alas.
Or least by Lime-twigs they be foyl'd,
Or by some greedy hawks be spoyl'd.
O would my young, ye saw my breast,
And knew what thoughts there sadly rest,
Great was my pain when I you bred,
Great was my care, when I you fed,
Long did I keep you soft and warm,
And with my wings kept off all harm,
My cares are more, and fears then ever,
My throbs such now, as 'fore were never:
Alas my birds, you wisdome want,

Of perils you are ignorant,
Oft times in grass, on trees, in flight,
Sore accidents on you may light.
O to your safety have an eye,
So happy may you live and die:
Mean while my dayes in tunes Ile spend,
Till my weak layes with me shall end.
In shady woods I'le sit and sing,
And things that past, to mind I'le bring.
Once young and pleasant, as are you,
But former toyes (no joyes) adieu.
My age I will not once lament,
But sing, my time so near is spent.
And from the top bough take my flight,
Into a country beyond sight,
Where old ones, instantly grow young,
And there with Seraphims set song:
No seasons cold, nor storms they see;
But spring lasts to eternity,
When each of you shall in your nest
Among your young ones take your rest,
In chirping language, oft them tell,
You had a Dam that lov'd you well,
That did what could be done for young,
And nurst you up till you were strong,
And 'fore she once would let you fly,
She shew'd you joy and misery;
Taught what was good, and what was ill,
What would save life, and what would kill?
Thus gone, amonst you I may live,
And dead, yet speak, and counsel give:
Farewel my birds, farewel adieu,
I happy am, if well with you.

3

Mary Rowlandson (c. 1635–1711)

from *A True History of the Captivity and Restoration of Mrs. Mary Rowlandson*

Beyond what she tells in this narrative, little is known of Mary Rowlandson. The wife of the Reverend Joseph Rowlandson of Lancaster, Massachusetts, she was captured in a raid on Lancaster in February, 1675/76, while her husband was on a journey to Boston to obtain aid for the town's defense. She was ransomed in Princeton, Massachusetts, May 2. The following year she and her husband moved to Wethersfield, Connecticut, where he returned to the ministry. He died in 1678, and she married Captain Samuel Talcott of Connecticut.

A careful and patient reader of this narrative, however, can learn a lot about her and about Puritanism. The full title of the first American edition, Boston, 1682, was *The Soveraignty and Goodness of God, Together with the Faithfulness of his Promises Displayed; Being a Narrative of the Captivity and Restauration of Mrs. Mary Rowlandson*—a title which assigns all the credits to the deity. God willed all these events as punishments for her sin, tests of her faith, and signs of his mercy. These lessons are reinforced in her numerous quotations from scripture. Even the Indians are part of the plan: they are devils unknowingly serving as agents of God.

The full title of the English edition, also 1682, was *A True History of the Captivity and Restoration of Mrs. Mary Rowlandson, A Minister's Wife in New-England: Wherein is set forth, The Cruel and Inhumane Usage she underwent amongst the Heathens for Eleven Weeks time: And her Deliverance from them. Written by her own Hand, for her Private Use: and now made Public at the earnest Desire of some Friends, for the Benefit of the Afflicted.* This second title places more emphasis on Indian cruelty and her suffering.

The careful reader can also see that Mary Rowlandson was one tough lady, a woman who kept up her courage and did not just wilt in self-pity. In the course of her captivity and its "removes" from place to place, she learned to eat food she would once have scorned. She knitted and did other kinds of work, sometimes to please her captors and sometimes to be independent of them. She even began to take a certain interest in Indian manners, finding King Philip rather polite and appreciating the fact that no one physically molested her. Even her turning down of the chance to run away may be a sign of her fortitude and good sense, rather than meek passivity, as some people have thought. She "desired to wait God's time."

Thus Puritanism not only exalted God, it also exalted the individual and the individual's experience as the microcosm in which, as in Puritan society and Puritan history generally, the workings of God could be examined. This gave Mary Rowlandson both the strength to endure her captivity and the reason to write about it.

The text, including bracketed editorial notes and preserving original punctuation, spelling, and italics, is from the selection edited by Amy Schrager Lang, in *Journeys in New Worlds: Early American Women's Narratives,* ed. William L. Andrews (Madison: Univ. of Wisconsin Press, 1990). For critical commentary, see Lang's introduction to the selection in that volume and *Held Captive by Indians: Selected Narratives, 1642–1836,* ed. Richard VanDerBeets (Knoxville: Univ. of Tennessee Press, 1973).

On the tenth of February, 1675, came the *Indians* with great number upon Lancaster. Their first coming was about Sun-rising. Hearing the noise of some guns, we looked out; several Houses were burning, and the smoke ascending to Heaven. There were five persons taken in one House, the Father and the Mother, and a sucking Child, they knock'd on the head; the other two they took, and carried away alive. There were two others, who, being out of their Garrison upon some occasion, were set upon; one was knock'd on the head, the other escaped. Another there was, who, running along, was shot and wounded, and fell down; he begged of them his Life, promising them Money, (as they told me;) but they would not hearken to him, but knock'd him on the head, stripped him naked, and split open his Bowels. Another, seeing many of the *Indians* about his Barn, ventured and went out, but was quickly shot down. There were three others belonging to the same Garrison who were killed. The *Indians,* getting up upon the Roof of the Barn, had advantage to shoot down upon them over their Fortification. Thus these murtherous Wretches went on, burning and destroying before them.

At length they came and beset our own House, and quickly it was the dolefullest day that ever mine eyes saw. The House stood upon the edge of a Hill; some of the *Indians* got behind the Hill, others into the Barn, and others behind any thing that would shelter them; from all which Places they shot against the House, so that the Bullets seemed to fly like Hail; and quickly they wounded one Man among us, then another, and then a third. About two Hours (according to my observation in that amazing time) they had been about the House before they could prevail to fire it, (which they did with flax and Hemp, which they brought out of the Barn, and there being no Defence about the House, only two Flankers,[1] at two opposite Corners, and one of them not finished). They fired it once, and one ventured out and quenched

1. "Flankers": projecting fortifications.

it; but they quickly fired it again, and that took. Now is that dreadful Hour come that I have often heard of, (in the time of the War, as it was the Case of others,) but now mine Eyes see it. Some in our House were fighting for their Lives, others wallowing in their Blood; the House on fire over our Heads, and the bloody Heathen ready to knock us on the Head if we stirred out. Now might we hear Mothers and Children crying out for themselves and one another, *Lord, what shall we do?* Then I took my Children (and one of my Sisters, hers) to go forth and leave the House; but as soon as we came to the Door and appeared, the *Indians* shot so thick that the Bullets rattled against the House as if one had taken an handful of Stones and threw them; so that we were fain to give back. We had six stout Dogs belonging to our Garrison, but none of them would stir, though another time, if an *Indian* had come to the Door, they were ready to fly upon him, and tear him down. The Lord hereby would make us the more to acknowledge his Hand, and to see that our Help is always in him. But out we must go, the Fire increasing and coming along behind us roaring, and the *Indians* gaping before us with their Guns, Spears, and Hatchets to devour us. No sooner were we out of the House but my Brother-in-Law (being before wounded, in defending the House, in or near the Throat) fell down dead, whereat the *Indians* scornfully shouted and hallowed, and were presently upon him, stripping off his Clothes. The Bullets flying thick, one went thorow my side, and the same (as would seem) thorow the Bowels and Hand of my dear Child in my Arms.[2] One of my eldest Sister's Children (named William) had then his Leg broken, which the *Indians* perceiving, they knock'd him on the head. Thus were we butchered by those merciless Heathen, standing amazed, with the Blood running down to our Heels. My elder sister, being yet in the House, and seeing those woful Sights, the Infidels hauling Mothers one way and Children another, and some wallowing in their Blood, and her elder son telling her that (her Son) William was dead, and myself was wounded; she said, *And, Lord, let me die with them!* which was no sooner said but she was struck with a Bullet, and fell down dead over the Threshold. I hope she is reaping the Fruit of her good Labours, being faithful to the Service of God in her Place. In her younger years she lay under much trouble upon Spiritual accounts, till it pleased God to make that precious Scripture take hold of her Heart, 2 *Cor.* xii. 9, *And he said unto me, My grace is sufficient for thee.* More than twenty years after, I have heard her tell how sweet and comfortable that Place was to her. But to return: the *Indians* laid hold of us, pulling me one way and the Children another, and said, *Come, go along with us.* I told them they would kill me. They answered, *If I were willing to go along with them, they would not hurt me.*

O the doleful Sight that now was to behold at this House! *Come, behold the works of the Lord, what desolation he has made in the earth.* Of thirty seven

---

2. "My dear child in my arms": Sarah, age six.

Persons who were in this one House, none escaped either present Death or a bitter Captivity, save only one, who might say as he, *Job* i. 15, *And I only am escaped alone to tell the news.* There were twelve killed, some shot, some stabb'd with their Spears, some knock'd down with their Hatchets. When we are in prosperity, oh the Little that we think of such dreadful Sights; and to see our dear Friends and Relations lie bleeding out their Heart-blood upon the Ground! There was one who was chopped into the Head with a Hatchet, and stripp'd naked, and yet was crawling up and down. It was a solemn Sight to see so many Christians lying in their Blood, some here and some there, like a company of Sheep torn by Wolves; all of them stript naked by a company of hell-hounds, roaring, singing, ranting, and insulting, as if they would have torn our very hearts out; yet the Lord, by his Almighty power, preserved a number of us from death, for there were twenty-four of us taken alive; and carried Captive.

I had often before this said, that if the *Indians* should come, I should chuse rather to be killed by them than taken alive; but when it came to the trial my mind changed; their glittering Weapons so daunted my Spirit, that I chose rather to go along with those (as I may say) ravenous Bears, than that moment to end my daies. And that I may the better declare what happened to me during that grievous Captivity, I shall particularly speak of the several Removes we had up and down the Wilderness.

The first Remove.—Now away we must go with those Barbarous Creatures, with our bodies wounded and bleeding, and our hearts no less than our bodies. About a mile we went that night; up upon a hill, within sight of the Town, where they intended to lodge. There was hard by a vacant house; (deserted by the English before for fear of the *Indians;*) I asked them whether I might not lodge in the house that night? to which they answered, What, will you love *English-men* still? This was the dolefullest night that ever my eyes saw: oh the roaring, and singing, and dancing, and yelling of those black creatures in the night, which made the place a lively resemblance of hell! And as miserable was the waste that was there made of Horses, Cattle, Sheep, Swine, Calves, Lambs, Roasting Pigs, and Fowls, (which they had plundered in the Town,) some roasting, some lying and burning, and some boyling, to feed our merciless Enemies; who were joyful enough, though we were disconsolate. To add to the dolefulness of the former day, and the dismalness of the present night, my thoughts ran upon my losses and sad bereaved condition. All was gone; my Husband gone, (at least separated from me, he being in the Bay; and, to add to my grief, the *Indians* told me they would kill him as he came homeward,) my Children gone, my Relations and Friends gone, our house and home, and all our comforts within door and without, all was gone, (except my life,) and I knew not but the next moment that might go too.

There remained nothing to me but one poor wounded Babe, and it seemed at present worse than death that it was in such a pitiful condition, bespeaking Compassion, and I had no refreshing for it, nor suitable things to revive it. Little do many think what is the savageness and brutishness of this barbarous Enemy, even those that seem to profess[3] more than others among them, when the *English* have fallen into their hands.

Those seven that were killed at Lancaster the summer before, upon a Sabbath-day, and the one that was afterward killed upon a week day, were slain and mangled in a barbarous manner by one-eyed John, and Marlberough's Praying *Indians*,[4] which Capt. Mosely[5] brought to Boston, as the *Indians* told me.

The second Remove.—But now (the next morning) I must turn my back upon the Town, and travel with them into the vast and desolate Wilderness, I know not whither. It is not my tongue or pen can express the sorrows of my heart and bitterness of my spirit that I had at this departure: but God was with me in a wonderful manner, carrying me along, and bearing up my Spirit, that it did not quite fail. One of the *Indians* carried my poor wounded Babe upon a horse: it went moaning all along, I shall die, I shall die! I went on foot after it, with sorrow that cannot be exprest. At length I took it off the horse, and carried it in my arms, till my strength failed, and I fell down with it. Then they set me upon a horse, with my wounded Child in my lap; and there being no Furniture upon the horse back; as we were going down a steep hill, we both fell over the horse's head, at which they, like inhuman creatures, laught, and rejoiced to see it, though I thought we should there have ended our dayes, as overcome with so many difficulties. But the Lord renewed my strength still, and carried me along, that I might see more of his power, yea, so much that I could never have thought of had I not experienced it.

After this it quickly began to Snow; and when night came on they stopt; and now down I must sit in the Snow, (by a little fire and a few boughs behind me,) with my sick Child in my lap; and calling much for water, being now (thorough the wound) fallen into a violent Fever; (my own wound also growing so stiff that I could scarce sit down or rise up;) yet so it must be, that I must sit all this cold winter night upon the cold snowy ground, with my sick Child in my arms, looking that every hour would be the last of its life; and having no Christian Friend near me, either to comfort or help me. Oh I may see the wonderful power of God, that my Spirit did not utterly sink under my affliction!—still the Lord upheld me with his gracious and merciful Spirit, and we were both alive to see the light of the next morning.

3. "Profess": that is, profess Christianity.
4. "One-eyed John, and Marlberough's Praying Indians": Rowlandson refers here to a raid on the outskirts of Lancaster the previous August led by "One-eyed" John Monoco, chief of the Nashaway Indians, and involving the Christian Indians who owned 150 acres in the town of Marlborough, ten miles from Lancaster.
5. "Capt. Mosely": an ex-Jamaica privateer and a notorious Indian-hater, Samuel Mosely was one of the most popular and cruelest officers in the English army.

The third Remove.—The morning being come, they prepared to go on their way. One of the Indians got up upon a horse, and they set me up behind him, with my poor sick Babe in my lap. A very wearisome and tedious day I had of it; what with my own wound, and my Child's being so exceeding sick, and in a lamentable Condition with her wound. It may easily be judged what a poor feeble condition we were in, there being not the least crumb of refreshing that came within either of our mouths from Wednesday night to Saturday night, except only a little cold water. This day in the afternoon, about an hour by Sun, we came to the place where they intended, *viz.* an *Indian town* called Wenimesset, Northward of Quabaug. When we were come, Oh the number of Pagans (now merciless Enemies) that there came about me, that I may say as *David,* Psal. xxvii. 13. *I had fainted, unless I had believed,* &c. The next day was the Sabbath: I then remembered how careless I had been of God's holy time; how many Sabbaths I had lost and mispent, and how evilly I had walked in God's sight; which lay so close upon my Spirit, that it was easie for me to see how righteous it was with God to cut off the thread of my life, and cast me out of his presence for ever. Yet the Lord still shewed mercy to me, and upheld me; and as he wounded me with one hand, so he healed me with the other. This day there came to me one Robert Pepper, (a Man belonging to Roxbury,) who was taken in Capt. Beers his fight; and had been now a considerable time with the *Indians;* and up with them almost as far as Albany, to see King Philip, as he told me, and was now very lately come with them into these parts. Hearing, I say, that I was in this *Indian* Town, he obtained leave to come and see me. He told me he himself was wounded in the Leg, at Capt. Beers his fight; and was not able sometime to go, but as they carried him, and that he took oaken leaves and laid to his wound, and through the blessing of God he was able to travel again. Then I took oaken leaves and laid to my side, and with the blessing of God it cured me also; yet before the cure was wrought, I may say as it is in *Psal.* xxxviii. 5, 6, *My wounds stink and are corrupt, I am troubled, I am bowed down greatly, I go mourning all the day long.* I sate much alone with a poor wounded Child in my lap, which mourned night and day, having nothing to revive the body or chear the Spirits of her; but, instead of that, sometimes one Indian would come and tell me one hour, And your Master will knock your Child in the head, and then a second, and then a third, Your Master will quickly knock your Child in the head.

This was the Comfort I had from them; miserable comforters are ye all, as he said. Thus nine dayes I sat upon my knees, with my babe in my lap, till my flesh was raw again. My child, being even ready to depart this sorrowful world, they bad me carry it out to another Wigwam; (I suppose because they would not be troubled with such spectacles;) whither I went with a very heavy heart, and down I sate with the picture of death in my lap. About two hours in the Night, my sweet Babe, like a Lamb, departed this life, on Feb. 18, 1675 [1676] it being about six years and five months old. It was nine dayes (from the first wounding) in this Miserable condition, without any refreshing of one nature or other, except a little cold water. I cannot but take notice how, at another time, I could not bear to be in the room where any dead person was; but now the case is changed; I must and could lye down by my dead Babe, side by side, all the night after. I have thought since of the wonderful goodness of God to me, in preserving me so in the use of my reason and senses in that distressed time, that I did not use wicked and violent means to end my own miserable life. In the morning, when they understood that my child was dead, they sent for me home to my Master's Wigwam; (by my Master, in this writing, must be understood Quannopin, who was a Saggamore, and married King Philip's wife's Sister; not that he first took me, but I was sold to him by another *Narrhaganset Indian,* who took me when first I came out of the Garrison). I went to take up my dead Child in my arms to carry it with me, but they bid me let it alone; there was no resisting, but go I must and leave it. When I had been a while at my Master's wigwam, I took the first opportunity I could get to go look after my dead child. When I came, I asked them what they had done with it. They told me it was upon the hill; then they went and shewed me where it was, where I saw the ground was newly digged, and there they told me they had buried it; there I left that child in the Wilderness, and must commit it, and myself also, in this wilder-ness condition, to Him who is above all. God having taken away this dear child, I went to see my daughter Mary, who was at the same *Indian Town,* at a Wigwam not very far off, though we had little liberty or opportunity to see one another: she was about ten years old, and taken from the door at first by a Praying *Indian,* and afterward sold for a gun. When I came in sight she would fall a-weeping; at which they were provoked, and would not let me come near her, but bade me be gone, which was a heart-cutting word to me. I had one child dead, another in the wilderness I knew not where, the third they would not let me come near to: *Me* (as he said) *have ye bereaved of my children; Joseph is not, and Simeon is not, and ye will take Benjamin also, all these things are against me.* I could not sit still in this condition, but kept walking from one place to another: and as I was going along, my heart was even overwhelmed with the thoughts of my condition, and that I should have Children and a Nation which I knew not ruled over them; whereupon I earnestly intreated the Lord that he would consider my low estate, and shew me a token for good, and, if it were his blessed will, some sign and hope of some relief: and indeed quickly the Lord answered, in some measure, my poor Prayer; for, as I was going up and down, mourning and lamenting my condition, my Son came to me, and asked me how I did. I had not seen him before since the destruction of the Town; and I knew not where he was till I was informed by himself, that he was amongst a smaller parcel of *Indians,* whose place was about six miles off. With tears in his eyes, he asked me whether his sister Sarah was dead, and told me he had seen his Sister Mary; and prayed me that I would not be troubled in reference to himself. The occasion of his coming to see me at this time was this: There was, as I said, about six miles from us a small Plantation of *Indians,* where it seems he had been during his Captivity; and at this time there were some Forces of the *Indians* gathered out of our company, and some also from them, (amongst whom was my Son's Master,) to go to assault and burn Medfield: in this time of the absence of his Master, his Dame brought him to see me. I took this to be some gracious Answer to my earnest and unfeigned desire. The next day, *viz.* to this, the *Indians* returned from Medfield, (all the Company, for those that belonged to the other smaller company came thorow the Town that now we were at). But before they came to us, Oh the outragious roaring and hopping that there was! They began their din about a mile before they came to us. By their noise and hooping, they signified how many they had destroyed; (which was at that time twenty-three). Those that were with us at home were gathered together as soon as they heard the hooping, and every time that the other went over their number, these at home gave a shout, that the very Earth rang again; and thus they continued till those that had been upon the expedition were come up to the Saggamore's Wigwam; and then, Oh the hideous insulting and triumphing that there was over some *English-men's* Scalps that they had taken (as their manner is) and brought with them! I cannot but take notice of the wonderful mercy of God to me in those afflictions, in sending me a Bible: one of the *Indians* that came from Medfield fight, and had brought some plunder; came to me, and asked me if I would have a Bible, he had got one in his Basket. I was glad of it, and asked him whether he thought the *Indians* would let me read. He answered, yes. So I took the Bible, and in that melancholy time it came into my mind to read first the 28th *Chapter* of *Deuteronomie,* which I did; and when I had read it, my dark heart wrought on this manner, that there was no mercy for me; that the blessings were gone, and the curses came in their room, and that I had lost my opportunity. But the Lord helped me to go on reading till I came to *Chap.* xxx, the seven first verses; where I found there was mercy promised again, if we would return to him by repentance; and though we were scattered from one end of the earth to the other, yet the Lord would gather us together, and turn all those curses upon our Enemies. I do not desire to live to forget this Scripture, and what comfort it was to me.

Now the *Indians* began to talk of removing from this place, some one way and some another. There were now, besides myself, nine *English* Captives in this place, (all of them Children, except one Woman). I got an opportunity to go and take my leave of them; they being to go one way and I another. I asked them whether they were earnest with God for deliverance; they all told me they did as they were able; and it was some comfort to me that the Lord stirred up Children to look to him. The Woman, *viz.* Good wife Joslin, told me she should never see me again, and that she could find in her heart to run away. I wisht her not to run away by any means, for we were near thirty miles from any *English* Town, and she very big with Child, and had but one week to reckon; and another Child in her arms two years old; and bad rivers there were to go over, and we were feeble with our poor and coarse entertainment. I had my Bible with me; I pulled it out; and asked her whether she would read; we opened the Bible, and lighted on *Psal.* xxvii, in which Psalm we especially took notice of that, *ver. ult. Wait on the Lord, be of good courage, and he shall strengthen thine heart; wait, I say, on the Lord.*

. . .

The seventh Remove.—After a restless and hungry night there, we had a wearisome time of it the next day. The Swamp by which we lay was, as it were, a deep Dungeon, and an exceeding high and steep hill before it. Before I got to the top of the hill, I thought my heart and legs and all would have broken and failed me; what through faintness and soreness of Body, it was a grievous day of Travel to me. As we went along, I saw a place where *English* Cattle had been; that was a comfort to me, such as it was. Quickly after that we came to an *English* path, which so took with me that I thought I could there have freely lyen down and died. That day, a little after noon, we came to Squaukheag; where the *Indians* quickly spread themselves over the deserted *English* Fields, gleaning what they could find; some pickt up Ears of Wheat that were crickled down; some found ears of *Indian Corn;* some found Ground-nuts, and others sheaves of wheat, that were frozen together in the Shock, and went to threshing of them out. Myself got two Ears of *Indian Corn;* and whilst I did but turn my back, one of them was stollen from me, which much troubled me. There came an *Indian* to them at that time with a Basket of *Horse-liver.* I asked him to give me a piece. What, (says he) can you eat Horse-liver? I told him I would try, if he would give me a piece; which he did; and I laid it on the coals to roast; but before it was half ready, they got half of it away from me; so that I was fain to take the rest, and eat it as it was, with the blood about my mouth, and yet a savory bit it was to me; for to the hungry soul every bitter thing is sweet. A solemn sight me thought it was to see whole fields of Wheat and *Indian Corn* forsaken and spoiled; and the remainders of them to be food for our merciless Enemies. That night we had a mess of Wheat for our supper.

The eighth Remove.—On the morrow morning we must go over the River, *i.e.* Connecticut, to meet with King Philip. Two Cannoos full they had carried over, the next turn I myself was to go; but as my foot was upon the Cannoo to step in, there was a sudden outcry among them, and I must step back; and, instead of going over the River, I must go four or five miles up the River farther northward. Some of the *Indians* ran one way, and some another. The cause of this rout was, as I thought, their espying some *English* Scouts who were thereabout.

In this travel up the River, about noon the Company made a stop, and sat down; some to eat, and others to rest them. As I sate amongst them, musing of things past, my Son Joseph unexpectedly came to me; we asked of each others welfare; bemoaning our doleful condition, and the change that had come upon us: we had Husband and Father, and Children and Sisters, and Friends and Relations, and House and Home, and many Comforts of this life; but now we might say as *Job, Naked came I out of my mother's womb, and naked shall I return; the Lord gave, and the Lord hath taken away, blessed be the name of the Lord.* I asked him, whether he would read? he told me he earnestly desired it. I gave him my Bible, and he lighted upon that comfortable Scripture, *Psal.* cxviii. 17, 18, *I shall not die, but live, and declare the works of the Lord: the Lord hath chastened me sore, yet he hath not given me over to death.* Look here, *Mother,* (says he) did you read this? And here I may take occasion to mention one principal ground of my setting forth these few Lines; even as the Psalmist says, To declare the works of the Lord, and his wonderful power in carrying us along, preserving us in the Wilderness, while under the Enemies hand, and returning of us in safety again; and his goodness in bringing to my hand so many comfortable and suitable Scriptures in my distress. But, to Return: we travelled on till night, and, in the morning, we must go over the River to Philip's Crew. When I was in the Cannoo, I could not but be amazed at the numerous Crew of Pagans that were on the Bank on the other side. When I came ashore, they gathered all about me, I sitting alone in the midst; I observed they asked one another Questions, and laughed, and rejoyced over their Gains and Victories; then my heart began to faile; and I fell a-weeping; which was the first time, to my remembrance, that I wept before them. Although I had met with so much Affliction, and my heart was many times ready to break, yet could I not shed one tear in their sight; but rather had been all this while in a maze, and like one astonished; but now I may say, as *Psal.* cxxxvii. 1, *By the rivers of* Babylon, *there we sate down, yea we wept when we remembered Zion.* There one of them asked me, why I wept? I could hardly tell what to say; yet I answered, they would kill me: No, said he, none will hurt you. Then came one of them and gave me two spoonfuls of Meal to comfort me, and another gave me half a pint of Pease, which was more worth than many Bushels at another time. Then I went to see King Philip; he bade me come in and sit down, and asked me, whether I would smoak it? (an usual Compliment now-a-days amongst Saints and Sinners.) But this no way suited me; for though I had formerly used Tobacco, yet I had left it ever since I was first taken. *It seems to be a Bait the Devil layes to make men lose their precious time.* I remember with shame, how, formerly, when I had taken two or three Pipes, I was presently ready for another, such a bewitching thing it is; but I thank God he has now given me power over it; surely there are many who may be better imployed than to lye sucking a stinking Tobacco-pipe.

Now the *Indians* gather their Forces to go against North-hampton; over night one went about yelling and hooting to give notice of the design; whereupon they fell to boyling of Ground Nuts, and parching of Corn, (as many as had it) for their Provision; and, in the morning, away they went. During my abode in this place Philip spake to me to make a shirt for his Boy, which I did; for which he gave me a shilling; I offered the money to my Master, but he bade me keep it; and with it I bought a piece of Horse flesh. Afterwards I made a Cap for his Boy, for which he invited me to Dinner; I went, and he gave me a Pancake about as big as two fingers; it was made of parched Wheat, beaten and fryed in Bears grease, but I thought I never tasted pleasanter meat in my life. There was a Squaw who spake to me to make a shirt for her Sannup;[6] for which she gave me a piece of Bear. Another asked me to knit a pair of Stockings, for which she gave me a quart of Pease. I boyled my Pease and Bear together, and invited my Master and Mistress to Dinner; but the proud Gossip, because I served them both in one Dish, would eat nothing, except one bit that he gave her upon the point of his Knife. Hearing that my Son was come to this place, I went to see him, and found him lying flat upon the ground; I asked him how he could sleep so? he answered me, that he was not asleep, but at Prayer; and lay so, that they might not observe what he was doing. I pray God he may remember these things, now he is returned in safety. At this place (the Sun now getting higher) what with the beams and heat of the Sun, and the smoak of the Wigwams, I thought I should have been blind: I could scarce discern one Wigwam from another. There was here one Mary Thurston of Medfield, who, seeing how it was with me, lent me a Hat to wear; but as soon as I was gone, the Squaw (who owned that Mary Thurston) came running after me, and got it away again. Here there was a Squaw who gave me one spoonful of Meal; I put it in my Pocket to keep it safe; yet, notwithstanding, somebody stole it, but put five *Indian Corns* in the room of it; which Corns were the greatest Provision I had in my travel for one day.

The *Indians* returning from North-hampton, brought with them some Horses and Sheep, and other things which they had taken; I desired them that they would carry me to Albany upon one of those Horses, and sell me for Powder; for so they had sometimes discoursed. I was utterly hopeless of getting home on foot the way that I came. I could hardly bear to think of the many weary steps I had taken to come to this place.

. . .

The seventeenth Remove.—A comfortable Remove it was to me, because of my hopes. They gave me my pack, and along we went cheerfully; but quickly my Will proved more than my strength; having little or no refreshing, my strength failed, and my spirits were almost quite gone. Now may I say as *David,* Psal. cix. 22, 23, 24, *I am poor and needy, and my heart is wounded within*

6. "Sannup": Algonquin for "husband."

me. I am gone like the shadow when it declineth: I am tossed up and down like the Locust: my knees are weak through fasting, and my flesh faileth of fatness. At night we came to an *Indian Town,* and the *Indians* sate down by a Wigwam discoursing, but I was almost spent, and could scarce speak. I laid down my load, and went into the Wigwam, and there sate an *Indian* boiling of *Horses feet:* (they being wont to eat the flesh first, and when the feet were old and dried, and they had nothing else, they would cut off the feet and use them.) I asked him to give me a little of his Broth, or Water they were boiling in: he took a Dish, and gave me one spoonful of Samp,[7] and bid me take as much of the Broth as I would. Then I put some of the hot water to the Samp, and drank it up, and my spirit came again. He gave me also a piece of the Ruffe or Ridding[8] of the small Guts, and I broiled it on the coals; and now may I say with *Jonathan, See, I pray you, how mine eyes have been enlightened, because I tasted a little of this honey,* I Sam. xiv. 29. Now is my Spirit revived again: though means be never so inconsiderable, yet if the Lord bestow his blessing upon them, they shall refresh both Soul and Body.

The eighteenth Remove.—We took up our packs, and along we went; but a wearisome day I had of it. As we went along I saw an *English-man* stript naked, and lying dead upon the ground, but knew not who it was. Then we came to another Indian Town, where we stayed all night: In this Town there were four *English Children,* Captives: and one of them my own Sister's: I went to see how she did, and she was well, considering her Captive condition. I would have tarried that night with her, but they that owned her would not suffer it. Then I went to another Wigwam, where they were boiling Corn and Beans, which was a lovely sight to see; but I could not get a taste thereof. Then I went into another Wigwam, where there were two of the *English Children:* The Squaw was boiling horses feet; then she cut me off a little piece, and gave one of the *English Children* a piece also: Being very hungry, I had quickly eat up mine; but the Child could not bite it, it was so tough and sinewy, but lay sucking, gnawing, chewing, and slobbering it in the mouth and hand; then I took it of the Child, and eat it myself; and savoury it was to my taste.

That I may say as *Job,* chap. vi. 7, *The things that my Soul refused to touch are as my sorrowful meat.* Thus the Lord made that pleasant and refreshing which another time would have been an Abomination. Then I went home to my Mistress's Wigwam; and they told me I disgraced my Master with begging; and if I did so any more they would knock me on the head: I told them, they had as good knock me on the head as starve me to death.

• • •

On Tuesday morning they called their General Court (as they stiled it) to consult and determine whether I should go home or no: And they all as one

---

7. "Samp": porridge made from coarsely ground Indian corn.
8. "Ruffe" or "Ridding": the refuse or waste portion.

man did seemingly consent to it, that I should go home; except Philip, who would not come among them.

But before I go any further, I would take leave to mention a few remarkable passages of Providence; which I took special notice of in my afflicted time.

1. Of the fair opportunity lost in the long March, a little after the Fortfight, when our *English* Army was so numerous, and in pursuit of the Enemy; and so near as to overtake several and destroy them; and the Enemy in such distress for Food, that our men might track them by their rooting in the Earth for Ground-nuts, whilst they were flying for their lives: I say, that then our Army should want Provision, and be forced to leave their pursuit, and return homeward; and the very next week the Enemy came upon our Town like Bears bereft of their whelps, or so many ravenous Wolves, rending us and our Lambs to death. But what shall I say? God seemed to leave his People to themselves, and ordered all things for his own holy ends. *Shall there be evil in the City and the Lord hath not done it? They are not grieved for the affliction of Joseph, therefore they shall go captive with the first that go Captive. It is the Lord's doing, and it should be marvellous in our Eyes.*

2. I cannot but remember how the *Indians* derided the slowness and dulness of the *English* Army in its setting out: For, after the desolations at Lancaster and Medfield, as I went along with them, they asked me when I thought the *English* Army would come after them? I told them I could not tell: it may be they will come in May, said they. Thus did they scoffe at us, as if the *English* would be a quarter of a Year getting ready.

3. Which also I have hinted before; when the *English* Army with new supplies were sent forth to pursue after the Enemy, and they understanding it; fled before them till they came to Baquaug River, where they forthwith went over safely: that that River should be impassable to the *English,* I cannot but admire to see the wonderful providence of God in preserving the Heathen for farther affliction to our poor Country. They could go in great numbers over, but the *English* must stop: God had an overruling hand in all those things.

4. It was thought, if their Corn were cut down, they would starve and die with hunger: and all their Corn that could be found was destroyed, and they driven from that little they had in store into the Woods in the midst of Winter; and yet how to admiration did the Lord preserve them for his holy ends, and the destruction of many still amongst the *English!* strangely did the Lord provide for them, that I did not see (all the time I was among them) one Man, or Woman, or Child, die with Hunger.

Though many times they would eat that that a hog or a dog would hardly touch, yet by that God strengthened them to be a scourge to his people.

Their chief and commonest food was Ground-nuts; they eat also Nuts and Acorns, Hartychoaks, Lilly-roots, Ground-beans, and several other weeds and roots that I know not.

They would pick up old bones, and cut them in pieces at the joynts, and if they were full of worms and magots, they would scald them over the fire to make the vermine come out; and then boyle them, and drink up the Liquor, and then beat the great ends of them in a Mortar, and so eat them. They would eat Horses guts and ears, and all sorts of wild birds which they could catch; also Bear, Venison, Beavers, Tortois, Frogs, Squirrels, Dogs, Skunks, Rattlesnakes; yea, the very Barks of Trees; besides all sorts of creatures and provision which they plundered from the *English*. I cannot but stand in admiration to see the wonderful power of God, in providing for such a vast number of our Enemies in the Wilderness, where there was nothing to be seen but from hand to mouth. Many times in the morning the generality of them would eat up all they had, and yet have some farther supply against they wanted. It is said, *Psal.* lxxxi. 13, 14, *Oh that my people had hearkened to me, and Israel had walked in my wayes, I should soon have subdued their Enemies, and turned my hand against their adversaries.* But now our perverse and evil carriages in the sight of the Lord have so offended him; that, instead of turning his hand against them, the Lord feeds and nourishes them up to be a scourge to the whole land.

5. Another thing that I would observe is, the strange providence of God in turning things about when the *Indians were at the highest,* and the *English at the lowest.* I was with the Enemy eleven weeks and five days; and not one Week passed without the fury of the Enemy, and some desolation by fire and sword upon one place or other. They mourned (with their black faces) for their own losses; yet triumphed and rejoyced in their inhumane (and many times devilish cruelty) to the *English.* They would boast much of their Victories; saying, that in two hours time, they had destroyed such a Captain and his Company in such a place; and such a Captain and his Company in such a place; and such a Captain and his Company in such a place: and boast how many Towns they had destroyed, and then scoff, and say, they had done them a good turn to send them to Heaven so soon. Again they would say, this Summer they would knock all the Rogues in the head, or drive them into the Sea, or make them flie the Country: thinking surely, *Agag-like, The bitterness of death is past.* Now the *Heathen* begin to think that all is their own, and the poor *Christians* hopes to fail (as to man) and now their eyes are more to God, and their hearts sigh heaven-ward; and to say in good earnest, *Help, Lord, or we perish;* when the Lord had brought his People to this, that they saw no help in any thing but himself; then he takes the quarrel into his own hand; and though they had made a pit (in their own imaginations) as deep as hell for the *Christians* that Summer; yet the Lord hurl'd themselves into it. And the Lord had not so many wayes before to preserve them, but now he hath as many to destroy them.

But to return again to my going home; where we may see a remarkable change of Providence: At first they were all against it, except my Husband would come for me; but afterwards they assented to it, and seemed much to rejoyce in it; some asking me to send them some Bread, others some Tobacco, others shaking me by the hand, offering me a Hood and Scarf to ride in; not one moving hand or tongue against it. Thus hath the Lord answered my poor desires, and the many requests of others put up unto God for me. In my Travels an *Indian* came to me, and told me, if I were willing, he and his Squaw would run away, and go home along with me. I told him, No, I was not willing to run away, but desired to wait God's time, that I might go home quietly, and without fear. And now God hath granted me my desire. O the wonderful power of God that I have seen, and the experiences that I have had! I have been in the midst of those roaring Lions and Savage Bears, that feared neither God nor Man, nor the Devil, by night and day, alone and in company, sleeping all sorts together; and yet not one of them ever offered the least abuse or unchastity to me in word or action. Though some are ready to say I speak it for my own credit; but I speak it in the presence of God, and to his Glory. God's power is as great now, and as sufficient to save, as when he preserved *Daniel* in the Lions Den, or the three Children in the Fiery Furnace. I may well say, as he, *Psal.* cvii. 1, 2, *Oh give thanks unto the Lord, for he is good, for his mercy endureth for ever. Let the Redeemed of the Lord say so, whom he hath redeemed from the hand of the Enemy;* especially that I should come away in the midst of so many hundreds of Enemies quietly and peaceably, and not a Dog moving his tongue. So I took leave of them, and in coming along my heart melted into Tears, more than all the while I was with them, and I was almost swallowed up with the thoughts that ever I should go home again. About the Sun's going down, Mr Hoar and myself, and the two *Indians,* came to Lancaster; and a solemn sight it was to me. There had I lived many comfortable years amongst my Relations and Neighbours; and now not one *Christian* to be seen, nor one House left standing. We went on to a Farm-house that was yet standing, where we lay all night; and a comfortable lodging we had, though nothing but straw to lye on. The Lord preserved us in safety that night, and raised us again in the morning, and carried us along, that before noon we came to Concord. Now was I full of joy, and yet not without sorrow: joy to see such a lovely sight, so many *Christians* together, and some of them my Neighbours: There I met with my Brother, and my Brother-in-Law, who asked me, if I knew where his Wife was? Poor heart! he had helped to bury her, and knew it not; she being shot down by the house, was partly burnt: so that those who were at Boston at the desolation of the Town, and came back afterward, and buried the dead, did not know her.

· · ·

I have seen the extreme vanity of this World; one hour I have been in health and wealth, wanting nothing; but the next hour in sickness, and wounds, and death, having nothing but sorrow and affliction.

Before I knew what affliction meant I was ready sometimes to wish for it. When I lived in prosperity; having the comforts of this World about me, my Relations by me, and my heart chearful; and taking little care for any thing; and yet seeing many (whom I preferred before myself) under many trials and afflictions, in sickness, weakness, poverty, losses, crosses, and cares of the World, I should be sometimes jealous least I should have my portion in this life; and that Scripture would come to my mind, *Heb.* xii 6, *For whom the Lord loveth he chasteneth, and scourgeth every Son whom he receiveth;* but now I see the Lord had his time to scourge and chasten me. The portion of some is to have their Affliction by drops, now one drop and then another; but the dregs of the Cup, the wine of astonishment, like a sweeping rain that leaveth no food, did the Lord prepare to be my portion. Affliction I wanted, and Affliction I had, full measure, (I thought) pressed down and running over; yet I see when God calls a person to any thing, and through never so many difficulties, yet he is fully able to carry them through, and make them see and say they have been gainers thereby. And I hope I can say in some measure as *David* did, *It is good for me that I have been afflicted.* The Lord hath shewed me the vanity of these outward things, that they are the *vanity of vanities, and vexation of spirit,* that they are but a shadow, a blast, a bubble, and things of no continuance; that we must rely on God himself, and our whole dependence must be upon him. If trouble from smaller matters begin to arise in me, I have something at hand to check myself with, and say when I am troubled, it was but the other day, that if I had had the world, I would have given it for my Freedom, or to have been a Servant to a *Christian.* I have learned to look beyond present and smaller troubles, and to be quieted under them, as *Moses* said, *Exod.* xiv. 13, *Stand still, and see the salvation of the Lord.*

4

Samuel Sewall (1652–1730)
from the *Diary*

Samuel Sewall was born in England and brought to America at age nine, although his father had first come to New England in 1634. He graduated from Harvard in 1671, then decided not to go into the ministry. He married Hannah Hull, daughter of one of the wealthiest men in Massachusetts, and devoted himself to managing her property, to scholarly hobbies, and to public life. From 1692 to 1728 he was a judge on the highest court in the colony, serving for the last ten years as chief justice. In 1693 he was made a member of the special court that tried witchcraft cases, consenting to the hanging of nineteen people. But in 1697, as shown below, he publicly recanted before the congregation of Boston's Old South Church.

He started his diary on December 3, 1673, and continued it almost unbroken until October 13, 1729—nearly fifty-six years. Such a span puts his diary in a class with those of George Templeton Strong, the nineteenth-century New Yorker, and Anaïs Nin (see below, Part 7). It is an invaluable record of his own works and days and also of his culture, although it was not published until the late nineteenth century. Excerpts describing his "Courtship of Madam Winthrop," in 1720, were once in all American literature anthologies.

The following excerpts, however, show the earnest, middle-aged Puritan leader rather than the somewhat comic, or pathetic, widower in his late sixties. Is he a sympathetic figure? As with other diaries, one can further ask whether he did or did not write for eventual publication, and for whom he wrote.

Sewall also wrote *The Selling of Joseph* (1700), the first American pamphlet against slavery.

The full text of the *Diary* is in *Collections of the Massachusetts Historical Society*, 5th series, vols. 5–7 (1878–82). For a biography, see Ola Elizabeth Winslow, *Samuel Sewall of Boston* (New York: Macmillan, 1964).

Jan. 13, 1677. Giving my chickens meat, it came to my mind that I gave them nothing save Indian corn and water, and yet they eat it and thrived very well, and that that food was necessary for them, how mean soever, which much affected me and convinced what need I stood in of spiritual food, and that I should not nauseat daily duties of Prayer, &c.

Nov. 6, 1692. Joseph threw a knop of Brass and hit his Sister Betty on the forhead so as to make it bleed and swell; upon which, and for his playing at Prayer-Time, and eating when Return Thanks, I whipd him pretty smartly. When I first went in (call'd by his Grandmother) he sought to shadow and hide himself from me behind the head of the Cradle: which gave me the sorrowfull remembrance of Adam's carriage.

April 29, 1695. The morning is very warm and Sunshiny; in the Afternoon there is Thunder and Lightening, and about 2. P.M. a very extraordinary Storm of Hail, so that the ground was made white with it, as with the blossoms when fallen; 'twas as bigg as pistoll and Musquet Bullets; It broke of the Glass of the new House about 480 Quarrels of the Front; of Mr. Sergeant's about as much; Col. Shrimpton, Major General, Govr. Bradstreet, New Meetinghouse, Mr. Willard, &c. Mr. Cotton Mather dined with us, and was with me in the new Kitchen when this was; He had just been mentioning that more Ministers Houses than others proportionably had been smitten with Lightening; enquiring what the meaning of God should be in it. Many Hail-Stones broke throw the Glass and flew to the middle of the Room, or farther: People afterward Gazed upon the House to see its Ruins. I got Mr. Mather to pray with us after this awfull Providence; He told God He had broken the brittle part of our house, and prayd that we might be ready for the time when our Clay-Tabernacles should be broken. Twas a sorrowfull thing to me to see the house so far undon again before twas finish'd.

Jan. 13, 1696. When I came in, past 7. at night, my wife met me in the Entry and told me Betty had surprised them. I was surprised with the abruptness of the Relation. It seems Betty Sewall had given some signs of dejection and sorrow; but a little after dinner she burst out into an amazing cry, which caus'd all the family to cry too; Her Mother ask'd the reason; she gave none; at last said she was afraid she should goe to Hell, her Sins were not pardon'd. She was first wounded by my reading a Sermon of Mr. Norton's, about the 5th of Jan. Text Jn° 7. 34. Ye shall seek me and shall not find me. And those words in the Sermon, Jn° 8. 21. Ye shall seek me and shall die in your sins, ran in her mind, and terrified her greatly. And staying at home Jan. 12. she read out of Mr. Cotton Mather—Why hath Satan filled thy heart, which increas'd her Fear. Her Mother ask'd her whether she pray'd. She answer'd, Yes; but feared her prayers were not heard because her Sins not pardon'd. Mr. Willard though sent for timelyer, yet not being told of the message, . . . He came not till after I came home. He discoursed with Betty who could not give a distinct account, but was confused as his phrase was, and as had experienced in himself. Mr. Willard pray'd excellently. The Lord bring Light and Comfort out of this dark and dreadful Cloud, and Grant that Christ's being formed in my dear child, may be the issue of these painfull pangs.

Dec. 25, 1696. We bury our little daughter. In the chamber, Joseph in course reads Ecclesiastes 3^d a time to be born and a time to die—Elisabeth, Rev. 22. Hanah, the 38th Psalm. I speak to each, as God helped, to our mutual comfort I hope. I order'd Sam. to read the 102. Psalm. Elisha Cooke, Edw. Hutchinson, John Baily, and Josia Willard bear my little daughter to the Tomb.

Note. Twas wholly dry, and I went at noon to see in what order things were set; and there I was entertain'd with a view of, and converse with, the Coffins of my dear Father Hull, Mother Hull, Cousin Quinsey, and my Six Children: for the little posthumous was now took up and set in upon that that stands on John's: so are three, one upon another twice, on the bench at the end. My Mother ly's on a lower bench, at the end, with head to her Husband's head: and I order'd little Sarah to be set on her Grandmother's feet. 'Twas an awfull yet pleasing Treat; Having said, The Lord knows who shall be brought hether next, I came away.

Jan. 14, 1697. Copy of the Bill I put up on the Fast day; giving it to Mr. Willard as he pass'd by, and standing up at the reading of it, and bowing when finished; in the Afternoon.

Samuel Sewall, sensible of the reiterated strokes of God upon himself and family; and being sensible, that as to the Guilt contracted upon the opening of the late commission of Oyer and Terminer at Salem (to which the order for this Day relates) he is, upon many accounts, more concerned than any that he knows of, Desires to take the Blame and shame of it, Asking pardon of men, And especially desiring prayers that God, who has an Unlimited Authority, would pardon that sin and all other his sins; personal and Relative: And according to his infinite Benignity, and Sovereignty, Not Visit the sin of him, or of any other, upon himself or any of his, nor upon the Land: But that He would powerfully defend him against all Temptations to Sin, for the future; and vouchsafe him the efficacious, saving Conduct of his Word and Spirit.

Jan. 26, 1697. I lodged at Charlestown, at Mrs. Shepards, who tells me Mr. Harvard built that house. I lay in the chamber next the street. As I lay awake past midnight, In my Meditation, I was affected to consider how long agoe God had made provision for my comfortable Lodging that night; seeing that was Mr. Harvards house: And that led me to think of Heaven the House not made with hands, which God for many Thousands of years has been storing with the richest furniture (saints that are from time to time placed there), and that I had some hopes of being entertain'd in that Magnificent Convenient Palace, every way fitted and furnished. These thoughts were very refreshing to me.

Oct. 1, 1697. Jer. Balchar's sons came for us to go to the Island. My Wife, through Indisposition, could not goe: But I carried Sam. Hannah, Elisa, Joseph, Mary and Jane Tapan: I prevail'd with Mr. Willard to goe, He carried Simon, Elisabeth, William, Margaret, and Elisa Tyng: Had a very comfortable Passage thither and home again; though against Tide: Had first Butter, Honey, Curds and Cream. For Dinner, very good Rost Lamb, Turkey, Fowls, Applepy. After Dinner sung the 121 Psalm. Note. A Glass of spirits my Wife sent stood upon a Joint-Stool which, Simon W. jogging, it fell down and broke all to shivers: I said twas a lively Emblem of our Fragility and Mortality. . . .

Jan. 14, 1701. Having been certified last night about 10. oclock of the death of my dear Mother at Newbury, Sam. and I set out with John Sewall, the Messenger, for that place. Hired Horses at Charlestown: set out about 10. aclock in a great Fogg. Din'd at Lewis's with Mr. Cushing of Salisbury. Sam. and I kept on in Ipswich Rode, John went to accompany Bro^r from Salem. About Mr. Hubbard's in Ipswich farms, they overtook us. Sam. and I lodg'd at Cromptons in Ipswich. Bro^r and John stood on for Newbury by Moonshine. Jany. 15th Sam. and I set forward. Brother Northend meets us. Visit Aunt Northend, Mr. Payson. With Bro^r and sister we set forward for Newbury: where we find that day appointed for the Funeral: twas a very pleasant Comfortable day.

Bearers, Jno Kent of the Island, Lt Cutting Noyes, Deacon William Noyes, Mr. Peter Tappan, Capt. Henry Somersby, Mr. Joseph Woodbridge. I follow'd the Bier single. Then Bro^r Sewall and sister Jane, Bro^r Short and his wife, Bro^r Moodey and his wife, Bro^r Northend and his wife, Bro^r Tappan and sister Sewall, Sam. and cous. Hannah Tappan. Mr. Payson of Rowley, Mr. Clark, Minister of Excester, were there. Col. Pierce, Major Noyes &c. Cous. John, Richard and Betty Dummer. Went ab^t 4. p.m. Nathan^l Bricket taking in hand to fill the Grave, I said, Forbear a little, and suffer me to say That amidst our bereaving sorrows We have the Comfort of beholding this Saint put into the rightfull possession of that Happiness of Living desir'd and dying Lamented. She liv'd commendably Four and Fifty years with her dear Husband, and my dear Father: And she could not well brook the being divided from him at her death; which is the cause of our taking leave of her in this place. She was a true and constant Lover of Gods Word, Worship, and Saints: And she always, with a patient cheerfullness, submitted to the divine Decree of providing Bread for her self and others in the sweat of her Brows. And now her infinitely Gracious and Bountiful Master has promoted her to the Honor of higher Employments, fully and absolutely discharged from all manner of Toil, and Sweat. My honoured and beloved Friends and Neighbours! My dear Mother never thought much of doing the most frequent and homely offices of Love for me; and lavish'd away many Thousands of Words upon me, before I could return one word in Answer: And therefore I ask and hope that none will be offended that I have now ventured to speak one word in her behalf; when shee her self is become speechless. Made a Motion with my hand for the filling of the Grave. Note, I could hardly speak for passion and Tears.

Jan. 24, 1704. Took 24^s in my pocket, and gave my Wife the rest of my cash £4. 3–8, and tell her she shall now keep the Cash; if I want I will borrow of her. She has a better faculty than I at managing Affairs: I will assist her;

and will endeavour to live upon my Salary; will see what it will doe. The Lord give his Blessing.

April 3, 1711. I dine with the Court at Pullin's. Mr. Attorney treats us at his house with excellent Pippins, Anchovas, Olives, Nuts. I said I should be able to make no Judgment on the Pippins without a Review, which made the Company Laugh. Spake much of Negroes; I mention'd the problem, whether they should be white after the Resurrection: Mr. Bolt took it up as absurd, because the body should be void of all Colour, spake as if it should be a Spirit. I objected what Christ said to his Disciples after the Resurrection. He said twas not so after his Ascension.

April 11, 1712. I saw Six Swallows together flying and chippering very rapturously.

May 5, 1713. Dr. Cotton Mather makes an Excellent Dedication-Prayer in the New Court-Chamber. Mr. Pain, one of the Overseers of the Work wellcom'd us, as the Judges went up Stairs. Dr. Cotton Mather having ended Prayer, The Clark went on and call'd the Grand-Jury: Giving their Charge, which was to enforce the Queen's Proclamation, and especially against Travailing on the Lord's Day; God having return'd to give us Rest. I said, You ought to be quickened to your Duty, in that you have so Convenient, and August a Chamber prepared for you to doe it in. And what I say to you, I would say to my self, to the Court, and to all that are concern'd. Seeing the former decay'd Building is consum'd, and a better built in the room, Let us pray, May that Proverb, Golden Chalices and Wooden Priests, never be transfer'd to the Civil order; that God would take away our filthy Garments, and cloath us with Change of Raiment; That our former Sins may be buried in the Ruins and Rubbish of the former House, and not be suffered to follow us into this; That a Lixivium may be made of the Ashes, which we may frequently use in keeping ourselves Clean: Let never any Judge debauch this Bench, by abiding on it when his own Cause comes under Trial; May the Judges always discern the Right, and dispense Justice with a most stable, permanent Impartiality; Let this large, transparent, costly Glass serve to oblige the Attornys alway to set Things in a True Light, And let the Character of none of them be *Impar sibi;* Let them Remember they are to advise the Court, as well as plead for their clients. The Oaths that prescribe our Duty run all upon Truth; God is Truth. Let Him communicat to us of His Light and Truth, in Judgment, and in Righteousness. If we thus improve this House, they that built it, shall inhabit it; the days of this people shall be as the days of a Tree, and they shall long enjoy the work of their hands. The Terrible Illumination that was made, the third of October was Twelve moneths, did plainly shew us that our GOD is a Consuming Fire: but it hath repented Him of the Evil. And since He has declar'd that He takes delight in them that hope in his Mercy, we firmly believe that He will be a Dwelling place to us throughout all Generations.

Saturday, Feb. 6, 1714 [Queen Anne's birthday]. . . . My neighbour Colson knocks at our door about 9. or past to tell of the Disorders at the Tavern at the Southend in Mr. Addington's house, kept by John Wallis. He desired me that I would accompany Mr. Bromfield and Constable Howell thither. It was 35. Minutes past Nine at Night before Mr. Bromfield came; then we went. I took Æneas Salter with me. Found much Company. They refus'd to go away. Said were there to drink the Queen's Health, and they had many other Healths to drink. Call'd for more Drink: drank to me, I took notice of the Affront to them. Said must and would stay upon that Solemn occasion. Mr. John Netmaker drank the Queen's Health to me. I told him I drank none; upon that he ceas'd. Mr. Brinley put on his Hat to affront me. I made him take it off. I threaten'd to send some of them to prison; that did not move them. They said they could but pay their Fine, and doing that they might stay. I told them if they had not a care, they would be guilty of a Riot. Mr. Bromfield spake of raising a number of Men to Quell them, and was in some heat, ready to run into Street. But I did not like that. Not having Pen and Ink, I went to take their Names with my Pensil, and not knowing how to Spell their Names, they themselves of their own accord writ them. Mr. Netmaker, reproaching the Province, said they had not made one good Law.

At last I address'd myself to Mr. Banister. I told him he had been longest an Inhabitant and Freeholder, I expected he should set a good Example in departing thence. Upon this he invited them to his own House, and away they went; and we, after them, went away. The Clock in the room struck a pretty while before they departed. I went directly home, and found it 25. Minutes past Ten at Night when I entred my own House. . . .

Monday, Feb. 8. Mr. Bromfield comes to me, and we give the Names of the Offenders at John Wallis's Tavern last Satterday night, to Henry Howell, Constable, with Direction to take the Fines of as many as would pay; and warn them that refus'd to pay, to appear before us at 3. p.m. that day. Many of them pay'd. The rest appear'd; and Andrew Simpson, Ensign, Alexander Gordon, Chirurgeon, Francis Brinley, Gent. and John Netmaker, Gent., were sentenc'd to pay a Fine of 5^s each of them, for their Breach of the Law Entituled, An Act for the better Observation, and Keeping the Lord's Day. They all Appeal'd, and Mr. Thomas Banister was bound with each of them in a Bond of 20^s upon Condition that they should prosecute their Appeal to effect.

Capt. John Bromsal, and Mr. Thomas Clark were dismiss'd without being Fined. The first was Master of a Ship just ready to sail, Mr. Clark a stranger of New York, who had carried it very civilly, Mr. Jekyl's Brother-in-Law.

Dec. 23, 1714. Dr. C. Mather preaches excellently from Ps. 37. Trust in the Lord &c. only spake of the Sun being in the centre of our System. I think it inconvenient to assert such Problems.

Oct. 15, 1717. My Wife got some Relapse by a new Cold and grew very bad; Sent for Mr. Oakes, and he sat up with me all night.

Oct. 16. The Distemper increases; yet my Wife speaks to me to goe to Bed.

Oct. 17. Thursday, I asked my wife whether twere best for me to go to Lecture: She said, I can't tell; so I staid at home. put up a Note. It being my Son's Lecture, and I absent, twas taken much notice of. Major Gen¹ Winthrop and his Lady visit us. I thank her that she would visit my poor Wife.

Oct. 18. My wife grows worse and exceedingly Restless. Pray'd God to look upon her. Ask'd not after my going to bed. Had the advice of Mr. Williams and Dr. Cutler.

Oct. 19. Call'd Dr. C. Mather to pray, which he did excellently in the Dining Room, having Suggested good Thoughts to my wife before he went down. After, Mr. Wadsworth pray'd in the Chamber when 'twas suppos'd my wife took little notice. About a quarter of an hour past four, my dear Wife expired in the Afternoon, whereby the Chamber was fill'd with a Flood of Tears. God is teaching me a new Lesson; to live a Widower's Life. Lord help me to Learn; and be a Sun and Shield to me, now so much of my Comfort and Defense are taken away.

Oct. 20. I goe to the publick Worship forenoon and Afternoon. My Son has much adoe to read the Note I put up, being overwhelm'd with tears.

PART TWO

Great Awakenings,
New Individuals, 1700–1775

The seventy-five-year period from 1700 to the beginning of the Revolution is one which tends to be neglected in American history and American literature courses. The stories of exploration and discovery that came before seem more exciting, while what came after seems much more important to the actual development of the new nation.

In the development of American autobiography and the emergence of the concepts of self that are so essential to autobiography, however, this is a vital period. In it lived the men who wrote three of the country's major, full-length autobiographical classics: Benjamin Franklin (1706–90), John Woolman (1720–72), and J. Hector St. John de Crevecoeur (1735–1813). Three short classics also come from this period: *The Journal of Sarah Kemble Knight,* Jonathan Edwards's "Personal Narrative," and the more recently discovered *Some Account of the Fore Part of the Life of Elizabeth Ashbridge* (all included here). Adding further to the vitality of this period is the publication of *A Narrative of the Uncommon Sufferings, and Surprizing Deliverance of Briton Hammon, A Negro man,—Servant to General Winslow of Marshfield, in New-England* (1760), "the first black autobiography in America." [1]

What was going on in this first three-quarters of the eighteenth century which inspired these people to write these autobiographies? The best way of answering this question may be to look at the autobiographies themselves, at the events they describe and how and why they describe them.

Sarah Kemble Knight's *Journal* describes a journey she made from Boston to New Haven and New York and back, starting in October, 1704, and ending in January, 1705. At first glance, this does not seem to be a very significant event or one worth writing about. But the very fact that an educated, middle-class woman was travelling alone at that time, and travelling to handle some matter of family business, tells us remarkable things. New England culture now permitted a woman to undertake such a journey, a journey we cannot

---

1. William L. Andrews, *To Tell a Free Story: The First Century of Afro-American Autobiography, 1760–1865* (Urbana: Univ. of Illinois Press, 1988), p. 32.

imagine Anne Bradstreet or Mary Rowlandson would have taken. She had the freedom, and travel conditions, though bad, as she vividly tells us, were not impossible. She could also look upon this as a practical, secular journey, not a spiritual one with all kinds of religious allegory to be packed in (or unpacked) at every point. Freed of this religious baggage, Madam Knight had all kinds of other things to do, observe, and report. She could describe the crude places she slept, the bad food, the manners of her guides and inn-keepers, her nervousness sitting in a canoe, and so on. This makes her story earthy and amusing. Chances are, as a recent editor has suggested, that she kept her notes on the trip and wrote them up in order to read or show to friends. Thus the trials of her patience, strength, and taste bring out her char-acter, to have it confirmed with the laughter and approval of an audience.[2] Her *Journal* is, in this sense, even an early illustration of one of the most basic types of American humor, in which a cultivated outsider ridicules the gross-ness of country bumpkins. For a New England woman, perhaps for any New Englander, this is both a new self and a new way of expressing it. It is secular, partially comic, sophisticated, and dramatic.

For most Americans, however, religion remained the dominant issue in their personal and social lives. This is very evident in the religious revival called the Great Awakening, which began in the 1730s and lasted through the 1740s. Prosperity and the beginnings of a scientific rationalism had cooled the religious fervor of early American Puritanism, as is illustrated in the *Journal* of Madam Knight. But poorer, less educated people, such as the members of Jonathan Edwards's congregation in Northampton, Massachusetts, remained attached to Puritanism and wanted more emotion in their religious faith and practice. They were also receptive to a more emotional style of preaching, that evoked their fears of God and made them anxious to renew their religious commitment.

But the Great Awakening was more than just a revival movement among latter-day Puritans. Although it can be said to have started in Jonathan Edwards's congregation in Northampton, Massachusetts, it soon spread to many other denominatons, from New England to Georgia. Indeed, there were concurrent expressions of emotional, popular piety in Germany, Switzer-land, Holland, and France. The Wesleyan and Methodist movements were the major English expressions, and they had direct impact on the Awakening in the colonies. When George Whitefield, a follower of John and Charles Wesley, came to Philadelphia in 1739, he immediately drew such crowds, Benjamin Franklin recalled, that "the Multitudes of all Sects and Denominations that attended his Sermons were enormous." People "admir'd and respected him, notwithstanding his common Abuse of them, by assuring them they were

2. Sargent Bush, Jr., "Introduction" to *The Journal of Madam Knight*, in *Journeys in New Worlds: Early American Women's Narratives*, ed. William L. Andrews (Madison: Univ. of Wisconsin Press, 1990), p. 75.

naturally *half Beasts and half Devils.*" Suddenly "it seem'd as if all the World were growing Religious; so that one could not walk thro' the Town in an Evening without Hearing Psalms sung in different Families of every Street."[3]

The Great Awakening crossed boundaries between "Sects and Denominations," spread throughout the diverse and separate colonies, and had a mass appeal. With people everywhere experiencing what Edwards called "surprising conversions," it also challenged the authority of the established churches. The clergy in Philadelphia soon resented Whitefield so much, wrote Franklin, that they "refus'd him their Pulpits and he was oblig'd to preach in the Fields."[4] The older, more conservative clergy in Boston also came to resent the uproar which Jonathan Edwards had started in the Connecticut Valley, as eventually did leaders of Edwards's own congregation, which dismissed him in 1750. But the disputes which the Great Awakening caused also led to the breakup of many denominations and the founding of new ones. The Presbyterians split briefly into the "Old Side Presbyterians," who opposed revivalism, and the "New Side Presbyterians," then later into the "Old Light" and "New Light." Methodist and Baptist churches grew.[5] The autobiography most directly related to the Great Awakening is Jonathan Edwards's "Personal Narrative," although circumstantially or metaphorically nearly all the autobiographical writing of this period can be related to it. Franklin, as we have just seen, wrote about it. Charles Woodmason, when he went to preach in the interior of the Carolinas in the 1760s, competed with different sects of Baptists and various forms of "New Lights" who vigorously carried on the emotional styles of the Awakening. In a broader way, the Awakening led to or stood for a discovery of the egalitarian individual.

As a leader of the Great Awakening, Edwards seems to have written the "Personal Narrative" as a way of studying in himself the religious affections which were exerting such a powerful influence in the members of his Northampton church. Many of them, by the late 1730s and early '40s, had told him the stories of their conversions—so many that he had come to question his own conversion and perhaps question the sincerity of theirs. He writes towards the end: "That my sins appear to me so great, don't seem to me to be, because I have so much more conviction of sin than other Christians, but because I am so much worse, and have so much more wickedness to be convinced of." The sentence urgently reflects the sense of sin that was so powerful in driving the revival and urging people to repent. Yet it also reflects the paradox that being convinced of one's "wickedness" was therefore beneficial. Caught in this paradox, Edwards alternated between confessions

3. *The Autobiography of Benjamin Franklin,* ed. Leonard W. Labaree et al. (New Haven: Yale Univ. Press, 1964), pp. 175–76.
4. Labaree et al., ed., *Autobiography of Franklin,* p. 175.
5. Alan Heimert and Perry Miller, *The Great Awakening: Documents Illustrating the Crisis and Its Consequences* (Indianapolis: Bobbs-Merril, 1967), pp. xxix–xxxv.

of his wickedness and confessions of his "dependence on God's grace," between weeping and rejoicing, and the "Narrative" breaks off unresolved. It has no true ending, and, without a resolution, none is possible.

Edwards's "Narrative" also has a brilliant, lyrical side, however, as in his descriptions of his innocent, early love of God and his delight in the physical world as God's creation. In this sense, it expresses another kind of "awakening" that is closer to the scientific revolutions of the eighteenth century and to his contemporaries like Franklin, Woolman, and even the dowdy humorist Sarah Kemble Knight. Indeed, some people have seen a much finer sensibility and true love of nature in Edwards and Woolman than in the practical Benjamin Franklin. Nature and the world, for Franklin, seem just stuff to experiment on and turn into instruments for human comfort and progress.

"The Spiritual Travels of Nathan Cole," written between 1740 and 1765, makes a very instructive contrast with Edwards's "Narrative." As a farmer and carpenter with no higher education and no degrees in divinity, Cole was the kind of person whom the Awakening empowered to think for himself and protest against the pride and complacency he saw in the mid-century Congregational establishment. Once "born again," Cole became far more conscious of his sins and his precarious spiritual life. In this sense, the Awakening brought him some of the same inner insecurity it gave Edwards. But his new-found piety also led him, as he says, "to see the Old Standing Churches were not in a gospel order." So he and his friends formed a separate fellowship in which they felt more comfortable and in which, inevitably, they had more control over church services and governance. At the same time, Cole's diary gave him a means of recording his "spiritual travels" and so examining himself and maintaining his resolution and purpose. He learned, he spoke, and he kept a record what he said and thought. The diary helped him to become the kind of Christian he believed he should become. In the process, it also contributed to his and his fellows' partial overthrow of those "Old Standing Churches" which were in many respects the most powerful governments in eighteenth-century America. Cole's diary is a record and an agent of the revolution the Awakening had set off. Yet, in being a revolution of diarists and autobiographers, it was also one that stressed piety, humility, and self-control.

Quakers such as John Woolman and Elizabeth Ashbridge were not directly involved in the Great Awakening. They had never subscribed to the Calvinist doctrines of election and predestination, and by the seventeenth century, the wealthier Quakers of Philadelphia had ceased to be enthusiasts. They did not believe in the "new lights" of sudden salvation but "the inner light"—the light of conscience which burned, brightly or obscurely, in all people. Their earthly pilgrimages were long, careful efforts to follow this light themselves and discern it in others, and they held aloof from the frenzies of revivalists like Whitefield. This is humorously illustrated by Benjamin

Franklin's story of being at a service where Whitefield appealed for funds for an orphanage in Georgia. Franklin had been so moved that he contributed all the money he had with him. A Quaker friend, who had anticipated such an appeal, had left his own money home. But this man, too, was moved and "apply'd to a Neighbour who stood near him to borrow some Money for the Purpose." But that man, also a Quaker, answered, "At any other time, Friend Hopkinson, I would lend to thee freely; but not now; for thee seems to be out of thy right Senses."[6]

Quakers could avoid the frenzy of the Great Awakening because they had already had their own private awakening, or awakenings. They had already established more independence from church authority and doctrine than any of the other churches, and they already acknowledged the individual "inner light." Thus their concepts of self were already implicitly egalitarian.

Readers of John Woolman's *Journal* (1774) can see this on almost every page. For Woolman thinks as independently as any man who ever lived. His very choice of words is independent: based on profound, exacting consultation of the inner light. Yet he is respectful of other people's rights and scrupulously avoids being vain or inflammatory. As the *Journal* testifies, he campaigned calmly but effectively against the social injustices which most men of his time took for granted. He persuaded other Quakers to free their slaves, simplified his dress and diet so as to avoid exploiting laborers, called attention to the hardships of sailors, opposed military conscription, and defended the interests and actions of Indians. The Quaker concept of the "inner light" as a divine light within all persons led to the concept of all persons being equal in their political rights and human needs.

Woolman's attention to Indians grew not only from Quaker pacifism but also from the nearly constant conflict in this period between the British-American colonists, the Indians, and the French. Following King William's War (1689–97), there was what Americans called Queen Anne's War, from 1702 to 1713, during which the French and Indians destroyed several towns in northern New England—and took more captives, some of whom wrote captivity narratives. King George's War, 1744–48, was not so long or so consequential, but the French and Indian War of 1755–63 definitely was. It was the war in which General Braddock was defeated in 1755 trying to capture Fort Duquesne (at the site of present-day Pittsburgh), demonstrating to Americans such as George Washington that British power in America was not invincible. There were other major battles in the north and in Canada—at Fort William Henry (on Lake George in 1757), Ticonderoga (on Lake Champlain in 1759), and Montreal, in 1760. These battles brought about the ceding of Canada to England. They also led to greater unity among the

6. Labaree et al., ed., *Autobiography of Franklin,* pp. 177–78.

American colonies, while leaving the British government so much in debt that taxation of the colonies was increased—two additional factors leading to the American Revolution.

Warfare, therefore, was another major influence in the shaping of the American life of the period. We see Franklin finding a way to raise money for forts and gunpowder, serving in the militia, and helping to supply Braddock's army. We also see Charles Woodmason's awareness of how frontier Carolinians were used by coastal Carolinians as a buffer against Indian attacks.

All through the period, in the midst of the Great Awakening and the recurrent border wars, the population of the American colonies continued to grow. In 1700 it had been a quarter of a million. By 1760 it was 1,600,000. In New England, new fortunes were made in shipbuilding, lumbering, and the slave trade. In Virginia, tobacco became the great cash crop, employing ever larger numbers of enslaved Africans. Much of the growth in the white population, too, was in the form of indentured English and Irish servants (who were in some ways like slaves until their indentures were paid), of prisoners sent to Georgia, and of German and Dutch immigrants. The colonies were growing in diversity as well as just numbers of people, and this is also illustrated in the autobiographies.

In addition to being a Quaker convert, Elizabeth Ashbridge was an indentured servant. She had run away from home, married, lost her husband, gone to Ireland, and then signed a contract to go to America. There she served three years with a cruel master and was on the verge of suicide. She "bought off the remainder of my Time," but soon afterwards lost her freedom again by marrying an oppressive, unreliable man she met while dancing in an alehouse. He was a restless schoolteacher and took her to Boston, then Long Island. He drank too much, abused her, and resented her attraction to the Quakers, especially because Quakers allowed women to preach. She does not go into all this in great detail, because her religious history is the primary subject of her narrative, yet we can imagine that there were many women and men in America in this period who were like Ashbridge and her husband. Even though only a comparatively small number joined the Quakers and an even smaller number became woman preachers, the pattern of finding one's fulfillment and also finding one's freedom through a religious experience and commitment was very common. The dislocations of immigration, settling, and resettling encouraged many people to take up new religious faiths. Even where people did not change religions, the religions themselves changed, accommodating their members' new conditions. In that way, religious "awakenings" and the other awakenings of immigration, new cultures, and new ways of life were related.

The role of immigration in building up both the number and character of eighteenth-century Americans is most brilliantly developed in St. Jean de Crevecoeur's *Letters from an American Farmer,* published in 1782. As a French military officer who had travelled around both French and British America,

then finally bought land in Orange County, New York, in 1769, Crevecoeur
had lived a life which may have been like a number of other people's of the
period, but which was not appropriate for an autobiography, as autobiography was then practiced. He had not been an expedition leader and had
not experienced a religious conversion. In composing his *Letters,* however,
he seized upon new conceptions of himself as *immigrant* and *farmer* which
fitted in with the experiences of tens of thousands of other Americans and
which both Europeans and Americans were glad to read about. Generalizing
his experiences, he turned himself into a spokesman for the new American. The "American Farmer" was a figure from old-world literary pastoralism
coming out of a new-world melting pot. The "American," said Crevecoeur, is
a "strange mixture of blood, which you will find in no other country." He had
also "[left] behind him all his ancient prejudices and manners, [and received]
new ones from the new mode of life he has embraced, the new government
he obeys, and the new rank he holds."[7]

The "Farmer" received the best of these new influences. People living on
the coasts, in Crevecoeur's vision of the country, "see and converse with a
variety of people; their intercourse with mankind becomes extensive." They
develop from "bold and enterprising" fishers and fish-eaters into traders and
then into merchants. "Those who inhabit the middle settlements," he went
on, "must be very different; the simple cultivation of the earth purifies them."
They have just enough government and religion to shelter them and restrain them. They will be proud "freeholders"—sharp bargainers, litigious,
informed, and critical of government. As farmers and tradesmen they will
also be thrifty and independent. Finally, said Crevecoeur, as "we arrive near
the great woods, near the last inhabited districts," we will find men who are
"beyond the reach of government," left to themselves, and therefore idle,
wasteful, quarrelsome, and wild.[8]

In making the "Farmer" from "the middle settlements" the ideal figure,
Crevecoeur was appealing to the sentiments of most European-Americans
of his time. He was also giving birth to a kind of geographic-historic account of American character which has been reshaped and extended by many
later scholars, publicists, artists, and political leaders. The frontier thesis of
Frederick Jackson Turner is latent in what we might call Crevecoeur's auto-
bio-geography.

But the most influential new American concept of self to come from this
period may be Benjamin Franklin's concept of the prudent, industrious, successful tradesman. His awakening may be the greatest of all. His life spans
nearly the whole period. There is a legend, though undocumented, that Sarah

---

7. *Letters from an American Farmer* . . . , ed. Albert E. Stone (New York: Penguin Books, 1981),
pp. 71–72.
8. Crevecoeur, *Letters,* p. 72.

Kemble Knight was one of his school teachers. He himself tells of visiting Cotton Mather, the heir to the early Puritan theocracy. As we have noted, he also knew George Whitefield and helped Pennsylvania Quakers build defenses against Indians. His business and other interests reached throughout the colonies. His *Autobiography* was begun in 1771, at a time when he was living in England but could also see the signs of an eventual break between the two countries.[9] The character of the benevolent but also shrewd self-made man that he celebrated in those "Memoirs," as he called them, was his own vision of the representative American and the vision enlarged upon by his followers. In the *Autobiography,* he also drew upon nearly all of the earlier traditions of American autobiography which we have noted. The religious conversion narrative, in his handling, became a secular one, "from the Poverty and Obscurity in which I was born and bred, to a State of Affluence and some Degree of Reputation in the World."[10] Nominally, at least, he wrote the *Autobiography* as a letter to his son, just as Anne Bradstreet had written to her children. Franklin's work included accounts of his own travel, beginning with his journey from Boston to Philadelphia, a journey necessitated by his running away from his apprenticeship to his older brother.

The importance of the autobiographies of this period, then, is enormous. Before them, autobiography was still bound to its early Christian past, going back to St. Augustine, and to its classical and early Renaissance traditions of governors' or travellers' journals. In these early eighteenth-century autobiographies, women write about their travels while away from their husbands, and celebrate their independent immigration to America. They also celebrate religious experiences which are quite separate from their husbands' lives and demands. Men, at the same time, begin to describe and celebrate their lives as tradesmen and farmers, their work, and their careers. In Charles Woodmason's *Journal,* even religious autobiography takes a new turn, as he narrates not his conversion but his career as an itinerant, backwoods preacher. After these autobiographies, therefore, modern autobiography is possible. In them is the discovery of the modern individual life.

9. James Cox, *Recovering Literature's Lost Ground: Essays in American Autobiography* (Baton Rouge: Louisiana State Univ. Press, 1989), p. 16.
10. Labaree et al., *Autobiography of Franklin*, p. 43.

5

Sarah Kemble Knight (1666–1727)
The Journal of Madam Knight

Sarah Kemble Knight's *Journal* was not published until 1825, when it was brought out by Theodore Dwight (1796–1866). Dwight was a New York teacher and journalist who wrote travel essays, histories, and biographies, and who wanted, like others of his generation, to contribute to building American literature. His father, Theodore Dwight, Sr. (1764–1846), and uncle, Timothy Dwight, were grandsons of Jonathan Edwards and members of the Connecticut Wits. Knight's *Journal,* he said elegantly, would "please those who have particularly studied the progressive history of our country."

In his brief introduction to the 1825 edition, Dwight described Knight as "a resident of Boston, and a lady of uncommon literary attainments, as well as great taste and strength of mind," and he noted that "she was called Madam Knight, out of respect to her character, according to a custom once common in New England. . . ." The *Journal,* he said, was "a faithful copy from a diary in the author's own hand-writing, compiled soon after her return home, as it appears, from notes recorded daily, while on the road." [1]

Unfortunately, the original text is now lost, and little more is known about Knight. A modern editor, however, has learned that when she hastily began her journey, "she left behind a fifteen-year-old daughter, whose father was apparently travelling on business abroad, and an elderly mother. . . . The road she took was the established one between Boston and New Haven; just three months earlier Connecticut's governor, Fitz-John Winthrop, and his son and daughter had taken the same road from Connecticut to Boston. But it must have been the rare woman who undertook the journey alone." [2]

The text is from *The Journal of Madam Knight,* ed. Sargent Bush, Jr., in *Journeys in New Worlds: Early American Women's Narratives,* ed. William L. Andrews (Madison: Univ. of Wisconsin Press, 1990). Bush retained the footnotes of 1825, by Theodore Dwight, which have been modified for the present volume. Bush's own editorial commentary, however, which appears in brackets, has not

1. Theodore Dwight, "Introduction to the Edition of 1825," in *The Journal of Madam Knight,* ed. Sargent Bush, Jr., in *Journeys in New Worlds,* ed. William L. Andrews, p. 85.
2. Bush, "Introduction" to *The Journal of Madam Knight,* p. 69.

been changed. In his introduction to the selection in *Journeys in New Worlds*, Bush summarizes what else is known of Knight, as well as other critical writing about her.

Monday, Octb'r. the second, 1704.—About three o'clock afternoon, I begun my Journey from Boston to New-Haven; being about two Hundred Mile. My Kinsman, Capt. Robert Luist, waited on me as farr as Dedham, where I was to meet the Western post.

I vissitted the Reverd. Mr. Belcher, the Minister of the town, and tarried there till evening, in hopes the post would come along. But he not coming, I resolved to go to Billingses where he used to lodg, being 12 miles further. But being ignorant of the way, Madm Billings,[3] seing no persuasions of her good spouses or hers could prevail with me to Lodg there that night, Very kindly went wyth me to the Tavern, where I hoped to get my guide, And desired the Hostess to inquire of her guests whether any of them would go with mee. But they being tyed by the Lipps to a pewter engine, scarcely allowed themselves time to say what clownish [Dwight's note: Here half a page of the MS is gone.] . . . Peices of eight, I told her no, I would not be accessary to such extortion.

Then John shan't go, sais shee. No, indeed, shan't hee; And held forth at that rate a long time, that I began to fear I was got among the Quaking tribe, beleeving not a Limbertong'd sister among them could out do Madm. Hostes.

Upon this, to my no small surprise, son John arrose, and gravely demanded what I would give him to go with me? Give you, sais I, are you John? Yes, says he, for want of a Better; And behold! this John look't as old as my Host, and perhaps had bin a man in the last Century. Well, Mr. John, sais I, make your demands. Why, half a pss. of eight and a dram, sais John. I agreed, and gave him a Dram (now) in hand to bind the bargain.

My hostess catechis'd John for going so cheep, saying his poor wife would break her heart [Dwight's note: Here another half page of the MS is gone.] . . . His shade on his Hors resembled a Globe on a Gate post. His habitt, Hors and furniture, its looks and goins Incomparably answered the rest.

Thus Jogging on with ·an easy pace, my Guide telling mee it was dangero's to Ride hard in the Night, (whch his horse had the sence to avoid,) Hee entertained me with the Adventurs he had passed by late Rideing, and eminent Dangers he had escaped, so that, Remembring the Hero's in Parismus and the Knight of the Oracle, I didn't know but I had mett wth a Prince disguis'd.

When we had Ridd about an how'r, wee come into a thick swamp, wch.

3. "Madm Billings": Knight meant to write "Madm Belcher"—Abigail Tompson Belcher, a daughter of the poet Benjamin Tompson.

by Reason of a great fogg, very much startled mee, it being now very Dark. But nothing dismay'd John: Hee had encountered a thousand and a thousand such Swamps, having a Universall Knowledge in the woods; and readily Answered all my inquiries wch. were not a few.

In about an how'r, or something more, after we left the Swamp, we come to Billinges, where I was to Lodg. My Guide dismounted and very Complasantly help't me down and shewd the door, signing to me wth his hand to Go in; wch I Gladly did—But had not gone many steps into the Room, ere I was Interogated by a young Lady I understood afterwards was the Eldest daughter of the family, with these, or words to this purpose, (viz.) Law for mee—what in the world brings You here at this time a night?—I never see a woman on the Rode so Dreadfull late, in all the days of my versall life. Who are You? Where are You going? I'me scar'd out of my witts—with much now of the same Kind. I stood aghast, Prepareing to reply, when in comes my Guide—to him Madam turn'd, Roreing out: Lawfull heart, John, is it You?—how de do! Where in the world are you going with this woman? Who is she? John made no Ansr. but sat down in the corner, fumbled out his black Junk,[4] and saluted that instead of Debb; she then turned agen to mee and fell anew into her silly questions, without asking me to sitt down.

I told her shee treated me very Rudely, and I did not think it my duty to answer her unmannerly Questions. But to get ridd of them, I told her I come there to have the post's company with me to-morrow on my Journey, &c. Miss star'd awhile, drew a chair, bid me sitt, And then run up stairs and putts on two or three Rings, (or else I had not seen them before,) and returning, sett herself just before me, showing the way to Reding,[5] that I might see her Ornaments, perhaps to gain the more respect. But her Granam's new Rung sow,[6] had it appeared, would [have] affected me as much. I paid honest John wth money and dram according to contract, and Dismist him, and pray'd Miss to shew me where I must Lodg. Shee conducted me to a parlour in a little back Lento, wch was almost fill'd wth the bedsted, wch was so high that I was forced to climb on a chair to gitt up to the wretched bed that lay on it; on wch having Stretcht my tired Limbs, and lay'd my head on a Sad-coulord pillow, I began to think on the transactions of the past day.

Tuesday, October the third, about 8 in the morning, I with the Post proceeded forward without observing any thing remarkable; And about two, afternoon, Arrived at the Post's second stage, where the western Post mett him and exchanged Letters. Here, having called for something to eat, the woman bro't in a Twisted thing like a cable, but something whiter; and laying it on the bord, tugg'd for life to bring it into a capacity to spread; wch having

---

4. "Junk": old rope; a comment on John's tobacco.
5. "Showing the way to Reding": gesturing with hands and arms.
6. "Rung sow": a "rung," or ringed, sow has a ring in its nose to prevent it from rooting.

wth great pains accomplished, shee serv'd in a dish of Pork and Cabage, I suppose the remains of Dinner. The sause was of a deep Purple, wch I tho't was boil'd in her dye Kettle; the bread was Indian, and every thing on the Table service Agreeable to these. I, being hungry, gott a little down; but my stomach was soon cloy'd, and what cabbage I swallowed serv'd me for a Cudd the whole day after.

Having here discharged the Ordnary for self and Guide, (as I understood was the custom,) About Three afternoon went on with my Third Guide, who Rode very hard; and having crossed Providence Ferry, we come to a River wch they Generally Ride thro'. But I dare not venture; so the Post got a Ladd and Cannoo to carry me to tother side, and hee rid thro' and Led my hors. The Cannoo was very small and shallow, so that when we were in she seem'd redy to take in water, which greatly terrified mee, and caused me to be very circumspect, sitting with my hands fast on each side, my eyes stedy, not daring so much as to lodg my tongue a hair's breadth more on one side of my mouth then tother, nor so much as think on Lott's wife, for a wry thought would have oversett our wherey:[7] But was soon put out of this pain, by feeling the Cannoo on shore, wch I as soon almost saluted with my feet; and Rewarding my sculler, again mounted and made the best of our way forwards. The Rode here was very even and the day pleasant, it being now near Sunsett. But the Post told mee we had neer 14 miles to Ride to the next Stage, (where we were to Lodg.) I askt him of the rest of the Rode, foreseeing wee must travail in the night. Hee told mee there was a bad River we were to Ride thro', wch was so very firce a hors could sometimes hardly stem it: But it was but narrow, and wee should soon be over. I cannot express The concern of mind this relation sett me in: no thoughts but those of the dang'ros River could entertain my Imagination, and they were as formidable as varios, still Tormenting me with blackest Ideas of my Approching fate—Sometimes seing my self drowning, otherwhiles drowned, and at the best like a holy Sister Just come out of a Spiritual Bath in dripping Garments.

Now was the Glorious Luminary, wth his swift Coursers arrived at his Stage, leaving poor me wth the rest of this part of the lower world in darkness, with which *wee* were soon Surrounded. The only Glimering we now had was from the spangled Skies, Whose Imperfect Reflections rendered every Object formidable. Each lifeless Trunk, with its shatter'd Limbs, appear'd an Armed Enymie; and every little stump like a Ravenous devourer. Nor could I so much as discern my Guide, when at any distance, which added to the terror.

Thus, absolutely lost in Thought, and dying with the very thoughts of drowning, I come up wth the post, who I did not see till even with his Hors: he told mee he stopt for mee; and wee Rode on Very deliberatly a few paces, when we entred a Thickett of Trees and Shrubbs, and I perceived by the Hors's going, we were on the descent of a Hill, w^{ch}, as wee come neerer the

7. "Wherey": a light riverboat.

bottom, 'twas totaly dark wth the Trees that surrounded it. But I knew by the Going of the Hors wee had entred the water, wch my Guide told mee was the hazzardos River he had told me off; and hee, Riding up close to my Side, Bid me not fear—we should be over Imediatly. I now ralyed all the Courage I was mistriss of, Knowing that I must either Venture my fate of drowning, or be left like the Children in the wood. So, as the Post bid me, I gave Reins to my Nagg; and sitting as Stedy as Just before in the Cannoo, in a few minutes got safe to the other side, which hee told mee was the Narragansett country.[8]

Here We found great difficulty in Travailing, the way being very narrow, and on each side the Trees and bushes gave us very unpleasent welcomes wth their Branches and bow's, wch wee could not avoid, it being so exceeding dark. My Guide, as before so now, putt on harder than I, wth my weary bones, could follow; so left mee and the way beehind him. Now Returned my distressed aprehensions of the place where I was: the dolesome woods, my Company next to none, Going I knew not wither, and encompased wth Terrifying darkness; The least of which was enough to startle a more Masculine courage. Added to which the Reflections, as in the afternoon of the day that my Call[9] was very Questionable, wch till then I had not so Prudently as I ought considered. Now, coming to the foot of a hill, I found great difficulty in ascending; But being got to the Top, was there amply recompenced with the friendly Appearance of the Kind Conductress of the night, Just then Advancing above the Horisontall Line. The Raptures wch the Sight of that fair Planett produced in mee, caus'd mee, for the Moment, to forgett my present wearyness and past toils; and Inspir'd me for most of the remaining way with very divirting tho'ts, some of which, with the other Occurances of the day, I reserved to note down when I should come to my Stage. My tho'ts on the sight of the moon were to this purpose:

> Fair Cynthia, all the Homage that I may
> Unto a Creature, unto thee I pay;
> In Lonesome woods to meet so kind a guide,
> To Mee's more worth than all the world beside.
> Some Joy I felt just now, when safe got or'e
> Yon Surly River to this Rugged shore,
> Deeming Rough welcomes from these clownish Trees,
> Better than Lodgings wth Nereidees.
> Yet swelling fears surprise; all dark appears—
> Nothing but Light can disipate those fears.
> My fainting vitals can't lend strength to say,

8. "Narragansett country": a large area of southwestern Rhode Island whose exact boundaries were still in doubt in 1704 because of conflicting deeds between the native Narragansett tribe and the white colonists.
9. "My Call": her spiritual "vocation," which in the Calvinist understanding of the process of salvation leads the sinner to grace and redemption. She suggests she has treated this matter less seriously than it requires.

> But softly whisper, O I wish 'twere day.
> The murmer hardly warm'd the Ambient air,
> E're thy Bright Aspect rescues from dispair:
> Makes the old Hagg her sable mantle loose,
> And a Bright Joy do's through my Soul diffuse.
> The Boistero's Trees now Lend a Passage Free,
> And pleasent prospects thou giv'st light to see.

From hence wee kept on, with more ease th^n before: the way being smooth and even, the night warm and serene, and the Tall and thick Trees at a distance, especially w^n the moon glar'd light through the branches, fill'd my Imagination wth the pleasent delusion of a Sumpteous citty, fill'd wth famous Buildings and churches, wth their spiring steeples, Balconies, Galleries and I know not what: Granduers wch I had heard of, and wch the stories of foreign countries had given me the Idea of.

> Here stood a Lofty church—there is a steeple,
> And there the Grand Parade—O see the people!
> That Famouse Castle there, were I but nigh,
> To see the mote and Bridg and walls so high—
> They'r very fine! sais my deluded eye.

Being thus agreably entertain'd without a thou't of any thing but thoughts themselves, I on a suden was Rous'd from these pleasing Imaginations, by the Post's sounding his horn, which assured mee hee was arrived at the Stage, where we were to Lodg: and that musick was then most musickall and agreeable to mee.

Being come to mr. Havens', I was very civilly Received, and courteously entertained, in a clean comfortable House; and the Good woman was very active in helping off my Riding clothes, and then ask't what I would eat. I told her I had some Chocolett, if shee would prepare it; which with the help of some Milk, and a little clean brass Kettle, she soon effected to my satisfaction. I then betook me to my Apartment, wch was a little Room parted from the Kitchen by a single bord partition; where, after I had noted the Occurrances of the past day, I went to bed, which, tho' pretty hard, Yet neet and handsome. But I could get no sleep, because of the Clamor of some of the Town tope-ers in next Room, Who were entred into a strong debate concerning the Signifycation of the name of their Country, (viz.) *Narraganset*. One said it was named so by the Indians, because there grew a Brier there, of a prodigious Highth and bigness, the like hardly ever known, called by the Indians Narragansett; And quotes an Indian of so Barberous a name for his Author, that I could not write it. His Antagonist Replyed no—It was from a Spring it had its name, wch hee well knew where it was, which was extreem cold in summer, and as Hott as could be imagined in the winter, which was much resorted too by the natives, and by them called Narragansett, (Hott and Cold,) and that was the originall of their places name—with a thousand Impertinances not worth notice, wch He utter'd with such a Roreing voice and Thundering blows with the fist of wickedness on the Table, that it peirced my very head. I heartily fretted, and wish't 'um tongue tyed; but wth as little succes as a freind of mine once, who was (as shee said) kept a whole night awake, on a Jorny, by a country Left.[10] and a Sergent, Insigne and a Deacon, contriving how to bring a triangle into a Square. They kept calling for tother Gill, wch while they were swallowing, was some Intermission; But presently, like Oyle to fire, encreased the flame. I set my Candle on a Chest by the bed side, and setting up, fell to my old way of composing my Resentments, in the following manner:

> I ask thy Aid, O Potent Rum!
> To Charm these wrangling Topers Dum.
> Thou hast their Giddy Brains possest—
> The man confounded wth the Beast—
> And I, poor I, can get no rest.
> Intoxicate them with thy fumes:
> O still their Tongues till morning comes!

And I know not but my wishes took effect; for the dispute soon ended w^th 'tother Dram; and so Good night!

Wedensday, Octob^r 4th. About four in the morning, we set out for Kingston (for so was the Town called) with a french Docter in our company. Hee and the Post put on very furiously, so that I could not keep up with them, only as now and then they'd stop till they see mee. This Rode was poorly furnished wth accommodations for Travellers, so that we were forced to ride 22 miles by the post's account, but neerer thirty by mine, before wee could bait so much as our Horses, wch I exceedingly complained of. But the post encourag'd mee, by saying wee should be well accommodated anon at mr. Devills, a few miles further. But I questioned whether we ought to go to the Devil to be helpt out of affliction. However, like the rest of Deluded souls that post to the Infernal denn, Wee made all posible speed to this Devil's Habitation; where alliting, in full assurance of good accommodation, wee were going in. But meeting his two daughters, as I suposed twins, they so neerly resembled each other, both in features and habit, and look't as old as the Divel himselfe, and quite as Ugly, We desired entertainm't, but could hardly get a word out of 'um, till with our Importunity, telling them our necesity, &c. they call'd the old Sophister, who was as sparing of his words as his daughters had bin, and no, or none, was the reply's hee made us to our demands. Hee differed only in this from the old fellow in to'ther Country: hee let us depart. However, I

10. "Left.": abbreviation for leftenant, now lieutenant.

thought it proper to warn poor Travailers to endeavour to Avoid falling into circumstances like ours, wch at our next Stage I sat down and did as followeth:

> May all that dread the cruel feind of night
> Keep on, and not at this curs't Mansion light.
> 'Tis Hell; 'tis Hell! and Devills here do dwell:
> Here dwells the Devill—surely this's Hell.
> Nothing but Wants: a drop to cool yo'r Tongue
> Cant be procur'd these cruel Feinds among.
> Plenty of horrid Grins and looks sevear,
> Hunger and thirst, But pitty's bannish'd here—
> The Right hand keep, if Hell on Earth you fear!

Thus leaving this habitation of cruelty, we went forward; and arriving at an Ordinary about two mile further, found tollerable accommodation. But our Hostes, being a pretty full mouth'd old creature, entertain'd our fellow travailer, the french Docter, wth Inumirable complaints of her bodily infirmities; and whisperd to him so lou'd, that all the House had as full a hearing as hee: which was very divirting to the company, (of which there was a great many,) as one might see by their sneering. But poor weary I slipt out to enter my mind in my Jornal, and left my Great Landly with her Talkative Guests to themselves.

From hence we proceeded (about ten forenoon) through the Narragansett country, pretty Leisurely; and about one afternoon come to Paukataug River, wch was about two hundred paces over, and now very high, and no way over to to'ther side but this. I darid not venture to Ride thro, my courage at best in such cases but small, And now at the Lowest Ebb, by reason of my weary, very weary, hungry and uneasy Circumstances. So takeing leave of my company, tho' wth no little Reluctance, that I could not proceed wth them on my Jorny, Stop at a little cottage Just by the River, to wait the Waters falling, wch the old man that lived there said would be in a little time, and he would conduct me safe over. This little Hutt was one of the wretchedest I ever saw a habitation for human creatures. It was suported with shores[11] enclosed with Clapbords, laid on Lengthways, and so much asunder, that the Light come throu' every where; the doore tyed on wth a cord in the place of hinges; The floor the bear earth; no windows but such as the thin covering afforded, nor any furniture but a Bedd wth a glass Bottle hanging at the head on't; an earthan cupp, a small pewter Bason, A Bord wth sticks to stand on, instead of a table, and a block or two in the corner instead of chairs. The family were the old man, his wife and two Children; all and every part being the picture of poverty. Notwithstanding both the Hutt and its Inhabitance were very clean and tydee: to the crossing the Old Proverb, that bare walls make giddy hows-wifes.

11. "Shores": props or buttresses to support a building; here, upright posts.

I Blest myselfe that I was not one of this misserable crew; and the Impressions their wretchedness formed in me caused mee on the very Spott to say:

> Tho' Ill at ease, A stranger and alone,
> All my fatigu's shall not extort a grone.
> These Indigents have hunger with their ease;
> Their best is wors behalfe then my disease.
> Their Misirable hutt wch Heat and Cold
> Alternately without Repulse do hold;
> Their Lodgings thyn and hard, their Indian fare,
> The mean Apparel which the wretches wear,
> And their ten thousand ills wch can't be told,
> Makes nature er'e 'tis midle age'd look old.
> When I reflect, my late fatigues do seem
> Only a notion or forgotten Dreem.

I had scarce done thinking, when an Indian-like Animal come to the door, on a creature very much like himselfe, in mien and feature, as well as Ragged cloathing; and having 'litt, makes an Awkerd Scratch wth his Indian shoo, and a Nodd, sitts on the block, fumbles out his black Junk, dipps it in the Ashes, and presents it piping hott to his muscheeto's, and fell to sucking like a calf, without speaking, for near a quarter of an hower. At length the old man said how do's Sarah do? who I understood was the wretches wife, and Daughter to the old man: he Replyed—as well as can be expected, &c. So I remembred the old say, and suposed I knew Sarah's case. Butt hee being, as I understood, going over the River, as ugly as hee was, I was glad to ask him to show me the way to Saxtons, at Stoningtown; wch he promising, I ventur'd over wth the old mans assistance; who having rewarded to content, with my Tattertailed guide, I Ridd on very slowly thro' Stoningtown, where the Rode was very Stony and uneven. I asked the fellow, as we went, divers questions of the place and way, &c. I being arrived at my country Saxtons, at Stonington, was very well accommodated both as to victuals and Lodging, the only Good of both I had found since my setting out. Here I heard there was an old man and his Daughter to come that way, bound to N. London; and being now destitute of a Guide, gladly waited for them, being in so good a harbour, and accordingly, Thirsday, Octobr the 5th, about 3 in the afternoon, I sat forward with neighbor Polly and Jemima, a Girl about 18 Years old, who hee said he had been to fetch out of the Narragansetts, and said they had Rode thirty miles that day, on a sory lean Jade, wth only a Bagg under her for a pillion, which the poor Girl often complain'd was very uneasy.

Wee made Good speed along, wch made poor Jemima make many a sow'r face, the mare being a very hard trotter; and after many a hearty and bitter Oh, she at length Low'd out: Lawful Heart father! this bare mare hurts mee Dingeely, I'me direfull sore I vow; with many words to that purpose: poor

Child sais Gaffer—she us't to serve your mother so. I don't care how mother us't to do, quoth Jemima, in a pasionate tone. At which the old man Laught, and kik't his Jade o' the side, which made her Jolt ten times harder.

About seven that Evening, we come to New London Ferry: here, by reason of a very high wind, we mett with great difficulty in getting over—the Boat tos't exceedingly, and our Horses capper'd at a very surprizing Rate, and set us all in a fright; especially poor Jemima, who desired her father to say so jack to the Jade, to make her stand. But the careless parent, taking no notice of her repeated desires, She Rored out in a Passionate manner: Pray suth father, Are you deaf? Say so Jack to the Jade, I tell you. The Dutiful Parent obey's; saying so Jack, so Jack, as gravely as if hee'd bin to saying Catechise after Young Miss, who with her fright look't of all coullers in the Rain Bow.

Being safely arrived at the house of Mrs. Prentices in N. London, I treated neighbour Polly and daughter for their divirting company, and bid them farewell; and between nine and ten at night waited on the Rev^d Mr. Gurdon Saltonstall, minister of the town, who kindly Invited me to Stay that night at his house, where I was very handsomely and plentifully treated and Lodg'd; and made good the Great Character I had before heard concerning him: viz. that hee was the most affable, courteous, Genero's and best of men.

Friday, Octo^r 6th. I got up very early, in Order to hire somebody to go with mee to New Haven, being in Great parplexity at the thoughts of proceeding alone; which my most hospitable entertainer observing, himselfe went, and soon return'd wth a young Gentleman of the town, who he could confide in to Go with mee; and about eight this morning, wth Mr. Joshua Wheeler my new Guide, takeing leave of this worthy Gentleman, Wee advanced on towards Seabrook. The Rodes all along this way are very bad, Incumbred wth Rocks and mountainos passages, wch were very disagreeable to my tired carcass; but we went on with a moderate pace wch made the Journy more pleasent. But after about eight miles Rideing, in going over a Bridge under wch the River Run very swift, my hors stumbled, and very narrowly 'scaped falling over into the water; wch extreemly frightened mee. But through God's Goodness I met with no harm, and mounting agen, in about half a miles Rideing, come to an ordinary, were well entertained by a woman of about seventy and vantage, but of as Sound Intellectuals as one of seventeen. Shee entertain'd Mr. Wheeler wth some passages of a Wedding awhile ago at a place hard by, the Brides-Groom being about her Age or something above, Saying his Children was dredfully against their fathers marrying, wch shee condemned them extreemly for.

From hence wee went pretty briskly forward, and arriv'd at Saybrook ferry about two of the Clock afternoon; and crossing it, wee call'd at an Inn to Bait, (foreseeing we should not have such another Opportunity till we come to Killingsworth.) Landlady come in, with her hair about her ears, and hands at full pay scratching. Shee told us shee had some mutton wch shee would broil, wch I was glad to hear; But I supose forgot to wash her scratchers; in a little time shee brot it in; but it being pickled, and my Guide said it smelt strong of head sause,[12] we left it, and p^d sixpence a piece for our Dinners, wch was only smell.

So wee putt forward with all speed, and about seven at night come to Killingsworth, and were tollerably well with Travillers fare, and Lodgd there that night.

Saturday, Oct. 7th, we sett out early in the Morning, and being something unaquainted wth the way, having ask't it of some wee mett, they told us wee must Ride a mile or two and turne down a Lane on the Right hand; and by their Direction wee Rode on but not Yet comeing to the turning, we mett a Young fellow and ask't him how farr it was to the Lane which turn'd down towards Guilford. Hee said wee must Ride a little further, and turn down by the Corner of uncle Sams Lott. My Guide vented his Spleen at the Lubber; and we soon after came into the Rhode, and keeping still on, without any thing further Remarkabell, about two a clock afternoon we arrived at New Haven, where I was received with all Posible Respects and civility. Here I discharged Mr. Wheeler with a reward to his satisfaction, and took some time to rest after so long and toilsome a Journey; and Inform'd myselfe of the manners and customs of the place, and at the same time employed myselfe in the afair I went there upon.

They are Govern'd by the same Laws as wee in Boston, (or little differing,) thr'out this whole Colony of Connecticot, And much the same way of Church Government, and many of them good, Sociable people, and I hope Religious too: but a little too much Independant in their principalls, and, as I have been told, were formerly in their Zeal very Riggid in their Administrations towards such as their Lawes made Offenders, even to a harmless Kiss or Innocent merriment among Young people. Whipping being a frequent and counted an easy Punishment, about wch as other Crimes, the Judges were absolute in their Sentences. They told mee a pleasant story about a pair of Justices in those parts, wch I may not omit the relation of.

A negro Slave belonging to a man in the Town, stole a hogs head from his master, and gave or sold it to an Indian, native of the place. The Indian sold it in the neighbourhood, and so the theft was found out. Thereupon the Heathen was Seized, and carried to the Justices House to be Examined. But his worship (it seems) was gone into the feild, with a Brother in office, to gather in his Pompions.[13] Whither the malefactor is hurried, And Complaint made, and satisfaction in the name of Justice demanded. Their Worships

---

12. "Head sause": pickled pig's head (or sometimes calf's head), including ears, jowls, and other parts. Also called head souse or, in a jelled form, head cheese.
13. "Pompions": pumpkins.

cann't proceed in form without a Bench: whereupon they Order one to be Imediately erected, which, for want of fitter materials, they made with pompions—which being finished, down setts their Worships, and the Malefactor call'd, and by the Senior Justice Interrogated after the following manner. You Indian why did You steal from this man? You sho'dn't do so—it's a Grandy wicked thing to steal. Hol't Hol't cryes Justice Junr. Brother, You speak negro to him. I'le ask him. You sirrah, why did You steal this man's Hoggshead? Hoggshead? (replys the Indian,) me no stomany.[14] No? says his Worship; and pulling off his hatt, Patted his own head with his hand, sais, Tatapa[15]—You, Tatapa—you; all one this. Hoggshead all one this. Hah! says Netop, now me stomany that. Whereupon the Company fell into a great fitt of Laughter, even to Roreing. Silence is comanded, but to no effect: for they continued perfectly Shouting. Nay, sais his worship, in an angry tone, if it be so, *take mee off the Bench.*

Their Diversions in this part of the Country are on Lecture days and Training days mostly: on the former there is Riding from town to town.

And on training dayes The Youth divert themselves by Shooting at the Target, as they call it, (but it very much resembles a pillory,) where hee that hitts neerest the white has some yards of Red Ribbin presented him, wch being tied to his hattband, the two ends streeming down his back, he is Led away in Triumph, wth great applausé, as the winners of the Olympiack Games. They generally marry very young: the males oftener as I am told under twentie than above; they generally make public wedings, and have a way something singular (as they say) in some of them, viz. Just before Joyning hands the Bridegroom quitts the place, who is soon followed by the Bridesmen, and as it were, dragg'd back to duty—being the reverse to the former practice among us, to steal m^s Pride.[16]

There are great plenty of Oysters all along by the sea side, as farr as I Rode in the Collony, and those very good. And they Generally lived very well and comfortably in their famelies. But too Indulgent (especially the farmers) to their slaves: sufering too great familiarity from them, permitting th^m to sit at Table and eat with them, (as they say to save time,) and into the dish goes the black hoof as freely as the white hand. They told me that there was a farmer lived nere the Town where I lodgd who had some difference wth his slave, concerning something the master had promised him and did not punctualy perform; wch caused some hard words between them; But at length they put the matter to Arbitration and Bound themselves to stand to the award of such

---

14. "Stomany": understand.
15. "Tatapa": the same as, equal to. The humor in the following story lies in the junior justice's failure to realize that, in pointing to his own head to help convey the concept "hogshead" to the "Netop" (Indian man), he is inadvertently insulting himself.
16. "Steal Mistress Pride": a familiar expression for the popular wedding ritual in which the bride was "stolen away" to a local tavern where she was later redeemed by the purchase of dinner for the captors.

as they named—wch done, the Arbitrators Having heard the Allegations of both parties, Order the master to pay 40^s to black face, and acknowledge his fault. And so the matter ended: the poor master very honestly standing to the award.

There are every where in the Towns as I passed, a Number of Indians the Natives of the Country, and are the most salvage of all the salvages of that kind that I had ever Seen: little or no care taken (as I heard upon enquiry) to make them otherwise. They have in some places Landes of their owne, and Govern'd by Law's of their own making;—they marry many wives and at pleasure put them away, and on the least dislike or fickle humour, on either side, saying *stand away* to one another is a sufficient Divorce. And indeed those uncomely *Stand aways* are too much in Vougue among the English in this (Indulgent Colony) as their Records plentifully prove; and that on very trivial matters, of which some have been told me, but are not proper to be Related by a Female pen, tho some of that foolish sex have had too large a share in the story.

If the natives committ any crime on their own precincts among themselves, the English takes no Cognezens of. But if on the English ground, they are punishable by our Laws. They mourn for their Dead by blacking their faces, and cutting their hair, after an Awkerd and frightfull manner; But can't bear You should mention the names of their dead Relations to them: they trade most for Rum, for wch they^d hazzard their very lives; and the English fit them Generally as well, by seasoning it plentifully with water.

They give the title of merchant to every trader; who Rate their Goods according to the time and spetia they pay in: viz. Pay, mony, Pay as mony, and trusting. *Pay* is Grain, Pork, Beef, &c. at the prices sett by the General Court that Year; *mony* is pieces of Eight, Ryalls, or Boston or Bay shillings (as they call them,) or Good hard money, as sometimes silver coin is termed by them; also Wampom, vizt. Indian beads wch serves for change. *Pay as mony* is provisions, as afores^d one Third cheaper then as the Assembly or Gene^l Court sets it; and *Trust* as they and the merch^t agree for time.

Now, when the buyer comes to ask for a comodity, sometimes before the merchant answers that he has it, he sais, *is Your pay redy?* Perhaps the Chap Reply's Yes: what do You pay in? say's the merchant. The buyer having answered, then the price is set; as suppose he wants a sixpenny knife, in pay it is 12d—in pay as money eight pence, and hard money its own price, viz. 6d. It seems a very Intricate way of trade and what Lex Mercatoria [17] had not thought of.

Being at a merchants house, in comes a tall country fellow, wth his alfogeos [18] full of Tobacco; for they seldom Loose their Cudd, but keep Chewing

17. "Lex Mercatoria": mercantile law.
18. "Alfogeos": probably an approximate spelling of *alforjas,* the Spanish word for "saddlebags," here used colloquially for cheeks.

and Spitting as long as they'r eyes are open,—he advanc't to the midle of the Room, makes an Awkward Nodd, and spitting a Large deal of Aromatick Tincture, he gave a scrape with his shovel like shoo, leaving a small shovel full of dirt on the floor, made a full stop, Hugging his own pretty Body with his hands under his arms, Stood staring rown'd him, like a Catt let out of a Baskett. At last, like the creature Balaam Rode on, he opened his mouth and said: have You any Ribinen for Hatbands to sell I pray? The Questions and Answers about the pay being past, the Ribin is bro't and opened. Bumpkin Simpers, cryes its confounded Gay I vow; and beckning to the door, in comes Jone Tawdry, dropping about 50 curtsees, and stands by him: hee shows her the Ribin. *Law, You,* sais shee, *its right Gent,* do You, take it, *tis dreadfull pretty.* Then she enquires, *have You any hood silk I pray?* wch being brought and bought, Have You any *thred silk to sew it* wth says shee, wch being accomodated wth they Departed. They Generaly stand after they come in a great while speachless, and sometimes dont say a word till they are askt what they want, which I Impute to the Awe they stand in of the merchants, who they are constantly almost Indebted too; and must take what they bring without Liberty to choose for themselves; but they serve them as well, making the merchants stay long enough for their pay.

We may Observe here the great necessity and bennifitt both of Education and Conversation; for these people have as Large a portion of mother witt, and sometimes a Larger, than those who have bin brought up in Citties; But for want of emprovements, Render themselves almost Ridiculos, as above. I should be glad if they would leave such follies, and am sure all that Love Clean Houses (at least) would be glad on't too.

They are generaly very plain in their dress, throuout all the Colony, as I saw, and follow one another in their modes; that You may know where they belong, especially the women, meet them where you will.

Their Cheif Red Letter day is St. Election, wch is annualy Observed according to Charter, to choose their Goven^r: a blessing they can never be thankfull enough for, as they will find, if ever it be their hard fortune to loose it. The present Govenor in Conecticott is the Honble John Winthrop Esq. A Gentleman of an Ancient and Honourable Family, whose Father was Govenor here sometime before, and his Grand father had bin Govr of the Massachusetts. This gentleman is a very curteous and afable person, much Given to Hospitality, and has by his Good services Gain'd the affections of the people as much as any who had bin before him in that post.

Decr 6th. Being by this time well Recruited and rested after my Journy, my business lying unfinished by some concerns at New York depending thereupon, my Kinsman, Mr. Thomas Trowbridge of New Haven, must needs take a Journy there before it could be accomplished, I resolved to go there in company wth him, and a man of the town wch I engaged to wait on me there. Accordingly, Dec. 6th we set out from New Haven, and about 11 same morning came to Stratford ferry; wch crossing, about two miles on the other side Baited our horses and would have eat a morsell ourselves, But the Pumpkin and Indian mixt Bred had such an Aspect, and the Bare-legg'd Punch so awkerd or rather Awfull a sound, that we left both, and proceeded forward, and about seven at night come to Fairfield, where we met with good entertainment and Lodg'd; and early next morning set forward to Norowalk, from its halfe Indian name *North-walk,* when about 12 at noon we arrived, and Had a Dinner of Fryed Venison, very savoury. Landlady wanting some pepper in the seasoning, bid the Girl hand her the spice in the little *Gay* cupp on the shelfe. From hence we Hasted towards Rye, walking and Leading our Horses neer a mile together up a prodigios high Hill; and so Riding till about nine at night, and there arrived and took up our Lodgings at an ordinary, wch a French family kept. Here being very hungry, I desired a fricasee, wch the Frenchman undertakeing, mannaged so contrary to my notion of Cookery, that I hastned to Bed superless; And being shewd the way up a pair of stairs wch had such a narrow passage that I had almost stopt by the Bulk of my Body; But arriving at my apartment found it to be a little Lento Chamber furnisht amongst other Rubbish with a High Bedd and a Low one, a Long Table, a Bench and a Bottomless chair,—Little Miss went to scratch up my Kennell wch Russelled as if shee'd bin in the Barn amongst the Husks, and supose such was the contents of the tickin—nevertheless being exceeding weary, down I laid my poor Carkes (never more tired) and found my Covering as scanty as my Bed was hard. Annon I heard another Russelling noise in The Room— called to know the matter—Little miss said shee was making a bed for the men; who, when they were in Bed, complained their leggs lay out of it by reason of its shortness—my poor bones complained bitterly not being used to such Lodgings, and so did the man who was with us; and poor I made but one Grone, which was from the time I went to bed to the time I Riss, which was about three in the morning, Setting up by the Fire till Light, and having discharged our ordinary wch was as dear as if we had had far Better fare— wee took our leave of Monsier and about seven in the morn come to New Rochell a french town, where we had a good Breakfast. And in the strength of that about an how'r before sunsett got to York. Here I applyd myself to Mr. Burroughs, a merchant to whom I was recommended by my Kinsman Capt. Prout, and received great Civilities from him and his spouse, who were now both Deaf but very agreeable in their Conversation, Diverting me with pleasant stories of their knowledge in Brittan from whence they both come, one of which was above the rest very pleasant to me viz. my Lord Darcy had a very extravagant Brother who had mortgaged what Estate hee could not sell, and in good time dyed leaving only one son. Him his Lordship (having none of his own) took and made him Heir of his whole Estate, which he was to receive at the death of his Aunt. He and his Aunt in her widowhood held a right understanding and lived as become such Relations, shee being a discreat Gentlewoman and he an Ingenios Young man. One day Hee fell into some Company though far his inferiors, very freely told him of the Ill circumstances his fathers Estate lay under, and the many Debts he left unpaid to the wrong of poor people with whom he had dealt. The Young gentleman was put out of countenance—no way hee could think of to Redress himself—his whole dependance being on the Lady his Aunt, and how to speak to her he knew not—Hee went home, sat down to dinner and as usual sometimes with her when the Chaplain was absent, she desired him to say Grace, wch he did after this manner:

> Pray God in Mercy take my Lady Darcy
> Unto his Heavenly Throne,
> That Little John may live like a man,
> And pay every man his own.

The prudent Lady took no present notice, But finishd dinner, after wch having sat and talk't awhile (as Customary) He Riss, took his Hatt and Going out she desired him to give her leave to speak to him in her Clossett, Where being come she desired to know why hee prayed for her Death in the manner afore-said, and what part of her deportment towards him merritted such desires. Hee Reply'd, none at all, But he was under such disadvantages that nothing but that could do him service, and told her how he had been affronted as above, and what Impressions it had made upon him. The Lady made him a gentle reprimand that he had not informed her after another manner, Bid him see what his father owed and he should have money to pay it to a penny, And always to lett her know his wants and he should have a redy supply. The Young Gentleman charm'd with his Aunts Discrete management, Beggd her pardon and accepted her kind offer and retrieved his fathers Estate, &c. and said Hee hoped his Aunt would never dye, for shee had done better by him than hee could have done for himself.—Mr. Burroughs went with me to Ven-due where I bought about 100 Rheem of paper wch was retaken in a fly-boat from Holland and sold very Reasonably here—some ten, some Eight shillings per Rheem by the Lott wch was ten Rheem in a Lott. And at the Vendue I made a great many acquaintances amongst the good women of the town, who curteosly invited me to their houses and generously entertained me.

The Cittie of New York is a pleasant, well compacted place, situated on a Commodius River wch is a fine harbour for shipping. The Buildings Brick Generaly, very stately and high, though not altogether like ours in Boston. The Bricks in some of the Houses are of divers Coullers and laid in Checkers, being glazed look very agreeable. The inside of them are neat to admiration, the wooden work, for only the walls are plasterd, and the Sumers and Gist [19] are plained and kept very white scowr'd as so is all the partitions if made of

---

19. "Sumers and Gist": summers and joists. The summer beam was a central floor timber holding the crossbeams, or joists, which were set into it. In early colonial homes the absence of plaster ceilings made these beams supporting the floor of the second story visible from the ground floor.

Bords. The fire places have no Jambs (as ours have) But the Backs run flush with the walls, and the Hearth is of Tyles and is as farr out into the Room at the Ends as before the fire, wch is Generally Five foot in the Low'r rooms, and the peice over where the mantle tree should be is made as ours with Joyners work, and as I supose is fasten'd to iron rodds inside. The House where the Vendue was, had Chimney Corners like ours, and they and the hearths were laid wth the finest tile that I ever see, and the stair cases laid all with white tile which is ever clean, and so are the walls of the Kitchen wch had a Brick floor. They were making Great preparations to Receive their Govenor, Lord Cornbury from the Jerseys, and for that End raised the militia to Gard him on shore to the fort.

They are Generaly of the Church of England and have a New England Gentleman for their minister, and a very fine church set out with all Customary requsites. There are also a Dutch and Divers Conventicles as they call them, viz. Baptist, Quakers, &c. They are not strict in keeping the Sabbath as in Boston and other places where I had bin, But seem to deal with great exactness as farr as I see or Deall with. They are sociable to one another and Curteos and Civill to strangers and fare well in their houses. The English go very fasheonable in their dress. But the Dutch, especially the middling sort, differ from our women, in their habitt go loose, were French muches wch are like a Capp and a head band in one, leaving their ears bare, which are sett out wth Jewells of a large size and many in number. And their fingers hoop't with Rings, some with large stones in them of many Coullers as were their pendants in their ears, which You should see very old women wear as well as Young.

They have Vendues very frequently and make their Earnings very well by them, for they treat with good Liquor Liberally, and the Customers Drink as Liberally and Generally pay for't as well, by paying for that which they Bidd up Briskly for, after the sack has gone plentifully about, tho' sometimes good penny worths are got there. Their Diversions in the Winter is Riding Sleys about three or four Miles out of Town, where they have Houses of entertainment at a place called the Bowery, and some go to friends Houses who handsomely treat them. Mr. Burroughs cary'd his spouse and Daughter and myself out to one Madame Dowes, a Gentlewoman that lived at a farm House, who gave us a handsome Entertainment of five or six Dishes and choice Beer and metheglin, Cyder, &c. all which she said was the produce of her farm. I believe we mett 50 or 60 slays that day—they fly with great swiftness and some are so furious that they'le turn out of the path for none except a Loaden Cart. Nor do they spare for any diversion the place affords, and sociable to a degree, they'r Tables being as free to their Naybours as to themselves.

Having here transacted the affair I went upon and some other that fell in the way, after about a fortnight's stay there I left New-York with no Little regrett, and Thursday, Dec. 21, set out for New Haven wth my Kinsman Trowbridge, and the man that waited on me about one afternoon, and about three come to half-way house about ten miles out of town, where we Baited and went forward, and about 5 come to Spiting Devil,[20] Else Kings bridge, where they pay three pence for passing over with a horse, which the man that keeps the Gate set up at the end of the Bridge receives.

We hoped to reach the french town and Lodg there that night, but unhapily lost our way about four miles short, and being overtaken by a great storm of wind and snow which set full in our faces about dark, we were very uneasy. But meeting one Gardner who lived in a Cottage thereabout, offered us his fire to set by, having but one poor Bedd, and his wife not well, &c. or he would go to a House with us, where he thought we might be better accommodated—thither we went, But a surly old shee Creature, not worthy the name of woman, who would hardly let us go into her Door, though the weather was so stormy none but shee would have turnd out a Dogg. But her son whose name was gallop, who lived Just by Invited us to his house and shewed me two pair of stairs, viz. one up the loft and tother up the Bedd, wch was as hard as it was high, and warmed it with a hott stone at the feet. I lay very uncomfortably, insomuch that I was so very cold and sick I was forced to call them up to give me something to warm me. They had nothing but milk in the house, wch they Boild, and to make it better sweetened wth molasses, which I not knowing or thinking oft till it was down and coming up agen wch it did in so plentifull a manner that my host was soon paid double for his portion, and that in specia. But I believe it did me service in Cleering my stomach. So after this sick and weary night at East Chester, (a very miserable poor place,) the weather being now fair, Friday the 22^d Dec. we set out for New Rochell, where being come we had good Entertainment and Recruited ourselves very well. This is a very pretty place well compact, and good handsome houses, Clean, good and passable Rodes, and situated on a Navigable River, abundance of land well fined and Cleerd all along as wee passed, which caused in me a Love to the place, wch I could have been content to live in it. Here wee Ridd over a Bridge made of one entire stone of such a Breadth that a cart might pass with safety, and to spare—it lay over a passage cutt through a Rock to convey water to a mill not farr off. Here are three fine Taverns within call of each other, very good provision for Travailers.

Thence we travailed through Merrinak,[21] a neet, though little place, wth a navigable River before it, one of the pleasantest I ever see—Here were good Buildings, Especialy one, a very fine seat, wch they told me was Col. Hethcoats, who I had heard was a very fine Gentleman. From hence we

---

20. "Spiting Devil": Spuyten Duyvil, a Dutch name still used for the place where the Hudson and Harlem rivers join at the northernmost tip of Manhattan Island.
21. "Merrinak": Mamaroneck, New York.

come to Hors Neck, where wee Baited, and they told me that one Church of England parson officiated in all these three towns once every Sunday in turns throughout the Year; and that they all could but poorly maintaine him, which they grudg'd to do, being a poor and quarelsome crew as I understand by our Host; their Quarelling about their choice of Minister, they chose to have none—But caused the Government to send this Gentleman to them. Here wee took leave of York Government, and Descending the Mountainos passage that almost broke my heart in ascending before, we come to Stamford, a well compact Town, but miserable meeting house, wch we passed, and thro' many and great difficulties, as Bridges which were exceeding high and very tottering and of vast Length, steep and Rocky Hills and precipices, (Buggbears to a fearful female travailer)[.] About nine at night we come to Norrwalk, having crept over a timber of a Broken Bridge about thirty foot long, and perhaps fifty to the water. I was exceeding tired and cold when we come to our Inn, and could get nothing there but poor entertainment, and the Impertinant Bable of one of the worst of men, among many others of which our Host made one, who, had he bin one degree Impudenter, would have outdone his Grandfather. And this I think is the most perplexed night I have yet had. From hence, Saturday, Dec. 23, a very cold and windy day, after an Intolerable night's Lodging, wee hasted forward only observing in our way the Town to be situated on a Navigable river wth indiferent Buildings and people more refind than in some of the Country towns wee had passed, tho' vicious enough, the Church and Tavern being next neighbours. Having Ridd thro a difficult River wee come to Fairfield where wee Baited and were much refreshed as well with the Good things wch gratified our appetites as the time took to rest our wearied Limbs, wch Latter I employed in enquiring concerning the Town and manners of the people, &c. This is a considerable town, and filld as they say with wealthy people—have a spacious meeting house and good Buildings. But the Inhabitants are Litigious, nor do they well agree with their minister, who (they say) is a very worthy Gentleman.

They have aboundance of sheep, whose very Dung brings them great gain, with part of which they pay their Parsons sallery, And they Grudg that, prefering their Dung before their minister. They Lett out their sheep at so much as they agree upon for a night; the highest Bidder always caries them, And they will sufficiently Dung a Large quantity of Land before morning. But were once Bitt by a sharper who had them a night and sheared them all before morning—From hence we went to Stratford, the next Town, in which I observed but few houses, and those not very good ones. But the people that I conversed with were civill and good natured. Here we staid till late at night, being to cross a Dangerous River ferry, the River at that time full of Ice; but after about four hours waiting with great difficulty wee got over. My fears and fatigues prevented my here taking any particular observation. Being got to Milford, it being late in the night, I could go no further; my fellow travailer going forward, I was invited to Lodg at Mrs. ——, a very kind and civill Gentlewoman, by whom I was handsomely and kindly entertained till the next night. The people here go very plain in their apparel (more plain than I had observed in the towns I had passed) and seem to be very grave and serious. They told me there was a singing Quaker lived there, or at least had a strong inclination to be so, His Spouse not at all affected that way. Some of the singing Crew come there one day to visit him, who being then abroad, they sat down (to the woman's no small vexation) Humming and singing and groneing after their conjuring way—Says the woman are you singing quakers? Yea says They—Then take my squalling Brat of a child here and sing to it says she for I have almost split my throat wth singing to him and cant get the Rogue to sleep. They took this as a great Indignity, and mediately departed. Shaking the dust from their Heels left the good woman and her Child among the number of the wicked.

This is a Seaport place and accomodated with a Good Harbour, But I had not opportunity to make particular observations because it was Sabbath day—This Evening.

December 24. I set out with the Gentlewomans son who she very civilly offered to go with me when she see no parswasions would cause me to stay which she pressingly desired, and crossing a ferry having but nine miles to New Haven, in a short time arrived there and was Kindly received and well accommodated amongst my Friends and Relations.

The Government of Connecticut Collony begins westward towards York at Stanford [22] (as I am told) and so runs Eastward towards Boston (I mean in my range, because I dont intend to extend my description beyond my own travails) and ends that way at Stonington—And has a great many Large towns lying more northerly. It is a plentiful Country for provisions of all sorts and its Generally Healthy. No one that can and will be dilligent in this place need fear poverty nor the want of food and Rayment.

January 6th. Being now well Recruited and fitt for business I discoursed the persons I was concerned with, that we might finnish in order to my return to Boston. They delay^d as they had hitherto done hoping to tire my Patience. But I was resolute to stay and see an End of the matter let it be never so much to my disadvantage—So January 9th they come again and promise the Wednesday following to go through with the distribution of the Estate which they delayed till Thursday and then come with new amusements. But at length by the mediation of that holy good Gentleman, the Rev. Mr. James

22. "Stanford": that is, Stamford, Connecticut.

Pierpont, the minister of New Haven, and with the advice and assistance of other our Good friends we come to an accommodation and distribution, which having finished though not till February, the man that waited on me to York taking the charge of me I sit out for Boston. We went from New Haven upon the ice (the ferry being not passable thereby) and the Rev. Mr. Pierpont wth Madam Prout Cuzin Trowbridge and divers others were taking leave wee went onward without any thing Remarkabl till wee come to New London and Lodged again at Mr. Saltonstalls—and here I dismist my Guide, and my Generos entertainer provided me Mr. Samuel Rogers of that place to go home with me—I stayed a day here Longer than I intended by the Commands of the Honble Govenor Winthrop to stay and take a supper with him whose wonderful civility I may not omitt. The next morning I Crossed the Ferry to Groton, having had the Honor of the Company, of Madam Livingston (who is the Govenors Daughter) and Mary Christophers and divers others to the boat—And that night Lodg^d at Stonington and had Rost Beef and pumpkin sause for supper. The next night at Haven's and had Rost fowle, and the next day wee come to a river which by Reason of The Freshetts coming down was swell'd so high wee fear^d it impassable and the rapid stream was very terryfying—However we must over and that in a small Cannoo. Mr. Rogers assuring me of his good Conduct, I after a stay of near an how'r on the shore for consultation went into the Cannoo, and Mr. Rogers paddled about 100 yards up the Creek by the shore side, turned into the swift stream and dexterously steering her in a moment wee come to the other side as swiftly passing as an arrow shott out of the Bow by a strong arm. I staid on the shore till Hee returned to fetch our horses, which he caused to swim over himself bringing the furniture in the Cannoo. But it is past my skill to express the Exceeding fright all their transactions formed in me. Wee were now in the colony of the Massachusetts and taking Lodgings at the first Inn we come too had a pretty difficult passage the next day which was the second of March by reason of the sloughy ways then thawed by the Sunn. Here I mett Capt. John Richards of Boston who was going home, So being very glad of his Company we Rode something harder than hitherto, and missing my way going up a very steep Hill, my horse dropt down under me as Dead; this new surprize no little hurt me meeting it Just at the Entrance into Dedham from whence we intended to reach home that night. But was now obliged to gett another Hors there and leave my own, resolving for Boston that night if possible. But in going over the Causeway at Dedham the Bridge being overflowed by the high waters comming down I very narrowly escaped falling over into the river Hors and all wch twas almost a miracle I did not—now it grew late in the afternoon and the people having very much discouraged us about the sloughy way wch they said wee should find very difficult and hazardous it so wrought on mee being tired and dispirited and disapointed of my desires of going home that I agreed to Lodg there that night wch wee did at the house of one Draper, and the next day being March 3d wee got safe home to Boston, where I found my aged and tender mother and my Dear and only Child in good health with open arms redy to receive me, and my Kind relations and friends flocking in to welcome mee and hear the story of my transactions and travails I having this day bin five months from home and now I cannot fully express my Joy and Satisfaction. But desire sincearly to adore my Great Benefactor for thus graciously carying forth and returning in safety his unworthy handmaid.

6

Elizabeth Ashbridge (1713–1755)

Some Account of the Fore Part
of the Life of Elizabeth Ashbridge

Though long known among Quaker readers, this fascinating autobiography did not acquire a larger readership until discussed by Daniel Shea in *Spiritual Autobiography in Early America* in 1968. Since then it has attracted further attention as a very sympathetic early woman's autobiography.

What makes the *Account* so sympathetic is Ashbridge's vitality and modernity. She in no way fits the stereotype of the pious Quaker woman, dressed in somber gray and speaking softly in "thee's" and "thou's." She was wild. She eloped. She wanted to be an actress, and delighted her second husband with her spirited singing and dancing. What's more, she writes with spirit, using excited colloquial language. (Once one gets accustomed to the eighteenth-century syntax, her writing is also quite easy to follow.) Yet as a bright, energetic, high-spirited woman, she still had considerable trouble breaking out of gender stereotypes, and that is Ashbridge's modernity.

She becomes a little tamer once she becomes a Quaker. She loses the urge to dance, and eventually alters her dress. But the spirit remains, sublimated in the energy of her faith and her works. She even temporarily reforms her husband.

The *Account* ends in about 1741 or 1742, with the news of his death. Post-scripts by her third husband (Aaron Ashbridge) and other people say that she paid off her second husband's debts, amounting to eighty pounds, and then supported herself by "School keeping" and "her Needle." Aaron was a Quaker, and they married "in the 9 mo 1746" in Burlington, New Jersey. She also travelled as a visitor to other Meetings. In 1753, she went to visit Meetings in England and Ireland, where she became ill from her exhausting travels. Daniel Shea has discovered from an Ashbridge family genealogy that her name at the time of her last marriage was Elizabeth Sampson Sullivan. He also learned that Aaron Ashbridge's later life "reversed the pattern" of Mr. Sullivan's. "He was twice complained of in the Goshen [Pennsylvania] Meeting for drinking to excess,"[1] and in 1775 the Meeting disowned him.

1. Daniel Shea, "Introduction" to *Some Account of the Fore Part of the Life of Elizabeth Ashbridge . . .*, in *Journeys in New Worlds: Early American Women's Narratives*, ed. William L. Andrews, p. 141.

The text is from *Some Account of the Fore Part of the Life of Elizabeth Ashbridge . . .* , ed. Daniel Shea, in *Journeys in New Worlds: Early American Women's Narratives,* ed. William L. Andrews (Madison: Univ. of Wisconsin Press, 1990). In his introduction, Shea provides biographical information as well as criticism. Shea's notes have been shortened to save space.

My Life being attended with many uncommon Occurences, some of which I through disobedience brought upon myself, and others I believe were for my Good, I therefore thought proper to make some remarks on the Dealings of Divine Goodness to me, and have often had cause with David to say, it was good for me that I have been afflicted &c.[2] and most earnestly I desire that whosoever reads the following lines, may take warning and shun the Evils that I have thro' the Deceitfulness of Satan been drawn into.

To begin with my beginning. I was born in Middlewich in Cheshire in the year 1713 of Honest Parents, my Father a Doctor of Physick or Surgeon; his name was Thomas Sampson, my Mother's name was Mary. My Father was a Man that bore a good Character, but not so Strictly religious as my Mother, who was a pattern of Virtue to me. I was the only Child of my Father but not of my Mother, she being a Widow when my Father married her, and had two Children by her former Husband, a Son & a daughter. Soon after my birth, my Father took to the sea & followed his Profession on board a ship, in many long voyages, till I arrived to the Age of twelve years, & then left off; so that my Education lay mostly on my Mother, in which She discharged her duty by endeavoring to instill in me, in my tender Age, the principles of virtue; for which I have since had Cause to be thankful to the Lord, & that he blessed me with such a parent, whose good Advice and Counsel to me has been as Bread cast on the Waters, & may all Parents have the same Testimony in their Children's breasts; in a word She was a good Example to all about her, and Beloved by most that Knew her, Tho' not of the same religious perswasion I am now of. But Alas for me, as soon as the time came that she might reasonably have expected the benefit of her Labours, & have had Comfort in me, I left her—of which I shall speak in its place.

In my very Infancy, I had an awful regard for religion & a great love for religious people, particularly the Ministers, and sometimes wept with Sorrow, that I was not a boy that I might have been one; believing them all Good Men & so beloved of God. Also I had a great Love for the Poor, remembering I had read that they were blessed of the Lord; this I took to mean such as were poor in this World. I often went to their poor Cottages to see them, and used to think they were better off than me, and if I had any money or any thing else I would give it to them, remembering that those that gave to such, lent to the Lord; for I had when very young earnest desires to be beloved

2. "It was good . . . afflicted": "It is good for me that I have been afflicted, that I may learn your statutes" (Psalm 119: 71).

by him, and used to make remarks on those that pretended to religion; and when I heard the Gentlemen swear it made me sorry, for my Mother told me, if I used any Naughty words God would not love me.

As I grew up, I took notice there were several different religious societies, wherefore I often went alone and wept; with desires that I might be directed to the right. Thus my young years were attended with these & such like tender desires tho' I was sometimes guilty of faults incident to Children; and then I always found something in me that made me sorry. From my Infancy till fourteen years of age I was as innocent as most Children, about which time my Sorrows began, and have continued for the most part of my life ever since; by giving way to a foolish passion, in Setting my affections on a young man who Courted me without my Parents' consent; till I consented, and with sorrow of Heart may say, I suffered myself to be carried off in the night, and before my Parents found me, was married, tho' as soon as they missed me, all possible search was made, but all in vain till too late to recover me.

This precipitate action plunged me into a deal of Sorrow. I was soon smote with remorse, for thus leaving my parents, whose right it was to have disposed of me to their contents, or at least to have been consulted in the Affair. I was soon Chastised for my disobedience—Divine Providence let me see my error. In five months I was stripped of the Darling of my Soul, and left a young & disconsolate Widow. I had then no home to fly to. My Husband was poor, had nothing but his Trade, which was a Stocking Weaver, & my Father was so displeased, he would do nothing for me. My Dear Mother had some Compassion & used to keep me Amongst the Neighbours. At last by her Advice I went over to Dublin, to a relation of hers in hopes that Absence would regain my Father's Affection. But he continued Inflexible, & would not send for me again & I durst not return without it.

This relation was one of the People called Quakers; his Conduct was so different from the Manner of my Education (which was in the way of the Church of England) that it proved very disagreeable to me for tho' (as I have said) I had a Religious Education, yet I was allowed to sing & dance, which my Cousin disallow'd of, & I having great Vivacity in my Natural Disposition, could not bear to give way to the Gloomy Sense of Sorrow & Convictions; therefore let it have the wrong effect, so gave up to be more Wild & Airy than ever, for which he often reproved me. But I then thought (as many do now of this Society), 'Twas the Effect of Singularity, & therefore would not bear it, nor be controuled, & having a distant relation in the West of Ireland, left Dublin and went thither; And here I might take my Swing, for what rendered me disagreeable to the former, was quite pleasing to the latter.

Between these two relations I spent Three Years and three Months. While I was in Ireland, I contracted an intimate Acquaintance with a Widow & her Daughter that were Papists, with whom I used to have a deal of discourse about religion, they in defence of their Faith & I of mine. And tho' I was then wild, yet it often made me very thoughtful. The Old Woman would tell me of such mighty miracles done by their Priests, that I began to be shaken, & thought if these things were so they must of a Truth be the Apostles' Successors.

The Old woman perceived it & one day in a rapture said "Oh! if I can under God, be the happy Instrument to convert you to the Holy Catholick Faith, all the sins that ever I committed will be forgiven." In a while it got so far that the priest came to converse with me, & I being young & my Judgment weak, was ready to believe what they said, and wild as I was, it cost me many Tears, with desires that I might be rightly directed; for some time I frequented their place of Worship, but none of my Relations knew what was my motive. At length I concluded never to be led darkly into their Belief, & if their Articles of Faith are good, they'll not be against my Knowing them, so the next time I had an Opportunity with the priest I told him I had some thoughts of becoming one of his flock but did not care to join till I knew all I must agree to; I therefore desired him to let me see their principles. He answered I must first confess my Sins to him: & gave me till the next day to consider them.

I was not much against it, for thought I, "I have done nothing if all the World Knew that any can hurt me for: And if what this Man says be true, it will be for my Good," & when he came again I told him all that I could remember, which for my part I thought bad enough, but he thought me (as he said) the most Innocent Creature that ever made Confession to him. When I had done, He took a book out & read it; all which I was to swear to, if I joined with them; and tho' young made my remarks[3] as he went on, but I shall neither give myself the Trouble of Writing, nor any of reading a deal of the ridiculous stuff it contained; But what made me sick of my new intention (I believe I should have swallowed the rest) was to swear that I believed the Pretender to be the true heir to the Crown of England; & that he was King James' Son and also that whosoever died out of the Pale of that Church was damned.

As to the first, I did not believe it essential to Salvation, whether I believed it or not, and to take an Oath to any such thing would be very unsafe; And the Second struck directly against Charity, which The Apostle preferred before all other Graces, & Besides I had a religious Mother who was not of that opinion. I thought it therefore barbarous in me, to believe she would be damned, Yet concluded to take it into Consideration.—But before I saw him again a Sudden Turn Took hold, which put a final end to it.

My Father still keeping me at such a distance that I thought myself quite shut out of his Affections, I therefore Concluded since my Absence was so

3. "Made my remarks": noticed, remarked privately.

Agreeable, he should have it; and getting acquainted with a Gentlewoman that then lately came from Pensilvania (& was going back again) where I had an Uncle, my Mother's Brother, I soon agreed with her for my passage & being ignorant of the Nature of an Indenture soon became bound, tho' in a private manner, (for fear I should be found out) tho' this was repugnant to law.—As soon as this was over, She invited me to go & see the Vessel I was to go in, to which I readily consented, not Knowing what would follow, & when I came on board, I found a Young Woman I afterward understood was of a very good Family and had been deluded away by this creature. I was extremely pleased to think I should have such an agreeable Companion & while we were in discourse, our Kidnapper left us & went on shore, & when I wanted to go, was not permitted.

Here I was kept near three weeks; at the end thereof the Friends of the other young Woman found her out & fetched her on shore; by which means mine found me, & sent the Water Bailif, who took me also on shore. Our Gentlewoman was forced to keep Incog[nito] or she would have been laid fast.[4]

I was Kept close for two weeks, but at last found means to get away, for I was so filled with the thought of coming to America, that I could not give it up, & meeting with the Captain I enquired when they sailed. He told me, I got on board & came in the same ship, & have cause to believe there was a Providential hand in it.

There was Sixty Irish Servants on board (I came now unindentured) & several English Passengers, but not one of them understood the Irish language but myself: I had taken no small pains to learn it. I could understand so much as to discover any thing they discoursed upon, which was of great service to us all. There was also on board the Gentlewoman beforementioned & a Young Man her Husband's Brother (Twenty of those Servants belonged to her). While we were on the Coast of Ireland (For the Wind kept us there some weeks) I overheard those Creatures contriving how they should be free when they came to America; to accomplish their design they concluded to rise & kill the Ship's crew & all the English on board, & the abovementioned Young Man was to navigate the Vessel. The same night I discovered their barbarous design privately to the Captain, who let the English know it. The next day they bore for the shore & some small distance off the Cove of Cork lowered sail & dropped Anchor under pretence that the Wind was not fair to stand their Course; so hoisted out the Boat, and invited the Passengers to go on shore to divert themselves, & among the rest the Rebels' Captain; he did, which was all they wanted. As soon as he was on shore the rest left him and came on board. Our Captain immediately ordered to weigh Anchor and hoist Sail, but there were great Outcries for the Young Man on Shore. The

---

4. "Laid fast": that is, imprisoned—possibly for tricking the others into prostitution.

Captain told them the Wind freshened up, & that he would not stay for his own Son. So their Treachery was betrayed in good time; & in such a manner that they did not mistrust it, for it was thought most advisable to keep it private, least any of them should do me a mischief; but at Length they found out that I understood Irish, by my Smiling at an Irish Story they were telling, and from that time they Devised many ways to hurt me, & several of them were corrected and Put in Irons for it.

In Nine Weeks from the time I left Ireland we arrived at New York, (viz) on the 15th of the 7 mo 1732 & then those to whom I had been Instrumental under Providence to save Life, proved Treacherous to me: I was a Stranger in a Strange Land.[5] The Captain got an Indenture wrote & Demanded of me to Sign it, withal Threatning a Gaol if I refused; I told him I could find means to Satisfy him for my Passage without becoming bound: they then told me I might take my Choice Either to Sign that, or have that I had signed in Ireland in force aginst me (by this time I had learned the Character of the afforesaid Woman, that she was a Vile Creature, & feared that if ever I was in her Power she would use me Ill on her Brother's Account). I therefore in a fright Signed that, & tho' there was no Magistrate present, I being Ignorant In such Cases, it Did well enough to Make me a Servant four Years.

In Two Weeks time I was Sold, & Were it Possible to Convey in Characters a sense of the Sufferings of my Servitude, it would make the most strong heart pity the Misfortunes of a young creature as I was, who had a Tender Education; for tho' my Father had no great Estate, yet he Lived well. I had been used to Little but my School, but now it had been better for me if I had been brought up to more hardship. For a While at first I was Pretty well used, but in a Little time the Scale turned, Occasioned by a Difference that happened between my Master & me, wherein I was Innocent: from that time he set himself against me and was Inhuman. He would not suffer me to have Clothes to be Decent in, having to go barefoot in his Service in the Snowey Weather & the Meanest drudgery, wherein I Suffered the Utmost Hardship that my Body was able to Bear, which, with the afforesaid Troubles, had like to have been my Ruin to all Eternity had not Almighty God in Mercy Interposed.

My Master would seem to be a Very Religious Man, taking the Sacrament (so called),[6] & used to Pray every Night in his family, except when his Prayer Book was Lost, for he never Pray'd without it that I knew of. The

---

5. "A Stranger in a Strange Land": Moses so describes himself living among the Egyptians (see Exodus 2: 22).
6. "The Sacrament (so called)": the sacrament of the Lord's Supper, or Communion. Quakers rejected the sacraments of the Church of England as empty outward forms, as when Elizabeth Ashbridge refers disparagingly to baptism as sprinkling, or to confirmation as merely passing under a bishop's hands. She mistrusts the set prayer of the Church of England's Book of Common Prayer for the same reason.

Afforesaid Difference was of Such a kind that it made me Sick of his Religion; for tho' I had but little my Self yet I had an Idea what sort of People they should be that were so.—At Length the old Enemy by insinuations made me believe there was no such thing as Religion, & that the Convictions I had felt from my Infancy was no other than the prejudice of Education, which Convictions were at times so Strong that I have gone alone & fallen with my face to the Ground crying for mercy: but now I began to be hardened, and for Some months I do not Remember that I felt any such thing, so was Ready to Conclude that there was no God; that such thoughts were foolish & all but Priest Craft: and though I had a Great Veneration for that set of men in my youth, I now looked on them in another Manner: & what corroborated me in my Atheistical opinion was, my Master's house used to be a place of Great resort of the Clergy, which gave me much opportunity to make my Remarks. Sometimes those that Came out of the Country lodged there & their Evening Diversion used to be Cards & Singing, & a few minutes after, Prayers and Singing Psalms to Almighty God. I used to think, if there be a God he is a pure being, & will not hear the Prayers of Polluted Lips: But he that hath in an abundant manner shewn mercy to me (as will be seen in the sequel) did not Long Suffer me to Doubt in this Matter, but in a moment, when my feet were near the Bottomless Pit, Pluckt me Back.

To one Woman (& no other) I had Discovered the Nature of the Difference which Two years before had happened between my Master & Me; by her means he heard of it, & tho' he knew it was True yet he sent for the Town Whipper to Correct me. I was Called In; he never asked me Whether I had told any such thing but ordered me to strip; at which my heart was ready to burst; for I could as freely have given up my Life as Suffer such Ignominy. I then said if there be a God, be graciously Pleased to Look down on one of the most unhappy Creatures & plead my Cause for thou knows what I have said is the truth; and were it not for a principle more noble than he was Capable of I would have told it before his wife. I then fixed my Eyes on the Barbarous man, & in a flood of Tears said: "Sir, if you have no Pity on me, yet for my Father's Sake spare me from this Shame (for before this time he had heard of my Father &C. several ways) & if you think I deserve such punishment, do it your Self." He then took a turn over the Room & bid the Whipper go about his business, and I came off without a blow, which I thought something Remarkable, but now I began to think my Credit was gone (for they said many things of me which I blessed God were not True) & here I suffer so much Cruelty I cannot bear it.

The Enemy Immediately Came in & put me in a way how to be rid of it all & tempted me to End my Miserable Life: I joyn'd with it & for that Purpose went into the garret to hang my Self. Now it was I was convinced there was a God, for as my feet Entered the Place Horrour seized to that degree, I trembled much, and as I stood like one in Amaze, it seemed as tho'

I heard a Voice say, "there is a Hell beyond the grave;" at which I was greatly astonished, & now Convinced that there was an almighty Power, to whom I then Prayed, saying, "God be merciful & Enable me to bear what thou in thy Providence shall bring or Suffer to Come upon me for my Disobedience." I then went Down again but Let none know what I had been about. Soon after this I had a Dream, & tho' some make a ridicule of Dreams, yet this seemed a significant one to me & therefore shall mention it. I thought somebody knocked at the Door, by which when I had opened it there stood a Grave woman, holding in her right hand an oil lamp burning, who with a Solid Countenance fixed her Eyes upon me & said—"I am sent to tell thee that If thou'l return to the Lord thy God, who hath Created thee, he will have mercy on thee, & thy Lamp shall not be put out in obscure darkness;" upon which the Light flamed from the Lamp in an extraordinary Manner, & She left me and I awoke.

But alas! I did not give up nor Comply with the heavenly Vision, as I think I may Call it, for after this I had like to have been caught in another Snare, which if I had would Probably have been my Ruin, from which I was also preserved. I was Counted a fine Singer & Dancer, in which I took great Delight, and once falling in with some of the Play house company then at New York, they took a Great fancy to me, as they said, & Perswaded me to become an Actress amongst them, & they would find means to get me from my cruel Servitude, & I should Live Like a Lady—The Proposal took with me & I used no small Pains to Qualify my Self for it in Reading their Play Books, even when I should have Slept, yet was put to the Demur when I came to Consider what my Father would say who had forgiven my Disobedience in marrying and earnestly desiring to see me again had sent for me home, but my proud heart would not Consent to return in so mean a Condition; therefore I chose Bondage rather.

So when I had Served near three years, I bought off the remainder of my Time & then took to my Needle, by which I could maintain my Self handsomely: but, alas, I was not Sufficiently Punished; I had got released from one cruel Servitude & then not Contented got into another, and this for Life. A few months after, I married a young man that fell in Love with me for my Dancing, a Poor Motive for a man to Choose a Wife, or a Woman a Husband. But for my Part I fell in Love with nothing I saw in him and it seems unaccountable that I who had refused several, both in this Country & Ireland, at Last married a man I had no Value for.

In a few Days after we were Married he took me from [New] York. Being a Schoolmaster he had hired in the Country to keep school; he led me to New England and there settled in a place called Westerly in Rhode Island Government. With regard to Religion he was much like my Self, without any, and when in Drink would use the worst of Oaths. I do not mention this to

Expose my husband; but to Shew the Effect it had on me, for I now saw my Self ruined as I thought, being joyned to a man I had no Love for & that was a Pattern of no good to me; then I began to think what a Couple we were, like two joyning hands and going to destruction, & there upon Concluded if I was not forsaken of heaven to alter my Course of Life. But to Set my Affections upon the Divine being & not Love my husband seemed Impossible: therefore I Daily Desired with Tears that my Affections might be in a right manner set upon my husband, and can say in a little time my Love was Sincere to him.

I now resolved to do my Duty to God; & Expecting I must come to the knowledge of it by the Scriptures I took to reading them with a Resolution to follow their Directions, but the more I read the more uneasy I grew, especially about Baptism; for altho' I had reason to believe I had been Sprinkled in my Infancy, because at the age of Thirteen I Passed under the Bishop's hands for Confirmation (as twas Called) yet I could not find any Precedent for that Practice & lighting on that place where it is said, "he that believes & is Baptized" &C.,[7] here I observed Belief went before Baptism, which I was not Capable of when Sprinkled: hence grew much Dissatisfied, & Living in a Neighbourhood that were mostly Seventh day Baptists, I Conversed much with them. At Length thinking it my Real Duty, I was In the Winter time Baptised by one of their Teachers, but Did not joyn Strictly with them, tho' I began to think the Seventh Day was the true Sabbath, & for some time kept it. My husband Did not Oppose me, for he saw I grew more Affectionate to him. I did not Leave off Singing & Dancing so, but that I could divert him when he'd ask me. But I did not find that Satisfaction in what I had done as I Expected.

Soon after this my husband & I concluded to go for England & for that End went to Boston & there found a Ship bound for Liverpool. We agreed for our Passage & Expected to Sail in two Weeks:—but my time was not to go yet, for there Came a Gentleman who hired the Ship to Carry him & his Attendance to Philadelphia & to take no other Passengers; & there being no other Ship near Sailing we for that time gave it out. We stayed Several weeks in Boston, & I still continued Dissatisfy'd as to Religion; tho' I had reformed my Conduct so as to be accounted by those that knew me a sober Woman yet was not Content, for Even then I expected to find the Sweets of Such a Change, & though several thought me Religious, I durst not think so my Self, but what to Do to be so was an utter Stranger. I used to Converse with People of all societies as Opportunity offer'd & like many others had got a Pretty Deal of Head Knowledge, & Several Societies thought me of their

7. "He . . . is Baptized": "He who believes and is baptized shall be saved, but he who does not believe shall be condemned" (Mark 16: 16).

Opinions severally; But I joyned Strictly with none, resolving never to leave Searching till I had found the truth: this was in the Twenty Second year of my age.

While we were in Boston I one Day went into the Quaker Meeting not Expecting to find what I wanted, but out of Curiosity. At this Meeting there was a Woman friend spoke, at which I was a Little surprised, for tho' I had heard of Women's preaching I had never heard one before. I looked on her with Pity for her Ignorance (as I thought) & Contempt of her Practise, saying to my self, "I am sure you are a fool, for if ever I should turn Quaker, which will never be, I would not be a preacher."—In these and such like thoughts, I sat while She was Speaking; after she had done there Stood up a man, which I could better Bear. He spoke well & I thought raised sound Doctrine from good Joshua's resolution (Viz) "as for me and my house we will serve the Lord,"[8] & C. After he had sat silent a while he went to prayer, which was something so awful & Affecting as drew tears from my Eyes yet a Stranger to the Cause.

Soon after this we Left Boston, & my husband being Given to ramble, which was very Disagreeable to me, but I must submit, we Came to Rhode Island by Water, from thence to the East End of Long Island, where we hired to keep School. This Place was mostly Settled with Presbyterians. I soon got Acquainted with some of the most Religious of them, for tho' I was poor yet was favoured with Reception amongst People of the Best Credit, & had frequent Discourses with them, but the more I was acquainted, the worse I liked their Opinions, so Remained Dissatisfy'd; & the old Enemy of my Happiness knowing that I was Resolved to Abandon him and Seek peace for my Soul, he fresh Assaults me & laid a bait, with which I had like to have been caught. One Day having been Abroad, at my return home I found the People at whose house we had taken a room had left some flax in an apartment thro' which I Passed to my own, at sight of which I was Immediately tempted to steal some to make me some thread. I went to it & took a small Bunch in my hand, at which I was smote with remorse. Being of such a kind that my Very Nature abhored it, I laid it Down, saying, "Lord keep me from such a Vile Action as this"; but the twisting serpent did not Leave me yet, but Assaulted again so strong & prevalent that I took it into my own Room; but when I came there Horror Seized me, & bursting into Tears Cryed, "Oh thou God of Mercy, enable me to resist this Temptation," which he in his Mercy did, and gave me power to say, "get thee behind me Satan, I'll resist till I'll die before I'll yield"; & then I Carryed it back, and returning to my Room was fill'd with thanksgiving to God, and wrapt in such a frame, as I have not words to Express, neither can any guess but those who have resisted Temptations;

8. "As for me . . . serve the Lord": Joshua 24: 15.

these have it in their own Experience to taste the sweet Peace that flows to the Soul.

My Husband soon hired further up the Island where we were nearer a Church of England to which I used to go, for tho' I Disliked some of their ways, yet I liked them best; but now a fresh Exercise fell upon me, and of such a Sort as I had never heard of any being in the like, & while under it I thought my self alone.—I was in the Second month sitting by a fire in Company with Several, my Husband also present; there arose a Thunder Gust, & with the Noise that struck my Ear, a voice attended, even as the Sound of a mighty Trumpet, piercing thro' me with these words, "O! Eternity, Eternity, the Endless term of Long Eternity:" at which I was Exceedingly Surprized, sitting speechless as in a trance, and in a moment saw my Self in such a state as made me Despair of ever being in a happy one. I seemed to see a Long Roll wrote in Black Characters, at sight whereof I heard a Voice say to me, "this is thy Sins;" I then saw Sin to be Exceeding Sinful, but this was not all, for Immediately followed another Saying, "and the Blood of Christ is not Sufficient to wash them out; this is shewn thee that thou mays't Confess thy Damnation is just & not in order that they should be forgiven."

All this while I sat Speechless; at Last I got up trembling, & threw my self on a Bed: the Company thought my Indisposition proceeded only from a fright at the Thunder, but Alas, it was of another kind, and from that time for several months I was in the utmost Despair, and if any time I would endeavour to hope or lay hold of any Gracious promise, the old Accuser would Come in, telling me, it was now too Late, I had withstood the day of Mercy till it was over, & that I should add to my Sins by praying for Pardon & provoke Divine Vengeance to make a Monument of Wrath of me. I was like one already in torment; my Sleep Departed from me, I Eat little, I became extremely melancholy, and took no delight in any thing. Had all the world been mine & the Glory of it, I would now have Gladly a given it for one glimpse of hope; My husband was Shock'd, to See me so changed, I that once Could divert him with a Song (in which he greatly delighted), nay after I grew Religious as to the outward, could now Do it no longer. My Singing now was turned into mourning & my Dancing into Lamentations: my Nights and Days were one Continual Scene of Sorrows: I let none know my Desperate Condition—My husband used all means in his power to divert my Melancholy, but in vain, the wound was too Deep to be healed with any thing short of the true Balm of Gilead.[9] I Durst not go much alone for fear

9. "Balm of Gilead": literally, an ointment, as in the rhetorical question of Jeremiah 8: 22, "Is there no balm in Gilead?" But by extension the phrase suggests a spiritual annointing, as in Jeremiah 46: 11: "Go up to Gilead and take balm, O virgin daughter of Egypt! In vain you have used many medicines; there is no healing for you." In the Christian typological tradition the balm of Gilead suggests the grace of conversion.

of Evil Spirits, but when I did my husband would not Suffer it, & if I took the Bible, he would take it from me saying, "how you are altered, you used to be agreeable Company but now I have no Comfort of you." I endeavoured to bear all with Patience, expecting soon to bear more than man could inflict upon me.

At Length I went to the Priest to see if he Could relieve me, but he was a Stranger to my Case: he advised me to take the Sacrament & use some innocent diversions, & lent me a Book of prayers, which he said was fit for my Condition, but all was in Vain. As to the Sacrament, I thought my Self in a State very unfit to receive it worthily, and could not use the Prayers, for I then thought if Ever my Prayers would be acceptable, I should be enabled to pray without form. Diversions were burdensome, for as I said above, my husband used all means tending that way to no Purpose, yet he with some others once perswaded me to go to the Raising of a building (where such Company were Collected) in Expectation of Aleviating my grief, but contrarywise it proved a means of adding to my Sorrow: for in the mean time there came an officer to summon a jury to Enquire concerning the Body of a man that had hanged himself, which as soon as I understood seemed to be attended with a Voice saying, "thou shall be the next Monument of such Wrath, for thou art not worthy to Die a natural Death," and for Two Months was Daily tempted to destroy myself, and some times so strong that I could hardly resist, thro' fear of that sort when I went alone, I used to throw off my apron & garters, & if I had a knife cast it from me Crying, "Lord keep me from taking that Life thou gave, & which thou Would have made happy if I had on my Part joyned with the Offers of Thy Grace, and had regarded the Convictions attending me from my youth: the fault is my own, thou O Lord art clear;" & yet so great was my Agony that I desired Death that I might know the worst of my Torments, of which I had so sharp a foretaste. All this while I Could not shed a Tear; my heart was as hard as a Stone & my Life Miserable, but God that's full of Mercy and Long forbearance, in his own good time delivered my Soul out of this Thraldom.

For one night as I Lay in Bed (my husband by me a Sleep) bemoaning my Miserable Condition, I had strength to Cry, "O, my God, hast thou no mercy left, Look Down, I beseech thee, for Christ's Sake, who has promised that all manner of Sins & blasphemies Shall be forgiven; Lord, if thou will graciously please to Extend this Promise to me an unWorthy Creature trembling before thee; there is nothing thou shalt Command but I will obey."— In an Instant my heart was tendered, & I dissolved in a flow of tears, abhoring my Past Offences, & admiring the mercy of God, for I now was made to hope in Christ my Redeemer, & Enabled to Look upon him with an Eye of Faith, & saw fulfilled what I believed when the Priest lent me his Book, (Viz.) that if ever my Prayers would be Acceptable I should be Enabled to pray without form & so used form no more.

Nevertheless I thought I ought to join with Some religious Society but met with none I liked in everything; yet the Church of England seeming nearest, I joined with them & took the Sacrament (So called) & can say in truth, I did it with reverence & fear. Being now released from Deep Distress I seemed Like another Creature, and often went alone without fear, & tears abundantly flowed from my Eyes & once as I was abhorring my Self in great Humility of mind, I heard a gracious Voice full of Love, saying, "I will never Leave thee, nor forsake thee, only obey what I shall make known to thee." I then entered into Covenant saying: "My soul Doth Magnify thee the God of mercy, if thou'l Vouchsafe thy Grace the rest of my Days shall be Devoted to thee, & if it be thy Will that I beg my Bread, I'll be content and Submit to thy Providence."

I now began to think of my Relations in Pennsylvania whom I had not yet seen; and having a great Desire that way, Got Leave of my Husband to go & also a Certificate from the Priest on Long Island in order that if I made any stay, I might be receiv'd as a Member wherever I came; Then Setting out, my husband bore me Company to the Blazing Star Ferry, saw me Safe over & then returned. On the way near a place called Maidenhead [New Jersey] I fell from my horse & I was Disabled from Traveling for some time: In the interval I abode at the house of an Honest Like Dutchman, who with his wife were very kind to me, & tho' they had much trouble going to the Doctor and waiting upon me, (for I was Several Days unable to help my self) yet would have nothing for it (which I thought Exceeding kind) but Charged me if ever I came that way again to call and Lodge there.—I mention this because by and by I shall have occasion to remark this Place again.

Hence I came to Trenton [New Jersey] Ferry, where I met with no small Mortification upon hearing that my Relations were Quakers, & what was the worst of all my Aunt a Preacher. I was Sorry to hear it, for I was Exceedingly prejudiced against these People & have often wondered with what face they Could Call them Selves Christians. I Repented my Coming and had a mind to have turned back. At Last I Concluded to go & see them since I was so far on my journey, but Expected little Comfort from my Visit. But see how God brings unforeseen things to Pass, for by my going there I was brought to my Knowledge of his Truth.—I went from Trenton to Philadelphia by Water, thence to my Uncle's on Horseback, where I met with very kind reception; for tho' my Uncle was dead and my Aunt married again, yet both her husband and She received me in a very kind manner.

I had not been there three Hours before I met with a Shock, & my opinion began to alter with respect to these People.—For seeing a Book lying on the Table (& being much for reading) I took it up: My Aunt Observing said, "Cousin that is a Quakers' Book," for Perceiving I was not a Quaker, I suppose she thought I would not like it: I made her no answer but revolving in my mind, "what can these People write about, for I have heard that they Deny the Scriptures & have no other bible but George Fox's Journal, & Deny all the holy Ordinances?" So resolved to read, but had not read two Pages before my very heart burned within me and Tears Issued from my Eyes, which I was Afraid would be seen; therefore with the Book (Saml. Crisp's Two Letters) I walked into the garden, sat Down, and the piece being Small, read it through before I went in; but Some Times was forced to Stop to Vent my Tears, my heart as it were uttering these involuntary Expressions; "my God must I (if ever I come to the true knowledge of thy Truth) be of this man's Opinion, who has sought thee as I have done & join with these People that a few hours ago I preferred the Papists before? O thou, the God of my Salvation & of my Life, who hast in an abundant manner manifested thy Long Suffering & tender Mercy, Redeeming me as from the Lowest Hell, a Monument of thy grace: Lord, my soul beseecheth thee to Direct me in the right way & keep me from Error, & then According to thy Covenant, I'll think nothing too near to Part with for thy name's Sake. If these things be so, Oh! happy People thus beloved of God."

After I came a little to my Self again I washed my face least any in the House should perceive I had been weeping. But this night got but Little Sleep, for the old Enemy began to Suggest that I was one of those that wavered & was not Steadfast in the faith, advancing several Texts of Scripture against me & them, as, in the Latter Days there should be those that would deceive the very Elect:[10] & these were they, & that I was in danger of being deluded. Here the Subtile Serpent transformed himself so hiddenly that I verily believed this to be a timely Caution from a good Angel—so resolved to beware of the Deceiver, & for Some weeks Did not touch any of their Books.

The next Day being the first of the week I wanted to have gone to Church, which was Distant about four Miles, but being a Stranger and having nobody to go along with me, was forced to Give it out, & as most of the Family was going to Meeting, I went with them, but with a resolution not to like them, & so it was fully Suffered: for as they sat in silence I looked over the Meeting, thinking with my self, "how like fools these People sit, how much better would it be to stay at home & read the Bible or some good Book, than to come here and go to Sleep." For my Part I was very Sleepy & thought they were no better than my Self. Indeed at Length I fell a sleep, and had like to fallen Down, but this was the last time I ever fell asleep in a Meeting, Tho' often Assaulted with it.

Now I began to be lifted up with Spiritual Pride & thought my Self better than they, but thro' Mercy this did not Last Long, for in a Little time I was brought Low & saw that these were the People to whom I must join.— It may seem strange that I who had Lived so long with one of this Society in

10. "Those that would deceive the very Elect": "For false Christs and false prophets will arise, and will show great signs and wonders, so as to lead astray if possible, even the elect" (Matthew 24: 24).

Dublin, should yet be so great a Stranger to them. In answer let it be Considered that During the time I was there I never read one of their Books nor went to one Meeting, & besides I had heard such ridiculous stories of them as made me Esteem them the worst of any Society of People; but God that knew the Sincerity of my heart looked with Pity on my Weakness & soon Let me see my Error.

In a few weeks there was an afternoon's Meeting held at my Uncle's to which came that Servant of the Lord Wm. Hammans who was made then Instrumental to the Convincing me of the truth more Perfectly, & helping me over Some great Doubts: tho' I believe no one did ever sit in Greater opposition than I did when he first stood up; but I was soon brought Down for he preached the Gospel with such Power I was forced to give up & Confess it was the truth. As soon as meeting Ended I Endeavoured to get alone, for I was not fit to be seen, I being So broken; yet afterward the Restless adversary assaulted me again, on this wise. In the morning before this meeting, I had been Disputing with my Uncle about Baptism, which was the subject this good Man Dwelt upon, which was handled so Clearly as to answer all my Scruples beyond all objection: yet the Crooked Serpent alleged that the Sermon that I had heard did not proceed from divine Revelation but that my Uncle and Aunt had acquainted the Friend of me; which being Strongly Suggested, I fell to Accusing them with it, of which they both cleared themselves, saying they had not seen him Since my Coming into these Parts until he came into the meeting. I then Concluded he was a messenger sent of God to me, & with fervent Cryes Desired I might be Directed a right and now Laid aside all Prejudice & set my heart open to receive the truth in the Love of it. And the Lord in his own good time revealed to my Soul not only the Beauty there is in truth, & how those should shine that continue faithful to it, but also the Emptiness of all shadows, which in the day were Gloryous, but now he the Son of Glory was come to put an end to them all, & to Establish Everlasting Righteousness in the room thereof, which is a work in the Soul. He likewise let me see that all I had gone through was to prepare me for this Day & that the time was near that he would require me to go forth & declare to others what he the God of Mercy had done for my Soul; at which I was Surprized & begged to be Excused for fear I should bring dishonour to the truth, and cause his Holy name to be Evil spoken of.

All the while, I never Let any know the Condition I was in, nor did I appear like a Friend, & fear'd a Discovery. I now began to think of returning to my husband but found a restraint to stay where I was. I then Hired to keep School & hearing of a place for him, wrote desiring him to come to me, but Let him know nothing how it was with me. I loved to go to meetings, but did not like to be seen to go on week days, & therefore to Shun it used to go from my school through the Woods, but notwithstanding all my care the Neighbours that were not friends began to revile me, calling me Quaker, saying they supposed I intended to be a fool and turn Preacher; I then receiv'd the same censure that I (a little above a year before) had Passed on one of the handmaids of the Lord at Boston, & so weak was I, alas! I could not bear the reproach, & in order to Change their Opinions got into greater Excess in Apparel than I had freedom to Wear for some time before I came Acquainted with Friends.

In this Condition I continued till my Husband came, & then began the Tryal of my Faith. Before he reached me he heard I was turned Quaker, at which he stampt, saying, "I'd rather heard She had been dead as well as I Love her, for if so, all my comfort is gone." He then came to me & had not seen me before for four Months. I got up & met him saying, "My Dear, I am glad to see thee," at which he flew in a Passion of anger & said, "the Divel thee thee, don't thee me." I used all the mild means I could to pacify him, & at Length got him fit to go & Speak to my Relations, but he was Alarmed, and as soon as we got alone said, "so I see your Quaker relations have made you one." I told him they had not, which was true, nor had I ever told him how it was with me: But he would have it that I was one, & therefore would not let me stay among them; & having found a place to his mind, hired and came Directly back to fetch me hence, & in one afternoon walked near thirty Miles to keep me from Meeting, the next Day being first Day; & on the Morrow took me to the Afforesaid Place & hired Lodgings at a churchman's house; who was one of the Wardens, & a bitter Enemy to Friends & used to Do all he could to irritate my Husband against them, & would tell me abundance of Ridiculous Stuff; but my Judgement was too Clearly convinced to believe it.

I still did not appear like a Friend, but they all believed I was one. When my Husband and he Used to be making their Diversion & reviling, I used to sit in Silence, but now and then an involuntary Sigh would break from me: at which he would tell my husband: "there, did not I tell you that your wife was a Quaker; & She will be a preacher." Upon which My Husband once in a Great rage came up to me, & Shaking his hand over me, said, "you had better be hanged in that Day." I then, Peter like, in a panick denied my being a Quaker, at which great horror seized upon me, which Continued near three Months: so that I again feared that by Denying the Lord that Bought me, the heavens were Shut against me; for great Darkness Surrounded, & I was again plunged into Despair. I used to Walk much alone in the Wood, where no Eye saw nor Ear heard, & there Lament my miserable Condition, & have often gone from Morning till Night and have not broke my Fast.

Thus I was brought so Low that my Life was a burden to me; the Devil seem'd to Vaunt that tho' the Sins of my youth were forgiven, yet now he was sure of Me, for that I had Committed the unpardonable Sin & Hell inevitable would be my portion, & my Torment would be greater than if I had hanged my Self at first. In this Doleful State I had none to bewail my Doleful Condition; & Even in the Night when I Could not Sleep under the painful Distress of mind, if my husband perceived me weeping he would revile me for it. At Length when he and his Friends thought themselves too weak to over Set me (tho' I feared it was all ready done) he went to the Priest at Chester [Pennsylvania] to Advise what to Do with me. This man knew I was a member of the Church, for I had Shewn him my Certificate: his advice was to take me out of Pennsylvania, and find some place where there was no Quakers; and then it would wear off. To this my Husband Agreed saying he did not Care where he went, if he Could but restore me to that Livelyness of Temper I was naturally of, & to that Church of which I was a member. I on my Part had no Spirit to oppose the Proposal, neither much cared where I was, For I seemed to have nothing to hope for, but Dayly Expected to be made a Spectacle of Divine Wrath, & was Possessed with a Thought that it would be by Thunder ere long.

The time of Removal came, & I must go. I was not Suffered to go to bid my Relations farewell; my husband was Poor & kept no horse, so I must travel on foot; we came to Wilmington [Delaware] (fifteen Miles) thence to Philadelphia by Water; here he took me to a Tavern where I soon became the Spectacle & discourse of the Company. My Husband told them, "my wife is a Quaker," & that he Designed if Possible to find out some Place where there was none. "O," thought I, "I was once in a Condition deserving that name, but now it is over with me. O! that I might from a true hope once more have an Opportunity to Confess to the truth;" tho' I was Sure of Suffering all manner of Crueltys, I would not Regard it.

These were my Concerns while he was Entertaining the Company with my Story, in which he told them that I had been a good Dancer, but now he Could get me neither to Dance nor Sing, upon which one of the Company stands up saying, "I'll go fetch my Fiddle, & we'll have a Dance," at which my husband was much pleased. The fiddle came, the sight of which put me in a sad Condition for fear if I Refused my husband would be in a great Passion: however I took up this resolution, not to Comply whatever be the Consequence. He comes to me, takes me by the hand saying, "come my Dear, shake off that Gloom, & let's have a civil Dance; you would now and then when you was a good Churchwoman, & that's better than a Stiff Quaker." I trembling desired to be Excused; but he Insisted on it, and knowing his Temper to be exceeding Cholerick, durst not say much, yet did not Consent. He then pluck'd me round the Room till Tears affected my Eyes, at Sight whereof the Musician Stopt and said, "I'll play no more, Let your wife alone," of which I was Glad.

There was also a man in Company who came from Freehold in East Jersey: he said, "I see your Wife is a Quaker, but if you will take my advice you need not go so far (for my husband's design was for Staten Island); come & live amonst us, we'll soon cure her of her Quakerism, for we want a School Master & Mistress Too" (I followed the Same Business); to which he agreed,

& a happy turn it was for me, as will be seen by and by: and the Wonderfull turn of Providence, who had not yet Abandoned me, but raised a glimmering hope, affording the Answer of peace in refusing to Dance, for which I was more rejoyced than to be made Mistress of much Riches; & in floods of Tears said, "Lord, I dread to ask and yet without thy gracious Pardon I'm Miserable; I therefore fall Down before thy Throne, imploring Mercy at thine hand. O Lord once more I beseech thee, try my Obedience, & then what soever thou Commands, I will Obey, & not fear to Confess thee before men."

Thus was my Soul Engaged before God in Sincerity & he in tender Mercy heard my cries, & in me has Shewn that he Delights not in the Death of a Sinner, for he again set my mind at Liberty to praise him & I longed for an Opportunity to Confess to his Truth, which he shewed me should come, but in what manner I did not see, but believed the word that I had heard, which in a little time was fulfilled to me.—My Husband as afforesaid agreed to go to Freehold, & in our way thither we came to Maidenhead, where I went to see the kind Dutchman before mentioned, who made us welcome & Invited us to stay a day or Two.

While we were here, there was held a great Meeting of the Presbyterians, not only for Worship but Business also: for one of their preachers being Charged with Drunkenness, was this day to have his Trial before a great number of their Priests, &c. We went to it, of which I was afterwards glad. Here I perceived great Divisions among the People about who Should be their Shepherd: I greatly Pitied their Condition, for I now saw beond the Men made Ministers, & What they Preached for: and which those at this Meeting might have done had not the prejudice of Education, which is very prevalent, blinded their Eyes. Some Insisted to have the old Offender restored, some to have a young man they had upon trial some weeks, a third Party was for sending for one from New England. At length stood up one & Directing himself to the Chief Speaker said "Sir, when we have been at the Expence (which will be no Small Matter) of fetching this Gentleman from New England, may be he'll not stay with us." *Answer,* "don't you know how to make him stay? *Reply,* "no Sir." "I'll tell you then," said he (to which I gave good attention), "give him a good Salary & I'll Engage he'll Stay." "O" thought I, "these Mercenary creatures: they are all Actuated by one & the same thing, even the Love of Money, & not the regard of Souls." This (Called Reverend) Gentleman, whom these People almost adored, to my knowledge had left his flock on Long Island & moved to Philadelphia where he could get more money. I my self have heard some of them on the Island say that they almost Impoverished themselves to keep him, but not being able to Equal Philadelphia's Invitation he left them without a Shepherd. This man therefore, knowing their Ministry all proceeded from one Cause, might be purchased with the Same thing; surely these and Such like are the Shepherd that regards the fleece more than the flock, in whose mouths are Lies; saying the Lord had sent them, &

that they were Christ's Ambassadors, whose Command to those he sent was, "Freely ye have receiv'd, freely give; & Blessed be his holy Name;"[11] so they do to this day.

I durst not say any Thing to my Husband of the Remarks I had made, but laid them up in my heart, & they Served to Strengthen me in my Resolution. Hence we set forward to Freehold, & Coming through Stony Brook [New Jersey] my Husband turned towards me tauntingly & Said, "Here's one of Satan's Synagogues, don't you want to be in it? O I hope to See you Cured of this New Religion." I made no answer but went on, and in a little time, we came to a large run of Water over which was no Bridge, & being Strangers knew no way to escape it, but thro' we must go: he Carried over our Clothes, which we had in Bundles. I took off my Shoes and waded over in my Stockings, which Served some what to prevent the Chill of the Water, being Very Cold & a fall of Snow in the 12 Mo.[12] My heart was Concerned in Prayer that the Lord would Sanctify all my Afflictions to me & give me Patience to bear whatsoever should be suffered to come upon me. We Walked the most part of a mile before we came to the first house, which was a sort of a Tavern. My husband Called for Some Spiritous Liquors, but I got some weakened Cider Mull'd, which when I had Drank of (the Cold being struck to my heart) made me Extremely sick, in so much that when we were a Little past the house I expected I should have Fainted, & not being able to stand, fell Down under a Fence. My husband Observing, tauntingly said, "What's the Matter now; what, are you Drunk; where is your Religion now?" He knew better & at that time I believe he Pitied me, yet was Suffered grievously to Afflict me. In a Little time I grew Better, & going on We came to another Tavern, where we Lodged: the next Day I was Indifferent well, so proceeded, and as we Journeyed a young man Driving an Empty Cart overtook us. I desired my husband to ask the young man to Let us Ride; he did, twas readily granted.

I now thought my Self well off, & took it as a great favour, for my Proud heart was humbled, & I did not regard the Looks of it, tho' the time had been that I would not have been seen in one; this Cart belonged to a man at Shrewsbury [New Jersey] & was to go thro' the place we Designed for, so we rode on (but soon had the Care of the team to our Selves from a failure in the Driver) to the place where I was Intended to be made a prey of; but see how unforeseen things are brought to Pass, by a Providential hand. Tis said and answered, "shall we do Evil that good may Come?" God forbid, yet hence good came to me. Here my husband would have had me Stay while we went to see the Team Safe at home: I Told him, no, since he had led me thro'

---

11. "Freely ye have received . . . his holy Name": Matthew 10: 8.
12. "in the 12 Mo.": Quakers numbered the days of the week, beginning with Sunday, as well as the months of the year, in order to avoid giving even perfunctory honor to the pagan deities. After the Gregorian calendar reform of 1752, January rather than March became first month. Writing before that date, Elizabeth Ashbridge would have designated February as twelfth month.

the Country like a Vagabond, I would not stay behind him, so went on, & Lodged that Night at the man's house who owned the Team. Next morning in our Return to Freehold, we met a man riding on full Speed, Stopping said to my Husband, "Sir, are you a School Master?" *Answer,* "Yes." "I came to tell you," replied the Stranger, "of Two new School Houses, & want a Master in Each, & are two miles apart." How this Stranger came to hear of us, who Came but the night before, I never knew, but I was glad he was not one Called a Quaker, Least my husband might have thought it had been a Plot; and then turning to my husband I said, "my Dear, look on me with Pity; if thou has any Affections left for me, which I hope thou hast, for I am not Conscious of having Done anything to Alienate them; here is (continued I) an Opportunity to Settle us both, for I am willing to do all in my Power towards getting an Honest Livelihood."

My Expressions took place, & after a Little Pause he consented, took the young man's Directions, & made towards the place, & in our way came to the house of a Worthy Friend, Whose wife was a Preacher, tho' we did not know it. I was Surprized to see the People so kind to us that were Strangers; we had not been long in the house till we were Invited to Lodge there that night, being the Last in the Week.—I said nothing but waited to hear my Master Speak; he soon Consented saying, "My wife has had a Tedious Travel & I pity her"; at which kind Expression I was Affected, for they Were now very Seldom Used to me. The friends' kindness could not proceed from my appearing in the Garb of a Quaker, for I had not yet altered my dress: The Woman of the house, after we had Concluded to Stay, fixed her Eyes upon me & Said, "I believe thou hast met with a deal of Trouble," to which I made but Little Answer. My husband, Observing they were of that sort of people he had so much Endeavoured to shun, would give us no Opportunity for any discourse that night, but the next morning I let the friend know a Little how it was with me. Meeting time came, to which I longed to go, but durst not ask my husband leave for fear of Disturbing him, till we were Settled, & then thought I, "if ever I am favoured to be in this Place, come Life or Death, I'll fight through, for my Salvation is at Stake." The Friend getting ready for Meeting, asked my husband if he would go, saying they knew who were to be his Employers, & if they were at Meeting would Speak to them. He then consented to go; then said the Woman Friend, "& wilt thou Let thy Wife go?," which he denied, making Several Objections, all which She answered so prudently that he Could not be angry, & at Last Consented; & with Joy I went, for I had not been at one for near four Months, & an Heavenly Meeting This was: I now renewed my Covenant & Saw the Word of the Lord made Good, that I should have another Opportunity to Confess his Name, for which my Spirit did rejoice in the God of my Salvation, who had brought Strange things to Pass: May I ever be preserved in Humility, never forgetting his tender Mercies to me.

Here According to my Desire we Settled; my husband got one School & I the Other, & took a Room at a Friend's house a Mile from Each School and Eight Miles from the Meeting House:—before next first day we were got to our new Settlement: & now Concluded to Let my husband to see I was determined to joyn with friends. When first day Came I directed my Self to him in this manner, "My Dear, art thou willing to let me go to a Meeting?," at which he flew into a rage, saying, "No you shan't." I then Drew up my resolution & told him as a Dutyfull Wife ought, So I was ready to obey all his Lawfull Commands, but where they Imposed upon my Conscience, I no longer Durst: For I had already done it too Long, & wronged my Self by it, & tho' he was near & I loved him as a Wife ought, yet God was nearer than all the World to me, & had made me sensible this was the way I ought to go, the which I Assured him was no Small Cross to my own will, yet had Given up My heart, & hoped that he that Called for it would Enable me the residue of my Life to keep it steadyly devoted to him, whatever I Suffered for it, adding I hoped not to make him any the worse Wife for it. But all I could Say was in vain; he was Inflexible & Would not Consent.

I had now put my hand to the Plough, & resolved not to Look back, so went without Leave; but Expected to be immediately followed & forced back, but he did not: I went to one of the neighbours & got a Girl to Show me the way, then went on rejoicing & Praising God in my heart, who had thus far given me Power & another Opportunity to Confess to his Truth. Thus for some time I had to go Eight Miles on foot to Meetings, which I never thought hard; My Husband soon bought a Horse, but would not Let me ride him, neither when my Shoes were worn out would he Let me have a new Pair, thinking by that means to keep me from going to meetings, but this did not hinder me, for I have taken Strings & tyed round to keep them on.

He finding no hard Usage could alter my resolution, neither threatening to beat me, nor doing it, for he several times Struck me with sore Blows, which I Endeavoured to bear with Patience, believing the time would Come when he would see I was in the right (which he Accordingly Did), he once came up to me & took out his pen knife saying, "if you offer to go to Meeting tomorrow, with this knife I'll cripple you, for you shall not be a Quaker." I made him no Answer, but when Morning came, set out as Usual & he was not Suffered to hurt me. In Despair of recovering me himself, he now flew to the Priest for help and told him I had been a very Religious Woman in the way of the Church of England, was a member of it, & had a good Certificate from Long Island, but now was bewitched and turn'd Quaker, which almost broke his heart. He therefore Desired as he was one who had the Care of souls, he would Come and pay me a Visit and use his Endeavours to reclaim me & hoped by the Blessing of God it would be done. The Priest Consented to Come, the time was Set, which was to be that Day two Weeks, for he said he could not come Sooner. My Husband Came home extremely Pleased, &

told me of it, at which I smiled Saying, "I hope to be Enabled to give him a reason for the hope that is in me," at the same time believing the Priest would never Trouble me (nor ever did).

Before his Appointed time came it was required of me in a more Publick manner to Confess to the world what I was and to give up in Prayer in a Meeting, the sight of which & the power that attended it made me Tremble, & I could not hold my Self still. I now again desired Death & would have freely given up my Natural Life a Ransom; & what made it harder to me I was not yet taken under the care of Friends, & what kept me from requesting it was for fear I might be overcome & bring a Scandal on the Society. I begged to be Excused till I was joyned to Friends & then I would give up freely, to which I receiv'd this Answer, as tho' I had heard a Distinct Voice: "I am a Covenant keeping God, and the word that I spoke to thee when I found thee In Distress, even that I would never leave thee nor forsake thee If thou would be obedient to what I should make known to thee, I will Assuredly make good: but if thou refuse, my Spirit shall not always strive; fear not, I will make way for thee through all thy difficulties, which shall be many for my name's Sake, but be thou faithfull & I will give thee a Crown of Life." I being then Sure it was God that Spoke said, "thy will O God, be done, I am in thy hand; do with me according to thy Word," & gave up. But after it was over the Enemy came in like a flood, telling me I had done what I ought not, & Should now bring Dishonour to this People. This gave me a Little Shock, but it did not at this time Last Long.

This Day as Usual I had gone on foot. My Husband (as he afterwards told me) lying on the Bed at home, these Words ran thro' him, "Lord where shall I fly to shun thee &C.,"[13] upon which he arose and seeing it Rain got his horse and Came to fetch me; and Coming just as the Meeting broke up, I got on horseback as quick as possible, least he Should hear what had happened. Nevertheless he heard of it, and as soon as we were got into the woods he began, saying, "What do you mean thus to make my Life unhappy? What, could you not be a Quaker without turning fool after this manner?" I Answered in Tears saying, "my Dear, look on me with Pity, if thou hast any. Canst thou think, that I in the Bloom of my Days, would bear all that thou knowest of & a great deal more that thou knowest not of if I did not believe it to be my Duty?" This took hold of him, & taking my hand he said, "Well, I'll E'en give you up, for I see it don't avail to Strive. If it be of God I can't over throw it, & if it be of your self it will soon fall." I saw tears stand in his Eyes, at which my heart was overcome with Joy, and I would not have Changed Conditions with a Queen.

I already began to reap the fruits of my Obedience, but my Tryal Ended not here, the time being up that the Priest was to come; but no Priest Ap-

13. "To shun thee": Psalm 139: 7.

peared. My Husband went to fetch him, but he would not come, saying he was busy; which so Displeased my husband, that he'd never go to hear him more, & for Some time went to no place of Worship.—Now the Unwearied adversary found out another Scheme, and with it wrought so Strong that I thought all I had gone through but a little to this: It came upon me in such an unexpected manner, in hearing a Woman relate a book she had read in which it was Asserted that Christ was not the son of God. As soon as She had Spoke these words, if a man had spoke I could not have more distinctly heard these words, "no more he is, it's all a fancy & the Contrivance of men," & an horrour of Great Darkness fell upon me, which Continued for three weeks.

The Exercise I was under I am not Able to Express, neither durst I let any know how it was with me. I again sought Desolate Places where I might make my moan, & have Lain whole nights, & don't know that my Eyes were Shut to Sleep. I again thought my self alone, but would not let go my Faith in him, often saying in my heart, "I'll believe till I Die," & kept a hope that he that had Delivered me out of the Paw of the Bear & out of the jaws of the Devouring Lion, would in his own time Deliver me out of his temptation also; which he in Mercy Did, and let me see that this was for my good, in order to Prepare me for future Service which he had for me to Do & that it was Necessary his Ministers should be dipt into all States, that thereby they might be able to Speak to all Conditions, for which my Soul was thankfull to him, the God of Mercies, who had at Several times redeemed me from great distress, & I found the truth of his Words, that all things should work together for good to those that Loved & feared him, which I did with my whole heart & hope ever shall while I have a being. This happened just after my first appearance, & Friends had not been to talk with me, nor did they know well what to do till I had appeared again, which was not for some time, when the Monthly Meeting appointed four Friends to give me a Visit, which I was Glad of; and gave them Such Satisfaction, that they left me well Satisfy'd. I then joyned with Friends.

My Husband still went to no place of Worship. One day he said, "I'd go to Meeting, only I am afraid I shall hear you Clack, which I cannot bear." I used no persuasions, yet when Meeting time Came, he got the horse, took me behind him & went to Meeting: but for several months if he saw me offer to rise, he would go out, till once I got up before he was aware and then (as he afterwards said) he was ashamed to go, & from that time never did, nor hindered me from going to Meetings. And tho' he (poor man) did not take up the Cross, yet his judgement was Convinced: & sometimes in a flood of tears would say, "My Dear, I have seen the Beauty there is in the Truth, & that thou art in the Right, and I Pray God Preserve thee in it. But as for me the Cross is too heavy, I cannot Bear it." I told him, I hoped he that had given me strength Would also favour him: "O!" said he, "I can't bear the Reproach thou Doest, to be Called turncoat & to become a Laughing Stock to the World; but I'll no Longer hinder thee," which I looked on as a great favour, that my way was thus far made easy, and a little hope remained that my Prayers would be heard on his account.

In this Place he had got linked in with some, that he was afraid would make game of him, which Indeed they already Did, asking him when he Designed to Commence Preacher, for that they saw he Intended to turn Quaker, & seemed to Love his Wife better since she did than before (we were now got to a little house by our Selves which tho' Mean, & little to put in it, our Bed no better than Chaff, yet I was truly Content & did not Envy the Rich their Riches; the only Desire I had now was my own preservation, & to be Bless'd with the Reformation of my husband). These men used to Come to our house & there Provoke my husband to Sit up and Drink, some times till near day, while I have been sorrowing in a Stable. As I once sat in this Condition I heard my husband say to his Company, "I can't bear any Longer to Afflict my Poor Wife in this manner, for whatever you may think of her, I do believe she is a good Woman," upon which he came to me and said, "Come in, my Dear; God has Given thee a Deal of Patience. I'll put an End to this Practice;" and so he did, for this was the Last time they sat up at Night.

My Husband now thought that if he was in any Place where it was not known that he'd been so bitter against Friends, he Could do better than here. But I was much against his Moving; fearing it would tend to his hurt, having been for some months much Altered for the Better, & would often in a broken and Affectionate Manner condemn his bad Usage to me: I told him I hoped it had been for my Good, even to the Better Establishing me in the Truth, & therefore would not have him to be Afflicted about it, & According to the Measure of Grace received did what I could both by Example and advice for his good: & my Advice was for him to fight thro' here, fearing he would Grow Weaker and the Enemy Gain advantage over him, if he thus fled: but All I could say did not prevail against his Moving; & hearing of a place at Bordentown [New Jersey] went there, but that did not suit; he then Moved to Mount Holly [New Jersey] & there we Settled. He got a good School & So Did I.

Here we might have Done very well; we soon got our house Prettily furnished for Poor folks; I now began to think I wanted but one thing to complete my Happiness, Viz. the Reformation of my husband, which Alas! I had too much reason to Doubt; for it fell out according to my Fears, & he grew worse here, & took much to Drinking, so that it Seem'd as if my Life was to be a Continual scene of Sorrows & most Earnestly I Pray'd to Almighty God to Endue me with Patience to bear my Afflictions & submit to his Providence, which I can say in Truth I did without murmuring or ever uttering an unsavoury expression to the Best of my Knowledge; except once, my husband Coming home a little in drink (in which frame he was very fractious) & finding me at Work by a Candle, came to me, put it out &

fetching me a box on the Ear said, "you don't Earn your light;" on which unkind Usage (for he had not struck me for Two Years so it went hard with me) I utter'd these Rash Expressions, "thou art a Vile Man," & was a little angry, but soon recovered & was Sorry for it; he struck me again, which I received without so much as a word in return, & that likewise Displeased him: so he went on in a Distracted like manner uttering Several Expressions that bespoke Despair, as that he now believed that he was predestinated to damnation, & he did not care how soon God would Strike him Dead, & the like. I durst say but Little; at Length in the Bitterness of my Soul, I Broke out in these Words, "Lord look Down on mine Afflictions and deliver me by some means or Other." I was answered, I Should Soon be, & so I was, but in such a manner, as I Verily thought It would have killed me.—In a little time he went to Burlington where he got in Drink, & Enlisted him Self to go a Common soldier to Cuba anno 1740.

I had drank many bitter Cups—but this Seemed to Exceed them all for indeed my very Senses Seemed Shaken; I now a Thousand times blamed my Self for making Such an unadvised request, fearing I had Displeased God in it, & tho' he had Granted it, it was in Displeasure, & Suffered to be in this manner to Punish me; Tho' I can truly say I never Desired his Death, no more than my own, nay not so much. I have since had cause to believe his mind was benefitted by the Undertaking, (which hope makes up for all I have Suffered from him) being Informed he did in the army what he Could not Do at home (Viz) Suffered for the Testimony of Truth. When they Came to prepare for an Engagement, he refused to fight; for which he was whipt and brought before the General, who asked him why he Enlisted if he would not fight; "I did it," said he, "in a drunken frolick, when the Divel had the Better of me, but my judgment is convinced that I ought not, neither will I whatever I Suffer; I have but one Life, & you may take that if you Please, but I'll never take up Arms."—They used him with much Cruelty to make him yield but Could not, by means whereof he was So Disabled that the General sent him to the Hospital at Chelsea, where in Nine Months time he Died & I hope made a Good End, for which I prayed both night & Day, till I heard of his Death.

Thus I thought it my duty to say what I could in his Favour, as I have been obliged to say so much of his hard usage to me, all which I hope Did me good, & altho' he was so bad, yet had Several Good Properties, & I never thought him the Worst of Men. He was one I Lov'd & had he let Religion have its Perfect work, I should have thought my Self Happy in the Lowest State of Life; & I've Cause to bless God, who Enabled me in the Station of a Wife to Do my Duty & now a Widow to Submit to his Will, always believing everything he doeth to be right. May he in all Stations of Life so Preserve me by the arm of Divine Power, that I may never forget his tender mercies to me, the Rememberance whereof doth often Bow my Soul, in Humility before his Throne, saying, "Lord, what was I; that thou should have reveal'd to me the Knowledge of thy Truth, & do so much for me, who Deserved thy Displeasure rather, But in me has thou shewn thy Long Suffering & tender Mercy; may thou O God be Glorifyed and I abased for it is thy own Works that praise thee, and of a Truth to the humble Soul thou Makest every bitter thing Sweet.—The End.—

Jonathan Edwards (1703–1758)
Personal Narrative

Although probably the most famous American Puritan autobiography, by one of the most famous American Puritans, Edwards's "Personal Narrative" does not follow the conventions of a Puritan confession. The established sequence of events, as summarized by Edmund S. Morgan, is "knowledge [of sin], conviction, faith, combat, and true, imperfect assurance [of salvation]."[1] Edwards's path, extending from his childhood to the point where this narrative stops in January, 1739, is from piety to doubt and then to alternations between lyric adoration and a fear of corruption, ending in "a vastly greater sense of my own wickedness," though the latter is tempered by faith "that God reigned, and that his will was done." Yet this very difference from the norms is part of what makes Edwards's story so intriguing and, for some people, so lifelike. He is introspective to the point of gloom. He is also like a psalmist when describing the "delight" and "sweetness" and "glory" of God's world.

Further, more definite interpretation of the "Narrative" would be aided by our knowing more about the circumstances of its writing. For whom was it written, and when? It was not published until 1765 in his friend Samuel Hopkins's *The Life and Character of the Late Rev. Mr. Jonathan Edwards*, where it appeared in a chapter called "An account of his conversion, experiences, and religious exercises, given by himself."

The inwardness of the writing suggests that it was not meant for publication in Edwards's lifetime. Yet the comparisons of his experiences and "affections" with other people's suggest that he was definitely mindful of his neighbors and parishioners, including those swept up in the emotions of the Great Awakening of 1740–50, which began with the revival at his church in Northampton, Massachusetts, in 1734–35. Was he testing their religious sincerity against his own? Was he, even somewhat pridefully, asserting his greater "wickedness"? Or was he trying to review his history and humble himself? Whatever the answers, such intensity was hard to bear (and have bared). By 1750 the residents of Northampton had had enough religious fervor, and they dismissed Edwards from his church. He went across the mountains to Stockbridge, where he was a missionary to the Indians

1. Edmund S. Morgan, *Visible Saints: The History of a Puritan Idea* (Ithaca: Cornell Univ. Press, 1963), p. 72.

until 1757, when he was invited to become President of the College of New Jersey (later Princeton) and where he died of smallpox in March of 1758.

Edwards's "Narrative" has long been contrasted with Franklin's *Autobiography* and John Woolman's *Journal*. The writings of Calvinist, Deist, and Quaker; of revivalist, of merchant-philanthropist-scientist, and of pacifist-reformer: the three allow for an illuminating range of comparisons. It is also instructive to compare Edwards and Charles Woodmason, noting, for example, how both are on "errands in the wilderness," but how Woodmason, despite his hardships, seems so much more psychologically settled and sure of himself. Woodmason, we might say, wrote his *Journal* in order to preserve his sense of himself and sense of propriety and control amid the misbehavior of others. He never questioned himself. Edwards constantly questioned himself, seeking salvation, not just social order. But these autobiographies also have some features in common. Each, we might say, espouses a particular virtue, and so aims, to use Franklin's term, at "the art of virtue." Piety, pragmatism, pacificism, and Episcopalianism were different virtues, but the autobiographies of these four individuals were used to explain and promote each.

The text is from *The Works of President Edwards*, ed. S. Austin, 8 vols., published in 1808, in which spelling and punctuation were much modernized, and from which the bracketed information of the present selection is derived. The classic biography of Edwards is Perry Miller, *Jonathan Edwards*, published in 1949. David Levin's *Jonathan Edwards: A Profile* (New York: Hill and Wang, 1969) reprints Hopkins's *Life and Character*.

I had a variety of concerns and exercises about my soul from my childhood; but had two more remarkable seasons of awakening, before I met with that change, by which I was brought to those new dispositions, and that new sense of things, that I have since had. The first time was when I was a boy, some years before I went to college, at a time of remarkable awakening in my father's congregation. I was then very much affected for many months, and concerned about the things of religion, and my soul's salvation; and was abundant in duties. I used to pray five times a day in secret, and to spend much time in religious talk with other boys; and used to meet with them to pray together. I experienced I know not what kind of delight in religion. My mind was much engaged in it, and had much self-righteous pleasure; and it was my delight to abound in religious duties. I, with some of my schoolmates joined together, and built a booth in a swamp, in a very secret and retired place, for a place of prayer. And besides, I had particular secret places of my own in the woods, where I used to retire by myself; and used to be from time to time much affected. My affections seemed to be lively and easily moved, and I seemed to be in my element, when engaged in religious duties. And I am ready to think, many are deceived with such affections, and such a kind of delight, as I then had in religion, and mistake it for grace.

But in process of time, my convictions and affections wore off; and I entirely lost all those affections and delights, and left off secret prayer, at least as to any constant performance of it; and returned like a dog to his vomit, and went on in ways of sin.

Indeed, I was at some times very uneasy, especially towards the latter part of the time of my being at college. 'Till it pleas'd God, in my last year at college, at a time when I was in the midst of many uneasy thoughts about the state of my soul, to seize me with a pleurisy; in which he brought me nigh to the grave, and shook me over the pit of hell.

But yet, it was not long after my recovery, before I fell again into my old ways of sin. But God would not suffer me to go on with any quietness; but I had great and violent inward struggles: 'till after many conflicts with wicked inclinations, and repeated resolutions, and bonds that I laid myself under by a kind of vows to God, I was brought wholly to break off all former wicked ways, and all ways of known outward sin; and to apply myself to seek my salvation, and practice the duties of religion: But without that kind of affection and delight, that I had formerly experienced. My concern now wrought more by inward struggles and conflicts, and self-reflections. I made seeking my salvation the main business of my life. But yet it seems to me, I sought after a miserable manner: Which has made me some times since to question, whether ever it issued in that which was saving; being ready to doubt, whether such miserable seeking was ever succeeded. But yet I was brought to seek salvation, in a manner that I never was before. I felt a spirit to part with all things in the world, for an interest in Christ. My concern continued and prevailed, with many exercising thoughts and inward struggles; but yet it never seemed to be proper to express my concern that I had, by the name of terror.

From my childhood up, my mind had been wont to be full of objections against the doctrine of God's sovereignty, in choosing whom he would to eternal life, and rejecting whom he pleased; leaving them eternally to perish, and be everastingly tormented in hell. It used to appear like a horrible doctrine to me. But I remember the time very well, when I seemed to be convinced, and fully satisfied, as to this sovereignty of God, and his justice in thus eternally disposing of men, according to his sovereign pleasure. But never could give an account, how, or by what means, I was thus convinced; not in the least imagining, in the time of it, nor a long time after, that there was any extraordinary influence of God's spirit in it; but only that now I saw further, and my reason apprehended the justice and reasonableness of it. However, my mind rested in it; and it put an end to all those cavils and objections, that had 'till then abode with me, all the preceding part of my life. And there has been a wonderful alteration in my mind, with respect to the doctrine of God's sovereignty, from that day to this; so that I scarce ever have found so much as the rising of an objection against God's sovereignty, in the most absolute sense, in showing mercy to whom he will show mercy, and hardening and eternally damning whom he will. God's absolute sovereignty, and justice, with respect to salvation and damnation, is what my mind seems to rest assured of, as much as of any thing that I see with my eyes; at least it is so at times. But I have often times since that first conviction, had quite another kind of sense of God's sovereignty, than I had then. I have often since, not only had a conviction, but a *delightful* conviction. The doctrine of God's sovereignty has very often appeared, an exceeding pleasant, bright and sweet doctrine to me: and absolute sovereignty is what I love to ascribe to God. But my first conviction was not with this.

The first that I remember that ever I found any thing of that sort of inward, sweet delight in God and divine things, that I have lived much in since, was on reading those words, I Tim. i. 17. "Now unto the king eternal, immortal, invisible, the only wise God, be honor and glory for ever and ever, Amen." As I read the words, there came into my soul, and was as it were diffused thro' it, a sense of the glory of the Divine Being; a new sense, quite different from any thing I ever experienced before. Never any words of scripture seemed to me as these words did. I thought with myself, how excellent a being that was; and how happy I should be, if I might enjoy that God, and be wrapt up to God in Heaven, and be as it were swallowed up in Him. I kept saying, and as it were singing over these words of scripture to myself; and went to prayer, to pray to God that I might enjoy him; and prayed in a manner quite different from what I used to do; with a new sort of affection. But it never came into my thought, that there was any thing spiritual, or of a saving nature in this.

From about that time, I began to have a new kind of apprehensions and ideas of Christ, and the work of redemption, and the glorious way of salvation by Him. I had an inward, sweet sense of these things, that at times came into my heart; and my soul was led away in pleasant views and contemplations of them. And my mind was greatly engaged, to spend my time in reading and meditating on Christ; and the beauty and excellency of His person, and the lovely way of salvation, by free grace in Him. I found no books so delightful to me, as those that treated of these subjects. Those words Cant. ii. I. used to be abundantly with me: *I am the Rose of Sharon, the lily of the valleys.* The words seemed to me, sweetly to represent, the loveliness and beauty of Jesus Christ. And the whole Book of Canticles used to be pleasant to me; and I used to be much in reading it, about that time. And found, from time to time, an inward sweetness, that used, as it were, to carry me away in my contemplations; in what I know not how to express otherwise, than by a calm, sweet abstraction of soul from all the concerns of this world; and a kind of vision, or fix'd ideas and imaginations, of being alone in the mountains, or some solitary wilderness, far from all mankind, sweetly conversing with Christ, and wrapt and swallowed up in God. The sense I had of divine things, would often of a sudden as it were, kindle up a sweet burning in my heart; an ardor of my soul, that I know not how to express.

Not long after I first began to experience these things, I gave an account to my father, of some things that had pass'd in my mind. I was pretty much affected by the discourse we had together. And when the discourse was ended, I walked abroad alone, in a solitary place in my father's pasture, for contemplation. And as I was walking there, and looked up on the sky and clouds; there came into my mind, a sweet sense of the glorious majesty and grace of God, that I know not how to express. I seemed to see them both in a sweet conjunction: majesty and meekness join'd together: it was a sweet and gentle, and holy majesty; and also a majestic meekness; an awful sweetness; a high, and great, and holy gentleness.

After this my sense of divine things gradually increased, and became more and more lively, and had more of that inward sweetness. The appearance of every thing was altered: there seem'd to be, as it were, a calm, sweet cast, or appearance of divine glory, in almost every thing. God's excellency, his wisdom, his purity and love, seemed to appear in every thing; in the sun, moon and stars; in the clouds, and blue sky; in the grass, flowers, trees; in the water, and all nature; which used greatly to fix my mind. I often used to sit and view the moon, for a long time; and so in the day time, spent much time in viewing the clouds and sky, to behold the sweet glory of God in these things: in the mean time, singing forth with a low voice, my contemplations of the Creator and Redeemer. And scarce any thing, among all the works of nature, was so sweet to me as thunder and lightning. Formerly, nothing had been so terrible to me. I used to be a person uncommonly terrified with thunder: and it used to strike me with terror, when I saw a thunder-storm rising. But now, on the contrary, it rejoiced me. I felt God at the first appearance of a thunderstorm. And used to take the opportunity at such times to fix myself to view the clouds, and see the lightnings play, and hear the majestic and awful voice of God's thunder: which often times was exceeding entertaining, leading me to sweet contemplations of my great and glorious God. And while I viewed, used to spend my time, as it always seem'd natural to me, to sing or chant forth my meditations; to speak my thoughts in soliloquies, and speak with a singing voice.

I felt then a great satisfaction as to my good estate. But that did not content me. I had vehement longings of soul after God and Christ, and after more holiness; wherewith my heart seemed to be full, and ready to break: which often brought to my mind, the words of the psalmist, Psal. cxix. 28. *My soul breaketh for the longing it hath.* I often felt a mourning and lamenting in my heart, that I had not turned to God sooner, that I might have had more time to grow in grace. My mind was greatly fix'd on divine things; I was almost perpetually in the contemplation of them. Spent most of my time

129

in thinking of divine things, year after year. And used to spend abundance of my time, in walking alone in the woods, and solitary places, for meditation, soliloquy and prayer, and converse with God. And it was always my manner, at such times, to sing forth my contemplations. And was almost constantly in ejaculatory prayer, wherever I was. Prayer seem'd to be natural to me; as the breath, by which the inward burnings of my heart had vent.

The delights which I now felt in things of religion, were of an exceeding different kind, from those forementioned, that I had when I was a boy. They were totally of another kind; and what I then had no more notion or idea of, than one born blind has of pleasant and beautiful colors. They were of a more inward, pure, soul-animating and refreshing nature. Those former delights, never reached the heart; and did not arise from any sight of the divine excellency of the things of God; or any taste of the soul-satisfying, and life-giving good, there is in them.

My sense of divine things seemed gradually to increase, 'till I went to preach at New York; which was about a year and a half after they began. While I was there, I felt them, very sensibly, in a much higher degree, than I had done before. My longings after God and holiness, were much increased. Pure and humble, holy and heavenly Christianity, appeared exceeding amiable to me. I felt in me a burning desire to be in every thing a complete Christian; and conformed to the blessed image of Christ: and that I might live in all things, according to the pure, sweet and blessed rules of the gospel. I had an eager thirsting after progress in these things. My longings after it, put me upon pursuing and pressing after them. It was my continual strife day and night, and constant inquiry, How I should be more holy, and live more holily, and more becoming a child of God, and disciple of Christ. I sought an increase of grace and holiness, and that I might live an holy life, with vastly more earnestness, than ever I sought grace, before I had it. I used to be continually examining myself, and studying and contriving for likely ways and means, how I should live holily, with far greater diligence and earnestness, than ever I pursued any thing in my life: But with too great a dependence on my own strength; which afterwards proved a great damage to me. My experience had not then taught me, as it has done since, my extreme feebleness and impotence, every manner of way; and the innumerable and bottomless depths of secret corruption and deceit, that there was in my heart. However, I went on with my eager pursuit after more holiness; and sweet conformity to Christ.

The Heaven I desired was a heaven of holiness; to be with God, and to spend my eternity in divine love, and holy communion with Christ. My mind was very much taken up with contemplations on heaven, and the enjoyments of those there; and living there in perfect holiness, humility and love. And it used at that time to appear a great part of the happiness of heaven, that there the saints could express their love to Christ. It appear'd to me a great clog and hindrance and burden to me, that what I felt within, I could not express to God, and give vent to, as I desired. The inward ardor of my soul, seem'd to be hindered and pent up, and could not freely flame out as it would. I used often to think, how in heaven, this sweet principle should freely and fully vent and express itself. Heaven appeared to me exceeding delightful as a world of love. It appeared to me, that all happiness consisted in living in pure, humble, heavenly, divine love.

I remember the thoughts I used then to have of holiness. I remember I then said sometimes to myself, I do certainly know that I love holiness, such as the gospel prescribes. It appeared to me, there was nothing in it but what was ravishingly lovely. It appeared to me, to be the highest beauty and amiableness, above all other beauties: that it was a *divine* beauty; far purer than any thing here upon earth; and that every thing else, was like mire, filth and defilement, in comparison of it.

Holiness, as I then wrote down some of my contemplations on it, appeared to me to be of a sweet, pleasant, charming, serene, calm nature. It seemed to me, it brought an inexpressible purity, brightness, peacefulness and ravishment to the soul: and that it made the soul like a field or garden of God, with all manner of pleasant flowers; that is all pleasant, delightful and undisturbed; enjoying a sweet calm, and the gently vivifying beams of the sun. The soul of a true Christian, as I then wrote my meditations, appear'd like such a little white flower, as we see in the spring of the year; low and humble on the ground, opening its bosom, to receive the pleasant beams of the sun's glory; rejoicing as it were, in a calm rapture; diffusing around a sweet fragrancy; standing peacefully and lovingly, in the midst of other flowers round about; all in like manner opening their bosoms, to drink in the light of the sun.

There was no part of creature-holiness, that I then, and at other times, had so great a sense of the loveliness of, as humility, brokenness of heart and poverty of spirit: and there was nothing that I had such a spirit to long for. My heart as it were panted after this, to lie low before God, and in the dust; that I might be nothing, and that God might be all; that I might become as a little child.

While I was there at New York, I sometimes was much affected with reflections on my past life, considering how late it was, before I began to be truly religious; and how wickedly I had lived 'till then: and once so as to weep abundantly, and for a considerable time together.

On January 12, 1722–3, I made a solemn dedication of myself to God, and wrote it down; giving up myself, and all that I had to God; to be for the future in no respect my own; to act as one that had no right to himself, in any respect. And solemnly vowed to take God for my whole portion and felicity; looking on nothing else as any part of my happiness, nor acting as if it were: and his law for the constant rule of my obedience: engaging to fight with all my might, against the world, the flesh and the devil, to the end of my life. But have reason to be infintely humbled, when I consider, how much I have fail'd of answering my obligation.

I had then abundance of sweet religious conversation in the family where I lived, with Mr. John Smith, and his pious mother. My heart was knit in affection to those, in whom were appearances of true piety; and I could bear the thoughts of no other companions, but such as were holy, and the disciples of the blessed Jesus.

I had great longings for the advancement of Christ's kingdom in the world. My secret prayer used to be in great part taken up in praying for it. If I heard the least hint of any thing that happened in any part of the world, that appear'd to me, in some respect or other, to have a favorable aspect on the interest of Christ's kingdom, my soul eagerly catch'd at it; and it would much animate and refresh me. I used to be earnest to read public news-letters, mainly for that end; to see if I could not find some news favorable to the interest of religion in the world.

I very frequently used to retire into a solitary place, on the banks of Hudson's river, at some distance from the city, for contemplation on divine things, and secret converse with God; and had many sweet hours there. Sometimes Mr. Smith and I walked there together, to converse of the things of God; and our conversation used much to turn on the advancement of Christ's kingdom in the world, and the glorious things that God would accomplish for his church in the latter days.

I had then, and at other times, the greatest delight in the holy Scriptures, of any book whatsoever. Often-times in reading it, every word seemed to touch my heart. I felt an harmony between something in my heart, and those sweet and powerful words. I seem'd often to see so much light, exhibited by every sentence, and such a refreshing ravishing food communicated, that I could not get along in reading. Used often-times to dwell long on one sentence, to see the wonders contained in it; and yet almost every sentence seemed to be full of wonders.

I came away from New York in the month of April, 1723, and had a most bitter parting with Madam Smith and her son. My heart seemed to sink within me, at leaving the family and city, where I had enjoyed so many sweet and pleasant days. I went from New York to Weathersfield by water. As I sail'd away, I kept sight of the city as long as I could; and when I was out of sight of it, it would affect me much to look that way, with a kind of melancholy mixed with sweetness. However, that night after this sorrowful parting, I was greatly comforted in God at Westchester, where we went ashore to lodge: and had a pleasant time of it all the voyage to Saybrook. It was sweet to me to think of meeting dear Christians in heaven, where we should never part more. At Saybrook we went ashore to lodge on Saturday, and there kept sabbath; where I had a sweet and refreshing season, walking alone in the fields.

After I came home to Windsor, remained much in a like frame of my mind, as I had been in at New York, but only sometimes felt my heart ready to sink, with the thoughts of my friends at New York. And my refuge and support was in contemplations on the heavenly state; as I find in my diary of May 1, 1723. It was my comfort to think of that state, where there is fulness of joy; where reigns heavenly, sweet, calm and delightful love, without alloy; where there are continually the dearest expressions of this love; where is the enjoyment of the persons loved, without ever parting; where these persons that appear so lovely in this world, will really be inexpressibly more lovely, and full of love to us. And how sweetly will the mutual lovers join together to sing the praises of God and the Lamb! How full will it fill us with joy, to think, that this enjoyment, these sweet exercises will never cease or come to an end; but will last to all eternity!

Continued much in the same frame in the general, that I had been in at New York, till I went to New Haven, to live there as tutor of the college; having some special seasons of uncommon sweetness: particularly once at Boston, in a journey from Boston, walking out alone in the fields. After I went to New Haven, I sunk in religion; my mind being diverted from my eager and violent pursuits after holiness, by some affairs that greatly perplexed and distracted my mind.

In September, 1725, was taken ill at New Haven; and endeavoring to go home to Windsor, was so ill at the North Village, that I could go no further: where I lay sick for about a quarter of a year. And in this sickness, God was pleased to visit me again with the sweet influences of His spirit. My mind was greatly engaged there on divine, pleasant contemplations, and longings of soul. I observed that those who watched with me, would often be looking out for the morning, and seemed to wish for it. Which brought to my mind those words of the psalmist, which my soul with sweetness made its own language. *My soul waitest for the Lord, more than they that watch for the morning, I say, more than they that watch for the morning.* And when the light of the morning came, and the beams of the sun came in at the windows, it refreshed my soul from one morning to another. It seemed to me to be some image of the sweet light of God's glory.

I remember, about that time, I used greatly to long for the conversion of some that I was concerned with. It seem'd to me, I could gladly honor them, and with delight be a servant to them, and lie at their feet, if they were but truly holy.

But some time after this, I was again greatly diverted in my mind, with some temporal concerns, that exceedingly took up my thoughts, greatly to the wounding of my soul: and went on through various exercises, that it would be tedious to relate, that gave me much more experience of my own heart, than ever I had before.

Since I came to this town [Northampton], I have often had sweet complacency in God, in views of his glorious perfections, and the excellency of Jesus Christ. God has appeared to me, a glorious and lovely being, chiefly on the account of His holiness. The holiness of God has always appeared to me the most lovely of all His attributes. The doctrines of God's absolute sovereignty, and free grace, in showing mercy to whom He would show mercy; and man's absolute dependence on the operations of God's Holy Spirit, have very often appeared to me as sweet and glorious doctrines. These doctrines have been much my delight. God's sovereignty has ever appeared to me, as great part of His glory. It has often been sweet to me to go to God, and adore Him as a sovereign God, and ask sovereign mercy of Him.

I have loved the doctrines of the gospel: They have been to my soul like green pastures. The gospel has seem'd to me to be the richest treasure; the treasure that I have most desired, and longed that it might dwell richly in me. The way of salvation by Christ, has appeared in a general way, glorious and excellent, and most pleasant and beautiful. It has often seem'd to me, that it would in a great measure spoil heaven, to receive it in any other way. That Text has often been affecting and delightful to me, Isai. xxxii. 2. *A man shall be an hiding place from the wind, and a covert from the temptest etc.*

It has often appear'd sweet to me, to be united to Christ; to have Him for my head, and to be a member of His body: and also to have Christ for my teacher and prophet. I very often think with sweetness and longings and pantings of soul, of being a little child, taking hold of Christ, to be led by Him through the wilderness of this world. That text, Matth. xviii. at the beginning, has often been sweet to me, *Except ye be converted, and become as little children etc.* I love to think of coming to Christ, to receive salvation of Him, poor in spirit, and quite empty of self; humbly exalting Him alone; cut entirely off from my own root, and to grow into, and out of Christ: to have God in Christ to be all in all; and to live by faith on the Son of God, a life of humble, unfeigned confidence in Him. That Scripture has often been sweet to me, Psal. cxv. I. *Not unto us, O Lord, not unto us, but unto Thy name give glory, for Thy mercy, and for Thy truth's sake.* And those words of Christ, *Luk. x. 21. In that hour Jesus rejoiced in spirit, and said, I thank thee, O Father, Lord of heaven and earth, that Thou hast hid these things from the wise and prudent, and hast revealed them unto babes: Even so Father, for so it seemed good in Thy sight.* That sovereignty of God that Christ rejoiced in, seemed to me to be worthy to be rejoiced in; and that rejoicing of Christ, seemed to me to show the excellency of Christ, and the spirit that He was of.

Sometimes only mentioning a single word, causes my heart to burn within me: or only seeing the Name of Christ, or the name of some attribute of God. And God has appeared glorious to me, on account of the Trinity. It has made me have exalting thoughts of God, that he subsists in three persons; Father, Son, and Holy Ghost.

The sweetest joys and delights I have experienced, have not been those that have arisen from a hope of my own good estate; but in a direct view of the glorious things of the gospel. When I enjoy this sweetness, it seems to carry me above the thoughts of my own safe estate. It seems at such times a loss that I cannot bear, to take off my eye from the glorious, pleasant object I behold without me, to turn my eye in upon myself, and my own good estate.

My heart has been much on the advancement of Christ's kingdom in the world. The histories of the past advancement of Christ's kingdom, have been sweet to me. When I have read histories of past ages, the pleasantest thing in all my reading has been, to read of the kingdom of Christ being promoted. And when I have expected in my reading, to come to any such thing, I have lotted upon it [counted on it] all the way as I read. And my mind has been much entertained and delighted, with the Scripture promises and prophecies, of the future glorious advancement of Christ's kingdom on earth.

I have sometimes had a sense of the excellent fulness of Christ, and His meetness and suitableness as a Saviour; whereby He has appeared to me, far above all, the chief of ten thousands. And His blood and atonement has appeared sweet, and His righteousness sweet; which is always accompanied with an ardency of spirit, and inward strugglings and breathings and groanings, that cannot be uttered, to be emptied of myself, and swallowed up in Christ.

Once, as I rid out into the woods for my health, *Anno* 1737; and having lit from my horse in a retired place, as my manner commonly has been, to walk for divine contemplation and prayer; I had a view, that for me was extraordinary, of the glory of the Son of God; as mediator between God and man; and his wonderful, great, full, pure and sweet grace and love, and meek and gentle condescension. This grace, that appear'd to me so calm and sweet, appear'd great above the heavens. The person of Christ appear'd ineffably excellent, with an excellency great enough to swallow up all thought and conception, which continued, as near as I can judge, about an hour; which kept me, the bigger part of the time, in a flood of tears, and weeping aloud. I felt withal, an ardency of soul to be, what I know not otherwise how to express, than to be emptied and annihilated; to lie in the dust, and to be full of Christ alone; to love Him with a holy and pure love; to trust in Him; to live upon Him; to serve and follow Him, and to be totally wrapt up in the fullness of Christ; and to be perfectly sanctified and made pure, with a divine and heavenly purity. I have several other times, had views very much of the same nature, and that have had the same effects.

I have many times had a sense of the glory of the third person in the Trinity, in His office of sanctifier; in His holy operations communicating divine light and life to the soul. God in the communications of His Holy Spirit, has appear'd as an infinite fountain of divine glory and sweetness;

being full and sufficient to fill and satisfy the soul: pouring forth itself in sweet communications, like the sun in its glory, sweetly and pleasantly diffusing light and life.

I have sometimes had an affecting sense of the excellency of the word of God, as a word of life; as the light of life; a sweet, excellent, life-giving word: accompanied with a thirsting after that word, that it might dwell richly in my heart.

I have often since I lived in this town, had very affecting views of my own sinfulness and vileness; very frequently so as to hold me in a kind of loud weeping, sometimes for a considerable time together: so that I have often been forced to shut myself up. I have had a vastly greater sense of my own wickedness, and the badness of my heart, since my conversion, than ever I had before. It has often appeared to me, that if God should mark iniquity against me, I should appear the very worst of all mankind; of all that have been since the beginning of the world to this time: and that I should have by far the lowest place in hell. When others that have come to talk with me about their soul concerns, have expressed the sense they have had of their own wickedness, by saying that it seem'd to them, that they were as bad as the devil himself; I thought their expressions seemed exceeding faint and feeble, to represent my wickedness. I thought I should wonder, that they should content themselves with such expressions as these, if I had any reason to imagine, that their sin bore any proportion to mine. It seemed to me, I should wonder at myself, if I should express *my* wickedness in such feeble terms as they did.

My wickedness, as I am in myself, has long appear'd to me perfectly ineffable, and infinitely swallowing up all thought and imagination; like an infinite deluge, or infinite mountains over my head. I know not how to express better, what my sins appear to me to be, than by heaping infinite upon infinite, and multiplying infinite by infinite. I go about very often, for this many years, with these expressions in my mind, and in my mouth, "Infinite upon infinite. Infinite upon infinite!" When I look into my heart, and take a view of my wickedness, it looks like an abyss infinitely deeper than hell. And it appears to me, that were it not for free grace, exalted and raised up to the infinite height of all the fulness and glory of the great Jehovah, and the arm of His power and grace stretched forth, in all the majesty of His power, and in all the glory of His sovereignty; I should appear sunk down in my sins infinitely below hell itself, far beyond sight of every thing, but the piercing eye of God's grace, that can pierce even down to such a depth, and to the bottom of such an abyss.

And yet, I ben't in the least inclined to think, that I have a greater conviction of sin than ordinary. It seems to me, my conviction of sin is exceeding small, and faint. It appears to me enough to amaze me, that I have no more sense of my sin. I know certainly, that I have very little sense of my sinfulness.

That my sins appear to me so great, don't seem to me to be, because I have so much more conviction of sin than other Christians, but because I am so much worse, and have so much more wickedness to be convinced of. When I have had these turns of weeping and crying for my sins, I thought I knew in the time of it, that my repentance was nothing to my sin.

I have greatly longed of late, for a broken heart, and to lie low before God. And when I ask for humility of God, I can't bear the thoughts of being no more humble, than other Christians. It seems to me, that tho' their degrees of humility may be suitable for them; yet it would be a vile self-exaltation in me, not to be the lowest in humility of all mankind. Others speak of their longing to be humbled to the dust. Tho' that may be a proper expression for them, I always think for myself, that I ought to be humbled down below hell. 'Tis an expression that it has long been natural for me to use in prayer to God. I ought to lie infinitely low before God.

It is affecting to me to think, how ignorant I was, when I was a young Christian, of the bottomless, infinite depths of wickedness, pride, hypocrisy and deceit left in my heart.

I have vastly a greater sense, of my universal, exceeding dependence on God's grace and strength, and mere good pleasure, of late, than I used formerly to have; and have experienced more of an abhorrence of my own righteousness. The thought of any comfort or joy, arising in me, on any consideration, or reflection on my own amiableness, or any of my performances or experiences, or any goodness of heart or life, is nauseous and detestable to me. And yet I am greatly afflicted with a proud and self-righteous spirit; much more sensibly, than I used to be formerly. I see that serpent rising and putting forth it's head, continually, everywhere, all around me.

Tho' it seems to me, that in some respects I was a far better Christian, for two or three years after my first conversion, than I am now; and lived in a more constant delight and pleasure: yet of late years, I have had a more full and constant sense of the absolute sovereignty of God, and a delight in that sovereignty; and have had more of a sense of the glory of Christ, as a mediator, as revealed in the gospel. On one Saturday night in particular, had a particular discovery of the excellency of the gospel of Christ, above all other doctrines; so that I could not but say to myself; "This is my chosen light, my chosen doctrine": and of Christ, "This is my chosen prophet." It appear'd to me to be sweet beyond all expression, to follow Christ, and to be taught and enlighten'd and instructed by Him; to learn of Him, and live to Him.

Another Saturday night, January, 1738–9, had such a sense, how sweet and blessed a thing it was, to walk in the way of duty, to do that which was right and meet to be done, and agreeable to the holy mind of God; that it caused me to break forth into a kind of a loud weeping, which held me some time; so that I was forced to shut myself up, and fasten the doors. I could not but as it were cry out, "How happy are they which do that which is right in the sight of God! They are blessed indeed, they are the happy ones!" I had at the same time, a very affecting sense, how meet and suitable it was that God should govern the world, and order all things according to his own pleasure; and I rejoiced in it, that God reigned, and that his will was done.

Nathan Cole (1711–1783)

from *The Spiritual Travels of Nathan Cole*

A farmer and carpenter from Kensington in central Connecticut (now a part of the town of Berlin), Nathan Cole was among the thousands of people aroused by the Great Awakening. On October 23, 1740, he went to nearby Middletown to hear George Whitefield preach, and his life was never the same. Before, as he says, he had been an Arminian, a believer that people's own moral choices rather than God's grace determine their salvation. This belief, named for Jacobus Arminius (1560–1609), a Dutch theologian, was considered a heresy by orthodox Calvinists because it downplayed the ultimate power of God, but it had been a comfort to an economically prosperous and independent people.

Cole's description of the crowds rushing to hear Whitefield could be a description of the end of the world. For Cole it was, indeed, the end of his old complacency, for he immediately became tormented by his sense of sin and his dependence on God's omnipotence. He wept, sobbed, and was tempted by Satan to commit suicide. In 1748 his wife also went through a conversion crisis. Yet from these experiences he became sufficiently dissatisfied with what he thought was the continued looseness and hyprocrisy of the Congregational establishment that he refused to pay his "rates," the tax that all citizens owed to the church. (The Congregational Church was then a state church.) He and his fellow Separatists set up their own fellowship that met in people's houses, until they joined other new churches. Meanwhile, their combined piety and disobedience troubled their neighbors.

Cole's "Travels," which he wrote in 1765, thus illustrate a paradox of the Awakening: a fear and abasement before a harsh, omnipotent God, but a new independence from ecclesiastical and civil authority.

The text is from Michael J. Crawford, ed., "The Spiritual Travels of Nathan Cole," *William and Mary Quarterly*, 3d series, 33 (1976): 89–126. Crawford's short introduction and notes, edited here and sometimes transposed into brackets, supply additional information about Cole. Not included here are the source references Crawford supplied for Cole's many biblical citations and paraphrasings. For

Reprinted by permission of *The William and Mary Quarterly* from "The Spiritual Travels of Nathan Cole," *The William and Mary Quarterly,* 3d series, vol. 33, January 1976.

a further interpretation of "Spiritual Travels," see the chapter on Cole in Daniel B. Shea, *Spiritual Autobiography in Early America* (Princeton: Princeton Univ. Press, 1968; reprint, Madison: Univ. of Wisconsin Press, 1988). The original manuscript is in the holdings of the Connecticut Historical Society.

I was born Feb 15th 1711 and born again octo 1741—

When I was young I had very early Convictions; but after I grew up I was an Arminian untill I was *near* 30 years of age; I intended to be saved by my own works such as prayers and good deeds.

[George Whitefield at Middletown]

Now it pleased God to send Mr Whitefield into this land; and my hearing of his preaching at Philadelphia, like one of the Old apostles, and many thousands flocking to hear him preach the Gospel; and great numbers were converted to Christ; I felt the Spirit of God drawing me by conviction; I longed to see and hear him, and wished he would come this way. I heard he was come to New York and the Jerseys and great multitudes flocking after him under great concern for their Souls which brought on my Concern more and more hoping soon to see him but next I heard he was at long Island; then at Boston and next at Northampton.

Then on a Sudden, in the morning about 8 or 9 of the Clock there came a messenger and said Mr Whitfield preached at Hartford and Weathersfield yesterday and is to preach at Middletown this morning [Thursday, Oct. 23, 1740] at ten of the Clock. I was in my field at Work, I dropt my tool that I had in my hand and ran home to my wife telling her to make ready quickly to go and hear Mr Whitfield preach at Middletown, then run to my pasture for my horse with all my might; fearing that I should be too late; as having my horse I with my wife soon mounted the horse and went forward as fast as I thought the horse could bear, and when my horse got *much* out of breath I would get down and put my wife on the Saddle and bid her ride as fast as she could and not Stop or Slack for me except I bad her and so I would run untill I was *much* out of breath; and then mount my horse again, and so I did several times to favour my horse; we improved every moment to get along as if we were fleeing for our lives; all the while fearing we should be too late to hear the Sermon, for we had twelve miles to ride double in little more than an hour and we went round by the upper housen parish [the present town of Cromwell].

And when we came within about half a mile or a mile of the Road that comes down from Hartford weathersfield and Stepney to Middletown; on high land I saw before me a Cloud or fogg rising; I first thought it came from the great River, but as I came nearer the Road, I heard a noise something like a low rumbling thunder and presently found it was the noise of Horses feet coming down the Road and this Cloud was a Cloud of dust made by the Horses feet; it arose some Rods into the air over the tops of Hills and trees and when I came within about 20 *rods* of the Road, I could see men and horses Sliping along in the Cloud like shadows and as I drew nearer it seemed like a steady Stream of horses and their riders, scarcely a horse more than his length behind another, all of a Lather and foam with sweat, their breath rolling out of their nostrils every Jump; every horse seemed to go with all his might to carry his rider to hear news from heaven for the saving of Souls, it made me tremble to see the Sight, how the world was in a Struggle; I found a Vacance between two horses to Slip in mine and my Wife said law our Cloaths will be all spoiled see how they look, for they were so Covered with dust, that they looked almost all of a Colour Coats, hats, Shirts, and horses.

We went down in the Stream but heard no man speak a word all the way for 3 miles but every one pressing forward in great haste and when we got to Middletown old meeting house there was a great Multitude *it was said to be 3 or 4000* of people Assembled together; we dismounted and shook of[f] our Dust; and the ministers were then Coming to the meeting house; I turned and looked towards the Great River and saw the ferry boats Running swift backward and forward bringing over loads of people and the Oars Rowed nimble and quick; every thing men horses and boats seemed to be Struggling for life; *The land and banks over the river looked black with people and horses* all along the 12 miles I saw no man at work in his field, but all seemed to be gone.

When I saw Mr Whitfield come upon the Scaffold he Lookt almost angelical; a young, Slim, slender, youth before some thousands of people with a bold undaunted Countenance, and my hearing how God was with him every where as he came along it Solemnized my mind; and put me into a trembling fear before he began to preach; for he looked as if he was Cloathed with authority from the Great God; *and a sweet sollome solemnity sat upon his brow* And my hearing him preach, gave me a heart wound; By Gods blessing: my old Foundation was broken up, and I saw that my righteousness would not save me; then I was convinced of the doctrine of Election: and went right to quarrelling with God about it; because that all I could do would not save me; and he had decreed from Eternity who should be saved and who not.

[Conversion Crisis]

I began to think I was not Elected, and that God made some for heaven and me for hell. And I thought God was not Just in so doing, I thought I did not stand on even Ground with others, if as I thought; I was made to be damned; My heart then rose against God exceedingly, for his making me for hell; Now this distress lasted Almost two years:—Poor—Me—Miserable me.—It pleased God to bring on my Convictions more and more, and I was loaded with the guilt of Sin, I saw I was undone for ever; I carried Such a weight of Sin in my breast or mind, that it seemed to me as if I should sink into the ground every step; and I kept all to my self as much as I could; I went month after month mourning and begging for mercy, I tryed every way I could think to help my self but all ways failed:—Poor me it took away *most* all my Comfort of eating, drinking, Sleeping, or working. Hell fire was most always in my mind; and I have hundreds of times put my fingers into my pipe when I have been smoaking to feel how fire felt: And to see how my Body could bear to lye in Hell fire for ever and ever. Now my countenance was sad so that others took notice of it.

Sometimes I had some secret hope in the mercy of God; that some time or other he would have mercy on me; And so I took some hopes, and thought I would do all that I could do, and remove all things out of the way that might possibly be an hindrance; and I thought I must go to my Honoured Father and Mother and ask their forgiveness for every thing I had done amiss toward them in all my life: if they had any thing against me; I went and when I came near the house one of my Brothers was there, and asked me what was the matter with me: I told him I did not feel well, and passed by; But he followed and asked again what was the matter. I gave him the same answer, but said he something is the matter more than Ordinary for I see it in your Countenance: I refused to tell at present—Poor me—I went to my Father and Mother and told them what I came for: and asked them to forgive me every think [*sic*] they had against me concerning my disobedience or whatsoever else it might be; they said they had not any thing against me, and both fell aweeping like Children for Joy to see me so concerned for my Soul.

Now when I went away I made great Resolutions that I would forsake every thing that was Sinfull; And do to my uttermost every thing that was good; And at once I felt a calm in my mind, and I had no desire to any thing that was sin as I thought; But here the Devil thought to Catch me on a false hope, for I began to think that I was converted, for I thought I felt a real Change in me. But God in his mercy did not leave me here to perish; but in the space of ten days I was made to see that I was yet in the Gall of bitterness; my Convictions came on again more smart than ever—poor me—Oh then I long'd to be in the Condition of some good Man.

There was then a very Mortal disease in the land, the fever and bloody flux; and I was possest with a notion that if I had it I should die and goe right to hell, but I presently had it and very hard too: then my heart rose against God again for making me for hell, when he might as well have made me for heaven; or not made me at all:—Poor me—Oh that I could be a Dog or a toad or any Creature but Man: I thought that would be a happy Change for they had no Souls and I had. Oh what will become of me was the language of my mind; for now I was worse than ever, my heart was as hard as a Stone: my Eyes were dry, once I could weep for my Self but now cannot shed one tear; I was as it were in the very mouth of hell. The very flashes of hell fire were in my Mind; Eternity before me, and my time short here. Now when all ways failed me then I longed to be annihilated; or to have my Soul die with my body; but that way failed too. Hell fire hell fire ran Swift in my mind and my distemper grew harder and harder upon me, and my nature was just wore out—Poor me—poor Soul.

One night my brother Elisha came in to see me, and I spake to him and said I should certainly die within two or three days at the out Side for my Nature cannot possibly hold it any longer; and I shall certainly goe right to hell: And do you always remember that your poor brother is in hell; don't you never think that I am in heaven but take care of your self and always remember every day that your poor brother is in hell fire.—Misery—Miserable me; my brother got out of his Chair and went to speak to me, but he could not for weeping and went out of the house; and went away home and told my Father and Mother what I had said to him, and they were greatly distressed for me, and thought in the morning they would come and see me; but their distress grew so great for me that they could not stay but Came in the night.

And when they came into the house Mother seem'd to bring heaven into the house; but there was no heaven for me: She said Oh Nathan will you despair of the mercy of God, do not for a thousand of worlds, don't despair of the mercy of God, for he can have mercy at the very last gasp; I told her there was no mercy for me, I was going right down to hell, for I cannot feel grieved for my self, I can't relent, I can't weep for my self, I cannot shed one tear for my Sins; I am a gone Creature: Oh Nathan says she I have been so my self that I could not shed one tear if I might have had all the world for it; And the next moment I could cry as freely for Joy as ever I could for any thing in the world: Oh said she I know how you feel now, O if God should Shine into your Soul now it would almost take away your life, it would almost part soul and body; I beg of you not to despair of the mercy of God. I told her I could not bear to hear her talk so; for I cannot pray, my heart is as hard as a stone, do be gone, let me alone: do go home; you cannot do me any good, I am past all help of men or means, either for soul or Body, and after some time I perswaded them to go away; and there I lay all night in such a Condition untill sometime the next day with pining thoughts in my mind that my Soul might die with my Body.

And there came some body in with a great Arm full of dry wood and laid it on the fire, *and went out* and it burnt up very briskly as I lay on my Bed with my face toward the fire looking on, with these thoughts in my mind, Oh that I might creep into that fire and lye there and burn to death and die for ever Soul and Body; Oh that God would suffer it—Oh that God would suffer it.—Poor Soul.

And while these thoughts were in my mind God appeared unto me and made me Skringe: before whose face the heavens and the earth fled away; and I was Shrinked into nothing; I knew not whether I was in the body or out, I seemed to hang in open Air before God, and he seemed to Speak to me in an angry and Sovereign way what won't you trust your Soul with God; My heart answered O yes, yes, yes; before I could stir my tongue or lips, And then He seemed to speak again, and say, may not God make one Vessel to honour and an other to dishonour and not let you know it; My heart answered again O yes yes before I cou'd stir my tongue or lips. Now while my Soul was viewing God, my fleshly part was working imaginations and saw many things which I will omitt to tell at this time.

When God appeared to me every thing vanished and was gone in the twinkling of an Eye, as quick as A flash of lightning; But when God disappeared or in some measure withdrew, every thing was in its place again and I was on my Bed. My heart was broken; my burden was fallen of[f] my mind; I was set free, my distress was gone, and I was filled with a pineing desire to see Christs own words in the bible; and I got up off my bed being alone; And by the help of Chairs I got along to the window where my bible was and I opened it and the first place I saw was the 15th Chap: John—on Christs own words and they spake to my very heart and every doubt and scruple that rose in my heart about the truth of Gods word was took right off; and I saw the whole train of Scriptures all in a Connection, and I believe I felt just as the Apostles felt the truth of the word when they writ it, every leaf line and letter smiled in my face; I got the bible up under my Chin and hugged it; it was sweet and lovely; the word was nigh me in my hand, then I began to pray and to praise God.

. . .

[Separation]

Now I began to see the Old Standing Churches were not in a gospel order. I was called a member of this old Church for 14 or 15 years; but now I saw Ichabod was written upon it, the Glory of the Lord was departed, for they held several things contrary to the Gospel; I will mention one Viz—that unconverted men had a divine right to come to the ordinance of the Lords supper; and to give themselves up in Covenant to the Lord: whereas the Lord says to the wicked what hast thou to do to take my Covenant into thy mouth[?] I saw here that every unconverted person that came there to give themselves up did solemnly lye unto God; and my mind run thus, that the person in owning the Covenant did as much as to say *and ye Chh* [Church] *too that* he was a Child of God, when many times there was no room for such a belief: So according to the true sence and meaning of the thing, there was lying on both sides; I tryed a long time to have these things mended but all in vain: Then I came out and separated or dissented from them, for I could not see them to be a Gospel Church, or Christs spouse, Christs bride, Christs beloved one Or Christs garden well enclosed [1747].

Now I was called to give up what the world calls a fine reputation, and to become the offs[c]ouring of the Earth, and to lose my own life as it were in the world, for my religion. Oh this was hard to nature; this was like death to the flesh; but God gave me grace according to my day: and in a little time he made every bitter thing sweet: I was many times loaded with Scoffs, reproaches, and mockerys; but the light of Gods countenance sweetned all, now many of my old friends grew Shy of me and forsook me: my being acquainted and having Conversation with the weathersfield and eastern brethren was A great help to me in my Taravels [travails, travels?], and I often saw and felt the movings of Gods spirit among them in their religious meetings All in love seemingly with Christ.

[Wife's Crisis]

[1748] But one that was very near and dear to me, seeing these other Christians so much before us even just out of sight as it were, it caused Great darkness and distress in her mind, and great fears that she had never entered that strait gate of Conversion, and one day as she was so far borne down with it that she was at her wits end while she was talking about it, so that she screamed out three or four times as loud as she could which surpriz'd me, and she said it will fall on me, I said what will fall, she said a great Cloud, I said it won't, She screamed out and said it will, it will, it is close to my head now, a great black Cloud; I said it was not, She said where be I. I told her she was here in the house; she said Oh I am raving distracted what shall I do, I told her *i hope* not; She said I never shall have my reason again; I told her she wou'd *i hope,* She said Oh I shall faint away, I said no you wont *i hope* but I helped her unto the bed as fast as I cou'd and gave her some water.

Now no body can tell how my heart sunk down for fear Satan should get the victory and drive her into total despair; or clear out of her witts, Oh my heart went up to God for her with all my might, for I saw that Satan worked strongly upon her immaginations, but after she was composed again I told her to give me a relation of all her experience, which she did, and I told her that She told a very Clear gospel Conversion, for I thought it my duty to lift up the hands that hung down, and to strengthen the feeble knees, She brought in some objections, but I took them of[f] with Scriptures, but while I was gone out a few hours Satan came with many temptations to her, as his manner is to young Christians in the wilderness they are lead into, and he told her not to tell me of them; for I should throw her away at once as to being a Christian, if I were to know what thoughts and temptations she had.

But I had Charged her before to tell me all her troubles from time to time, and so she thought she wou'd, but was afraid; thinking that I shou'd say at once she was no convert, and so she concluded with her self that she was not, but yet she thought she wou'd tell me but when she had told me, I told her these were blessed evidences of heaven, these words came so unexpected that she almost fainted away, and the love of God broke Clearly into her Soul.

But after a few weeks Satan comes again with a drove of temptations and horrible thoughts, and threw them into her mind, and then told her she was a dreadfull Sinner to have such thoughts and blasphemous temptations against God, they are dreadfull Sins says he; and you are no Christian because you have such temptations; she labour'd under these things some time and at length she told me; and here I had a very Close dispute with Satan; I knew his voice and knew his run pretty well for I was not altogether ignorant of his devices; here I had 3 or 4 hours dispute with satan, for as he put these things into her mind so she spake them to me; And as he tempted by Scripture, I answered by Scripture, and he stove to make the Scriptures Clash one against another, Satan all the while said they were her Sins, and strove to prove it by Scripture; but I proved by Scripture they were not hers; I asked her if they were a burden to her or a delight, She said Oh. a burden I would give all the world to be sett at liberty from them said she, I told her if her heart acted freely in them then it left a guilt upon her Conscience; but if her heart strove against them then they were not her Sins; but Satan labourd hard to make her think they were her sins, My heart trembled for fear he would get the Victory, but I thought there was no better weapon to fight the Devil with than the sword of the Spirit which is the word of God; and I told her it was no sin to be tempted, but it was sin to yeild to the temptation, So that the Sin of temptation was not hers but *ye* Devils sin; for if it were a sin to be tempted then Christ must be a Sinner, for Christ was tempted and yet without Sin; The Devil fled and She seemed to feel him go away as plain as she could feel a burden taken from of[f] her back; for he was fairly worsted. And a Ray of Divine light broke into her Soul, and she was set at liberty "Glory be to God.["] But I will return and leave this; yet I told *her* she never honoured God so much in all her life as she did in this War.

[Separate Fellowship]

Now I learned more by discoursing with Weathersfield Brethren a little time, than I learnt in all my Life before by discoursing with any in the world, Concerning the true Worship of God. And I have had many sweet meetings with them; I was glad of all opportunity of being with them and so I am to this day; for my soul is much knit to some of them. Dear Children of God.

Now I was very steady at Conference meetings for the space of Seven years past, once a week steadily in a general way and great part of the time twice a week, and sometimes we had our religious meetings three times a week. Now I saw that nothing was acceptable to God in worship, but what was done by the help of his spirit; and I believe that when God designs to do any thing for his poor Creatures, he first gives some of his saints a spirit of prayer for that very thing that he intends speedily to do: there has been some persons that lay at the point of Death and the Doctors have given them over to die, and at my hearing of it I have carried their case to the Lord; and he has given to me to pray in spirit for their recovery and I had real satisfaction that it wou'd be so; and them persons did get well again beyond *their* expectation. At other times I have had freedom to pray for other some persons Souls and not for their recovery; and at other times I have had no freedom at all to pray for Some.

But here some may mistake and take the Natural flowing of affections to be the assistance of the Spirit of God. But if the Spirit of God prays with a Saint that prayer is not in Vain; and every Creature that Christ pray'd for will certainly be saved, for Christ never pray'd in vain; Christians know much by prayers: Christ says I will send the Comforter and when he is come he will teach you all things, that is the Spirit of truth [I John 2: 27]. The Saints have meat to eat that the world knows not of [John 4: 32]; I am not a Stranger to such things as these, the Saints feeling one another when they are together or when they are some miles apart. I was once with A Christian that was on a Journey and after he was gone some hours from me I told a man that was at work with me, that *i thought* such A man was then athinking of me and was then aweeping: for I was then in the same posture about him and felt his Tryals and burden; And 3 days after I saw the same Christian again and told him that I felt him after he had been gone from me some hours. And I had told a man that he was thinking on me and weeping and he said it was very true.

At another time I seemed to feel that a number of Saints some miles from me were distresd and in the dark about some things, and wanted to converse with other certain Saints; and while I was plowing in the field my mind ran so upon them that at unawares I broke out into a prayer with a loud voice not thinking but that I was in the midst of them, and I believe they were then praying that I might be sent to them. I finished my days work, and went and found them together: I had not been there long before there came an other from nine or ten miles of[f] on the same Errand. And said that the saints in that town felt the Distress of the saints in this Town: and sent him to see how it was; and I believe that Saints have been fetched from town to town many a time by the strength of prayer.

•   •   •

[Trouble with the Standing Church]

[1756] Now I have for many years refused to pay rates to the hireling Ministers and am often threatned by them to be carried to prison and time has been set by Collectors when they wou'd do it.[1] Once a Collector [in] *1756* which I had no reason to expect any mercy from set a time for to take me at a Society meeting and carry me right to prison, and I believe he did really intend to do it; and I found my flesh to Shrink at the Cross; and I had some thoughts of not going to the meeting, but after a little consideration I concluded I would not forsake the Cause of Christ for a Cross which I should take up, so gave my self and case up to God that I might submit to his will in the matter, and went to the meeting praying all the way as I went that I might by no means be left to Dishonour the Cause of Christ, and that my corrupt nature might not rise against any person, and that I might have a loving Christian temper; and that I might humbly Submit to Gods will in the matter; So I continued praying untill I came near the meeting house with all my might, and some standing at the door saw me coming and one man came and met me a few steps from the Door. I asked him if the meeting was begun; he said yes; I asked him what they had done, he said nothing but trying my Case about my rate, and that they had abated it for this year; I asked him if he spake true, he said yes, soon came another friend to me and told me the same, so I was set free at that time—All Glory be to God.

[1758] At another time—*1758* 4 Collectors threatned hard to carry me to prison, I told them I was in their hands as to Mans law and lay at their mercy; but not according to Gods law; I told them if they carryed me to prison I must suffer as patiently as I could; and hoped God would keep down my Corrupt nature, and not to seek revenge upon them; and many other Soft words; but one of them was very resolute and told some of my friends he would have carried me to prison long ago, if it had not been for my Morals, but I hate (said he) to carry such a moral Man to prison, as I heard afterwards from a friend, but they urged me to go to the Society meeting and ask them to abate my rates.

I went and asked and gave my reasons supported by Scripture. the Moderator desired the people to speak their minds about it: and then Deacon [Thomas Hart] Esqr riseth up and said as to Brother Cole his morals are lovely, and I love them but as to his rates we have a law, and by our law I do not know why he ought not pay as well as We then up riseth another man and said as to what the Esqr. has said Concerning brother Cole is true, for I have

1. The ministers of the standing churches of Connecticut were supported by a tax levied by the government. Some protection existed for members of such recognized dissenting groups as Baptists and Anglicans, but this protection was not extended to Separates until after 1770. See Williston Walker, *The Creeds and Platforms of Congregationalism* (Boston, 1960 [orig. publ. New York, 1893]), pp. 502–7.

lived near him some years—and he is not only a man of good Morals but a faithfull man that may be depended on, but as to his rate the Law obliges him to pay here as much as it does me; then another A Capt. [*militia officer*] rose up and says in as much as part of brother Coles family come here to meeting I do not see why he may not pay part of his rate here, but I am quite willing to abate as much as his head in the list or rate—and to him they agreed and Voted it So for the time past.

God made their Cheif men or speakers confess in the open meeting my morals; this was contrary to my expectation and my heart was drawn out with love and thankfulness to God for his Goodness to me in keeping me from many great and open Sins; which would be stains and blots to my life before the World: I felt my self to be a poor unworthy weak helpless creature; and saw it was all Gods goodness to me, I rejoyce to stand a witness for the Cause of God: all the Glory be to God: Blessed be his name.

· · ·

[Defense of Freewill Offerings]

Now two Collectors came for Ministers rates; which I refused to pay; and told them to get them abated at the next Society meeting; *and* at the next Society meeting these Collectors told me they tryed four times to have the Committee and Moderator try a vote to abate my rates; but they refused and at last bid them hold their Tongues for they would not hear a word about it; immediately at once there was such a confusion fell upon the people that men would not vote for the very thing they wanted to have voted for as they told me—and that they never saw such a meeting before: they could get no more votes that day; but contended till night; and then adjourned the meeting to another day.

Now the Collectors came and attached to the Value of ten pounds of my Estate; for little more than one pound; which they put to me for a rate and posted over to farmington in order for Sale; but I went to the adjourned meeting; which when the meeting was opened I put in a paper and when it was Read; then the minister desired to speak to the Case and fixing his eyes on me he said Mr Cole you ought to pay Rates here out of obedience to the Civil Authority; for they have set bounds to Societys and all within them bounds must pay to that Minister for God has placed that order of men as a Civil Authority; and they ought to be obeyed Even Christ payd tribute to the Civil authority; out of obedience to them etc. Therefore it was duty to do it and many other words which were not to the Case; then I asked liberty to answer the Minister and I said this Law of Society bounds is mans law; not Gods Law; and God says men frame mischief by their laws; etc. But God says submit to every ordinance of Man for the Lords sake; now mark it is for the

Lords sake; therefore when mans law agreeth with Gods law then submit to mans law; why; because it agreeth with Gods law; but if mans law disagreeth with Gods law then disobey mans law for the Lords sake, and why, because it disagreeth with Gods law, and again the Lord says the powers that be are ordained of God; and there is no power but of God; therefore mark; that Law that is contrary to Gods Law, hath no power in it; why, because God never gave man any power to make laws against himself; now Gods law to support the Gospel is free will offerings all over the Bible; and not by a force of law from men; for if men do not help to support the Gospel, God reserves that punishment to himself; And never set men to punish one an other by force of law, for the Gospel is a Gospel of peace, and is not to be forced on any; I also told them, that Gods law is, let every man bare his own burden, and where doth God mean but in that Church where he goeth to Worship; and God says let him that is taught minister to him that teacheth in all good things; not to one that doth not teach him, and now I have done ten times more to support the Gospel by free will offering this last year than any man in Kensintom [*sic*] according to his list; and yet you must fall to Robbing your neighbour Churches by force of law, to get money to pay your ministers; which the Church of Christ never did, in all the whole bible, no nor no saints in all the whole book of God, *and yet you call your selves a Church of Christ* and as to what your Minister says about Christ paying tribute to Cesar; I told them that Cesar was a king, and it was the kings rate, it was not to Support the Gospel, but it was the kings Rate and I pay the kings rate my country Rate; and that I had rather have my head cut off than brake Gods Law, knowingly and willingly, and now you have sent your Servants the Collectors, and they have taken ten pounds in Value of my estate, to make A merchandize of me; and now I ask for mercy, I am under great afflictions at home as to my wife etc.

Now it was put to vote to abate my rates that were past and they were abated by a great Majority Blessed be the Lord; Now one says the Minister lookt pale; and others say it killed the minister stone dead; but a Certain Esqr. said I wonder he would come to us in such a spirit as he doth; to reflect so hard upon us.—One asked him if Mr Cole made any reflections but what was according to Scripture, he made no answer; others say they never heard them Scriptures and laws opened before, and seemed much pleased at it but I came away, and as I came round in the Ally [aisle] to come at the door, the faces and eyes of the Assembly turned as I went round, with a sober amaze in the Countenance; as if I had been some strange Creature, from some other nation or World.

Charles Woodmason (c. 1720–1776?)

from the *Journal of C. W., Clerk,*
Itinerant Minister in South Carolina

Very little is known about Charles Woodmason, and his writings were not published until 1953, when Richard J. Hooker brought together his journal, letters, and sermons in *The Carolina Backcountry on the Eve of the Revolution.* Yet we know equally little of other early American autobiographers like Madam Knight and Elizabeth Ashbridge. Their autobiographies stand as their only biographies.

According to Richard Hooker, Woodmason was born in England about 1720 and grew up, probably in London, as a member of the gentry class and the Anglican church. In about 1752 he went to South Carolina, probably expecting his wife and family to join him later. A fall from a horse and "a Kick received in the Scrotum" made him impotent, however, and his wife "refus'd coming over to America." But Woodmason stayed, and during the next seven or eight years he bought over 2100 acres of land and 18 slaves. He became a member of the wealthy class of planters and merchants who ruled the colony. In 1762 he returned briefly to England, probably because his wife had died, but then came back and moved to Charleston, and entered into its civic and political life.

In 1765, misjudging the depth of the popular opposition to the Stamp Act, Woodmason applied to be distributor of stamps, and suddenly found himself treated as "a faithless fellow—one that is a betrayer of the Country, and of the Rights and Privileges of America." Perhaps as a result, he then gave up political life to become an itinerant Anglican minister. He had long regretted the lack of Anglican ministers in the backcountry and absence of support the backcountry got from the wealthy residents of the coast, who used its residents merely as a buffer against the Indians. But this was a radical change in life for an educated, upperclass South Carolinian. So he made a short trip to England to be ordained, then started back in June, 1766, the point at which the *Journal* begins.

As the reader can see, Charles Woodmason's *Journal* makes a fascinating contrast to other, more familiar or canonical American religious autobiographies. It is not a conversion story; it is not very introspective; it does not even concern itself with God. It is a social document, a powerful, often humorous, moving

Reprinted from *The Carolina Backcountry on the Eve of the Revolution,* ed. Richard J. Hooker (Chapel Hill: Univ. of North Carolina Press, 1953). Reprinted by permission of the University of North Carolina Press and Nancy Hooker.

description of frontier poverty, ignorance, and brutishness, told from the point of view of a cultivated gentleman. Christianity, to Woodmason, does not mean salvation; it means a minimum of physical comfort and social refinement—and an end to nakedness, drunkenness, brawling, lechery, dirt, and hunger. Yet different as Woodmason's *Journal* is from, say, Edwards's "Personal Narrative," its values are all the closer to the mainstream of the American middle class. Woodmason might almost have been an ancestor to Caroline Kirkland's Mary Clavers in *A New Home.* Though writing from an establishmentarian perspective, he also bears comparison with the great Methodist frontier preacher, Peter Cartwright.

But the first and last brilliance of Woodmason is the energy, frankness, and roughness of his language. He kept this journal as a record of his travels and sacrifices (counting up the miles travelled and people baptized), as a record to show to his friends, perhaps, and an account (which he somehow anticipated) of how his anger and outrage at the backcountry gave way to sympathy and support. But he must also have kept his journal as a way of keeping his own sanity. The long lists of debauchery and notes on frontier trickery, like drowning out sermons with dogfights, are a kind of mental defense. As the ruffians tried to drown him out with the dogfights, he drowned them in words.

The text, including all notes and editorial matter in brackets, edited slightly for the present selection, is from Richard J. Hooker, ed., *The Carolina Backcountry on the Eve of the Revolution* (Chapel Hill: Univ. of North Carolina Press, 1953).

1766 . *June 10*

Sail'd down to Gravesend, and embark'd on board the Portland, a Snow, G. H.[1] Master, and same Evening went down the River.

The Passengers were, 3 London Bucks—5 or 6 Tradesmen, and some Ladies of Pleasure, seeking a Retreat.

June 11

Came to Anchor in the Downs. 12th Went on Shore at Deal, 13th Sail'd down Channel: Address'd the Passengers to join in Prayer for a prosp'rous Voyage. Refus'd.

12th

Pass'd by the Isle of Wight. 13th off Plymouth. 15th Clear'd Channel, and bid adieu to Old England.

From this Time to the 21t the Passengers Sea-Sick and on

Sunday 22d

Collected them together at Divine Service—Refus'd attending in the afternoon. Captain and Londoners went to Cards.

1. The master of the "Portland" was George Higgins. *South Carolina Gazette and Country-Journal,* Aug. 19, 1766.

Sunday 29

All the Ships Company attended Sermon—save two Scotsmen—Captain and Gentlemen invited the Ladies in the afternoon to drink Tea—Would not suffer them to come into the Cabbin: Which affronted the Bucks.

A Criminal Commerce enter'd into between the Gentlemen and Ladies— Read them Lectures of Continence and Temperance. Laughed at and Ridiculed.

Sunday July 6th

Ships Company attended—Behaved ludicrously.

Sunday July 13th

Not half the People attended—One of the Bucks absented.

Sunday July 20th

The Commen People attended—Captain and Women to themselves.

Sunday July 27th

All the passengers at Divine Service—Captain and Women behav'd indecently.

Sunday August 3d

Refus'd to officiate any more, as they turn'd both the Sermon and Service to Raillery.

August 12th

Landed in Charlestown: A dangerous Fever in the Place carries off 8 or 10 persons ev'ry Day—Carried by Gentleman to his Country Seat on Ashley River.

August 17th

Officiated at St. Andrews Church. Weather excessive hot and Sultry, and Country very Sickly—Multitudes of New Imported Irish People die daily.

August 24

The Ministers of St Andrews, St James', St John's, and other Parishes down in the Fever. Officiated at St Andrews. Received Intelligence of the Death of 4 Episcopal Ministers, and 3 of the Kirk of Scotland. About 40 Persons in these Churches, which is more than usual.

August 31

Continued at the Gentlemans Seat, and pray'd with them most days, they being of the Baptist Congregation—Did Duty this Day at St. James Church —Two other Ministers died this Week, and all in the Country very ill of the

Fever. The Clerk of the Board of Church Commissioners sick—No Board as yet met to receive my Credentials, and give me my Commission.

September 7

Officiated at St. Andrews—On the 12th the Board of Commissioners (25 in number) met at the Council Chamber, and sign'd my Commission. Left me to move as I thought proper without any Restrictions but would not allow my Salary to commence from the Day of my Landing (as the Law expressly appoints) but from the day of my Commission. Deliv'd Mr. Broughtons Letters and Parcel of Books to the Reverend Mr. Hart.[2] Miles rode to St Andrews and St James.——50 [miles traveled] *

September 12th

Sett off from Charlestown to enter on my Mission—Wet to the Skin in several claps of Thunder—and greatly fatigu'd thro' Horses failing during this hot Weather.

Sunday 14th

Officiated at St Marks Church 80 Miles from Town—70 in Congregation— which is double the Number in Common——80 [miles]
The Roads hot and Sandy—and Weather excessive Sultry.

16th

Arriv'd at Pine Tree Hill and Centre of my Distric.[3] This Week employ'd in riding the Environs and baptizing.——50 [miles]; 40 [miles]

Sunday 21st[4]

Officiated in the Presbyterian Meeting House to about 200 Hearers, Chiefly Presbyterians. Offer'd to give Sermon twice on ev'ry Sunday. Rejected.
Beside this Meeting House, there is another of Quakers with a large

2. The Rev. Oliver Hart, minister of the Baptist Church in Charleston, was born in Bucks County, Pennsylvania, in 1723 and came to Charleston in 1749. William Rogers, *Sermon Occasioned by the Death of the Rev. Oliver Hart* . . . (Philadelphia, 1796), pp. 20–21.
*The number of miles which Woodmason traveled was recorded in the right-hand margin of the MS Journal and occasionally he inserted the total mileage up to a certain point. This information has been transferred to the end of the paragraph opposite which the original marginal note occurred. Hereafter [miles traveled] will appear simply as [miles], and [total miles traveled] will be [total miles].
3. By an act of 1756, a salary of £700 (or about £100 Sterling) was provided for a clergyman to preach at "Fredericksburgh, Pine Tree Creek, or such other centrical part in the Waterees as the said commissioners shall direct and appoint, and six times a year at least, at the most populous places within forty miles of the same." Thomas Cooper, ed., *The Statutes at Large of South Carolina* (Columbia, S.C., 1838), IV, p. 21.
4. Woodmason first wrote "28th," then corrected it to "21st." The change could have resulted either from error or from the delay of a week in making the entry.

Congregation[5]—But they have neither Pastor or Teacher or Speaker at Either.

The People around, of abandon'd Morals, and profligate Principles—Rude—Ignorant—Void of Manners, Education or Good Breeding—No genteel or Polite Person among them—save Mr. Kershaw an English Merchant settled here.[6] The people are of all Sects and Denominations—A mix'd Medley from all Countries and the Off Scouring of America. Baptized 20 Children this Week and rode about 40 Miles——Miles Brought over 220.

September 28

Officiated in the Meeting House—Promoted a Petition to the General Assembly to have a Chapel built, which ev'ry one of ev'ry Class and Sect sign'd. About 150 percons present at Service.

Received Great Civilities from Mr. Samuel Wyly,[7] an eminent Quaker in the Neighbourhood—who kindly rode about with me to make me known to the People.

Not a House to be hir'd—Nor even a single Room on all this River to be rented, fit to put my Head or Goods in—The People all new Settlers, extremely poor—Live in Logg Cabbins like Hogs—and their Living and Behaviour as rude or more so than the Savages. Extremely embarrassed how to subsist. Took up my Quarters in a Tavern—and exposed to the Rudeness of the Mobb. People continually drunk.

The Country being very Sickly, Mr. Kershaw would not permit me to move abroad much as this Week. Married a Couple—for the 1st Time—Woman very bigg.——20 [miles]

My English Servant Man whom I brought over, taken with the Fever. Excessive hot Weather for the Season.

5. A small immigration of Irish Quakers came to the Waterees in October, 1751, and took up land on both sides of the Wateree River above and below the future town of Pine Tree Hill, later Camden. A Quaker meeting was organized as early as 1753. Robert L. Meriwether, *The Expansion of South Carolina* (Kingsport, Tenn., 1940), pp. 103–5; Thomas J. Kirkland and Robert M. Kennedy, *Historic Camden* (Columbia, S.C., 1905), pp. 11–12, 73–74.

6. Joseph Kershaw, an Englishman and an Anglican, was a man of great importance in the entire region of the Wateree River. He was the son of Joseph Kershaw of Sowerby, Yorkshire, England, and emigrated to Charleston about 1750 with two brothers. Joseph Kershaw served as a clerk for James Laurens and Company and later worked for the firm of Ancrum, Lance and Loocock. In 1758 the latter firm sent him to establish a country branch on the Wateree River. Leila Sellers, *Charleston Business on the Eve of the Revolution* (Chapel Hill, 1934), pp. 89–90. Woodmason had known Kershaw earlier, when the latter was still a clerk in Charleston.

7. Samuel Wyly, one of the Irish Quakers, had come to the Waterees in 1752. He became a leader among the Quakers, established a store, became a justice of the peace, was placed in charge of the nearby Catawba Indians, and in January, 1766, attempted to take his seat in the Assembly to represent St. Mark's Parish. Since as a Quaker he refused to take the election oath, it was resolved that he could not be seated. Wyly died February 13, 1768, at the age of forty-six. Meriwether, *Expans. of S. C.*, pp. 104–5; *South Carolina Gazette*, Dec. 22, 1759; Kirkland and Kennedy, *Historic Camden*, p. 51; Commons Journal, Jan. 25, 1766; *The South Carolina and American General Gazette*, Mar. 4, 1768.

October 5th

The Season very dry—and people in Great distress for want of Provisions—Greatly relieved by the Kindness of Mr. Kershaw, who open'd all his Stores to them.

Offer'd to take 20 Boys and educate them Gratis would they fit up a Room for a School, which they promis'd to do.

About 100 People this day at Service—Offer'd to catchecise their Children in the Afternoon, but none brought—Do not find but one religious person among this Great Multitude.

The Weather comes more moderate. But my Horse quite worn down for want of Grass.——25 [miles]

October 8th

Received a Subpena from C. T. [Charles Town] to attend Court to give Evidence in a Suit at Law; Went down the Country. Preached at the High Hills of Santee. Met here with some serious Christians But the Generality very loose, dissolute, Idle People—Without either Religion or Goodness—The same may be said of the whole Body of the People in these Back Parts.—[total] miles 305

Received at St Marks by Col Richardson[8]—a Worthy sensible Gentleman and Pious Christian.—Once more in a Christian family.——50 [miles]

Sunday October 12

Did Duty at St. Marks Church—This Church has been destitute of a Minister these 3 Years—And so little do they care for Religion, that they'l not send to England for a Minister tho' this Church is on the Establishment.[9]

Their late Minister is remov'd to Pon pon—At his first Sermon 50 Persons attended—But they fell off to about 7 or 8 the Communicants only—Often when he gave Notice to celebrate None attended—At other times, No Elements provided—Wearied out, and vex'd at their Indifference, he quitted them.

The people solicited me to fill this Vacancy—but I declin'd, as could not

8. Richard Richardson, born in Virginia about 1704, became a leading South Carolinian. As early as 1757 he was named colonel of militia, and during the Cherokee wars of 1760–1761 he commanded a regiment. Richardson was repeatedly elected to the Assembly to represent St. Mark's Parish, and on the outbreak of war with England he played an important part in both political and military affairs. Joseph S. Ames, "The Cantey Family," *South Carolina Historical and Genealogical Magazine,* 11 (1910), pp. 225–26.

9. St. Mark's Parish had been established in 1757 by dividing the Parish of Prince Frederick. Richard Richardson was named as one of the commissioners to build the church and parsonage and to manage the affairs of the church. *Stat. at Large of S.C.,* IV, pp. 35–37; James M. Burgess, *Chronicles of St. Mark's Parish, Santee Circuit, and Williamsburg Township, South Carolina, 1731–1885* (Columbia, S.C., 1888), pp. 12–13.

to accept it with out leave of my Diocesan and it would be annulling the Orders of the Church Commissioners. Withal, I came to this Wild Country to support the Interests of the Church of England and the People of our Communion, trodden under foot by the Herds of Sectaries.

Sunday 26 [10] October

Returned from C. T. My Journey being thrown away—The plaintiff suffering a Nonsuit. My English Servant seduc'd from my Service.——210 [miles]

Sunday 19

Officiated at the parish of St Matthew on the upper part of Santee at Solicitation of the Inhabitants—A vast Congregation—In the Evening was carried down the Road to another Congregation who met at a Gentleman's where I preach'd and baptiz'd—Made it late (by our long singing) e're Service was over—Quite fatigued.——110 [miles]

Monday 20

The Minister of St John's being Sick, went down to that parish—and baptiz'd. But no Congregation assembled there not being an House wherein hardly a well person. All in the fever.——[total] miles 695

The same at St Andrews and St James—Went down with a party of Friends to the Sea Islands for fresh Air—Courteously and genteely treated by a very rich Gentleman of the Baptist Communion who promis'd to make handsome provision for me.——100 [miles]

October 29

My Friend, the Gentleman above, bit by a mad Dog—and died in four Days— A very Great Loss, and much Grief to Me. Invited to Charlestown by the Chief Justice, the Honorable Charles Shinner Esquire who treated me with Great Kindness and Humanity—Promis'd to be my Friend and to take me under his protection.

Accordingly he prepar'd to accompany me into the Country and to look out for a place to build me an House and Chapel at his own Expense, till public Affairs (now very fluctuating) were settled, and the Country in some Quiet—which was up in Arms thro' a Gang of Theives and Robbers that laid the province under Contribution.——10 [miles]

Mean time rode up to St Marks, and did Duty there on Sunday November 9. and returned to the Cheif Justice,—whom I found in Great afliction thro' loss of his two Sons, who died after few Hours Illness of a flux and fever.——160 [miles]

---

10. This entry is out of chronological order. The day and date are apparently correct.

Suffer'd great fatigues this Journey thro' bad and tir'd Horses walk'd 60 Miles on foot thro' the hot burning Sands and Sun. Obliged to lay by for a fortnight to recover Strength, and take Rest, till the Weather came cooler.

December 6

The Cheif Justice set off with me (with his attendants) for the Country. On Sunday the 7th preached at St Jame's before him and some other Gentlemen of the Council, and from Charlestown.——16 [miles]; [total] miles 981

December 8

Sett off for St Marks, and received with great kindness at Col. Richardsons.——64 [miles]

December 14

Officiated at St Marks Church—and on the 18th arrived at Pine Tree Hill. Mr. Kershaw took me to his House, till Lodgings could be fitted up for me.——50 [miles]

The Cheif Justice busied in concerting Measures to suppress the Gangs of Horse Theives—Depressing Vice, and bringing about a Reformation of Manners—As most of the low People around had Connexions with these Theives, this gave them the Alarm. The Robbers gather'd in a Body and stood on their defence.

December 21

Officiated in the Meeting House. By Influence of the Cheif Justice, had a Congregation, and preach'd in the Afternoon.

Found the School Room that was intended for me, turn'd by the Tavern Keeper into a Stable. Only 3 Boys offer'd, out of 2 or 300 that run wild here like Indians—But as their Parents are Irish Presbyterians, they rather chuse to let them run thus wild, than to have them instructed in the Principles of Religion by a Minister of the Church of England.

25. Christmas Day

Officiated as usual in the Meeting House, and would have celebrated with the C. J. but could raise no Communicants—Withal, the Elders would not consent to it, as to have in their Phrase, Mass said in their House. About 100 People, cheifly Church People from distant Parts—None of whom would consent to receive the Communion in a Meeting House. Hereby the Poor lost 100£ which the C. J. intended to give the Poor.

December 26

The Cheif Justice attempted to raise the Militia, and to attack the Gang of Theives—But the officers were too cowardly—All afraid to venture—Nor could he enlist any Volunteers.[11]

His intention was to cross the Country, to take me with Him, and to make a Circle back to C. T.—The Robbers hearing of his Intent laid in wait for to attack Him and his Retinue. So by perswasion he returned by the Road which he came up.[12]——1095 [total miles]

Could not purchase in Fee Simple a Piece of Ground for a Chapel or Dwelling House. Received a Petition from the People to the Assembly for to settle a fine Tract of 460 Acres of public Land on me, for a Glebe. This Land worth 500 Guineas

Sunday 28

Officiated as usual at Pine Tree. Congregation about 80 people Tho' they are so populous around, that 500 might attend if they would.

January 1, 1767

Gave them a Sermon suited to the Day—and set off to accompany the Cheif Justice in his Return—The Tavern Keeper[13] (who is a Rich fellow, and Who has made an Estate by encouraging Vice and Idleness) affronted at my Discourse against Immorality as if aim'd against Him—He cryed out like Demetrius that the Craft was in Danger—And (but behind our Backs) abus'd both my Self and Cheif Justice, vowing Vengeance on both.

Jan. 3) Took leave of my Hon'd Friend—and on Jan. 4.) assembled the People at the High Hills, and gave them Service.——25 [miles]

Had a large Congregation—but according to Custom, one half of them got drunk before they went home.

Next Day cross'd the River (Wateree) into the Fork to baptize several Children—A Shocking Passage. Obliged to cut the Way thro' the Swamp for 4 Miles, thro' Canes, and impenetrable Woods—Had my Cloaths torn to Pieces—After meeting some Religious People return'd back the same Way: and went down to St Marks Church w[h]ere I officiated on Sunday Jan. 11. and then returned back to Pine Tree Hill.——25 [miles]; 75 [miles] Jan. 18) Officiated as usual at Pine Tree—and received an Invitation from the people

---

11. In his "Memorandum" on the Regulator movement, written long after the events he described, Woodmason said that no one would "turn out or obey" Shinner "because he brought not Orders from the Governour." Sermon Book, IV, [372].

12. This incident played a part in the charges against Shinner which preceded his removal from office in 1767. According to Shinner, Govey Black, a notorious outlaw, and eleven men had lain in wait for him as he was "very credibly informed by many persons of good repute." Shinner's opponents appeared to disbelieve the story. Commons Journal, Apr. 9, May 27, 1767.

13. The tavernkeeper was John Canty.

on Pedee River to visit them—With Man and Horse to carry me, where (after many Difficulties,—much fatigue, and suffering Hunger, Cold, and no Bed to lye on, but only the Ground) I arrived the 22d—80 [miles]; 1300 [total miles]

Sunday January 25 . 1767

A Congregation at the Cheraws of above 500 People. Baptiz'd about 60 Children—Quite jaded out—standing and speaking 6 Hours together and nothing to refresh me, but Water—and their Provisions I could not touch— All the Cookery of these People being exceeding filthy, and most execrable.

Next Day, I returned and preached the 27th in my Way back at Lynch's Creek to a great Multitude of People assembled together, being the 1st Episcopal Minister they had seen since their being in the province—They complain'd of being eaten up by Itinerant Teachers, Preachers, and Imposters from New England and Pensylvania—Baptists, New Lights, Presbyterians, Independants, and an hundred other Sects—So that one day You might hear this System of Doctrine—the next day another—next day another, retrograde to both—Thus by the Variety of Taylors who would pretend to know the best fashion in which Christs Coat is to be worn none will put it on—And among the Various Plans of Religion, they are at Loss which to adapt, and consequently are without any Religion at all. They came to Sermon with Itching Ears only, not with any Disposition of Heart, or Sentiment of Mind— Assemble out of Curiosity, not Devotion, and seem so pleas'd with their native Ignorance, as to be offended at any Attempts to rouse them out of it.——40 [miles]

I was almost tir'd in baptizing of Children—and laid my Self down for the Night frozen with the Cold—without the least Refreshment—No Eggs, Butter, Flour, Milk, or anything, but fat rusty Bacon, and fair Water, with Indian Corn Bread, Viands I had never before seen or tasted.——1340 [total miles]

I set off next day for Pine Tree, glad to be once more under the Roof of the good Samaritan, Mr. Kershaw, who poured Wine and Oil into my Wounds, and would have prevented my moving from him for a Space: But I was obliged to travel upwards—having engaged my Self for next Sunday at the Settlement of Irish Presbyterians called the Waxaws, among whome were several Church People.——40 [miles]

This is a very fruitful fine Spot, thro' which the dividing Line between North and South Carolina runs—The Heads of P. D. [Peedee] River, Lynch's Creek, and many other Creeks take their Rise in this Quarter—so that a finer Body of Land is no where to be seen—But it is occupied by a Sett of the most lowest vilest Crew breathing—Scotch Irish Presbyterians from the North of Ireland—They have built a Meeting House and have a Pastor, a Scots Man among them [14]—A good Sort of Man—He once was of the Church of

---

14. The Rev. William Richardson, Presbyterian minister at the Waxhaws.

England, and solicited for Orders, but was refus'd—whereon he went to Pensylvania, and got ordained by the Presbytery there, who allow him a Stipend to preach to these People, who (in his Breast) he heartily contemns—They will not suffer him to use the Lords Prayer. He wants to introduce Watts'[15] Psalms in place of the barbarous Scotch Version—but they will not admit it—His Congregation is very large—This Tract of Land being most surprisingly thick settled beyond any Spot in England of its Extent—Seldom less than 9, 10, 1200 People assemble of a Sunday—They never heard an Episcopal Minister, or the Common Prayer, and were very curious—The Church people among them are thinly scatter'd but they had a numerous Progeny for Baptism—rather chusing they should grow up to Maturity without Baptism than they should receive it by the hands of Sectaries—So in Compliance with their Request to visit them, I appointed Sunday the 31st to go up to them— and the Presbyterian Minister was to come down to this Meeting House in my Absence.——1380 [total miles]

He came down on the Friday. I stay'd till Saturday till I moved—when there arose such a Storm of Wind, Rain, Hail and Storm, as I think I hardly ever before saw. I could not stir out of the House, and was obliged to keep close Quarters.

But above, it was Fair Weather, and more than a thousand people assembled to attend my coming—and returned greatly vex'd and disapointed— Whereon I sent them Word, I would attend them very soon.

Accordingly I wrote them (and enclosed advertisements) that I would be with them (if Health and Weather permitted) the last Sunday in February.[16]

Mean time went down to the High Hills where I officiated and baptiz'd on Sunday the 7th. Next day at St Marks—giving the people Sermons and Lectures, in various Places, and at different Houses as I went along—For I found it here, the same as at Lynch's Creek and the Cheraws—Wherever you went to a House to marry or baptize, a Multitude would assemble, and desire a Discourse; which I was more ready alway to give, than they to ask.

At all these Places I've been at, I read the King's Proclamation against Vice and Immorality,[17] which has had very good Effects. For thro' want of Ministers to marry and thro' the licentiousness of the People, many hundreds live in Concubinage—swopping their Wives as Cattel, and living in a State of Nature, more irregularly and unchastely than the Indians—I therefore made Public Notice ev'ry where be given, that whoever did not attend to be legally married, I would prosecute them at the Sessions—and that all who had liv'd

15. Isaac Watts (1674–1748) was an English theologian and hymn writer. Among his works are the *Hymns* (1707), and *The Psalms of David* (1719).

16. Woodmason never preached in the Waxhaws. Although he prepared a sermon to give there, some of the elders of the Waxhaw Presbyterian Church were opposed to his coming.

17. The Royal Proclamation "For the encouragement of piety and virtue, and the preventing and punishing of vice, prophaneness, and immorality" was issued October 31, 1760. *Bibliotheca Lindesiana, Vol. VIII. Handlist of Proclamations Issued by Royal and Other Constitutional Authorities 1714–1910 George I to Edward VII* (Wigan, 1913), col. 97.

in a State of Concubinage on application to me, I would marry Gratis—Numbers accepted of my Offer, and were married, and then I baptiz'd their Children—Several who were Episcopal, and who had been married by Itinerant Dissenting Ministers desir'd to be re-married by the Liturgy, as judging such their former Marriage invalid.——[total] Miles 1380

As there are no Clergy in North Carolina, the Magistrates are there permitted to Marry—and many of this Province travel over there for to be join'd—Several Couple married by them apply'd likewise to be re-married, as judging such their former Marriage temporary only.

From St Marks I returned to Pine Tree Hill, where my Good Samaritan had finish'd off two upper Rooms in a House belonging to an Old Widow Dutch Woman—And about this Time the Waggons with my Goods and Library came from C. T. the Carriage of which cost me Seven Guineas.——50 [miles]

Sunday Feb. 14

Officiated at Pine Tree—Find my Congregation here to be at a medium about 60 or 70 Persons—But no Clerk or Singing—none to make the Responses—they sit all the Time of Prayer and Sermon, and I have but one person (as yet) offer as a Communicant.

Friday 19. Journey'd upwards to Lynch's Creek, and did Duty there on Sunday the 21. A Crowd of People assembled, the Major Part Episcopals—Married several Couple on the Proclamation and Baptized 30 or 40 children and 2 Adults—A Great Number of Adults present—but all of them totally ignorant of the first Principles of things—So cannot baptize them—And what is worse, being oblig'd to be in perpetual Motion, I cannot have Time to instruct them, which is great Grief to me. In this Congregation was not a Bible or Common Prayer—None to respond. All very poor and extremely ignorant—Yet desirous of the Knowledge of God and of Christ. Their Case is truly pitiable, but out of my power to amend and the Legislature turn a deaf Ear to all Remonstrances on this Subject, and like *Gallio* care for none of these things.[18]——40 [miles]

From the lower part of Lynch's Creek I proceeded to the upper—and from the Greater to the Lesser; The Weather was exceeding Cold and piercing—And as these People live in open Logg Cabbins with hardly a Blanket to cover them, or Cloathing to cover their Nakedness, I endur'd Great Hardships and my Horse more than his Rider—they having no fodder, nor a Grain of Corn to spare.——[total] miles 1470

I had appointed a Congregation to meet me at the Head of Hanging Rock Creek[19]—Where I arriv'd on Tuesday Evening—Found the Houses

18. Acts 18: 12–17.
19. Hanging Rock is a hundred-foot cliff overhanging the branch of Little Lynch's River. Meriwether, *Expans. of S. C.*, p. 145.

filled with debauch'd licentious fellows, and Scot Presbyterians who had hir'd these lawless Ruffians to insult me, which they did with Impunity—Telling me, they wanted no D——d Black Gown Sons of Bitches among them— and threatning to lay me behind the Fire, which they assuredly would have done had not some travellers alighted very opportunely, and taken me under Protection—These Men sat up with, and guarded me all the Night—In the Morning the lawless Rabble moved off on seeing the Church People appear, of whom had a large Congregation. But the Service was greatly interrupted by a Gang of Presbyterians who kept hallooing and whooping without Door like Indians.——30 [miles]

From this Place I went upwards to Cane Creek where I had wrote to the Church People for to assemble—But when I came I found that all my Letters and Advertisements had been intercepted. I trac'd them into the hands of one John Gaston, an Irish Presbyterian Justice of Peace on Fishing Creek, on other Side the River. However, at a Days Notice, about 80 Church People were brought together on Sunday the 27th who behav'd very decently and orderly. One Elderly Gentleman stood Clerk—He brought 6 Sons and 4 Daughters with Him, all excellent Singers, so that the Service was regularly perform'd—Baptiz'd 27 Children.——20 [miles]

Here came Deputies from Camp Creek and Cedar Creek to adjoining Settlements—and Indeed, I was glad to get away from this starved place, where have lived all this Week on a little Milk and Indian Corn Meal, without any other Sustennance but Cold Water—and hardly any Fire to warm me tho' the Season bitter Cold indeed. Wood is exceeding plenty (for the Country is a Forest and Wilderness) but the people so very lazy, that they'l sit for Hours hovering over a few Embers, and will not turn out to cut a Stick of Wood.——1520 [total miles]

I preach'd and baptiz'd at these two Settlements and returned to Pine Tree, where officiated as usual on Sunday March 1.——55 [miles]

In my Absence, found that my Lod[g]ings had been robbed. About 30 Volumes of my Books—much Linen, my Letter folder Port Folio, Key of Desk, and many little Articles taken away. It appear'd to me that Search had been made after my private Papers—and MSS. But they were secur'd. This was some Device of the Presbyterians. By their hurry, they took what Books they first laid hands on, whereby several of my Setts are spoiled.

Set off this Week for St Marks Church and officiated as usual. The Weather very wet and Cold and Road intolerably bad. Gave Sermon at the High Hills both going down and coming up.——100 [miles]

Sunday 15) Officiated for the 1st time at Rafting Creek where married many agreeable to my Summons, and baptiz'd a Number of Children.

Proceeded from Pine Tree to Lynch's Creek, enduring the same hardships as before and more—The Creeks being full of Water and almost impassable— Obliged to swim both Self and Horse over Lynchs Creek, and Black Creek—

The Swamps full of Water—Bridges carried away, and riding for Miles to the Skirts in Mud and Water—So that the Horse gave out.

Obliged to stay a day in a dirty smoaky Cabbin without Sustenance.——50 [miles]

When I came to Thompsons Creek, found it so swelled and so exceeding Rapid, that I waited 2 days for subsiding of the Waters—Mean time the people collected together, and brought their Children for Baptism, and had Sermons. They entertained me very hospitably and took good Care of my Horse.——1680 [total miles]

Saturday came, and the Creek still very deep and rapid—I got a Sailor to make a Raft, on which he was to venture over and inform the People that I was come and could not get to them. The Man ventur'd on the Raft, but no sooner put off, but the Torrent ingulph'd him in a Moment, and both him and Raft were carried to the Bottom—I never was so frighten'd, sweat at ev'ry Pore, thinking that the Man was drowned, and my Self the occasion of his Death. But he rose again, and got hold of a Tree floating in the Stream—We threw him Ropes, by which we pull'd him on shore unhurt—and he was as unconcern'd and merry, as if nothing had happen'd to Him.

I then mounted Horse, and rode to and fro up and down the Creek to endeavor to find some narrow place, where to fall some Great Trees, and mount over by them—But the Stream was ev'ry where too Broad. So waited till Sunday Morning.——40 [miles]

When the Neighbours came again—and a Bold Man brought a very large strong and High Horse. We found a place where the Waters were not very rapid—and he made trial if he could swim it on his Horse, and happily effected it.

He then recross'd the Stream, took my Saddle and Baggage at Times on his Head, and carried them safe and dry to the opposite Bank.

The Women then stript me Naked, and gave Him my Cloaths which he carried on his Head in like Manner—They put their aprons around me—and when he returned, I got behind Him, and the Horse carried us both over very safe—but I never trembled more in my Life. The People placed themselves at Places below, to take me up if I slipt off, or that the Horse sank under me. The Man afterward brought over my Horse—but I was almost stiff and torpid with the Cold, and being in the Cold Water—the Wind blowing very sharp at N. E. and Ground cover'd with Ice.——2020 [total miles]

It was now but 12 Miles to Pedee River to the place of Rendezvous. Found the People not assembled—for they could form no Imagination that I could get to them—because none but those within the two Rivers could meet—All above and below were hinder'd—Yet in an Hours Time, I had 100 People in the Congregation.——10 [miles]

In the Afternoon, I drew up for them a Petition to the Legislature for this

Part of the Province to be rais'd into a Parish which petition was cheerfully sign'd. The Weather grew mild and Clear.

On Monday I returned to Thompsons Creek, and found it fordable and on Tuesday gave Sermon to another Congregation assembled there.———10 [miles]. From hence I set off across the Country for Hanging Rock—but for want of Guides and thro' not knowing the Country nor understanding their Directions, I lost my Self in the Woods for here are no Roads—only small paths, in many places grown up with Grass or cover'd with Leaves and undiscernable. I got to a Cabbin at Night, and sat up by the Fire—The poor Woman had nothing but Indian Corn Bread and Water. In the Morning I pursu'd my Journey, and after wand'ring the whole Day, and riding 30 Miles to and fro out of my Way, arriv'd at Hanging Rock at 3 in the afternoon. But the greater Part of the Congregation were gone—However I gave them Service and baptiz'd 6 Children.———80 [miles]; 2120 [total miles]

In the Morning came a large Body of people, ⅔ of them Presbyterians—They had prepared a Band of Ruffians as before to make disturbance—But a Neighbouring Magistrate came to Service and officiated as Clerk, bringing with Him a party of the Catawba Indians—These poor Wretches behaved more quiet and decent than the lawless Crew—who kept (as before) a great Noise without Door; The Indians resented their affronts and fought with several of them, which only made more Noises. I went home to the Magistrates House, and from thence next day to visit the Presbyterian Minister according to an Invitation made me when he was at my House at Pine Tree—We address'd some of the Elders, and represented the Insolence of some of their Congregation. They disown'd all Proceedings and the authors of them—tho' twas very visible that they set them on. I threatned them so severely that never afterward had any more disturbances in these Parts.———20 [miles]

Returned to Pine Tree, and gave Sermon as usual on Sunday April 5th. The Reason why my Congregation here is not larger, am told is That there are a Gang of Baptists or New Lights over the River to whom many on that Side resort—And that on Swift Creek 10 Miles below, a Methodist has set up to read and preach ev'ry Sunday—Both of them exceeding low and ignorant persons—Yet the lower Class chuse to resort to them rather than to hear a Well connected Discourse.———50 [miles]

All this obliges me to repeat the Liturgy by Heart and to use no Book but the Bible, when I read the Lessons. I have the whole Service and all the Offices at my fingers Ends. I also give an Extempore Prayer before Sermon—but cannot yet venture to give Extempore Discourses, tho' certainly could perform beyond any of these Poor Fools. I shall make Trial in a short time.

Received an Invitation from the People on other Side the River to visit them—who set a pilot to conduct me on Sunday April 12. The Path an entire Bogg and deep Swamp—Had a very genteel and polite Congregation;

50 Young Ladies all drest in White of their own Spinning—Many of them Baptists.——30 [miles]

From thence recross'd the River thro' a long deep miry Swamp, and on the Thursday gave Service at the High Hills—on Good Friday some Miles below, and on Easter Sunday administered the Holy Communion at St Marks Church—about 80 persons attended. Most of them Gentry from distant Parts—but had only eight Communicants—the most ever known here.——2220 [total miles]

Attended the next day at their Vestry, and drew up for them a Letter to my Lord of London to supply them with a Pastor—but could not prevail with them to sign it[20]—They seem'd to be all inclined to turn Baptists—and shewed no Regard for or to the Church.——40 [miles]

Received News that Mr. Shinner the Cheif Justice was suspended from his Office, by desire of the House of Assembly, who had an Implacable Resentment against Him on Account of his Endeavours to enforce the Stamp Act—In Him I lose a good Benefactor and the Poor, the Church and Religion, a strenuous and valuable Friend.

Employ'd this Week in going to different Houses to baptize Children—Preached a fine Sermon at Pine Tree to a large Congregation. Went back over the River again into the Fork and gave Service on Sunday April 26. Had a smart Congregation.——20 [miles]; 50 [miles]

Sunday May 3. Officiated at Pine Tree. 10th at Hanging Rock, where (being Sunday) had no Presbyterians or any Disturbance, on the 17th over the River in the Fork—on the 21st at Lynch's Creek, and the 24th on Pedee River.——30 [miles]; 60 [miles]; 80 [miles]

At P. D. The Sheriff and people of Anson County in North Carolina attended and conducted me up thither, and treated me with great Civility.——30 [miles]

A numerous Body of People attended at the Court House where I celebrated Divine Service and baptiz'd about 60 Children. A great Dinner was prepared by the Sheriff for the Company. They had ne'er seen an Episcopal Minister before. A Number of Well dressed people here—seem'd more an English than Carolina Congregation—A large Body of Baptists and New Lights with their Teachers attended—Wanted to preach before me, and to enter into Disputes—found them exceeding Vain and Ignorant—They rode down the Road 10 Miles with me to escort me, asking Questions on Divinity all the Way. I found their Reading to be of no greater Extent than the Pilgrims Progress and Works of John Bunyan.——50 [miles]

20. This petition, dated April 20, 1767, was sent to the Bishop of London without signatures. It informed the Bishop that St. Mark's Parish had been without a minister for two years, since the Rev. Mr. Evans had moved to St. Paul's Parish and asked a replacement. The duties would be "very easy, as the laborious Part is executed by an Itinerant Minister [Woodmason] plac'd about 50 Miles above us by the Church Commissioners." Fulham Palace Transcripts, S.C., No. 44, Library of Congress.

Tuesday gave Sermon to a Congregation of Baptists, Quakers, and a mix'd Multitude, at head of Thompsons Creek and baptiz'd several Children—and on Wednesday at Black Creek.——2380 [miles]

Holy Thursday the 21. Gave Sermon and baptized at Lynchs Creek. A large Body of people attended—But not a Bible among them. Married several Couple.

Crossed the Country to Hanging Rock, and on May 29th gave Service and Sermon speaking to a mix'd Company—Baptiz'd a Number of Children—Several Adults, and many whole families. A Great Many Presbyterians attended, who did not disturb me. Some Women attempted it, but were soon silenc'd—Many of the Men withdrew—Had no Clerk—Nor could raise a psalm. The next Day gave Sermon to a small Congregation on Camp Creek.——30 [miles]; 20 [miles]

In Consequence of an Appointment and Invitation, went over the River to Rocky Mount, w[h]ere was kindly received by the younger Mr. Kershaw.—10 [miles]

Rocky Mount is an Hill on the West Side Wateree River, about 20 Miles below the Province Line. It is very elevated, and a fine Situation. The Land is good, and plowed to the Summit, bringing Wheat Rye Indian Corn and all kind of Grain and Fruit Trees—This is [a] most delightful healthy part of this Country—No Bogs, Marshes, Swamps, Fogs, Insects to annoy you. Its but newly settled. But the People are already crowded together as thick as in England.

On the 31. (Sunday) I gave Service to about 400 people among whom a great Number of Baptists and Presbyterians. I had here a good Clerk, and excellent Singing. The Women sing as well or better than the Girls at the Magdalene Chapel, London—They all came from Virginia and Pensylvania—Not an English person or Carolinian among them—I baptiz'd 4 Children and promised to visit them Monthly.

Returned to Pine Tree and by the way, gave Sermon to another Body of People on Beaver Creek—on the 7th at Pine Tree—14th at Pine Tree the 21st St Marks, the 26. at Beaver Creek, the 28th Rocky Mt.——35 [miles]; 135 [miles]; [total] miles 2610

July 2. Returned from Rocky Mount—3d Gave Sermon at Beaver Creek and Baptiz'd several Negroes and Mullatoos. Married several Couple on the Proclamation—5th Gave Service at Pine Tree and 12th at Rafting Creek—the 19th at Lynch's Creek—where received an Invitation to preach to a Congregation on Granny Quarter Creek, which I attended next Day, and found about 100 people assembled together—More rude ignorant, and void of things, than any Circle hitherto among. Not a Bible or Prayer Book—Not the least Rudiments of Religion, Learning, Manners or Knowledge (save of Vice) among them.——65 [miles]; 60 [miles]

Such a Pack I never met with—Neither English, Scots Irish, or Carolinian by Birth—Neither of one Church or other or of any denomination by Profession, not having (like some of the Lynchs Creek people) ever seen a Minister—heard or read a Chapter in the Scriptures, or heard a Sermon in their days.——15 [miles]

Went down to Pine Tree, and on the Saturday following was accompanied up to Rocky Mount by several Gentlemen and Ladies—not from Motives of Religion, or Respect—But thro' Curiosity, and Itching Ears. My appearance among them being a Novelty—and none in the World so fond of Novelties, as the Carolinians—The difference between them and the Londoners, is, That the former are quickly tir'd of any thing, even what pleases their fancy— The latter never think they can have enough of what pleases them—Of the two, the Carolinians are the most fickle—and there is not a more fickle trite, superficial people in the World.[21]——15 [miles]

The 26. I gave Sermon at Rocky Mount to a numerous Audience, of various degrees, Countries, Complexions and Denominations—Baptiz'd 36 Children—and was quite exhausted thro' the Great Heat of the Weather and Length of the Service.

When we came from Sermon, My Company found two of their Horses carried off—While we were at Sermon, the Gang of Horse Theives paid a Visit to the Creatures—Their Intent was to carry off my Horses, by Way of Reprisal [I] having stirr'd up the Country against them, and brought up the Cheif Justice to raise the Country: But unluckily for my Friends, they carried off two of their Horses instead of mine, so that their Scheme of Pleasure was greatly disconcerted.——35 [miles]; [total] miles 2800

Tuesday following we proceeded downward, and gave Sermon and baptiz'd; and married many Rogues and Whores on Beaver Creek.——35 [miles]

Next day went down and gave Sermon at Rafting Creek and on August 2d at Pine Tree. Quite jaded and almost worn out thro' heat of the Weather, and dullness of the Horse, travelling over the hot Sands this dry Season.——15 [miles]; 15 [miles]

Went down this Week to St Marks Church, and from thence by Invitation to Santee River—where the Gentry assembled to hear me—but more out of Curiosity than Religion.——50 [miles]; 20 [miles]; 20 [miles]

Gave Sermon the 16th at Lynchs Creek. 17th at Granny's Quarter. 18th at Beaver Creek. 21 at Dutchmans Creek on the West Side of the Wateree. Lost my Self in the Woods in going from thence to Rocky Mount and stayed in the Woods the whole Night, quite famished and fatigued—Could find no

---

21. Such sweeping characterizations as this are not convincing. But for what it is worth, it may be mentioned that Henry Laurens wrote to a friend, the Rev. Mr. St. John, on November 11, 1747. "The people of this province are generally very fickle, especially as to Governors spiritual or temporal, soon pleased and soon disgusted." David D. Wallace, *The Life of Henry Laurens* (New York, 1915), p. 95.

Water—Would have given all the Mines of Peru (if had them) for a drop of Water.—In the Morning, found the right Path, and pursu'd my Journey.——80 [miles]; 35 [miles]

The 24. preached at Rocky Mount from whence the People carried me up the Country to Fishing Creek, settled cheifly by Presbyterians, but several worthy Church People among them.—Had a crowded Audience—but obliged to drive some of the Presbyterians away, who wanted to be Insolent. Returned to Rocky Mount.——10 [miles]; 10 [miles]

From Fishing Creek, the People conducted me to Sandy River, near Broad River—Gave Service the 30th to above 500 persons who had never seen a Minister before. Baptiz'd 50 Children and several Adults. Met with many serious and Religious persons—The Service perform'd this Day with as much pomp as if at St Pauls. Married several Couples—Quite exhausted with the heat of the Weather and Crowds of People—Went down from hence to Pine Tree.——30 [miles]; 65 [miles]; 3185 [total miles]

I forgot to set down that in the last Excursion from Lynchs Creek to the Cheraws, my Horse fail'd and was obliged to stay in the Woods, in the Night when he got from me and I got lost—wandering a Day and Night in the Wilderness, not knowing where I was, famished, and without any Sustenance.

Thus You have the Travels of a Minister in the Wild Woods of America—Destitute often of the very Necessaries of Life—Sometimes starved—Often famished—Exposed to the burning Sun and scorching Sands—Obliged to fight his Way thro' Banditti, profligates, Reprobates, and the lowest vilest Scum of Mankind on the one hand, and of the numerous Sectaries pregnant in these Countries, on the other—With few Friends, and fewer Assistants—and surmounting Difficulties, and braving Dangers, that ev'ry Clergyman that ever entered this Province shrinked even at the thoughts off—Which none, not even the meanest of the Scotch Clergy that have been sent here, would undertake, and for which he subjected himself to the Laughter of Fools and Ridicule of the Licentiousness [*sic*] for undertaking.

Number of Persons married this Year about   40 Couple
Children baptized about   760 ⎫ 782
Adults   10 ⎬ that took a
Negroes and Mullatoes   12 ⎭ Register off.

Beside many others, whose Names were not given in, or attended too.

No other Clergyman of the Church of England from the Sea to the Mountains, on the North Side of Santee River to the Province Line. Number of Miles rode this year (All perform'd by one Horse) 3185. May say, full four thousand Miles.

Observe that not above 2 or 3 out of any family can attend Divine Service at one Time, thro' want of Horses and Saddles—otherwise each Congregation would be doubled. They therefore come by turns.

Congregations rais'd, and attended occasionally. 1767

[Miles from Camden]				auditors more or less communicants
80	A	1	Great Swamp of Santee	80— 2
50	A	2	St. Marks Church	70— 6
26	A	3	High Hills of Santee	300— 1
18	B	4	Rafting Creek	200— 1
	C	5	Pine Tree Hill (The Centre)	200— 2
16	B	6	Granny Quarter Creek	90—
30	B	7	Hanging Rock Creek	50— 2
28	B	8	Little Lynchs Creek, Flat Creek &c	150—15
33	B	9	Great Lynch's Creek (2 Places)	100— 3
70	D	10	Thompsons Creek (2 Places)	150
96	E	11	Cheraws, on Pedee River	400— 2
125	D	13[22]	Anson Court House, North Carolina	300
36	F	14	Camp Creek, and Cedar Creek	40— 2
26	F	15	Beaver Creek, White Oak &c	120
32	F	16	Dutchmans Creek	50
34	B	17	Rocky Creek, Wateree Creek &c	300— 4
40	F	18	Fishing Creek	60— 2
42	F	19	Waxaws	70
96	E	20	Sandy River (near Broad River)	300
40	E	21	Fork of the Wateree and Broad River	100— 3

A—Attended ev'ry 2 Months. D—Once a Year.
B—Once ev'ry Month. E—Twice a Year.
C—Ev'ry other Sunday, by Law. F—Once a Quarter.

Could all these Congregations be regularly attended ev'ry Sunday, the Number set against each (say treble the Number) would attend. But it would employ 20 Ministers. The figures set before the Letters express the Number of Miles each Place is distant from my Centre.

These Congregations being settled—their Children Baptiz'd, and the people rouz'd from their Insensibility—A New System of Things, and an entire Alteration in the Minds of Individuals, seem'd to take place from this Period.

I will wave all Political Matters (leaving it to another Paper—which I have mention'd)[23] and proceed in my Journal just to set down Facts, and Occurences respecting my Self—and the State of Religion in this Country.

The fatigue and Pain—the Toil and Expense I have sustain'd in these Peregrinations are beyond Description—Few beside me could have born them. The Task deterr'd ev'ry one—None to be found to enter on it.

22. Woodmason skips from number 11 to number 13.
23. Woodmason has made no mention of a paper on political matters in his Journal. This reference to such a paper may be an error, or it could be evidence that Woodmason intended this Journal for the eyes of someone with whom he was in correspondence.

But[24] the people wearied out with being expos'd to the Depredations of Robbers—Set down here just as a Barrier between the Rich Planters and the Indians, to secure the former against the Latter—Without Laws or Government Churches Schools or Ministers—No Police established—and all Property quite insecure—Merchants as fearful to venture their Goods as Ministers their Persons—The Lands, tho' the finest in the Province unoccupied, and rich Men afraid to set Slave to work to clear them, lest they should become a Prey to the Banditti—No Regard had to the numberless petitions and Complaints of the people—Thus neglected and slighted by those in Authority, they rose in Arms—pursued the Rogues, broke up their Gangs—burnt the dwellings of all their Harbourers and Abettors—Whipp'd and drove the Idle, Vicious and Profligate out of the Province, Men and Women without Distinction and would have proceeded to Charlestown in a Regular Corps of 5000 Men, and hung up the Rogues before the State House in Presence of Governor and Council.

For the Mildness of Legislation here is so great and the Clemency of the Cheif in Authority has been carried to such Excess that when a notorious Robber was with Great Pains catch'd and sent to Town, and there try'd and Condemn'd he always got pardon'd by Dint of Money, and came back 50 times worse than before. The fellows thus pardon'd form'd themselves into a large Gang, ranging the province with Impunity.

It was with great Pains that I prevail'd with the Multitude to lay aside desperate Resolutions. I wrote to all in Authority—and received for answer, that if they would apply in a Constitutional Way, their Greivances should be redressed.

I drew up for them a Remonstrance, which was presented to the House. Many articles of a Civil Nature were granted. But those of a Religious remain as they were—save the raising of a large Distric big enough for 6 Parishes into one Parish, because they want not to increase the Number of Members of Assembly. But the Regulators (so the Populace call themselves) will not long be passive—If the next Sessions do not relieve them, they are determin'd to surround the Metropolis.

I now proceed in my Journal for the second Year. (but forgot to Note, that on the 20th November) I was at Beaver Creek where gave Sermon to a Body of about 2000 arm'd persons, of the Populace call'd Regulators—and it was happiness for many that I went there as I sav'd many Homes frm being burnt and stopped the Outrages of the Mobb—No Lives were lost nor Blood spilt.

24. This paragraph and those that follow up to the entry of September 6 were clearly added later, and out of chronological order, by Woodmason. The reference to the Remonstrance and to the sermon of November 20 would suggest that Woodmason wrote this passage in late November or early December, 1767. He probably erred in believing that the blank space in his Journal came at the end of the calendar year. Actually, it came at the end of his first year as clergyman on the South Carolina frontier.

PART THREE

National Identities: Patriots, Promoters, and Pretenders, 1776–1837

In the sixty years or so from the Revolution to the 1830s, autobiography in the United States became closely identified with the new nation. It was used to defend and promote the goals of the Revolutionary War. It enabled Americans to invent (or reinvent) themselves as the citizens of the new nation, at once defining themselves and defining it. After the war, autobiography helped to promote the settlement of the frontier, describing the country and the people. In turn, it also helped Indians justify their opposition to settlement. At the same time, however, autobiography was criticized by many people as a vain and deceitful kind of writing that modest, respectable folks should shun.

The association of autobiography with the Revolution might be said to have begun with Benjamin Franklin. He started writing his *Autobiography* in England in 1771, having already foreseen "a total disunion of the two countries,"[1] and foreseen his life as an anticipation of revolution and a preparation for it. The story of a young man's rise to wealth and fame by his own virtue and industry, combined with the mutual support of fellow tradesmen, was a new one—and potentially a very unsettling one for established orders. His pride in his achievement, while masked by a seemingly simple modesty, was even more unsettling. People had once been ashamed of humble origins, as John Adams noted in his *Discourses on Davila*. As Franklin went on to write in 1784 and 1788–90, that is, just after the Revolution, he took pride in his success and advised later generations on how they, too, could become civic leaders by promoting useful improvements through voluntary associations.

An even more forthright identification with the Revolution occurs in Thomas Jefferson's *Autobiography,* written in 1821, when Jefferson was seventy-seven. Focusing on the writing of *The Declaration of Independence* and then on his efforts, early in the war years, while he was in the Virginia House of Burgesses, to abolish primogeniture and to separate church and state, his

---

1. Quoted in James M. Cox, *Recovering Literature's Lost Ground* (Baton Rouge: Louisiana State Univ. Press, 1989), p. 18, from a letter written by Franklin to James Otis, Thomas Cushing, and Samuel Adams, July, 1771.

autobiography clearly reveals its author's sense that the Revolution was the great event of his life, and that these were the deeds for which he wanted and expected to be remembered. Without the Revolution, Jefferson might have been merely a scholarly and inventive Virginia gentleman. Because of it, however—because he helped to make it—he could conceive of himself in a much larger and loftier sense: as an American, a national leader, a spokesman for independence and liberty, and as, therefore, a man whose biography and autobiography would be historically important.

Yet Franklin and Jefferson were by no means the only people of this time to achieve these "national identities," this sense of themselves as citizens and representatives of a new nation, and as spokesmen and spokeswomen for it, whether by their own or someone else's designation. Their friend, associate, and occasional critic and rival John Adams showed a similar sense of history when, in Philadelphia in 1775 to attend the Continental Congress, he entered a stationery store and bought the letter book in which he would keep copies of all his future correspondence. Before, he had been simply a hard-working lawyer from Braintree and Boston, Massachusetts. On election to the Congress, he became a person with a historical destiny. He now needed to keep copies of his letters, for they performed official business and were valuable historical documents. Meanwhile, from his and his wife Abigail's longstanding love of each other's letters, which were not just signs of their mutual affection but a means of refining and expressing their sensibilities, he and she went on saving their private correspondence, too. Her letters informed him of the sacrifices women were making in the war and taunted him that independence and freedom should be for women as well as men. Later, her letters from Paris to her family back home gave her explicitly American reactions to French houses, housekeeping, and manners. Sometimes offended, sometimes amused, she always stood up for her native land.

Soldiers and seamen also wrote autobiographical accounts of their wartime experiences. Men such as Ethan Allen, who had been British captives, had stories to tell of the atrocities they witnessed and of how their faith in the American cause sustained them during months of hunger and sickness. Allen's *Narrative* was particularly inspiring to other patriots because it also told of his astonishing victory at Fort Ticonderoga and his even more amazing boldness during his two and one half years in captivity. His *Narrative* mythologized him as a symbol of "Yankee" determination and courage. Its publication in 1779 was a critical move in the war for the hearts and minds of the American people that was being fought in newspapers and pamphlets.

Other autobiographies of the Revolution would not be published until many years later, for there was simply not the money, the place, or the time and interest to print every person's letters or diaries during the war itself. One account must have seemed more or less like another. But, retrospectively, their significance grew. The nation grew and prospered, and it honored its past and its heroes at Fourth of July celebrations, militia musters, and grand patriotic occasions like the anniversary visit of General Lafayette in the 1820s. Publication of an ancestor's diary, sometimes privately and sometimes in the proceedings of a newly founded state or local historical society, became a combined act of patriotism and family piety. The first editor of the *Letters of Mrs. Adams,* for example, was her grandson Charles Francis Adams, who published them in 1840. In doing so, he also corrected her spelling and grammar and standardized her punctuation. The autobiographies of one's revered ancestors were being not just preserved for posterity but polished for it.

A unique further expression of this retrospective honoring of the heroes of the Revolution was the collection of still more of their stories during the 1830s as a part of their pension applications. As John C. Dann wrote in his introduction to a small selection from the thousands of these applications, the 1832 pension act was the first in which the federal government undertook to provide for all the veterans, not just those of the Continental Army or those who were disabled or poor. However, records of these men's service were missing and incomplete, so the aged veterans had to go to their local courtrooms and present sworn testimony about the battles they had been in, their units, officers, and the times and places where they had served. This was, in Dann's words, "one of the largest oral history projects ever undertaken."[2] It literally paid men to tell their stories of their service to their country; in effect, it paid them for composing their national identities. The American concept of self now had governmental approval.

Not all the post-Revolutionary autobiographers were so honorable, however. Another, less desirable effect of the Revolution—from official or respectable standpoints—was a change in manners that diminished respect for authority and encouraged some men to cloak their own unruliness in patriotic colors, while also celebrating their private deeds as they might not have done before. Thus rogue narratives like Stephen Burroughs's *Memoirs* (1798) and *A Narrative of the Life, Adventures, Travels, and Sufferings of Henry Tufts* (1807), which once would never have been published or would only have been published after re-writing by a minister or another member of the colonial establishment, were now written in the first person and became popular books. Burroughs had rebelled against his strict father, a Presbyterian minister, as the colonies had revolted against Great Britain—or so he claimed, using the same familial metaphors that had been used by defenders of the Revolution.[3] When he engaged in counterfeiting, he argued (like Benjamin Franklin promoting the printing of paper currency) that he was actually serving the

2. John C. Dann, ed., *The Revolution Remembered: Eyewitness Accounts of the War for Independence* (Chicago: Univ. of Chicago Press, 1980), p. xvii.
3. On the use of familial metaphors in defenses of the Revolution, see Jay Fliegelman, *Prodigals and Pilgrims: The American Revolution against Patriarchal Authority, 1750–1800* (New York: Cambridge Univ. Press, 1982).

public good by increasing the money supply. When he was sent to jail, he complained that he was being enslaved and held against his will. The more society punished an ingenious rationalizer like Burroughs, the more he could bend the rhetoric of the Revolution to make himself a hero and a martyr.[4]

Such men thus took to autobiography as their organ of self-justification and self-advertisement almost as readily as they took to crime! Autobiography was simply an extension of the same posturing and imposturing they were already engaged in. And the guardians of the new American republic did not like it, any more than they liked the crimes.

A vivid sense of this conservative reaction against revolution and, by implication, against autobiography can be had from reading John Adams's extensive digressions on emulation in his *Discourses on Davila*. Written in 1789–90, the first year of the new American federal government, in which Adams was Washington's vice-president (and also the first year of the French Revolution), the *Discourses* were Adams's warning to Americans against the dangers of excessive liberty and egalitarianism. Specifically, he saw the French abandonment of inherited titles and aristocratic rank as unleashing, instead of productively channelling, the powerful human instinct "to be observed, considered, esteemed, praised, beloved, and admired." A well-ordered state channeled this "instinct of emulation," as Adams called it, following Aristotle and other philosophers of government, so that men could gain fame and receive honors in accordance with their service in war or statecraft. Inherited titles, while not necessary or desirable in the United States, had been the French way of perpetuating the memory of its great men and so preserving social order. Without them, Adams feared, people would rush to gain fame by any means at hand—through crime, great wealth, usurpation of power, flattery, and deceit. The implicit immorality in autobiography, Adams might have gone on, was that it, too, might encourage men towards boasting, lying, and an emphasis on sensation and scandal. True achievement should be recognized and rewarded by other men and by the state and those one served. Praising one's self led to chaos.

The further importance of the *Discourses* to autobiography is that, paradoxically, they illustrate the very satisfaction and pride which Adams and other founding fathers took in the public recognition they received. The councils, town meetings, and congresses of the revolution and early republic, as Hannah Arendt argued in *On Revolution,* were the American equivalent of the Athenian *polis*. The right and glory of a free man was participation in the government of his town or state and then being recognized for what he had said and done. Thus, early American autobiography, as we have been saying, emphasized one's service to various public bodies: Franklin's Philadelphia,

---

4. See especially Daniel Williams, "In Defense of Self: Author and Authority in the Memoirs of Stephen Burroughs," *Early American Literature* 25 (1990): 96–122.

the army, Jefferson's Virginia, the new nation. The intensity with which the Adams family valued this civic service and the emulation given and gained from it underlies a lot of the ironies and despair in *The Education of Henry Adams,* with Henry's portrait of himself as a "failure."

The early American dislike of boastful and scandalous autobiography also shows up in the very low opinion Americans had of Rousseau's *Confessions.* The first American edition of this landmark in the history of autobiography was published in New York in 1796, and it was almost universally condemned. The book demonstrated, wrote Samuel Miller, a Presbyterian minister and member of the American Philosophical Society, that Rousseau's life was "an unnatural compound of vanity, meanness, and contemptible self-love, a suspicious, restless temper, bordering on insanity, and a prostration of every principle of duty, to his own aggrandisement and gratification."[5] Before 1789, Americans had admired Rousseau. His ideas and sentiments helped justify their revolution. But after the French Revolution and the reign of terror, the larger number of Americans "accounted [him] erratic and intolerant, foolish and indiscreet."[6] His character was seen to be symptomatic of French excesses, and, as this character was most visible in the *Confessions,* this text (as well as Goethe's *Sorrows of Young Werther*) seems to represent the dangers of egotism and sentimentalism. Some Americans, like Nathaniel Hawthorne and the families he addressed in his early children's stories, even had reservations about Benjamin Franklin's autobiography. Franklin was a great man and his book an exemplary tale, but did he have to be so cunning—and so smugly satisfied with himself?[7] Federalist Americans remained wary of the ego.

The conservative reaction against autobiographical vanity did not affect the writing of narratives of captivity, travel, and life on the frontier. The first two were already well established, and the third kind would become immensely important to the post-war opening of the West and the new national identities that would develop around the West and its settlement.

John Filson's life of Daniel Boone, told in the first person as if it were Boone's autobiography, was the earliest and most influential of these new frontier narratives. Yet it is also part captivity narrative and part war memoir. In it, Boone tells of repeated battles with Indians and being held captive from January to June, 1778. He is taken on "an uncomfortable journey, in very severe weather" all the way to Detroit and then held in Chelicothe (Chillicothe, Ohio) for several months. But unlike the Puritan captives, Boone becomes quite well adjusted to Indian life. They "entertained me well," he says,

---

5. Paul M. Spurlin, *Rousseau in America, 1760–1809* (Tuscaloosa: Univ. of Alabama Press, 1969), p. 98.
6. Spurlin, *Rousseau,* p. 99.
7. See Nathaniel Hawthorne, *True Stories from History and Biography* (Columbus: Ohio State Univ. Press, 1972), pp. 273–74. Also see Herman Melville's amusing attack on Franklin in *Israel Potter.*

and soon adopted him "according to their custom, into a family where I became a son, and had a great share in the affection of my new parents, brothers, sisters, and friends." Boone quickly reassures his readers of his greater loyalty to white Kentuckians: he escapes and goes to warn Boonsborough of an impending Indian attack. But his temporary adoption by the Indians has made him a still better scout and woodsman. He is not just a frontier adventurer; he straddles the frontier, as a spokesman for both sides of it and as someone who can put Indian skills into the service of the new settlers.

This willingness to learn from the Indians and even to respect them at times, while still keeping bright a vision of the eventual triumph of "civilization," made Boone an archetype for many later autobiographers, biographers, and novelists. James Fennimore Cooper's Leatherstocking is derived from Boone (along with a hunter from near Cooperstown whom Cooper had known as a boy), and spurious "autobiographies" of frontier heroes like Davy Crockett filled the newspapers and sporting magazines of the 1830s. The reading public was strongly attracted to the frontier type (in its proliferating manifestations), and resourceful writers searched for more people who might embody it. In the Genesee Valley of New York, James Everett Seaver, a school teacher, interviewed Mary Jemison, who had lived among the Seneca for forty years, and in 1824 he published the *Narrative* of her life. Seaver wanted to make her a sort of female Boone and an example of how the refinements of white womanhood endured in spite of long exposure to savage life. But Jemison had her own agenda too, and at moments her praise of the Seneca and what she learned from them also come through. As Annette Kolodny has said, *The Narrative of the Life of Mrs. Mary Jemison* is a "fascinating store of historical information" and also "an inconsistent, often perplexing document."[8] It is not nearly so well known as the other autobiographies mentioned here, but it is an important one, just the same, and a good one to read alongside these others.

Beyond the frontier lay the Indians themselves, and as they ceased to be a threat to white expansion (or could be absorbed symbolically by a border figure like Boone), they became all the more interesting and useful as symbols and historical relics. In 1832, Samuel Gardner Drake, a Boston antiquarian, published a *Biography and History of the Indians of North America,* which in the next twenty-five years went through ten revisions and re-publications. Benjamin Thatcher, another Bostonian, published a similar collection, *Indian Biography,* which was nearly as popular. Such encyclopedias contained brief biographies of scores of famous chiefs, as well as captivity narratives, speeches, anecdotes, and histories of Indian wars. The form of the life of a famous chief was very conventionalized. His tribe had once been a "powerful, warlike

8. Annette Kolodny, *The Land Before Her: Fantasy and Experience of the American Frontiers, 1630–1860* (Chapel Hill: Univ. of North Carolina Press, 1984), p. 73.

nation"; it was met and corrupted by white men; its land was purchased or lost in war; the chief rallied the people to resist; but he failed and now the tribe was almost extinct. Although repetitious, such stories had tragic grandeur, and the focus on the life of the chief gave them more immediacy and drama. His life embodied tribal experience and customs, which were difficult to understand and interpret, in a seemingly verifiable individual account. The individual noble Indian was also more appealing than a confusing, heterogeneous group of people. Meanwhile, the very repetition of the stories made them confirm one another: collectively, they all accounted for "the vanishing Indian."

Some editions of Thatcher's and Drake's books even used the word *autobiography* alongside biography. Calling a story an "autobiography" was a way of claiming greater authenticity for it (the same strategy used with the spurious "autobiographies" of Davy Crockett). The less true a "life" was, the more the necessity to call it an autobiography, as a way of claiming authenticity. (The same continues to happen with spurious works like *The Autobiography of Howard Hughes,* which might better have been called an unauthorized biography by Clifford Irving, and *The Education of Little Tree,* which was purported to be by a Cherokee named Forrest Carter but was actually by a white Southerner named Asa Earl Carter.[9])

There were authentic Indian autobiographies in this period, however, and we can now see that they anticipated later Indian autobiography. In 1831, William Apess, a man of mixed Pequot and white ancestry, published *A Son of the Forest,* in which he told of being raised by foster parents, serving in the War of 1812, and eventually coming to prize his Indian heritage. In 1833, Black Hawk, the Sac leader who had become the sentimental hero of the Black Hawk War, even though the enemy and loser, dictated his autobiography, through an interpreter, to a frontier journalist, using the opportunity to defend himself and tell his side of the story. Thus, at the very moment that white Americans were using autobiography to define their national identities, Apess and Black Hawk were using it to define a revived or preserved tribal identity—or ethnic identity, as we might call it today.

At nearly the same time, Carolyn Kirkland, using the pseudonym of Mary Clavers, published an autobiography about her and her husband's pioneering experiences in Michigan. It was considered improper for a lady to write and even more so for her to use her own name, just as some aristocratic gentlemen had once thought it beneath their dignity to attach their own names to their books and pamphlets.[10] Controversy was demeaning, especially with social

9. For a short history of the *Autobiography of Howard Hughes* affair, see G. Thomas Couser, *Altered Egos: Authority in American Autobiography* (New York: Oxford Univ. Press, 1989), pp. 3–12. For a discussion of the issues in the *Little Tree* fabrication, see Henry Louis Gates, Jr., " 'Authenticity,' or the Lesson of Little Tree," *New York Times Book Review* (November 24, 1991), pp. 1, 26–30.
10. Mary Kelley, *Private Woman, Public Stage* (New York: Oxford Univ. Press, 1984), pp. 111–37.

inferiors. It was also more gentlemanly to appear not to have to write, to be a dabbler and amateur, with the result that, following Washington Irving, the sketch had become a favorite upperclass (or pseudo-upperclass) literary form. The sketch mixed fact and whimsy, observation and fantasy, while the author's persona (or even more evasively, the pseudo-author's persona) was supposedly someone too light and frivolous to take seriously. The pseudonym also was a way of escaping the onus of vanity that was attached to autobiographical writing.

All of these conditions make it very difficult with respect to some of the writings of this period to distinguish between autobiography and fiction and between biography and autobiography, and to impose other later definitions. The American novel was new, and it often imitated autobiographies as a way of making the story seem more real and of making it (or pretending to make it) less sensational and scandalous. Novelists then as now drew on personal experience, but they went much further than novelists today in saying that they were writing to warn and advise their young readers—another way of passing the personal and societal censors who felt that novels misrepresented reality and wasted time. With one hand, therefore, "Mary Clavers" apologized for her "straggling and cloudy crayon sketches," acting modest and self-effacing, while, with the other, she wrote that these sketches "of life and manners in the remoter parts of Michigan" had "the merit of general truth of outline." The apology and the claim for truth appear in the same sentence, as if the "crayon" had been passed from one hand to the other.

Yet whether she was novelist or autobiographer is finally secondary to the fact that in writing of her frontier experience she, too, had adopted a new national identity. For her generation, the frontier was now the main locus of personhood and nationhood, as the Revolution had been for most members of the generation before. And her confidence that her generation wanted to hear about it from a woman's standpoint demonstrates that it wanted not just to settle the frontier but to domesticate it, to make it refined and a place for people with education and manners. Autobiography had taken Americans through revolution, had endured conservative reactions against it, and had gone on to help populate and refine the frontier, even while providing the dispossessed victims of the frontier with a place to publish their apologias and defenses.

Ethan Allen (1738–1789)

from *The Narrative of*
Colonel Ethan Allen's Captivity

The Narrative of Colonel Ethan Allen's Captivity was published first in 1779, in a Philadelphia newspaper, and it made such good anti-British propaganda that George Washington gave orders to his officers to read it to their troops. By 1780, it had gone through seven more printings and reprintings, all "in the shabby dress of a large and ragged pamphlet," as an 1807 editor described them. The *Narrative* remained popular until outdated by Civil War prison stories of the 1860s.

On first reading it may seem like the most egotistical autobiography ever written, and some people are put off by Allen's swaggering. He also seems inconsistent, at one moment acting rough and egalitarian and at another insisting upon his status as a gentleman—even serving as a British officer's "faithful second" in a duel. But there was strategy to Allen's boasting. As he notes, many of the British treated the Americans with contempt, especially early in the war, and many Americans were in awe of British power. By not showing fear, Allen attempted to "set an example of virtue and fortitude to our little commonwealth." Likewise, taking pride in being an officer and a gentleman was a way of irritating the enemy and inspiring his countrymen. So he demanded all the rights of an officer as dictated by eighteenth-century military customs (which, however, were not based on wars of revolution or ideological conflict). Demanding his rights might not only bring better treatment; it might also bring greater respect for him and the American cause.

The selections below all come from the beginning of his *Narrative,* when he showed himself as generally at his boldest. Later, following the imprisonment in Falmouth, England, he was sent back to America and spent over a year and a half in New York, part of the time on parole and part in jail. Conditions there, especially among the enlisted men starving and dying of disease in abandoned churches, were too severe and pathetic for Allen to change by any tough-talk. But he did cry out against such atrocities, while continuing to show himself as unsubdued by them. He was released in an exchange of prisoners in May, 1778.

The standard biographies of Ethan Allen are John Pell, *Ethan Allen* (Boston: Houghton Mifflin, 1929) and Charles A. Jellison, *Ethan Allen: Frontier Rebel* (Syracuse: Syracuse Univ. Press, 1969). A balanced, critical assessment of Allen is John McWilliams, "The Faces of Ethan Allen" (*New England Quarterly* 49 [1976]: 257–82).

Introduction

Induced by a sense of duty to my country, and by the application of many of my worthy friends, some of whom are of the first characters, I have concluded to publish the following narrative of the extraordinary scenes of my captivity, and the discoveries which I made in the course of the same, of the cruel and relentless disposition and behaviour of the enemy, towards the prisoners in their power; from which the state politician, and every gradation of character among the people, to the worthy tiller of the soil, may deduce such inferences as they shall think proper to carry into practice. Some men are appointed into office, in these States, who read the history of the cruelties of this war with the same careless indifference, as they do the pages of the Roman history; nay, some are preferred to places of trust and profit by the tory influence. The instances are (I hope) but rare; and it stands all freemen in hand, to prevent their further influence, which, of all other things, would be the most baneful to the liberties and happiness of this country; and so far as such influence takes place, robs us of the victory we have obtained, at the expense of so much blood and treasure.

I should have exhibited to the public a history of the facts herein contained, soon after my exchange, had not the urgency of my private affairs, together with more urgent public business, demanded my attention, till a few weeks before the date hereof. The reader will readily discern, that a narrative of this sort could not have been wrote when I was a prisoner: My trunk and writings were often searched under various pretences; so that I never wrote a syllable, or made even a rough minute, whereon I might predicate this narration, but trusted solely to my memory for the whole. I have, however, taken the greatest care and pains to recollect the facts, and arrange them; but as they touch a variety of characters and opposite interests, I am sensible that all will not be pleased with the relation of them: Be this as it will, I have made truth my invariable guide, and stake my honor on the truth of the facts. I have been very generous with the British, in giving them full and ample credit for all their good usage of any considerable consequence, which I met with among them, during my captivity; which was easily done, as I met with but little, in comparison of the bad, which by reason of the great plurality of it, could not be contained in so concise a narrative; so that I am certain that I have more fully enumerated the favours which I received, than the abuses I suffered. The critic will be pleased to excuse any inaccuracies in the performance itself, as the author has unfortunately missed a liberal education.

Ethan Allen
Bennington, March 25, 1779

A Narrative of
Colonel Ethan Allen's Observations
during His Captivity

Ever since I arrived to a state of manhood, and acquainted myself with the general history of mankind, I have felt a sincere passion for liberty. The history of nations doomed to perpetual slavery, in consesequence of yielding up to tyrants their natural born liberties, I read with a sort of philosophical horror; so that the first systematical and bloody attempt at Lexington, to enslave America, thoroughly electrified my mind, and fully determined me to take part with my country: And while I was wishing for an opportunity to signalize myself in its behalf, directions were privately sent to me from the then colony (now state) of Connecticut, to raise the Green Mountain Boys; (and if possible) with them to surprise and take the fortress Ticonderoga. This enterprise I cheerfully undertook; and, after first guarding all the several passes that led thither, to cut off all intelligence between the garrison and the country, made a forced march from Bennington, and arrived at the lake opposite to Ticonderoga, on the evening of the ninth day of May, 1775, with two hundred and thirty valiant Green Mountain Boys; and it was with the utmost difficulty that I procured boats to cross the lake: However, I landed eighty-three men near the garrison, and sent the boats back for the rear guard commanded by col. Seth Warner; but the day began to dawn, and I found myself under a necessity to attack the fort, before the rear could cross the lake; and, as it was viewed hazardous, I harangued the officers and soldiers in the manner following; "Friends and fellow soldiers, you have, for a number of years past, been a scourge and terror to arbitrary power. Your valour has been famed abroad, and acknowledged, as appears by the advice and orders to me (from the general assembly of Connecticut) to surprise and take the garrison now before us. I now propose to advance before you, and in person conduct you through the wicket-gate; for we must this morning either quit our pretensions to valour, or possess ourselves of this fortress in a few minutes; and, in as much as it is a desperate attempt, (which none but the bravest of men dare undertake) I do not urge it on any contrary to his will. You that will undertake voluntarily, poise your firelocks."

The men being (at this time) drawn up in three ranks, each poised his firelock. I ordered them to face to the right; and, at the head of the centre-file, marched them immediately to the wicket gate aforesaid, where I found a centry posted, who instantly snapped his fusee at me; I ran immediately toward him, and he retreated through the covered way into the parade within the garrison, gave a halloo, and ran under a bomb-proof. My party who followed me into the fort, I formed on the parade in such a manner as to face the two barracks which faced each other. The garrison being asleep, (except the centries) we gave three huzzas which greatly surprised them. One of the centries made a pass at one of my officers with a charged bayonet, and slightly wounded him: My first thought was to kill him with my sword; but, in an instant, altered the design and fury of the blow to a slight cut on the side of the head; upon which he dropped his gun, and asked quarter, which I readily granted him, and demanded of him the place where the commanding officer kept; he shewed me a pair of stairs in the front of a barrack, on the west part of the garrison, which led up to a second story in said barrack, to which I immediately repaired, and ordered the commander (capt. Delaplace) to come forth instantly, or I would sacrifice the whole garrison; at which the capt. came immediately to the door with his breeches in his hand, when I ordered him to deliver to me the fort instantly, who asked me by what authority I demanded it; I answered, "In the name of the great Jehovah, and the Continental Congress." (The authority of the Congress being very little known at that time) he began to speak again; but I interrupted him, and with my drawn sword over his head, again demanded an immediate surrender of the garrison; to which he then complied, and ordered his men to be forthwith paraded without arms, as he had given up the garrison; in the mean time some of my officers had given orders, and in consequence thereof, sundry of the barrack doors were beat down, and about one third of the garrison imprisoned, which consisted of the said commander, a lieut. Feltham, a conductor of artillery, a gunner, two serjeants, and forty four rank and file; about one hundred pieces of cannon, one 13 inch mortar, and a number of swivels. This surprise was carried into execution in the gray of the morning of the 10th day of May, 1775. The sun seemed to rise that morning with a superior lustre; and Ticonderoga and its dependencies smiled on its conquerors, who tossed about the flowing bowl, and wished success to Congress, and the liberty and freedom of America.

. . .

The officer I capitulated with, then directed me and my party to advance towards him, which was done, I handed him my sword, and in half a minute after a savage, part of whose head was shaved, being almost naked and painted, with feathers intermixed with the hair of the other side of his head, came running to me with an incredible swiftness; he seemed to advance with more than mortal speed (as he approached near me, his hellish visage was beyond all description, snakes eyes appear innocent in comparison of his, his features extorted, malice, death, murder, and the wrath of devils and damned spirits are the emblems of his countenance) and in less than twelve feet of me, presented his firelock; at the instant, of his present, I twitched the officer to whom I gave my sword, between me and the savage, but he flew round with great fury, trying to single me out to shoot me without killing the officer;

but by this time I was near as nimble as he, keeping the officer in such a position that his danger was my defence, but in less than half a minute, I was attacked by just such another imp of hell; then I made the officer fly around with incredible velocity, for a few seconds of time, when I perceived a Canadian (who had lost one eye, as appeared afterwards) taking my part against the savages; and in an instant an Irishman came to my assistance with a fixed bayonet, and drove away the fiends, swearing by Jasus he would kill them. This tragic scene composed my mind. The escaping from so awful a death, made even imprisonment happy, the more so as my conquerors on the field treated me with great civility and politeness.

The regular officers said that they were very happy to see Col. Allen, I answered them that I should rather chose to have seen them at Gen. Montgomery's camp; the gentlemen replied, that they gave full credit to what I said, and as I walked to the town, which was (as I should guess) more than two miles, a British officer walking at my right hand, and one of the French noblesse at my left; the latter of which in the action, had his eyebrow carried away by a glancing shot, but was nevertheless very merry and facetious, and no abuse was offered me till I came to the barrackyard at Montreal, where I met Gen. Prescott, who asked me my name, which I told him, he then asked me, whether I was that Col. Allen, who took Ticonderoga, I told him I was the very man; then he shook his cane over my head, calling many hard names, among which he frequently used the word rebel, and put himself in a great rage. I told him he would do well not to cane me, for I was not accustomed to it, and shook my fist at him, telling him that that was the beetle of mortality for him, if he offered to strike; upon which Capt. M'Cloud of the British, pulled him by the skirt, and whispered to him (as he afterwards told me) to this import; that it was inconsistent with his honor to strike a prisoner. He then ordered a sergeant's command with fixed bayonets to come forward and kill 13 Canadians, which were included in the treaty aforesaid.

It cut me to the heart to see the Canadians in so hard a case, in consequence of their having been true to me; they were wringing their hands, saying their prayers, (as I concluded) and expected immediate death. I therefore stepped between the executioners and the Canadians, opened my clothes, and told Gen. Prescott to thrust his bayonets into my breast, for I was the sole cause of the Canadians taking up arms.

The guard in the mean time, rolling their eyeballs from the General to me, as though impatient waiting his dread commands to sheath their bayonets in my heart; I could however plainly discern, that he was in a suspence and quandary about the matter: this gave me additional hopes of succeeding, for my design was not to die but save the Canadians by a finesse. The General stood a minute, when he made the following reply: "I will not execute you now, but you shall grace a halter at Tyburn, God damn ye."

• • •

The reader is now invited back to the time I was put in irons. I requested the privilege to write to Gen. Prescott, which was granted. I reminded him of the kind and generous manner of my treatment to the prisoners I took at Ticonderoga; the injustice and ungentleman like usage, which I had met with from him, and demanded gentleman like usage, but received no answer from him. I soon after wrote to Gen. Carlton, which met the same success. In the mean while many of those who were permitted to see me, were very insulting.

I was confined in the manner I have related, on board the Gaspee schooner, about six weeks; during which time I was obliged to throw out plenty of extravagant language, which answered certain purposes, (at that time) better than to grace a history.

To give an instance upon being insulted, in a fit of anger I twisted off a nail with my teeth, which I took to be a ten-penny nail; it went through the mortise of the bar of my hand cuff, and at the same time I swaggered over those who abused me; particularly a Doctor Dace, who told me that I was outlawed by New York, and deserved death for several years past; was at last fully ripened for the halter, and in a fair way to obtain it: when I challenged him, he excused himself in consequence, as he said, of my being a criminal; but I flung such a flood of language at him that it shocked him and the spectators, for my anger was very great. I heard one say, damn him can he eat iron? After that a small padlock was fixed to the hand cuff, instead of the nail, and as they were mean-spirited in their treatment to me; so it appeared to me, that they were equally timorous and cowardly.

I was after sent with the prisoners taken with me to an armed vessel in the river, which lay off against Quebec, under the command of Capt. M'Cloud of the British, who treated me in a very generous and obliging manner, and according to my rank; in about twenty-four hours I bid him farewell with regret; but my good fortune still continued; the name of the captain of the vessel I was put on board, was Little John, who, with his officers, behaved in a polite, generous and friendly manner. I lived with them in the cabin, and fared on the best, my irons being taken off, contrary to the order he had received from the commanding officer; but Capt. Little John swore, that a brave man should not be used as a rascal on board his ship.

Thus I found myself in possession of happiness once more, and the evils I had lately suffered, gave me an uncommon relish for it.

Captain Little John used to go to Quebec almost every day, in order to pay his respects to certain gentlemen and ladies; being there on a certain day, he happened to meet with some disagreeable treatment, as he imagined, from a lieutenant of a man of war, and one word brought on another till the lieutenant challenged him to a duel on the plains of Abraham. Captain Little

John was a gentleman, who entertained a high sense of honour, and could do no less than accept the challenge.

At nine o'clock the next morning they were to fight. The Captain returned in the evening, and acquainted his lieutenant and me with the affair: his lieutenant was a high-blooded Scotchman as well as himself, who replied to his captain that he should not want for a second. With this I interrupted him, and gave the captain to understand, that since an opportunity had presented, I would be glad to testify my gratitude to him, by acting the part of a faithful second, on which he gave me his hand, and said that he wanted no better man. Says he, "I am a king's officer, and you a prisoner under my care; you must therefore go with me to the place appointed, in disguise;" and added further, "You must engage to me, upon the honour of a gentleman, that whether I die or live, or whatever happens, provided you live, that you will return to my lieutenant, on board this ship." All this I solemnly engaged him; the combatants were to discharge each a pocket pistol, and then to fall on with their iron-hilted muckle whangers; and one of that sort was allotted for me; but some British officers, who interposed early in the morning, settled the controversy without fighting.

. . .

A few days before I was taken prisoner, I shifted my cloaths, by which I happened to be taken in a Canadian dress, viz. a short fawn skin jacket, double-breasted, an under vest and breeches of sagathy, worsted stockings, a decent pair of shoes, two plain shirts, and a red worsted cap; this was all the cloathing I had, in which I made my appearance in England.

When the prisoners were landed, multitudes of the citizens of Falmouth, excited by curiosity, crowded together to see us, which was equally gratifying to us. I saw numbers of people on the tops of houses, and the rising adjacent grounds were covered with them of both sexes; the throng was so great, that the king's officers were obliged to draw their swords, and force a passage to Pendennis castle, which was near a mile from the town, where we were closely confined, in consequence of orders from Gen. Carlton, who then commanded in Canada.

The rascally Brook Watson then set out for London in great haste, expecting the reward of his zeal; but the ministry received him (as I have been since informed) rather coolly; for the minority in parliament took advantage, arguing that the opposition of America to Great Britain, was not a rebellion. . . . "If it is," say they, "why do you not execute Col. Allen, according to law?" . . . But the majority argued, that I ought to be executed, and that the opposition was really a rebellion, but that policy obliged them not to do it, inasmuch as the Congress had then most prisoners in their power; so that my being sent to England for the purpose of being executed, and necessity restraining them, was rather a foil on their laws and authority, and they consequently disapproved of my being sent thither. . . . But I never had heard the least hint of those debates in parliament, or of the working of their policy, till some time after I left England.

Consequently the reader will readily conceive I was anxious about my preservation, knowing that I was in the power of a haughty and cruel nation, and considered as such; therefore the first proposition which I determined in my own mind was, that humanity and moral suasion would not be consulted in the determination of my fate; and those that daily came in great numbers, out of curiosity to see me, both gentle and simple united in this, that I would be hanged. A gentleman from America, by the name of Temple, and who was friendly to me, just whispered me in the ear, and told me, that bets were laid in London that I would be executed; he likewise privately gave me a guinea, but durst say but little to me.

However, agreeable to my first negative proposition, that moral virtue would not influence my destiny, I had recourse to stratagem, which I was in hopes would move in the circle of their policy. I requested of the commander of the castle the privilege of writing to Congress, who, after consulting with an officer that lived in town, of a superior rank, permitted me to write. I wrote, in the fore part of the letter, a short narrative of my ill treatment; but withal let them know, that though I was treated as a criminal in England, and continued in irons, together with those taken with me, yet it was in consequence of the orders which the commander of the castle received from Gen. Carlton; and therefore desired Congress to desist from matters of retaliation, till they should know the result of the government at England, respecting their treatment towards me, and the prisoners with me, and govern themselves accordingly; with a particular request, that if retaliation should be found necssary, that it might be exercised not according to the smallness of my character in America, but in proportion to the importance of the cause for which I suffered . . . this is, according to my present recollection, the substance of the letter, subscribed, "To the illustrious Continental Congress." This letter was wrote with a view that it should be sent to the ministry at London, rather than to Congres, with a design to intimidate the haughty English government, and screen my neck from the halter.

The next day the officer from whom I obtained licence to write, came to see me, and frowned on me on account of the impudence of the letter, (as he phrased it) and further added, "Do you think that we are fools in England, and would send your letter to Congress, with instructions to retaliate on our own people; I have sent your letter to Lord North." This gave me inward satisfaction, though I carefully concealed it with a pretended resentment, for I found I had come yankee over him, and that the letter had gone to the identical person I designed it for. Nor do I know, to this day, but that it had the desired effect, though I have not heard any thing of the letter since.

My personal treatment by lieutenant Hamilton, who commanded the castle, was very generous. He sent me every day a fine breakfast and dinner from his own table, and a bottle of good wine. Another aged gentleman, whose name I cannot recollect, sent me a good supper: but there was no distinction in public support between me and the privates; we all lodged on a sort of Dutch bunks, in one common apartment, and were allowed straw. The privates were well supplied with fresh provision, and, with me, took effectual measures to rid ourselves of lice.

I could not but feel inwardly extreme anxious for my fate; this I however carefully concealed from the prisoners, as well as from the enemy, who were perpetually shaking the halter at me. I nevertheless treated them with scorn and contempt; and having sent my letter to the ministry, could conceive of nothing more in my power but to keep up my spirits and behave in a daring soldier-like manner, that I might exhibit a good sample of American fortitude. Such a conduct I judged would have a more probable tendency to my preservation than concession and timidity. This, therefore, was my deportment, and I had lastly determined in my own mind, that if a cruel death must inevitably be my portion, I would face it undaunted, and though I greatly rejoice that I have returned to my country and friends, and to see the power and pride of Great Britain humbled, yet I am confident I could then die without the least appearance of dismay.

I now clearly recollect that my mind was so resolved, that I would not have trembled or shewn the least fear, as I was sensible it could not alter my fate, nor do more than reproach my memory, make my last act despicable to my enemies, and eclipse the other actions of my life. For I reasoned thus, that nothing was more common than for men to die, with their friends round them, weeping and lamenting over them, but not able to help them, which was in reality not different in the consequence of it from such a death as I was apprehensive of; and as death was the natural consequence of animal life to which the laws of nature subject mankind, to be timorous and uneasy as to the event or manner of it, was inconsistent with the character of a philosopher or soldier. The cause I was engaged in, I ever viewed worthy hazarding my life for, nor was I (at the critical moments of trouble) sorry that I engaged in it; and as to the world of spirits, though I knew nothing of the mode or manner of it, expected nevertheless, when I should arrive at such a world, that I should be as well treated as other gentlemen of my merit.

Among the great numbers of people, who came to the castle to see the prisoners, some gentlemen told me, that they had come 50 miles on purpose to see me, and desired to ask me a number of questions, and to make free with me in conversation. I gave for answer, that I chose freedom in every sense of the word: Then one of them asked me what my occupation in life had been? I answered him, that in my younger days I had studied divinity, but was a conjurer by passion. He replied, that I conjured wrong at the time that I was taken; and I was obliged to own, that I mistook a figure at that time, but that I had conjured them out of Ticonderoga. This was a place of great notoriety in England, so that the joke seemed to go in my favour.

It was a common thing for me to be taken out of close confinement, into a spacious green in the castle, or rather parade, where numbers of gentlemen and ladies were ready to see and hear me. I often entertained such audiences, with harangues on the impracticability of Great Britain's conquering the (then) colonies of America. At one of these times I asked a gentleman for a bowl of punch, and he ordered his servant to bring it, which he did, and offered it me, but I refused to take it from the hand of his servant; he then gave it to me with his own hand, refusing to drink with me in consequence of my being a state criminal: However I took the punch and drank it all down at one draught, and handed the gentleman the bowl: This made the spectators as well as myself merry.

I expatiated on American freedom: This gained the resentment of a young beardless gentleman of the company, who gave himself very great airs, and replied, that he "knew the Americans very well, and was certain that they could not bear the smell of powder." I replied, that I accepted it as a challenge, and was ready to convince him on the spot, that an American could bear the smell of powder; at which he answered he should not put himself on a par with me. I then demanded of him to treat the character of the Americans with due respect: He answered that I was an Irishman; but I assured him, that I was a *full blooded Yankee,* and in fine, bantered him so much, that he left me in possession of the ground, and the laugh went against him. Two clergymen came to see me, and inasmuch as they behaved with civility, I returned them the same: We discoursed on several parts of moral philosophy and christianity; and they seemed to be surprized, that I should be acquainted with such topics, or that I should understand a syllogism or regular mood of argumentation. I am apprehensive my Canadian dress contributed not a little to the surprize, and excitement of curiosity: To see a gentleman in England, regularly dressed and well behaved, would be no sight at all; but such a rebel, as they were pleased to call me, it is probable was never before seen in England.

11

Abigail (1744–1818) and John Adams (1735–1826)

Selected Letters

John Adams

from *Diary and Autobiography of John Adams* and *Discourses on Davila*

Letters and diaries, it has been said, are "serial autobiography." The writers compose and recompose themselves at short intervals and, in the case of letters, to an audience of just one other person, whose interests and viewpoints help shape the letter. Moreover, as forms much older than autobiography per se, letters and diaries provided precedents for it.

In the eighteenth century, the familiar letter became an extremely important means of self-improvement, self-invention, and liberation from the restrictions of Puritanism. Young New Englanders like John Adams and his wife-to-be Abigail Smith wrote letters to entertain themselves, to improve their penmanship and writing, and to cultivate their sentiments. To add to the game, and to show off their learning, they often chose classical pen names, making a pretense of hiding or altering identity, while also giving themselves more license to tease or be frank. Thus Abigail Smith, a minister's daughter from Weymouth, Massachusetts, early chose the name Diana, while John Adams became Lysander. Later Abigail became Portia, and John simply became John or, to Abigail, "My dearest Friend," but some of the teasing and playfulness, and the gentleness and gentility, remained throughout a correspondence which, because of the Revolution and John's subsequent diplomatic and governmental assignments, continued nearly all their lives.

The Revolution, along with their ambition and desire for recognition, also gave them both a profound sense of destiny. This sense underlies their correspondence and John Adams's diary/autobiography—even to the recording of his night with Benjamin Franklin and his reflections on colds. Their sense of destiny also intensified their identification with the creation of the American character. Their ideals were not just for themselves but for their children and the nation, as is clear in the remarkable exchange of letters, March 31 and April 14, 1776. These two letters are also known for Abigail's request that the declarers of "an independancy" "remember the Ladies," and for John's answer which notes "the Despotism of the Peticoat," a clash in which teasing may be present, too. But when John wrote "My dear Portia" in May, 1780, about how he "must study Politicks and War that my sons may have liberty to study Mathematicks and Philosophy . . . , in order to give their Children a right to study Painting, Poetry, Musick, . . . and Porcelaine," he was deadly serious. He, like leaders of other wars, liked to think his war would be the last war. America was to be a new kind of nation. (One can ask how the autobiographies of Henry and Charles, his great-grandsons, reply to this prophecy.) Similarly, when Abigail objected to French manners and the dirt of her house in Auteuil, she wrote to her American sister, Mrs. Richard Cranch, and niece, Lucy Cranch, as if writing to and for all American women. The irony in Abigail's experience, meanwhile, is that when she saw Madame Helvétius as the image of all French female depravity, Madame Helvétius's darling was at that moment Benjamin Franklin, the vastly popular image of new American worldly success.

Yet thanks to Charles Francis Adams's edition of his grandmother's letters in 1840, Abigail's style of letter-writing became a model for later American women. Her chattiness mixed with her acerbic wit and strong sense of self-worth is abundantly present in the letters of Marianne Hooper Adams, Henry Adams's wife. Her letters are also interesting to compare with Mary Boykin Chesnut's diary.

With Charles Francis Adams's publication of *Familiar Letters of John Adams and His Wife, during the Revolution* in 1876, as a tribute to the national Centennial, both writers were soon reprinted in anthologies. As the editors of *The Book of Abigail and John* wrote in their introduction: "their fortitude, their sacrifices, their public and private wisdom—and . . . their unexpected charm and humor" made them "the prototypical American couple"; "in the United States at its hundredth birthday, John and Abigail Adams were *everybody's* grandparents" (9).

No such popularity has ever fallen on John Adams's *Discourses on Davila*. They were written, as we noted above, in 1789–90, the first year of the French Revolution, and Adams wrote them to warn his fellow Americans of the dangers of an unchecked and unchanneled drive for fame. Wisdom in statecraft sublimated the instinct of emulation to the public good, Adams argued, and he believed that the American experiment had so far done this. But many of Adams's critics misread the *Discourses* as a plea for monarchy and inherited titles in America.

The *Discourses* thus illustrate the controversy in early Federalist America over the power of egotism and how to control it, whether by a stronger class system or through training in self-control and modesty. The work also illustrates the value which the Adams family placed on civic service and fame. John and Abigail Adams knew the power of the "instinct of emulation," because they felt it in themselves.

The selections below are from *The Book of Abigail and John: Selected Letters of the Adams Family, 1762–1784,* ed. L. H. Butterfield, Marc Friedlaender, and Mary-Jo Kline (Cambridge: Harvard Univ. Press, 1975); *Letters of Mrs. Adams . . . ,* ed. Charles Francis Adams (Boston: Little and Brown, 1840); *Diary and Autobiography of John Adams,* ed. L. H. Butterfield, vol. 3 (Cambridge: Harvard Univ. Press, 1962);

and *Discourses on Davila,* in *The Works of John Adams* . . . , ed. Charles Francis Adams, vol. 6 (Boston: Little and Brown, 1851). All editorial information in notes and brackets is given by the respective editors.

from The Book of Abigail and John:
Selected Letters*

[AA to JA]   *Braintree March 31 1776*

I wish you would ever write me a Letter half as long as I write you; and tell me if you may where your Fleet are gone? What sort of Defence Virginia can make against our common Enemy? Whether it is so situated as to make an able Defence? Are not the Gentery Lords and the common people vassals, are they not like the uncivilized Natives Brittain represents us to be? I hope their Riffel Men who have shewen themselves very savage and even Blood thirsty; are not a specimen of the Generality of the people.

I am willing to allow the Colony great merrit for having produced a Washington but they have been shamefully duped by a Dunmore.

I have sometimes been ready to think that the passion for Liberty cannot be Eaquelly Strong in the Breasts of those who have been accustomed to deprive their fellow Creatures of theirs. Of this I am certain that it is not founded upon that generous and christian principal of doing to others as we would that others should do unto us.

Do not you want to see Boston; I am fearfull of the small pox, or I should have been in before this time. I got Mr. Crane to go to our House and see what state it was in. I find it has been occupied by one of the Doctors of a Regiment, very dirty, but no other damage has been done to it. The few things which were left in it are all gone. Cranch has the key which he never deliverd up. I have wrote to him for it and am determined to get it cleand as soon as possible and shut it up. I look upon it a new acquisition of property, a property which one month ago I did not value at a single Shilling, and could with pleasure have seen it in flames.

The Town in General is left in a better state than we expected, more oweing to a percipitate flight than any Regard to the inhabitants, tho some individuals discoverd sense of honour and justice and have left the rent of the Houses in which they were, for the owners and the furniture unhurt, or if damaged suffcent to make it good.

Others have committed abominable Ravages. The Mansion House of your President is safe and the furniture unhurt whilst both the House and

Furniture of the Solisiter General have fallen prey to their own merciless party. Surely the very Fiends feel a Reverential awe for Virtue and patriotism, whilst they Detest the paricide and traitor.

I feel very differently at the approach of spring to what I did a month ago. We knew not then whether we could plant or sow with safety, whether when we had toild we could reap the fruits of our own industery, whether we could rest in our own Cottages, or whether we should not be driven from the sea coasts to seek shelter in the wilderness, but now we feel as if we might sit under our own vine and eat the good of the land.

I feel a gaieti de Coar to which before I was a stranger. I think the Sun looks brighter, the Birds sing more melodiously, and Nature puts on a more chearfull countanance. We feel a temporary peace, and the poor fugitives are returning to their deserted habitations.

Tho we felicitate ourselves, we sympathize with those who are trembling least the Lot of Boston should be theirs. But they cannot be in similar circumstances unless pusilanimity and cowardise should take possession of them. They have time and warning given them to see the Evil and shun it.—I long to hear that you have declared an independancy—and by the way in the new Code of Laws which I suppose it will be necessary for you to make I desire you would Remember the Ladies, and be more generous and favourable to them than your ancestors. Do not put such unlimited power into the hands of the Husbands. Remember all Men would be tyrants if they could. If perticuliar care and attention is not paid to the Laidies we are determined to foment a Rebelion, and will not hold ourselves bound by any Laws in which we have no voice, or Representation.

That your Sex are Naturally Tyrannical is a Truth so thoroughly established as to admit of no dispute, but such of you as wish to be happy willingly give up the harsh title of Master for the more tender and endearing one of Friend. Why then, not put it out of the power of the vicious and the Lawless to use us with cruelty and indignity with impunity. Men of Sense in all Ages abhor those customs which treat us only as the vassals of your Sex. Regard us then as Beings placed by providence under your protection and in immitation of the Supreem Being make use of that power only for our happiness.

[JA to AA]   *Ap. 14. 1776*
You justly complain of my short Letters, but the critical State of Things and the Multiplicity of Avocations must plead my Excuse.—You ask where the Fleet is. The inclosed Papers will inform you. You ask what Sort of Defence Virginia can make. I believe they will make an able Defence. Their Militia and minute Men have been some time employed in training them selves, and they have Nine Battallions of regulars as they call them, maintained among them, under good Officers, at the Continental Expence. They have set up a Number of Manufactories of Fire Arms, which are busily employed. They are

tolerably supplied with Powder, and are successfull and assiduous, in making Salt Petre. Their neighbouring Sister or rather Daughter Colony of North Carolina, which is a warlike Colony, and has several Battallions at the Continental Expence, as well as a pretty good Militia, are ready to assist them, and they are in very good Spirits, and seem determined to make a brave Resistance—The Gentry are very rich, and the common People very poor. This Inequality of Property, gives an Aristocratical Turn to all their Proceedings, and occasions a strong Aversion in their Patricians, to Common Sense. But the Spirit of these Barons, is coming down, and it must submit.

It is very true, as you observe they have been duped by Dunmore. But this is a Common Case. All the Colonies are duped, more or less, at one Time and another. A more egregious Bubble was never blown up, than the Story of Commissioners coming to treat with the Congress. Yet it has gained Credit like a Charm, not only without but against the clearest Evidence. I never shall forget the Delusion, which seized our best and most sagacious Friends the dear Inhabitants of Boston, the Winter before last. Credulity and the Want of Foresight, are Imperfections in the human Character, that no Politician can sufficiently guard against.

You have given me some Pleasure, by your Account of a certain House in Queen Street. I had burned it, long ago, in Imagination. It rises now to my View like a Phoenix.—What shall I say of the Solicitor General? I pity his pretty Children, I pity his Father, and his sisters. I wish I could be clear that it is no moral Evil to pity him and his Lady. Upon Repentance they will certainly have a large Share in the Compassions of many. But let Us take Warning and give it to our Children. Whenever Vanity, and Gaiety, a Love of Pomp and Dress, Furniture, Equipage, Buildings, great Company, expensive Diversions, and elegant Entertainments get the better of the Principles and Judgments of Men or Women there is no knowing where they will stop, nor into what Evils, natural, moral, or political, they will lead us.

Your Description of your own Gaiety de Coeur, charms me. Thanks be to God you have just Cause to rejoice—and may the bright Prospect be obscured by no Cloud.

As to Declarations of Independency, be patient. Read our Privateering Laws, and our Commercial Laws. What signifies a Word.

As to your extraordinary Code of Laws, I cannot but laugh. We have been told that our Struggle has loosened the bands of Government every where. That Children and Apprentices were disobedient—that schools and Colledges were grown turbulent—that Indians slighted their Guardians and Negroes grew insolent to their Masters. But your Letter was the first Intimation that another Tribe more numerous and powerfull than all the rest were grown discontented.—This is rather too coarse a Compliment but you are so saucy, I wont blot it out.

Depend upon it, We know better than to repeal our Masculine systems.

Altho they are in full Force, you know they are little more than Theory. We dare not exert our Power in its full Latitude. We are obliged to go fair, and softly, and in Practice you know We are the subjects. We have only the Name of Masters, and rather than give up this, which would compleatly subject Us to the Despotism of the Peticoat, I hope General Washington, and all our brave Heroes would fight. I am sure every good Politician would plot, as long as he would against Despotism, Empire, Monarchy, Aristocracy, Oligarchy, or Ochlocracy.—A fine Story indeed. I begin to think the Ministry as deep as they are wicked. After stirring up Tories, Landjobbers, Trimmers, Bigots, Canadians, Indians, Negroes, Hanoverians, Hessians, Russians, Irish Roman Catholicks, Scotch Renegadoes, at last they have stimulated the ___ to demand new Priviledges and threaten to rebell.

. . .

[JA to AA]   [Paris, post 12 May 1780]
My dear Portia

The inclosed Dialogue in the Shades was written by Mr. Edmund Jennings now residing at Brussells, a Native of Maryland. I will send you the Rest when I can get it.

How I lament the Loss of my Packets by Austin! There were I suppose Letters from Congress of great Importance to me. I know not what I shall do without them. I suppose there was Authority to draw &c. Mr. T[haxter]'s Letter from his father, hints that Mr. L. is coming here. This will be excellent.

Since my Arrival this time I have driven about Paris, more than I did before. The rural Scenes around this Town are charming. The public Walks, Gardens, &c. are extreamly beautifull. The Gardens of the Palais Royal, the Gardens of the Tuilleries, are very fine. The Place de Louis 15, the Place Vendome or Place de Louis 14, the Place victoire, the Place royal, are fine Squares, ornamented with very magnificent statues. I wish I had time to describe these objects to you in a manner, that I should have done, 25 Years ago, but my Head is too full of Schemes and my Heart of Anxiety to use Expressions borrowed from you know whom.

To take a Walk in the Gardens of the Palace of the Tuilleries, and describe the Statues there, all in marble, in which the ancient Divinities and Heroes are represented with exquisite Art, would be a very pleasant Amusement, and instructive Entertainment, improving in History, Mythology, Poetry, as well as in Statuary. Another Walk in the Gardens of Versailles, would be usefull and agreable.—But to observe these Objects with Taste and describe them so as to be understood, would require more time and thought than I can possibly Spare. It is not indeed the fine Arts, which our Country requires. The Usefull, the mechanic Arts, are those which We have occasion for in a young Country, as yet simple and not far advanced in Luxury, altho perhaps much too far for her Age and Character.

I could fill Volumes with Descriptions of Temples and Palaces, Paintings, Sculptures, Tapestry, Porcelaine, &c. &c. &c.—if I could have time. But I could not do this without neglecting my duty.—The Science of Government it is my Duty to study, more than all other Sciences: the Art of Legislation and Administration and Negotiation, ought to take Place, indeed to exclude in a manner all other Arts.—I must study Politicks and War that my sons may have liberty to study Mathematicks and Philosophy. My sons ought to study Mathematicks and Philosophy, Geography, natural History, Naval Architecture, navigation, Commerce and Agriculture, in order to give their Children a right to study Painting, Poetry, Musick, Architecture, Statuary, Tapestry and Porcelaine.

Adieu.

from Letters of Mrs. Adams

To Mrs. Cranch.

Auteuil, distant from Paris four miles.
5 September, 1784.

My Dear Sister,

It is now the 5th of September, and I have been at this place more than a fortnight; but I have had so many matters to arrange, and so much to attend to, since I left London, that I have scarcely touched a pen. I am now vastly behindhand in many things which I could have wished to have written down and transmitted to my American friends, some of which would have amused, and others diverted them. But such a rapid succession of events, or rather occurrences, have been crowded into the last two months of my life, that I can scarcely recollect them, much less recount them in detail. There are so many of my friends, who have demands upon me, and who I fear will think me negligent, that I know not which to address first. Abby has had less of care upon her, and therefore has been very attentive to her pen, and I hope will supply my deficiencies.

Auteuil is a village four miles distant from Paris, and one from Passy. The house we have taken is large, commodious, and agreeably situated, near the Woods of Boulogne, which belong to the King, and which Mr. Adams calls his park, for he walks an hour or two every day in them. The house is much larger than we have need of; upon occasion, forty beds may be made in it. I fancy it must be very cold in winter. There are few houses with the privilege which this enjoys, that of having the saloon, as it is called, the apartment where we receive company, upon the first floor. This room is very elegant, and about a third larger than General Warren's hall. The dining-room is upon the right hand, and the saloon upon the left, of the entry, which has large glass doors opposite to each other, one opening into the court, as they call it, the other into a large and beautiful garden. Out of the dining-room you pass through an entry into the kitchen, which is rather small for so large a house. In this entry are stairs which you ascend, at the top of which is a long gallery fronting the street, with six windows, and, opposite to each window, you open into the chambers which all look into the garden.

But with an expense of thirty thousand livres in looking glasses, there is no table in the house better than an oak board, nor a carpet belonging to the house. The floors I abhor, made of red tiles in the shape of Mrs. Quincy's floor-cloth tiles. These floors will by no means bear water, so that the method of cleaning them is to have them waxed, and then a man-servant with foot brushes drives round your room, dancing here and there like a Merry Andrew. This is calculated to take from your foot every atom of dirt, and leave the room in a few moments as he found it. The house must be exceedingly cold in winter. The dining-rooms, of which you make no other use, are laid with small stones, like the red tiles for shape and size. The servants' apartments are generally upon the first floor, and the stairs which you commonly have to ascend to get into the family apartments are so dirty, that I have been obliged to hold up my clothes, as though I was passing through a cow-yard.

I have been but little abroad. It is customary in this country for strangers to make the first visit. As I cannot speak the language, I think I should make rather an awkward figure. I have dined abroad several times with Mr. Adams's particular friends, the Abbés, who are very polite and civil, three sensible and worthy men. The Abbé de Mably has lately published a book, which he has dedicated to Mr. Adams. This gentleman is nearly eighty years old; the Abbé Chalut, seventy-five; and Arnoux, about fifty, a fine, sprightly man, who takes great pleasure in obliging his friends. Their apartments were really nice. I have dined once at Dr. Franklin's, and once at Mr. Barclay's, our consul, who has a very agreeable woman for his wife, and where I feel like being with a friend. Mrs. Barclay has assisted me in my purchases, gone with me to different shops, &c. To-morrow I am to dine at Monsieur Grand's; but I have really felt so happy within doors, and am so pleasingly situated, that I have had little inclination to change the scene. I have not been to one public amusement as yet, not even the opera, though we have one very near us.

You may easily suppose I have been fully employed, beginning house-keeping anew, and arranging my family to our no small expense and trouble; for I have had bed-linen and table-linen to purchase and make, spoons and forks to get made of silver, three dozen of each, besides tea furniture, china for the table, servants to procure, &c. The expense of living abroad, I always supposed to be high, but my ideas were nowise adequate to the thing. I could have furnished myself in the town of Boston, with every thing I have, twenty or thirty per cent. cheaper than I have been able to do it here. Every thing which will bear the name of elegant, is imported from England, and, if you will have it, you must pay for it, duties and all. I cannot get a dozen handsome wine-glasses under three guineas, nor a pair of small decanters for less than a guinea and a half. The only gauze fit to wear is English, at a crown a yard; so that really a guinea goes no further than a copper with us. For this house, garden, stables, &c., we give two hundred guineas a year. Wood is two guineas and a half per cord; coal, six livres the basket of about two bushels; this article of firing, we calculate at one hundred guineas a year. The difference between coming upon this negotiation to France and remaining at the Hague, where the house was already furnished at the expense of a thousand pounds sterling, will increase the expense here to six or seven hundred guineas; at a time, too, when Congress have cut off five hundred guineas from what they have heretofore given. For our coachman and horses alone, (Mr. Adams purchased a coach in England,) we give fifteen guineas a month. It is the policy of this country to oblige you to a certain number of servants, and one will not touch what belongs to the business of another, though he or she has time enough to perform the whole. In the first place, there is a coachman who does not an individual thing but attend to the carriages and horses; then the gardener, who has business enough; then comes the cook; then the *maître d'hôtel*; his business is to purchase articles in the family, and oversee, that nobody cheats but himself; a *valet de chambre*,—John serves in this capacity; a *femme de chambre*,—Esther serves in this line, and is worth a dozen others; a *coiffeuse*,—for this place, I have a French girl about nineteen, whom I have been upon the point of turning away, because Madame will not brush a chamber; "it is not de fashion, it is not her business." I would not have kept her a day longer, but found, upon inquiry, that I could not better myself, and hairdressing here is very expensive, unless you keep such a madam in the house. She sews tolerably well, so I make her as useful as I can. She is more particularly devoted to Mademoiselle. Esther diverted me yesterday evening, by telling me that she heard her go muttering by her chamber door after she had been assisting Abby in dressing. "Ah, mon Dieu, 't is provoking,"—(she talks a little English.)—"Why, what is the matter, Pauline, what is provoking?"—"Why, Mademoiselle look so pretty, I, so mauvais." There is another indispensable servant, who is called a *frotteur*; his business is to rub the floors.

We have a servant who acts as *maître d'hôtel*, whom I like at present, and who is so very gracious as to act as footman too, to save the expense of another servant, upon condition that we give him a gentleman's suit of clothes in lieu of a livery. Thus, with seven servants and hiring a charwoman upon occasion of company, we may possibly make out to keep house; with less, we should be hooted at as ridiculous, and could not entertain any company. To tell this in our own country, would be considered as extravagance; but would they send a person here in a public character to be a public jest? At lodgings in Paris last year, during Mr. Adams's negotiations for a peace, it was as expensive to him as it is now at house-keeping, without half the accommodations.

Washing is another expensive article; the servants are all allowed theirs, besides their wages; our own costs us a guinea a week. I have become steward and book-keeper, determined to know with accuracy what our expenses are, and to prevail with Mr. Adams to return to America, if he finds himself straitened, as I think he must be. Mr. Jay went home because he could not support his family here with the whole salary; what then can be done, curtailed as it now is, with the additional expense? Mr. Adams is determined to keep as little company as he possibly can, but some entertainments we must make, and it is no unusual thing for them to amount to fifty or sixty guineas at a time. More is to be performed by way of negotiation, many times, at one of these entertainments, than at twenty serious conversations; but the policy of our country has been, and still is, to be penny-wise and pound-foolish. We stand in sufficient need of economy, and, in the curtailment of other salaries, I suppose they thought it absolutely necessary to cut off their foreign ministers. But, my own interest apart, the system is bad; for that nation which degrades their own ministers by obliging them to live in narrow circumstances, cannot expect to be held in high estimation themselves. We spend no evenings abroad, make no suppers, attend very few public entertainments, or spectacles, as they are called, and avoid every expense that is not held indispensable. Yet I cannot but think it hard, that a gentleman who has devoted so great a part of his life to the service of the public, who has been the means, in a great measure, of procuring such extensive territories to his country, who saved their fisheries, and who is still laboring to procure them further advantages, should find it necessary so cautiously to calculate his pence, for fear of overrunning them. I will add one more expense. There is now a Court mourning, and every foreign minister, with his family, must go into mourning for a Prince of eight years old, whose father is an ally to the King of France. This mourning is ordered by the Court, and is to be worn eleven days only. Poor Mr. Jefferson had to hie away for a tailor to get a whole black silk suit made up in two days; and at the end of eleven days, should another death happen, he will be obliged to have a new suit of mourning, of cloth, because that is the season when silk must be left off. We may groan and scold, but these are expenses which cannot be avoided; for fashion is the deity every one worships in this country, and, from the highest to the lowest, you must submit. Even poor John and Esther had no comfort amongst the servants, being constantly the subjects of their ridicule, until we were obliged to direct them to have their hair dressed. Esther had several crying fits upon the occasion, that she should be forced to be so much of a fool; but there was no way to keep them from being trampled upon but this; and, now that they are *à la mode de Paris,* they are much respected. To be out of fashion is more criminal than to be seen in a state of nature, to which the Parisians are not averse.

Sunday here bears the nearest resemblance to our Commencement, and

Election days; every thing is jollity, and mirth, and recreation. But, to quit these subjects, pray tell me how you all do. I long to hear from you. House and garden, with all its decorations, are not so dear to me as my own little cottage, connected with the society I used there to enjoy; for, out of my own family, I have no attachments in Europe, nor do I think I ever shall have. As to the language, I speak it a little, bad grammar and all; but I have so many French servants, that I am under a necessity of trying.

Could you, my sister, and my dear cousins, come and see me as you used to do, walk in the garden, and delight yourselves in the alcoves and arbours, I should enjoy myself much better. When Mr. Adams is absent, I sit in my little writing-room, or the chamber I have described to Betsey, and read or sew. Abby is for ever at her pen, writing or learning French; sometimes company, and sometimes abroad, we are fully employed.

Who do you think dined with us the other day? A Mr. Mather and his lady, son of Dr. Mather, and Mrs. Hay, who have come to spend the winter in France. I regret that they are going to some of the provinces. To-day, Mr. Tracy, Mr. Williams, Mr. Jefferson, and Colonel Humphreys are to dine with us; and one day last week we had a company of twenty-seven persons; Dr. Franklin, Mr. Hartley and his secretaries, &c. &c. But my paper warns me to close. Do not let anybody complain of me. I am going on writing to one after another as fast as possible, and, if this vessel does not carry the letters, the next will. Give my love to one of the best men in the world.

Affectionately yours,

A. A.

To Miss Lucy Cranch.

Auteuil, 5 September, 1784.

My Dear Lucy,

I promised to write to you from the Hague, but your uncle's unexpected arrival at London prevented me. Your uncle purchased an excellent travelling coach in London, and hired a post-chaise for our servants. In this manner we travelled from London to Dover, accommodated through England with the best of horses, postilions, and good carriages; clean, neat apartments, genteel entertainment, and prompt attendance. But no sooner do you cross from Dover to Calais, than every thing is reversed, and yet the distance is very small between them.

The cultivation is by no means equal to that of England; the villages look poor and mean, the houses all thatched, and rarely a glass window in them; their horses, instead of being handsomely harnessed, as those in England are, have the appearance of so many old cart-horses. Along you go, with seven horses tied up with ropes and chains, rattling like trucks; two ragged postilions, mounted, with enormous jack-boots, add to the comic scene. And this is the style in which a duke or a count travels through this kingdom. You inquire of me how I like Paris. Why, they tell me I am no judge, for that I have not seen it yet. One thing, I know, and that is that I have smelt it. If I was agreeably disappointed in London, I am as much disappointed in Paris. It is the very dirtiest place I ever saw. There are some buildings and some squares, which are tolerable; but in general the streets are narrow, the shops, the houses, inelegant and dirty, the streets full of lumber and stone, with which they build. Boston cannot boast so elegant public buildings; but, in every other respect, it is as much superior in my eyes to Paris, as London is to Boston. To have had Paris tolerable to me, I should not have gone to London. As to the people here, they are more given to hospitality than in England, it is said. I have been in company with but one French lady since I arrived; for strangers here make the first visit, and nobody will know you until you have waited upon them in form.

This lady[1] I dined with at Dr. Franklin's. She entered the room with a careless, jaunty air; upon seeing ladies who were strangers to her, she bawled out, "Ah! mon Dieu, where is Franklin? Why did you not tell me there were ladies here?" You must suppose her speaking all this in French. "How I look!" said she, taking hold of a chemise made of tiffany, which she had on over a blue lutestring, and which looked as much upon the decay as her beauty, for she was once a handsome woman; her hair was frizzled; over it she had a small straw hat, with a dirty gauze half-handkerchief round it, and a bit of dirtier gauze, than ever my maids wore, was bowed on behind. She had a black gauze scarf thrown over her shoulders. She ran out of the room; when she returned, the Doctor entered at one door, she at the other; upon which she ran forward to him, caught him by the hand, "Helas! Franklin;" then gave him a double kiss, one upon each cheek, and another upon his forehead. When we went into the room to dine, she was placed between the Doctor and Mr. Adams. She carried on the chief of the conversation at dinner, frequently locking her hand into the Doctor's, and sometimes spreading her arms upon the backs of both the gentlemen's chairs, then throwing her arm carelessly upon the Doctor's neck.

I should have been greatly astonished at this conduct, if the good Doctor had not told me that in this lady I should see a genuine Frenchwoman, wholly free from affection or stiffness of behaviour, and one of the best women in the world. For this I must take the Doctor's word; but I should have set her down for a very bad one, although sixty years of age, and a widow. I own I was highly disgusted, and never wish for an acquaintance with any ladies of this cast. After dinner she threw herself upon a settee, where she showed more than her feet. She had a little lap-dog, who was, next to the Doctor, her favorite. This she kissed, and when he wet the floor she wiped it up with

1. This lady was Madame Helvétius, widow of the philosopher who had resided at Auteuil.

her chemise. This is one of the Doctor's most intimate friends, with whom he dines once every week, and she with him. She is rich, and is my near neighbour; but I have not yet visited her. Thus you see, my dear, that manners differ exceedingly in different countries, I hope, however, to find amongst the French ladies manners more consistent with my ideas of decency, or I shall be a mere recluse.

You must write to me, and let me know all about you; marriages, births, and preferments; every thing you can think of. Give my respects to the Germantown family. I shall begin to get letters for them by the next vessel.

Good night. Believe me

Your most affectionate aunt,

A. A.

from the Diary and Autobiography of John Adams *

[September 1776]

The Taverns were so full We could with difficulty obtain Entertainment. At Brunswick, but one bed could be procured for Dr. Franklin and me, in a Chamber little larger than the bed, without a Chimney and with only one small Window. The Window was open, and I, who was an invalid and afraid of the Air in the night (*blowing upon me*), shut it close. Oh! says Franklin dont shut the Window. We shall be suffocated. I answered I was afraid of the Evening Air. Dr. Franklin replied, the Air within this Chamber will soon be, and indeed is now worse than that without Doors: come! open the Window and come to bed, and I will convince you: I believe you are not acquainted with my Theory of Colds. Opening the Window and leaping into Bed, I said I had read his Letters to Dr. Cooper in which he had advanced, that Nobody ever got cold by going into a cold Church, or any other cold Air: but the Theory was so little consistent with my experience, that I thought it a Paradox: However I had so much curiosity to hear his reasons, that I would run the risque of a cold. The Doctor then began an harrangue, upon Air and cold and Respiration and Perspiration, with which I was so much amused that I soon fell asleep, and left him and his Philosophy together: but I believe they were equally sound and insensible, within a few minutes after me, for the last Words I heard were pronounced as if he was more than half asleep. . . . I remember little of the Lecture, except, that the human Body, by Respiration and Perspiration, destroys a gallon of Air in a minute: that two such Persons, as were now in that Chamber, would consume all the Air in it, in an hour or two: that by breathing over again the matter thrown off, by the Lungs and the Skin, We should imbibe the real Cause of Colds, not from abroad but from within. I am not inclined to introduce here a dissertation on this Subject. There is much Truth I believe, in some things he advanced: but they warrant not the assertion that a Cold is never taken from cold air. I have often conversed with him since on the same subject: and I believe with him that Colds are often taken in foul Air, in close Rooms: but they are often taken from cold Air, abroad too. I have often asked him, whether a Person heated with Exercise, going suddenly into cold Air, or standing still in a current of it, might not have his Pores suddenly contracted, his Perspiration stopped, and that matter thrown into the Circulations or cast upon the Lungs which he acknowledged was the Cause of Colds. To this he never could give me a satisfactory Answer. And I have heard that in the Opinion of his own able Physician Dr. Jones he fell a Sacrifice at last, not to the Stone but to his own Theory; having caught the violent Cold, which finally choaked him, by sitting for some hours at a Window, with the cool Air blowing upon him.

from Discourses on Davila

from II

. . . Men, in their primitive conditions, however savage, were undoubtedly gregarious; and they continue to be social, not only in every stage of civilization, but in every possible situation in which they can be placed. As nature intended them for society, she has furnished them with passions, appetites, and propensities, as well as a variety of faculties, calculated both for their individual enjoyment, and to render them useful to each other in their social connections. There is none among them more essential or remarkable, than the *passion for distinction*. A desire to be observed, considered, esteemed, praised, beloved, and admired by his fellows, is one of the earliest, as well as keenest dispositions discovered in the heart of man. If any one should doubt the existence of this propensity, let him go and attentively observe the journeymen and apprentices in the first workshop, or the oarsmen in a cockboat, a family or a neighborhood, the inhabitants of a house or the crew of a ship, a school or a college, a city or a village, a savage or civilized people, a hospital or a church, the bar or the exchange, a camp or a court. Wherever men, women, or children, are to be found, whether they be old or young, rich or poor, high or low, wise or foolish, ignorant or learned, every individual is seen to be strongly actuated by a desire to be seen, heard, talked of, approved and respected, by the people about him, and within his knowledge.

.   .   .

This passion, while it is simply a desire to excel another, by fair industry in the search of truth, and the practice of virtue, is properly called *Emulation*. When it aims at power, as a means of distinction, it is *Ambition*. When it is in a situation to suggest the sentiments of fear and apprehension, that another, who is now inferior, will become superior, it is denominated *Jealousy*. When it is in a state of mortification, at the superiority of another, and desires to bring him down to our level, or to depress him below us, it is properly called *Envy*. When it deceives a man into a belief of false professions of esteem or admiration, or into a false opinion of his importance in the judgment of the world, it is *Vanity*. These observations alone would be sufficient to show, that this propensity, in all its branches, is a principal source of the virtues and vices, the happiness and misery of human life; and that the history of mankind is little more than a simple narration of its operation and effects.

There is in human nature, it is true, simple *Benevolence*, or an affection for the good of others; but alone it is not a balance for the selfish affections. Nature then has kindly added to benevolence, the desire of reputation, in order to make us good members of society. *Spectemur agendo* expresses the great principle of activity for the good of others. Nature has sanctioned the law of self-preservation by rewards and punishments. The rewards of selfish activity are life and health; the punishments of negligence and indolence are want, disease, and death. Each individual, it is true, should consider, that nature has enjoined the same law on his neighbor, and therefore a respect for the authority of nature would oblige him to respect the rights of others as much as his own. But reasoning as abstruse, though as simple as this, would not occur to all men. The same nature therefore has imposed another law, that of promoting the good, as well as respecting the rights of mankind, and has sanctioned it by other rewards and punishments. The rewards in this case, in this life, are *esteem* and *admiration* of others; the punishments are *neglect* and *contempt;* nor may any one imagine that these are not as real as the others. The desire of the esteem of others is as real a want of nature as hunger; and the neglect and contempt of the world as severe a pain as the gout or stone. It sooner and oftener produces despair, and a detestation of existence; of equal importance to individuals, to families, and to nations. It is a principal end of government to regulate this passion, which in its turn becomes a principal means of government. It is the only adequate instrument of order and subordination in society, and alone commands effectual obedience to laws, since without it neither human reason, nor standing armies, would ever produce that great effect. Every personal quality, and every blessing of fortune, is cherished in proportion to its capacity of gratifying this universal affection for the esteem, the sympathy, admiration and congratulations of the public. Beauty in the face, elegance of figure, grace of attitude and motion, riches, honors, every thing is weighed in the scale, and desired, not so much for the pleasure they afford, as the attention they command. As this is a point of great importance, it may be pardonable to expatiate a little upon these particulars.

Why are the personal accomplishments of beauty, elegance, and grace, held in such high estimation by mankind? Is it merely for the pleasure which is received from the sight of these attributes? By no means. The taste for such delicacies is not universal; in those who feel the most lively sense of them, it is but a slight sensation, and of shortest continuance; but those attractions command the notice and attention of the public; they draw the eyes of spectators. This is the charm that makes them irresistible. Is it for such fading perfections that a husband or a wife is chosen? Alas, it is well known, that a very short familiarity totally destroys all sense and attention to such properties; and on the contrary, a very little time and habit destroy all the aversion to ugliness and deformity, when unattended with disease or ill temper. Yet beauty and address are courted and admired, very often, more than discretion, wit, sense, and many other accomplishments and virtues, of infinitely more importance to the happiness of private life, as well as to the utility and ornament of society. Is it for the momentous purpose of dancing and drawing, painting and music, riding or fencing, that men or women are destined in this life or any other? Yet those who have the best means of education bestow more attention and expense on those, than on more solid acquisitions. Why? Because they attract more forcibly the attention of the world, and procure a better advancement in life. Notwithstanding all this, as soon as an establishment in life is made, they are found to have answered their end, are neglected and laid aside.

Is there any thing in birth, however illustrious or splendid, which should make a difference between one man and another? If, from a common ancestor, the whole human race is descended, they are all of the same family. How then can they distinguish families into the more or the less ancient? What advantage is there in an illustration of an hundred or a thousand years? Of what avail are all these histories, pedigrees, traditions? What foundation has the whole science of genealogy and heraldry? Are there differences in the breeds of men, as there are in those of horses? If there are not, these sciences have no foundation in reason; in prejudice they have a very solid one. All that philosophy can say is, that there is a general presumption, that a man has had some advantages of education, if he is of a family of note. But this advantage must be derived from his father and mother chiefly, if not wholly; of what importance is it then, in this view, whether the family is twenty generations upon record, or only two?

The mighty secret lies in this:—An illustrious descent attracts the notice of mankind. A single drop of royal blood, however illegitimately scattered, will make any man or woman proud or vain. Why? Because, although it excites the indignation of many, and the envy of more, it still attracts the *attention* of the world. Noble blood, whether the nobility be hereditary or elective, and, indeed, more in republican governments than in monarchies, least of all in despotisms, is held in estimation for the same reason. It is a name and a race that a nation has been interested in, and is in the habit of respecting. Benevolence, sympathy, congratulation, have been so long associated to those names in the minds of the people, that they are become national habits. National gratitude descends from the father to the son, and is often stronger to the latter than the former. It is often excited by remorse, upon reflection on the ingratitude and injustice with which the former has been treated. When the names of a certain family are read in all the gazettes, chronicles, records, and histories of a country for five hundred years, they become known, respected, and delighted in by every body. A youth, a child of this extraction, and bearing this name, attracts the eyes and ears of all companies long before it is known or inquired whether he be a wise man or a fool. His name is often a greater distinction than a title, a star, or a garter. This it is which makes so many men proud, and so many others envious of illustrious descent. The pride is as irrational and contemptible as the pride of riches, and no more. A wise man will lament that any other distinction than that of merit should be made. A good man will neither be proud nor vain of his birth, but will earnestly improve every advantage he has for the public good. A cunning man will carefully conceal his pride; but will indulge it in secret the more effectually, and improve his advantage to greater profit. But was any man ever known so wise, or so good, as really to despise birth or wealth? Did you ever read of a man rising to public notice, from obscure beginnings, who was not reflected on? Although, with every liberal mind, it is an honor and a proof of merit, yet it is a disgrace with mankind in general. What a load of sordid obloquy and envy has every such man to carry! The contempt that is thrown upon obscurity of ancestry, augments the eagerness for the stupid adoration that is paid to its illustration.

This desire of the consideration of our fellow-men, and their congratulations in our joys, is not less invincible than the desire of their sympathy in our sorrows. It is a determination of our nature, that lies at the foundation of our whole moral system in this world, and may be connected essentially with our destination in a future state.

from VI

. . . As no appetite in human nature is more universal than that for honor, and real merit is confined to a very few, the numbers who thirst for respect, are out of all proportion to those who seek it only by merit. The great majority trouble themselves little about merit, but apply themselves to seek for honor, by means which they see will more easily and certainly obtain it, by displaying their taste and address, their wealth and magnificence, their ancient parchments, pictures, and statues, and the virtues of their ancestors; and if these fail, as they seldom have done, they have recourse to artifice, dissimulation, hypocrisy, flattery, imposture, empiricism, quackery, and bribery. What chance has humble, modest, obscure, and poor merit in such a scramble? Nations, perceiving that the still small voice of merit was drowned in the insolent roar of such dupes of impudence and knavery in national elections, without a possibility of a remedy, have sought for something more permanent than the popular voice to designate honor. Many nations have attempted to annex it to land, presuming that a good estate would at least furnish means of a good education; and have resolved that those who should possess certain territories, should have certain legislative, executive, and judicial powers over the people. Other nations have endeavored to connect honor with offices; and the names and ideas at least of certain moral virtues and intellectual qualities have been by law annexed to certain offices, as veneration, grace, excellence, honor, serenity, majesty. Other nations have attempted to annex honor to families, without regard to lands or offices. The Romans allowed none, but those who had possessed curule offices, to have statues or portraits. He who had images or pictures of his ancestors, was called noble. He who had no statue or pictures but his own, was called a new man. Those who had none at all, were ignoble. Other nations have united all those institutions; connected lands, offices, and families; made them all descend together, and honor, public attention, consideration, and congratulation, along with them.

This has been the policy of Europe; and it is to this institution she owes her superiority in war and peace, in legislation and commerce, in agriculture, navigation, arts, sciences, and manufactures, to Asia and Africa.* These families, thus distinguished by property, honors, and privileges, by defending themselves, have been obliged to defend the people against the encroachments of despotism. They have been a civil and political militia, constantly watching the designs of the standing armies, and courts; and by defending their own rights, liberties, properties, and privileges, they have been obliged, in some degree, to defend those of the people, by making a common cause with them. But there were several essential defects in this policy; one was, that the people took no rational measures to defend themselves, either against these great families, or the courts. They had no adequate representation of themselves in the sovereignty. Another was, that it never was determined where the sovereignty resided. Generally it was claimed by kings; but not admitted by the nobles. Sometimes every baron pretended to be sovereign in his own territory; at other times, the sovereignty was claimed by an assembly of nobles, under the name of States or Cortes. Sometimes the united authority of the king and states was called the sovereignty. The common people had no adequate and independent share in the legislatures, and found themselves harassed to discover who was the sovereign, and whom they ought to obey, as much as they ever had been or could be to determine who had the most merit. A thousand years of barons' wars, causing universal darkness, ignorance, and barbarity, ended at last in simple monarchy, not by express stipulation, but by

---

*This is a truth; but by no means a justification of the system of nobility in France, nor in other parts of Europe. Not even in England without a more equitable representation of the Commons in the legislature. J. A. 1812.

tacit acquiescence, in almost all Europe; the people preferring a certain sovereignty in a single person, to endless disputes, about merit and sovereignty, which never did and never will produce any thing but aristocratical anarchy; and the nobles contenting themselves with a security of their property and privileges, by a government of fixed laws, registered and interpreted by a judicial power, which they called sovereign tribunals, though the legislation and execution were in a single person.

In this system to control the nobles, the church joined the kings and common people. The progress of reason, letters, and science, has weakened the church and strengthened the common people; who, if they are honestly and prudently conducted by those who have their confidence, will most infallibly obtain a share in every legislature. But if the common people are advised to aim at collecting the whole sovereignty in single national assemblies, as they are by the Duke de la *Rochefoucauld* and the Marquis of *Condorcet;* or at the abolition of the regal executive authority; or at a division of the executive power, as they are by a posthumous publication of the Abbé de *Mably,* they will fail of their desired liberty, as certainly as emulation and rivalry are founded in human nature, and inseparable from civil affairs. It is not to flatter the passions of the people, to be sure, nor is it the way to obtain a present enthusiastic popularity, to tell them that in a single assembly they will act as arbitrarily and tyrannically as any despot, but it is a sacred truth, and as demonstrable as any proposition whatever, that a sovereignty in a single assembly must necessarily, and will certainly be exercised by a majority, as tyrannically as any sovereignty was ever exercised by kings or nobles. And if a balance of passions and interests is not scientifically concerted, the present struggle in Europe will be little beneficial to mankind,[†] and produce nothing but another thousand years of feudal fanaticism, under new and strange names.

from XIII

. . . The increase and dissemination of knowledge, instead of rendering unnecessary the checks of emulation and the balances of rivalry in the orders of society and constitution of government, augment the necessity of both. It becomes the more indispensable that every man should know his place, and be made to keep it. Bad men increase in knowledge as fast as good men; and science, arts, taste, sense, and letters, are employed for the purposes of injustice and tyranny, as well as those of law and liberty; for corruption, as well as for virtue.

FRENCHMEN! Act and think like yourselves! confessing human nature, be magnanimous and wise. Acknowledging and boasting yourselves to be men,

*Witness the quintuple directory and the triumvirate consulate. J. A.
†Witness France and Europe in 1813. J. A.

avow the feelings of men. The affectation of being exempted from passions is inhuman. The grave pretension to such singularity is solemn hypocrisy. Both are unworthy of your frank and generous natures. Consider that government is intended to set bounds to passions which nature has not limited; and to assist reason, conscience, justice, and truth, in controlling interests, which, without it, would be as unjust as uncontrollable.*

AMERICANS! Rejoice, that from experience you have learned wisdom; and instead of whimsical and fantastical projects, you have adopted a promising essay towards a well-ordered government. Instead of following any foreign example, to return to *the legislation of confusion,* contemplate the means of restoring decency, honesty, and order in society, by preserving and completing, if any thing should be found necessary to complete the balance of your government. In a well-balanced government, reason, conscience, truth, and virtue, must be respected by all parties, and exerted for the public good.** Advert to the principles on which you commenced that glorious self-defence, which, if you behave with steadiness and consistency, may ultimately loosen the chains of all mankind. If you will take the trouble to read over the memorable proceedings of the town of Boston, on the twenty-eighth day of October, 1772, when the Committee of Correspondence of twenty-one persons was appointed to state the rights of the colonists as men, as Christians, and as subjects, and to publish them to the world, with the infringements and violations of them,† you will find the great principles of civil and religious liberty for which you have contended so successfully, and which the world is contending for after your example. I could transcribe with pleasure the whole of this immortal pamphlet, which is a real picture of the sun of liberty rising on the human race; but shall select only a few words more directly to the present purpose.

"The first fundamental, positive law of all commonwealths or states is the establishment of the legislative power."   Page 9.

"It is absolutely necessary in a mixed government like that of this province, that a *due proportion or balance* of power should be established among the several branches of the legislative. Our ancestors received from King William and Queen Mary a charter, by which it was understood by both parties in the contract, that such a proportion or balance was fixed; and, therefore, every thing which renders any one branch of the legislative more independent of the other two than it was originally designed, is an alteration of the constitution."

---

*Frenchmen neither saw, heard, nor felt or understood this. J. A. 1813.

**Americans paid no attention or regard to this. And a blind, mad rivalry between the north and the south is destroying all morality and sound policy. God grant that division, civil war, murders, assassination, and massacres may not soon grow out of these rivalries of states, families, and individuals.

†This Boston pamphlet was drawn by the great James Otis. J. A. 1813.

12

John Filson
The Adventures of Col. Daniel Boon
(1734–1820)

Although written by John Filson (c. 1747–88) and first published as an appendix to Filson's *The Discovery, Settlement, and Present State of Kentucke* (1784), "The Adventures of Col. Daniel Boon" [sic] is an autobiography in that it is based on stories Boone told to Filson during Filson's two years in Kentucky as a surveyor and land speculator. Furthering the idea that it is Boone's own story, Filson has Boone narrate it in the first person. With the rest of his *Kentucke* being, as Richard Slotkin has said, "an elaborate real-estate promotion brochure designed to sell farm lands . . . to easterners and Europeans," Filson needed the direct testimony of an actual inhabitant. Even more important, Slotkin argues, Filson needed a heroic figure who would "portray the promise of the frontier" while also not "glossing over the obviously perilous realities of the pioneer's situation."[1] In 1784, right after the Revolution's many Indian attacks there, Kentucky was known as "the Dark and Bloody Ground"—a name that discouraged prospective settlers.

Boone, therefore, emerges as the "instrument ordained to settle the wilderness." With his references to "Providence" and "our Creator," he does indeed imply that he is on a divine, historic mission. With his almost emotionless chronicle of his travels and Indian fights, he also seems more like an "instrument" than a man. And yet behind the few and formulaic descriptions of feeling ("sorrows and sufferings vanish," "a long and fatiguing march"), readers can sense a person with vision and human concern, not just cold discipline. He is very fond of elegant, poetic diction for describing landscape, and this plays into his vision of Kentucky as a future site of great cities and fertile farms. He also respects his Indian enemies, even though sometimes calling them "barbarous savages." At moments such as his long captivity, he shows them coming to like and respect him. What keeps him from being more responsive and friendly, what makes him tricky and cautious, is his always underlying purpose "to settle the wilderness."

These complexities and tensions in Boone's character, which the "Adventures" are too short to work out and resolve, almost begged later novelists, playwrights, biographers, and mythologizers to study him, not just celebrate him.

1. Richard Slotkin, *Regeneration Through Violence: The Mythology of the American Frontier, 1600–1860* (Middletown, CT: Wesleyan Univ. Press, 1973), p. 268.

And they did, giving us as many later images of Boone as there are images of the frontier. He is heroic, but he is cold-blooded; he is folksy and illiterate, or he is educated and ambitious. He is tragic, jolly; sincere, ironic; handsome, scarred; young, old; sociable, solitary. A longer, more self-scrutinizing kind of autobiography might not have left so many questions open, so much room for the imagination to work and thus for myth-making. But one thing there is no doubt about is that by being published right at the end of the Revolution and the beginning of trans-Appalachian settlement, "The Adventures of Daniel Boon" made Boone the personification of American national expansion.

The modern edition of Filson's *Kentucke* is a facsimile edited, with notes, by W. R. Jillson (Louisville: Standard Printing Co., 1930). The most recent biography of Boone is by John Mack Faragher, *Daniel Boone: The Life and Legend of an American Pioneer* (New York: Holt, 1992).

Curiosity is natural to the soul of man, and interesting objects have a powerful influence on our affections. Let these influencing powers actuate, by the permission or disposal of Providence, from selfish or social views, yet in time the mysterious will of Heaven is unfolded, and we behold our conduct, from whatsoever motives excited, operating to answer the important designs of heaven. Thus we behold Kentucke, lately an howling wilderness, the habitation of savages and wild beasts, become a fruitful field; this region, so favourably distinguished by nature, now become the habitation of civilization, at a period unparalled in history, in the midst of a raging war, and under all the disadvantages of emigration to a country so remote from the inhabited parts of the continent. Here; where the hand of violence shed the blood of the innocent; where the horrid yells of savages, and the groans of the distressed, sounded in our ears, we now hear the praises and adorations of our Creator; where wretched wigwams stood, the miserable abodes of savages, we behold the foundations of cities laid, that, in all probability, will rival the glory of the greatest upon earth. And we view Kentucke situated on the fertile banks of the great Ohio, rising from obscurity to shine with splendor, equal to any other of the stars of the American hemisphere.

The settling of this region well deserves a place in history. Most of the memorable events I have myself been exercised in; and, for the satisfaction of the public, will briefly relate the circumstances of my adventures, and scenes of life, from my first movement to this country until this day.

It was on the first of May, in the year 1769, that I resigned my domestic happiness for a time, and left my family and peaceable habitation on the Yadkin River, in North-Carolina, to wander through the wilderness of America, in quest of the country of Kentucke, in company with John Finley, John Stewart, Joseph Holden, James Monay, and William Cool. We proceeded successfully, and after a long and fatiguing journey through a mountainous wilderness, in a westward direction, on the seventh day of June following, we found ourselves on Red-River, where John Finley had formerly been trading with the Indians, and, from the top of an eminence, saw with pleasure the beautiful level of Kentucke. Here let me observe, that for some time we had experienced the most uncomfortable weather as a prelibation of our future sufferings. At this place we encamped, and made a shelter to defend us from the inclement season, and began to hunt and reconnoitre the country. We found every where abundance of wild beasts of all sorts, through this vast forest. The buffaloes were more frequent than I have seen cattle in the settlements, browzing on the leaves of the cane, or croping the herbage on those extensive plains, fearless, because ignorant, of the violence of man. Sometimes we saw hundreds in a drove, and the numbers about the salt springs were amazing. In this forest, the habitation of beasts of every kind natural to America, we practiced hunting with great success until the twenty-second day of December following.

This day John Stewart and I had a pleasing ramble, but fortune changed the scene in the close of it. We had passed through a great forest, on which stood myriads of trees, some gay with blossoms, others rich with fruits. Nature was here a series of wonders, and a fund of delight. Here she displayed her ingenuity and industry in a variety of flowers and fruits, beautifully coloured, elegantly shaped, and charmingly flavoured; and we were diverted with innumerable animals presenting themselves perpetually to our view.— In the decline of the day, near Kentucke river, as we ascended the brow of a small hill, a number of Indians rushed out of a thick canebrake upon us, and made us prisoners. The time of our sorrow was now arrived, and the scene fully opened. The Indians plundered us of what we had, and kept us in confinement seven days, treating us with common savage usage. During this time we discovered no uneasiness or desire to escape, which made them less suspicious of us; but in the dead of night, as we lay in a thick cane brake by a large fire, when sleep had locked up their senses, my situation not disposing me for rest, I touched my companion and gently awoke him. We improved this favourable opportunity, and departed, leaving them to take their rest, and speedily directed our course towards our old camp, but found it plundered, and the company dispersed and gone home. About this time my brother, Squire Boon, with another adventurer, who came to explore the country shortly after us, was wandering through the forest, determined to find me, if possible, and accidentally found our camp. Notwithstanding the unfortunate circumstances of our company, and our dangerous situation, as surrounded with hostile savages, our meeting so fortunately in the wilderness made us reciprocally sensible of the utmost satisfaction. So much does friendship triumph over misfortune, that sorrows and sufferings vanish at the meeting not only of real friends, but of the most distant acquaintances, and substitutes happiness in their room.

Soon after this, my companion in captivity, John Stewart, was killed by the savages, and the man that came with my brother returned home by himself. We were then in a dangerous, helpless situation, exposed daily to perils and death amongst savages and wild beasts, not a white man in the country but ourselves.

Thus situated, many hundred miles from our families in the howling wilderness, I believe few would have equally enjoyed the happiness we experienced. I often observed to my brother, You see now how little nature requires to be satisfied. Felicity, the companion of content, is rather found in our own breasts than in the enjoyment of external things: And I firmly believe it requires but a little philosophy to make a man happy in whatsoever state he is. This consists in a full resignation to the will of Providence; and a resigned soul finds pleasure in a path strewed with briars and thorns.

We continued not in a state of indolence, but hunted every day, and prepared a little cottage to defend us from the Winter storms. We remained there undisturbed during the Winter; and on the first day of May, 1770, my brother returned home to the settlement by himself, for a new recruit of horses and ammunition, leaving me by myself, without bread, salt or sugar, without company of my fellow creatures, or even a horse or dog. I confess I never before was under greater necessity of exercising philosophy and fortitude. A few days I passed uncomfortably. The idea of a beloved wife and family, and their anxiety upon the account of my absence and exposed situation, made sensible impressions on my heart. A thousand dreadful apprehensions presented themselves to my view, and had undoubtedly disposed me to melancholy, if further indulged.

One day I undertook a tour through the country, and the diversity and beauties of nature I met with in this charming season, expelled every gloomy and vexatious thought. Just at the close of day the gentle gales retired, and left the place to the disposal of a profound calm. Not a breeze shook the most tremulous leaf. I had gained the summit of a commanding ridge, and, looking round with astonishing delight, beheld the ample plains, the beauteous tracts below. On the other hand, I surveyed the famous river Ohio that rolled in silent dignity, marking the western boundary of Kentucke with inconceivable grandeur. At a vast distance I beheld the mountains lift their venerable brows, and penetrate the clouds. All things were still. I kindled a fire near a fountain of sweet water, and feasted on the loin of a buck, which a few hours before I had killed. The sullen shades of night soon overspread the whole hemisphere, and the earth seemed to gasp after the hovering moisture. My roving excursion this day had fatigued my body, and diverted my imagination. I laid me down to sleep, and I awoke not until the sun had chased away the night. I continued this tour, and in a few days explored a considerable part of the country, each day equally pleased as the first. I returned again to my old camp, which was not disturbed in my absence. I did not confine my lodging to it, but often reposed in thick cane-brakes, to avoid the savages, who, I believe, often visited my camp, but fortunately for me, in my absence. In this situation I was constantly exposed to danger, and death. How unhappy such a situation for a man tormented with fear, which is vain if no danger comes, and if it does, only augments the pain. It was my happiness to be destitute of this afflicting passion, with which I had the greatest reason to be affected. The prowling wolves diverted my nocturnal hours with perpetual howlings; and the various species of animals in this vast forest, in the daytime, were continually in my view.

Thus I was surrounded with plenty in the midst of want. I was happy in the midst of dangers and inconveniences. In such a diversity it was impossible I should be disposed to melancholy. No populous city, with all the varieties of commerce and stately structures, could afford so much pleasure to my mind, as the beauties of nature I found here.

Thus, through an uninterrupted scene of sylvan pleasures, I spent the time until the 27th day of July following, when my brother, to my great felicity, met me, according to appointment, at our old camp. Shortly after, we left this place, not thinking it safe to stay there longer, and proceeded to Cumberland river, reconnoitring that part of the country until March, 1771, and giving names to the different waters.

Soon after, I returned home to my family with a determination to bring them as soon as possible to live in Kentucke, which I esteemed a second paradise, at the risk of my life and fortune.

I returned safe to my old habitation, and found my family in happy circumstances. I sold my farm on the Yadkin, and what goods we could not carry with us; and on the twenty-fifth day of September, 1773, bade a farewell to our friends, and proceeded on our journey to Kentucke, in company with five families more, and forty men that joined us in Powel's Valley, which is one hundred and fifty miles from the now settled parts of Kentucke. This promising beginning was soon overcast with a cloud of adversity; for up on the tenth day of October, the rear of our company was attacked by a number of Indians, who killed six, and wounded one man. Of these my eldest son was one that fell in the action. Though we defended ourselves, and repulsed the enemy, yet this unhappy affair scattered our cattle, brought us into extreme difficulty, and so discouraged the whole company, that we retreated forty miles, to the settlement on Clench river. We had passed over two mountains, viz. Powels and Walden's, and were approaching Cumberland mountain when this adverse fortune overtook us. These mountains are in the wilderness, as we pass from the old settlements in Virginia to Kentucke, are ranged in S. west and N. east direction, are of a great length and breadth, and not far distant from each other. Over these, nature hath formed passes, that are less difficult than might be expected from a view of such huge piles. The aspect of these cliffs is so wild and horrid, that it is impossible to behold them without terror. The spectator is apt to imagine that nature had formerly suffered some violent convulsion; and that these are the dismemembered remains of the dreadful shock; the ruins, not of Persepolis or Palmyra, but of the world!

I remained with my family on Clench until the sixth of June, 1774, when I and one Michael Stoner were solicited by Governor Dunmore, of Virginia, to go to the Falls of the Ohio, to conduct into the settlement a number of surveyors that had been sent thither by him some months before; this country having about this time drawn the attention of many adventurers. We immediately complied with the Governor's request, and conducted in the surveyors, compleating a tour of eight hundred miles, through many difficulties, in sixty-two days.

Soon after I returned home, I was ordered to take the command of three garrisons during the campaign, which Governor Dunmore carried on against the Shawanese Indians: After the conclusion of which, the Militia was discharged from each garrison, and I being relieved from my post, was solicited by a number of North-Carolina gentlemen, that were about purchasing the lands lying on the S. side of Kentucke River, from the Cherokee Indians, to attend their treaty at Wataga, in March, 1775, to negotiate with them, and, mention the boundaries of the purchase. This I accepted, and at the request of the same gentlemen, undertook to mark out a road in the best passage from the settlement through the wilderness to Kentucke, with such assistance as I thought necessary to employ for such an important undertaking.

I soon began this work, having collected a number of enterprising men, well armed. We proceeded with all possible expedition until we came within fifteen miles of where Boonsborough now stands, and where we were fired upon by a party of Indians that killed two, and wounded two of our number; yet, although surprised and taken at a disadvantage, we stood our ground. This was on the twentieth of March, 1775. Three days after, we were fired upon again, and had two men killed, and three wounded. Afterwards we proceeded on to Kentucke river without opposition; and on the first day of April began to erect the fort of Boonsborough at a salt lick, about sixty yards from the river, on the S. side.

On the fourth day, the Indians killed one of our men.—We were busily employed in building this fort, until the fourteenth day of June following, without any farther opposition from the Indians; and having finished the works, I returned to my family, on Clench.

In a short time, I proceeded to remove my family from Clench to this garrison; where we arrived safe without any other difficulties than such as are common to this passage, my wife and daughter being the first white women that ever stood on the banks of Kentucke river.

On the twenty-fourth day of December following we had one man killed, and one wounded, by the Indians, who seemed determined to persecute us for erecting this fortification.

On the fourteenth day of July, 1776, two of Col. Calaway's daughters, and one of mine, were taken prisoners near the fort. I immediately pursued the Indians, with only eight men, and on the sixteenth overtook them, killed two of the party, and recovered the girls. The same day on which this attempt was made, the Indians divided themselves into different parties, and attacked several forts, which were shortly before this time erected, doing a great deal of mischief. This was extremely distressing to the new settlers. The innocent husbandman was shot down, while busy cultivating the soil for his family's supply. Most of the cattle around the stations were destroyed. They continued their hostilities in this manner until the fifteenth of April, 1777, when they attacked Boonsborough with a party of above one hundred in number, killed one man, and wounded four—Their loss in this attack was not certainly known to us.

On the fourth day of July following, a party of about two hundred Indians attacked Boonsborough, killed one man, and wounded two. They besieged us forty-eight hours; during which time seven of them were killed, and at last, finding themselves not likely to prevail, they raised the siege, and departed.

The Indians had disposed their warriors in different parties at this time, and attacked the different garrisons to prevent their assisting each other, and did much injury to the distressed inhabitants.

On the nineteenth day of this month, Col. Logan's fort was besieged by a party of about two hundred Indians. During this dreadful siege they did a great deal of mischief, distressed the garrison, in which were only fifteen men, killed two, and wounded one. The enemies loss was uncertain, from the common practice which the Indians have of carrying off their dead in time of battle. Col. Harrod's fort was then defended by only sixty-five men, and Boonsborough by twenty-two, there being no more forts or white men in the country, except at the Falls, a considerable distance from these, and all taken collectively, were but a handful to the numerous warriors that were every where dispersed through the country, intent upon doing all the mischief that savage barbarity could invent. Thus we passed through a scene of sufferings that exceeds description.

On the twenty-fifth of this month a reinforcement of forty-five men arrived from North-Carolina, and about the twentieth of August following, Col. Bowman arrived with one hundred men from Virginia. Now we began to strengthen, and from hence, for the space of six weeks, we had skirmishes with Indians, in one quarter or other, almost every day.

The savages now learned the superiority of the Long Knife, as they call the Virginians, by experience; being out-generalled in almost every battle.

Our affairs began to wear a new aspect, and the enemy, not daring to venture on open war, practiced secret mischief at times.

On the first day of January, 1778, I went with a party of thirty men to the Blue Licks, on Licking River, to make salt for the different garrisons in the country.

On the seventh day of February, as I was hunting, to procure meat for the company, I met with a party of one hundred and two Indians, and two Frenchmen, on their march against Boonsborough, that place being particularly the object of the enemy.

They pursued, and took me; and brought me on the eighth day to the Licks, where twenty-seven of my party were, three of them having previously returned home with the salt. I knowing it was impossible for them to escape, capitulated with the enemy, and, at a distance in their view, gave notice to my men of their situation, with orders not to resist, but surrender themselves captives.

The generous usage the Indians had promised before in my capitulation, was afterwards fully complied with, and we proceeded with them as prisoners to old Chelicothe, the principal Indian town, on Little Miami, where we arrived, after an uncomfortable journey, in very severe weather, on the eighteenth day of February, and received as good treatment as prisoners could expect from savages—On the tenth day of March following, I, and ten of my men, were conducted by forty Indians to Detroit, where we arrived the thirtieth day, and were treated by Governor Hamilton, the British commander at that post, with great humanity.

During our travels, the Indians entertained me well; and their affection for me was so great, that they utterly refused to leave me there with the others, although the Governor offered them one hundred pounds Sterling for me, on purpose to give me a parole to go home. Several English gentlemen there, being sensible of my adverse fortune, and touched with human sympathy, generously offered a friendly supply for my wants, which I refused, with many thanks for their kindness; adding, that I never expected it would be in my power to recompense such unmerited generosity.

The Indians left my men in captivity with the British at Detroit, and on the tenth day of April brought me towards Old Chelicothe, where we arrived on the twenty-fifth day of the same month. This was a long and fatiguing march, through an exceeding fertile country, remarkable for fine springs and streams of water. At Chelicothe I spent my time as comfortably as I could expect; was adopted, according to their custom, into a family where I became a son, and had a great share in the affection of my new parents, brothers, sisters, and friends. I was exceedingly familiar and friendly with them, always appearing as chearful and satisfied as possible, and they put great confidence in me. I often went a hunting with them, and frequently gained their applause for my activity at our shooting-matches. I was careful not to exceed many of them in shooting; for no people are more envious than they in this sport. I could observe, in their countenances and gestures, the greatest expressions of joy when they exceeded me; and, when the reverse happened, of envy. The Shawanese king took great notice of me, and treated me with profound respect, and entire friendship, often entrusting me to hunt at my liberty. I frequently returned with the spoils of the woods, and as often presented some of what I had taken to him, expressive of duty to my sovereign. My food and lodging was, in common, with them, not so good indeed as I could desire, but necessity made every thing acceptable.

I now began to meditate an escape, and carefully avoided their suspicions, continuing with them at Old Chelicothe until the first day of June following, and then was taken by them to the salt springs on Sciotha, and kept there, making salt, ten days. During this time I hunted some for them, and found the land, for a great extent about this river, to exceed the soil of Kentucke, if possible, and remarkably well watered.

When I returned to Chelicothe, alarmed to see four hundred and fifty Indians, of their choicest warriors, painted and armed in a fearful manner, ready to march against Boonsborough, I determined to escape the first opportunity.

On the sixteenth, before sun-rise, I departed in the most secret manner, and arrived at Boonsborough on the twentieth, after a journey of one hundred and sixty miles; during which, I had but one meal.

I found our fortress in a bad state of defence, but we proceeded immediately to repair our flanks, strengthen our gates and posterns, and form double bastions, which we compleated in ten days. In this time we daily expected the arrival of the Indian army; and at length, one of my fellow prisoners, escaping from them, arrived, informing us that the enemy had an account of my departure, and postponed their expedition three weeks.—The Indians had spies out viewing our movements, and were greatly alarmed with our increase in number and fortifications. The Grand Councils of the nations were held frequently, and with more deliberation than usual. They evidently saw the approaching hour when the Long Knife would dispossess them of their desirable habitations; and anxiously concerned for futurity, determined utterly to extirpate the whites out of Kentucke. We were not intimidated by their movements, but frequently gave them proofs of our courage.

About the first of August, I made an incursion into the Indian country, with a party of nineteen men, in order to surprise a small town up Sciotha, called Paint-Creek-Town. We advanced within four miles thereof, where we met a party of thirty Indians, on their march against Boonsborough, intending to join the others from Chelicothe. A smart fight ensued betwixt us for some time: At length the savages gave way, and fled. We had no loss on our side: The enemy had one killed, and two wounded. We took from them three horses, and all their baggage; and being informed, by two of our number that went to their town, that the Indians had entirely evacuated it, we proceeded no further, and returned with all possible expedition to assist our garrison against the other party. We passed by them on the sixth day, and on the seventh, we arrived safe at Boonsborough.

On the eighth, the Indian army arrived, being four hundred and forty-four in number, commanded by Capt. Duquesne, eleven other Frenchmen, and some of their own chiefs, and marched up within view of our fort, with British and French colours flying; and having sent a summons to me, in his Britannick Majesty's name, to surrender the fort, I requested two days consideration, which was granted.

It was now a critical period with us.—We were a small number in the garrison:—A powerful army before our walls, whose appearance proclaimed inevitable death, fearfully painted, and marking their footsteps with desolation. Death was preferable to captivity; and if taken by storm, we must inevitably be devoted to destruction. In this situation we concluded to maintain our garrison, if possible. We immediately proceeded to collect what we could of our horses, and other cattle, and bring them through the posterns into the fort: And in the evening of the ninth, I returned answer, that we were determined to defend our fort while a man was living—Now, said I to their commander, who stood attentively hearing my sentiments, We laugh at all your formidable preparations: But thank you for giving us notice and time to provide for our defence. Your efforts will not prevail; for our gates shall for ever deny you admittance.—Whether this answer affected their courage, or not, I cannot tell; but, contrary to our expectations, they formed a scheme to deceive us, declaring it was their orders, from Governor Hamilton, to take us captives, and not to destroy us; but if nine of us would come out, and treat with them, they would immediately withdraw their forces from our walls and return home peaceably. This sounded grateful in our ears; and we agreed to the proposal.

We held the treaty within sixty yards of the garrison, on purpose to divert them from a breach of honour, as we could not avoid suspicions of the savages. In this situation the articles were formally agreed to, and signed; and the Indians told us it was customary with them, on such occasions, for two Indians to shake hands with every white-man in the treaty, as an evidence of entire friendship. We agreed to this also, but were soon convinced their policy was to take us prisoners.—They immediately grappled us; but, although surrounded by hundreds of savages, we extricated ourselves from them, and escaped all safe into the garrison, except one that was wounded, through a heavy fire from their army. They immediately attacked us on every side, and a constant heavy fire ensued between us day and night for the space of nine days.

In this time the enemy began to undermine our fort, which was situated sixty yards from Kentucke river. They began at the water-mark, and proceeded in the bank some distance, which we understood by their making the water muddy with the clay; and we immediately proceeded to disappoint their design, by cutting a trench a-cross their subterranean passage. The enemy discovering our counter-mine, by the clay we threw out of the fort, desisted from that stratagem: And experience now fully convincing them that neither their power nor policy could effect their purpose, on the twentieth day of August they raised the siege, and departed.

During this dreadful siege, which threatened death in every form, we had two men killed, and four wounded, besides a number of cattle. We killed of the enemy thirty-seven, and wounded a great number. After they were gone, we picked up one hundred and twenty-five pounds weight of bullets, besides what stuck in the logs of our fort; which certainly is a great proof of their industry. Soon after this, I went into the settlement, and nothing worthy of a place in this account passed in my affairs for some time.

During my absence from Kentucke, Col. Bowman carried on an expedition against the Shawanese, at Old Chelicothe, with one hundred and sixty men, in July, 1779. Here they arrived undiscovered, and a battle ensued, which lasted until ten o'clock, A.M. when Col. Bowman, finding he could not succeed at this time, retreated about thirty miles. The Indians, in the mean time, collecting all their forces, pursued and overtook him, when a smart fight continued near two hours, not to the advantage of Col. Bowman's party.

Col. Harrod proposed to mount a number of horse, and furiously to rush upon the savages, who at this time fought with remarkable fury. This desperate step had a happy effect, broke their line of battle, and the savages fled on all sides. In these two battles we had nine killed, and one wounded. The enemy's loss uncertain, only two scalps being taken.

On the twenty-second day of June, 1780, a large party of Indians and Canadians, about six hundred in number, commanded by Col. Bird, attacked Riddle's and Martin's stations, at the Forks of Licking River, with six pieces of artillery. They carried this expedition so secretly, that the unwary inhabitants did not discover them, until they fired upon the forts; and, not being prepared to oppose them, were obliged to surrender themselves miserable captives to barbarous savages, who immediately after tomahawked one man and two women, and loaded all the others with heavy baggage, forcing them along toward their towns, able or unable to march. Such as were weak and faint by the way, they tomahawked. The tender women, and helpless children, fell victims to their cruelty. This, and the savage treatment they received afterwards, is shocking to humanity, and too barbarous to relate.

The hostile disposition of the savages, and their allies, caused General Clark, the commandant at the Falls at the Ohio, immediately to begin an expedition with his own regiment, and the armed force of the country, against

Pecaway, the principal town of the Shawanese, on a branch of Great Miami, which he finished with great success, took seventeen scalps, and burnt the town to ashes, with the loss of seventeen men.

About this time I returned to Kentucke with my family; and here, to avoid an enquiry into my conduct, the reader being before informed of my bringing my family to Kentucke, I am under the necessity of informing him that, during my captivity with the Indians, my wife, who despaired of ever seeing me again, expecting the Indians had put a period to my life, oppressed with the distresses of the country, and bereaved of me, her only happiness, had, before I returned, transported my family and goods, on horses, through the wilderness, amidst a multitude of dangers, to her father's house, in North-Carolina.

Shortly after the troubles at Boonsborough, I went to them, and lived peaceably there until this time. The history of my going home, and returning with my family, forms a series of difficulties, an account of which would swell a volume, and being foreign to my purpose, I shall purposely omit them.

I settled my family in Boonsborough once more; and shortly after, on the sixth day of October, 1780, I went in company with my brother to the Blue Licks; and, on our return home, we were fired upon by a party of Indians. They shot him, and pursued me, by the scent of their dog, three miles; but I killed the dog, and escaped. The Winter soon came on, and was very severe, which confined the Indians to their wigwams.

The severity of this Winter caused great difficulties in Kentucke. The enemy had destroyed most of the corn, the Summer before. This necessary article was scarce, and dear; and the inhabitants lived chiefly on the flesh of buffaloes. The circumstances of many were very lamentable: However, being a hardy race of people, and accustomed to difficulties and necessities, they were wonderfully supported through all their sufferings, until the ensuing Fall, when we received abundance from the fertile soil.

Towards Spring, we were frequently harassed by Indians; and, in May, 1782, a party assaulted Ashton's station, killed one man, and took a Negro prisoner. Capt. Ashton, with twenty-five men, pursued, and overtook the savages, and a smart fight ensued, which lasted two hours; but they being superior in number, obliged Captain Ashton's party to retreat, with the loss of eight killed, and four mortally wounded; their brave commander himself being numbered among the dead.

The Indians continued their hostilities; and, about the tenth of August following, two boys were taken from Major Hoy's station. This party was pursued by Capt. Holder and seventeen men, who were also defeated, with the loss of four men killed, and one wounded. Our affairs became more and more alarming. Several stations which had lately been erected in the country were continually infested with savages, stealing their horses and killing the men at every opportunity. In a field, near Lexington, an Indian shot a man, and running to scalp him, was himself shot from the fort, and fell dead upon his enemy.

Every day we experienced recent mischiefs. The barbarous savage nations of Shawanese, Cherokees, Wyandots, Tawas, Delawares, and several others near Detroit, united in a war against us and assembled their choicest warriors at old Chelicothe, to go on the expedition, in order to destroy us, and entirely depopulate the country. Their savage minds were inflamed to mischief by two abandoned men, Captains McKee and Girty. These led them to execute every diabolical scheme; and, on the fifteenth day of August, commanded a party of Indians and Canadians, of about five hundred in number, against Briant's station, five miles from Lexington. Without demanding a surrender, they furiously assaulted the garrison, which was happily prepared to oppose them; and, after they had expended much ammunition in vain, and killed the cattle round the fort, not being likely to make themselves masters of this place, they raised the siege, and departed in the morning of the third day after they came, with the loss of about thirty killed, and the number of wounded uncertain.—Of the garrison four were killed, and three wounded.

On the eighteenth day Col. Todd, Col. Trigg, Major Harland, and myself, speedily collected one hundred and seventy-six men, well armed, and pursued the savages. They had marched beyond the Blue Licks to a remarkable bend of the main fork of Licking River, about forty-three miles from Lexington, as it is particularly represented in the map, where we overtook them on the nineteenth day. The savages observing us, gave way; and we, being ignorant of their numbers, passed the river. When the enemy saw our proceedings, having greatly the advantage of us in [our] situation, they formed the line of battle, as represented in the map, from one bend of Licking to the other, about a mile from the Blue Licks. An exceeding fierce battle immediately began, for about fifteen minutes, when we, being over-powered by numbers, were obliged to retreat, with the loss of sixty seven men; seven of whom were taken prisoners. The brave and much lamented Colonels Todd and Trigg, Major Harland and my second son, were among the dead. We were informed that the Indians, numbering their dead, found they had four killed more than we; and therefore, four of the prisoners they had taken, were, by general consent, ordered to be killed, in a most barbarous manner, by the young warriors, in order to train them up to cruelty; and then they proceeded to their towns.

On our retreat we were met by Col. Logan, hastening to join us, with a number of well armed men. This powerful assistance we unfortunately wanted in the battle; for, notwithstanding the enemy's superiority of numbers, they acknowledged that, if they had received one more fire from us, they should undoubtedly have given way. So valiantly did our small party fight, that, to the memory of those who unfortunately fell in the battle, enough of honour cannot be said. Had Col. Logan and his party been with us, it is highly probable we should have given the savages a total defeat.

I cannot reflect upon this dreadful scene, but sorrow fills my heart. A zeal for the defence of their country led these heroes to the scene of action, though with a few men to attack a powerful army of experienced warriors. When we gave way, they pursued us with the utmost eagerness, and in every quarter spread destruction. The river was difficult to cross, and many were killed in the flight, some just entering the river, some in the water, others after crossing in ascending the cliffs. Some escaped on horse-back, a few on foot; and, being dispersed every where, in a few hours, brought the melancholy news of this unfortunate battle to Lexington. Many widows were now made. The reader may guess what sorrow filled the hearts of the inhabitants, exceeding any thing that I am able to describe. Being reinforced, we returned to bury the dead, and found their bodies strewed every where, cut and mangled in a dreadful manner. This mournful scene exhibited a horror almost unparalleled: Some torn and eaten by wild beasts; those in the river eaten by fishes; all in such a putrified condition, that no one could be distinguished from another.

As soon as General Clark, then at the Falls of the Ohio, who was ever our ready friend, and merits the love and gratitude of all his country-men, understood the circumstances of this unfortunate action, he ordered an expedition, with all possible haste, to pursue the savages, which was so expeditiously effected, that we overtook them within two miles of their towns, and probably might have obtained a great victory, had not two of their number met us about two hundred poles before we come up. These returned quick as lightening to their camp with the alarming news of a mighty army in view. The savages fled in the utmost disorder, evacuated their towns, and reluctantly left their territory to our mercy. We immediately took possession of Old Chelicothe without opposition, being deserted by its inhabitants. We continued our pursuit through five towns on the Miami rivers, Old Chelicothe, Pecaway, New Chelicothe, Will's Towns, and Chelicothe, burnt them all to ashes, entirely destroyed their corn, and other fruits, and every where spread a scene of desolation in the country. In this expedition we took seven prisoners and five scalps, with the loss of only four men, two of whom were accidentally killed by our own army.

This campaign in some measure damped the spirits of the Indians, and made them sensible of our superiority. Their connections were dissolved, their armies scattered, and a future invasion put entirely out of their power; yet they continued to practice mischief secretly upon the inhabitants, in the exposed parts of the country.

In October following, a party made an excursion into that district called the Crab Orchard, and one of them, being advanced some distance before the others, boldly entered the house of a poor defenceless family, in which was only a Negro man, a woman and her children, terrified with the apprehensions of immediate death. The savage, perceiving their defenceless situation, without offering violence to the family attempted to captivate the Negro, who, happily proved an over-match for him, threw him on the ground, and, in the struggle, the mother of the children drew an ax from a corner of the cottage, and cut his head off, while her little daughter shut the door. The savages instantly appeared, and applied their tomahawks to the door. An old rusty gun-barrel, without a lock, lay in a corner, which the mother put through a small crevice, and the savages, perceiving it, fled. In the mean time, the alarm spread through the neighbourhood; the armed men collected immediately, and pursued the savages into the wilderness. Thus Providence, by the means of this Negro, saved the whole of the poor family from destruction. From that time, until the happy return of peace between the United States and Great-Britain, the Indians did us no mischief. Finding the great king beyond the water disappointed in his expectations, and conscious of the importance of the Long Knife, and their own wretchedness, some of the nations immediately desired peace; to which, at present, they seem universally disposed, and are sending ambassadors to General Clark, at the Falls of the Ohio, with the minutes of their Councils; a specimen of which, in the minutes of the Piankashaw Council, is subjoined.

To conclude, I can now say that I have verified the saying of an old Indian who signed Col. Henderson's deed. Taking me by the hand, at the delivery thereof, Brother, says he, we have given you a fine land, but I believe you will have much trouble in settling it.—My footsteps have often been marked with blood, and therefore I can truly subscribe to its original name. Two darling sons, and a brother, have I lost by savage hands, which have also taken from me forty valuable horses, and abundance of cattle. Many dark and sleepless nights have I been a companion for owls, separated from the chearful society of men, scorched by the Summer's sun, and pinched by the Winter's cold, an instrument ordained to settle the wilderness. But now the scene is changed: Peace crowns the sylvan shade.

What thanks, what ardent and ceaseless thanks are due to that all-superintending Providence which has turned a cruel war into peace, brought order out of confusion, made the fierce savages placid, and turned away their hostile weapons from our country! May the same Almighty Goodness banish the accursed monster, war, from all lands, with her hated associates, rapine and insatiable ambition. Let peace, descending from her native heaven, bid her olives spring amidst the joyful nations; and plenty, in league with commerce, scatter blessings from her copious hand.

This account of my adventures will inform the reader of the most remarkable events of this country.—I now live in peace and safety, enjoying the sweets of liberty, and the bounties of Providence, with my once fellow-sufferers, in this delightful country, which I have seen purchased with a vast expence of blood and treasure, delighting in the prospect of its being, in a short time, one of the most opulent and powerful states on the continent of North-America; which, with the love and gratitude of my country-men, I esteem a sufficient reward for all my toil and dangers.

DANIEL BOON
Fayette county, Kentucke.

13

Sarah Osborn (c. 1756–1854) and
Nathan B. Jennings (1754–1841)
Narratives of the Revolution

In 1832, Congress authorized pensions to all veterans of the Revolutionary War. Since this included people such as militia men and crewmen on privateers, for whom there were no official records, all applicants were asked to provide detailed information about "the time and place of service, the names of units and officers, and engagements in which [they] had participated," and to present this testimony in court, with at least two character witnesses.[1]

What this led to, as John C. Dann has explained, was the appearance, in towns and courthouses all over the United States, of several thousand veterans, by then in their late sixties and older, to tell their stories to clerks and court reporters, sometimes in open court with friends, family, and other townspeople listening. Whether or not Congress had foreseen this, these pension applications thus became, in Dann's words, "one of the largest oral history projects ever undertaken."[2] But unlike more general oral history projects, this one privileged just a certain set of speakers and subject matters. The Revolutionary veteran and his story became a sort of sanctified national treasure.

The further result was that the government officially preserved the stories of all kinds of men (and, in one case) women. These were not just officers or decorated heroes. They were also privates, noncommissioned officers, sailors, and "coast guards," and this led, inevitably, to a kind of democratizing of autobiographies.

The ones that follow, chosen from the seventy-nine stories which John C. Dann selected from National Archives microfilms, are by Nathan B. Jennings and Sarah Osborn. Such a pair, obviously, cannot be typical. Osborn's narrative, Dann says, "is the first known account by a female who traveled with the army,"[3] and Jennings appears to have been exceptionally ingenious and successful. But

---

The narratives of Sarah Osborn and Nathan B. Jennings are reprinted from *The Revolution Remembered: Eyewitness Accounts of the War for Independence*, ed. John C. Dann, copyright 1980 the University of Chicago. Reprinted by permission of the University of Chicago Press.

1. Dann, *Revolution*, p. xvii.
2. Dann, *Revolution*, xvii.
3. Dann, *Revolution*, xviii.

the reader should focus not just on the action but on the concepts of self that are discovered in it. In the beginning, Jennings repeatedly identifies himself with Sag Harbor, the place on eastern Long Island near which he was born, from which he embarked to New York, and to which he returned in his daring raid in 1777. But as a result of the raid, he does not dare go back and even changes his name: his Revolutionary success has in effect rebaptized him.

Sarah Osborn identifies herself by telling how she met her husband, by how well she knew Captain Gregg, including having seen "the bare spot on his head where he had been scalped," and by her memories of General Washington and the surrender at Yorktown. But she also recalls her children and calmly recounts her discovery of her husband's bigamy. Other people and events before and after the war seem to loom larger to her than to Jennings. Yet for both the war is *the* event, designated as much after the fact as at the time, which shaped their identity.

The texts, including all bracketed editorial material, are from John C. Dann, ed., *The Revolution Remembered: Eyewitness Accounts of the War for Independence* (Chicago: Univ. of Chicago Press, 1980). For additional background, see Dann's introduction.

Sarah Osborn

On this twentieth day of November, A.D. 1837, personally appeared before the Court of Common Pleas of said county of Wayne, Sarah Benjamin, a resident of Pleasant Mount in said county of Wayne and state of Pennsylvania, aged eighty-one years on the seventeenth day of the present month, who being first duly sworn according to law, doth on her oath make the following declaration in order to obtain the benefit of the provision made by the act of Congress passed July 4, 1836, and the act explanatory of said act, passed March 3, 1837.

That she was married to Aaron Osborn, who was a soldier during the Revolutionary War. That her first acquaintance with said Osborn commenced in Albany, in the state of New York, during the hard winter of 1780. That deponent then resided at the house of one John Willis, a blacksmith in said city. That said Osborn came down there from Fort Stanwix and went to work at the business of blacksmithing for said Willis and continued working at intervals for a period of perhaps two months. Said Osborn then informed deponent that he had first enlisted at Goshen in Orange County, New York. That he had been in the service for three years, deponent thinks, about one year of that time at Fort Stanwix, and that his time was out. And, under an assurance that he would go to Goshen with her, she married him at the house of said Willis during the time he was there as above mentioned, to wit, in January 1780. That deponent was informed by said Osborn that while he was at Fort Stanwix he served under Capt. James Gregg and Colonel Van Schaick, the former of whom she was informed by said Osborn was scalped by the Indians near Fort Stanwix while he was on an excursion pigeon hunting, which in the sequel proved to be true, as she will show hereafter.

That after deponent had married said Osborn, he informed her that he was returned during the war, and that he desired deponent to go with him. Deponent declined until she was informed by Captain Gregg that her husband should be put on the commissary guard, and that she should have the means of conveyance either in a wagon or on horseback. That deponent then in the same winter season in sleighs accompanied her husband and the forces under command of Captain Gregg on the east side of the Hudson river to Fishkill, then crossed the river and went down to West Point. There remained till the river opened in the spring, when they returned to Albany. Captain Gregg's company was along, and she thinks Captain Parsons, Lieutenant Forman, and Colonel Van Schaick, but is not positive.

Deponent, accompanied by her said husband and the same forces, returned during the same season to West Point. Deponent recollects no other females in company but the wife of Lieutenant Forman and of Sergeant Lamberson. Deponent was well acquainted with Captain Gregg and repeatedly saw the bare spot on his head where he had been scalped by the Indians. Captain Gregg had turns of being shattered in his mind and at such times would frequently say to deponent, "Sarah, did you ever see where I was scalped?" showing his head at the same time. Captain Gregg informed deponent also of the circumstances of his being scalped: that he and two more went out pigeon hunting and were surprised by the Indians, and that the two men that were with him were killed dead, but that he escaped by reason of the tomahawk glancing on the button of his hat; that when he came to his senses, he crept along and laid his [head near] one of the dead men, and while there, his dog came to his relief, and by means of his dog, [caught the attention of] the two fishermen who were fishing near the fort.

Deponent further says that she and her husband remained at West Point till the departure of the army for the South, a term of perhaps one year and a half, but she cannot be positive as to the length of time. While at West Point, deponent lived at Lieutenant Foot's, who kept a boardinghouse. Deponent was employed in washing and sewing for the soldiers. Her said husband was employed about the camp. She well recollects the uproar occasioned when word came that a British officer had been taken as a spy. She understood at the time that Major André was brought up on the opposite side of the river and kept there till he was executed. On the return of the bargemen who assisted Arnold to escape, deponent recollects seeing two of them, one by the name of Montecu, the other by the name of Clark. That they said Arnold told them to hang up their dinners, for he had to be at Stony Point in so many minutes, and when he got there he hoisted his pocket handkerchief and his sword and said, "Row on boys," and that they soon arrived in Haverstraw

Bay and found the British ship. That Arnold jumped on board, and they were all invited, and they went aboard and had their choice to go or stay. And some chose to stay and some to go and did accordingly.

When the army were about to leave West Point and go south, they crossed over the river to Robinson's Farms and remained there for a length of time to induce the belief, as deponent understood, that they were going to take up quarters there, whereas they recrossed the river in the nighttime into the Jerseys and traveled all night in a direct course for Philadelphia. Deponent was part of the time on horseback and part of the time in a wagon. Deponent's said husband was still serving as one of the commissary's guard. A man by the name of Burke was hung about this time for alleged treason, but more especially for insulting Adjutant Wendell, the prosecutor against Burke, as deponent understood and believed at the time. There was so' much opposition to the execution of Burke that it was deferred some time, and he was finally executed in a different place from what was originally intended.

In their march for Philadelphia, they were under command of Generals Washington and Clinton, Colonel Van Schaick, Captain Gregg, Captain Parsons, Lieutenant Forman, Sergeant Lamberson, Ensign Clinton, one of the general's sons. They continued their march to Philadelphia, deponent on horseback through the streets, and arrived at a place towards the Schuylkill where the British had burnt some houses, where they encamped for the afternoon and night. Being out of bread, deponent was employed in baking the afternoon and evening. Deponent recollects no females but Sergeant Lamberson's and Lieutenant Forman's wives and a colored woman by the name of Letta. The Quaker ladies who came round urged deponent to stay, but her said husband said, "No, he could not leave her behind." Accordingly, next day they continued their march from day to day till they arrived at Baltimore, where deponent and her said husband and the forces under command of General Clinton, Captain Gregg, and several other officers, all of whom she does not recollect, embarked on board a vessel and sailed down the Chesapeake. There were several vessels along, and deponent was in the foremost. General Washington was not in the vessel with deponent, and she does not know where he was till he arrived at Yorktown, where she again saw him. He might have embarked at another place, but deponent is confident she embarked at Baltimore and that General Clinton was in the same vessel with her. Some of the troops went down by land. They continued sail until they had got up the St. James River as far as the tide would carry them, about twelve miles from the mouth, and then landed, and the tide being spent, they had a fine time catching sea lobsters, which they ate.

They, however, marched immediately for a place called Williamsburg, as she thinks, deponent alternately on horseback and on foot. There arrived, they remained two days till the army all came in by land and then marched for Yorktown, or Little York as it was then called. The York troops were posted at the right, the Connecticut troops next, and the French to the left. In about one day or less than a day, they reached the place of encampment about one mile from Yorktown. Deponent was on foot and the other females above named and her said husband still on the commissary's guard. Deponent's attention was arrested by the appearance of a large plain between them and Yorktown and an entrenchment thrown up. She also saw a number of dead Negroes lying round their encampment, whom she understood the British had driven out of the town and left to starve, or were first starved and then thrown out. Deponent took her stand just back of the American tents, say about a mile from the town, and busied herself washing, mending, and cooking for the soldiers, in which she was assisted by the other females; some men washed their own clothing. She heard the roar of the artillery for a number of days, and the last night the Americans threw up entrenchments, it was a misty, foggy night, rather wet but not rainy. Every soldier threw up for himself, as she understood, and she afterwards saw and went into the entrenchments. Deponent's said husband was there throwing up entrenchments, and deponent cooked and carried in beef, and bread, and coffee (in a gallon pot) to the soldiers in the entrenchment.

On one occasion when deponent was thus employed carrying in provisions, she met General Washington, who asked her if she "was not afraid of the cannonballs?"

She replied, "No, the bullets would not cheat the gallows," that "It would not do for the men to fight and starve too."

They dug entrenchments nearer and nearer to Yorktown every night or two till the last. While digging that, the enemy fired very heavy till about nine o'clock next morning, then stopped, and the drums from the enemy beat excessively. Deponent was a little way off in Colonel Van Schaick's or the officers' marquee and a number of officers were present, among whom was Captain Gregg, who, on account of infirmities, did not go out much to do duty.

The drums continued beating, and all at once the officers hurrahed and swung their hats, and deponent asked them, "What is the matter now?"

One of them replied, "Are not you soldier enough to know what it means?"

Deponent replied, "No."

They then replied, "The British have surrendered."

Deponent, having provisions ready, carried the same down to the entrenchments that morning, and four of the soldiers whom she was in the habit of cooking for ate their breakfasts.

Deponent stood on one side of the road and the American officers upon the other side when the British officers came out of the town and rode up to the American officers and delivered up [their swords, which the deponent] thinks were returned again, and the British officers rode right on before the army, who marched out beating and playing a melancholy tune, their drums covered with black handkerchiefs and their fifes with black ribbands tied around them, into an old field and there grounded their arms and then returned into town again to await their destiny. Deponent recollects seeing a great many American officers, some on horseback and some on foot, but cannot call them all by name. Washington, Lafayette, and Clinton were among the number. The British general at the head of the army was a large, portly man, full face, and the tears rolled down his cheeks as he passed along. She does not recollect his name, but it was not Cornwallis. She saw the latter afterwards and noticed his being a man of diminutive appearance and having cross eyes.

On going into town, she noticed two dead Negroes lying by the market house. She had the curiosity to go into a large building that stood nearby, and there she noticed the cupboards smashed to pieces and china dishes and other ware strewed around upon the floor, and among the rest a pewter cover to a hot basin that had a handle on it. She picked it up, supposing it to belong to the British, but the governor came in and claimed it as his, but said he would have the name of giving it away as it was the last one out of twelve that he could see, and accordingly presented it to deponent, and she afterwards brought it home with her to Orange County and sold it for old pewter, which she has a hundred times regretted.

After two or three days, deponent and her husband, Captain Gregg, and others who were sick or complaining embarked on board a vessel from Yorktown, not the same they came down in, and set sail up the Chesapeake Bay and continued to the Head of Elk, where they landed. The main body of the army remained behind but came on soon afterwards. Deponent and her husband proceeded with the commissary's teams from the Head of Elk, leaving Philadelphia to the right, and continued day after day till they arrived at Pompton Plains in New Jersey. Deponent does not recollect the county. They were joined by the main body of the army under General Clinton's command, and they set down for winter quarters. Deponent and her husband lived a part of the time in a tent made of logs but covered with cloth, and a part of the time at a Mr. Manuel's near Pompton Meetinghouse. She busied herself during the winter in cooking and sewing as usual. Her said husband was on duty among the rest of the army and held the station of corporal from the time he left West Point.

In the opening of spring, they marched to West Point and remained there during the summer, her husband still with her. In the fall they came up a little back of Newburgh to a place called New Windsor and put up huts on Ellis's lands and again sat down for winter quarters, her said husband still along and on duty. The York troops and Connecticut troops were there. In the following spring or autumn they were all discharged. Deponent and her husband remained in New Windsor in a log house built by the army until the spring following. Some of the soldiers boarded at their house and worked round among the farmers, as did her said husband also. Deponent and her husband spent certainly more than three years in the service, for she recollects a part of one winter at West Point and the whole of another winter there, another winter at Pompton Plains, and another at New Windsor. And her husband was the whole time under the command of Captain Gregg as an enlisted soldier holding the station of corporal to the best of her knowledge.

In the winter before the army were disbanded at New Windsor, on the twentieth of February, deponent had a child by the name of Phebe Osborn, of whom the said Aaron Osborn was the father. A year and five months afterwards, on the ninth day of August at the same place, she had another child by the name of Aaron Osborn, Jr., of whom the said husband was the father. The said Phebe Osborn afterwards married a man by the name of William Rockwell and moved into the town of Dryden, Tompkins County, New York, where he died, say ten or twelve years ago, but her said daughter yet lives near the same place on the west side of Ithaca, in the town of Enfield. Her son Aaron Osborn, Jr., lived in Blooming Grove, Orange County, New York, had fits and was crazy, and became a town charge, and finally died there at the age of about thirty years.

About three months after the birth of her last child, Aaron Osborn, Jr., she last saw her said husband, who then left her at New Windsor and never returned. He had been absent at intervals before this from deponent, and at one time deponent understood he was married again to a girl by the name of Polly Sloat above Newburgh about fifteen or sixteen miles. Deponent got a horse and rode up to inquire into the truth of the story. She arrived at the girl's father's and there found her said husband, and Polly Sloat, and her parents. Deponent was kindly treated by the inmates of the house but ascertained for a truth that her husband was married to said girl. After remaining overnight, deponent determined to return home and abandon her said husband forever, as she found he had conducted in such a way as to leave no hope of reclaiming him. About two weeks afterwards, her said husband came to see deponent in New Windsor and offered to take deponent and her children to the northward, but deponent declined going, under a firm belief that he would conduct no better, and her said husband the same night absconded with two others, crossed the river at Newburgh, and she never saw him afterwards. This was about a year and a half after his discharge. Deponent heard of him afterwards up the Mohawk River and that he had married again. Deponent, after hearing of this second unlawful marriage of her said husband, married herself to John Benjamin of Blooming Grove, Orange County, New York, whose name she now bears.

About twenty years ago, deponent heard that her said husband Osborn died up the Mohawk, and she has no reason to believe to the contrary to this day. Deponent often saw the discharge of her said husband Osborn and understood that he drew a bounty in lands in the lake country beyond Ithaca, but her husband informed her that he sold his discharge and land together in Newburgh to a merchant residing there whose name she cannot recollect. Her son-in-law, said Rockwell, on hearing of the death of Osborn, went out to see the land and returned saying that it was a very handsome lot. But said Rockwell being now dead, she can give no further information concerning it. Deponent was informed more than forty years ago and believes that said Polly Sloat, Osborn's second wife above mentioned, died dead drunk, the liquor running out of her mouth after she was dead. Osborn's third wife she knows nothing about.

After deponent was thus left by Osborn, she removed from New Windsor to Blooming Grove, Orange County, New York, about fifty years ago, where she had been born and brought up, and, having married Mr. Benjamin as above stated, she continued to reside there perhaps thirty-five years, when she and her husband Benjamin removed to Pleasant Mount, Wayne County, Pennsylvania, and there she has resided to this day. Her said husband, John Benjamin, died there ten years ago last April, from which time she has continued to be and is now a widow.

Nathan B. Jennings

I, Nathan B. Jennings, was born in the township of Southampton, near Sag Harbor, on the east end of Long Island, in June, the sixteenth day in the year of our Lord 1754, and in the year 1775, in the month of April, I was drafted in the militia in Captain Holabord's company, in Colonel Dayton's regiment for the term of six months; then was ordered to march to Montauk Point on the very end of Long Island to prevent the British from taking off cattle and sheep, as part of their fleet then lay in Gardiner's Bay, within three-quarters of a mile of Long Island shore. Within about five weeks after we encamped there, we received orders to embark from Sag Harbor to New York and from New York to Albany. Then we was ordered to join General McDougall's brigade to prepare for a march to St. Johns. The very day that we received orders to march, the express came to our commander that the fort was taken. Then our troops was ordered back to New York and there continued until my six months was up; received my discharge, then returned back to my parents on Long Island; there continued till sometime in March 1776. My father and family all fled before the British and left a large stock of horses, cattle, and sheep behind us for want of vessels to carry them off. We left them in the power of the enemy. We went over to Connecticut River and went up the river near Middletown. A very short time after, I was recommended to His Excellency Governor Trumbull, Esq., for a warrant to take command of three whaleboats with ten men each to pilot them to Sag Harbor, and in Southold Sound to take vessels and boats that was found guilty of supplying the British with wood and any kind of stores. We soon captured three vessels loaded with flour and wood and took them up Connecticut River for trial, and they was condemned and sold according to law. Soon after, the British cutters prevented our crusing there.

Then I enlisted for six months in Captain Ely's company, Colonel Sage's regiment, commanded by General Putnam. We marched to New York and was stationed on Governor's Island. The British fleet lay in view of us at Staten Island about five miles of us. The twenty-fourth [*sic*] of August, 1776, was the Battle of Long Island fair in our view when General McDougall was defeated the twenty-eighth day. Our regiment retreated off Governor's Island to the city of New York in flat-bottom boats in the night, and, within a few days after, the whole British fleet came up to the city and parted. Some went up the East River and some up the North River; some of their troops landed at Harlem, above our army, which obliged us to fight our way through; then fought on our retreat to Kingsbridge, fourteen miles from city. There we stood our ground for some time. Then we was ordered to march to White Plains, and the twenty-eighth of October, 1776, we had a sharp battle with the British at White Plains, and I received two slight wounds, one musket ball in my right foot, and one in my right groin, cut four inches in length, but never applied for a pension until the fourteenth day of April, 1818, after the law of Congress was passed (a law of the eighteenth of March, 1818). The thirty-first of October, 1776, His Excellency General Washington give orders to march to Northcastle for winter quarters. There I continued until my time was out, then received my discharge and returned back to Connecticut to my parents. There remained until the spring following, sometime about the first of April [when I] enlisted for three years a sergeant in Captain Cole's company in the First Connecticut Regiment. Was ordered to march to New Haven. There we was stationed.

The twenty-fourth [*sic*] of May, 1777, I, said N. B. Jennings, volunteered myself to Colonel Meigs, stating the situation of Sag Harbor and the strength of the British guard and how easy they might be taken, and that I would pilot him and a detachment of troops across the sound to Long Island and carry our boats across Oysterpond Branch, about 150 yards, into Southold Bay. Then we could land and come on the back of the guard. The colonel was highly pleased with my plan. Then Colonel Meigs showed it to His Excellency General Washington. Then the general sent for me to come to headquarters with Colonel Meigs. Then, after asking me many questions, he was highly pleased with my conversation and plan.

The next day, the troops was ordered on the green at New Haven. The orders was read that about 110 men of good oarsmen to volunteer themselves to go on a private expedition, and when the word march was given there was upwards of 300 men stepped four paces in front in less than three minutes, and, after Colonel Meigs had picked out 110 men, the rest fell back in the ranks. At the same time, there was a number of whaleboat[s] lying at the Long Wharf at New Haven. Then we crossed over the sound to Long Island, carried our boats across the beach into Southold Bay, crossed bay, landed just before daylight on Joseph's Island, and carried our boats into a thicket of red cedars. There lay all day. The next night, I conducted the boats within about two miles and a half of Sag Harbor, on the back of the guardhouse. The guard was kept in a schoolhouse where I had gone to school. After landed, we left a few men to keep our boats afloat. Then I conducted our detachment a back way across fields and through thick brush until we came in sight of the guard-house. We kept under the side of a thick swamp within about fifty yards of the two sentries. We immediately surrounded the guard and sentries and took all except one sentry that made his escape through a piece of marsh. Then we left a guard with our prisoners and marched down about two hundred yards to my uncle. There we took a man by the name of Chew. The said Chew was appointed a commissary in Connecticut and went to the British with a large sum of the public money. Then we marched about one [hundred?] yards to their barracks. We made prisoners of all that was there. Then we went on the Long Wharf. There we took more prisoners and burnt twelve brigs and schooners, a quantity of hay and corn. Then the British was playing on us with grapeshot. Then we returned back to our boats with ninety prisoners the same way to the Oyster Point beach, carried our boats across the beach, then put our prisoners on board of two small vessels and guarded them across the sound to Black Rock, and from there we marched our prisoners to New Haven without the loss of a man.

There was not a man in the attachment that ever had been on Long Island except myself and one man who said that about twenty years ago he was ashore about two hours. And, in a few days after, we guarded our prisoners from New Haven to Hartford prison up Connecticut River, then returned back to New Haven. There I fell in with two young men that was looking for me. We had been schoolboys together. They had made their escape from Sag Harbor in a boat. They told me not to venture over there no more, for the Tories and the British swore that if they could take me, as I had been cruising about that shores and piloting Colonel Meigs with a detachment of troops a few days before, that if they could get hold of me, they swore they would put me to death without judge or jury. Then I asked the two young men to go with me to Colonel Meigs's lodging. We went together. They told the colonel the same that they had told me. The colonel asked me what my mother's maiden name was before she was married. I told him it was Bishop. Then he advised me to go to His Excellency Governor Trumbull, the governor of the state of Connecticut, with a recommendation which he would give me. Accordingly I procured a furlough and went to His Excellency the Governor Trumbull with my recommendation stating my danger in case I should fall in the hands of the enemy. He said in such a case it should be lawful for me, as my name was Elnathan, to leave out the two letters "El" and write it Nathan, and as my mother's maiden name was Bishop, to write my name Nathan B. Jennings, although it was wrote in the enlistment Elnathan Jennings, but ever since the governor decreeded it lawful, I have wrote my name Nathan B. Jennings, which is well known in this city for near thirty-eight years by the first gentlemen in Philadelphia.

And when we received orders to march from New Haven into the state of New York, we had several marches to different places in that state before we came into New Jersey, from Jersey to Whitemarsh in Pennsylvania and to Swedes Ford. From Swedes Ford, sometime in December 1777 we marched to Valley Forge, and soon after I was ordered to take charge of a stationed guard called the bullock guard under the directions of Commissary Conrad Huff. I had seven hundred head of cattle to guard besides other stores for the use of the United States army. There I continued on that guard till June 28, 1778, then followed the British to Monmouth in New Jersey sometime after the Battle of Monmouth, which was on the twenty-eighth of June, 1778. Some short time after, I joined the First Connecticut Regiment, which I enlisted in and continued there until our troops was ordered to march to Middlebrook in New York State for winter quarters. Soon after, I was struck with a fit of apperplacks [apoplexy] and lay three days in the fit. Then Dr. Holmes of the same regiment recommended me for a discharge from the service of the United States, which I received the latter end of December 1778. The above statement is true to the best of my knowledge.

14

Stephen Burroughs (1765–1840)

from *Memoirs of Stephen Burroughs*

In the early nineteenth century, Stephen Burroughs was a famous, or infamous, man. Fifteen different editions of his *Memoirs* came out between 1798 and 1861, plus eleven editions of a *Sketch of the Life of the Notorious Stephen Burroughs* and four pamphlet editions of the sermon he purportedly delivered from a hay-mow in Rutland, after being chased by the people of Pelham as an imposter. Who was he? Why was he so well known? And what interest does his autobiography have today?

His father, he says, was a clergyman in Hanover, New Hampshire, who raised him with a Presbyterian "rigor . . . which illy suited my volatile, impatient temper of mind." At age fourteen, he tried three times to enlist in the Continental Army, each time being withdrawn by his father. In 1781, his father enrolled him in Dartmouth College, but he was so undisciplined he had to quit. Next he went to Newburyport, Massachusetts, and sailed aboard a privateer, having picked up enough instruction from an elderly doctor to act as the ship's physician. But after a year at sea and in France, he was jailed for reportedly breaking open a chest of wine and distributing it to the crew.

Shortly afterwards comes the adventure he describes below, in which he successfully posed for awhile as a preacher. To judge by the number of times he later refers to it, this was also the act he became most famous for, the legend even springing up that he started by stealing a real minister's watch and clothes. So perhaps one reason for Burroughs's fame was this boldness in imitating, and thus in a way exposing and making fun of, the most revered of early American professions. None of his later tricks as counterfeiter, prison-escape artist, school teacher, and real estate shark were quite so brazen. Nor were they quite so ridiculous, which is another pleasure in reading Burroughs. He likes telling of his pranks, and defends them by sometimes confiding in the reader and sometimes acting very proper and offended (see the short second selection). Burroughs was a trickster who could both laugh and be laughed at. But we also wonder at how he deceived himself. Robert Frost, who wrote a short introduction to a twentieth-century printing of the *Memoirs*, called him not just a "knowing rascal" but a "naive hypocrite"—nearly contradictory personalities.

A further reason for Burroughs's fame may have been that the members of the early American republic were deeply worried by confidence men. As Karen Halttunen wrote in *Confidence Men and Painted Women: A Study of Middle-class Culture in America, 1830–1870,* the American emphasis on sincerity and benevolence made people fear and try to exclude all those who were insincere and too boldly, or too covertly, selfish. A whole system of manners and rituals grew up around protecting and yet properly displaying the depth and the goodness of individual feeling. A culture cannot establish such codes without painful repression, however, which repression is released in fascination with those who break them, as appears to have happened with Burroughs and would later happen with P. T. Barnum. In addition, the autobiographies of the confidence man, trickster, and prince of humbug are the books we read to try to learn the difference between sincerity and hypocrisy, the good man and the shyster, the true and the false.

Such autobiographies, however, also raise fundamental questions about autobiography. What credence can we place in Burroughs, when we know he lied? Autobiographies are written, we also believe, out of an impulse in the writers to know and examine themselves. But can hypocrites and, especially, naive hypocrites ever do that? Or to ask a very specific question, how is Burroughs's pretending to be a minister, a role he played reasonably well, different from Benjamin Franklin's game of pushing his goods in a wheelbarrow so as to convince his neighbors he was virtuous and industrious?

The text is adapted from the *Memoirs of Stephen Burroughs* (Albany, NY: B. D. Packard, 1811), chs. 7, 8, and 10. A new edition of the *Memoirs* has been edited by Philip Gura (Boston: Northeastern Univ. Press, 1988). For an informed and insightful critical article, see Daniel E. Williams, "In Defense of Self: Author and Authority in the Memoirs of Stephen Burroughs," *Early American Literature* 25 (1990): 96–122.

Chapter VII

"Fir'd is the muse? And let the muse be fir'd,
Who not inflam'd, when what he speaks, he feels?"

Weary with life, I returned to my father's, made some small arrangements, and left the country. One pistareen was all the ready cash I had on hand, and the suddenness with which I departed deprived me of a chance to raise more. Travelling on leisurely, I had time for reflection. What, said I, again an outcast among mankind? Where am I going? What can I do with myself in this world, where I meet with nothing but disappointment and chagrin? True it is, I am an outcast, but who cares for that? If I will not use the means for my own preservation and prosperity, what am I to expect? Is it to be supposed that whining over misfortunes is calculated to make them better? No, by no means. Then arouse, said I, for shame; use such means as you have in your power. The greater embarrassments, the more honor in overcoming them;

lay aside the idea of being any longer a child, and become a man. If others endeavor to throw obstacles in the way of your prosperity, show them that you can rise above them.

This dialogue with myself was productive of the most happy effects; I began to look about me, to see what was to be done in my present situation, to what business I could turn my attention.

The practice of Law, which would have been most to my mind, I could not undertake until I had spent some time in the study, which would be attended with expense far beyond my abilities; therefore, this object must be laid aside. Physic was under the same embarrassments: business of the mercantile line, I could not pursue for want of a capital; and even a school at this time of the year was hardly to be obtained.

Business of some kind I must enter into, and that immediately, in order to answer the present calls of nature. And what can that be? said I; have not I enumerated all the callings which are profitable for me to attend to? I might possibly write in an office or tend in a store, on wages, had I any person to recommend or introduce me into that business. But what can now be done? A stranger—moneyless and friendless. There is one thing, said contrivance, which you may do, and it will answer your purpose—preach! Preach? What a pretty fellow am I for a preacher! A pretty character mine, to tickle the ears of a grave audience! Run away from my own home for being connected in robbing a bee house, and for my attention to a married woman; having been through scenes of tumult, during my whole career, since I have exhibited on the active stage of life. Besides all this, what an appearance should I make in my present dress? which consisted of a light grey coat with silver-plated buttons, green vest, and red velvet breeches. This, said I, is a curious dress for me to offer myself in as a preacher; and I am by no means able to obtain a different suit.

These objections, truly, are weighty; many difficulties must be surmounted in order to enter into this business; but as this is the only kind you can attend to, said I to myself, under present circumstances, you can but be destitute of resource if you make the trial and do not succeed. At any rate, it is best to see what can be done; therefore, in order to obviate the first difficulty, viz., of disagreeable reports following you, it will be necessary to prevent, as much as possible, your being known where you offer yourself to preach; and in order to prevent that you must change your name. This being done, you must go some distance, where you are not personally known; and the probability is that you can continue in such business, till some opportunity may offer for your entering into other employment. As for your dress, you cannot alter that at present, and therefore, you must make the best of it you can. I do not think it will be an insurmountable obstacle; if you fail in one attempt, mind not to be discouraged, but repeat the trial until you succeed.

After I had held this parley with myself, I was determined to follow the foregoing plan according to the best of my abilities. I exchanged my horse for another, much worse, and received three dollars for the difference. This furnished me with money for my immediate expenses in travelling. I pursued my course down Connecticut river about one hundred and fifty miles, judging that by this time I was far enough from home to remain unknown. I concluded to begin my operations. Hearing of a place called Ludlow, not far distant, where they were destitute of a clergyman, I bent my course that way, it being Saturday, and intended to preach the next day if I proved successful. I arrived about noon, and put up at the house of one Fuller, whom I found to be a leading man in their religious society. I introduced myself to him as a clergyman, and he gave me an invitation to spend the sabbath with them and preach. You will readily conclude that I did not refuse this invitation. The greatest obstacle was now surmounted, as I conceived, viewing myself as fairly introduced into the ministerial function. I retired to rest at the usual time, and after I had composed my mind sufficiently for reflection, I began to consider under what situation my affairs now stood, and what was to be done under present circumstances. I had engaged to preach on the morrow. I had almost forgotten to tell you that my name here was Davis. People had been notified that a sermon would be delivered. This business I never had attempted. It is true, the study of divinity had come under my attention, together with every other subject of common concern, in a cursory manner. I concluded that sermonizing would not be so difficult as the other exercises of public worship. Many disagreeable possibilities arose into view. What, said I, would be my feelings, should I make some egregious blunder in travelling this unbeaten road? I must be exposed to the mortifying consideration of being observed by a whole assembly, in this ridiculous essay to preach, and not be able to carry my attempt into execution; and all those things possibly may happen. Those considerations made so dismal an appearance that I once concluded to get up, take my horse privately out of the stable and depart, rather than run the risk of the dangers which were before me. But upon more mature reflection, I found the hard hand of necessity compelled me to stay. When I awoke the next morning, my heart beat with anxious palpitation for the issue of the day. I considered this as the most important scene of my life—that in a great measure, my future happiness or wretchedness depended on my conduct through this day. The time for assembling approached! I saw people begin to come together. My feelings were all in arms against me, my heart would almost leap into my mouth.

What a strange thing, said I, is man! Why am I thus perturbated with these whimsical feelings? I know my dress is against me, and will cause some speculation; but I cannot help it, and why need I afflict myself with disagreeables before they arrive? I endeavored to calm my feelings by those reflections. I fortified my countenance with all my resolution, and set out with my bible and psalm book under my arm, those being the only insignia of a clergyman about me. When I made my appearance, I found a stare of universal surprise at my gay dress, which suited better the character of a beau than a clergyman. My eyes I could not persuade myself to raise from the ground till I had ascended the pulpit. I was doubtful whether I had the command of my voice, or even whether I had any voice. I sat a few minutes, collecting my resolution for the effort of beginning: I made the attempt—I found my voice at command—my anxiety was hushed, in a moment my perturbation subsided, and I felt all the serenity of a calm summer's morning. I went through the exercises of the forenoon without any difficulty. No monarch, when seated on the throne, had more sensible feelings of prosperity than what I experienced at this time.

During the intermission, I heard the whisper in swift circulation among the people, concerning my appearance in such a dress. The question was often asked with great emphasis, "Who is he?" but no one was able to give those answers which were satisfactory. A consultation took place among some leading members of the society, relative to hiring me to continue among them as a preacher, as I had intimated to Mr. Fuller that I should be willing to continue among them in that capacity, should such a matter meet with their approbation. I attended on the afternoon's exercises without any singular occurrence. The meeting being dismissed, and the people retired, I was informed by my landlord that they did not agree to hire me any longer; accordingly, I found my business here at an end.

I was advised by Mr. Fuller to make application to Mr. Baldwin, minister of Palmer, about twenty miles distant from Ludlow, for information where were vacancies, and for an introduction into those vacancies. I accordingly set out for Palmer on Monday morning, and arrived at Mr. Baldwin's about four o'clock in the afternoon. I introduced myself to him as a clergyman wanting employment. I saw he noticed my dress but asked no questions. He examined into my education, knowledge of divinity, tenets, etc., and finding all agreeing with his ideas of orthodoxy, he concluded to recommend me to a town called Pelham, eighteen miles distant from Palmer. The next morning I set off for Pelham, with a letter to one Deacon Gray. I arrived, and delivered my letter, and was hired, in consequence of the recommendation of Mr. Baldwin, without any hesitation, for four sabbaths: five dollars a sabbath; boarding, horse-keeping, etc., etc.—I now found myself, in some measure, settled in business. The want of an immediate relief to my temporary inconveniences was now supplied. I found the family into which I had fallen to be an agreeable, sociable circle, and I was much respected in the family, not only on account of my sacerdotal character, but likewise on account of the ease with which I mixed with them, in all their little social enjoyments.

Chapter VIII

"Companion of the wretched, come,
Fair Hope! and dwell with me awhile;
Thy heav'nly presence gilds the gloom,
While happier scenes in prospect smile."

Before I proceed to the relation of succeeding events, it will be necessary to give a description of the people inhabiting this town, as much will depend on knowing their character to rightly understand the relation of incidents which will follow.

The town of Pelham was settled with people chiefly from the north of Ireland. They were, of course, strict Presbyterians. They valued themselves much on being acquainted with the nice distinctions between orthodox and heterodox principles and practice. They likewise wished to be thought shrewd in their observations on ministers and preaching. A people generally possessing violent passions, which once disturbed, raged, uncontrolled by the dictates of reason; unpolished in their manners, possessing a jealous disposition; and either very friendly or very inimical, not knowing a medium between those two extremes. The first settled minister they had among them was one Abicrombie, from Scotland, a man of handsome abilities, but violent passions, resolute and persevering. Not many years after he was settled among them, a difficulty took place between him and the people, which was carried to considerable length, and ended in his dismission. After Mr. Abicrombie left this people, they made application to one Grayham, who at length settled among them, to their universal satisfaction, being a very handsome speaker, and otherwise possessed with popular talents as a preacher. Mr. Grayham was a man of very delicate feelings, of superior refinement, and inheriting a great desire for that peace which establishes the enjoyments of society.

After preaching a number of years to this people, he found an uneasiness prevailing among them, the chief cause of which was his practicing upon a system of manners more refined than what was prevalent in the place; consequently, they accused him of pride, of attention to the vanities of the world; of leaving the plain path of scripture, and following after the vices of Rome. Mr. Grayham labored to convince them of their mistake; of his wish to live with them upon the most intimate terms of equality; of his ever having it in view to pursue such measures as would, in their operation, conduce to their good and prosperity; and in that pursuit, he had expected his examples and precepts would answer a valuable purpose. His expostulations, remonstrances, and entreaties were all given to the wind. The difficulties increased, and the clamor grew louder. The mind of Mr. Grayham was too delicately strung to bear those strokes of misfortune; they insensibly wore upon his constitution, till at last he fell a sacrifice to the tumult, and sought his rest in the grave.

The town of Pelham remained destitute of a minister for a considerable time. They tried a number of candidates, but not finding any with whom they could agree, no one was yet settled. At length, a Mr. Merrill came among them. He was a man possessing the gift of utterance and flow of expression, perhaps equal to any. He was an eccentric genius, and imprudent to the last degree, possessing violent passions, headstrong and impetuous. The plausible part of his character was so captivating that the town agreed to settle him. He accordingly was installed. His imprudences soon made their appearance. Complaint was made, but they found one now who paid but little attention to their complaining. Both parties began to give way to passion. Their contention increased, and a flame was kindled which set the whole town in an uproar. Mr. Merrill refused to start from that foundation to which his legal contract entitled him; therefore, the other party determined to use extraordinary and violent measures. This attack Mr. Merrill dared not meet; therefore, he suddenly left the town. Matters were in this situation when I came to Pelham. From the information of Mr. Baldwin, and from the communications of my landlord and family, I soon gained a pretty thorough knowledge of the people whom I was amongst; and I endeavored to adapt my conduct to their genius as far as I was capable. I found myself soon able to dress in a habit fitting my calling. I soon found, likewise, that my endeavors to suit the people had not altogether failed. At the expiration of the four Sabbaths, they engaged me to preach sixteen more. I began to form an acquaintance in the neighboring towns, and with the neighboring ministers.

This happened to be a time of great mortality among women in childbed; consequently, I was called to preach many funeral sermons in this and the neighboring towns, many of which were destitute of a clergyman of their own. I always attended this business when I had a call. This circumstance began to raise a wonder in the minds of some, how I could be prepared for preaching so constantly, and on so short notice, being as yet only nineteen years of age. I had, in reality, ten sermons with me, written by my father.

At a certain time, being suddenly called to preach a funeral sermon, I had none of my own written, proper for the occasion. I took one of my father's, and delivered it to a crowded audience. As this sermon was delivered in a private house, it was in the power of any to look into my notes. One, who had wondered at my always being prepared to preach, took this opportunity of looking over my notes, and thought they appeared too old to be lately written. This circumstance was mentioned to a number, who began to grow uneasy with apprehension of my preaching sermons not my own. Mr. Baldwin coming to Pelham about this time, they mentioned the matter to him, that he might make some enquiry into the business, and inform them. He accordingly mentioned the matter to me, in a confidential manner, and desired to see the sermon alluded to. I was sensible the handwriting of my father was so different from my own that the first view must clearly convince any observer that this sermon was not written by myself; I therefore thought it the better way to treat the matter ingenuously, and tell him the simple matter of fact.

I told Mr. Baldwin that the sermon was a manuscript which I had in my possession, together with some others, written by another person, and that the want of time to prepare a discourse had induced me to take this, rather than refuse to preach. Mr. Baldwin made some observations with regard to my situation of the necessity of a great degree of prudence, and of the impropriety of using other sermons as a general thing. He returned to Palmer, without giving the men any account respecting the matter of their suspicion. Not gaining that intelligence by Mr. Baldwin which was expected, those who were uneasy spread their suspicions among others, until there became uneasiness pretty generally through the town. They proposed a number of ways to obtain that satisfaction, with regard to their suspicion, which would either clear me from the fact of which they were jealous, or else establish them in it. They at length agreed to this method, viz., to send one of their number to me on Sunday morning previous to my going into the meetinghouse, and desire me to preach from a passage of scripture, which he should give me. I was informed of all these circumstances previous to the time of trial. Their reasoning upon this subject was of this nature, viz., that if I was able on the shortest notice to preach on any occasion, I should be able likewise to preach on Sunday, from such a passage as should be given me on the morning of the same day; and should I not be able to preach, the evidence would be conclusive against me that I preached the sermons of others, and not my own.

The Sunday following, I was waited on by Mr. Clark, who desired me to oblige him by delivering a discourse from the first clause of the 5th verse of the 9th chapter of Joshua; the words were, "old shoes and clouted on their feet." I informed him I would deliver a discourse from that text, and accordingly he left me. I truly felt somewhat blanked at the nature of the passage I had to discourse upon. However, I was determined to do the best on the subject I was capable. I endeavored to make some arrangements in my mind on the subject. I had not thought long on it before the matter opened to my mind in such a manner, as to give me much satisfaction. As your patience would hardly endure the repetition of a tedious sermon, I will not trouble you with it; yet, sir, indulge me in giving you some general outlines of this discourse, as it was founded on a very singular passage, and delivered on a very extraordinary occasion.

Chapter X

"It was a season when the lingering night
Disputes her empire with the rising light;
A rosy blush here paints the doubtful morn,
There glimmering stars the uncertain shades adorn."

At the time fixed on, Joseph Huntington came to see me at Pelham; I introduced him to my acquaintance, and particularly to Lysander. We opened our schemes of aggrandizement to him, without reserve. He was pleased with our prospects, and in the overflowings of our friendship, we agreed to allow him, as the highest favor possible for us to communicate, to set his hand to our agreement, and so become a partner in our business. In the course of Huntington's remaining with me at Pelham, he made several unguarded mistakes, which reduced me to a very disagreeable situation. He called me by my proper name, a number of times, before the family where I lived. He excused himself by saying, that Burroughs was my nickname at College, and was given in consequence of my looking so much like one of that name. One Sunday morning, as people were going to meeting, I was leaning back in my chair, the pommel resting against the door case. Huntington, seeing the situation in which I was resting, put his staff against the chair and pushed it off the case, and down I fell on the floor. This impudent action done on Sunday by my known and intimate friend had a very disagreeable appearance, and made people look with astonishment at the circumstance; however, I reproved Huntington with some warmth, and he, seeing the nature of his folly, bore it with patience. The Monday following, Huntington was to proceed on to Coventry. I rode with him about twelve miles on his way, and then returned; but previous to my return, an affair took place which gave a new face to the scene of things.

As we were riding by the house of Mr. Forward, minister of Belchertown, he came out of his house, and desired us to call, alleging that Mr. Chapin, a minister from Windsor, was in the house, to whom he offered to introduce us. Mr. Chapin was a man well known to me, and I presumed I should be equally well known to him. I excused the matter, alleging that I was in haste, and therefore, could not do myself the pleasure of accepting his invitation. Mr. Forward was pressing for us to alight, and go in; and while this dialogue continued, Mr. Chapin came out of the house, and addressed me by the name of Burroughs. I endeavored to convince him of his mistake, but to no purpose; he insisted in a very peremptory manner that my name was not Davis, but was bona fide Burroughs. I replied that those insults were not grateful to my feelings, and what I should not bear. "Your humble servant, gentlemen." We then rode on, though repeatedly desired to stop. When Huntington and I were by ourselves, we were merry upon the circumstance of being driven into so short a corner.

After I had parted from Huntington, I was under the necessity of returning back the same road I came, and consequently, must pass again the house of Mr. Forward. Soon after I had gone by the house, I heard somebody calling after me, "Mr. Davis, Mr. Burroughs," but for reasons which you will easily conceive, I did not answer. As I rode on towards Pelham, I endeavored to concert measures of retreat against the storm, which was fast gathering, and would soon burst upon me if it were not averted. The news would soon come to Pelham of my real name, character, etc. This would serve to arouse the indignation of that people to its full height. To continue among them any longer would be out of the question; and to meet the rage of their resentment, after the whole matter of fact should be promulgated, I dared not, neither did I wish it. One Sunday more I was to preach among them before my time of engagement expired, and for this Sunday, I had already received my pay; but under existing circumstances, it was doubtful in my mind whether they would insist on my fulfilling my engagement. At all events, I was determined to leave them very suddenly. I accordingly came to my landlord's that evening, put my horse in the barn, and after the family were all retired to rest, I put my things in order, took my horse, and silently left the house. In this situation, I sought Lysander, related the circumstances which I was under, and concluded to lie by with him, till I should see what the event of those things would be.

The next morning, Mr. Davis was not to be found. My landlord was almost frantic with surprise and grief. The town was alarmed, and suddenly was all in a flame. About 11 o'clock P.M., a man came from Belchertown with information respecting the character who had been exhibited among them as a preacher. This blew the flame into a tenfold rage. No pen can describe the uproar there was in the town of Pelham. They mounted, hue and cries after me in every direction, with orders to spare not horseflesh. They perambulated the town, and anxiously asked every one for some circumstances, which would lead to a discovery where I was. All this took place whilst I lay snug in the corner, observing their operations. In holding a consultation upon these disagreeable matters, every one was anxious to clear himself of being the dupe to my artifice, as much as possible. "I never liked him," says one. "I always thought there was something suspicious about him," says another. "He ever had a very deceitful look," says a third. In fine, it had come to this, that not one now could discern anything which ever appeared good or commendable about me, except one good old lady, who said, "Well, I hope they will catch him, and bring him back among us, and we will make him a good man, and keep him for our preacher."

You may with propriety ask me what the people of Pelham expected they could do, should they overtake me in their pursuit? I know the question will naturally arise; but I cannot give you an answer, for I do not know their intentions or expectations. Perhaps they thought, for they were a people very ignorant, that I had broken the laws of the land, to the same amount as I had offended them.

About 12 o'clock the night following, I took my leave of Lysander, promising to return and see him again as soon as the tumult was hushed, and concert further measures for our prosecuting our schemes for gaining wealth by transmutation; being obliged so suddenly to leave the country, that we could not ripen our plans for the present. It was not without the most sensible pain I left this amiable family. Journeying on, I had time for reflection. At dead of night—all alone—reflection would have its operation.

A very singular scene have I now passed through, said I, and to what does it amount? Have I acted with propriety as a man, or have I deviated from the path of rectitude? I have had an unheard of, difficult, disagreeable part to act: I do not feel entirely satisfied with myself in this business, and yet I do not know how I should have done otherwise, and have made the matter better. The laws of the land I have not broken, in any instance; but my situation has been such, that I have violated that principle of veracity which we implicitly pledge ourselves to maintain towards each other, as a general thing in society; and whether my peculiar circumstances would warrant such a line of procedure is the question. I know many things may be said in favor of it, as well as against it. How I came into this disagreeable situation, is another matter. I know that the leading cause which produced it was founded in wrong. My giving countenance to an open breach of the laws of the land, in the case of the bees, was a matter in which I was justly reprehensible; but that matter is now past; the owner of the bees is remunerated to the utmost extent which is provided for by law, and therefore, I must take things as they now are, and under these circumstances do the best I can. I know the world will blame me, but I wish to justify my conduct to myself, let the world think what it may. Indeed, I know they are not capable of judging upon the matter, with any propriety, because they ever will and ever must remain ignorant of the particular causes which brought these events into existence. They understand the matter in the gross, that I have preached under a fictitious name and character, and consequently have roused many ideas in the minds of the people not founded in fact. Therefore, they concluded from this general view, the whole to be grounded in wrong. The name impostor is therefore easily fixed to my character. An impostor, we generally conceive, puts on feigned appearances, in order to enrich or aggrandize himself to the damage of others. That this is not the case with me, in this transaction, I think is clear. That I have aimed at nothing but a bare supply of the necessaries of life, is a fact. That I have never, in one instance, taken advantage of that confidence which the people of Pelham entertained towards me, to injure them and benefit myself, is a truth acknowledged by all. Under these circumstances, whether I ought to bear the name of imposture, according to the common acceptation, is the question.

That I have a good and equitable right to preach, if I choose, and others choose to hear me, is a truth of which I entertain no doubt: but whether any circumstance will justify my putting on a false appearance, in order to introduce myself into that business, is the only doubt remaining on my mind. I think it my duty, at least, to steer as clear of this base guise for the future as my safety will admit.

About 1 o'clock at night, leaving the confines of Pelham, I overtook

Powers, the person whom I have before mentioned, likewise coming out of Pelham. He knew me—I asked him where he had been. He was embarrassed about giving me an answer. I mistrusted he had been employed in searching after me; I laid it to his charge. After some hesitation, he owned the fact. I put on a fierce look, and commanded him to stop, in a very peremptory manner; he obeyed. Now, said I, Powers, you see my situation; you are the only person who knows where I am; therefore, I am determined to take measures for my own safety; and for that reason, promise me, with the solemnity of an oath, that you will give no information respecting me. Powers began to expostulate. I added still more terror to my looks, and commanded him to swear to secrecy immediately, if he ever wished for the opportunity. He was terrified. He began to imprecate curses on his head, of the most horrid nature, if he should divulge his having seen me, or knowing which way I had gone. We then fell into familiar chat on various topics, rode on together till we arrived at the place where he left me to go to his father's. I went on without suspicion of danger; but no sooner had I left Powers than he took his way back again with all speed, and informed the people of Pelham of his discovery. It was about the dawn of day when he had returned to Pelham, and gave this important information. The news was like an electric shock. It was communicated through the town with that rapidity which would have done honor to a cause of importance. The people were assembled, and a select number appointed to pursue me.

All these things were unknown to me, whilst I rode on leisurely and securely, thinking of no danger. I had determined to bend my course for Rutland (Mass.), where I expected to find an acquaintance of mine by the name of Frink, who was doing business in the mercantile line in that town; and if, fortunately, I could obtain business of some other kind, through his means, I determined to drop preaching, which subjected me to so many false appearances contrary to my inclination. I arrived about 8 o'clock A.M. at Rutland, and found Mr. Frink, according to my expectation, at his shop.

15

Caroline Kirkland (1801–1864)
from *A New Home—Who'll Follow?*

Caroline Kirkland's *A New Home—Who'll Follow?* (1839) is a work which straddles the fence between novel and autobiography. Though the book was written in the character of "Mary Clavers," the pseudonym that appeared on the title page, and though it was long recognized as a pioneer work in American realism (and so written about in histories of the American novel), most early readers soon knew that Caroline Kirkland was the real author and that the book was based on her and her husband's experience building the frontier town of Pinckney, Michigan (about fifty miles west of Detroit). Thus the book also is accepted as an autobiography and appears in Louis Kaplan's *Bibliography of American Autobiographies*.

Such a mixed status derives from the fact that in the early nineteenth century the line between autobiography and the novel was not so clear as some readers would like to make it today. Both were praised if they were faithful to real life, and Edgar Allan Poe, who knew Kirkland was the author, praised the book highly, saying that "to Mrs. Kirkland alone we were indebted for our acquaintance with the *home* and home-life of the backwoodsman."[1] The disadvantage to autobiography as such was that it was thought to be vain, while the advantage to a little fictionalizing, as of names and places, was that the writer would not be held exactly accountable and might keep her identity unknown. So the fence *A New Home* straddled was a kind of pioneer split-rail fence, not straight, not high, and not very rigid. Indeed, after publication, the residents of Pinckney recognized themselves in the "Montacute" of the book, and their displeasure was one of the reasons Kirkland returned to New York.

And New Yorker she was, eldest child of Samuel Stansbury, a cultivated bookseller, and granddaughter of Joseph Stansbury, who during the Revolution had been a Loyalist poet and satirist. She received an excellent education and then taught in her aunt's school. In 1828, she married William Kirkland, an instructor at Hamilton College, in Clinton, New York, and for a time they ran a girls' school in Geneva, New York. But in 1835 William became principal of the Detroit Female

---

1. "The Literati of New York City," in Edgar Allan Poe, *Essays and Reviews* (New York: Library of America, 1984), p. 1181.

Seminary, and he began buying Michigan land until he and his father owned 1300 acres. He then took his wife and children to settle it and build the town, hoping to grow up (and grow rich) with the expanding West.

A New Home thus invites comparison with Boone's autobiography and other explorers' and settlers' narratives, with the difference that it is written by a very bright and critical woman, one who is often much more realistic than the men. She also has both a sense of humor and a standard of taste, two qualities that complement each other beautifully in her case. So she wants by turns to refine the frontier and to make the new settlers adapt to it. She warns them of the "mud-holes" and the crude cabins, where a fine cabinet is likely to end up as a corn-crib. She urges them to be tolerant of frontier customs, understanding their purpose, and she mostly approves of frontier democracy. In all this she uses her own mistakes and successes as lessons to others, making her book an "Emigrant's Guide" to easterners going west. Seeing herself as an "emigrant," she thus identifies with this aspect of the nation's experience, as others had identified with the Revolution.

Perhaps the greatest irony in Kirkland's experience, however, is that the frontier did not in the end provide as much freedom and opportunity as the city. It was also not a good place to write, even though it was good material for a writer. So in 1843 she and her husband returned to New York, where she wrote more sketches about the West, as well as writing and editing travel letters, advice books, and literary anthologies.

The text below is from *A New Home—Who'll Follow* (1839), chapters 1 and 18. A recent edition is *A New Home—Who'll Follow?*, ed. William S. Osborne (New Haven: College & Univ. Press, 1965). William Osborne is also the author of the brief biography, *Caroline M. Kirkland* (New York: Twayne, 1972). For critical study and comparison of Kirkland to other women's writing about the frontier, see Annette Kolodny, *The Land Before Her: Fantasy and Experience of the American Frontiers, 1630–1860* (Chapel Hill: Univ. of North Carolina Press, 1984), pp. 131–58.

Chapter 1

Here are seen
No traces of man's pomp and pride; no silks
Rustle, nor jewels shine, nor envious eyes
Encounter . . .
Oh, there is not lost
One of earth's charms; upon her bosom yet
After the flight of untold centuries
The freshness of her far beginning lies.

Bryant

Our friends in the "settlements" have expressed so much interest in such of our letters to them, as happened to convey an account of the peculiar features

251

of western life, and have asked so many curious questions, touching particulars which we had not thought worthy of mention, that I have been for some time past contemplating the possibility of something like a detailed account of our experiences. And I have determined to give them to the world, in a form not very different from that in which they were originally recorded for our private delectation; nothing doubting, that a veracious history of actual occurrences, an unvarnished transcript of real characters, and an impartial record of every-day forms of speech (taken down in many cases from the lips of the speaker) will be pronounced "graphic," by at least a fair proportion of the journalists of the day.

'Tis true there are but meagre materials for anything which might be called a story. I have never seen a cougar—nor been bitten by a rattlesnake. The reader who has patience to go with me to the close of my desultory sketches, must expect nothing beyond a meandering recital of common-place occurrences—mere gossip about every-day people, little enhanced in value by any fancy or ingenuity of the writer; in short, a very ordinary pen-drawing; which, deriving no interest from coloring, can be valuable only for its truth.

A home on the outskirts of civilization—habits of society which allow the maid and her mistress to do the honors in complete equality, and to make the social tea visit in loving conjunction—such a distribution of the duties of life as compels all, without distinction, to rise with the sun or before him—to breakfast with the chickens—then,

> Count the slow clock and dine exact at noon—

to be ready for tea at four, and for bed at eight—may certainly be expected to furnish some curious particulars for the consideration of those whose daily course almost reverses this primitive arrangement—who "call night day and day night," and who are apt occasionally to forget, when speaking of a particular class, that "those creatures" are partakers with themselves of a common nature.

I can only wish, like other modest chroniclers, my respected prototypes, that so fertile a theme had fallen into worthier hands. If Miss Mitford, who has given us such charming glimpses of Aberleigh, Hilton Cross and the Loddon, had by some happy chance been translated to Michigan, what would she not have made of such materials as Tinkerville, Montacute, and the Turnip?

When my husband purchased two hundred acres of wild land on the banks of this to-be-celebrated stream, and drew with a piece of chalk on the bar-room table at Danforth's the plan of a village, I little thought I was destined to make myself famous by handing down to posterity a faithful record of the advancing fortunes of that favored spot.

"The madness of the people" in those days of golden dreams took more commonly the form of city-building; but there were a few who contented themselves with planning villages, on the banks of streams which certainly never could be expected to bear navies, but which might yet be turned to account in the more homely way of grinding or sawing—operations which must necessarily be performed somewhere for the well being of those very cities. It is of one of these humble attempts that it is my lot to speak, and I make my confession at the outset, warning any fashionable reader who may have taken up my book, that I intend to be "decidedly low."

Whether the purchaser of *our* village would have been moderate under all possible circumstances, I am not prepared to say, since, never having enjoyed a situation under government, his resources have not been unlimited;—and for this reason any remark which may be hazarded in the course of these my lucubrations touching the more magnificent plans of wealthier aspirants, must be received with some grains of allowance. "Il est plus aisé d'être sage pour les autres, que de l'être pour soi-même."

When I made my first visit to these remote and lonely regions, the scattered woods through which we rode for many miles were gay in their first gosling-green suit of half-opened leaves, and the forest odors which exhaled with the dews of morning and evening, were beyond measure delicious to one "long in populous cities pent." I desired much to be a little sentimental at the time, and feel tempted to indulge to some small extent even here—but I forbear; and shall adhere closely to matters more in keeping with my subject.

I think, to be precise, the time was the last, the very last of April, and I recollect well that even at that early season, by availing myself with sedulous application, of those times when I was fain to quit the vehicle through fear of the perilous mudholes, or still more perilous half-bridged marshes, I picked upwards of twenty varieties of wild-flowers—some of them of rare and delicate beauty;—and sure I am, that if I had succeeded in inspiring my companion with one spark of my own floral enthusiasm, one hundred miles of travel would have occupied a week's time.

The wild flowers of Michigan deserve a poet of their own. Shelley, who sang so quaintly of "the pied wind-flowers and the tulip tall," would have found many a fanciful comparison and deep-drawn meaning for the thousand gems of the road-side. Charles Lamb could have written charming volumes about the humblest among them. Bulwer would find means to associate the common three-leaved white lily so closely with the Past, the Present and the Future—the Wind, the Stars, and the tripod of Delphos, that all future botanists, and eke all future philosophers, might fail to unravel the "linked sweetness." We must have a poet of our own.

Since I have casually alluded to a Michigan mud-hole, I may as well enter into a detailed memoir on the subject, for the benefit of future travellers, who, flying over the soil on rail-roads, may look slightingly back upon the achievements of their predecessors. In the "settlements," a mud-hole is considered as apt to occasion an unpleasant jolt—a breaking of the thread of one's reverie—or in extreme cases, a temporary stand-still or even an overturn of the rash

253

or the unwary. Here, on approaching one of these characteristic features of the "West"—(How much does that expression mean to include? I never have been able to discover its limits,)—the driver stops—alights—walks up to the dark gulf—and around it if he can get round it. He then seeks a long pole and sounds it, measures it across to ascertain how its width compares with the length of his wagon—tries whether its sides are perpendicular, as is usually the case if the road is much used. If he find it not more than three feet deep, he remounts cheerily, encourages his team, and in they go, with a plunge and a shock rather apt to damp the courage of the inexperienced. If the hole be narrow the hinder wheels will be quite lifted off the ground by the depression of their precedents, and so remain until by unwearied chirruping and some judicious touches of "the string," the horses are induced to struggle as for their lives; and if the Fates are propitious they generally emerge on the opposite side, dragging the vehicle, or at least the fore wheels after them. When I first "penetrated the interior," (to use an indigenous phrase) all I knew of the wilds was from Hoffman's tour or Captain Hall's "graphic" delineations: I had some floating idea of "driving a barouche-and-four anywhere through the oak-openings"—and seeing "the murdered Banquos of the forest" haunting the scenes of their departed strength and beauty. But I confess, these pictures, touched by the glowing pencil of fancy, gave me but incorrect notions of a real journey through Michigan.

Our vehicle was not perhaps very judiciously chosen;—at least we have since thought so. It was a light high-hung carriage—of the description commonly known as a buggy or shandrydan—names of which I would be glad to learn the etymology. I seriously advise any of my friends who are about flitting to Wisconsin or Oregon, to prefer a heavy lumber-wagon, even for the use of the ladies of the family; very little aid or consolation being derived from making a "genteel" appearance in such cases.

At the first encounter of such a mud-hole as I have attempted to describe, we stopped in utter despair. My companion indeed would fain have persuaded me that the many wheel tracks which passed through the formidable gulf were proof positive that it might be forded. I insisted with all a woman's obstinacy that I could not and would not make the attempt, and alighted accordingly, and tried to find a path on one side or the other. But in vain, even putting out of the question my paper-soled shoes—sensible things for the woods. The ditch on each side was filled with water and quite too wide to jump over; and we were actually contemplating a return, when a man in an immense bear-skin cap and a suit of deer's hide, sprang from behind a stump just within the edge of the forest. He "poled" himself over the ditch in a moment, and stood beside us, rifle in hand, as wild and rough a specimen of humanity as one would wish to encounter in a strange and lonely road, just at the shadowy dusk of the evening. I did *not* scream, though I own I was prodigiously frightened. But our stranger said immediately, in a gentle tone and with a French accent, "Me watch deer—you want to cross?" On receiving an answer in the affirmative, he ran in search of a rail which he threw over the terrific mud-hole—aided me to walk across by the help of his pole—showed my husband where to plunge—waited till he had gone safely through and "slow circles dimpled o'er the quaking mud"—then took himself off by the way he came, declining any compensation with a most polite "rien, rien!" This instance of true and genuine and generous politeness I record for the benefit of all bearskin caps, leathern jerkins and cowhide boots, which ladies from the eastward world may hereafter encounter in Michigan.

Our journey was marked by no incident more alarming than the one I have related, though one night passed in a wretched inn, deep in the "timbered land"—as all woods are called in Michigan—was not without its terrors, owing to the horrible drunkenness of the master of the house, whose wife and children were in constant fear of their lives, from his insane fury. I can never forget the countenance of that desolate woman, sitting trembling and with white, compressed lips in the midst of her children. The father raving all night, and coming through our sleeping apartment with the earliest ray of morning, in search of more of the poison already boiling in his veins. The poor wife could not forbear telling me her story—her change of lot—from a well-stored and comfortable home in Connecticut to this wretched den in the wilderness—herself and children worn almost to shadows with the ague, and her husband such as I have described him. I may mention here, that not very long after I heard of this man in prison in Detroit, for stabbing a neighbor in a drunken brawl, and ere the year was out he died of delerium tremens, leaving his family destitute. So much for turning our fields of golden grain into "fire water"—a branch of business in which Michigan is fast improving.

Our ride being a deliberate one, I felt, after the third day, a little wearied, and began to complain of the sameness of the oak-openings and to wish we were fairly at our journey's end. We were crossing a broad expanse of what seemed at a little distance a smooth shaven lawn of the most brilliant green, but which proved on trial little better than a quaking bog—embracing within its ridgy circumference all possible varieties of

Muirs, and mosses, slaps and styles—

I had just indulged in something like a yawn, and wished that I could see our hotel. At the word, my companion's face assumed rather a comical expression, and I was preparing to inquire somewhat testily what there was so laughable—I was getting tired and cross, reader—when down came our good horse to the very chin in a bog-hole, green as Erin on the top, but giving way on a touch, and seeming deep enough to have engulphed us entirely if its width had been proportionate. Down came the horse—and this was not all—down came the driver; and I could not do less than follow, though at a little distance—our good steed kicking and floundering—covering us with hieroglyphics, which would be readily deciphered by any Wolverine we should meet, though perchance strange to the eyes of our friends at home. This mishap was soon amended. Tufts of long march grass served to assoilize our habiliments a little, and a clear stream which rippled through the marsh aided in removing the eclipse from our faces. We journeyed on cheerily, watching the splendid changes in the west, but keeping a bright look-out for bog-holes.

Chapter 18

Lend me your *ears*.   Shakespeare

Grant graciously what you cannot refuse safely.   Bacon

"Mother wants your sifter," said Miss Ianthe Howard, a young lady of six years' standing, attired in a tattered calico, thickened with dirt; her unkempt locks straggling from under that hideous substitute for a bonnet, so universal in the western country, a dirty cotton handkerchief, which is used, *ad nauseam,* for all sorts of purposes.

"Mother wants your sifter, and she says she guesses you can let her have some sugar and tea, 'cause you've got plenty."

This excellent reason, "'cause you've got plenty," is conclusive as to sharing with your neighbors. Whoever comes into Michigan with nothing, will be sure to better his condition; but woe to him that brings with him any thing like an appearance of abundance, whether of money or mere household conveniences. To have them, and not be willing to share them in some sort with the whole community, is an unpardonable crime. You must lend your best horse to *qui que ce soit,* to go ten miles over hill and marsh, in the darkest night, for a doctor; or your team to travel twenty after a "gal;" your wheel-barrows, your shovels, your utensils of all sorts, belong, not to yourself, but to the public, who do not think it necessary even to *ask* a loan, but take it for granted. The two saddles and bridles of Montacute spend most of their time travelling from house to house a-man-back; and I have actually known a stray martingale to be traced to four dwellings two miles apart, having been lent from one to another, without a word to the original proprietor, who sat waiting, not very patiently, to commence a journey.

Then within doors, an inventory of your plenishing of all sorts, would scarcely more than include the articles which you are solicited to lend. Not only are all kitchen utensils as much your neighbor's as your own, but bedsteads, beds, blankets, sheets, travel from house to house, a pleasant and effectual mode of securing the perpetuity of certain efflorescent peculiarities of the skin, for which Michigan is becoming almost as famous as the land "'twixt Maidenkirk and John o' Groat's." Sieves, smoothing irons, and churns, run about as if they had legs; one brass kettle is enough for a whole neighborhood; and I could point to a cradle which has rocked half the babies in Montacute. For my own part, I have lent my broom, my thread, my tape, my spoons, my cat, my thimble, my scissors, my shawl, my shoes; and have been asked for my combs and brushes: and my husband, for his shaving apparatus and his pantaloons.

But the cream of the joke lies in the manner of the thing. It is so straight-forward and honest, none of your hypocritical civility and servile gratitude! Your true republican, when he finds that you possess any thing which would contribute to his convenience, walks in with, "Are you going to use your horses *to-day?*" if horses happen to be the thing he needs.

"Yes, I shall probably want them."

"Oh, well; if you want them——I was thinking to get 'em to go up north a piece."

Or perhaps the desired article comes within the female department.

"Mother wants to get some butter: that 'ere butter you bought of Miss Barton this mornin'."

And away goes your golden store, to be repaid perhaps with some cheesy, greasy stuff, brought in a dirty pail, with, "Here's your butter!"

A girl came in to borrow a "wash-dish," "because we've got company." Presently she came back: "Mother says you've forgot to send a towel."

"The pen and ink, and a sheet o' paper and a wafer," is no unusual re-quest; and when the pen is returned, you are generally informed that you sent "an awful bad pen."

I have been frequently reminded of one of Johnson's humorous sketches. A man returning a broken wheel-barrow to a Quaker, with, "Here I've broke your rotten wheel-barrow usin' on't. I wish you'd get it mended right off, 'cause I want to borrow it again this afternoon." The Quaker is made to reply, "Friend, it shall be done:" and I wish I possessed more of his spirit.

But I did not intend to write a chapter on involuntary loans; I have a story to tell.

One of my best neighbors is Mr. Philo Doubleday, a long, awkward, honest, hard-working Maine-man, or Mainote I suppose one might say; so good-natured, that he might be mistaken for a simpleton; but that must be by those that do not know him. He is quite an old settler, came in four years ago, bringing with him a wife who is to him as vinegar-bottle to oil-cruet, or as mustard to the sugar which is used to soften its biting qualities. Mrs. Doubleday has the sharpest eyes, the sharpest nose, the sharpest tongue, the sharpest elbows, and above all, the sharpest voice that ever "penetrated the interior" of Michigan. She has a tall, straight, bony figure, in contour somewhat resembling two hard-oak planks fastened together and stood on end; and, strange to say! she was full five-and-thirty when her mature graces attracted the eye and won the affections of the worthy Philo. What eclipse had come over Mr. Doubleday's usual sagacity when he made choice of his

Polly, I am sure I never could guess; but he is certainly the only man in the wide world who could possibly have lived with her; and he makes her a most excellent husband.

She is possessed with a neat devil; I have known many such cases; her floor is scoured every night, after all are in bed but the unlucky scrubber, Betsey, the maid of all work; and woe to the unfortunate "indifiddle," as neighbor Jenkins says, who first sets dirty boot on it in the morning. If men come in to talk over road business, for Philo is much sought when "the public" has any work to do, or school-business, for that being very troublesome, and quite devoid of profit, is often conferred upon Philo, Mrs. Doubleday makes twenty errands into the room, expressing in her visage all the force of Mrs. Raddle's inquiry, "*Is* them wretches going?" And when at length their backs are turned, out comes the bottled vengeance. The sharp eyes, tongue, elbow, and voice, are all in instant requisition.

"Fetch the broom, Betsey! and the scrub broom, Betsey! and the mop, and that 'ere dish of soap, Betsey; and why on earth didn't you bring some ashes? You didn't expect to clean such a floor as this without ashes, did you?"—"What time are you going to have dinner, my dear?" says the imperturbable Philo, who is getting ready to go out.

"Dinner! I'm sure I don't know! there's no time to cook dinner in this house! nothing but slave, slave, slave, from morning till night, cleaning up after a set of nasty, dirty," &c. &c. "Phew!" says Mr. Doubleday, looking at his fuming helpmate with a calm smile, "It'll all rub out when it's dry, if you'll only let it alone."

"Yes, yes; and it would be plenty clean enough for you if there had been forty horses in here."

Philo on some such occasion waited till his Polly had stepped out of the room, and then with a bit of chalk wrote on the broad black-walnut mantel-piece:

> Bolt and bar hold gate of wood,
> Gate of iron springs make good,
> Bolt nor spring can bind the flame,
> Woman's tongue can no man tame.

and then took his hat and walked off.

This is the favorite mode of vengeance—"poetical justice" he calls it; and as he is never at a loss for a rhyme of his own or other people's, Mrs. Doubleday stands in no small dread of these efforts of genius. Once, when Philo's crony, James Porter, the blacksmith, had left the print of his blackened knuckles on the outside of the oft-scrubbed door, and was the subject of some rather severe remarks from the gentle Polly, Philo, as he left the house with his friend, turned and wrote over the offended spot:

Knock not here!
Or dread my dear.
P. D.

and the very next person that came was Mrs. Skinner, the merchant's wife, all
drest in her red merino, to make a visit. Mrs. Skinner, who did not possess an
unusual share of tact, walked gravely round to the back-door, and there was
Mrs. Doubleday up to the eyes in soap-making. Dire was the mortification,
and point-blank were the questions as to how the visitor came to go round
that way; and when the warning couplet was produced in justification, we
must draw a veil over what followed—as the novelists say.

Sometimes these poeticals came in aid of poor Betsey; as once, when
on hearing a crash in the little shanty-kitchen, Mrs. Doubleday called in her
shrillest tones, "Betsey! what on earth's the matter?" Poor Betsey, knowing
what was coming, answered in a deprecatory whine, "The cow's kicked over
the buckwheat batter!"

When the clear, hilarious voice of Philo from the yard, where he was
chopping, instantly completed the triplet—

"Take up the pieces and throw 'em at her!" for once the grim features of
his spouse relaxed into a smile, and Betsey escaped her scolding.

Yet, Mrs. Doubleday is not without her excellent qualities as a wife, a
friend, and a neighbor. She keeps her husband's house and stocking in unex-
ceptionable trim. Her *emptins* are the envy of the neighborhood. Her vinegar
is, as how could it fail? the *ne plus ultra* of sharpness; and her pickles are
greener than the grass of the field. She will watch night after night with the
sick, perform the last sad offices for the dead, or take to her home and heart
the little ones whose mother is removed forever from her place at the fireside.
All this she can do cheerfully, and she will not repay herself as many good
people do by recounting every word of the querulous sick man, or the desolate mourner, with added hints of tumbled drawers, closets all in heaps, or
awful dirty kitchens.

I was sitting one morning with my neighbor, Mrs. Jenkins, who is a sister of Mr. Doubleday, when Betsey, Mrs. Doubleday's "hired girl," came in
with one of the shingles of Philo's handiwork in her hand, which bore in
Mr. Doubleday's well-known chalk marks—

Come quick, Fanny!
And bring the granny,
For Mrs. Double-
day's in trouble.

And the next intelligence was of a fine new pair of lungs at that hitherto
silent mansion. I called very soon after to take a peep at the "latest found;"
and if the suppressed delight of the new papa was a treat, how much more

was the softened aspect, the womanized tone of the proud and happy mother. I never saw a being so completely transformed. She would almost forget to answer me in her absorbed watching of the breath of the little sleeper. Even when trying to be polite, and to say what the occasion demanded, her eyes would *not* be withdrawn from the tiny face. Conversation on any subject but the ever-new theme of "babies" was out of the question. Whatever we began upon whirled round sooner or later to the one point. The needle may tremble, but it turns not with the less constancy to the pole.

As I pass for an oracle in the matter of paps and possets, I had frequent communication with my now happy neighbor, who had forgotten to scold her husband, learned to let Betsey have time to eat, and omitted the nightly scouring of the floor, lest so much dampness might be bad for the baby. We were in deep consultation one morning on some important point touching the well-being of this sole object of Mrs. Doubleday's thoughts and dreams, when the very same little Ianthe Howard, dirty as ever, presented herself. She sat down and stared awhile without speaking, *à l' ordinaire;* and then informed us that her mother "wanted Miss Doubleday to let her have her baby for a little while, 'cause Benny's mouth's so sore that"——but she had no time to finish the sentence.

"Lend my baby!!!"—and her utterance failed. The new mother's feelings were fortunately too big for speech, and Ianthe wisely disappeared before Mrs. Doubleday found her tongue. Philo, who entered on the instant, burst into one of his electrifying laughs with—

> Ask my Polly,
> To lend her dolly!

—and I could not help thinking that one must come "west" in order to learn a little of every thing.

The identical glass tube which I offered Mrs. Howard, as a substitute for Mrs. Doubleday's baby, and which had already, frail as it is, threaded the country for miles in all directions, is, even as I write, in demand; a man on horseback comes from somewhere near Danforth's, and asks in mysterious whispers for——but I shall not tell what he calls it. The reader must come to Michigan.

16

Black Hawk (1767–1838)
from *Life of MA-KA-TAI-ME-SHE-KIA-KIAK*

By the 1830s, for millions of white Americans, Indian Americans were sentimental heroes. Popular novels like Lydia Maria Child's *Hobomok* (1824) and Catharine Maria Sedgwick's *Hope Leslie* (1827) portrayed Indians as saintly and benevolent, and popular dramas like John Augustus Stone's *Metamora, or, the Last of the Wampanoags* (1828) had transformed feared and hated Indian leaders like King Philip into tragic heroes nobly defending their homelands. This sympathy in turn made Andrew Jackson's Indian removal policy highly controversial—supported by most frontier settlers but vigorously opposed by many easterners and religious groups.

Such was the context for the Black Hawk War (1832) and then the publication of Black Hawk's *Life of MA-KA-TAI-ME-SHE-KIA-KIAK* (1833), the first or nearly the first full-length Indian autobiography. Black Hawk, though defeated, captured, and imprisoned after the fifteen-week war, had later been taken east with other Sauks, and huge crowds had turned out to see him and applaud his bravery. In August, 1833, following his return to the Sac and Fox Agency on Rock Island in the Mississippi, Black Hawk therefore called upon Antoine LeClair, the U.S. Interpreter on the Agency, and "express[ed] a great desire to have a History of his Life written and published, in order . . . 'that the people of the United States . . . might know the *causes* that had impelled him to act as he has done, and the *principles* by which he was governed' " (3). Thus did LeClair "certify" in a brief preface, swearing to the book's accuracy, and similar accounts of the origin and purpose of the book are given in Black Hawk's dedication of it and the Advertisement of it by the editor, a newspaperman named John B. Patterson. Black Hawk was therefore not asked or paid to dictate his life history (as later happened with other Indian autobiographers). His story must have been heavily edited, for the translation is sometimes even embellished with phrases from English poetry, but the sixty-six-year-old Black Hawk did succeed in giving sympathetic white readers his motives and reasons for having fought and in "vindicat[ing] my character from misrepresentation" (7). David Brumble, in *American Indian Autobiography*, has recently argued that such "self-vindications" had long been a purpose of Indian autobiographical discourse. The medium and context were new, but the tradition of a defeated warrior justifying himself and his supporters was probably an old one.

The selection below is from near the middle of the book. Before it, Black Hawk tells of his ancestors, how the people came to live on Rock Island in the Mississippi River (near present-day Rock Island, Illinois), his early battles, and the injustice of an 1804 treaty which was an underlying cause of the war. In the remainder of the book he criticizes Keokuk, leader of the peace band, explains how the war began, and narrates its events. He also describes his journey east in 1833.

As the passage opens, it is 1816 on the U.S. calendar, and Black Hawk has just been forced to sign a treaty in St. Louis and then gone back to his village. The description of the cycles of village life, his sorrow over the deaths of his son and daughter, and the "difficulty with the Ioways" and how it was peacefully resolved all build respect for him and for the Sauk people. He is also eloquent in defending the Sauk attitude towards land. Therefore, in spite of the sentimental benevolence both sides attempted to express towards each other, the facts of white-Indian cultural differences cannot be ignored. This, and his emphasis on the difficulties of adjustment, place the text in the mainstream of what is now called ethnic autobiography. Where other autobiographers of this period stressed their new national identity, Black Hawk stressed his tribal one, and his success in defending it makes this a compelling story.

Black Hawk died in Iowa, near the Des Moines River. The selection of his story below is from *Life of MA-KA-TAI-ME-SHE-KIA-KIAK or Black Hawk,* ed. J. B. Patterson (Boston, 1834). A modern edition, *Black Hawk, an Autobiography,* edited by Donald Jackson, was published by the University of Illinois Press in 1955.

We were friendly treated by the white chiefs, and started back to our village on Rock river. Here we found that troops had arrived to build a fort at Rock Island. This, in our opinion, was a contradiction to what we had done—"to prepare for war in time of peace." We did not, however, object to their building the fort on the island, but we were very sorry, as this was the best island on the Mississippi, and had long been the resort of our young people during the summer. It was our garden (like the white people have near to their big villages) which supplied us with strawberries, blackberries, gooseberries, plums, apples, and nuts of different kinds; and its waters supplied us with fine fish, being situated in the rapids of the river. In my early life, I spent many happy days on this island. A good spirit had care of it, who lived in a cave in the rocks immediately under the place where the fort now stands, and has often been seen by our people. He was white, with large wings like a *swan's,* but ten times larger. We were particular not to make much noise in that part of the island which he inhabited, for fear of disturbing him. But the noise of the fort has since driven him away, and no doubt a *bad spirit* has taken his place!

Our village was situated on the north side of Rock river, at the foot of its rapids, and on the point of land between Rock river and the Mississippi. In its front, a prairie extended to the bank of the Mississippi; and in our rear, a continued bluff, gently ascending from the prairie. On the side of this bluff we had our cornfields, extending about two miles up, running parallel with the Mississippi; where we joined those of the Foxes, whose village was on the bank of the Mississippi, opposite the lower end of Rock island, and three miles distant from ours. We had about eight hundred acres in cultivation, including what we had on the islands of Rock river. The land around our village, uncultivated, was covered with blue-grass, which made excellent pasture for our horses. Several fine springs broke out of the bluff, near by, from which we were supplied with good water. The rapids of Rock river furnished us with an abundance of excellent fish, and the land, being good, never failed to produce good crops of corn, beans, pumpkins, and squashes. We always had plenty—our children never cried with hunger, nor our people were never in want. Here our village had stood for more than a hundred years, during all which time we were the undisputed possessors of the valley of the Mississippi, from the Ouisconsin to the Portage des Sioux, near the mouth of the Missouri, being about seven hundred miles in length.

At this time we had very little intercourse with the whites, except our traders. Our village was healthy, and there was no place in the country possessing such advantages, nor no hunting grounds better than those we had in possession. If another prophet had come to our village in those days, and told us what has since taken place, none of our people would have believed him! What! to be driven from our village and hunting grounds, and not even permitted to visit the graves of our forefathers, our relations and friends?

This hardship is not known to the whites. With us it is a custom to visit the graves of our friends, and keep them in repair for many years. The mother will go alone to weep over the grave of her child! The brave, with pleasure, visits the grave of his father, after he has been successful in war, and re-paints the post that shows where he lies! There is no place like that where the bones of our forefathers lie, to go to when in grief. Here the Great Spirit will take pity on us!

But, how different is our situation now, from what it was in those days! Then we were as happy as the buffalo on the plains—but now, we are as miserable as the hungry, howling wolf in the prairie! But I am digressing from my story. Bitter reflection crowds upon my mind, and must find utterance.

When we returned to our village in the spring, from our wintering grounds, we would finish trading with our traders, who always followed us to our village. We purposely kept some of our fine furs for this trade; and, as there was great opposition among them, who should get these skins, we always got our goods cheap. After this trade was over, the traders would give us a few kegs of rum, which was generally promised in the fall, to encourage us to make a good hunt, and not go to war. They would then start with their furs and peltries for their homes. Our old men would take a frolic, (at this time our young men never drank.) When this was ended, the next thing to be done was to bury our dead, (such as had died during the year.) This is a great *medicine feast*. The relations of those who have died, give all the goods they have purchased, as presents to their friends—thereby reducing themselves to poverty, to show the Great Spirit that they are humble, so that he will take pity on them. We would next open the cashes, and take out corn and other provisions, which had been put up in the fall,—and then commence repairing our lodges. As soon as this is accomplished, we repair the fences around our fields, and clean them off, ready for planting corn. This work is done by our women. The men, during this time, are feasting on dried venison, bear's meat, wild fowl, and corn, prepared in different ways; and recounting to each other what took place during the winter.

Our women plant the corn, and as soon as they get done, we make a feast, and dance the *crane* dance, in which they join us, dressed in their best, and decorated with feathers. At this feast our young braves select the young woman they wish to have for a wife. He then informs his mother, who calls on the mother of the girl, when the arrangement is made, and the time appointed for him to come. He goes to the lodge when all are asleep, (or pretend to be,) lights his matches, which have been provided for the purpose, and soon finds where his intended sleeps. He then awakens her, and holds the light to his face that she may know him—after which he places the light close to her. If she blows it out, the ceremony is ended, and he appears in the lodge next morning, as one of the family. If she does not blow out the light, but leaves it to burn out, he retires from the lodge. The next day he places himself in full view of it, and plays his flute. The young women go out, one by one, to see who he is playing for. The tune changes, to let them know that he is not playing for them. When his intended makes her appearance at the door, he continues his *courting* tune, until she returns to the lodge. He then gives over playing, and makes another trial at night, which generally turns out favorable. During the first year they ascertain whether they can agree with each other, and can be happy—if not, they part, and each looks out again. If we were to live together and disagree, we should be as foolish as the whites! No indiscretion can banish a woman from her parental lodge—no difference how many children she may bring home, she is always welcome—the kettle is over the fire to feed them.

The crane dance often lasts two or three days. When this is over, we feast again, and have our *national* dance. The large square in the village is swept and prepared for the purpose. The chiefs and old warriors, take seats on mats which have been spread at the upper end of the square—the drummers and singers come next, and the braves and women form the sides, leaving a large space in the middle. The drums beat, and the singers commence. A warrior enters the square, keeping time with the music. He shows the manner he started on a war party—how he approached the enemy—he strikes, and describes the way he killed him. All join in applause. He then leaves the square, and another enters and takes his place. Such of our young men as have not been out in war parties, and killed an enemy, stand back ashamed—not being able to enter the square. I remember that I was ashamed to look where our young women stood, before I could take my stand in the square as a warrior.

What pleasure it is to an old warrior, to see his son come forward and relate his exploits—it makes him feel young, and induces him to enter the square, and "fight his battles o'er again."

This national dance makes our warriors. When I was travelling last summer, on a steam-boat, on a large river, going from New York to Albany, I was shown the place where the Americans dance their national dance [West Point]; where the old warriors recount to their young men, what they have done, to stimulate them to go and do likewise. This surprised me, as I did not think the whites understood our way of making braves.

When our national dance is over—our corn-fields hoed, and every weed dug up, and our corn about knee-high, all our young men would start in a direction towards sun-down, to hunt deer and buffalo—being prepared, also, to kill Sioux, if any are found on our hunting grounds—a part of our old men and women to the lead mines to make lead—and the remainder of our people start to fish, and get mat stuff. Every one leaves the village, and remains about forty days. They then return: the hunting party bringing in dried buffalo and deer meat, and sometimes *Sioux scalps,* when they are found trespassing on our hunting grounds. At other times they are met by a party of Sioux too strong for them, and are driven in. If the Sioux have killed the Sacs last, they expect to be retaliated upon, and will fly before them, and vice versa. Each party knows that the other has a right to retaliate, which induces those who have killed last, to give way before their enemy—as neither wish to strike, except to avenge the death of their relatives. All our wars are predicated by the relatives of those killed; or by aggressions upon our hunting grounds.

The party from the lead mines bring lead, and the others dried fish, and mats for our winter lodges. Presents are now made by each party; the first, giving to the others dried buffalo and deer, and they, in exchange, presenting them with lead, dried fish and mats. This is a happy season of the year—having plenty of provisions, such as beans, squashes, and other produce, with our dried meat and fish, we continue to make feasts and visit each other, until our corn is ripe. Some lodge in the village makes a feast daily, to the Great Spirit. I cannot explain this so that the white people would comprehend me, as we have no regular standard among us. Every one makes his feast as he thinks best, to please the Great Spirit, who has the care of all beings created. Others believe in two Spirits; one good and one bad, and make feasts for the Bad Spirit, *to keep him quiet!* If they can make peace with him, the Good

265

Spirit will not hurt them. For my part, I am of opinion, that so far as we have *reason*, we have a right to use it, in determining what is right or wrong; and should pursue that path which we believe to be right—believing that, "whatever is, is right." If the Great and Good Spirit wished us to believe and do as the whites, he could easily change our opinions, so that we would see, and think, and act as they do. We are *nothing* compared to His power, and we feel and know it. We have men among us, like the whites, who pretend to know the right path, but will not consent to show it without *pay!* I have no faith in their paths—but believe that every man must make his own path!

When our corn is getting ripe, our young people watch with anxiety for the signal to pull roasting ears—as none dare touch them until the proper time. When the corn is fit to use, another great ceremony takes place, with feasting, and returning thanks to the Great Spirit for giving us corn.

I will here relate the manner in which corn first came. According to tradition, handed down to our people, a beautiful woman was seen to descend from the clouds, and alight upon the earth, by two of our ancestors, who had killed a deer, and were sitting by a fire, roasting a part of it to eat. They were astonished at seeing her, and concluded that she must be hungry, and had smelt the meat—and immediately went to her, taking with them a piece of the roasted venison. They presented it to her, and she eat—and told them to return to the spot where she was sitting, at the end of one year, and they would find a reward for their kindness and generosity. She then ascended to the clouds, and disappeared. The two men returned to their village, and explained to the nation what they had seen, done, and heard—but were laughed at by their people. When the period arrived, for them to visit this consecrated ground, where they were to find a reward for their attention to the beautiful woman of the clouds, they went with a large party, and found, where her right hand had rested on the ground, *corn* growing—and where the left hand had rested, *beans*—and immediately where she had been seated, *tobacco*.

The two first have, ever since, been cultivated by our people, as our principal provisions—and the last used for smoking. The white people have since found out the latter, and seem to relish it as much as we do—as they use it in different ways, viz. smoking, snuffing and eating!

We thank the Great Spirit for all the benefits he has conferred upon us. For myself, I never take a drink of water from a spring, without being mindful of his goodness.

We next have our great ball play—from three to five hundred on a side, play this game. We play for horses, guns, blankets, or any other kind of property we have. The successful party take the stakes, and all retire to our lodges in peace and friendship.

We next commence horse-racing, and continue our sport and feasting, until the corn is all secured. We then prepare to leave our village for our hunting grounds. The traders arrive, and give us credit for such articles as we want to clothe our families, and enable us to hunt. We first, however, hold a council with them, to ascertain the price they will give us for our skins, and what they will charge us for goods. We inform them where we intend hunting—and tell them where to build their houses. At this place, we deposit part of our corn, and leave our old people. The traders have always been kind to them, and relieved them when in want. They were always much respected by our people—and never since we have been a nation, has one of them been killed by any of our people.

We disperse, in small parties, to make our hunt, and as soon as it is over, we return to our traders' establishment, with our skins, and remain feasting, playing cards and other pastimes, until near the close of the winter. Our young men then start on the beaver hunt; others to hunt raccoons and musk-rats—and the remainder of our people go to the sugar camps to make sugar. All leave our encampment, and appoint a place to meet on the Mississippi, so that we may return to our village together, in the spring. We always spent our time pleasantly at the sugar camp. It being the season for wild fowl, we lived well, and always had plenty, when the hunters came in, that we might make a feast for them. After this is over, we return to our village, accompanied, sometimes, by our traders. In this way, the year rolled round happily. But these are times that were!

On returning, in the spring, from our hunting ground, I had the pleasure of meeting our old friend, the trader of Peoria, at Rock Island. He came up in a boat from St. Louis, not as a trader, as in times past, but as our *agent*. We were all pleased to see him. He told us, that he narrowly escaped falling into the hands of Dixon. He remained with us a short time, gave us good advice, and then returned to St. Louis.

The Sioux having committed depredations on our people, we sent out war parties that summer, who succeeded in killing *fourteen*. I paid several visits to fort Armstrong during the summer, and was always well treated. We were not as happy then in our village as formerly. Our people got more liquor than customary. I used all my influence to prevent drunkenness, but without effect. As the settlements progressed towards us, we became worse off, and more unhappy. Many of our people, instead of going to their old hunting grounds, where game was plenty, would go near to the settlements to hunt—and, instead of saving their skins to pay the trader for goods furnished them in the fall, would sell them to the settlers for whiskey! and return in the spring with their families, almost naked, and without the means of getting any thing for them.

About this time my eldest son was taken sick and died. He had always been a dutiful child, and had just grown to manhood. Soon after, my youngest daughter, an interesting and affectionate child, died also. This was a hard stroke, because I loved my children. In my distress, I left the noise of the village, and built my lodge on a mound in my corn-field, and enclosed it with a fence, around which I planted corn and beans. Here I was with my family alone. I gave every thing I had away, and reduced myself to poverty. The only covering I retained, was a piece of buffalo robe. I resolved on blacking my face and fasting, for two years, for the loss of my two children—drinking only of water in the middle of the day, and eating sparingly of boiled corn at sunset. I fulfilled my promise, hoping that the Great Spirit would take pity on me.

My nation had now some difficulty with the Ioways, with whom we wished to be at peace. Our young men had repeatedly killed some of the Ioways; and these breaches had always been made up by giving presents to the relations of those killed. But the last council we had with them, we promised that, in case any more of their people were killed by ours, instead of presents, we would give up the person, or persons, that had done the injury. We made this determination known to our people; but, notwithstanding, one of our young men killed an Ioway the following winter.

A party of our people were about starting for the Ioway village to give the young man up. I agreed to accompany them. When we were ready to start, I called at the lodge for the young man to go with us. He was sick, but willing to go. His brother, however, prevented him, and insisted on going to die in his place, as he was unable to travel. We started, and on the seventh day arrived in sight of the Ioway village, and when within a short distance of it, halted and dismounted. We all bid farewell to our young brave, who entered the village alone, singing his *deathsong,* and sat down in the square in the middle of the village. One of the Ioway chiefs came out to us. We told him that we had fulfilled our promise—that we had brought the brother of the young man who had killed one of their people—that he had volunteered to come in his place, in consequence of his brother being unable to travel from sickness. We had no further conversation, but mounted our horses and rode off. As we started, I cast my eye towards the village, and observed the Ioways coming out of their lodges with spears and war clubs. We took our trail back, and travelled until dark—then encamped and made a fire. We had not been here long, before we heard the sound of horses coming towards us. We seized our arms; but instead of an enemy, it was our young brave with two horses. He told me that after we had left him, they menaced him with death for some time—then gave him something to eat—smoked the pipe with him—and made him a present of the two horses and some goods, and started him after us. When we arrived at our village, our people were much pleased; and for the noble and generous conduct of the Ioways, on this occasion, not one of their people has been killed since by any of our nation.

That fall I visited Malden with several of my band, and were well treated by the agent of our British father, who gave us a variety of presents. He also gave me a medal, and told me there never would be war between England and America again; but, for my fidelity to the British during the war that had terminated sometime before, requested me to come with my band every year and get presents, as Col. Dixon had promised me.

I returned, and hunted that winter on the Two-Rivers. The whites were now settling the country fast. I was out one day hunting in a bottom, and met three white men. They accused me of killing their hogs; I denied it; but they would not listen to me. One of them took my gun out of my hand and fired it off—then took out the flint, gave back my gun, and commenced beating me with sticks, and ordered me off. I was so much bruised that I could not sleep for several nights.

Some time after this occurrence, one of my camp cut a bee-tree, and carried the honey to his lodge. A party of white men soon followed, and told him that the bee-tree was theirs, and that he had no right to cut it. He pointed to the honey, and told them to take it; they were not satisfied with this, but took all the packs of skins that he had collected during the winter, to pay his trader and clothe his family with in the spring, and carried them off!

How could we like such people, who treated us so unjustly? We determined to break up our camp, for fear that they would do worse—and when we joined our people in the spring, a great many of them complained of similar treatment.

This summer our agent came to live at Rock Island. He treated us well, and gave us good advice. I visited him and the trader very often during the summer, and, for the first time, heard talk of our having to leave my village. The trader explained to me the terms of the treaty that had been made, and said we would be obliged to leave the Illinois side of the Mississippi, and advised us to select a good place for our village, and remove to it in the spring. He pointed out the difficulties we would have to encounter, if we remained at our village on Rock river. He had great influence with the principal Fox chief, his adopted brother, and persuaded him to leave his village, and go to the west side of the Mississippi river, and build another—which he did the spring following.

Nothing was now talked of but leaving our village. Ke-o-kuck had been persuaded to consent to go; and was using all his influence, backed by the war chief at fort Armstrong, and our agent and trader at Rock Island, to induce others to go with him. He sent the crier through the village to inform our people that it was the wish of our Great Father that we should remove to the west side of the Mississippi—and recommended the Ioway river as a good place for the new village—and wished his party to make such arrangements, before they started out on their winter's hunt, as to preclude the necessity of their returning to the village in the spring.

The party opposed to removing, called upon me for my opinion. I gave it freely—and after questioning Quàsh-quà-me about the sale of the lands, he assured me that he "never had consented to the sale of our village." I now promised this party to be their leader, and raised the standard of opposition

269

to Ke-o-kuck, with a full determination not to leave my village. I had an interview with Ke-o-kuck, to see if this difficulty could not be settled with our Great Father—and told him to propose to give other land, (any that our Great Father might choose, even our *lead mines,*) to be peaceably permitted to keep the small point of land on which our village and fields were situate. I was of opinion that the white people had plenty of land, and would never take our village from us. Ke-o-kuck promised to make an exchange if possible, and applied to our agent, and the great chief at St. Louis, (who has charge of all the agents,) for permission to go to Washington to see our Great Father for that purpose. This satisfied us for some time. We started to our hunting grounds, in good hopes that something would be done for us. During the winter, I received information that three families of whites had arrived at our village, and destroyed some of our lodges, and were making fences and divid-ing our corn-fields for their own use—*and were quarreling among themselves about their lines, in the division!* I immediately started for Rock river, a distance of ten days' travel, and on my arrival, found the report to be true. I went to my lodge, and saw a family occupying it. I wished to talk with them, but they could not understand me. I then went to Rock Island, and (the agent being absent,) told the interpreter what I wanted to say to those people, viz: "Not to settle on our lands—nor trouble our lodges or fences—that there was plenty of land in the country for them to settle upon—and they must leave our village, as we were coming back to it in the spring." The interpreter wrote me a paper, and I went back to the village, and showed it to the intruders, but could not understand their reply. I expected, however, that they would re-move, as I requested them. I returned to Rock Island, passed the night there, and had a long conversation with the trader. He again advised me to give up, and make my village with Ke-o-kuck, on the Ioway river. I told him that I would not. The next morning I crossed the Mississippi, on very bad ice—but the Great Spirit made it strong, that I might pass over safe. I travelled three days farther to see the Winnebago sub-agent, and converse with him on the subject of our difficulties. He gave me no better news than the trader had done. I started then, by way of Rock river, to see the prophet, believing that he was a man of great knowledge. When we met, I explained to him every thing as it was. He at once agreed that I was right, and advised me never to give up our village, for the whites to plough up the bones of our people. He said, that if we remained at our village, the whites would not trouble us—and advised me to get Ke-o-kuck, and the party that had consented to go with him to the Ioway in the spring, to return, and remain at our village.

I returned to my hunting ground, after an absence of one moon, and related what I had done. In a short time we came up to our village, and found that the whites had not left it—but that others had come, and that the greater part of our corn-fields had been enclosed. When we landed, the whites appeared displeased because we had come back. We repaired the lodges that had been left standing, and built others. Ke-o-kuck came to the village; but his object was to persuade others to follow him to the Ioway. He had accomplished nothing towards making arrangements for us to remain, or to exchange other lands for our village. There was no more friendship existing between us. I looked upon him as a coward, and no brave, to abandon his village to be occupied by strangers. What *right* had these people to our village, and our fields, which the Great Spirit had given us to live upon?

My reason teaches me that *land cannot be sold*. The Great Spirit gave it to his children to live upon, and cultivate, as far as is necessary for their subsistence; and so long as they occupy and cultivate it, they have the right to the soil—but if they voluntarily leave it, then any other people have a right to settle upon it. Nothing can be sold, but such things as can be carried away.

In consequence of the improvements of the intruders on our fields, we found considerable difficulty to get ground to plant a little corn. Some of the whites permitted us to plant small patches in the fields they had fenced, keeping all the best ground for themselves. Our women had great difficulty in climbing their fences, (being unaccustomed to the kind,) and were ill-treated if they left a rail down.

PART FOUR

Self-Liberators, 1836-1865

Although the autobiographical writers of the Revolution and years following had achieved (and helped the nation to achieve) national identities, they had not necessarily achieved or helped others to achieve personal and cultural independence. Approximately one-ninth of the population was, in fact, enslaved, and the native Indian population was not regarded as a part of the nation at all. They were not citizens and could not vote. Women could not vote either, and their rights to property were in most cases tightly restricted. Even white males frequently chafed against the nation's psychic bondage to English and European traditions and its lack of a literature and culture of its own. When Emerson said in his now famous Phi Beta Kappa address at Harvard in 1837, "We have listened too long to the courtly muses of Europe" and lamented that "The spirit of the American freeman is already suspected to be timid, imitative, tame," he was only saying what scores of American commencement speakers had said before. The United States were no longer colonies, but many people still had a colonial mentality.

What was new and liberating in Emerson's message to the Harvard graduates of 1837, however, was the linkage of a cultural independence for the nation with individual freedom from social conventions. He lined up Europe, tradition, the past, oppression, conformity, and society on one side, and America, innovation, the future, the individual, and freedom on the other. "Society everywhere is in conspiracy against the manhood of every one of its members," he later said in "Self-Reliance." "Whoso would be a man, must be a nonconformist," he also said, and, "Nothing is at last sacred but the integrity of your own mind." Such sentences were intentionally short. Emerson, that "winged Franklin" (as one of his contemporaries called him), replaced Poor Richard's prudential maxims with a whole new almanac of inspirational sayings that for his generation (and after) were to become personal mottoes, icons of the ego.

In the Emersonian vision, autobiography occupied a very large and lofty place, as the short selections on it that are given here indicate. Emerson saw the new age, the nineteenth century, as an age of introspection. Kant, Goethe, and Coleridge appealed most to him for their individualism, as expressed in their journals and conversations and "aids to reflection," and he valued his own journal accordingly. He also advised journal-keeping to friends, as a means of discipline and self-discovery. From his journals would later come his lectures and essays, which were unified more by their inspirational tone than by sequential logic. Indeed, one often feels that he wrote first of all to inspire people to freedom—starting with himself. Thus, his whole literary production seems an ongoing experiment in inspirational autobiography. Yet his lectures and essays inspired his audiences, too, from associations of young mechanics in Boston to farmers and lawyers in Illinois. His private reflections expressed the aspirations of pre-Civil War America, or at least the northern half of it. Thus he himself realized the comparison to Dante (or Dante as he saw him) that he made in the essay "The Poet": "he dared to write his autobiography in colossal cipher, or into universality."

The apposition "into universality" indicates, however, the paradox in Emerson's concepts of autobiography, as in his concepts of self. The Emersonian or Transcendental "self" was not a mean or selfish ego. It was more like the Christian soul. It was "part or parcel of God," as Emerson wrote in the beginning of his first book, *Nature*. It was "a transparent eyeball," and when he suddenly transcended his ordinary being and reached this state, he said he felt "the currents of the Universal Being circulate through me." True autobiography should be the expression of this more noble, purer, universal self—a restriction that almost idealized it into thin air. One can read all day in Emerson's essays and never learn who his parents were, where he went to college, or how he earned his living.

Thoreau and Whitman and Margaret Fuller were equally concerned about universals and transcendence but much more inclusive of particulars in their definitions of self. The self had to have a location, like a house and a pond (and a book), a *Walden*. It could not just stand "on a bare common." Indeed, Thoreau was unlikely to see *bare* commons, or *bare* woods; he described their history, their botany and zoology, and he appropriated all these details as parts or mirrors of the self. For Whitman, the self thrived on its relations to other selves, the great democratic multitudes which he celebrated and appropriated in his poetry. For Margaret Fuller, the self had to be a woman and had to be revolutionary. It was what drove her to be different, to seek greater fulfillment, and to contend with the status quo.

In their own ways, then, all of these decidedly autobiographical writers continue to reflect some of the prejudices against autobiography which ruled during the late eighteenth and early nineteenth centuries. None wrote autobiographies in the manner of Franklin, Goethe, or Rousseau, and all had reservations about the specific egotism those autobiographies reflected. The New Englanders, in the tradition of their Federalist ancestors, also had reservations about rowdy democratic individualism, including manifestations of it in autobiography. And thus we have the curious paradox of American Transcendentalism that, as Lawrence Buell put it, "The most egoistic movement in American literary history produced no first-rate autobiography, unless one counts *Walden* as such."[1] One answer, of course, is that the kinds of autobiographies Emerson, Thoreau, Whitman and Margaret Fuller (as well as Hawthorne, Melville, and Dickinson) *did* write are decidedly better and more characteristic of them than if they had written imitations of Franklin, Rousseau, and Goethe. But the fact remains that autobiography of this more lengthy and directly individualistic and particular sort continued in disrepute, at least among the class of Americans who were well educated and became writers, artists, and leaders in political or professional life.

In this respect, it is interesting to note that none of the eleven U.S. presidents between Jefferson and James Buchanan wrote an autobiography (see Louis Kaplan's *Bibliography of American Autobiographies*), and Buchanan's was only a thirty-page reminiscence of his early years. Lincoln, his successor, was the first president to write what might be called campaign autobiographies, and those, one of which is included here, were primarily sketches for use by newspapermen preparing biographies of him. The first literary autobiography, Lawrence Buell believes, in the sense of an autobiography written by someone whose major work was writing poetry or fiction, was Lydia Sigourney's *Letters of Life* of 1866, an excerpt of which is included below.

But stories of religious experience and stories of adventure, like travel books and narratives of enslavement, captivity, and escape, did continue to be written, and it was out of these traditions that the new kinds of popular autobiography grew. The religious autobiographies, by and large, were "a gentry-class product,"[2] such as Orestes Brownson's *The Convert* (1857). Brownson told of his spiritual odyssey from Presbyterian to Roman Catholic, passing through Universalism, Unitarianism, Transcendentalism, and various reformist and utopian programs like Saint-Simonianism. The adventure narratives were mainly lower-class, coming from sailors, escaped slaves, and victims of Indian captivity. These lines were not rigid, however, and one of the most interesting of the full-length religious autobiographies of the period is Peter Cartwright's *Autobiography* (1856). Cartwright (1785–1872) was a backwoods preacher who joined the Methodist Episcopal Church in Kentucky at age sixteen and soon began speaking at camp meetings, one-room schoolhouses, and new churches all through the Ohio valley. Such men faced the same kinds of physical obstacles that Charles Woodmason had, as well as resistance and rivalry from atheists, agnostics, other churchmen, drunks, and

1. Lawrence Buell, *Literary Transcendentalism: Style and Vision in the American Renaissance* (Ithaca: Cornell Univ. Press, 1973), p. 268.
2. Lawrence Buell, "Autobiography in the American Renaissance," in *American Autobiography: Retrospect and Prospect,* ed. Paul John Eakin (Madison: Univ. of Wisconsin Press, 1991), p. 48.

frontier bullies. Thus, autobiographies of frontier preachers like Cartwright combine religion and uproarious adventure. Cartwright was no intellectual like Jonathan Edwards, and his sectarian prejudices are narrow and dated, but such autobiographies are extremely revealing documents of frontier life and culture. It was the frontier that gave American Protestant churches the room to expand and to develop a more democratic liturgy and governance, and the autobiographies of their ministers are one of their most characteristic forms of history and expression.

The frontier also provided the setting for a lot of the travel narratives of the period. Men and women travelling the overland trails to California and Oregon in the 1840s and '50s very often kept diaries in which they recorded the number of miles travelled each day, encounters with Indians, the hardships of the journey, and the deaths of their friends and family members from diseases like cholera. A recent annotated bibliography of the diaries and memoirs of just the Platte River route contains hundreds of entries. *Women's Diaries of the Overland Trail,* edited by Lillian Schlissel, comments on the differences between the men's and women's experiences and the ways of writing about them. At the same time, upperclass easterners undertook journeys to the West as a way of breaking free from social conventions, recuperating from illness, and learning (and writing) about the new country. Washington Irving helped establish this convention with *A Tour on the Prairies* (1835) about his journey into present-day Oklahoma in 1832, after seventeen years of living in Europe. Margaret Fuller went to Illinois, via the Great Lakes, in 1843 and published her *Summer on the Lakes* in 1844. Francis Parkman followed with *The Oregon Trail* in 1849. Richard Henry Dana, meanwhile, had been one of the most daring of these eastern adventurers when he sailed for California as a seaman in 1834 and spent over a year loading hides off the beaches, before returning to Boston and graduating from Harvard Law School. His *Two Years Before the Mast* (1840) encouraged Herman Melville to write about his seafaring adventures and helped arouse public sympathy for the plight of sailors.

What these many kinds of first-person accounts of travel and adventure illustrate is that by the 1840s and '50s Americans of many backgrounds did, in fact, have the freedom and the opportunity to go to many new places and engage in a much more expansive life. Their autobiographical writings became more diverse and extensive because their lives were. Meanwhile, P. T. Barnum, as impresario and entrepreneur, capitalized on such adventures and the curiosities they discovered by setting up his American Museum in New York in 1842. His *Life of P. T. Barnum,* which in turn capitalized on the curiosity millions of Americans had about his own tricks and adventures, was published in 1855, just in time for a reviewer in the *Knickerbocker Magazine* to write about it and *Walden* in the same column, under the title "Town and Rural Humbugs"! The contrast between Barnum and Thoreau is stunning.

But in radically different ways they had shown the range of personal freedom and freedom of enterprise in the mid-century United States.

The black and the women autobiographers of this period, however, did not have such freedoms, or had to earn them in even more daring and subversive ways. Yet, as some commentators like William L. Andrews and Jean Fagan Yellin have noticed, this makes the slave narrators and the feminist writers the period's most representative lives, in the full Emersonian sense of people who experienced in the greatest intensity and wrote most movingly about what all men and women knew. They spoke for more than just themselves.

Jarena Lee appears first in this group because her *Life and Religious Experience* was published in 1836, and because she was one of those who made religious autobiography a means of both religious witness and personal liberation. Like Peter Cartwright, she was of the Methodist Episcopal Church, but she belonged to the African-American branch of it founded in 1794 by Richard Allen, a former slave who had been born in Philadelphia in 1760 and who purchased his own freedom in 1777. Lee had not been born a slave, but, even so, "at the age of seven years I was parted from my parents and went to live as a servant maid. . . ." At age twenty-one, she began her emancipation from this work when she became aware of, or "convicted" of, her sins. Gradually but relentlessly, she gained the rights to exhort and then to preach, finally becoming a travelling revivalist like Cartwright, operating mainly in New Jersey, Pennsylvania, and Ohio, also helping "to set the world on fire" for Methodism (Cartwright's words). Even more than Cartwright's *Autobiography,* her *Life* was an important part of her liberation. She sold it to help support herself; it was proof of her conversion and an example to her followers; and the fact that she had written it and published it was further evidence of her mastery of the written language—what had previously been the master's language.

Mastery of the master's language, his "script," so to speak, is also a very important theme in the writing of ex-slaves, as readers of Frederick Douglass's *Narrative* or Harriet Jacobs's *Incidents in the Life of Slave Girl* know. Just to write one's autobiography was "to tell a free story"—to tell a story of (relative) freedom, in (relative) freedom. Yet there were still some things which the ex-slave could not relate, and one frequently was the specific story of how he or she had escaped. Frederick Douglass censors himself at this point in both his *Narrative* (1845) and *My Bondage and My Freedom* (1855), though he does tell the story in his *Life and Times* . . . (1881), the last of his three autobiographies. An excerpt from this work appears in the next section of this anthology.

Another representative life from this period of the American Renaissance, as F. O. Matthiessen called it over fifty years ago, was the life of Fanny Fern. Matthiessen and his contemporary discoverers of the "great" American literature would never have called her so significant. They dismissed her as just a tearful newspaper columnist. But her fight to support herself and her children, as told in her autobiographical novel *Ruth Hall*, is a story of the trials and prejudices a woman faced. Writing newspaper columns was her way up from poverty. The columns were also autobiographical, and they were so moving and so satirical and sassy that they made her "the first woman columnist in the United States" and also one of the best-paid writers in the United States.[3] Just as for ex-slaves, therefore, autobiography for Fanny Fern was a means of protest. Within her columns and her novels, she could attack the men who had struck the poses of sentimental regard for women without delivering the substance. She could also expose their demeaning condescension and misinformed notions of women's experience and sensibility, while boldly writing about her own true feelings.

For those who like to collect telling historical trivia, there is an unexpected coincidence in the lives of Fanny Fern and Harriet Jacobs. Nathaniel P. Willis, Fanny Fern's selfish brother, who would not help support her when she was destitute, who printed her columns without paying her, and whom she satirized as "Apollo Hyacinth," was Harriet Jacobs's employer. Willis and his wife had hired Jacobs as a children's nurse, shortly after her escape from North Carolina. When his first wife died, Willis took her to England with his children, and she continued working for him after he remarried. But all this time Jacobs sensed that he was pro-slavery, so she hid her manuscript of *Incidents* and only worked on it in secret.[4] Thus, for both Fanny Fern and Harriet Jacobs (or "Linda Brent," to use her pseudonym), autobiography was not only a means of protest but something written under circumstances of secrecy or subversion, also something that had to be written under a "nom de plume," as book reviewers elegantly said.

Lydia Sigourney did not face such immediate physical and familial obstacles. As her autobiography makes abundantly clear, she led a highly privileged, financially secure life, and her parents and husband did not oppose her literary activity. Still, she had anxieties about writing her own life history, just as forty years before, in 1815, she says, she had had compunctions about publishing her first book. That book, *Moral Pieces in Prose and Verse,* had been published at the urging of Daniel Wadsworth, the backer of the school she ran in Hartford, Connecticut, and Wadsworth "took upon himself the whole responsibility of contracting with publishers, gathering subscriptions, and even correcting the proof-sheets."[5] Publishing a book was then "a novel enterprise for a female," as she puts it, and Wadsworth, whom she calls

3. Joyce W. Warren, "Introduction" to Fanny Fern, *Ruth Hall and Other Writings* (New Brunswick, NJ: Rutgers Univ. Press, 1986), p. xv.
4. Harriet Jacobs, Letter to Amy Post, c. 1852, in *Incidents in the Life of a Slave Girl,* ed. Jean Fagan Yellin (Cambridge: Harvard Univ. Press, 1987), p. 232.
5. Lydia Sigourney, *Letters of Life* (New York: D. Appleton, 1866), p. 325. Further references are given in text.

"my kind patron" and the book's "disinterested prompter," shielded her from these sordid details (325). Such were the restrictions of gender and gentility in 1815!

By 1865, when she wrote *Letters of Life,* many of those restrictions had fallen. The descriptive catalogue of her own books which she gives in the last chapter of *Letters of Life* lists fifty-five titles. She had also edited religious journals and children's magazines, until what she delicately calls "the financial feature . . . which at first supplied only my indulgences, my journeyings, or my charities, became eventually a form of subsistence" (378). But she still had hesitations about writing an autobiography. "You request of me, my dear friend, a particular account of my own life," she begins, thus adopting the formula of a series of letters written to oblige someone else. She is also cautious to be modest and to insist that as in all her writing "two principles" are "ever kept in view." The writing will not "interfere with the discharge of womanly duty" and will "aim at being an instrument of good" (324). In addition, as the record of her "earthly pilgrimage," this book "might impart some instruction to the future traveller, and set forth His praise, whose mercies are 'new every morning, and fresh every moment'" (5).

Lydia Sigourney thereby made domesticity, beneficence, and piety the ends of the first American literary autobiography—a woman's equivalent of Benjamin Franklin's promotion of industry, doing good, and modestly instructing his "son" (or sons) in the ways of Providence. But where Franklin repeatedly stressed his active roles of going into business, promoting good causes, and seizing one opportunity after another, there is a heavy passivity in the life and style of Lydia Sigourney.[6] She accepts responsibilities because she is asked; she writes because she was a lonely child; and she publishes to oblige Wadsworth, as she later wrote many obituary poems because someone asked her. Indeed, at the end of her list of her fifty-five books, she adds nearly ten pages listing some of the requests she has had from readers asking for odes, elegies, epitaphs, book dedications, and hymns for them, their families, and charities! No other kind of laborer, she protests, gets asked for such donations. And yet her sense of women's literature, like women's work, as a service to others inflicted these obligations on her.

Nevertheless, Lydia Sigourney's *Letters of Life* also projects her solid satisfaction with her domestic and literary accomplishments. There is a difference, after all, between just being passive—serving others, being genteel, and living a life of self-control—and successfully writing books commending the woman's passive role. The writing is active, and the success leads to a greater pride, to financial independence, and to a sense of individual fulfillment. As Jarena Lee had gone into the pulpit and preached, and as prominent early feminists like Susan B. Anthony and Elizabeth Cady Stanton had stepped

6. Buell, "Autobiography," p. 60.

onto the platforms and begun to lecture, so had Sigourney walked into the literary marketplace (however hesitantly at first), using her own name and becoming famous. Moreover, unlike most women of her time, she had written histories and biographies on public events and figures, and not merely on women's matters. As Nina Baym has pointed out, Lydia Sigourney became a major voice in the interpretation and celebration of the American Revolution, providing her readers with images of patriotism, dedication, and sacrifice. Thus, despite her modesty and caution, she was a public figure herself; and in *Letters of Life,* she claimed the public figure's right to tell her own story, in her own words, from childhood to old age. It was a new freedom, both for women and for American authors.

17

Jarena Lee (1783–1849?)

The Life and Religious Experience of
Jarena Lee, A Coloured Lady

The Life and Religious Experience of Jarena Lee, A Coloured Lady, Giving an Account of Her Call to Preach the Gospel, was first printed in Philadelphia in 1836, Lee paying thirty-eight dollars for a thousand copies which she could distribute at camp meetings and other places where she preached. A second edition, published in 1849, added her record of these places, with the scriptural texts she preached from, miles travelled, and number of converts. But otherwise very little is known of her. She was one of hundreds of itinerant preachers and "exhorters" who roamed the United States in the first half of the nineteenth century. They held revivals, established new congregations, and also helped to establish social order on the frontier and in urban areas unrepresented by other churches.

One of these churches was the African Methodist Episcopal church, which had been founded by Richard Allen, the man who converted Lee in 1804. Allen was also glad to accept her as someone who could hold prayer meetings and "exhort," that is, encourage congregations to heed the sermons and the scriptures; but like other clergymen of the time, he resisted accepting women preachers.

Lee's autobiography, therefore, is both a spiritual autobiography, with powerful accounts of her visions and her promptings to speak and pray, and also an account of her progress in attaining greater social autonomy, until she becomes one of the first non-Quaker woman preachers in America. Indeed, the two stories come together at many points. The visions *call* her out of a life of submissiveness, and once they are answered and described, they give her power. Religion liberates her from a life of sin (and the status of a "servant maid"). Religion provides her with a way of supporting herself after her minister-husband dies and of having a very active, eventful life. In 1827, for example, she gave 178 sermons, travelling 2325 miles. The religious autobiography allows her to repeat this story—and make her plea for women preachers.

The text is from *Sisters of the Spirit: Three Black Women's Autobiographies of the Nineteenth Century,* ed. William L. Andrews (Bloomington: Indiana Univ. Press, 1986). For discussion of Lee in the context of other black autobiographers, see Andrews's *To Tell a Free Story: The First Century of Afro-American Autobiography, 1760–1865* (Urbana: Univ. of Illinois Press, 1986).

And it shall come to pass . . . that I will pour out my Spirit upon all flesh; and your sons, and your *daughters* shall prophecy.

Joel 2: 28

I was born February 11th, 1783, at Cape May, state of New Jersey. At the age of seven years I was parted from my parents, and went to live as a servant maid, with a Mr. Sharp, at the distance of about sixty miles from the place of my birth.

My parents being wholly ignorant of the knowledge of God, had not therefore instructed me in any degree in this great matter. Not long after the commencement of my attendance on this lady, she had bid me do something respecting my work, which in a little while after, she asked me if I had done, when I replied, Yes—but this was not true.

At this awful point, in my early history, the spirit of God moved in power through my conscience, and told me I was a wretched sinner. On this account so great was the impression, and so strong were the feelings of guilt, that I promised in my heart that I would not tell another lie.

But notwithstanding this promise my heart grew harder, after a while, yet the spirit of the Lord never entirely forsook me, but continued mercifully striving with me, until his gracious power converted my soul.

The manner of this great accomplishment was as follows: In the year 1804, it so happened that I went with others to hear a missionary of the Presbyterian order preach. It was an afternoon meeting, but few were there, the place was a school room; but the preacher was solemn, and in his countenance the earnestness of his master's business appeared equally strong, as though he were about to speak to a multitude.

At the reading of the Psalms, a ray of renewed conviction darted into my soul. These were the words, composing the first verse of the Psalms for the service:

> Lord, I am vile, conceived in sin,
> Born unholy and unclean.
> Sprung from man, whose guilty fall
> Corrupts the race, and taints us all.

This description of my condition struck me to the heart, and made me to feel in some measure, the weight of my sins, and sinful nature. But not knowing how to run immediately to the Lord for help, I was driven of Satan, in the course of a few days, and tempted to destroy myself.

There was a brook about a quarter of a mile from the house, in which there was a deep hole, where the water whirled about among the rocks; to this place it was suggested, I must go and drown myself.

At the time I had a book in my hand; it was on a Sabbath morning, about ten o'clock; to this place I resorted, where on coming to the water I sat down on the bank, and on my looking into it; it was suggested, that drowning would be an easy death. It seemed as if some one was speaking to me, saying put your head under, it will not distress you. But by some means, of which I can give no account, my thoughts were taken entirely from this purpose, when I went from the place to the house again. It was the unseen arm of God which saved me from self murder.

But notwithstanding this escape from death, my mind was not at rest—but so great was the labour of my spirit and the fearful oppressions of a judgment to come, that I was reduced as one extremely ill. On which account a physician was called to attend me, from which illness I recovered in about three months.

But as yet I had not found him of whom Moses and the prophets did write, being extremely ignorant: there being no one to instruct me in the way of life and salvation as yet. After my recovery, I left the lady, who during my sickness, was exceedingly kind, and went to Philadelphia. From this place I soon went a few miles into the country, where I resided in the family of a Roman Catholic. But my anxiety still continued respecting my poor soul, on which account I used to watch my opportunity to read in the Bible; and this lady observing this, took the Bible from me and hid it, giving me a novel in its stead—which when I perceived, I refused to read.

Soon after this I again went to the city of Philadelphia; and commenced going to the English Church, the pastor of which was an Englishman, by the name of Pilmore, one of the number, who at first preached Methodism in America, in the city of New York.

But while sitting under the ministration of this man, which was about three months, and at the last time, it appeared that there was a wall between me and a communion with that people, which was higher than I could possibly see over, and seemed to make this impression upon my mind, *this is not the people for you.*

But on returning home at noon I inquired of the head cook of the house respecting the rules of the Methodists, as I knew she belonged to that society, who told me what they were; on which account I replied, that I should not be able to abide by such strict rules not even one year;—however, I told her that I would go with her and hear what they had to say.

The man who was to speak in the afternoon of that day, was the Rev. Richard Allen, since bishop of the African Episcopal Methodists in America. During the labors of this man that afternoon, I had come to the conclusion, that this is the people to which my heart unites, and it so happened, that as soon as the service closed he invited such as felt a desire to flee the wrath to come, to unite on trial with them—I embraced the opportunity. Three weeks from that day, my soul was gloriously converted to God, under preaching, at the very outset of the sermon. The text was barely pronounced, which was: "I perceive thy heart is not right in the sight of God," when there appeared to *my* view, in the centre of the heart *one* sin; and this was *malice,* against one particular individual, who had strove deeply to injure me, which I resented. At this discovery I said, *Lord* I forgive *every* creature. That instant, it appeared to me, as if a garment, which had entirely enveloped my whole person, even to my fingers ends, split at the crown of my head, and was stripped away from me, passing like a shadow, from my sight—when the glory of God seemed to cover me in its stead.

That moment, though hundreds were present, I did leap to my feet, and declare that God, for Christ's sake, had pardoned the sins of my soul. Great was the ecstasy of my mind, for I felt that not only the sin of *malice* was pardoned, but all other sins were swept away together. That day was the first when my heart had believed, and my tongue had made confession unto salvation—the first words uttered, a part of that song, which shall fill eternity with its sound, was *glory to God*. For a few moments I had power to exhort sinners, and to tell of the wonders and of the goodness of him who had clothed me with *his* salvation. During this, the minister was silent, until my soul felt its duty had been performed, when he declared another witness of the power of Christ to forgive sins on earth, was manifest in my conversion.

From the day on which I first went to the Methodist church, until the hour of my deliverance, I was strangely buffetted by that enemy of all righteousness—the devil.

I was naturally of a lively turn of disposition; and during the space of time from my first awakening until I knew my peace was made with God, I rejoiced in the vanities of this life, and then again sunk back into sorrow.

For four years I had continued in this way, frequently labouring under the awful apprehension, that I could never be happy in this life. This persuasion was greatly strengthened, during the three weeks, which was the last of Satan's power over me, in this peculiar manner: on which account, I had come to the conclusion that I had better be dead than alive. Here I was again tempted to destroy my life by drowning; but suddenly this mode was changed, and while in the dusk of the evening, as I was walking to and fro in the yard of the house, I was beset to hang myself, with a cord suspended from the wall enclosing the secluded spot.

But no sooner was the intention resolved on in my mind, than an awful dread came over me, when I ran into the house; still the tempter pursued me. There was standing a vessel of water—into this I was strongly impressed to plunge my head, so as to extinguish the life which God had given me. Had I have done this, I have been always of the opinion that I should have been unable to have released myself; although the vessel was scarcely large enough to hold a gallon of water. Of me may it not be said, as written by Isaiah, (chap. 65, verses 1,2.) "I am sought of them that asked not for me; I am found of them that sought me not." Glory be to God for his redeeming power, which saved me from the violence of my own hands, from the malice of Satan, and from eternal death; for had I have killed myself, a great ransom could not have delivered me; for it is written—"No murderer hath eternal life abiding in him." How appropriately can I sing—

> Jesus sought me, when a stranger,
>   Wandering from the fold of God;
> He to rescue me from danger,
>   Interposed his precious blood.

But notwithstanding the terror which seized upon me, when about to end my life, I had no view of the precipice on the edge of which I was tottering, until it was over, and my eyes were opened. Then the awful gulf of hell seemed to be open beneath me, covered only, as it were, by a spider's web, on which I stood. I seemed to hear the howling of the damned, to see the smoke of the bottomless pit, and to hear the rattling of those chains, which hold the impenitent under clouds of darkness to the judgment of the great day.

I trembled like Belshazzar, and cried out in the horror of my spirit, "God be merciful to me a sinner." That night I formed a resolution to pray; which, when resolved upon, there appeared, sitting in one corner of the room, Satan, in the form of a monstrous dog, and in a rage, as if in pursuit, his tongue protruding from his mouth to a great length, and his eyes looked like two balls of fire; it soon, however, vanished out of my sight. From this state of terror and dismay, I was happily delivered under the preaching of the Gospel as before related.

This view, which I was permitted to have of Satan, in the form of a dog, is evidence, which corroborates in my estimation, the Bible account of a hell of fire, which burneth with brimstone, called in Scripture the bottomless pit; the place where all liars, who repent not, shall have their portion; as also the Sabbath breaker, the adulterer, the fornicator, with the fearful, the abominable, and the unbelieving, this shall be the portion of their cup.

This language is too strong and expressive to be applied to any state of suffering in *time*. Were it to be thus applied, the reality could no where be found in human life; the consequence would be, that *this* scripture would be found a false testimony. But when made to apply to an endless state of perdition, in eternity, beyond the bounds of human life, then this language is found not to exceed our views of a state of eternal damnation.

During the latter part of my state of conviction, I can now apply to my case, as it then was, the beautiful words of the poet:

> The more I strove against its power,
> I felt its weight and guilt the more;
> Till late I hear'd my Saviour say,
> Come hither soul, I am the way.

This I found to be true, to the joy of my disconsolate and despairing heart, in the hour of my conversion to God.

During this state of mind, while sitting near the fire one evening, after

I had heard Rev. Richard Allen, as before related, a view of my distressed condition so affected my heart, that I could not refrain from weeping and crying aloud; which caused the lady with whom I then lived, to inquire, with surprise, what ailed me; to which I answered, that I knew not what ailed me. She replied that I ought to pray. I arose from where I was sitting, being in an agony, and weeping convulsively, requested her to pray for me; but at the very moment when she would have done so, some person rapped heavily at the door for admittance; it was but a person of the house, but this occurrence was sufficient to interrupt us in our intentions; and I believe to this day, I should then have found salvation to my soul. This interruption was, doubtless, also the work of Satan.

Although at this time, when my conviction was so great, yet I knew not that Jesus Christ was the Son of God, the second person in the adorable trinity. I knew him not in the pardon of my sins, yet I felt a consciousness that if I died without pardon, that my lot must inevitably be damnation. If I would pray—I knew not how. I could form no connexion of ideas into words; but I knew the Lord's prayer; this I uttered with a loud voice, and with all my might and strength. I was the most ignorant creature in the world; I did not even know that Christ had died for the sins of the world, and to save sinners. Every circumstance, however, was so directed as still to continue and increase the sorrows of my heart, which I now know to have been a godly sorrow which wrought repentance, which is not to be repented of. Even the falling of the dead leaves from the forests, and the dried spires of the mown grass, showed me that I too must die, in like manner. But my case was awfully different from that of the grass of the field, or the wide spread decay of a thousand forests, as I felt within me a living principle, an immortal spirit, which cannot die, and must forever either enjoy the smiles of its Creator, or feel the pangs of ceaseless damnation.

But the Lord led me on; being gracious, he took pity on my ignorance; he heard my wailings, which had entered into the ear of the Lord of Sabaoth. Circumstances so transpired that I soon came to a knowledge of the being and character of the Son of God, of whom I knew nothing.

My strength had left me. I had become feverish and sickly through the violence of my feelings, on which account I left my place of service to spend a week with a coloured physician, who was a member of the Methodist society, and also to spend this week in going to places where prayer and supplication was stately made for such as me.

Through this means I had learned much, so as to be able in some degree to comprehend the spiritual meaning of the text, which the minister took on the Sabbath morning, as before related, which was, "I perceive thy heart is not right in the sight of God." Acts, chap. 8, verse 21.

This text, as already related, became the power of God unto salvation to me, because I believed. I was baptized according to the direction of our Lord, who said, as he was about to ascend from the mount, to his disciples, "Go ye into all the world and preach my gospel to every creature, he that believeth and is baptized shall be saved."

I have now passed through the account of my conviction, and also of my conversion to God; and shall next speak of the blessing of sanctification.

A time after I had received forgiveness flowed sweetly on; day and night my joy was full, no temptation was permitted to molest me. I could say continually with the psalmist, that "God had separated my sins from me, as far as the east is from the west." I was ready continually to cry,

> Come all the world, come sinner thou,
> All things in Christ are ready now.

I continued in this happy state of mind for almost three months, when a certain coloured man, by name William Scott, came to pay me a religious visit. He had been for many years a faithful follower of the Lamb; and he had also taken much time in visiting the sick and distressed of our colour, and understood well the great things belonging to a man of full stature in Christ Jesus.

In the course of our conversation, he inquired if the Lord had justified my soul. I answered, yes. He then asked me if he had sanctified me. I answered, no; and that I did not know what that was. He then undertook to instruct me further in the knowledge of the Lord respecting this blessing.

He told me the progress of the soul from a state of darkness, or of nature, was threefold; or consisted in three degrees, as follows:—First, conviction for sin. Second, justification from sin. Third, the entire sanctification of the soul to God. I thought this description was beautiful, and immediately believed in it. He then inquired if I would promise to pray for this in my secret devotions. I told him, yes. Very soon I began to call upon the Lord to show me all that was in my heart, which was not according to his will. Now there appeared to be a new struggle commencing in my soul, not accompanied with fear, guilt, and bitter distress, as while under my first conviction for sin; but a labouring of the mind to know more of the right way of the Lord. I began now to feel that my heart was not clean in his sight; that there yet remained the roots of bitterness, which if not destroyed, would ere long sprout up from these roots, and overwhelm me in a new growth of the brambles and brushwood of sin.

By the increasing light of the Spirit, I had found there yet remained the root of pride, anger, self-will, with many evils, the result of fallen nature. I now became alarmed at this discovery, and began to fear that I had been deceived in my experience. I was now greatly alarmed, lest I should fall away from what I knew I had enjoyed; and to guard against this I prayed almost incessantly, without acting faith on the power and promises of God to keep me from falling. I had not yet learned how to war against temptation of this kind. Satan well knew that if he could succeed in making me disbelieve my conversion, that he would catch me either on the ground of complete despair, or on the ground of infidelity. For if all I had passed through was to go for nothing, and was but a fiction, the mere ravings of a disordered mind, then I would naturally be led to believe that there is nothing in religion at all.

From this snare I was mercifully preserved, and led to believe that there was yet a greater work than that of pardon to be wrought in me. I retired to a secret place (after having sought this blessing, as well as I could, for nearly three months, from the time brother Scott had instructed me respecting it) for prayer, about four o'clock in the afternoon. I had struggled long and hard, but found not the desire of my heart. When I rose from my knees, there seemed a voice speaking to me, as I yet stood in a leaning posture—"Ask for sanctification." When to my surprise, I recollected that I had not even thought of it in my whole prayer. It would seem Satan had hidden the very object from my mind, for which I had purposely kneeled to pray. But when this voice whispered in my heart, saying, "Pray for sanctification," I again bowed in the same place, at the same time, and said, "Lord *sanctify* my soul for Christ's sake?" That very instant, as if lightning had darted through me, I sprang to my feet, and cried, "The Lord has sanctified my soul!" There was none to hear this but the angels who stood around to witness my joy—and Satan, whose malice raged the more. That Satan was there, I knew; for no sooner had I cried out, "The Lord has sanctified my soul," than there seemed another voice behind me, saying, "No, it is too great a work to be done." But another spirit said, "Bow down for the witness—I received it—*thou art sanctified!*" The first I knew of myself after that, I was standing in the yard with my hands spread out, and looking with my face toward heaven.

I now ran into the house and told them what had happened to me, when, as it were, a new rush of the same ecstasy came upon me, and caused me to feel as if I were in an ocean of light and bliss.

During this, I stood perfectly still, the tears rolling in a flood from my eyes. So great was the joy, that it is past description. There is no language that can describe it, except that which was heard by St. Paul, when he was caught up to the third heaven, and heard words which it was not lawful to utter.

My Call to Preach the Gospel

Between four and five years after my sanctification, on a certain time, an impressive silence fell upon me, and I stood as if some one was about to speak to me, yet I had no such thought in my heart. But to my utter surprise there seemed to sound a voice which I thought I distinctly heard, and most certainly understood, which said to me, "Go preach the Gospel!" I immediately replied aloud, "No one will believe me." Again I listened, and again the same voice seemed to say, "Preach the Gospel; I will put words in your mouth, and will turn your enemies to become your friends."

At first I supposed that Satan had spoken to me, for I had read that he could transform himself into an angel of light, for the purpose of deception. Immediately I went into a secret place, and called upon the Lord to know if he had called me to preach, and whether I was deceived or not; when there appeared to my view the form and figure of a pulpit, with a Bible lying thereon, the back of which was presented to me as plainly as if it had been a literal fact.

In consequence of this, my mind became so exercised that during the night following, I took a text, and preached in my sleep. I thought there stood before me a great multitude, while I expounded to them the things of religion. So violent were my exertions, and so loud were my exclamations, that I awoke from the sound of my own voice, which also awoke the family of the house where I resided. Two days after, I went to see the preacher in charge of the African Society, who was the Rev. Richard Allen, the same before named in these pages, to tell him that I felt it my duty to preach the gospel. But as I drew near the street in which his house was, which was in the city of Philadelphia, my courage began to fail me; so terrible did the cross appear, it seemed that I should not be able to bear it. Previous to my setting out to go to see him, so agitated was my mind, that my appetite for my daily food failed me entirely. Several times on my way there, I turned back again; but as often I felt my strength again renewed, and I soon found that the nearer I approached to the house of the minister, the less was my fear. Accordingly, as soon as I came to the door, my fears subsided, the cross was removed, all things appeared pleasant—I was tranquil.

I now told him, that the Lord had revealed it to me, that I must preach the gospel. He replied by asking, in what sphere I wished to move in? I said, among the Methodists. He then replied, that a Mrs. Cook, a Methodist lady, had also some time before requested the same privilege; who it was believed, had done much good in the way of exhortation, and holding prayer meetings; and who had been permitted to do so by the verbal license of the preacher in charge at the time. But as to women preaching, he said that our Discipline knew nothing at all about it—that it did not call for women preachers. This I was glad to hear, because it removed the fear of the cross—but not no sooner did this feeling cross my mind, than I found that a love of souls had in a measure departed from me; that holy energy which burned within me, as a fire, began to be smothered. This I soon perceived.

O how careful ought we to be, lest through our by-laws of church government and discipline, we bring into disrepute even the word of life. For as unseemly as it may appear now-a-days for a woman to preach, it should be remembered that nothing is impossible with God. And why should it be thought impossible, heterodox, or improper, for a woman to preach? seeing the Saviour died for the woman as well as the man.

If a man may preach, because the Saviour died for him, why not the woman? seeing he died for her also. Is he not a whole Saviour, instead of a half one? as those who hold it wrong for a woman to preach, would seem to make it appear.

Did not Mary *first* preach the risen Saviour, and is not the doctrine of the resurrection the very climax of Christianity—hangs not all our hope on this, as argued by St. Paul? Then did not Mary, a woman, preach the gospel? for she preached the resurrection of the crucified Son of God.

But some will say, that Mary did not expound the Scripture, therefore, she did not preach, in the proper sense of the term. To this I reply, it may be that the term *preach,* in those primitive times, did not mean exactly what it is now *made* to mean; perhaps it was a great deal more simple then, than it is now:—if it were not, the unlearned fishermen could not have preached the gospel at all, as they had no learning.

To this it may be replied, by those who are determined not to believe that it is right for a woman to preach, that the disciples, though they were fishermen, and ignorant of letters too, were inspired so to do. To which I would reply, that though they were inspired, yet that inspiration did not save them from showing their ignorance of letters, and of man's wisdom; this the multitude soon found out, by listening to the remarks of the envious Jewish priests. If then, to preach the gospel, by the gift of heaven, comes by inspiration solely, is God straitened; must he take the man exclusively? May he not, did he not, and can he not inspire a female to preach the simple story of the birth, life, death, and resurrection of our Lord, and accompany it too, with power to the sinner's heart. As for me, I am fully persuaded that the Lord called me to labour according to what I have received, in his vineyard. If he has not, how could he consistently bear testimony in favour of my poor labours, in awakening and converting sinners?

In my wanderings up and down among men, preaching according to my ability, I have frequently found families who told me that they had not for several years been to a meeting, and yet, while listening to hear what God would say by his poor coloured female instrument, have believed with trembling—tears rolling down their cheeks, the signs of contrition and repentance towards God. I firmly believe that I have sown seed, in the name of the Lord, which shall appear with its increase at the great day of accounts, when Christ shall come to make up his jewels.

At a certain time, I was beset with the idea, that soon or late I should fall from grace, and lose my soul at last. I was frequently called to the throne of grace about this matter, but found no relief; the temptation pursued me still. Being more and more afflicted with it, till at a certain time when the spirit strongly impressed it on my mind to enter into my closet, and carry my case once more to the Lord; the Lord enabled me to draw nigh to him, and to his mercy seat, at this time, in an extraordinary manner; for while I wrestled

with him for the victory over this disposition to doubt whether I should per-
severe, there appeared a form of fire, about the size of a man's hand, as I was
on my knees; at the same moment, there appeared to the eye of faith a man
robed in a white garment, from the shoulders down to the feet; from him a
voice proceeded, saying: "Thou shalt never return from the cross." Since that
time I have never doubted, but believe that god will keep me until the day of
redemption. Now I could adopt the very language of St. Paul, and say that
nothing could have separated my soul from the love of god, which is in Christ
Jesus [Rom. 8:35–39]. From that time, 1807, until the present, 1833, I have
not yet doubted the power and goodness of God to keep me from falling,
through sanctification of the spirit and belief of the truth.

My Marriage

In the year 1811, I changed my situation in life, having married Mr. Joseph
Lee, Pastor of a Coloured Society at Snow Hill, about six miles from the city
of Philadelphia. It became necessary therefore for me to remove. This was a
great trial at first, as I knew no person at Snow Hill, except my husband; and
to leave my associates in the society, and especially those who composed the
band of which I was one. Not but those who have been in sweet fellowship
with such as really love God, and have together drank bliss and happiness
from the same fountain, can tell how dear such company is, and how hard it
is to part from them.

At Snow Hill, as was feared, I never found that agreement and closeness
in communion and fellowship, that I had in Philadelphia, among my young
companions, nor ought I to have expected it. The manners and customs at
this place were somewhat different, on which account I became discontented
in the course of a year, and began to importune my husband to remove to
the city. But this plan did not suit him, as he was the Pastor of the Society;
he could not bring his mind to leave them. This afflicted me a little. But the
Lord soon showed me in a dream what his will was concerning this matter.

I dreamed that as I was walking on the summit of a beautiful hill, that I
saw near me a flock of sheep, fair and white, as if but newly washed; when
there came walking toward me, a man of a grave and dignified countenance,
dressed entirely in white, as it were in a robe, and looking at me, said emphatically, "Joseph Lee must take care of these sheep, or the wolf will come
and devour them." When I awoke, I was convinced of my error, and immediately, with a glad heart, yielded to the right way of the Lord. This also greatly
strengthened my husband in his care over them, for fear the wolf should by
some means take any of them away. The following verse was beautifully suited
to our condition, as well as to all the little flocks of God scattered up and
down this land:

Us into Thy protection take,
    And gather with Thine arm;
Unless the fold we first forsake,
    The wolf can never harm.

After this, I fell into a state of general debility, and in an ill state of health, so much so, that I could not sit up; but a desire to warn sinners to flee the wrath to come, burned vehemently in my heart, when the Lord would send sinners into the house to see me. Such opportunities I embraced to press home on their consciences the things of eternity, and so effectual was the word of exhortation made through the Spirit, that I have seen them fall to the floor crying aloud for mercy.

From this sickness I did not expect to recover, and there was but one thing which bound me to earth, and this was, that I had not as yet preached the gospel to the fallen sons and daughters of Adam's race, to the satisfaction of my mind. I wished to go from one end of the earth to the other, crying, Behold, behold the Lamb! To this end I earnestly prayed the Lord to raise me up, if consistent with his will. He condescended to hear my prayer, and to give me a token in a dream, that in due time I should recover my health. The dream was as follows: I thought I saw the sun rise in the morning, and ascend to an altitude of about half an hour high, and then become obscured by a dense black cloud, which continued to hide its rays for about one third part of the day, and then it burst forth again with renewed splendour.

This dream I interpreted to signify my early life, my conversion to God, and this sickness, which was a great affliction, as it hindered me, and I feared would forever hinder me from preaching the gospel, was signified by the cloud; and the bursting forth of the sun, again, was the recovery of my health, and being permitted to preach.

I went to the throne of grace on this subject, where the Lord made this impressive reply in my heart, while on my knees: "Ye shall be restored to thy health again, and worship God in full purpose of heart."

This manifestation was so impressive, that I could but hide my face, as if someone was gazing upon me, to think of the great goodness of the Almighty God to my poor soul and body. From that very time I began to gain strength of body and mind, glory to God in the highest, until my health was fully recovered.

For six years from this time I continued to receive from above, such baptisms of the Spirit as mortality could scarcely bear. About that time I was called to suffer in my family, by death—five, in the course of about six years, fell by his hand; my husband being one of the number, which was the greatest affliction of all.

I was now left alone in the world, with two infant children, one of the age of about two years, the other six months, with no other dependance than the promise of Him who hath said—"I will be the widow's God, and a father to the fatherless." Accordingly, he raised me up friends, whose liberality comforted and solaced me in my state of widowhood and sorrows. I could sing with the greatest propriety the words of the poet.

> He helps the stranger in distress,
> The widow and the fatherless,
> And grants the prisoner sweet release.

I can say even now, with the Psalmist, "Once I was young, but now I am old, yet I have never seen the righteous forsaken, nor his seed begging bread." I have ever been fed by his bounty, clothed by his mercy, comforted and healed when sick, succoured when tempted, and every where upheld by his hand.

The Subject of My Call to Preach Renewed

It was now eight years since I had made application to be permitted to preach the gospel, during which time I had only been allowed to exhort, and even this privilege but seldom. This subject now was renewed afresh in my mind; it was as a fire shut up in my bones. About thirteen months passed on, while under this renewed impression. During this time, I had solicited of the Rev. Bishop Richard Allen, who at this time had become Bishop of the African Episcopal Methodists in America, to be permitted the liberty of holding prayer meetings in my own hired house, and of exhorting as I found liberty, which was granted me. By this means, my mind was relieved, as the house was soon filled when the hour appointed for prayer had arrived.

I cannot but relate in this place, before I proceed further with the above subject, the singular conversion of a very wicked young man. He was a coloured man, who had generally attended our meetings, but not for any good purpose; but rather to disturb and to ridicule our denomination. He openly and uniformly declared that he neither believed in religion, nor wanted anything to do with it. He was of a Gallio disposition, and took the lead among the young people of colour. But after a while he fell sick, and lay about three months in a state of ill health; his disease was consumption. Toward the close of his days, his sister who was a member of the society, came and desired me to go and see her brother, as she had no hopes of his recovery; perhaps the Lord might break into his mind. I went alone, and found him very low. I soon commenced to inquire respecting his state of feeling, and how he found his mind. His answer was, "O tolerable well," with an air of great indifference. I asked him if I should pray for him. He answered in a sluggish and careless manner, "O yes, if you have time." I then sung a hymn, kneeled down and prayed for him, and then went my way.

Three days after this, I went again to visit the young man. At this time there went with me two of the sisters in Christ. We found the Rev. Mr. Cornish, of our denomination, labouring with him. But he said he received but little satisfaction from him. Pretty soon, however, brother Cornish took his leave; when myself, with the other two sisters, one of which was an elderly woman named Jane Hutt, the other was younger, both coloured, commenced conversing with him, respecting his eternal interest, and of his hopes of a happy eternity, if any he had. He said but little; we then kneeled down together and besought the Lord in his behalf, praying that if mercy were not clear gone forever, to shed a ray of softening grace upon the hardness of his heart. He appeared now to be somewhat more tender, and we thought we could perceive some tokens of conviction, as he wished us to visit him again, in a tone of voice not quite as indifferent as he had hitherto manifested.

But two days had elapsed after this visit, when his sister came for me in haste, saying, that she believed her brother was then dying, and that he had *sent* for me. I immediately called on Jane Hutt, who was still among us as a mother in Israel, to go with me. When we arrived there, we found him sitting up in his bed, very restless and uneasy, but he soon laid down again. He now wished me to come to him, by the side of his bed. I asked him how he was. He said, "Very ill;" and added, "Pray for me, quick?" We now perceived his time in this world to be short. I took up the hymn-book and opened to a hymn suitable to his case, and commenced to sing. But there seemed to be a *horror* in the room—a darkness of a mental kind, which was felt by us all; there being five persons, except the sick young man and his nurse. We had sung but one verse, when they all gave over singing, on account of this unearthly sensation, but myself. I continued to sing on alone, but in a dull and heavy manner, though looking up to God all the while for help. Suddenly, I felt a spring of energy awake in my heart, when darkness gave way in some degree. It was but a glimmer from above. When the hymn was finished, we all kneeled down to pray for him. While calling on the name of the Lord, to have mercy on his soul, and to grant him repentance unto life, it came suddenly into my mind never to rise from my knees until God should hear prayer in his behalf, until he should convert and save his soul.

Now, while I thus continued importuning heaven, as I felt I was led, a ray of light, more abundant, broke forth among us. There appeared to my view, though my eyes were closed, the Saviour in full stature, nailed to the cross, just over the head of the young man, against the ceiling of the room. I cried out, brother look up, the Saviour is come, he will pardon you, your sins he will forgive. My sorrow for the soul of the young man was gone; I could no longer pray—joy and rapture made it impossible. We rose up from our knees, when lo, his eyes were gazing with ecstasy upward; over his face there was an expression of joy; his lips were clothed in a sweet and holy smile; but no sound came from his tongue; it was heard in its stillness of bliss, full of hope and immortality. Thus, as I held him by the hand his happy and purified soul soared away, without a sign or a groan, to its eternal rest.

I now closed his eyes, straightened out his limbs, and left him to be dressed for the grave. But as for me, I was filled with the power of the Holy Ghost—the very room seemed filled with glory. His sister and all that were in the room rejoiced, nothing doubting but he had entered into Paradise; and I believe I shall see him at the last and great day, safe on the shores of salvation.

But to return to the subject of my call to preach. Soon after this, as above related, the Rev. Richard Williams was to preach at Bethel Church, where I with others were assembled. He entered the pulpit, gave out the hymn, which was sung, and then addressed the throne of grace; took his text, passed through the exordium, and commenced to expound it. The text he took is in Jonah, 2d chap. 9th verse,—"Salvation is of the Lord." But as he proceeded to explain, he seemed to have lost the spirit; when in the same instant, I sprang, as by an altogether supernatural impulse, to my feet, when I was aided from above to give an exhortation on the very text which my brother Williams had taken.

I told them that I was like Jonah; for it had been then nearly eight years since the Lord had called me to preach his gospel to the fallen sons and daughters of Adam's race, but that I had lingered like him, and delayed to go at the bidding of the Lord, and warn those who are as deeply guilty as were the people of Ninevah.

During the exhortation, God made manifest his power in a manner sufficient to show the world that I was called to labour according to my ability, and the grace given unto me, in the vineyard of the good husbandman.

I now sat down, scarcely knowing what I had done, being frightened. I imagined, that for this indecorum, as I feared it might be called, I should be expelled from the church. But instead of this, the Bishop rose up in the assembly, and related that I had called upon him eight years before, asking to be permitted to preach, and that he had put me off; but that he now as much believed that I was called to that work, as any of the preachers present. These remarks greatly strengthened me, so that my fears of having given an offence, and made myself liable as an offender, subsided, giving place to a sweet serenity, a holy job of a peculiar kind, untasted in my bosom until then.

The next Sabbath day, while sitting under the word of the gospel, I felt moved to attempt to speak to the people in a public manner, but I could not bring my mind to attempt it in the church. I said, Lord, anywhere but here. Accordingly, there was a house not far off which was pointed out to me, to this I went. It was the house of a sister belonging to the same society with myself. Her name was Anderson. I told her I had come to hold a meeting in her house, if she would call in her neighbours. With this request she immediately complied. My congregation consisted of but five persons. I commenced by reading and singing a hymn, when I dropped to my knees by the side of a table to pray. When I arose I found my hand resting on the Bible, which I had not noticed till that moment. It now occurred to me to take a text. I opened the Scripture, as it happened, at the 141st Psalm, fixing my eye on the 3d verse, which reads: "Set a watch, O Lord, before my mouth, keep the door of my lips." My sermon, such as it was, I applied wholly to myself, and added an exhortation. Two of my congregation wept much, as the fruit of my labour this time. In closing I said to the few, that if any one would open a door, I would hold a meeting the next sixth-day evening; when one answered that her house was at my service. Accordingly I went, and God made manifest his power among the people. Some wept, while others shouted for joy. One whole seat of females, by the power of God, as the rushing of a wind, were all bowed to the floor at once, and screamed out. Also a sick man and woman in one house, the Lord convicted them both; one lived, and the other died. God wrought a judgment—some were well at night, and died in the morning. At this place I continued to hold meetings about six months. During that time I kept house with my little son, who was very sickly. About this time I had a call to preach at a place about thirty miles distant, among the Methodists, with whom I remained one week, and during the whole time, not a thought of my little son came into my mind; it was hid from me, lest I should have been diverted from the work I had to, to look after my son. Here by the instrumentality of a poor coloured woman, the Lord poured forth his spirit among the people. Though, as I was told, there were lawyers, doctors, and magistrates present, to hear me speak, yet there was mourning and crying among sinners, for the Lord scattered fire among them of his own kindling. The Lord gave his handmaiden power to speak for his great name, for he arrested the hearts of the people, and caused a shaking amongst the multitude, for God was in the midst.

I now returned home, found all well; no harm had come to my child, although I left it very sick. Friends had taken care of it which was of the Lord. I now began to think seriously of breaking up housekeeping, and forsaking all to preach the everlasting Gospel. I felt a strong desire to return to the place of my nativity, at Cape May, after an absence of about fourteen years. To this place, where the heaviest cross was to be met with, the Lord sent me, as Saul of Tarsus was sent to Jerusalem, to preach the same gospel which he had neglected and despised before his conversion. I went by water, and on my passage was much distressed by sea sickness, so much so that I expected to have died, but such was not the will of the Lord respecting me. After I had disembarked, I proceeded on as opportunities offered, toward where my mother lived. When within ten miles of that place, I appointed an evening meeting. There were a goodly number came out to hear. The Lord was pleased to give me light and liberty among the people. After meeting, there came an elderly lady to me and said, she believed the Lord had sent me among them; she then appointed me another meeting there two weeks from that night. The next day I hastened forward to the place of my mother, who was happy to see me, and the happiness was mutual between us. With her I left my poor sickly boy, while I departed to do my Master's will. In this neighborhood I had an uncle, who was a Methodist, and who gladly threw open his door for meetings to be held there. At the first meeting which I held at my uncle's house, there was, with others who had come from curiosity to hear the coloured woman preacher, an old man, who was a deist, and who said he did not believe the coloured people had any souls—he was sure they had none. He took a seat very near where I was standing, and boldly tried to look me out of countenance. But as I laboured on in the best manner I was able, looking to God all the while, though it seemed to me I had but little liberty, yet there went an arrow from the bent bow of the gospel, and fastened in his till then obdurate heart. After I had done speaking, he went out, and called the people around him, said that my preaching might seem a small thing, yet he believed I had the worth of souls at heart. This language was different from what it was a little time before, as he now seemed to admit that coloured people had souls, whose good I had in view, his remark must have been without meaning. He now came into the house, and in the most friendly manner shook hands with me, saying, he hoped God had spared him to some good purpose. This man was a great slave holder, and had been very cruel; thinking nothing of knocking down a slave with a fence stake, or whatever might come to hand. From this time it was said of him that he became greatly altered in his ways for the better. At that time he was about seventy years old, his head as white as snow; but whether he became a converted man or not, I never heard.

The week following, I had an invitation to hold a meeting at the Court House of the County, when I spoke from the 53d chap. of Isaiah, 3d verse. It was a solemn time, and the Lord attended the word; I had life and liberty, though there were people there of various denominations. Here again I saw the aged slaveholder, who notwithstanding his age, walked about three miles to hear me. This day I spoke twice, and walked six miles to the place appointed. There was a magistrate present, who showed his friendship, by saying in a friendly manner, that he had heard of me: he handed me a hymn-book, pointing to a hymn which he had selected. When the meeting was over, he invited me to preach in a schoolhouse in his neighbourhood, about three miles distant from where I then was. During this meeting one backslider was reclaimed. This day I walked six miles, and preached twice to large congregations, both in the morning and evening. The Lord was with me, glory be to his holy name. I next went six miles and held a meeting in a coloured friend's house, at eleven o'clock in the morning, and preached to a well behaved congregation of both coloured and white. After service I again walked back, which was in all twelve miles in the same day. This was on Sabbath, or as I sometimes call it, seventh-day; for after my conversion I preferred the plain language of the quakers: On fourth-day, after this, in compliance with an invitation received by note, from the same magistrate who had heard me at the above place, I preached to a large congregation, where we had a precious time: much weeping was heard among the people. The same gentleman, now at the close of the meeting, gave out another appointment at the same place, that day week. Here again I had liberty, there was a move among the people. Ten years from that time, in the neighbourhood of Cape May, I held a prayer meeting in a school house, which was then the regular place of preaching for the Episcopal Methodists; after service, there came a white lady of the first distinction, a member of the Methodist Society, and told me that at the same school house, ten years before, under my preaching, the Lord first awakened her. She rejoiced much to see me, and invited me home with her, where I staid till the next day. This was bread cast on the waters, seen after many days.

From this place I next went to Dennis Creek meeting house, where at the invitation of an elder, I spoke to a large congregation of various and conflicting sentiments, when a wonderful shock of God's power was felt, shown everywhere by groans, by sighs, and loud and happy amens. I felt as if aided from above. My tongue was cut loose, the stammerer spoke freely; the love of God, and of his service, burned with a vehement flame within me—his name was glorified among the people.

But here I feel myself constrained to give over, as from the smallness of this pamphlet I cannot go through with the whole of my journal, as it would probably make a volume of two hundred pages; which, if the Lord be willing, may at some future day be published. But for the satisfaction of such as may follow after me, when I am no more, I have recorded how the Lord called me to his work, and how he has kept me from falling from grace, as I feared I should. In all things he has proved himself a God of truth to me; and in his service I am now as much determined to spend and be spent, as at the very first. My ardour for the progress of his cause abates not a whit, so far as I am able to judge, though I am now something more than fifty years of age.

As to the nature of uncommon impressions, which the reader cannot but have noticed, and possibly sneered at in the course of these pages, they may be accounted for in this way: It is known that the blind have the sense of hearing in a manner much more acute than those who can see: also their sense of feeling is exceedingly fine, and is found to detect any roughness on the smoothest surface, where those who can see can find none. So it may be with such as [I] am, who has never had more than three months schooling; and wishing to know much of the way and law of God, have therefore watched the more closely the operations of the Spirit, and have in consequence been led thereby. But let it be remarked that [I] have never found that Spirit to lead me contrary to the Scriptures of truth, as I understand them. "For as many as are led by the Spirit of God are the sons of God."—Rom. viii. 14.

I have now only to say, May the blessing of the Father, and of the Son, and of the Holy Ghost, accompany the reading of this poor effort to speak well of his name, wherever it may be read. AMEN.

Ralph Waldo Emerson (1803–1882)

from *The American Scholar,* *The Poet,* and *History*

On the surface, Emerson was the least revolutionary of men. One of eight children of a Unitarian minister, who died when Emerson was still a boy, he was raised by his mother and his father's sister, went to Harvard, and became a Unitarian minister, too. In September, 1832, however, he announced to his congregation that he could no longer in good conscience serve communion, or the "Lord's Supper." He had decided that it was a form which Christ did not intend should be continued for century after century, and, resigning from his post, left in December for Europe.

Such "independent judgement," as Alexis de Tocqueville might have called it, was highly characteristic of Emerson and can be seen in most of his early writing. He was impatient with tradition, formalism, and orthodoxy; and he sought inspiration and individual freedom. The "duties" of the American scholar, he told the students at Harvard in 1837, consciously turning the words of John Calvin and his own Puritan ancestors downside up, "may all be comprised in self-trust."

A faith in "self-trust" and "self-reliance," as he later called it, made Emerson a predestined journal-keeper. The first edition of his own *Journal,* published 1909–14, filled ten volumes, and the modern, scholarly edition fills over twice as many. Equally important, from the perspective of American autobiography, was his role as a sort of propagandist for all kinds of personal writing. It was he who urged Thoreau to keep a journal, which he started in 1837 and kept till 1861 (1st ed. 1906, 14 volumes). And Emerson's enthusiastic endorsements of transcendental individualism and autobiographical poetry (see below) helped inspire the young Walt Whitman.

The paradox of Emersonian individualism is that he and his fellow Transcendentalists expected the fully developed individual to be universal. The individual would become a part and an expression of a transcendent mind or soul or spirit that ran through all individuals, present and past. "There is one mind common to all individual men," he says in "History." How one can be one's self and also be like all others is a problem. Nevertheless, the underlying self-confidence and optimism are very clear.

There are many biographies of Emerson. For a searching discussion of Emerson and other Transcendentalists' relation to the autobiographical tradition, see Lawrence Buell, *Literary Transcendentalism: Style and Vision in the American Renaissance* (Ithaca: Cornell Univ. Press, 1973).

from The American Scholar

MR. PRESIDENT AND GENTLEMEN:

I greet you on the recommencement of our literary year. Our anniversary is one of hope, and, perhaps, not enough of labor. We do not meet for games of strength or skill, for the recitation of histories, tragedies, and odes, like the ancient Greeks; for parliaments of love and poesy, like the Troubadours; nor for the advancement of science, like our contemporaries in the British and European capitals. Thus far, our holiday has been simply a friendly sign of the survival of the love of letters amongst a people too busy to give to letters any more. As such it is precious as the sign of an indestructible instinct. Perhaps the time is already come when it ought to be, and will be, something else; when the sluggard intellect of this continent will look from under its iron lids and fill the postponed expectation of the world with something better than the exertions of mechanical skill. Our day of dependence, our long apprenticeship to the learning of other lands, draws to a close. The millions that around us are rushing into life, cannot always be fed on the sere remains of foreign harvests. Events, actions arise, that must be sung, that will sing themselves. Who can doubt that poetry will revive and lead in a new age, as the star in the constellation Harp, which now flames in our zenith, astronomers announce, shall one day be the polestar for a thousand years?

In this hope I accept the topic which not only usage but the nature of our association seem to prescribe to this day,—the AMERICAN SCHOLAR. Year by year we come up hither to read one more chapter of his biography. Let us inquire what light new days and events have thrown on his character and his hopes.

It is one of those fables which out of an unknown antiquity convey an unlooked-for wisdom, that the gods, in the beginning, divided Man into men, that he might be more helpful to himself; just as the hand was divided into fingers, the better to answer its end.

The old fable covers a doctrine ever new and sublime; that there is One Man,—present to all particular men only partially, or through one faculty; and that you must take the whole society to find the whole man. Man is not a farmer, or a professor, or an engineer, but he is all. Man is priest, and scholar, and statesman, and producer, and soldier. In the *divided* or social state these functions are parcelled out to individuals, each of whom aims to do his stint of the joint work, whilst each other performs his. The fable implies that the individual, to possess himself, must sometimes return from his own labor to embrace all the other laborers. But, unfortunately, this original unit, this

fountain of power, has been so distributed to multitudes, has been so minutely subdivided and peddled out, that it is spilled into drops, and cannot
be gathered. The state of society is one in which the members have suffered
amputation from the trunk, and strut about so many walking monsters,—a
good finger, a neck, a stomach, an elbow, but never a man.

Man is thus metamorphosed into a thing, into many things. The planter,
who is Man sent out into the field to gather food, is seldom cheered by any
idea of the true dignity of his ministry. He sees his bushel and his cart, and
nothing beyond, and sinks into the farmer, instead of Man on the farm. The
tradesman scarcely ever gives an ideal worth to his work, but is ridden by the
routine of his craft, and the soul is subject to dollars. The priest becomes a
form; the attorney a statute-book; the mechanic a machine; the sailor a rope
of the ship.

In this distribution of functions the scholar is the delegated intellect. In
the right state he is *Man Thinking*. In the degenerate state, when the victim
of society, he tends to become a mere thinker, or still worse, the parrot of
other men's thinking.

In this view of him, as Man Thinking, the theory of his office is contained. Him Nature solicits with all her placid, all her monitory pictures; him
the past instructs; him the future invites. Is not indeed every man a student,
and do not all things exist for the student's behoof? And, finally, is not the
true scholar the only true master? But the old oracle said, "All things have two
handles: beware of the wrong one." In life, too often, the scholar errs with
mankind and forfeits his privilege. Let us see him in his school, and consider
him in reference to the main influences he receives.

I. The first in time and the first in importance of the influences upon
the mind is that of nature. Every day, the sun; and, after sunset, Night and
her stars. Ever the winds blow; ever the grass grows. Every day, men and
women, conversing—beholding and beholden. The scholar is he of all men
whom this spectacle most engages. He must settle its value in his mind. What
is nature to him? There is never a beginning, there is never an end, to the
inexplicable continuity of this web of God, but always circular power returning into itself. Therein it resembles his own spirit, whose beginning, whose
ending, he never can find,—so entire, so boundless. Far too as her splendors
shine, system on system shooting like rays, upward, downward, without center, without circumference,—in the mass and in the particle, Nature hastens
to render account of herself to the mind. Classification begins. To the young
mind every thing is individual, stands by itself. By and by, it finds how to
join two things and see in them one nature; then three, then three thousand;
and so, tyrannized over by its own unifying instinct, it goes on tying things
together, diminishing anomalies, discovering roots running under ground
whereby contrary and remote things cohere and flower out from one stem.

It presently learns that since the dawn of history there has been a constant accumulation and classifying of facts. But what is classification but the perceiving that these objects are not chaotic, and are not foreign, but have a law which is also a law of the human mind? The astronomer discovers that geometry, a pure abstraction of the human mind, is the measure of planetary motion. The chemist finds proportions and intelligible method throughout matter; and science is nothing but the finding of analogy, identity, in the most remote parts. The ambitious soul sits down before each refractory fact; one after another reduces all strange constitutions, all new powers, to their class and their law, and goes on forever to animate the last fiber of organization, the outskirts of nature, by insight.

Thus to him, to this schoolboy under the bending dome of day, is suggested that he and it proceed from one root; one is leaf and one is flower; relation, sympathy, stirring in every vein. And what is that root? Is not that the soul of his soul? A thought too bold; a dream too wild. Yet when this spiritual light shall have revealed the law of more earthly natures,—when he has learned to worship the soul, and to see that the natural philosophy that now is, is only the first gropings of its gigantic hand, he shall look forward to an ever expanding knowledge as to a becoming creator. He shall see that nature is the opposite of the soul, answering to it part for part. One is seal and one is print. Its beauty is the beauty of his own mind. Its laws are the laws of his own mind. Nature then becomes to him the measure of his attainments. So much of nature as he is ignorant of, so much of his own mind does he not yet possess. And, in fine, the ancient precept, "Know thyself," and the modern precept, "Study nature," become at last one maxim.

II. The next great influence into the spirit of the scholar is the mind of the Past,—in whatever form, whether of literature, of art, of institutions, that mind is inscribed. Books are the best type of the influence of the past, and perhaps we shall get at the truth,—learn the amount of this influence more conveniently,—by considering their value alone.

The theory of books is noble. The scholar of the first age received into him the world around; brooded thereon; gave it the new arrangement of his own mind, and uttered it again. It came into him life; it went out from him truth. It came to him short-lived actions; it went out from him immortal thoughts. It came to him business; it went from him poetry. It was dead fact; now, it is quick thought. It can stand, and it can go. It now endures, it now flies, it now inspires. Precisely in proportion to the depth of mind from which it issued, so high does it soar, so long does it sing.

Or, I might say, it depends on how far the process had gone, of transmuting life into truth. In proportion to the completeness of the distillation, so will the purity and imperishableness of the product be. But none is quite perfect. As no air-pump can by any means make a perfect vacuum, so neither can any artist entirely exclude the conventional, the local, the perishable from his book, or write a book of pure thought, that shall be as efficient, in all respects, to a remote posterity, as to contemporaries, or rather to the second age. Each age, it is found, must write its own books; or rather, each generation for the next succeeding. The books of an older period will not fit this.

Yet hence arises a grave mischief. The sacredness which attaches to the act of creation, the act of thought, is transferred to the record. The poet chanting was felt to be a divine man: henceforth the chant is divine also. The writer was a just and wise spirit: henceforward it is settled the book is perfect; as love of the hero corrupts into worship of his statue. Instantly the book becomes noxious: the guide is a tyrant. The sluggish and perverted mind of the multitude, slow to open to the incursions of Reason, having once so opened, having once received this book, stands upon it, and makes an outcry if it is disparaged. Colleges are built on it. Books are written on it by thinkers, not by Man Thinking; by men of talent, that is, who start wrong, who set out from accepted dogmas, not from their own sight of principles. Meek young men grow up in libraries, believing it their duty to accept the views which Cicero, which Locke, which Bacon, have given; forgetful that Cicero, Locke, and Bacon were only young men in libraries when they wrote these books.

Hence, instead of Man Thinking, we have the bookworm. Hence the book-learned class, who value books, as such; not as related to nature and the human constitution, but as making a sort of Third Estate with the world and the soul. Hence the restorers of readings, the emendators, the bibliomaniacs of all degrees.

Books are the best of things, well used; abused, among the worst. What is the right use? What is the one end which all means go to effect? They are for nothing but to inspire. I had better never see a book than to be warped by its attraction clean out of my own orbit, and made a satellite instead of a system. The one thing in the world, of value, is the active soul. This every man is entitled to; this every man contains within him, although in almost all men obstructed and as yet unborn. The soul active sees absolute truth and utters truth, or creates. In this action it is genius; not the privilege of here and there a favorite, but the sound estate of every man. In its essence it is progressive. The book, the college, the school of art, the institution of any kind, stop with some past utterance of genius. This is good, say they,—let us hold by this. They pin me down. They look backward and not forward. But genius looks forward: the eyes of man are set in his forehead, not in his hindhead: man hopes: genius creates. Whatever talents may be, if the man create not, the pure efflux of the Deity is not his;—cinders and smoke there may be, but not yet flame. There are creative manners, there are creative actions, and creative words; manners, actions, words, that is, indicative of no custom or authority, but springing spontaneous from the mind's own sense of good and fair.

On the other part, instead of being its own seer, let it receive from another mind its truth, though it were in torrents of light, without periods of solitude, inquest, and self-recovery, and a fatal disservice is done. Genius is always sufficiently the enemy of genius by over-influence. The literature of every nation bears me witness. The English dramatic poets have Shakespearized now for two hundred years.

Undoubtedly there is a right way of reading, so it be sternly subordinated. Man Thinking must not be subdued by his instruments. Books are for the scholars' idle times. When he can read God directly, the hour is too precious to be wasted in other men's transcripts of their readings. But when the intervals of darkness come, as come they must,—when the sun is hid and the stars withdraw their shining,—we repair to the lamps which were kindled by their ray, to guide our steps to the East again, where the dawn is. We hear, that we may speak. The Arabian proverb says, "A fig tree, looking on a fig tree, becometh fruitful."

It is remarkable, the character of the pleasure we derive from the best books. They impress us with the conviction that one nature wrote and the same reads. We read the verses of one of the great English poets, of Chaucer, of Marvell, of Dryden, with the most modern joy,—with a pleasure, I mean, which is in great part caused by the abstraction of all *time* from their verses. There is some awe mixed with the joy of our surprise, when this poet, who lived in some past world, two or three hundred years ago, says that which lies close to my own soul, that which I also had well-nigh thought and said. But for the evidence thence afforded to the philosophical doctrine of the identity of all minds, we should suppose some preëstablished harmony, some foresight of souls that were to be, and some preparation of stores for their future wants, like the fact observed in insects, who lay up food before death for the young grub they shall never see.

I would not be hurried by any love of system, by any exaggeration of instincts, to underrate the Book. We all know, that as the human body can be nourished on any food, though it were boiled grass and the broth of shoes, so the human mind can be fed by any knowledge. And great and heroic men have existed who had almost no other information than by the printed page. I only would say that it needs a strong head to bear that diet. One must be an inventor to read well. As the proverb says, "He that would bring home the wealth of the Indies, must carry out the wealth of the Indies." There is then creative reading as well as creative writing. When the mind is braced by labor and invention, the page of whatever book we read becomes luminous with manifold allusion. Every sentence is doubly significant, and the sense of our author is as broad as the world. We then see, what is always true, that as the seer's hour of vision is short and rare among heavy days and months, so is its record, perchance, the least part of his volume. The discerning will read, in his Plato or Shakespeare, only that least part,—only the authentic utterances of the oracle;—all the rest he rejects, were it never so many times Plato's and Shakespeare's.

Of course there is a portion of reading quite indispensable to a wise man. History and exact science he must learn by laborious reading. Colleges, in like manner, have their indispensable office,—to teach elements. But they can only highly serve us when they aim not to drill, but to create; when they gather from far every ray of various genius to their hospitable halls, and by the concentrated fires, set the hearts of their youth on flame. Thought and knowledge are natures in which apparatus and pretension avail nothing. Gowns and pecuniary foundations, though of towns of gold, can never countervail the least sentence of syllable of wit. Forget this, and our American colleges will recede in their public importance, whilst they grow richer every year.

III. There goes in the world a notion that the scholar should be a recluse, a valetudinarian,—as unfit for any handiwork or public labor as a penknife for an axe. The so-called "practical men" sneer at speculative men, as if, because they speculate or *see,* they could do nothing. I have heard it said that the clergy,—who are always, more universally than any other class, the scholars of their day,—are addressed as women; that the rough, spontaneous conversation of men they do not hear, but only a mincing and diluted speech. They are often virtually disfranchised; and indeed there are advocates for their celibacy. As far as this is true of the studious classes, it is not just and wise. Action is with the scholar subordinate, but it is essential. Without it he is not yet man. Without it thought can never ripen into truth. Whilst the world hangs before the eye as a cloud of beauty, we cannot even see its beauty. Inaction is cowardice, but there can be no scholar without the heroic mind. The preamble of thought, the transition through which it passes from the unconscious to the conscious, is action. Only so much do I know, as I have lived. Instantly we know whose words are loaded with life, and whose not.

The world,—this shadow of the soul, or *other me,*—lies wide around. Its attractions are the keys which unlock my thoughts and make me acquainted with myself. I run eagerly into this resounding tumult. I grasp the hands of those next me, and take my place in the ring to suffer and to work, taught by an instinct that so shall the dumb abyss be vocal with speech. I pierce its order; I dissipate its fear; I dispose of it within the circuit of my expanding life. So much only of life as I know by experience, so much of the wilderness have I vanquished and planted, or so far have I extended my being, my dominion. I do not see how any man can afford, for the sake of his nerves and his nap, to spare any action in which he can partake. It is pearls and rubies to his discourse. Drudgery, calamity, exasperation, want, are instructors in eloquence and wisdom. The true scholar grudges every opportunity of action past by, as a loss of power. It is the raw material out of which the intellect molds her splendid products. A strange process too, this by which experience is converted into thought, as a mulberry leaf is converted into satin. The manufacture goes forward at all hours.

The actions and events of our childhood and youth are now matters of calmest observation. They lie like fair pictures in the air. Not so with our recent actions,—with the business which we now have in hand. On this we are quite unable to speculate. Our affections as yet circulate through it. We no more feel or know it than we feel the feet, or the hand, or the brain of our body. The new deed is yet a part of life,—remains for a time immersed in our unconscious life. In some contemplative hour it detaches itself from the life like a ripe fruit, to become a thought of the mind. Instantly it is raised, transfigured; the corruptible has put on incorruption. Henceforth it is an object of beauty, however base its origin and neighborhood. Observe too the impossibility of antedating this act. In its grub state, it cannot fly, it cannot shine, it is a dull grub. But suddenly, without observation, the selfsame thing unfurls beautiful wings, and is an angel of wisdom. So is there no fact, no event, in our private history, which shall not, sooner or later, lose its adhesive, inert form, and astonish us by soaring from our body into the empyrean. Cradle and infancy, school and playground, the fear of boys, and dogs, and ferules, the love of little maids and berries, and many another fact that once filled the whole sky, are gone already; friend and relative, profession and party, town and country, nation and world, must also soar and sing.

Of course, he who has put forth his total strength in fit actions has the richest return of wisdom. I will not shut myself out of this globe of action, and transplant an oak into a flower-pot, there to hunger and pine; nor trust the revenue of some single faculty, and exhaust one vein of thought, much like those Savoyards, who, getting their livelihood by carving shepherds, shepherdesses, and smoking Dutchmen, for all Europe, went out one day to the mountain to find stock, and discovered that they had whittled up the last of their pine trees. Authors we have, in numbers, who have written out their vein, and who, moved by a commendable prudence, sail for Greece or Palestine, follow the trapper into the prairie, or ramble round Algiers, to replenish their merchantable stock.

If it were only for a vocabulary, the scholar would be covetous of action. Life is our dictionary. Years are well spent in country labors; in town; in the insight into trades and manufactures; in frank intercourse with many men and women; in science; in art; to the one end of mastering in all their facts a language by which to illustrate and embody our perceptions. I learn immediately from any speaker how much he has already lived, through the poverty or the splendor of his speech. Life lies behind us as the quarry from whence we get tiles and copestones for the masonry of today. This is the way to learn grammar. Colleges and books only copy the language which the field and the work-yard made.

But the final value of action, like that of books, and better than books, is that it is a resource. That great principle of Undulation in nature, that shows itself in the inspiring and expiring of the breath; in desire and satiety; in the ebb and flow of the sea; in day and night; in heat and cold; and, as yet more deeply ingrained in every atom and every fluid, is known to us under the name of Polarity,—these "fits of easy transmission and reflection," as Newton called them, are the law of nature because they are the law of spirit.

The mind now thinks, now acts, and each fit reproduces the other. When the artist has exhausted his materials, when the fancy no longer paints, when thoughts are no longer apprehended and books are a weariness,—he has always the resource to *live*. Character is higher than intellect. Thinking is the function. Living is the functionary. The stream retreats to its source. A great soul will be strong to live, as well as strong to think. Does he lack organ or medium to impart his truths? He can still fall back on this elemental force of living them. This is a total act. Thinking is a partial act. Let the grandeur of justice shine in his affairs. Let the beauty of affection cheer his lowly roof. Those "far from fame," who dwell and act with him, will feel the force of his constitution in the doings and passages of the day better than it can be measured by any public and designed display. Time shall teach him that the scholar loses no hour which the man lives. Herein he unfolds the sacred germ of his instinct, screened from influence. What is lost in seemliness is gained in strength. Not out of those on whom systems of education have exhausted their culture, comes the helpful giant to destroy the old or to build the new, but out of unhandselled savage nature; out of terrible Druids and Berserkers come at last Alfred and Shakespeare.

I hear therefore with joy whatever is beginning to be said of the dignity and necessity of labor to every citizen. There is virtue yet in the hoe and the spade, for learned as well as for unlearned hands. And labor is everywhere welcome; always we are invited to work; only be this limitation observed, that a man shall not for the sake of wider activity sacrifice any opinion to the popular judgments and modes of action.

. . .

from The Poet

There was this perception in him which makes the poet or seer an object of awe and terror, namely that the same man or society of men may wear one aspect to themselves and their companions, and a different aspect to higher intelligences. Certain priests, whom he describes as conversing very learnedly together, appeared to the children who were at some distance, like dead horses; and many the like misappearances. And instantly the mind inquires whether these fishes under the bridge, yonder oxen in the pasture, those dogs in the yard, are immutably fishes, oxen and dogs, or only so appear to me, and perchance to themselves appear upright men; and whether I appear as a man to all eyes. The Brahmins and Pythagoras propounded the same question, and if any poet has witnessed the transformation he doubtless found it in harmony with various experiences. We have all seen changes as considerable in wheat and caterpillars. He is the poet and shall draw us with love and terror, who sees through the flowing vest the firm nature, and can declare it.

I look in vain for the poet whom I describe. We do not with sufficient plainness or sufficient profoundness address ourselves to life, nor dare we chaunt our own times and social circumstance. If we filled the day with bravery, we should not shrink from celebrating it. Time and nature yield us many gifts, but not yet the timely man, the new religion, the reconciler, whom all things await. Dante's praise is that he dared to write his autobiography in colossal cipher, or into universality. We have yet had no genius in America, with tyrannous eye, which knew the value of our incomparable materials, and saw, in the barbarism and materialism of the times, another carnival of the same gods whose picture he so much admires in Homer; then in the Middle Age; then in Calvinism. Banks and tariffs, the newspaper and caucus, Methodism and Unitarianism, are flat and dull to dull people, but rest on the same foundations of wonder as the town of Troy and the temple of Delphi, and are as swiftly passing away. Our log-rolling, our stumps and their politics, our fisheries, our Negroes and Indians, our boats and our repudiations, the wrath of rogues and the pusillanimity of honest men, the northern trade, the southern planting, the western clearing, Oregon and Texas, are yet unsung. Yet America is a poem in our eyes; its ample geography dazzles the imagination, and it will not wait long for meters. If I have not found that excellent combination of gifts in my countrymen which I seek, neither could I aid myself to fix the idea of the poet by reading now and then in Chalmer's collection of five centuries of English poets. These are wits more than poets, though there have been poets among them. But when we adhere to the ideal of the poet, we have our difficulties even with Milton and Homer. Milton is too literary, and Homer too literal and historical.

. . .

from History

There is no great and no small
To the Soul that maketh all:
And where it cometh, all things are;
And it cometh everywhere.

I am owner of the sphere,
Of the seven stars and the solar year,

Of Cæsar's hand, and Plato's brain,
Of Lord Christ's heart, and Shakespeare's strain.

There is one mind common to all individual men. Every man is an inlet to the same and to all of the same. He that is once admitted to the right of reason is made a freeman of the whole estate. What Plato has thought, he may think; what a saint has felt, he may feel; what at any time has befallen any man, he can understand. Who hath access to this universal mind is a party to all that is or can be done, for this is the only and sovereign agent.

Of the works of this mind history is the record. Its genius is illustrated by the entire series of days. Man is explicable by nothing less than all his history. Without hurry, without rest, the human spirit goes forth from the beginning to embody every faculty, every thought, every emotion which belongs to it, in appropriate events. But the thought is always prior to the fact; all the facts of history preëxist in the mind as laws. Each law in turn is made by circumstances predominant, and the limits of nature give power to but one at a time. A man is the whole encyclopædia of facts. The creation of a thousand forests is in one acorn, and Egypt, Greece, Rome, Gaul, Britain, America, lie folded already in the first man. Epoch after epoch, camp, kingdom, empire, republic, democracy, are merely the application of his manifold spirit to the manifold world.

This human mind wrote history, and this must read it. The Sphinx must solve her own riddle. If the whole of history is in one man, it is all to be explained from individual experience. There is a relation between the hours of our life and the centuries of time. As the air I breathe is drawn from the great repositories of nature, as the light on my book is yielded by a star a hundred millions of miles distant, as the poise of my body depends on the equilibrium of centrifugal and centripetal forces, so the hours should be instructed by the ages and the ages explained by the hours. Of the universal mind each individual man is one more incarnation. All its properties consist in him. Each new fact in his private experience flashes a light on what great bodies of men have done, and the crises of his life refer to national crises. Every revolution was first a thought in one man's mind, and when the same thought occurs to another man, it is the key to that era. Every reform was once a private opinion, and when it shall be a private opinion again it will solve the problem of the age. The fact narrated must correspond to something in me to be credible or intelligible. We, as we read, must become Greeks, Romans, Turks, priest and king, martyr and executioner; must fasten these images to some reality in our secret experience, or we shall learn nothing rightly. What befell Asdrubal or Cæsar Borgia is as much an illustration of the mind's powers and depravations as what has befallen us. Each new law and political movement has a meaning for you. Stand before each of its tablets and say, "Under this mask did my Proteus nature hide itself." This remedies the defect of our too great nearness to ourselves. This throws our actions into perspective—and as crabs, goats, scorpions, the balance and the waterpot lose their meanness when hung as signs in the zodiac, so I can see my own vices without heat in the distant persons of Solomon, Alcibiades, and Catiline.

It is the universal nature which gives worth to particular men and things. Human life, as containing this, is mysterious and inviolable, and we hedge it round with penalties and laws. All laws derive hence their ultimate reason; all express more or less distinctly some command of this supreme, illimitable essence. Property also holds of the soul, covers great spiritual facts, and instinctively we at first hold to it with swords and laws and wide and complex combinations. The obscure consciousness of this fact is the light of all our day, the claim of claims; the plea for education, for justice, for charity; the foundation of friendship and love and of the heroism and grandeur which belong to acts of self-reliance. It is remarkable that involuntarily we always read as superior beings. Universal history, the poets, the romancers, do not in their stateliest pictures—in the sacerdotal, the imperial palaces, in the triumphs of will or of genius—anywhere lose our ear, anywhere make us feel that we intrude, that this is for better men; but rather is it true that in their grandest strokes we feel most at home. All that Shakspeare says of the king, yonder slip of a boy that reads in the corner feels to be true of himself. We sympathize in the great moments of history, in the great discoveries, the great resistances, the great prosperities of men; because there law was enacted, the sea was searched, the land was found, or the blow was struck, *for us,* as we ourselves in that place would have done or applauded.

We have the same interest in condition and character. We honor the rich because they have externally the freedom, power, and grace which we feel to be proper to man, proper to us. So all that is said of the wise man by Stoic or Oriental or modern essayist, describes to each reader his own idea, describes his unattained but attainable self. All literature writes the character of the wise man. Books, monuments, pictures, conversation, are portraits in which he finds the lineaments he is forming. The silent and the eloquent praise him and accost him, and he is stimulated wherever he moves, as by personal allusions. A true aspirant therefore never needs look for allusions personal and laudatory in discourse. He hears the commendation, not of himself, but, more sweet, of that character he seeks, in every word that is said concerning character, yea further in every fact and circumstance—in the running river and the rustling corn. Praise is looked, homage tendered, love flows, from mute nature, from the mountains and the lights of the firmament.

These hints, dropped as it were from sleep and night, let us use in broad day. The student is to read history actively and not passively; to esteem his own life the text, and books the commentary. Thus compelled, the Muse of history will utter oracles, as never to those who do not respect themselves.

I have no expectation that any man will read history aright who thinks that what was done in a remote age, by men whose names have resounded far, has any deeper sense than what he is doing to-day.

The world exists for the education of each man. There is no age or state of society or mode of action in history to which there is not somewhat corresponding in his life. Every thing tends in a wonderful manner to abbreviate itself and yield its own virtue to him. He should see that he can live all history in his own person. He must sit solidly at home, and not suffer himself to be bullied by kings or empires, but know that he is greater than all the geography and all the government of the world; he must transfer the point of view from which history is commonly read; from Rome and Athens and London, to himself, and not deny his conviction that he is the court, and if England or Egypt have anything to say to him he will try the case; if not, let them forever be silent. He must attain and maintain that lofty sight where facts yield their secret sense, and poetry and annals are alike. The instinct of the mind, the purpose of nature, betrays itself in the use we make of the signal narrations of history. Time dissipates to shining ether the solid angularity of facts. No anchor, no cable, no fences avail to keep a fact a fact. Babylon, Troy, Tyre, Palestine, and even early Rome are passing already into fiction. The Garden of Eden, the sun standing still in Gibeon, is poetry thenceforward to all nations. Who cares what the fact was, when we have made a constellation of it to hang in heaven an immortal sign? London and Paris and New York must go the same way. "What is history," said Napoleon, "but a fable agreed upon?" This life of ours is stuck round with Egypt, Greece, Gaul, England, War, Colonization, Church, Court and Commerce, as with so many flowers and wild ornaments grave and gay. I will not make more account of them. I believe in Eternity. I can find Greece, Asia, Italy, Spain and the Islands—the genius and creative principle of each and of all eras, in my own mind.

We are always coming up with the emphatic facts of history in our private experience and verifying them here. All history becomes subjective; in other words there is properly no history, only biography. Every mind must know the whole lesson for itself—must go over the whole ground. What it does not see, what it does not live, it will not know. What the former age has epitomized into a formula or rule for manipular convenience, it will lose all the good of verifying for itself, by means of the wall of that rule. Somewhere, sometime, it will demand and find compensation for that loss, by doing the work itself. Ferguson discovered many things in astronomy which had long been known. The better for him.

19

Lewis Clarke (dates unknown)

from *Leaves from a Slave's Journal of Life*

One of the most stirring moments at anti-slavery meetings was when recently escaped slaves told their own stories. Their testimony was specific and fresh, and anti-slavery writers often reported it in abolitionist papers. As a result, there are actually far more of these shorter, oral or dictated autobiographies than there are book-length slave narratives, making them an important source of information about slavery. They also provide insight into the interests and attitudes of abolitionists.

This speech has all these values. First, it was written by Lydia Maria Child, a long-time white abolitionist who was later the editor of Harriet Jacobs's *Incidents in the Life of a Slave Girl*. Her opening description of Lewis Tappan, a founder of the American Anti-Slavery Society, reveals some of his mannerisms as well as her differences from him. Yet both she and Tappan are directly concerned with the credibility of Clarke, which builds up to Clarke's still more emphatic points about slavery, manhood, and truth. "A SLAVE CAN'T BE A MAN!"—because "He daren't tell what's in him," because "slavery's the father of lies." In turn, these points not only justify Clarke's testimony, they underscore the great importance of testimony to Clarke in establishing his freedom and manhood.

Clarke's speech and Child's account also reveal many other features of slavery and the southern and northern white interests in it, such as the treatment of women and girls, the vicious "patter-rollers," the prurience of some anti-slavery "boys," and the misery of slave children.

Child's report of Clarke's speech was originally printed in two issues of the *National Anti-Slavery Standard*, October 20 and 27, 1842. We have cut most of the second part, except for Clarke's memories of his childhood experiences.

For a complete text of "Leaves from a Slave's Journal of Life," see John W. Blassingame, ed., *Slave Testimony: Two Centuries of Letters, Speeches, Interviews, and Autobiographies* (Baton Rouge: Louisiana State Univ. Press, 1977), pp. 151–64. Blassingame also supplies further information about general conditions and about the conventions of speeches by ex-slaves.

from **Part 1**

A polite note from Lewis Tappan, last week, informed me that a fugitive slave, nearly as white as himself, would address an audience at Brooklyn; and having curiosity to hear what he would say, I crossed the ferry, at the time appointed for the meeting. I have seldom been more entertained by any speaker. His obvious want of education was one guaranty of the truth of his story; and the uncouth awkwardness of his language had a sort of charm, like the circuitous expression, and stammering utterance, of a foreign tongue, striving to speak our most familiar phrases. His mind was evidently full of ideas, which he was eager to express; but the medium was wanting. "I've got it in *here*," said he, laying his hand on his heart; "but I don't know how to get it out." How-ever, in his imperfect way, I believe he conveyed much information to many minds; and that few who heard him went away without being impressed by the conviction that he was sincerely truthful, and testified of things which he did know.

Lewis Tappan introduced him to the meeting, as Lewis Clarke, from Kentucky; saying that he brought highly satisfactory letters from Ohio, where Judge King, and General Somebody, and Esquire Somebody, had called meet-ings for him, and certified their full belief of his story. I would record the individuals, if I remembered them; but my organ of reverence, though pretty largely developed, never occupies itself with great *names*. I should be ex-tremely unpopular in Great Britain; for I should be as likely to recognize the true queen of the nation in a washerwoman, as any way. Lewis Tappan, luckily, had more adaptation to the state of the public mind, and doubtless gained the ear of many, by thus propping up his *protegé* with *magnates* on either side. Many in the audience, of course, would not perceive, so readily as I did, that the man spoke truth, from *what* he spoke, and the *way* in which he spoke it; and I bade them a hearty welcome to all the aid they could derive from judges and generals.

The fugitive informed us that his father was a soldier of the revolution. Though he was quite a little boy when separated from his parents, he remem-bered hearing his father tell about fighting battles for freedom; and that he thought all the while that *he* was to have a share in the freedom, as well as the white folks. But in *that*, he found himself mistaken. "He thought it was a hard case," said he; "and I, that come after him, had reason to think it was a hard case, too. My grandmother was her master's daughter; and my mother was her master's daughter; and I was my master's son; so you see I han't got but one-eighth of the blood. Now, admitting it's right to make a slave of a full black nigger, I want to ask gentlemen acquainted with business, whether because I owe a shilling, I ought to be made to pay a dollar?"

I was very much struck with the fact, that he seemed to think much less of the physical sufferings of the slave, than of his moral and intellectual degradation. The great idea, which formed the basis of Dr. Channing's abolition, and which he expressed in such various forms of eloquence, inspired likewise the soul of this fugitive slave, and shone through his awkward language, like fragments of rainbow through a fog. "I an't a going to tell you first about the whippings," said he; "though I'm the boy that's got 'em, times a plenty. But as I was saying, 'tan't the slave's sufferings I care so much to tell about; though they do suffer, some of them a big, vast quantity." The audience laughed audibly, and he at once understood its meaning. He smiled, as he said, "Now, you oughtn't to expect words out of the grammar from me; for how should I know what's in the grammar?"

"Your words are plenty good enough," said a friendly voice; "go on—never mind your words."

"So I will, as well as I can. I want to tell you, not so much about the slave's being whipped, or about his not having enough to eat; though I could tell you enough of that, too, if I had a chance. But what I want to make you understand is, that A SLAVE CAN'T BE A MAN! Slavery makes a brute of man; I don't mean that he *is* a brute, neither. But a horse *can't* speak; and he *daren't*. He daren't tell what's in him; it wouldn't do. The worse he's treated, the more he must smile; the more he's kicked the lower he must crawl. For you see the master *knows* when he's treated his slave too bad for human nature; and he *suspects* the slave will resent; and he watches him the closer, and so the slave has to be more deceitful. Folks from hereabouts go down to Kentucky, and they send you word that the slaves say they don't *want* their freedom.— Well, I suppose they do. I daren't swear I han't done that thing myself. I had the privilege of letting myself out, and sending my master twelve dollars a month.—This was a sort of taste of freedom; for I went round about, and made my own little contracts, and so on.—Now, if some Yankee had come along and said, 'Do you want to be free?' what do you suppose I'd have told him? Now, what do you *suppose* I'd tell him? Why, I'd tell him, to be sure, that I didn't want to be free; that I was very well off as I was. If I didn't, its precious few contracts I should be allowed to make, I'm thinking. And if a woman slave had a husband and children, and somebody asked her if she would like her freedom? Would she tell 'em, yes? If she did, she'd be down the river to Louisiana, in no time; and her husband and children never know what become of her. Of course, the slaves don't tell folks what's passing in their minds about freedom; for they know what'll come of it, if they do. I said a slave was like a brute; and so he is, in many things; but he an't altogether that much like a brute, neither. The fact is, slavery's the father of lies. The slave knows he ought to have his freedom; and his master knows it, jest as well as he does; but they both *say* they don't; and they tell me some folks this way believe 'em. The master says the slave don't want his freedom, and the slave says he don't want it; but they both of 'em lie, and know it. There never was anything beat slavery for lying; and of all folks in the world, there's nobody deceived quite so bad, as the masters down South; for the slaves deceive them, and they deceive themselves. Some have thought their slaves were so much attached to them, that nobody could coax them away; and them very slaves now reside in Canada. Others think the slaves are too brutified to think or care anything about freedom; and them's the worst deceived of any. The masters say the slaves are a lying and thieving set; and so they are; for slavery makes a man lie and steal. It won't let him be honest, if he would.

"Some folks go down to Kentucky, and tell fine stories about how well the slaves live; that they dress as nice as anybody, and have horses to ride a Sunday.—Well, so it is with many of them slaves that are favorites in rich families; but I tell you them favorite slaves are most to be pitied of all. They are obliged to cringe a little lower than any of the others. They must mind and please master and mistress in everything; and please the children, and the uncles, and the aunts, and the cousins, and all the relations; for the master wants him to feel that it is all along of his will that he is better off than others, and that he has the power at any moment, to cut his comb; and he is always sort of jealous, too, that the slave will think he has a *right* to any of the privileges he has been used to having. So he has to mind his P's and Q's right smart; for if he says or does anything that any of the relations don't like, he's pushed right down below all the slaves. I've seen this, many a time. The brighter a slave is, the more he has to lie; for the more the master is jealous of what's working in his mind, and the harder he has to try to hide it. It an't the lightest colored that are always the brightest and best; for a man's disposition an't in his skin. Yes, it is in his skin, too; because it is in his heart, and his heart is inside his skin; but what I mean is, that it an't in the *color* of his skin.—The slaves used to debate together sometimes, what could be the reason that the yellow folks couldn't be trusted like the dark ones could. As a general rule, they seemed to be dissipated, devil-may-care fellows; and I'll tell you what we concluded was the reason—we concluded it was because they was sons of their masters,and took after their fathers. You laugh; but that's what the *slaves* concluded was the reason; and I declare to you I have heard 'em talk on about it, and bring up this here one, and that ere one, that was the son of a dissipated master, till I felt ashamed of the white blood that was in me. And I tell you, the man that bears the best character in all Kentucky, in respect of his morals, has a face as black as the inside of a blacking box. He is engaged in the public works, and takes hundreds and hundreds of dollars. He might run away with the money, if he would; but ever since he was a boy he was walked right ahead, as straight as any crack in this floor. You might ask anybody, from highest to lowest, and they'd all tell you that they'd trust him afore any man in Kentucky. White men trust one-another, I know; but mind ye, they always have *bond and security;* now, it would be no use for this man to give bond and security—for he's a slave."

One of the audience here interrupted, saying, "I thought you observed, a little while ago, that slaves *couldn't* be honest; that they were *obliged* to lie and steal?"

"So I did; and it was true. But this man, you see, was a slave, and then again he warn't a slave. He was a first-rate blacksmith, and worked for the public works, and had money trusted to him; and this made him feel somehow like a man, though he was a slave, too. They *trusted* him a good deal, you see."

"You mean," said a friendly voice, "that if you trust a man, it makes him worthy to be trusted."

This seemed a little too grammatical for him to understand; and another one said, "You mean that if a slave feels that he is trusted, he may be trusted with anything."

"Not exactly that, neither," replied he, with an arch look; "when a slave knows that he is trusted, he may be trusted with *almost* anything—except *himself!*"

When the laugh subsided, he continued: "But the smarter he is, the more they [are] jealous [of] him, and the more they like to hold him for a slave; and the whiter he is, the grander they feel. As a general thing, if a Kentuckian has a little money, he'd a deal rather vest it in slaves than in any other property. A horse don't *know* that he's property, and a man does. There's a sort of satisfaction in thinking 'You're a man, but you're *mine*. You're as white as I am, but you're *mine*.' Many a time I've had 'em say to me, 'You're my property. If I tell you to hold your hand in the fire till it burns off, you've got to do it.' Not that they *meant* to make me put my hand in the fire; but they like to let me know they had the *power*. The whiter a man is, the lower down they keep him. I knew a slave that was *all* white. I might tell you his name, and where he lived. I believe I will. No, I won't either; for if I do, you may perhaps ask me whether *I* came from his neighborhood; and I don't care to have you know any more than that I came from Kentucky. Her borders are pretty broad, you know, and it's not so easy to guess what part I come from. But what I wanted to say was, that this white slave was stolen from Virginia when he was a very little boy, and he had been kept in slavery ever since. He was brought up more ignorant than any of the slaves, and if any whipping was to be done on the plantation, he was sure to catch it. The slaves used to say to him, 'Massa had a great deal rather whip you than Steve.' Now Steve was the blackest man of the whole lot. Knowing he was a white man, I suppose they was afraid he'd find out his rights, if they didn't keep him down right hard.

"Kentucky is the best of the slave States, in respect to the laws; but the masters manage to fix things pretty much to their own liking. The law don't allow 'em to brand a slave, or cut off his ear; but if they happen to switch it off with a cow-hide, nobody says anything about it. Though the laws are better than in other States, they an't anyways equal. If a negro breaks open a house, he is hung for it; but if a white man does the same thing, he is put in the penitentiary, unless he has money enough to buy himself off. And there is one crime for which more black men are hung than for any other; and if a white man does it, it is no crime at all. The law gives him full swing; and he don't fail to use his privilege, I can tell you. Now, if there was nothing else but this, it would make a slave's life as bad as death, many times. I can't tell these respectable people as much as I would like to; but jest think for a minute how you would like to have *your* sisters, and *your* wives, and *your* daughters, completely, teetotally, and altogether, in the power of a master.— You can picture to yourselves a little, how you would feel; but oh, if I could *tell* you! A slave woman an't allowed to respect herself, if she would. I had a pretty sister; she was whiter than I am, for she took more after her father. When she was sixteen years old, her master sent for her. When he sent for her again, she cried, and didn't want to go. She told mother her troubles, and she tried to encourage her to be decent, and hold up her head above such things, if she could. Her master was so mad, to think she complained to her mother, that he sold her right off to Louisiana; and we heard afterward that she died there of hard usage.

"There was a widower in Kentucky, who took one of his women slaves into the house. She told her master one day that seven of the young girls had poked fun at her for the way she was living. This raised his *ambition*. 'I'll teach 'em to make fun!' said he. So he sent the woman away, and ordered the young girls to come to him, one by one." (An ill-mannered and gross laughter, among the boys of the audience, here seemed to embarrass him.) "Perhaps I had better not try to tell this story," he continued; "for I cannot tell it as it was; though surely it is more shameful to have such things *done*, than it is to *tell* of 'em. He got mad with the girls, because they complained to their mothers; but he didn't like to punish 'em for that, for fear it would make a talk. So he ordered 'em to go out into the field to do work that was too hard for 'em. Six of 'em said they couldn't do it; but the mother of the seventh, guessing what it was for, told her to go, and do the best she could. The other six was every one of 'em tied up naked, and flogged, for disobeying orders. Now, who would like to be a slave, even if there was nothing bad about it but such treatment of his sisters and daughters? But there's a worse thing yet about slavery; the worst thing in the whole lot; though it's all bad, from the butt end to the *pint*. I mean the *patter-rollers* (patrols.) I suppose you know that they have patter-rollers to go round o' nights, to see that the slaves are all in, and not planning any mischief? Now, these are jest about the worst fellows that can be found; as bad as any you could pick up on the wharves. The reason is, you see, that no decent man will undertake the business.— Gentlemen in Kentucky are ready enough to hire such jobs done; but if you was to ask any of them to *be* a patter-roller, he would look upon it as a right down insult, and likely enough would blow out your brains for an answer. They're mighty handy with pistols down there; and if a man don't resent anything that's put upon him, they call him Pokeeasy. The slaves catch it, too: and them as won't fight, is called Pokeeasy.—But as I was telling ye, they hire those patter-rollers, and they have to take the meanest fellows above ground; and because they are so mortal sure the slaves don't want their freedom, they have to put all power into their hands to do with the niggers jest as they like. If a slave don't open his door to them at any time of night they break it down. They steal his money if they can find it, and act just as they please with his wives and daughters. If a husband dares to say a word, or even look as if he wasn't quite satisfied, they tie him up and give him thirty-nine lashes. If there's any likely young girls in a slave's hut, they're mighty apt to have business there; especially if they think any colored young man takes a fancy to any of 'em. Maybe he'll get a pass from his master, and go to see the young girl for a few hours. The patter-rollers break in and find him there. They'll abuse the girl as bad as they can, a purpose to provoke him. If he looks cross, they give him a flogging, tear up his pass, turn him out of doors, and then take him up and whip him for being out without a pass. If the slave says they tore it up, they swear he lies: and nine times out of ten the master won't come out agin 'em; for they say it won't *do* to let the niggers suppose they may complain of the patter-rollers; they must be taught that it's their business to obey 'em in everything; and the patter-roller knows that very well. Oh, how often I've seen the poor girls sob and cry, when there's been such goings on! Maybe you think, because they're slaves, they an't got no feeling and no shame? A woman's being a slave, don't stop her having genteel ideas; that is, according to their way, and as far as they can. They know they must submit to their masters; besides, their masters, maybe, dress 'em up, and make 'em little presents, and give 'em more privileges, while the whim lasts; but that an't like having a parcel of low, dirty, swearing, drunk patter-rollers let loose among 'em, like so many hogs. This breaks down their spirits dreadfully, and makes 'em wish they was dead.

"Now who among you would like to have your wives, and daughters, and sisters, in such a situation? This is what every slave in all these States is exposed to.—Yet folks go from these parts down to Kentucky, and come back, and say the slaves have enough to eat and drink, and they are very happy, and they wouldn't mind it much to be slaves themselves. I'd like to have 'em try it; it would teach 'em a little more than they know now. I'm not going to deny that Kentucky is better than other slave States, in respect of her laws; and she has the best name, too, about treating her slaves. But one great reason of that is, they are proud about punishing in *public*. If a man ties his slave up in the marketplace, and flogs him till he can't stand, the neighbors all cry out, 'What a shame! The man has no regard to his character. What an abominable thing to have that nigger screaming where *everybody can hear!* Shame on him, to do such things in public!'

"But if the same man flogs his slave ten times as bad, up garret, or down cellar, with his mouth stopped, that he mayn't make a noise, or off in the woods out of hearing—it's all well enough. If his neighbors hear of it, they only say, 'Well, of course there's no managing niggers without letting 'em know who's master.' And there's an end of the business. The law, to be sure, don't allow such cruel floggings; but how's a slave going to get the law of his master? The law won't let him, nor any of the slaves, testify; and if the neighbors know anything about it, they *won't* testify. For it won't *do* to let the slaves think they would be upheld in complaining of master or overseer. I told you in the beginning, that it wouldn't *do* to let the slave think he is a *man*. That would spoil slavery, clean entirely.—No; this is the cruelty of the thing—A SLAVE CAN'T BE A MAN. He *must* be made a brute; but he an't a brute, neither, if he had a chance to act himself out. Many a one of 'em is right smart, I tell you. But a horse *can't* speak, and slave *darn't;* and that's the best way I can tell the story."

Next week, I will continue the remarks by this ignorant but naturally intelligent slave. They are valuable for their honest directness and simplicity, and as sketches of scenes from one who dwelt in the midst of them. As he stood side by side with Lewis Tappan, one could hardly perceive that he was a shade darker. Many a New England farmer, tanned by the sun, is as brown as he. What he *might* have been, with common advantages for education, is shown by his shrewd conclusions, and the large ideas which his soul struggled so hard to utter in imperfect language. He lectured three evenings. Toward the close of the second, Isaac T. Hopper rose and repeated some of his anecdotes of fugitive slaves. The audience were evidently much entertained; and the Kentuckian refugee seemed as if touched by an electric chain. "The more that old gentleman says," exclaimed he, "the more it puts me in mind of."

As there seemed some danger of talking all night, an adjournment was proposed, and carried.

The audience continually increased each successive evening, and listened throughout with great attention, and without the slightest demonstration of disrespect, or impatience. A slaveholder from Mississippi was present, and was requested to declare openly if any of the statements appeared to him incorrect. He said nothing in the meeting; and Mr. Tappan declared that he admitted, out of doors, that he had heard nothing incredible. He *says* he is going to emancipate his slaves forthwith. God give him grace to keep his word! His person was not pointed out to the audience, nor was he addressed by name; for the same reason that one would not like to point out a reformed man, who had been in the penitentiary for stealing horses. Men are beginning to blush at being slaveholders, unless they have a throng of slaveholders around them, to keep them in countenance.—L.M.C.

from Part II

"The suffering of children in slavery will never the half of it be told; especially if the mistress suspects that the child is a little too nearly connected with master. It's a nateral thing that she shouldn't feel very pleasant, in such a case; and sometimes the slave mother and child had better both be dead, than lead the life they do. My mistress had a little slave girl, about seven years old, that used to get terribly abused. She used to beat her head up against the chimney, till it was in a dreadful state, and kick her about for any little thing, as if she was a dog. This poor child died of bad treatment. Mistress did her best to kill me, but I lived through it. She set me to spinning flax when I was five years old. She didn't show me how; but every time I made any mistake, she switched me. Every year when the trees were trimmed, she had all the switches laid up, to whip the slaves. She used to sit over her toddy, trying to invent some new way to punish 'em.—Master was a little too fond of grog; she used to keep it locked up from him; and he had to coax her to get any. Sometimes, when he came home, she would whine and groan about what a hard time she had of it; and tell how the slaves acted so unruly she couldn't manage 'em. 'Well, give me a dram,' he'd say, 'and I'll beat 'em for you.' She used to pull the hair out of my head, and tell the children to pull it. In several places, they pulled it all out of my head. Folks noticed the looks of it, and asked what ailed me. She told 'em I had a scald head; but one of the neighbors said it didn't look at all like scald head; and so for fear of making a talk, she left off doing that. One day, she sent me to get a pitcher out of the closet. It stood above my head, and had some spoons in front of it. Trying to get the pitcher, I knocked down the spoons. She gave me a blow over the head with a dusting brush, and I fell senseless on the floor. There is a dent in my skull now, which any gentleman can feel, if he has a mind to put his hand on my head. They brought me to; and after I got a little over it, she whipped me for pretending to be dead.

"I used to have to get up at all times o' night, to make fires, or rock the children, or bring 'em water, or something or other; and as I had to work smart all day, it used to make me dreadful drowsy, to be so broke of my rest. I used to bring the bed-clothes down stairs, and warm them before the fire, for the children to sleep on. One night I was bringing down an armfull, and having rather more than I could well manage, I set down on the landing of the stairs to rest. I was scarcely down, before I was sound asleep. I don't know how long I staid there. The first thing I knew, mistress waked me up with a bunch of switches. I had forgot all about where I was, and set out to run straight ahead. I pitched right over mistress, and we both rolled down stairs together. She was mad enough; and I got a good flogging. This all happened when I was quite a little boy."

20

Margaret Fuller (1810–1850)

from *Mariana*

Like many other New England writers, Margaret Fuller kept diaries and wrote lengthy letters. She also wrote a very important book in the history of feminism, *Woman in the Nineteenth Century* (1845), and a very good travel book, *Summer on the Lakes* (1844), about a trip to the Middle West in 1843. But as autobiography none of these writings seems as original as the following romantic sketch, which she included in *Summer on the Lakes*, introducing it as about "an old schoolmate" back East. By using such a frame and such other fictional devices as the third-person narration and the Shakespearean name (Mariana was Angelo's rejected but forgiving betrothed in *Measure for Measure*), Fuller managed to talk about her adolescent anguish without seeming to be morbidly self-conscious or self-pitying.

Today the bildungsroman is a common form. Fuller, however, had only one example to follow, Goethe's *Wilhelm Meisters Lehrjahre,* and upright Americans looked askance on it, just as they disapproved of Fuller's feminism and thought her interest in Goethe and German philosophy an affectation. So "Mariana" is in some ways primitive: a sketch rather than an intensely written short story or confessional essay. But the story of Mariana's misery at boarding school, arising from her ardor and her friends' conformity and cruelty, is archetypal. Nothing in "Mariana" is better drawn than the moment at dinner when she looks up and sees all the other girls wearing her rouge!

Fuller thus opened the way for countless later stories of adolescence, and in the process extended our very concept of individual uniqueness and the necessity for freedom of self-expression. The romantic individual is like (and partially derived from) the plight of a bright adolescent in a company of peers who are all boorish and mean.

The story is taken from *Summer on the Lakes, in 1843* (Boston and New York, 1844), and omits the less autobiographical ending about Mariana's marriage. For more on Fuller, see Bell Gale Chevigny, *The Woman and the Myth: Margaret Fuller's Life and Writings* (Old Westbury, NY: Feminist Press, 1976).

Among those whom I met in a recent visit at Chicago was Mrs. Z., the aunt of an old schoolmate, to whom I impatiently hasted, to demand news of Mariana. The answer startled me. Mariana, so full of life, was dead. That form, the most rich in energy and coloring of any I had ever seen, had faded from the hearth. The circle of youthful associations had given way in the part that seemed the strongest. What I now learned of the story of this life, and what was by myself remembered, may be bound together in this slight sketch.

At the boarding school to which I was too early sent, a fond, a proud, and timid child, I saw among the ranks of the gay and graceful, bright or earnest girls, only one who interested my fancy or touched my young heart; and this was Mariana. She was, on the father's side, of Spanish Creole blood, but had been sent to the Atlantic coast, to receive a school education under the care of her aunt, Mrs. Z.

This lady had kept her mostly at home with herself, and Mariana had gone from her house to a day school; but the aunt being absent for a time in Europe, she had now been unfortunately committed for some time to the mercies of a boarding school.

A strange bird she proved there—a lonely one, that could not make for itself a summer. At first, her schoolmates were captivated with her ways, her love of wild dances and sudden song, her freaks of passion and of wit. She was always new, always surprising, and, for a time, charming.

But after a while, they tired of her. She could never be depended on to join in their plans, yet she expected them to follow out hers with their whole strength. She was very loving, even infatuated in her own affections, and exacted from those who had professed any love for her, the devotion she was willing to bestow.

Yet there was a vein of haughty caprice in her character; and a love of solitude, which made her at times wish to retire entirely; and at these times she would expect to be thoroughly understood, and let alone, yet to be welcomed back when she returned. She did not thwart others in their humors, but she never doubted of great indulgence from them.

Some singular ways she had, which, when new, charmed, but, after acquaintance, displeased her companions. She had by nature the same habit and power of excitement that is described in the spinning dervishes of the East. Like them she would spin until all around her were giddy, while her own brain, instead of being disturbed, was excited to great action. Pausing, she would declaim verses of others, or her own; perform many parts, with strange catch-words and burdens that seemed to act with mystical power on her own fancy, sometimes stimulating her to convulse the hearer with laughter, sometimes to melt him to tears. When her power began to languish, she would spin again till fired to recommence her singular drama, into which she wove figures from the scenes of her earlier childhood, her companions, and the dignitaries she sometimes saw, with fantasies unknown to life, unknown to heaven or earth.

This excitement, as may be supposed, was not good for her. It usually came on in the evening, and often spoiled her sleep. She would wake in the night, and cheat her restlessness by inventions that teased, while they sometimes diverted her companions.

She was also a sleep-walker; and this one trait of her case did somewhat alarm her guardians, who, otherwise, showed the same profound stupidity, as to this peculiar being, usual in the overseers of the young. They consulted a physician, who said she would outgrow it, and prescribed a milk diet.

Meantime, the fever of this ardent and too early stimulated nature was constantly increased by the restraints and narrow routine of the boarding school. She was always devising means to break in upon it. She had a taste, which would have seemed ludicrous to her mates, if they had not felt some awe of her, from a touch of genius and power, that never left her, for costume and fancy dresses; always some sash twisted about her, some drapery, something odd in the arrangement of her hair and dress; so that the methodical preceptress dared not let her go out without a careful scrutiny and remodelling, whose soberizing effects generally disappeared the moment she was in the free air.

At last, a vent for her was found in private theatricals. Play followed play, and in these and the rehearsals she found entertainment congenial with her. The principal parts, as a matter of course, fell to her lot; most of the good suggestions and arrangements came from her, and for a time she ruled masterly and shone triumphant.

During these performances the girls had heightened their bloom with artificial red; this was delightful to them—it was something so out of the way. But Mariana, after the plays were over, kept her carmine saucer on the dressing table, and put on her blushes regularly as the morning.

When stared and jeered at, she at first said she did it because she thought it made her look prettier; but, after a while, she became petulant about it— would make no reply to any joke, but merely kept on doing it.

This irritated the girls, as all eccentricity does the world in general, more than vice or malignity. They talked it over among themselves, till they were wrought up to a desire of punishing, once for all, this sometimes amusing, but so often provoking nonconformist.

Having obtained leave of the mistress, they laid, with great glee, a plan, one evening, which was to be carried into execution the next day at dinner.

Among Mariana's irregularities was a great aversion to the meal-time ceremonial. So long, so tiresome she found it, to be seated at a certain moment, to wait while each one was served at so large a table, and one where there was scarcely any conversation; from day to day it became more heavy to sit there, or go there at all. Often as possible she excused herself on the ever-convenient plea of headache, and was hardly ever ready when the dinner-bell rang.

To-day the summons found her on the balcony, lost in gazing on the beautiful prospect. I have heard her say afterwards, that she had scarcely in her life been so happy—and she was one with whom happiness was a still rapture. It was one of the most blessed summer days; the shadows of great white clouds empurpled the distant hills for a few moments only to leave them more golden; the tall grass of the wide fields waved in the softest breeze. Pure blue were the heavens, and the same hue of pure contentment was in the heart of Mariana.

Suddenly on her bright mood jarred the dinner bell. At first rose her usual thought, I will not, cannot go; and then the *must*, which daily life can always enforce, even upon the butterflies and birds, came, and she walked reluctantly from her room. She merely changed her dress, and never thought of adding the artificial rose to her cheek.

When she took her seat in the dining-hall, and was asked if she would be helped, raising her eyes, she saw the person who asked her was deeply rouged, with a bright glaring spot, perfectly round, in either cheek. She looked at the next—the same apparition! She then slowly passed her eyes down the whole line, and saw the same, with a suppressed smile distorting every countenance. Catching the design at once, she deliberately looked along her own side of the table, at every schoolmate in turn; every one had joined in the trick. The teachers strove to be grave, but she saw they enjoyed the joke. The servants could not suppress a titter.

When Warren Hastings stood at the bar of Westminster Hall; when the Methodist preacher walked through a line of men, each of whom greeted him with a brickbat or rotten egg,—they had some preparation for the crisis, and it might not be very difficult to meet it with an impassive brow. Our little girl was quite unprepared to find herself in the midst of a world which despised her, and triumphed in her disgrace.

She had ruled like a queen in the midst of her companions; she had shed her animation through their lives, and loaded them with prodigal favors, nor once suspected that a popular favorite might not be loved. Now, she felt that she had been but a dangerous plaything in the hands of those whose hearts she never had doubted.

Yet the occasion found her equal to it; for Mariana had the kind of spirit, which, in a better cause, had made the Roman matron truly say of her death wound, "It is not painful, Poetus." She did not blench—she did not change countenance. She swallowed her dinner with apparent composure. She made remarks to those near her as if she had no eyes.

The wrath of the foe of course rose higher, and the moment they were freed from the restraints of the dining room, they all ran off, gayly calling, and sarcastically laughing, with backward glances, at Mariana, left alone.

Alone she went to her room, locked the door, and threw herself on the floor in strong convulsions. These had sometimes threatened her life, as a child, but of later years she had outgrown them. School hours came, and she was not there. A little girl, sent to her door, could get no answer. The teachers became alarmed, and broke it open. Bitter was their penitence and that of her companions at the state in which they found her. For some hours terrible anxiety was felt; but at last Nature, exhausted, relieved herself by a deep slumber.

From this Mariana arose an altered being. She made no reply to the expressions of sorrow from her companions, none to the grave and kind, but undiscerning comments of her teacher. She did not name the source of her anguish, and its poisoned dart sank deeply in. It was this thought which stung her so.—"What, not one, not a single one, in the hour of trial, to take my part! not one who refused to take part against me!" Past words of love, and caresses little heeded at the time, rose to her memory, and gave fuel to her distempered heart. Beyond the sense of universal perfidy, of burning resentment, she could not get. And Mariana, born for love, now hated all the world.

The change, however, which these feelings made in her conduct and appearance bore no such construction to the careless observer. Her gay freaks were quite gone, her wildness, her invention. Her dress was uniform, her manner much subdued. Her chief interest seemed now to lie in her studies and in music. Her companions she never sought; but they, partly from uneasy, remorseful feelings, partly that they really liked her much better now that she did not oppress and puzzle them, sought her continually. And here the black shadow comes upon her life—the only stain upon the history of Mariana.

They talked to her as girls, having few topics, naturally do of one another. Then the demon rose within her, and spontaneously, without design, generally without words of positive falsehood, she became a genius of discord among them. She fanned those flames of envy and jealousy which a wise, true word from a third person will often quench forever; by a glance, or a seemingly light reply, she planted the seeds of dissension, till there was scarce a peaceful affection or sincere intimacy in the circle where she lived, and could not but rule, for she was one whose nature was to that of the others as fire to clay.

It was at this time that I came to the school, and first saw Mariana. Me she charmed at once, for I was a sentimental child, who, in my early ill health, had been indulged in reading novels till I had no eyes for the common greens and browns of life. The heroine of one of these, "the Bandit's Bride," I immediately saw in Mariana. Surely the Bandit's Bride had just such hair, and such strange, lively ways, and such a sudden flash of the eye. The Bandit's Bride, too, was born to be "misunderstood" by all but her lover. But Mariana, I was determined, should be more fortunate; for, until her lover appeared, I myself would be the wise and delicate being who could understand her.

It was not, however, easy to approach her for this purpose. Did I offer to run and fetch her handkerchief, she was obliged to go to her room, and would rather do it herself. She did not like to have people turn over for her the leaves of the music book as she played. Did I approach my stool to her feet, she moved away, as if to give me room. The bunch of wild flowers which I timidly laid beside her plate was left there.

After some weeks my desire to attract her notice really preyed upon me, and one day, meeting her alone in the entry, I fell upon my knees, and kissing her hand, cried, "O Mariana, do let me love you, and try to love me a little." But my idol snatched away her hand, and laughing more wildly than the Bandit's Bride was ever described to have done, ran into her room. After that day her manner to me was not only cold, but repulsive; I felt myself scorned, and became very unhappy.

Perhaps four months had passed thus, when, one afternoon, it became obvious that something more than common was brewing. Dismay and mystery were written in many faces of the older girls; much whispering was going on in corners.

In the evening, after prayers, the principal bade us stay; and, in a grave, sad voice summoned Mariana to answer charges to be made against her.

Mariana came forward, and leaned against the chimneypiece. Eight of the older girls came forward, and preferred against her charges—alas! too well founded—of calumny and falsehood.

My heart sank within me, as one after the other brought up their proofs, and I saw they were too strong to be resisted. I could not bear the thought of this second disgrace of my shining favorite. The first had been whispered to me, though the girls did not like to talk about it. I must confess, such is the charm of strength to softer natures, that neither of these crises could deprive Mariana of hers in my eyes.

At first, she defended herself with self-possession and eloquence. But when she found she could no more resist the truth, she suddenly threw herself down, dashing her head, with all her force, against the iron hearth, on which a fire was burning, and was taken up senseless.

The affright of those present was great. Now that they had perhaps killed her, they reflected it would have been as well if they had taken warning from the former occasion, and approached very carefully a nature so capable of any extreme. After a while she revived, with a faint groan, amid the sobs of her companions. I was on my knees by the bed, and held her cold hand. One of those most aggrieved took it from me to beg her pardon, and say it was impossible not to love her. She made no reply.

Neither that night, nor for several days, could a word be obtained from her, nor would she touch food; but, when it was presented to her, or any one drew near from any cause she merely turned away her head, and gave no sign. The teacher saw that some terrible nervous affection had fallen upon her— that she grew more and more feverish. She knew not what to do.

Meanwhile, a new revolution had taken place in the mind of the passionate but nobly-tempered child. All these months nothing but the sense of injury had rankled in her heart. She had gone on in one mood, doing what the demon prompted, without scruple and without fear.

But at the moment of detection, the tide ebbed, and the bottom of her soul lay revealed to her eye. How black, how stained and sad! Strange, strange, that she had not seen before the baseness and cruelty of falsehood, the loveliness of truth! Now, amid the wreck, uprose the moral nature, which never before had attained the ascendant. "But," she thought, "too late sin is revealed to me in all its deformity, and sin-defiled, I will not, cannot live. The main-spring of life is broken."

And thus passed slowly by her hours in that black despair of which only youth is capable. In older years men suffer more dull pain, as each sorrow that comes drops its leaden weight into the past, and, similar features of character bringing similar results, draws up the heavy burden buried in those depths. But only youth has energy, with fixed, unwinking gaze, to contemplate grief, to hold it in the arms and to the heart, like a child which makes it wretched, yet is indubitably its own.

The lady who took charge of this sad child had never well understood her before, but had always looked on her with great tenderness. And now love seemed—when all around were in greatest distress, fearing to call in medical aid, fearing to do without it—to teach her where the only blame was to be found that could have healed this wounded spirit.

One night she came in, bringing a calming draught. Mariana was sitting, as usual, her hair loose, her dress the same robe they put on her at first, her eyes fixed vacantly upon the whited wall. To the proffers and entreaties of her nurse, she made no reply.

The lady burst into tears, but Mariana did not seem even to observe it.

The lady then said, "O, my child, do not despair; do not think that one great fault can mar a whole life! Let me trust you; let me tell you the griefs of my sad life. I will tell you, Mariana, what I never expected to impart to any one."

And so she told her tale: it was one of pain, of shame, borne, not for herself, but for one near and dear as herself. Mariana knew the lady—knew the pride and reserve of her nature. She had often admired to see how the cheek, lovely, but no longer young, mantled with the deepest blush of youth, and the blue eyes were cast down at any little emotion: she had understood the proud sensibility of the character. She fixed her eyes on those now raised to hers, bright with fast-falling tears. She heard the story to the end, and then, without saying a word, stretched out her hand for the cup.

She returned to life, but it was as one who had passed through the valley of death. The heart of stone was quite broken in her, the fiery life fallen from flame to coal. When her strength was a little restored, she had all her companions summoned, and said to them,—"I deserved to die, but a generous trust has called me back to life. I will be worthy of it, nor ever betray the truth, or resent injury more. Can you forgive the past?"

And they not only forgave, but, with love and earnest tears, clasped in their arms the returning sister. They vied with one another in offices of humble love to the humbled one; and let it be recorded, as an instance of the pure honor of which young hearts are capable, that these facts, known to forty persons, never, so far as I know, transpired beyond those walls.

It was not long after this that Mariana was summoned home. She went thither a wonderfully instructed being, though in ways those who had sent her forth to learn little dreamed of.

21

Fanny Fern (1811–1872)
from *Fern Leaves from Fanny's Portfolio*

"Fanny Fern" was the pen name of Sara Payson Willis Eldredge Farrington Parton
(to add the names of her first, second, and third husbands to her family and
given names). Her father, Nathaniel Willis, was a Presbyterian deacon and the
founder of *The Recorder,* the nation's first religious newspaper, and also of *The
Youth's Companion,* the first children's paper. Her brother, N. P. Willis, became a
very popular poet and journalist. But Sara did not start writing for money until
left practically destitute by the death of her first husband, Charles Harrington
Eldredge (in 1846) and her separation from her second, Samuel P. Farrington (in
January, 1851). She could make no more than seventy-five cents a week as a seam-
stress and could obtain no post as a teacher. Her wealthy father had remarried,
and he contributed very little to her. Nor did her first husband's parents help
her much, despite their being grandparents to her children. But on June 18, 1851,
she published her first sketch, anonymously, in a Boston paper called the *Olive
Branch,* which paid her fifty cents. In September, she began using the pen name
Fanny Fern, and her sketches were being pirated by other papers, including her
brother N. P. Willis's *Home Journal,* which had turned them down when Sara had
sent them to Willis under her own name! Moving to other papers, at increasingly
better pay, she was soon one of the best-paid columnists in the country—and
the first woman columnist. In June, 1853, the first collection of her pieces was
published, *Fern Leaves from Fanny's Portfolio,* and in the next year it earned her
nearly ten thousand dollars.

As a columnist, she both wrote in the first person and told other stories
that were often disguised autobiography. In the persona of Fanny Fern, she also
developed the style of a woman who was vulnerable to sentiment and yet leery of
it and, frequently, sharp-tongued and irreverent. At times she cried and brought
tears to her readers; at other times she shocked. "A Widow's Trials" is tearful
and obviously based on the cruel treatment she had received from her father.
"Apollo Hyacinth," June 18, 1853, satirized her well-known brother N. P. Willis
as a self-centered, dandified hypocrite. But while "Fanny Fern" acquired fame and
notoriety, Sara's own identity was safely secret—until December, 1854, when one
of the people satirized in *Ruth Hall,* the autobiographical novel she had just published, started a series of articles exposing her. Male journalists soon attacked her

for being so vindictive towards the father, brother, and in-laws who had refused to support her when she was a poor widow, and though interest in *Ruth Hall* as a scandal grew and sales zoomed, the game was over . . . or the rules had changed. The hurt and sensitive Sara, who had once hidden behind the pseudonym, now used it as both shield and sword. She also was a personage in it, Fanny Fern come to life.

This change shows up in later sketches like "A Law More Nice than Just" (1858) and "How I Look" (1870). In the first, James Parton, whom she had married in 1856, appears as "Mr. Fern," assisting in her experiment in wearing men's clothes. In that piece, incidentally, the man to whom she bears such a close resemblance is her brother. In the second, she enjoys the mistake a man makes in identifying her as another woman, dressed in diamonds and lace. (In other sketches, too, she alludes to "Fanny Fern" as being dark and sinister, while she, the real Fanny, is blonde.) Thus, even though she increasingly called herself "Fanny Fern" (and this is the name now used in most library catalogues), the mystery over who this autobiographer really was continued. Indeed, until the recent rediscovery of nineteenth-century women's writing, literary historians cast her as just "sentimental," the "grandmother of all sob sisters." They seem to have judged her only by the flowery name, without bothering to read her books. She and her writings are fascinating studies in the interactions of autobiography, fictions, and pseudonyms.

A further selection of sketches is in *Ruth Hall and Other Writings*, ed. Joyce W. Warren (New Brunswick, NJ: Rutgers Univ. Press, 1986). For a biographical and critical study, see Nancy Walker, *Fanny Fern* (New York: Twayne, 1992).

A Widow's Trials

The funeral was over, and Janie Grey came back to her desolate home. There were the useless drugs, the tempting fruits and flowers, which came all too late for the sinking sufferer. Wherever her eye fell, there was some sad reminiscence to torture her. They, whose life had been all sunshine, came in from cheerful homes, whose threshold death's shadow had never darkened, to offer consolation. All the usual phrases of stereotyped condolence had fallen upon her ear; and now they had all gone, and the world would move on just the same that there was one more broken heart in it. She must bear her weary weight of woe alone. She knew that her star had set. Earth, sea, and sky had no beauty now, since the eye that worshipped them with her was closed and rayless.

"Whom the Lord loveth, he chasteneth," said Uncle John, joining the tips of the fingers of either hand, and settling himself in a vestry attitude, to say his lesson. "Afflictions come not out of the ground. Man is cut down like a flower. God is the God of the widow and the fatherless. I suppose you find it so?" said he, looking into the widow's face.

"I can scarcely tell," said Janie. "This was a lightning flash from a summer cloud. My eyes are blinded. I cannot see the bow of promise."

"Wrong; all wrong," said Uncle John. "The Lord gave, and the Lord has taken away. You ought to be resigned. I'm afraid you don't enjoy religion. Afflictions are mercies in disguise. I'll lend you this volume of 'Dew-Drops' to read. You must get submissive, somehow, or you will have some other trouble sent upon you. Good-morning."

Uncle John was a rigid sectarian, of the bluest school of divinity; enjoyed an immense reputation for sanctity, than which nothing was dearer to him, save the contents of his pocket-book. It was his glory to be the Alpha and Omega of parish gatherings and committees; to be consulted on the expediency of sending tracts to the Kangaroo Islands; to be present at the laying of corner-stones for embryo churches; to shine conspicuously at ordinations, donation visits, Sabbath-school celebrations, colporteur meetings,—in short, anything that smacked of a church-steeple, or added one inch to the length and breadth of his pharisaical skirt. He pitied the poor, as every good Christian should; but he never allowed them to put their hands in his pocket;—that was a territory over which the church had no control—it belonged entirely to the other side of the fence.

Uncle John sat in his counting-room, looking very satisfactorily at the proof-sheets of "The Morning Star," of which he was editor. He had just glanced over his long list of subscribers, and congratulated himself that matters were in such a prosperous condition. Then he took out a large roll of bank bills, and fingered them most affectionately; then he frowned ominously at a poor beggar child, who peeped in at the door; smoothed his chin, and settled himself comfortably in his rocking-chair.

A rap at the door of the counting-room. "May I come in, uncle?" and Janie's long, black veil was thrown back from her sad face.

"Y-e-s," said Uncle John, rather frigidly. "Pretty busy,—'spose you won't stay long?" and he pushed his portemonnaie further down in his pocket.

"I came to ask," said Janie, timidly, "if you would employ me to write for your paper. Matters are more desperate with me than I thought, and there is a necessity for my doing something immediately. I believe I have talents that I might turn to account as a writer. I have literally nothing, Uncle John, to depend upon."

"Your husband was an extravagant man;—lived too fast,—that's the trouble,—lived too fast. Ought to have been economical as I was, when I was a young man. Can't have your cake and eat it, too. Can't expect me to make up for other people's deficiencies. You must take care of *yourself.*"

"Certainly, that's just what I wish to do," said Janie, struggling to restrain her tears. "I—I—" but she only finished the sentence with sobs; the contrast between the sunny past and the gloomy present was too strong for her troubled heart.

Now, if there was anything Uncle John mortally hated, it was to see a woman cry. In all such cases he irritated the victim till she took a speedy and frenzied leave. So he remarked again that "Mr. May was extravagant, else there would have been something left. He was sorry he was dead; but that was a thing *he* wasn't to blame for—and he didn't know any reason why he should be bothered about it. The world was full of widows;—they all went to work, he supposed, and took care of themselves."

"If you will tell me whether you can employ me to write for you," said the widow, "I will not trouble you longer."

"I have plenty who will write for nothing," said the old man. "Market is overstocked with that sort of thing. Can't afford to pay contributors, especially new beginners. Don't think you have any talent that way, either. Better take in sewing or something," said he, taking out his watch, by way of a reminder that she had better be going.

The young widow could scarcely see her way out through her fast-falling tears. It was her first bitter lesson in the world's selfishness. She, whose tender feet had been so love-guided, to walk life's thorny path alone; she, for whom no gift was rich, or rare, or costly enough; she, who had leaned so trustingly on the dear arm now so powerless to shield her; she, to whom love was life, breath, being, to meet only careless glances,—nay, more, harsh and taunting words. O, where should that stricken heart find rest, this side heaven?

Yet she might not yield to despair; there was a little, innocent, helpless one, for whom she must live on, and toil, and struggle. Was the world all darkness? Bent every knee at Mammon's shrine? Beat every human heart only for its own joys and sorrows?

Days and months rolled on. Uncle John said his prayers, and went to church, and counted over his dear bank bills; and the widow sat up till the stars grew pale, and bent wearily over long pages of manuscript; and little Rudolph lay with his rosy cheek nestled to the pillow, crushing his bright ringlets, all unconscious of the weary vigil the young mother was keeping. And now it was New-Year's night; and, as she laid aside her pen, memory called her back to rich, sunny days,—to a luxurious home. Again she was leaning on that broad, true breast. Troops of friends were about them. O, where were they now? Then she looked upon her small, plainly furnished room, so unattractive to the eye of taste and refinement;—then it fell upon her child, too young to remember that father, whose last act was to kiss his baby brow.

Still the child slumbered on,—his red lips parted with a smile,—and, for the first time, she noted the little stocking, yet warm from the dimpled foot, hung close by the pillow, with childhood's beautiful trust in angel hands to fill it; and, covering her face with her hands, she wept aloud, that this simple luxury must be denied a mother's heart. Then, extinguishing her small lamp, she laid her tearful cheek against the rosy little sleeper, with that instinctive yearning for sympathy, which only the wretched know. In slumber there is, at least, forgetfulness. Kind angels whisper hope in dreams.

The golden light of New-Year's morning streamed through the partially opened shutters upon the curly head that already nestled uneasily on its pillow. The blue eyes opened slowly, like violets kissed by the sun, and the little hand was outstretched to grasp the empty stocking. His lip quivered, and tears of disappointment forced themselves through his tiny fingers; while his mother rose, sad and unrefreshed, to meet another day of toil. And Uncle John, oblivious of everything that might collapse his purse, sat comfortably in his rocking-chair, "too busy" to call on his niece. Treading, not in his Lord's footsteps, where sorrow, and misery, and want made foot-tracks, but where the well-warmed, well-clad, and well-filled sat at Dives' table.

Time flew on. A brighter day dawned for Janie. She had triumphed over disappointments and discouragements before which stouter hearts than hers had quailed. Comfort and independence were again hers,—earned by her own untiring hand. Uncle John was not afraid of her now. He turned no more short corners to avoid her. She needed no assistance. Uncle John liked to notice that sort of people. He grew amiable, even facetious; and one day, in his uproariousness, actually sent a threecent piece to his nephew, whom he had not inquired for for three long years.

Janie's praises reached him from every quarter; and he took a great deal of pains to let people know that this new literary light was *his niece*. Had he known she would have turned out such a star, he would have employed her. Now she was swelling other editors' subscription lists, instead of his. That was a feature of the case he was fully prepared to understand!

"No talent that way!" said Janie to herself, as she saw him, at last, very coolly transfer, with his editorial hand, her articles to "The Morning Star," without credit, without remuneration to herself. Sanctimonious, avaricious Uncle John! Did you count the weary vigils they cost the writer? Did you count the tears which blistered their pages? Did you dream of the torturing process by which the bird was blinded, ere it could be learned to sing so sweetly? Knew you that those gushing notes reached you, through prison bars, from a weary captive's throat? No, no, Uncle John! how should you? For where your heart should have been, there was a decided vacuum.

Apollo Hyacinth

> There is no better test of moral excellence, than the keenness of one's sense, and the depth of one's love, of all that is beautiful.
>
> *Donohue.*

I don't endorse that sentiment. I am acquainted with Apollo Hyacinth. I have read his prose, and I have read his poetry; and I have cried over both, till my heart was as soft as my head, and my eyes were as red as a rabbit's. I have listened to him in public, when he was, by turns, witty, sparkling, satirical, pathetic, till I could have added a codicil to my will, and left him all my worldly possessions; and possibly you have done the same. He has, perhaps, grasped you cordially by the hand, and, with a beaming smile, urged you, in his musical voice, to "call on him and Mrs. Hyacinth;" and you have called; but, did you ever find him "in?" You have invited him to visit you, and have received a "gratified acceptance," in his elegant chirography; but, *did he ever come?* He has borrowed money of you, in the most elegant manner possible; and, as he deposited it in his beautiful purse, he has assured you, in the choicest and most happily chosen language, that he "should never forget your kindness;" but, *did he ever pay?*

Should you die to-morrow, Apollo would write a poetical obituary notice of you, which would raise the price of pocket-handkerchiefs; but should your widow call on him in the course of a month, to solicit his patronage to open a school, she would be told "he was out of town," and that it was "quite uncertain when he would return."

Apollo has a large circle of relatives; but his "keenness of perception, and deep love, of the beautiful" are so great, that none of them *exactly* meet his views. His "moral excellence," however, does not prevent his making the most of them. He has a way of dodging them adroitly, when they call for a reciprocation, either in a business or a social way; or, if, at any time, there is a necessity for inviting them to his house, he does it when he is at his *country* residence, where their *greenness* will not be out of place.

Apollo never says an uncivil thing—never; he prides himself on that, as well as on his perfect knowledge of human nature; therefore, his sins are all sins of omission. His tastes are very exquisite, and his nature peculiarly sensitive; consequently, he cannot bear trouble. He will tell you, in his elegant way, that trouble "annoys" him, that it "bores" him; in short, that it unfits him for life—for business; so, should you hear that a friend or relative of his, even a brother or a sister, was in distress, or persecuted in any manner, you could not do Apollo a greater injury (in his estimation) than to inform him of the fact. It would so grate upon his sensitive spirit,—it would so "annoy" him; whereas, did he not hear of it until the friend, or brother, or sister, were relieved or buried, he could manage the matter with his usual urbanity and without the slightest draught upon his exquisitely sensitive nature, by simply writing a pathetic and elegant note, expressing the keenest regret at not having known "all about it" in time to have "flown to the assistance of his dear"—&c.

Apollo prefers friends who can stand grief and annoyance, as a rhinoceros can stand flies—friends who can bear their own troubles and all his—friends who will stand between him and everything disagreeable in life, and never ask anything in return. To such friends he clings with the most touching tenacity—as long as he can use them; but let their good name be assailed, let misfortune once overtake them, and his "moral excellence" compels him, at once, to ignore their existence, until they have been extricated from all their troubles, and it has become perfectly safe and *advantageous* for him to renew the acquaintance.

Apollo is keenly alive to the advantages of social position, (not having always enjoyed them;) and so, his Litany reads after this wise: From all questionable, unfashionable, unpresentable, and vulgar persons, Good Lord, deliver us!

A Law More Nice Than Just

Here I have been sitting twiddling the morning paper between my fingers this half hour, reflecting upon the following paragraph in it: "Emma Wilson was arrested yesterday for wearing man's apparel." Now, why this should be an actionable offense is past my finding out, or where's the harm in it, I am as much at a loss to see. Think of the old maids (and weep) who have to stay at home evening after evening, when, if they provided themselves with a coat, pants and hat, they might go abroad, instead of sitting there with their noses flattened against the window-pane, looking vainly for "the Coming Man." Think of the married women who stay at home after their day's toil is done, waiting wearily for their thoughtless, truant husbands, when they might be taking the much needed independent walk in trousers, which custom forbids to petticoats. And this, I fancy, may be the secret of this famous law—who knows? It *wouldn't* be pleasant for some of them to be surprised by a touch on the shoulder from some dapper young fellow, whose familiar treble voice belied his corduroys. That's it, now. What a fool I was not to think of it—not to remember that men who make the laws, make them to meet all these little emergencies.

Everybody knows what an everlasting drizzle of rain we have had lately, but nobody but a woman, and a woman who lives on fresh air and out-door exercise, knows the thraldom of taking her daily walk through a three weeks' rain, with skirts to hold up, and umbrella to hold down, and puddles to skip over, and gutters to walk round, and all the time in a fright lest, in an unguarded moment, her calves should become visible to some one of those rainy-day philanthropists who are interested in the public study of female anatomy.

One evening, after a long rainy day of scribbling, when my nerves were in double-twisted knots, and I felt as if myriads of little ants were leisurely traveling over me, and all for want of the walk which is my daily salvation, I stood at the window, looking at the slanting, persistent rain, and took my resolve: "*I'll do it,*" said I, audibly, planting my slipper upon the carpet. "Do what?" asked Mr. Fern, looking up from a big book. "Put on a suit of your clothes and take a tramp with you," was the answer. "You dare not," was the rejoinder; "you are a little coward, only saucy on paper." It was the work of a moment, with such a challenge, to fly up stairs and overhaul my philosopher's wardrobe. Of course we had fun. Tailors must be a stingy set, I remarked, to be so sparing of their cloth, as I struggled into a pair of their handiwork, un-deterred by the vociferous laughter of the wretch who had solemnly vowed to "cherish me" through all my tribulations. "Upon my word, everything seems to be narrow where it ought to be broad, and the waist of this coat might be made for a hogshead; and, ugh! this shirt collar is cutting my ears off, and you have not a decent cravat in the whole lot, and your vests are frights, and what am I to do with my hair?" Still no reply from Mr. Fern, who lay on the floor, faintly ejaculating, between his fits of laughter, "Oh, my! by Jove!—oh! by Jupiter!"

Was that to hinder me? Of course not. Strings and pins, women's never-failing resort, soon brought broadcloth and kerseymere to terms. I parted my hair on one side, rolled it under, and then secured it with hairpins; chose the best fitting coat, and cap-ping the climax with one of those soft, cosy hats, looked in the glass, where I beheld the very fac-simile of a certain musical gentleman, whose photograph hangs this minute in Brady's entry.

Well, Mr. Fern seized his hat, and out we went together. "Fanny," said he, "you must not take my arm; you are a fellow." "True," said I. "I forgot; and you must not help me over puddles, as you did just now, and do, for mercy's sake, stop laughing. There, there goes your hat—I mean *my* hat; confound the wind! and down comes my hair; lucky 'tis dark, isn't it?" But oh, the deli-cious freedom of that walk; after we were well started! No skirts to hold up, or to draggle their wet folds against my ankles; no stifling vail flapping in my face, and blinding my eyes; no umbrella to turn inside out, but instead, the cool rain driving slap into my face, and the resurrectionized blood coursing through my veins, and tingling in my cheeks. To be sure, Mr. Fern occa-sionally loitered behind, and leaned up against the side of a house to enjoy a little private "guffaw," and I could now and then hear a gasping "Oh, Fanny! Oh, my!" but none of these things moved me, and if I don't have a nicely-fitting suit of my own to wear rainy evenings, it is because—well, there *are* difficulties in the way. Who's the best tailor?

Now, if any male or female Miss Nancy who reads this feels shocked, let 'em! Any woman who likes, may stay at home during a three weeks' rain, till her skin looks like parchment, and her eyes like those of a dead fish, or she may go out and get a consumption dragging round wet petticoats; I won't—I positively declare I won't. I shall begin *evenings* when *that* suit is made, and take private walking lessons with Mr. Fern, and they who choose may crook their backs at home for fashion, and then send for the doctor to straighten them; I prefer to patronize my shoe-maker and tailor. I've as good a right to preserve the healthy body God gave me, as if I were not a woman.

How I Look

A correspondent inquires how I look? Am I tall? have I dark, or light complexion? and what color are my eyes?

I should be very happy to answer these questions, did I know myself. I proceed to explain why I cannot tell whether "I be I."

First—one evening I was seated at the opera, waiting patiently for the performances to begin. In two orchestra chairs, directly in front of me, sat a lady and gentleman, both utter strangers to me. Said the *gentleman* to his companion, "Do you see the lady who has just entered yonder box?" pointing, as he did so, to the gallery; "well, that is Fanny Fern."—"You know her, then?" asked the lady.—"Intimately," replied this strange gentleman—"*intimately*. Observe how expensively she is dressed. See those diamonds, and that lace! Well, I assure you, that every cent she has ever earned by her writings goes straightway upon her back." Naturally desiring to know how I did look, I used my opera-glass. The lady was tall, handsome, graceful, and beautifully dressed. The gentleman who accompanied me began to grow red in the face, at the statement of my "intimate" acquaintance, and insisted on a word with him; but the fun was too good to be spoiled, and the game too insignificant to hunt; so, in hope of farther revelations, I laughingly observed my "double" during the evening, who looked as I have just described, for your benefit.

Again—in a list of pictures announced to be sold lately, was one labelled "Fanny Fern." Having lost curiosity concerning that lady myself, I did not go on a tour of inspection; but a gentleman friend of mine who did, came back in high glee at the manner in which the purchaser thereof, if any should be found, would be swindled—as "I was *not* I" in that case either.

Some time ago "Fanny Fern" was peddled round California, or at least, so I was informed by letter. In this instance they had given her, by way of variety, black eyes and hair, and a brunette complexion. I think she was also taken smiling. A friend, moreover, informed me that he had seen me, with an angelic expression, seated upon a rosy cloud, with wings at my back. This last fact touched me. Wings are what I sigh for. It was too cruel a mockery.

You will see from the above, how impossible it is, for such a chameleon female, to describe herself, even to one "who likes my writings." If it will throw any light on the subject, however, I will inform you that a man who got into my parlor under cover of "New-Year's calls," after breathlessly inspecting me, remarked, "Well, now, I *am* agreeably disappointed! I thought from the way you *writ,* that you were a great six-footer of a woman, with snapping black eyes and a big waist, and I *am* pleased to find you looking so soft and so femi-*nine!*"

I would have preferred, had I been consulted, that he should have omitted the word "soft;" but after the experiences narrated above, this was a trifle.

22

P. T. Barnum (1810–1891)
from *The Life of P. T. Barnum* and
Struggles and Triumphs

P[hineas] T[aylor] Barnum is crucial to the history of American autobiography, both for what he wrote and for what he did to establish enduring popular attitudes towards truth and deception, self-advertisement and commerce, and other values surrounding it. One of the great national tricksters, he helped define appearance and reality in America.

On the simplest level, his life is a success story. Born in the little town of Bethel, Connecticut, in 1810, he rose from being a clerk in country stores to being the owner of "Barnum's American Museum" in New York City, to being the greatest impresario of his time (ushering Jenny Lind, the "Swedish Nightingale," on her famous 1850–52 tour), and to being co-owner of the Barnum and Bailey Circus. But where Benjamin Franklin somewhat deceptively attributed his success to virtue and industry, Barnum, in *The Life of P. T. Barnum* (1855), virtuously attributed his to deception. Half rogue that he was, he realized (as had Stephen Burroughs and as would later tricksters like Richard Nixon) that a rogue admitting his tricks is taken as a sinner repenting—he is believed. Or if he is not, he is still discussed, and as a great showman, Barnum watched the crowds come.

But there are still deeper levels to Barnum's understanding of the American psyche and the American public's responses to him. At a time when Americans were very eager to gain refinement and education, as expressed in appreciation of art and nature, Barnum still recognized their insecurities and their need for relaxation and fun. Thus he made his American Museum an attractive palace where wonders and curiosities of all kinds were assembled: in his words, "educated dogs, industrious fleas, automatons, jugglers, ventriloquists, living statuary, tableaux, gipsies, Albinoes, fat boys, giants, dwarfs, rope-dancers, live 'Yankees,' pantomime, . . . models of Niagara, . . . fancy glass-blowing, knitting machines and other triumphs of the mechanical arts. . . ." In such a collection, the popular issue, as Neil Harris has written, came to be "an aesthetic of the operational, a delight in observing process and examining for literal truth."[1] Visitors did not have to think about beauty or taste or spirituality, values with which they felt uncertain. Instead, they

1. Neil Harris, *Humbug: The Art of P. T. Barnum* (Boston: Little, Brown, 1973), p. 79.

focused just on the facts and the problem of truth—where a freak came from, how a machine worked, whether something was fake or genuine.

The consequence in Barnum's autobiography is a similarly overwhelming flood of anecdotes, giving the story of each curiosity and wonder, and a confession of how it was found, authenticated (or not), and publicized. The Fejee Mermaid story is an example. But as the story of the great Hoboken Buffalo Hunt illustrates, audiences also came to like Barnum's tricks. Being able to shout that the hunt "was the biggest humbug you ever heard of!" was part of the pleasure. Barnum was likewise quite willing and proud to reveal several days later that he had made his money by chartering the ferry boats. It won him further respect (and publicity) and gave those who told the story the thrill of feeling in the know. All the while, as perhaps the first story of Ivy Island best demonstrates, there is an important moral lesson to be learned from having been deceived, or from having believed inflated promises, from having false hopes, and then seeing the modest truth. The boy-innocent finds he is not rich and privileged but like everyone else.

In 1869, Barnum published a second version of his autobiography, *Struggles and Triumphs,* which did not paint himself as quite such a confidence man—an interesting difference. Adding chapter after chapter, he republished it so many times that one scholar has estimated that after the Bible, Barnum's autobiography was the most widely read book in America. Copies were given away free with circus tickets, as if the book was a part of, or the background to, the circus. Thus did Barnum further contribute to the popular expectation (a mainstay of auto-biography) that behind every appearance is a reality in the form of yet another personal story.

Copies of the 1855 *Life* are rare. This text is taken from the reprint, *Barnum's Own Story,* edited by Waldo R. Browne (New York: Dover Publications, 1961), which also contains the material from *Struggles and Triumphs.* For biography and criticism, see G. Thomas Couser, *Altered Egos: Authority in American Autobiography* (New York: Oxford Univ. Press, 1989), 52–69; and Neil Harris, *Humbug: The Art of P. T. Barnum* (Boston: Little, Brown, 1973).

from Ivy Island

Previous to my visit to New York, I think it was in 1820, when I was ten years of age, I made my first expedition to my landed property, "Ivy Island." This, it will be remembered, was the gift of my grandfather, from whom I derived my name. From the time when I was four years old I was continually hearing of this "property." My grandfather always spoke of me (in my presence) to the neighbors and to strangers as the richest child in town, since I owned the whole of "Ivy Island," one of the most valuable farms in the State. My father and mother frequently reminded me of my wealth and hoped I would do something for the family when I attained my majority. The neighbors pro-fessed to fear that I might refuse to play with their children because I had inherited so large a property.

These constant allusions, for several years, to "Ivy Island" excited at once my pride and my curiosity and stimulated me to implore my father's permission to visit my property. At last, he promised I should do so in a few days, as we should be getting some hay near "Ivy Island." The wished for day at length arrived and my father told me that as we were to mow an adjoining meadow, I might visit my property in company with the hired man during the "nooning." My grandfather reminded me that it was to his bounty I was indebted for this wealth, and that had not my name been Phineas I might never have been proprietor of "Ivy Island." To this my mother added:

"Now, Taylor, don't become so excited when you see your property as to let your joy make you sick, for remember, rich as you are, that it will be eleven years before you can come into possession of your fortune."

She added much more good advice, to all of which I promised to be calm and reasonable and not to allow my pride to prevent me from speaking to my brothers and sisters when I returned home.

When we arrived at the meadow, which was in that part of the "Plum Trees" known as "East Swamp," I asked my father where "Ivy Island" was.

"Yonder, at the north end of this meadow, where you see those beautiful trees rising in the distance."

All the forenoon I turned grass as fast as two men could cut it, and after a hasty repast at noon, one of our hired men, a good natured Irishman, named Edmund, took an axe on his shoulder and announced that he was ready to accompany me to "Ivy Island." We started, and as we approached the north end of the meadow we found the ground swampy and wet and were soon obliged to leap from bog to bog on our route. A mis-step brought me up to my middle in water. To add to the dilemma a swarm of hornets attacked me. Attaining the altitude of another bog I was cheered by the assurance that there was only a quarter of a mile of this kind of travel to the edge of my property. I waded on. In about fifteen minutes more, after floundering through the morass, I found myself half-drowned, hornet-stung, mud-covered, and out of breath, on comparatively dry land.

"Never mind, my boy," said Edmund, "we have only to cross this little creek, and ye'll be upon your own valuable property."

We were on the margin of a stream, the banks of which were thickly covered with alders. I now discovered the use of Edmund's axe, for he felled a small oak to form a temporary bridge to my "Island" property. Crossing over, I proceeded to the centre of my domain; I saw nothing but a few stunted ivies and straggling trees. The truth flashed upon me. I had been the laughing-stock of the family and neighborhood for years. My valuable "Ivy Island" was an almost inaccessible, worthless bit of barren land, and while I stood deploring my sudden downfall, a huge black snake (one of my tenants) approached me with upraised head. I gave one shriek and rushed for the bridge.

This was my first, and, I need not say, my last visit to "Ivy Island." My father asked me how I liked my property, and I responded that I would sell it pretty cheap. My grandfather congratulated me upon my visit to my property as seriously as if it had been indeed a valuable domain. My mother hoped its richness had fully equalled my anticipations. The neighbors desired to know if I was not now glad I was named Phineas, and for five years forward I was frequently reminded of my wealth in "Ivy Island."

from **The Fejee Mermaid**

The "Fejee Mermaid" was by many supposed to be a curiosity manufactured by myself, or made to my order. This is not the fact. I certainly had much to do in bringing it before the public, and as I am now in the confessional mood, I will "make a clean breast" of the ways and means I adopted for that purpose. I must first relate how it came into my possession and its alleged history.

Early in the summer of 1842, Moses Kimball, Esq., the popular proprietor of the Boston Museum, came to New York and exhibited to me what purported to be a mermaid. He stated that he had bought it of a sailor whose father, while in Calcutta in 1817 as captain of a Boston ship (of which Captain John Ellery was principal owner), had purchased it, believing it to be a preserved specimen of a veritable mermaid, obtained, as he was assured, from Japanese sailors. Not doubting that it would prove as surprising to others as it had been to himself, and hoping to make a rare speculation of it as an extraordinary curiosity, he appropriated $6000 of the ship's money to the purchase of it, left the ship in charge of the mate, and went to London.

He did not realize his expectations, and returned to Boston. Still believing that his curiosity was a genuine animal and therefore highly valuable, he preserved it with great care, not stinting himself in the expense of keeping it insured, though re-engaged as ship's captain under his former employers to reimburse the sum taken from their funds to pay for the mermaid. He died possessing no other property, and his only son and heir, who placed a low estimate on his father's purchase, sold it to Mr. Kimball, who brought it to New York for my inspection.

Such was the story. Not trusting my own acuteness on such matters, I requested my naturalist's opinion of the genuineness of the animal. He replied that he could not conceive how it was manufactured; for he never knew a monkey with such peculiar teeth, arms, hands, etc., nor had he knowledge of a fish with such peculiar fins.

"Then why do you suppose it is manufactured?" I inquired.

"Because I don't believe in mermaids," replied the naturalist.

"That is no reason at all," said I, "and therefore I'll believe in the mermaid, and hire it."

This was the easiest part of the experiment. How to modify general incredulity in the existence of mermaids, so far as to awaken curiosity to see and examine the specimen, was now the all-important question. Some extraordinary means must be resorted to, and I saw no better method than to "start the ball a-rolling" at some distance from the centre of attraction.

In due time a communication appeared in the New York *Herald,* dated and mailed in Montgomery, Ala., giving the news of the day, trade, the crops, political gossip, etc., and also an incidental paragraph about a certain Dr. Griffin, agent of the Lyceum of Natural History in London, recently from Pernambuco, who had in his possession a most remarkable curiosity, being nothing less than a veritable mermaid taken among the Fejee Islands, and preserved in China, where the Doctor had bought it at a high figure for the Lyceum of Natural History.

A week or ten days afterwards, a letter of similar tenor, dated and mailed in Charleston, S. C., varying of course in the items of local news, was published in another New York paper.

This was followed by a third letter, dated and mailed in Washington city, published in still another New York paper—there being in addition the expressed hope that the editors of the Empire City would beg a sight of the extraordinary curiosity before Dr. Griffin took ship for England.

A few days subsequently to the publication of this thrice-repeated announcement, Mr. Lyman (who was my employee in the case of Joice Heth) was duly registered at one of the principal hotels in Philadelphia as Dr. Griffin of Pernambuco for London. His gentlemanly, dignified, yet social manners and liberality gained him a fine reputation for a few days, and when he paid his bill one afternoon, preparatory to leaving for New York the next day, he expressed his thanks to the landlord for special attention and courtesy. "If you will step to my room," said Lyman, alias Griffin, "I will permit you to see something that will surprise you." Whereupon the landlord was shown the most extraordinary curiosity in the world—a mermaid. He was so highly gratified and interested that he earnestly begged permission to introduce certain friends of his, including several editors, to view the wonderful specimen.

"Although it is no interest of mine," said the curiosity-hunter, "the Lyceum of Natural History, of which I am agent, will not be injured by granting the courtesy you request." And so an appointment was made for the evening.

The result might easily be gathered from the editorial columns of the Philadelphia papers a day or two subsequently to that interview with the mermaid. Suffice it to say, that the plan worked admirably, and the Philadelphia press aided the press of New York in awakening a wide-reaching and increasing curiosity to see the mermaid.

I may as well confess that those three communications from the South were written by myself, and forwarded to friends of mine, with instructions respectively to mail them, each on the day of its date. This fact and the corresponding post-marks did much to prevent suspicion of a hoax, and the New York editors thus unconsciously contributed to my arrangements for bringing the mermaid into public notice.

Lyman then returned to New York with his precious treasure, and putting up at the Pacific Hotel in Greenwich Street as Dr. Griffin, it soon reached the ears of the wide-awake reporters for the press that the mermaid was in town. They called at the Pacific Hotel, and the polite agent of the British Lyceum of Natural History kindly permitted them to gratify their curiosity. The New York newspapers contained numerous reports of these examinations, all of which were quite satisfactory.

I am confident that the reporters and editors who examined this animal were honestly persuaded that it was what it purported to be—a veritable mermaid. Nor is this to be wondered at, since, if it was a work of art, the monkey and fish were so nicely conjoined that no human eye could detect the point where the junction was formed. The spine of the fish proceeded in a straight and apparently unbroken line to the base of the skull—the hair of the animal was found growing several inches down on the shoulders of the fish, and the application of a microscope absolutely revealed what seemed to be minute fish scales lying in myriads amidst the hair. The teeth and formation of the fingers and hands differed materially from those of any monkey or orang-outang ever discovered, while the location of the fins was different from those of any species of the fish tribe known to naturalists. The animal was an ugly, dried-up, black-looking, and diminutive specimen, about three feet long. Its mouth was open, its tail turned over, and its arms thrown up, giving it the appearance of having died in great agony.

Assuming, what is no doubt true, that the mermaid was manufactured, it was a most remarkable specimen of ingenuity and untiring patience. For my own part I really had scarcely cared at the time to form an opinion of the origin of this creature, but it was my impression that it was the work of some ingenious Japanese, Chinaman, or other eastern genius, and that it had probably been one among the many hideous objects of Buddhist or Hindoo worship.

However, in reading myself up on the history of Japan, I found the following article in a work entitled "Manners and Customs of the Japanese in the Nineteenth Century, from the accounts of recent Dutch residents in Japan, and from the German work of Dr. Ph. Fr. Von Siebold":

Another Japanese fisherman displayed his ingenuity in a less honorable and useful form than Kiyemon, to make money out of his countrymen's passion for whatever is odd and strange. He contrived to unite the upper half of a monkey to the lower half of a fish, so neatly as to defy ordinary inspection. He then gave out that he had caught the creature alive in his net, but that it had died shortly after being taken out of the water: and he derived considerable pecuniary profit from his device in more ways than one The exhibition of the sea monster to Japanese curiosity paid well; but yet more productive was the assertion that the half-human fish had spoken during the few minutes it existed out of its native element, predicting a certain number of years of wonderful fertility, to be followed by a fatal epidemic, the only remedy against which would be possession of the marine prophet's likeness. The sale of these pictured mermaids was immense. Either this composite animal, or another, the offspring of the success of the first, was sold to the Dutch factory and transmitted to Batavia, where it fell into the hands of a shrewd American, who brought it to Europe, and there, in the years 1822–3, exhibited his purchase as a real mermaid, at every capital, to the admiration of the ignorant, the perplexity of the learned, and the filling of his own purse.

Is it not a plausible conjecture that this account relates to the identical mermaid exhibited in the American Museum? Certainly the method adopted to induce people to buy the likeness, as related by Siebold, fairly entitles my Japanese *confrère* to the palm and title of "Prince of Humbugs."

Smaller specimens, purporting to be mermaids, but less elaborately gotten up, have been seen in various museums. I believe they are all made in Japan. I purchased one in the Peale collection in Philadelphia. It was burnt at the time the Museum opened by me in that city was destroyed by fire in 1851.

While Lyman was preparing public opinion on mermaids at the Pacific Hotel, I was industriously at work (though of course privately) in getting up wood-cuts and transparencies, as well as a pamphlet, proving the authenticity of mermaids, all in anticipation of the speedy exhibition of Dr. Griffin's specimen. I had three several and distinct pictures of mermaids engraved, and with a peculiar description written for each, had them inserted in 10,000 copies of the pamphlet which I had printed and quietly stored away in a back office until the time came to use them.

I then called respectively on the editors of the New York *Herald*, and two of the Sunday papers, and tendered to each the free use of a mermaid cut, with a well-written description, for their papers of the ensuing Sunday. I informed each editor that I had hoped to use this cut in showing the Fejee Mermaid, but since Mr. Griffin had announced that, as agent for the Lyceum of Natural History, he could not permit it to be exhibited in America, my chance seemed dubious, and therefore he was welcome to the use of the engraving and description. The three mermaids made their appearance in the three different papers on the morning of Sunday, July 17, 1842. Each editor supposed he was giving his readers an exclusive treat in the mermaid line, but when they came to discover that I had played the same game with the three different papers, they pronounced it a *scaly* trick.

The mermaid fever was now getting pretty well up. Few city readers had missed seeing at least one of the illustrations, and as the several printed descriptions made direct allusion to *the* mermaid of Mr. Griffin now in town, a desire to see it was generally prevailing. My 10,000 mermaid pamphlets were then put into the hands of boys, and sold at a penny each (half the cost) in all the principal hotels, stores, etc., etc.

When I thought the public was thoroughly "posted up" on the subject of mermaids, I sent an agent to engage Concert Hall, Broadway, for the exhibition, and the newspapers immediately contained the following advertisement:

THE MERMAID, AND OTHER WONDERFUL SPECIMENS OF THE ANIMAL CREATION.—The public are respectfully informed that, in accordance with numerous and urgent solicitations from scientific gentlemen in this city, Mr. J. GRIFFIN, proprietor of the Mermaid, recently arrived from Pernambuco, S. A., has consented to exhibit it to the public, *positively for one week only!* For this purpose he has procured the spacious saloon known as Concert Hall, 404 Broadway, which will open on Monday, August 8, 1842, and will positively close on Saturday the 13th inst.

This animal was taken near the Fejee Islands, and purchased for a large sum by the present proprietor, for the Lyceum of Natural History in London, and is exhibited for this short period more for the gratification of the public than for gain. The proprietor having been engaged for several years in various parts of the world in collecting wonderful specimens in Natural History, has in his possession, and will at the same time submit to public inspection, THE ORNITHORHINCHUS, from New Holland, being the connecting link between the Seal and the Duck. THE FLYING FISH, two distinct species, one from the Gulf Stream, and the other from the West Indies. This animal evidently connects the Bird with the Fish. THE PADDLE-TAIL SNAKE from South America. THE SIREN, or MUD IGUANA, an intermediate animal between the Reptile and the Fish. THE PROTEUS SANGUIHUS, a subterraneous animal from a grotto in Australia—with other animals forming connecting links in the great chain of Animated Nature.

Tickets of admission 25 cents each.

A large number of visitors attended Concert Hall, and Lyman, alias Griffin, exhibited the mermaid with much dignity. I could not help fearing that some of the Joice Heth victims would discover in Professor Griffin the exhibitor of the "nurse of Washington," but happily no such catastrophe occurred. Lyman, surrounded by numerous connecting links in nature, as set forth in the advertisement, and with the hideous-looking mermaid firmly secured from the hands of visitors by a glass vase, enlightened his audiences by curious accounts of his travels and adventures, and by scientific harangues upon the works of nature in general, and mermaids in particular.

The public appeared to be satisfied, but as some persons always *will* take things literally, and make no allowance for poetic license even in mermaids, an occasional visitor, after having seen the large transparency in front of the hall, representing a beautiful creature half woman and half fish, about eight feet in length, would be slightly surprised in finding that the reality was a black-looking specimen of dried monkey and fish that a boy a few years old could easily run away with under his arm.

The mermaid remained a single week at Concert Hall, and was then advertised to be seen at the American Museum, "without extra charge." Numerous transparencies had been prepared; showbills were posted with a liberal hand; and on Monday morning, a flag representing a mermaid eighteen feet in length was streaming directly in front of the Museum. Lyman saw it as he was slowly approaching to commence operations. He quickened his pace, entered my office, and demanded, "What in the name of all conscience is that immense flag out for?"

"In order that nobody shall enter Broadway without knowing where to find the mermaid," I replied.

"Well, that flag must come in. Nobody can satisfy the public with our dried-up specimen *eighteen inches long,* after exhibiting a picture representing it as *eighteen feet.* It is preposterous."

"Oh, nonsense," I replied; "that is only to catch the eye. They don't expect to see a mermaid of that size."

"I tell you it won't do," replied Lyman, "I think I ought to know something of the public 'swallow' by this time, and I tell you the mermaid won't go down if that flag remains up."

"That flag cost me over seventy dollars, and it must remain up," I replied.

Lyman deliberately buttoned his coat, and said as he slowly walked towards the door, "Well, Mr. Barnum, if you like to fight under that flag, you can do so, but *I* won't."

"What! you are a deserter, then!" I replied, laughing.

"Yes, I desert false colors when they are too strong," said Lyman; "and *you* will desert them before night," he continued.

I could not spare "Professor Griffin," and was reluctantly compelled to take down the flag. It never saw the light again.

That her "ladyship" was an attractive feature, may be inferred from these facts and figures: The receipts of the American Museum for the four weeks immediately preceding the exhibition of the mermaid, amounted to $1272. During the first four weeks of the mermaid's exhibition, the receipts amounted to $3341.93.

I used my mermaid mainly to advertise the regular business of the Museum, and this effective indirect advertising is the only feature I can commend, in a special show of which, I confess, I am not proud. I might have published columns in the newspapers, presenting and praising the great collection of genuine specimens of natural history in my exhibition, and they would not have attracted nearly so much attention as did a few paragraphs about the mermaid which was only a small part of my show. Newspapers throughout the country copied the mermaid notices, for they were novel and caught the attention of readers. Thus was the fame of the Museum, as well as the mermaid, wafted from one end of the land to the other. I was careful to keep up the excitement, for I knew that every dollar sown in advertising would return in tens, and perhaps hundreds in a future harvest, and after obtaining all the notoriety possible by advertising and by exhibiting the mermaid at the Museum, I sent the curiosity throughout the country, directing my agent to everywhere advertise it as "From Barnum's Great American Museum, New

York." The effect was immediately felt; money flowed in rapidly and was readily expended in more advertising.

The Buffalo Hunt

I attended the great Bunker Hill celebration, June 17, 1843, and heard Mr. Webster's oration. I found exhibiting near the monument, under an old canvas tent, a herd of calf buffaloes a year old. There were fifteen in number, and I purchased the lot for $700. I had an idea in my head which, if I could carry it out, would make buffaloes a profitable investment, and I was determined to try it. The animals were poor and remarkably docile, having been driven from the plains of the Great West. I had them brought to New York, and placed in a farmer's barn in New Jersey, near Hoboken. Mr. C. D. French, of whom I purchased them, understood throwing the *lasso,* and I hired him for $30 per month to take care of the buffaloes, until such time as I had matured my plans.

Paragraphs were soon started in the papers announcing that a herd of wild buffaloes, caught by the lasso when quite young, were now on their way from the Rocky Mountains to Europe, *via* New York, in charge of the men who captured them. In a few days communications appeared in several papers, suggesting that if the buffaloes could be safely secured in some race course, and a regular buffalo chase given by their owners, showing the use of the *lasso,* etc., it would be a treat worth going many miles to see. One correspondent declared it would be worth a dollar to see it; another asserted that fifty thousand persons would gladly pay to witness it, etc. One suggested the Long Island Race Course; another thought a large plot of ground at Harlem, inclosed expressly for the purpose, would be better; and a third suggested Hoboken as just the place. In due time, the following advertisement appeared in the public prints and handbills and posters of the same purport, illustrated by a picture of wild buffaloes pursued by Indians on horseback, were simultaneously circulated, far and near, with a liberal hand:

GRAND BUFFALO HUNT, FREE OF CHARGE.—At Hoboken, on Thursday, August 31, at 3, 4, and 5 o'clock P. M. ☞Mr. C. D. French, one of the most daring and experienced hunters of the West, has arrived thus far on his way to Europe, with a HERD OF BUFFALOES, captured by himself, near Santa Fé. He will exhibit the method of hunting the Wild Buffaloes, and throwing the lasso, by which the animals were captured in their most wild and untamed state. This is perhaps one of the most exciting and difficult feats that can be performed, requiring at the same time the most expert horsemanship and the greatest skill and dexterity. Every man, woman and child can here witness *the wild sports of the Western Prairies,* as the exhibition is to be free to all, and will take place on the extensive grounds and Race Course of the Messrs. Stevens, within a few rods of the Hoboken Ferry, where at least fifty thousand ladies and gentlemen can conveniently witness the interesting sport. The Grand Chase will be repeated at three distinct hours. At 3 o'clock P. M., from twelve to twenty Buffaloes will be turned loose, and Mr. French will appear dressed as an Indian, mounted on a Prairie Horse and Mexican saddle, chase the Buffaloes around the Race Course, and capture one with the lasso. At 4 and 5 o'clock, the race will be repeated, and the intervals of time will be occupied with various other sports. The City Brass Band is engaged.

"No possible danger need be apprehended, as a double railing has been put around the whole course, to prevent the possibility of the Buffaloes approaching the multitude. Extra ferry-boats will be provided, to run from Barclay, Canal, and Christopher streets. If the weather should be stormy, the sport will come off at the same hours the first fair day."

The mystery of a free exhibition of the sort, though not understood at the time, is readily explained. I had engaged all the ferryboats to Hoboken, at a stipulated price, and all the receipts on the day specified were to be mine.

The assurance that no danger need be apprehended from the buffaloes was simply ridiculous. The poor creatures were so weak and tame that it was doubtful whether they would run at all, notwithstanding my man French had been cramming them with oats to get a little extra life into them.

The eventful day arrived. Taking time by the forelock, multitudes of people crossed to Hoboken before ten o'clock, and by noon the ferryboats were constantly crowded to their utmost capacity. An extra boat, the "Passaic," was put on, and the rush of passengers continued until five o'clock. Twenty-four thousand persons went by the ferryboats to Hoboken that day. Each paid six and a quarter cents going, and as much returning, and the aggregate receipts, including the ferriage of carts and carriages, and the hire for refreshment-stands on the ground, were $3500. Many thousand persons were present from various parts of New Jersey, and these, though bringing "grist to my mill," of course escaped my "toll" at the ferries.

The band of music engaged for the occasion did its best to amuse the immense crowd until three o'clock. At precisely that hour the buffaloes emerged from a shed in the center of the inclosure—my man French having previously administered a punching with a sharp stick, hoping to excite them to a trot on their first appearance. He immediately followed them, painted and dressed as an Indian, mounted on a fiery steed, with lasso in one hand and a sharp stick in the other, but the poor little calves huddled together, and refused to move! This scene was so wholly unexpected, and so perfectly ludicrous, that the spectators burst into uncontrollable uproarious laughter. The shouting somewhat startled the buffaloes, and goaded by French and his assistants, they started off in a slow trot. The uproar of merriment was renewed, and the multitude swinging their hats and hallooing in wild disorder, the buffaloes broke into a gallop, ran against a panel of the low fence, (consisting of two narrow boards), tumbled over, and scrambled away as fast as they could. The crowd in that quarter offered no obstruction. Seeing the animals approach, and not being sufficiently near to discover how harmless they were, men, women and children scattered pell-mell! Such a scampering I never saw before. The buffaloes, which were as badly frightened as the people, found shelter in a neighboring swamp, and all efforts to disengage them proved ineffectual. French, however, captured one of them with his lasso, and afterwards amused the people by lassoing horses and riders—and good-humor prevailed.

No one seemed to suspect the ferry-boat arrangement—the projector was *incog.*—the exhibition had been free to the public—there had been much amusement for twelve and a half cents each, and no one complained. It was, however, nearly midnight before all the visitors found ferry accommodations to New York.

N. P. Willis, of the *Home Journal,* wrote an article illustrating the perfect good nature with which the American public submits to a clever humbug. He said that he went to Hoboken to witness the Buffalo Hunt. It was nearly four o'clock when the boat left the foot of Barclay Street, yet it was so densely crowded that many persons were obliged to stand upon the railings and hold on to the awning posts. When they reached the Hoboken side, a boat equally crowded was leaving that wharf. The passengers of the boat just arriving cried out to those in the boat just returning, "Is the Buffalo Hunt over?" To which came the reply, "Yes, and it was the biggest humbug you ever heard of!" Willis added, that the passengers on the boat with him were so delighted that they instantly gave three cheers for the author of the humbug, whoever he might be.

The same experiment was subsequently tried successfully at Camden, N. J., opposite Philadelphia; after which a number of the buffaloes were sent to England and sold, and the rest were fattened and disposed of in steaks in Fulton Market at fifty cents per pound.

It is but justice to myself to remind the reader that, at the time of their occurrence, the public did not suspect that I had any connection whatever with the exhibition of the Woolly Horse, or the herd of Buffaloes. The entire facts in these cases came to light only through my own voluntary admissions.

23

Abraham Lincoln (1809–1865)
To Jesse W. Fell, Enclosing Autobiography

Lincoln's humility and brevity are legendary, and at first glance this "little sketch" seems to confirm both. But we might also ask how this sketch illustrates the condition of autobiography in America in 1859.

According to Louis Kaplan's *Bibliography of American Autobiographies,* none of the eleven U.S. presidents between Jefferson and James Buchanan (Lincoln's immediate predecessor) wrote an autobiography. There are many possible reasons for this, but one is that autobiographies were often the objects of suspicion. Of the roughly eight hundred written between 1800 and 1870, approximately seventy per cent were written by either clergymen or people who had experienced some unusual adventure or distress.[1] Persons in the mainstream of American life, including political leaders, did not write their life stories. Lincoln's reticence, therefore, may be due more to social-literary conventions than to inherent modesty.

Jesse W. Fell was secretary of the Illinois Republican State Central Committee and a Lincoln backer. He asked for this biographical information for use by a newspaper in Pennsylvania. The article based on it was published February 11, 1860, and reprinted by other papers. As a man who had not held previous national office (except for one term in Congress, 1847–49) and who had not acquired a national reputation until his debates with Stephen Douglas in 1858, Lincoln needed to be better known. In June, 1860, following his nomination for President (on May 18, 1860), he wrote a second sketch much like this one for a Chicago newspaperman, and it was used in preparing a campaign biography. Significantly, it was four times longer, but written in the third person. So Lincoln appears to have gladly cooperated with the publicists who were helping to advance his candidacy, but he also wanted to make sure that the publicity "must not appear to have been written by myself."

There are many other interesting features to this sketch, such as the emphasis on his humble education, his frontier background, and his pleasure in being elected captain by his fellow volunteers in the Black Hawk War. The sketch skillfully per-

1. Lawrence Buell, "Autobiography in the American Renaissance," in *American Autobiography: Retrospect and Prospect,* ed. Paul John Eakin (Madison: Univ. of Wisconsin Press, 1991), p. 48.

forms self-promotion by means of the self-irony and humor that are sympathetic to his audience.

There are many Lincoln biographies. For a documentary of his life, see Earl Schenck Miers, et al., *Lincoln Day by Day: A Chronology*, 3 vols. (Washington, D.C.: Lincoln Sesquicentennial Commission, 1960).

J. W. Fell, Esq   Springfield,
My dear Sir: Dec. 20. 1859

Herewith is a little sketch, as you requested. There is not much of it, for the reason, I suppose, that there is not much of me.

If any thing be made out of it, I wish it to be modest, and not to go beyond the materials. If it were thought necessary to incorporate any thing from any of my speeches, I suppose there would be no objection. Of course it must not appear to have been written by myself. Yours very truly

I was born Feb. 12, 1809, in Hardin County, Kentucky. My parents were both born in Virginia, of undistinguished families—second families, perhaps I should say. My mother, who died in my tenth year, was of a family of the name of Hanks, some of whom now reside in Adams, and others in Macon counties, Illinois. My paternal grandfather, Abraham Lincoln, emigrated from Rockingham County, Virginia, to Kentucky, about 1781 or 2, where, a year or two later, he was killed by indians, not in battle, but by stealth, when he was laboring to open a farm in the forest. His ancestors, who were quakers, went to Virginia from Berks County, Pennsylvania. An effort to identify them with the New-England family of the same name ended in nothing more definite, than a similarity of Christian names in both families, such as Enoch, Levi, Mordecai, Solomon, Abraham, and the like.

My father, at the death of his father, was but six years of age; and he grew up, litterally without education. He removed from Kentucky to what is now Spencer county, Indiana, in my eighth year. We reached our new home about the time the State came into the Union. It was a wild region, with many bears and other wild animals still in the woods. There I grew up. There were some schools, so called; but no qualification was ever required of a teacher, beyond *"readin, writin, and cipherin,"* to the Rule of Three. If a straggler supposed to understand latin, happened to sojourn in the neighborhood, he was looked upon as a wizzard. There was absolutely nothing to excite ambition for education. Of course when I came of age I did not know much. Still somehow, I could read, write, and cipher to the Rule of Three; but that was all. I have not been to school since. The little advance I now have upon this store of education, I have picked up from time to time under the pressure of necessity.

I was raised to farm work, which I continued till I was twenty two. At twenty one I came to Illinois, and passed the first year in Macon county. Then

I got to New-Salem (at that time in Sangamon, now in Menard county, where I remained a year as a sort of Clerk in a store. Then came the Black-Hawk war; and I was elected a Captain of Volunteers—a success which gave me more pleasure than any I have had since. I went the campaign, was elated, ran for the Legislature the same year (1832) and was beaten—the only time I ever have been beaten by the people. The next, and three succeeding biennial elections, I was elected to the Legislature. I was not a candidate afterwards. During this Legislative period I had studied law, and removed to Springfield to practice it. In 1846 I was once elected to the lower House of Congress. Was not a candidate for re-election. From 1849 to 1854, both inclusive, practiced law more assiduously than ever before. Always a whig in politics, and generally on the whig electoral tickets, making active canvasses. I was losing interest in politics, when the repeal of the Missouri Compromise aroused me again. What I have done since then is pretty well known.

If any personal description of me is thought desirable, it may be said, I am, in height, six feet, four inches, nearly; lean in flesh, weighing, on an average, one hundred and eighty pounds; dark complexion, with coarse black hair, and grey eyes—no other marks or brands recollected. Yours very truly

24

Lydia Sigourney (1791–1865)
from *Letters of Life*

Lydia Sigourney was born in Norwich, Connecticut, where her father, Ezekiel Huntley, was the head gardener for a wealthy widow who set the social and moral tone for the town. She published her first book in 1815, *Moral Pieces in Prose and Verse,* and went on to write over fifty more—histories, biography (many honoring Revolutionary War patriots), a long descriptive poem on American Indians, children's books, travel sketches, and religious verse. Nevertheless, what she later was known for was the writing of lugubrious funeral verses, in the manner of *Huckleberry Finn*'s Emeline Grangerford, who was said to be modeled after her. New research in women's literature is reassessing her work.

Letters of Life (1866) is especially important because it was "the first full-dress autobiography written by an American author of either sex whose primary vocation was creative writing."[1] Before Sigourney, American poets, novelists, and essayists—however autobiographical their work—did not write autobiographies, at least not in the sense of a full-length biography written about one's self. *Letters of Life,* therefore, is a landmark in the history of American autobiography and the remote forerunner of works like Henry James's *A Small Boy and Others* or Lillian Hellman's *Pentimento.*

One justification of her project, which she notably refuses to make herself, is that she was in her time an extremely popular writer. Her meticulously correct grammar and diction and unassailable character were models for genteel women. In England, she was compared to the popular Mrs. Felicia Hemans; in America she was deluged with fan mail, and an Iowa town was even named after her. (In response she donated fifty volumes to the town library and directed the planting of trees around the courthouse square.) So she could presume interest in her life. But her declared strategy in the autobiography was to write "letters" to a "dear friend" who had requested "a particular account of my own life." Her goal was to be instructive and, as in all her writing, "not to interfere with the discharge of womanly duty, and to aim at being an instrument of good."[2] In these ways, she nominally placed autobiography within a kind of personal writing which women

1. Lawrence Buell, "Autobiography in the American Renaissance," in *American Autobiography: Retrospect and Prospect,* ed. Paul John Eakin (Madison: Univ. of Wisconsin Press, 1991), p. 60.
2. Lydia Sigourney, *Letters of Life* (New York: D. Appleton and Co., 1866), pp. 5, 324.

had already published (letters and travel narratives) and also made it line up with the kinds of didactic literature she had already written.

The *Letters* is about evenly divided between a narrative of her childhood and education, leading up to her first experiments in writing (chapters 1–8) and (chapters 9–14), a record of her experiences as a teacher of young ladies, her marriage to Charles Sigourney (a Hartford, Connecticut, hardware merchant and banker), their happy life together till his death in 1854, and an account of her other books. Throughout, she presents herself as extremely cognizant of social proprieties, pious, frugal, hard-working, self-disciplined, and eager to educate and improve herself. In some ways she seems like a terrible prig, just as her language seems insufferably polished. But she also seems highly aware that all these virtues are expected of her and that, having acquired them, she has the authority to play.

In this chapter, "Letter V," subtitled "Removal—Household Employments," she describes the responsibilities she had at age fourteen when her parents moved from Mrs. Lathrop's mansion to their own "new abode." A confident young lady, she supervises the moving in of the furniture and then resumes her domestic occupations, the ultimate of which is making clothes for her father. In addition to telling about being a dutiful, loving daughter, however, the author also has a little fun, as in her riddling description of the "quadruped member of our establishment . . . scarcely mentionable to ears polite." In this playfulness she might be compared to Franklin, Caroline Kirkland, or Fanny Fern. She is also very aware of her responsibility as a social historian: *Letters of Life* is a veritable time capsule of her culture.

The text of "Letter V," given here in its entirety, is from *Letters of Life* (New York: D. Appleton and Co., 1866). An important critical essay is Nina Baym's "Reinventing Lydia Sigourney," *American Literature* 62 (September 1990): 385–404.

It was in the bloom and beauty of a most glorious June that we made our first removal. The new abode was at a short distance from my birthplace, less aristocratic in its appointments, but perfectly comfortable, and our own. My father, according to his invariable system, paid every cent of the purchase-money, and all the workmen who had been employed to put it in complete repair, ere we entered on the premises.

On the morning of leaving the spot endeared by so many tender recollections, my young heart was too exultingly filled with the present to summon mournful shadows from the past. Greatly was my housekeeping ambition gratified, by obtaining permission to receive and arrange all the furniture— my mother superintending its departure, and my father alternating between the two habitations, as the benefit of both might require. This deputed trust was executed with immense zeal, and as much judgment as might be expected from a girl of fourteen, the men who drove the carts aiding in the transfer of the heavier articles, according to my direction. After the more laborious parts of the mission were completed, I amused myself by disposing, in a closet with a glass door, our slender stores of silver and china, to the best possible advantage. The satisfactions of that day, and the responsibilities entrusted to me, come back fresh and unimpaired over the expanse of half a century. Wearied as my limbs were at last, I managed to course all over the garden, and fill a large vase of roses, to greet my beautiful mother. At the sunset she came, herself as blooming as they. Methought I had never before appreciated her comeliness. Though nearly forty, she might have passed for half that age, so brilliant was her complexion, so elastic her movements. Proud was I of her aspect of youth, and the charm of her animated manner.

Great Pussy, an integral part of our household, arrived ignobly tied in a sack, lest, taking note of the way, he might be tempted surreptitiously to return. After his liberation, and a slight flurry of anger at the indignity to which he had been subjected, he ran about, applying his olfactories to the various floors and thresholds, and apparently approving their odor, finding also his old friends, and, still more, a good supper, made up his mind contentedly to become a citizen.

Our house was after the plan of the convenient structures of that day, comprising, on the first floor, two parlors, a bedroom, a spacious kitchen, with a wing for pantry and milk-room; on the second, five chambers; in the attic, one, and that delightful appendage to old-fashioned mansions, a large garret. The garden, which had been planted and prepared for our reception, contained the finest vegetables, in luxuriant beds; while the borders were enriched with fruits—pears, peaches, and the clustering grape-vines. The interstices were filled with the currant, gooseberry, and strawberry; concerning the latter of which Sydney Smith has said, "Without doubt God *might* have made a better berry, but without doubt He *never did*."

This garden, whose fertile soil and admirable cultivation rendered it remarkably productive for its size, was skirted by a small, green meadow, swelling at its extremity into a knoll, where apple trees flourished, and refreshed by a clear brooklet. It furnished an abundance of winter food for our fair cow, who in autumn, after the second mowing, might be seen grazing there with great delight, or ruminating, after a rich repast, "alone in her glory." She seemed also well satisfied with her new quarters in a nice barn; and our fine flock of poultry, being equally well accommodated, strutted, and crowed, and paraded their hopeful offspring, as if they had held tenure there from the beginning.

Our domain comprised, at the distance of a couple of miles from the city, several acres of excellent woodland. There, majestic forest trees spread a broad canopy, and younger ones interlaced their boughs, melodious with the nesting people, their feet laved by a busy, whispering burnie, as clear as crystal. Every autumn the master designated, with his usual judgment, a sufficient quantity of wood for our yearly expenditure, which, after being cut in proper lengths, was stored to dry in a basement room with glass windows, which might have been easily fitted up for a kitchen, had the size of the family required it. Those piles were pleasant objects, from their mathematical symmetry as well as the vision of the cheerful warmth their glowing coals and dancing flame would diffuse around the wintry hearth-stone. How much more poetical than the black stove and the coal-fed furnace!

The man who depended on the regular commission of transporting these loads of wood in his team, was an old Revolutionary soldier. He had been in the battle of Bunker Hill, and maintained his post at that sanguinary spot called the "Rail-fence," whence so few escaped. Weather-beaten and wiry was he, like one who had seen and could bear hardships. No skill had he in narration. His taste was for deeds. He would not have been apt to waste powder in a poor aim, and might be a tight hand at the bayonet.

"I fired seventeen times," said he, "till my cartridges giv' out; and I guess some on 'em told, for I looked out sharp afore I spent my ammunition."

A mixture of the Yankee and the Spartan character he seemed. I should not like to have had him for a foe. His oxen, like himself, looked as if used to hard knocks, and, at his slightest monosyllable, started off at a more rapid rate than is common to their contemplative race.

In this new abode I was elevated to a higher rank, as an assistant to my mother. This gratified both my filial love and my desire to learn new things. She was an adept in that perfect system of New England housekeeping which allots to every season its peculiar work, to every day its regular employment, to every article its place; which allows no waste of aught committed to its charge; which skills to prolong the existence of whatever may need repair, and builds up the comfort of a family on the solid basis of industry and economy. Under her training I had already acquired some elements of this science; now I was installed in the dignity of a prime minister. In those days of simplicity of living, when the use of the hands was accounted honorable, it was the custom of households far more wealthy than ourselves to take some poor child, and bring it up as a domestic assistant, or hire occasional aid, as their needs might require. The latter was our choice. Thus we enjoyed the luxury of living without turning a key. The women who could be readily called in when additional labor or unexpected company rendered such aid desirable, were generally small householders, who considered it a privilege to earn something for the comfort of those at home. Thus the mutual benefit had in it a feature of philanthropy.

If Lord Bacon is correct in his position that the mind needs no recreation save change of employment, our sex have a favored sphere, for it admits of an unending variety. Very happy were my mother and myself in our light and constantly recurring household occupations. Up with the lark, we wrought with a spontaneous song. Broom and duster were our calisthenics, and every apartment was kept in the speckless sanctity of neatness. Somewhat enterprising were we too, and made excursions out of the orbit of regular feminine rotation. We papered walls when we chose, and refreshed the wood-work of our parlors with fresh coats of paint, purchasing pots of such shades as pleased us. I was honored by having particular charge of the sashes, which required a delicate brush, lest the panes of glass should be soiled. I cut silhouette likenesses, and executed small landscapes, and bunches of flowers in water-colors, to embellish the rooms.

In culinary compounds, and the preparation of the golden butter, I was only subaltern; but in some other departments an equal partner and perhaps a little more. The needlework of the household was especially my forte. I became expert in those arts by which the structure of garments is varied, and their existence prolonged. From the age of eight I had been promoted to the office of shirt-maker for my father. I now adventured upon his vests, cutting to pieces an old one as a pattern.

For a hall in the second story, which was carpetless, I cut squares of flannel, about the size of the compartments in a marble pavement, and sewed on each a pattern of flowers and leaves cut from broadcloth, of appropriate colors. The effect of the whole was that of rich, raised embroidery. With the true New England spirit of turning fragments to good account, I constructed of the pieces which were too small for the carpet a gay counterpane for a little bed, used when we had children among our nightly guests. I also braided white chip, and fine split straw, for the large and very pretty hats which were then in vogue.

It was the custom, in many families, to supply by their own spinning-wheels what the Scotch call *napery*. The sound of the flax-wheel of my diligent grandmother was among the melodies of my infancy. Her hands, with those of my mother, thus made the linen of the household. Our six beds, with the exception of one in the guest-chamber, which exhibited what were then called "Holland sheets," were thus furnished, the manufacture of cotton being then unknown in this region. Comely were those fabrics to my unsophisticated eye, and durable, some of them being in existence even at this date.

This branch of internal revenue received a remarkable impulse after our removal to this new habitation. On our premises was a small house, whose sole tenant was a widow and a weaver, who desired to pay her rent in her own work. To accommodate her, my mother enlarged this sphere of productive industry, and taught me the use of the great-wheel. Always shall I be grateful to her for this new source of pleasure. It is one of the most healthful and effective forms of feminine exercise. It gives muscular vigor, and has power in removing pulmonary tendencies. But no eulogy of mine may hope to call again from the shades that which Fashion has proscribed and made obsolete.

A stated period in the morning was allotted to me for this employment. I was sorry when it expired, and ever mingled it with a cheerful song. Flannel sheets, with table-cloths, and towels woven in a rude form of damask, soon abounded among us. Then we betook ourselves to the manufacture of carpets, the warp being spun wool of various colors, and the woof economically made of cast-off winter clothing, or remnants purchased from the tailor's shop, cut in narrow strips, sewed strongly, and dyed black. Truly respectable were they, and, in those days of simplicity, praised.

Growing ambitious in proportion to our success, we spun for ourselves each a dress out of fine cotton, carded in long, beautiful rolls by my mother. A portion of the yarn was bleached to a snowy whiteness, and the remainder dyed a beautiful fawn or salmon color. It was woven in small, even checks, and made a becoming costume, admired even by the tasteful. I wore mine with more true satisfaction than I have since worn brocades, or court costume at presentations to royalty.

The antique tenant, for whose convenience in the matter of rent we so much bestirred ourselves, was quite a character. Wrinkled was her visage, yet rubicund with healthful toil; and when she walked in the streets, which was seldom, her bow-like body, and arms diverging toward a crescent form, preserved the altitude in which she sprung the shuttle and heaved the beam. Her cumbrous, old-fashioned loom contained a vast quantity of timber, and monopolized most of the space in the principal apartment of her cottage: Close under her window were some fine peach trees, which she claimed as her own, affirming that she planted the kernels from whence they sprung. So their usufruct was accorded her by the owner of the soil. As the large, rich fruit approached its blush of ripeness, her watchfulness became intense. Her cap, yellow with smoke, and face deepening to a purple tinge of wrathful emotion, might be seen protruding from her casement, as she vituperated the boys who manifested a hazardous proximity to the garden wall. Not perfectly lamblike was her temperament, as I judge from the shriek of the objurgations she sometimes addressed to them; while they, more quiescent, it would seem, than boy-nature in modern times, returned no rude reply. I opine that the lady might have been both exacting and tyrannical, if power on a large scale had been vouchsafed her. She was mollified by our mode of treatment, which was a reverse of the code of paying tribute to Cæsar. My principal intercourse with her was in giving her something to read—for she read on "Sabba-day," as she called it, and on the yearly fastday—in carrying her pudding on Sunday noons, and baked beans on Saturday nights.

Of the last-named dish, which was so symbolical of the early customs of Norwich that a large province of the township was christened Bean-hill, it is fitting that I should speak particularly. It made its appearance on the supper-table of every householder who was able to compass its ingredients, at the closing day of the week; and with the setting sun that announced to the Israelite the termination of his Sabbath, warned these descendants of the Pilgrims that theirs had begun. A little boy of our acquaintance said honestly,

"We never missed having baked beans but one Saturday night, and then our oven fell down"—a penal result which seemed to him both natural and just.

This nutritious and canonical dish of our forefathers was always received by the weaver-widow with complacence. A little conversation was wont to ensue, in which she evinced a good measure of intelligence and shrewdness, with those true Yankee features, keen observation of other people, and a latent desire to manage them. Her strongest sympathies hovered around the majesty and mystery of her trade, and her highest appreciation was reserved for those who promoted it. The kindness that dwelt in her nature was most palpably called forth by a quadruped member of our establishment which has not been mentioned, and is, I suppose, scarcely mentionable to ears polite. Yet I could never understand why it should be an offence to delicacy to utter the name of an animal which the Evangelists have recorded on their pages as plunging, in a dense herd, "down a steep place into the sea, and perishing in the waters." Neither do I know why they should be made the personification of all that is mean and gormandizing, because they chance to have a good appetite, and a digestion that a dyspeptic might envy. Wolves and bears are not more abstinent or refined, yet they freely figure in elegant writing and parlance. Such treatment is peculiarly ungrateful in a people who allow this scorned creature to furnish a large part of their subsistence, to swell the gains of commerce, and to share with the monarch of ocean the honor of lighting their evening lamp. He is justly styled the poor man's friend, and the adjunct of every economical household. Happy to feed on the refuse of our table, he liberally replaces it by luxuries purchased with his life. Our creed in this matter is more inconsistent than that of the Jews; for we do not hesitate to profit by his death, though we have made his life despicable. He is not originally destitute of grace, as those who have seen his infancy, in the peaceful sphere of a rural farmyard, can testify. That he is capable of mental progress, has been proved by those who, with the epithet of "learned," have been exhibited in public. Yet, without aiming to advance any extraordinary pretensions on the part of this stigmatized animal, it would seem but common compassion as well as justice to make comfortable the short span allotted him among the living. Our own formed quite a friendship for the elegant cow, welcoming her when she entered the yard to which his mansion had access, frisking, and looking in her calm face with an affectionate guttural language reserved for her alone. She was far less demonstrative, but not wholly indifferent to his attentions. His skill in making his bed was amusing, shaking and arranging the fresh straw until the smooth pillow suited his epicurean taste. White and clean was he in his person, having water at his command, and happy in regular and ample rations. He regarded those who bestowed on him his favorite viand of greens from the garden with a loving twinkle in his eye, as if sympathizing with that large class of higher humanities mentioned by Southey, "the most direct road to whose heart was through the stomach." Our lady-tenant was never more interesting to me than when, presenting her slender libations to this humble retainer, she exulted to see how readily he came at the call of her cracked voice. She was prone, however, to modify the effect of her disinterested attentions, by computing the weight which might be expected to accrue from his increasing corpulence, and hinting some personal claim, or future prospect of a dividend of bacon, on the principle of joint investment.

My highest entrustment to her skill as an artisan, and indeed the Ultima Thule of my ambition in the line of constructiveness, was a suit of clothes for my father. The choicest wool was obtained, and each thread drawn out to the utmost fineness consistent with strength, was carefully evened and smoothed with the fingers, ere it received the final twist, and was run upon the spindle. The yarn was arranged in skeins of twenty knots, vernacularly called a *run*, each knot containing forty strands around the reel, which was two yards in circumference. The addition of every skein to the mass hanging upon the panels of the spinning apartment, heightened my happiness. When committed to our lady of the loom, she incessantly complained of its "awful fineness," and demanded a higher price for weaving, which we deemed it equitable to accord. Released from her manipulations, its texture was tested in a fulling-mill, where I believe its contraction was onefourth of its original dimensions. When brought home from the cloth-dresser a beautiful, lustrous black, and made into a complete suit, surmounted by a handsome overcoat, or surtout, methought I was never so perfectly happy. The filial sentiment was mingled with a pride and tenderness which I had never felt before.

Another part of his wardrobe, the knitting of his stockings, I claimed as my especial province. It had been so considered since the death of his mother, and until his own, at the age of eighty-seven. I think no other shared with me that privilege, and am sure than none were purchased. It was the habit of our family, and not a peculiarity at that day, that this article of dress should be of domestic manufacture. With us the yarn of which they were made emanated from our own wheels, and was more durable, because more carefully wrought, than what was for sale in the shops. We produced cotton of various degrees of fineness—linen thread for summer, and wool for the colder seasons. To the hose destined for my father I devoted particular attention, because short breeches and buckles being essential to the full dress of a gentleman, the encasing of the lower limbs was more conspicuous than since the easier regency of the pantaloon. I took pleasure in making his ribbed, viz., knitting two stitches and seaming one, which, though a slower process, rendered them more adhesive, and better revealed the symmetry of his well-shaped limbs.

Great was his complacence in my various little works to please him. Yet always calm and equable, he never boasted of them or praised me. I cannot recollect that he ever thanked me. I would not have had him; it would have troubled me. The holy intonation of his voice when he said *"My child,"* was enough. The sweetest tears swelled under my eyelids when I thought of him. Methinks the love of a daughter for a father is distinct and different from all other loves.

He liked to have me with him in his ministrations among the green, living things, whose welfare he scientifically understood. How kindly would he ask my opinion about pruning or grafting, as if I were able to counsel him. He wished to cultivate a correct judgment, and increase my admiration of the works of Him whose beneficence is seen in the grass blade, and the herb which hides under its rough coat the spirit of health. I well remember, and could even now weep, as I recall his serene, approving look, when at the close of some summer's day, if rain had been withheld, I refreshed with my bright watering-pot not only my own flowers but his trenches of celery and beds of salad.

If he planted a tree, my hand must hold it steadily while he arranged the fibrous roots, and pressed around it the earth of its new abiding place. I recollect his calling me to assist in setting out two apple trees in our front yard. To the rallying remarks of some of his more fashionable friends, he replied it was better to fill the space with something useful, than with un-productive shade. His utilitarian decision was rewarded with bushels of the finest greenings and russets—and also with what he had affirmed might be secured, the symmetrical form of the trees, which were judiciously pruned as their growth advanced. The fragrance which they diffused through the whole house in their time of efflorescence, was delightful, and not impaired by the sight of the clustering bees, burying themselves in the calyx, or glancing from petal to petal of the pink and white flowers, with their busy song of gain and gladness.

The productiveness of his fruit trees was the wonder of his neighbors. He devoted to them almost a florist's care. During the fervors of summer their trunks and principal boughs were occasionally refreshed with a bath of soap-suds. He had an office of kindness for them as they mournfully shed their leaves, preparing for the discipline of winter. If any moss, or unsightly excres-cences adhered to their bodies, they were removed by friction, and a plentiful lavation administered, a love token till a better season, like the stirrup-cup of our British ancestors to the parting guest. Its ingredients, if I recollect right, were in the following proportions: three gallons of lye from wood ashes, a pint of soft-soap, a quarter of a pound of nitre, with a handful of common salt. The nitre was dissolved in warm water, and after the mixture was well incorporated, it was applied with a brush to the trunks and principal limbs. When spring revivified their roots, another hydropathic welcome awaited them. The elements of the medicated bath were one quart of soap and of salt, and one pound of flour of sulphur, with a sufficient quantity of soft water. As an additional tonic the earth was opened in a circle around each tree to the depth of two inches, and a prescription of compost, mingled with two quarts of wood-ashes, one quart of salt, and the same quantity of pulverized plaster added, to quicken their appetite, and the whole neatly raked over. The recipients repaid these attentions by their healthful condition. Since almost every person likes good fruit, and does not object to a large quantity, I make no apology for mentioning to you, dear friend, the old-fashioned modes by which those results were promoted.

Busy and merry was the autumnal ingathering from our small domain. The vegetables accepted a winter shelter in the spacious cellar, where each genus was arranged in due order; and the savoy cabbage, standing erect in its bed of sand, might have pleased a Dutch burgomaster by its unfading greenness. Apples were to be cut and dried for tarts, pears and peaches for confections and pastry, and boiled sweet corn exposed to the sun for the dish of succotash, whose richness was learned from the poor Indians. Sage, and the red heads of thyme, and the rough leaves of the burdock, were to be saved for the domestic pharmacopeia; tansy and peppermint for distillation, as the fragrant damask-rose had already been, and the luxuriant hop, for beer, which sometimes burst the bottles with its luscious effervescence. The finest apples were to be thoroughly wiped, and wrapped in paper, ere they were committed to their reservoirs, the rough-coated pear that served the oven until spring, comfortably accommodated, and the large, golden quince, embalmed with sugar to regale the guest. Heavy sheaves of maize covered with a formidable depth the garret floor, as a field was appropriated to the culture of this majestic plant, with its humbler adjunct, the potato, having their interstices filled with the graceful bean and ponderous pumpkin, without the favor of whose yellow face our Puritan forefathers dared not adventure on their Thanksgiving. There was a rural independence in our style of living which pleased us all. Our poultry and eggs were abundant and fine, our cow furnished an overflow of the richest milk, cream, and butter, and our hams, etc., preserved by a recipe of my father's, were proverbial for their delicacy. It is something to know what you are eating. More than this, we knew what *they* had eaten, upon whom we fed, and their aliment had been healthful and ample. Butchers' meat, of which we were no great consumers, could be obtained daily from carts, there being then no regularly established market.

The provisions for our table, though simple, were always admirably prepared. Let no one esteem this a matter of slight importance, or to be confidently trusted to careless hirelings. Ill-cooked and over-seasoned viands may serve to help the physicians; and all trades must live. Neither should the appointments of a board round which the family gather thrice during one diurnal revolution, be viewed with aught of stoical indifference. Good food, neatly presented, has something to do with a good character. You can tell the merchant on 'change who has had a nice breakfast, and expects a still better dinner. Gourmands are disgusting, but very abstinent people are prone to be crabbed and provoked to see others enjoying what they deny themselves. Whoever has wholesome viands, and a hearty appetite, and a good conscience, let him eat and be thankful. I have observed that ladies who understand the science of table-comfort and economy, whose bread is always light, who know the ingredients of every important dish, and are not afraid or ashamed actually to compound it, possess the high respect of their husbands. Let those look to this "who love their lords."

The principle of our little household was not "living to eat, but eating to live," and honestly taking the enjoyment which the Creator has kindly connected with that on which existence depends. The hours appointed for our repasts were as primitive as our opinions. Breakfast was soon after sunrise, dinner at twelve, and supper somewhat varied by the seasons. From so vulgar a dining-hour the fashionable city people might be moved to count us barbarians. Yet I recollect hearing a French physician of eminence say at a banquet in Paris, that there was a quickening, a rise of tide in the human system at high noon, that concurred with the reception of the principal meal, and that the increase of paralysis in that region since the dining-hour had approached evening, was marked and manifest. Perhaps he might have endorsed the proverb which was used in his native clime, as early as the tenth and eleventh centuries:

> Lever à cinq, dîner à neuf,
> Souper à cinq, coucher à neuf,
> Fait vivre ans nonante et neuf.

The translation is particularly quaint:

> To rise at five, and dine at nine,
> To sup at five, and sleep at nine,
> Will make one live to ninety-nine.

This adage of the Carlovingian dynasty is extreme both in premises and promise. Not having exactly its *nonante-neuf* in view, the point which principally harmonized with our creed was the hour for retiring, in whose memory we were always aided by the sonorous voice of the bell, pealing from the church tower, and reverberating from rock to rock. Regularity in periods of rest, rising, and refreshment, were considered among the elements of health. Led by my father, who had a deep sense of the value of the fleeting hours, we were distinguished by punctuality, especially at meals, which I think seldom varied for years five minutes from their allotted time, except from calls or unavoidable interruptions. I have already mentioned that they combined simplicity with comfort. Yet though not studious of luxury, and never making the devices to pamper appetite a subject of conversation, it was an object to secure a commendable variety. In this we were aided by our proximity to the sea, which brought to our board different races of the finny people, and the oysters from the Norwich cove, which were proverbially excellent. For all our household expenses and wardrobe the invariable rule was, to "pay as you go." Hence, whatever we used was our own. There was no charge against us on any merchant's ledger, and no bills brought in to impede the festivities of the New Year. What was needful for our comfort that our domain did not furnish, was supplied by the interest of money, which my father had saved and invested. Our income from all sources, prudently managed, left us perfectly at ease, and indulged us in the pleasure of aiding the poor. I cannot imagine a happier domestic condition. Not annoyed by watchfulness over the doubtful fidelity of servants, the employments that devolved upon us aided health and cheerfulness.

Voltaire, using as homely a simile as Socrates was fond of adopting, has compared the different grades of society to a cup of beer: "The top is froth, the bottom, dregs, the middle, pure and good." This mediocrity, removed from the vanity of wealth and the pain of poverty, it was our lot to share. Our united happiness is sketched in a few simple lines, written during one of our quiet evenings at home:

> Loud roars the hoarse storm from the angry North,
> As though the winter-spirit loath to leave
> His wonted haunts, came rudely rushing back
> Fast by the steps of the defenceless spring,
> To hurl his frost-spear at her shrinking flowers.
>
> Yet while the tempest o'er the charms of May
> Sweeps dominant, and with discordant tone
> Wild uproar rules without—peace reigns within.
> Bright glows the hearthstone, while the taper clear
> Alternate aids the needle, or illumes
> The page sublime, inciting the rapt soul
> To rise above all warring elements.
> The gentle kitten at my footstool breathes
> A song monotonous and full of joy.
> Close by my side my tender mother sits,
> Industriously bent; her brow still fair
> With lingering beams of youth, while he, the sire—
> The faithful guide, listens indulgently
> To our discourse, or wakes the tuneful hymn
> With full, rich voice of manly melody.
>
> Fountain of life and light, to Thee I turn,
> Father Supreme! from whom our joys descend
> As streams flow from their source; and unto whom
> All good on earth shall finally return
> As to a natural centre—praise is due
> To Thee, from all thy works—nor least from me,
> Though in thy scale of being, light and low.
> From Thee descends whate'er of joy or peace

Sparkles in my full cup—health, hope, and bliss,
And pure parental love; beneath whose smile
A heart call'd lonely, doth not feel the loss
Of brother, or of sister, or of friend.

So, unto Thee be all the honor given,
Whether young Morning with her vestal lamp
Warn from my couch—or sober twilight gray
Yield to advancing Night; or summer sky
Spread its smooth azure; or contending storms
Muster their wrath; or whether in the shade
Of much-loved solitude, deep-wove and close
I rest; or gayly share the social scene,
Or wander wide to wake in stranger-hearts
New sympathies; or wheresoever else
Thy hand shall lead, still let my steadfast eye
Behold Thee, and my heart attune Thy praise.

To Thee alone, in humble trust I come
For strength and wisdom. Leaning on thine arm
Oh let me pass this intermediate state,
This vale of discipline; and when its mists
Shall fleet away, I trust Thou wilt not leave
My soul in darkness, for Thy word is truth,
Nor are Thy thoughts like the vain thoughts of man,
Nor Thy ways like his ways.
                              Therefore I rest
In peace—and sing Thy praise, Father Supreme.

PART FIVE

Survivors and Self-Teachers, 1865–1915

When the Civil War ended in 1865, approximately two million men had served in the Union Army, out of a population of twenty-three million: 750,000 had served in the Army of the Confederacy, out of a population of nine million, which included 3,500,000 slaves. Northern casualties had been 640,000 dead and wounded; those of the South, 450,000. In addition, 220,000 Confederates had been captured by the North and 200,000 Union soldiers had been captured by the South. Measured against the size and wealth of the country, it was the bloodiest and most expensive war in American history.[1]

It was also a war that was recorded and remembered in hundreds of memoirs, diaries, letters, and other kinds of autobiographical writing. The index to Louis Kaplan's *Bibliography of American Autobiographies* (1961) lists 542 autobiographies from the Civil War, roughly 8½ percent of all the 6377 books listed. That, of course, does not include shorter pieces or unpublished material, and a great many more Civil War diaries, letters, and autobiographies have been published since 1945, the cut-off year for the *Bibliography*.

The classic Civil War memoir has long been Grant's *Personal Memoirs*. Thanks to Mark Twain, whose American Book Company published it by subscription in 1885–86, its two volumes had an immense sale, and they became, in a sense, the Union veterans' official history. But the *Memoirs* also received critical praise from contemporaries like Matthew Arnold and Henry James; and many later readers have praised it, too, notably Gertrude Stein and Edmund Wilson. Its plain style, its unromantic view of war, and Grant's own directness and lack of military pomp make it a very appropriate record of a war that was won by the endurance and sacrifices of common men. No novels written about the war, with the exception of John William DeForest's autobiographical novel *Miss Ravenel's Conversion*, and Stephen Crane's *Red Badge of Courage*, are nearly so sobering and realistic.

Nevertheless, a general's memoirs cannot possibly give the common sol-

1. Shelby Foote, *The Civil War: A Narrative* (New York: Random House, 1974), p. 1040.

dier's or civilian's view of a war. He gave the orders: the soldiers and civilians had to carry them out and bear the suffering. It was they who were most likely to become casualties and prisoners, or to lose their homes and families. Writing their own stories was their way of insuring that these experiences would not be forgotten and that the parts which they played in the great epic struggle would be suitably recognized. Writing their own stories, which, thanks to increased literacy, a large portion of the population now could do, was also a way of helping themselves to remember and of leaving physical records for their children and other readers. Some diarists like Mary Boykin Chesnut and Cornelia Peake McDonald also went on to *rewrite* their stories, because parts of the original diary were lost and because they wanted to edit and polish them and make them more worthy of publication and thus celebration and preservation.

So much writing not only contributed to the total body of American autobiography, it also had a marked effect on concepts of the self and so on the history of autobiography.

Before the Civil War, as we have already noted, most Americans were reluctant to write their personal histories. It took the leadership of Transcendentalists, escaped slaves, abolitionists, feminists, and other people of outstanding talent who had had unusual experiences to start the ante-bellum self-liberation movement. Americans may have been inclined, as Tocqueville observed, towards "independent judgement," towards thinking for themselves and judging the world from their own perspective, but they were equally inclined, he noted, to conformity and a fear of appearing different from or better than their neighbors.[2] And their concepts of self corresponded to this fear. "The self stood as no accommodating channel to enhancement or perfection," Lewis O. Saum said in his study of *The Popular Mood of Pre-Civil War America,* "it stood rather as an endlessly frustrating, dark-hued impediment."[3] The shadow of Puritanism was long and dark, and the newer, more optimistic lights of religious and political liberalism did not fully penetrate its gloom, because liberalism taught that for the self to become generous, refined, and sincere it also had to be disciplined. These virtues might be natural; but they still required nurture.

Veterans of the Civil War, however, were likely to have a very different view, if not of human nature, then at least of themselves and their comrades. The very fact of disinterested sacrifice for a noble cause—for preservation of the Union and emancipation of slaves, or for the Right of Secession and love of country—was proof of some higher kind of benevolence. The war's polarization of opinion further encouraged each side to celebrate its own heroes

2. Alexis de Tocqueville, *Democracy in America,* ed. Phillips Bradley (New York: Vintage, 1960), vol. 2, pp. 4, 11.
3. Lewis O. Saum, *The Popular Mood of Pre-Civil War America* (Westport, CT: Greenwood, 1980), p. 108.

in these terms, leaving the enemy as the embodiment of evil: of selfishness, ignorance, crudity, and the forces of darkness. One's own motives and character were generous, sincere, and noble; the enemy's were the opposite. In this way, in fact, it was even possible to maintain both the old Puritan and the new liberal views of human nature. From the northern perspective the northern self was selfless, enlightened, and modern, while the southern self was dark and sinister. Contrariwise, the Southerner saw himself as noble and free and the Northerner as a tricky, deceptive, money-grubbing Yankee.

Because testimonies about wars inevitably require a way of dealing with one's own pain and suffering, as well as the suffering and death of others, these views of self and non-self, or Self and Other, were deeply inscribed into Civil War autobiographies. They were an integral part of the whole elegiac strategy with which writers justified pain and death and tried to make sense of the war. Here is the way, for instance, that Warren Lee Goss, a Massachusetts sergeant and the author of *The Soldier's Story,* elegized a man in his company who died at Andersonville, the Georgia prison, where nearly 13,000 men died in 1864–65.

C. H. A. Moore was a drummer . . . the only son of a widowed mother. . . . In him all her hopes were centred, and it was with great reluctance that she finally agreed to his enlistment. A soldier's life, to one thus reared, is at best hard; but to plunge one so young and unaccustomed even to the rudiments of hardships into the unparalleled miseries of Andersonville, seemed cruelty inexpressible. . . . The day previous to his death I saw and conversed with him, tried to encourage him; but a look of premature age had settled over his youthful face, which bore but little semblance to the bright, expressive look he wore when he enlisted. . . . He spoke of home and of his mother, but his words were all in the same key, monotonous and weary, with a stony, unmoved expression of countenance. . . . It seems to me that God's everlasting curse must surely rest upon those who thus knowingly allowed hundreds of innocent young lives to be blotted out of existence by cruelties unheard of before in the annals of civilized warfare. It seems to me that in the future the South, who abetted so great a crime against civilization and humanity, against Christianity and even decency, must stand condemned by the public opinion of the world. . . .[4]

The drummerboy is thus eulogized for his youth, innocence, and devotion to the cause. He was also a symbol of his mother's hopes and goodness, so that his suffering and death are all the worse because they are by extension violations of her, the person from whom he received his virtuous sentiments. The South, on the other hand, by "knowingly" allowing such "innocent young lives to be blotted out" has offended "civilization and humanity," "Christianity and even decency"—all the forces of good that Goss can list.

Conversely, here is the way Cornelia Peake McDonald described her home in Virginia in February, 1863, after it had been occupied by the invading Union army:

4. Warren Lee Goss, *The Soldier's Story of His Captivity at Andersonville, Belle Isle, and Other Rebel Prisons* (Boston: Lee and Shepard, 1868), pp. 99–100. Further references are given in text.

I sit every day and see this lovely place converted into a wagon yard. The smooth green turf has disappeared, and roads go over and across in every direction. Under the dining room windows runs one, and mules and horses continually pass, driven by men cursing and swearing, uttering oaths that make my blood curdle. . . .

Under the parlour windows goes another road. Those windows used to look out on a sweet shrubbery of syringas, mock orange, white lilacs and purple . . . everything old fashioned and lovely that I delight in. . . . [Now] all the long day through [pass] wagons, artillery horses, . . . soldiers and camp women, gay officers on foot and on horseback, and most sickening sight of all, Yankee "Ladies" in dainty riding habits, hats and plumes, pace by as if the ground they passed over was their own; and chatting with their beaux, glance around at us if they chance to see us as if we were intruders on their domain.[5]

"Yankees" are "cursing and swearing" mule drivers and disgusting, supercillious "camp women," and Mrs. McDonald is too angry to stop and qualify these images with any further reflection that this is war and that soldiers and their camp followers are not genteel. Rather, she excuses herself for her "resentful and revengeful" feelings towards them. She wishes that "our artillery could, from some near point, sweep them all away."[6]

The powerful emotions in these Civil War autobiographies helped to keep this war alive for generations after it was supposedly over, and this, in turn, perpetuated the need for publishing more autobiographies, as apologists for North and South continued to build up the evidence for heroism or horror. In the ten years from 1862 through 1871, for example, seventy-four memoirs of Civil War prisoners were published. Interest apparently dropped off from 1872 to 1881, when only seventeen were published, but from 1882 through 1891, fifty-eight more appeared, followed by thirty-two in the decade 1892–1901, fifty-one in the period 1901–10, and twenty-seven between 1912 and 1921.[7] There were other reasons for this increase, too. Just as with the Revolution, there were controversies over pension legislation; elderly veterans wished to publish their stories before they died; and their descendants wished to honor them after they died. But ongoing rivalry of North and South continued to promote interest in the war and in the personal experiences of its participants.

Another significant difference between the prison story of Warren Goss and the narratives of Revolutionary prisoners, Indian captives, and others, is in Goss's interpretation of the meaning of his experience. Like other prisoners and captives, Goss saw it as a test of faith. He and his fellows had

5. Cornelia Peake McDonald, *A Woman's Civil War: A Diary, with Reminiscences of the War, from March 1862*, ed. Minrose C. Gwin (Madison: Univ. of Wisconsin Press, 1992), pp. 120–21.
6. McDonald, *A Woman's Civil War,* p. 121.
7. William Best Hesseltine, *Civil War Prisons: A Study in War Psychology*. Ohio State University Contributions in History and Political Science, no. 12 (Columbus: Ohio State Univ. Press, 1930), pp. 247–48. Hesseltine counted both books and magazine articles, from both the North and South, for a total of 259.

remained true to the cause and not accepted offers from the enemy to gain release by becoming turncoats. But the awful conditions of Andersonville— hunger, exposure, disease, and almost unimaginable overcrowding, with over twenty thousand men confined in an area of ten acres—pitted the prisoners against each other. Not all could survive, however strong their faith. Thus, as Goss shows, they fought among themselves, and "the strong often tyrannized over the weak" (104). To protect themselves, the prisoners developed ways of punishing offenders. To raise money for a little extra food, they developed simple kinds of businesses. The prison became a grotesque microcosm of nineteenth-century capitalist society, where "rough native force or talent showed itself by ingenious devices for making the most of little" (104). This was a world, as Goss describes it, where what later became known as social Darwinism definitely prevailed. Only the fittest survived, and Goss devoted great attention to explaining the techniques of his own survival, both physical and psychological. He needed a bucket in which to cook, wash, and carry water—and with which to trade such services to others, for their services to him. He needed to sustain his spirit, by humor and some pleasant thoughts, and by keeping up his hopes of escape, exchange, or parole, but without becoming unrealistic. Finally, he had to restrain his humanitarian impulses to help those who were weaker, sicker, and hungrier than himself, since, if he did not, he would die, too. With these lessons, Goss also justified his survival, overcoming the guilt arising from the fact that he had survived where others had not. Then he went on, directly and indirectly, to teach similar lessons to the post-war American society.

In these Civil War autobiographies, therefore, we see the emergence of a demonstrably different concept of self. The universalism of Transcendentalists, abolitionists, and revivalists has been eliminated or subdued. Not even Walt Whitman retains the optimism he had before the war. *Specimen Days* is a book of much more detail, of the speci-men and other specifics, rather than glorious universals. And when he celebrates himself, it is the tireless, gray-headed, middle-aged male nurse whom he celebrates, not the boisterous young democract. This self, then, is a survivor and a teacher and a self-historian more than a great liberator. Similarly, Frederick Douglass in his last volume of autobiography, the *Life and Times . . .* , devotes much more attention to the unique record of his own life as a public figure than to himself as a victim of slavery. To some extent, of course, these differences are due to the fact that by the 1880s and 1890s Whitman and Douglass were older, well-recognized public men, which they had not been before the war. Their individual stories now held significant interest for many readers. However, what gave them the license to tell these stories, and the forms in which to tell them, were the developments in autobiography which had been introduced by books like Goss's *Story* and Grant's *Memoirs*. The mundane particulars— what Whitman had referred to in "Song of Myself" as "dinner, dress, associates, looks, compliments, dues"—which had once *not* been the real self, the "Me myself," and supposedly could not be recounted—were now a very large part of this new self, and could be, even had to be, recounted. Goss, Grant, Douglass, and Whitman had all survived to tell their tales, their *own* tales, and they could tell them with the expectation that book-buyers would want to read about them. Even people who had not been famous but had witnessed great events and survived could feel that their stories were important. Mary Boykin Chesnut, the wife of a Confederate leader, worked for years at revising and improving her diary and preparing it for publication, which it first received in 1905, nineteen years after her death. Other manuscripts were left with children and grandchildren or privately published and then placed in attics and state historical societies, preserved from a sense of patriotism and family piety. Cornelia Peake McDonald's story was first passed on just to her children. Her children then published a private edition of it for *their* children, but it was not printed in a public edition until 1992. Nevertheless, McDonald, like Chesnut and Goss, had felt that her story deserved being recorded and saved. Just having been a witness to the war and played a small part in it was reason enough.

The Self could become this more specific historical self because, as we noted before, these later autobiographers had less shame about it. The dark, evil self was no longer within but outside: in the shape, first, of the wartime enemy, and later in the shape simply of others different from "one's self" by virtue of race, sex, religion, class, education, or status. Autobiography and the Self had become, or were about to become, more racial, ethnic, and status-conscious.

These cultural and political valences of the self, as we might call them, were not new. They can be seen, for instance, in Thoreau's distinctions between himself and John Field, the impoverished Irish bogger, as also between Harriet Jacobs-Linda Brent and Mr. Flint, her mean and insensitive white master. But starting in the late 1880s with Lucy Larcom's *New England Girl-hood,* these valences also become associated with the past and with differences between the past of childhood and one's origins and the present, the time of composition, in a very different world. A wave of nostalgia was about to break on many Americans, and with it a discovery or rediscovery of childhood. And much of this nostalgia identified childhood with an innocent time before the war and before the ethnic multiplicity that had come with late nineteenth-century immigration.

Lucy Larcom did not have as sheltered and idyllic a girlhood as Lydia Sigourney's or Catherine Sedgwick's (whose *Life and Letters* was published in 1871). She grew up in the declining sailing port of Beverly, Massachusetts. The old New England Calvinism was also dying, and she did not regret it, though she fondly remembered the old hymns. The death of her father, a retired shipmaster, in 1835 when she was eleven, was a drastic blow to family status and security, and her mother moved to the milltown of Lowell, where she became housekeeper in one of the boardinghouses for the girl millworkers. Lucy, for her part, went to work in the mills.

Working in the mills of Lowell, Massachusetts, in the 1830s and '40s, before the arrival of thousands of immigrants, was a utopian experience, however. The girls came from farms and hilltowns from all over New England, and, according to Larcom, they were glad to leave those confined places, where the only paying jobs had been as serving girls. In this new, relatively cosmopolitan world they made more friends, and, thanks to the benevolence of the factory owners, went to lectures, night schools, and music classes. They also had a chance to write poems and edit their own magazines, which was Lucy's particular delight. In 1846, she had a chance to go to Illinois, where she completed her formal education, then returned to New England, where she later became a teacher at Wheaton Seminary in Norton, Massachusetts, and an editor for children's magazines. But the account given in *New England Girlhood* ends with 1852.

Although barely noticed, this is a significant date. Since the setting is nine years before the Civil War, Larcom could omit her later Unionist passions. It was also before the period of mass immigration that began in 1848 and became even greater in the 1880s. Larcom could, as it were, preserve, or recall the lost innocence of her "girlhood" in 1824–52. This faraway, almost utopian world was also the utopian "girlhood" of New England, just as Mark Twain's *Adventures of Tom Sawyer* (1876), *Life on the Mississippi* (1883), and *Adventures of Huckleberry Finn* (1884) evoked the "boyhood" of the Mississippi valley. Collectively, such autobiographies and autobiographical novels of childhood took their middle-class, Anglo-Saxon readers back to a seeming childhood of America, where there were no rumblings of war, immigrants, strikes, labor agitators, or tenements.

The next two or three decades saw the appearance of many of these nostalgic autobiographies of growing up: William Dean Howells's *My Year in a Log Cabin* (1893) and *Boy's Town* (1904), Edward Everett Hale's *New England Boyhood* (1893), Hamlin Garland's *Boy Life on the Prairie* (1899), Charles Eastman's *Indian Boyhood* (1902), and John Muir's *Story of My Boyhood and Youth* (1912). The early chapters of *The Education of Henry Adams* (written in 1906–7) and the whole of Henry James's *A Small Boy and Others* (1913) and *Notes of a Son and Brother* (1914) belong in this genre, too. The anti-Semitism of the *Education* and parts of James's *American Scene* are, therefore, not unique to James and Adams and their upperclass cohorts, but aspects of ethnic linkage and prejudice which had begun to be widespread. Ethnicity was presumably a matter of parentage and was normally simplest or purest in childhood. Yet, for ethnicity to be an issue, there had to be an awareness or later awareness of other ethnic heritages and types—valences to avoid as well as valences to bond to. Therefore, "native" ethnic pride, be it New

England, small-town Ohio, Prairie, Indian, or Negro, was but one feature among others involving various forms of ethno-centrism, ethnic anxiety, and ethnic prejudice.

Ethnicity was by no means the only theme in these reminiscences of girlhood and boyhood. A much older tradition, the success story, still endured, having been handed down from Franklin to Barnum to Horatio Alger's novels about Ragged Dick (a series started in 1867), Luck and Pluck (started in 1869), and Tattered Tom (started in 1871). This was the tradition picked up by Andrew Carnegie, perhaps because as a Scottish immigrant he wasn't so prepared to write what reviewers liked to call a "delightful reminiscence" of a native-born childhood. The memory Carnegie begins with is one which was also a "lesson": his father, who was a hand-loom weaver in Dunfermline, Scotland, returning "to our little home greatly distressed because there was no more work for him to do." Then and there, writes Carnegie the millionaire, "I resolved . . . that the wolf of poverty should be driven from our door someday, if I could do it."[8]

"How I Served My Apprenticeship" (1894) is thus not only a success story, but also a grim, bare-knuckled account of what Carnegie learned in the worlds of nineteenth-century capitalism and technological development. The story was archetypal: from bobbin boy to messenger boy to telegraph operator to assistant to the superintendent of the Pennsylvania Railroad. There is more to the story, however, because Carnegie's even greater pleasure was his investment in "ten shares in the Adams Express Company." This required his parents' mortgaging their house, but it succeeded, and it taught "how money could make money"—the lesson of a real businessman, by Carnegie's lights. Thus his "apprenticeship" was not in an old-fashioned handicraft or trade in the traditional sense, but in capitalism, which was a success story of its own, at least to its persuasive advocates and apologists.

Comparison of Carnegie's little autobiographical essay with these others and with the autobiographies of earlier generations could be lengthy. His autobiography does not celebrate America or virtue or religion or nature or benevolence and civic improvement so much as it celebrates business and capitalism. Carnegie's aim, as he notes in the closing passages of his story, is to be "working upon my own account . . . being my own master, . . . manufacturing something and giving employment to many men." This aim was apparently so socially accepted and easy to learn that he could direct his story even to children, for it appeared in *Youth's Companion*. Autobiography was again didactic, although, some people would say, no longer very moral. And any successful, surviving, self-teacher could write it.

8. Andrew Carnegie, "How I Served My Apprenticeship," *Youth's Companion* (April 23, 1896). See below, p. 436.

25

Warren Lee Goss (1835–1925)

from *The Soldier's Story*

The Soldier's Story was first published in 1866 and went through two more editions and fourteen additional printings, the last in 1876. Many editions included an appendix "containing the names of the Union soldiers who died at Andersonville," and some had a "presentation page," indicating that the book was used as a gift and memorial.

Goss was born in Brewster, Massachusetts, and educated at Pierce Academy in Middleboro. In 1860–61, he spent one year at Harvard Law School, after which he enlisted as a private in the engineer corps. *The Soldier's Story,* however, tells only of his military experience, beginning with his enlistment, his capture in 1862, and his first imprisonment at Libby Prison in Richmond, Virginia. Exchanged in the fall of 1862, he regained his health, and reenlisted in November, 1863, as a sergeant. In the spring of 1864, he was captured again and this time taken to Andersonville in southern Georgia.

Andersonville prison was one of the worst atrocities of the Civil War. It was still being written about in the 1950s, in MacKinlay Kantor's best-selling novel *Andersonville* and in *The Andersonville Trial,* a play based upon the trial and execution of Colonel Wirz, the commander. Goss satisfied the great curiosity about it and appealed to post-war, pro-Union and anti-Confederate sentiments, while generally avoiding sensationalism.

He describes Andersonville as a bare compound surrounded by a stockade fence. Most of the prisoners had no more shelter than tattered blankets supported by sticks. They cooked on open fires, eating meager rations of dried corn, beans, and sometimes a little meat. The barracks that once had been planned were built very late and in insufficient number (the South by that time being very short of men, funds, and supplies). The compound soon became massively overcrowded, and by August, 1864, held 31,000 men, nearly 3000 of whom died in that month alone. To escape, Goss and others dug tunnels, feigned death, and tried running off while outside on wood-gathering forays. Few succeeded, though Goss did once escape for a few days. In the fall he was among the "lucky ones" moved to a prison in Charleston, South Carolina, from which he was exchanged in December.

The chapter below, describing events near the beginning of his account of Andersonville, is typical in its emphasis on not just the conditions of the prison but also on the society and the survival strategies that grew up among the prisoners. As can be seen, he also attacks southern character and praises the prisoners' loyalty to the Union. But the overall message is that "Yankee ingenuity" and the New England and western character are what have been tested and have endured.

After the war, Goss became an editor and magazine writer and an author of children's novels and children's biographies of Grant and Sherman. He also held offices in veterans' organizations.

The selection here is Chapter 5 of *The Soldier's Story* (Boston: Lee and Shepard, 1866). There is no biography of Goss, though he did write a second autobiography, *Recollections of a Private* (1890).

> Prison Vocabulary.—Punishment of Larcenies.—Scenes of Violence.
> —Destitution provocative of Troubles.—Short Rations.—More
> Fights.—Advantages of Strength of Body and Mind.—New Stan-
> dards of Merit.—Ingenuity profitable.—Development of Faculties.—
> New Trades and Kinds of Business.—Cures for all Ills and Diseases.—
> Trading to get more Food.—Burden of Bad Habits.—Experience in
> Trade.—Stock in Trade eaten up by Partner.—A Shrewd Dealer de-
> stroys the Business.—Trading Exchange.—Excitement in the Issue of
> Rations.—A Starving Man killed.—His Murderer let off easy through
> Bribery.—Considerable Money in the Camp.—Tricks upon Rebel
> Traders in Prison.—Counterfeit or Altered Money disposed of.

The prison had a vocabulary of words peculiarly its own, which, if not new in themselves, were novel in their significance. A thief, for instance, was termed a "flanker," or a "half shave," the latter term originating in a wholesome custom, which prevailed in prison, of shaving the heads of those who were caught pilfering, on one side, leaving the other untouched. Thus they would remain sufficiently long to attract universal attention and derision. The shaving was a less punishment in itself than its final consequences, for a fellow with half-shaven crown was lucky if he escaped a beating or a ducking every hour of the day. Where a thief had the boldness to steal in open daylight, and by a dash, grab and run, to get off with his booty, he was termed a "raider," which was considered one grade above the sneaking "flanker." The articles stolen were usually cooking utensils, or blankets, for the want of which, many a man died. Either epithet, "flanker" or "raider," hurled at a fast-retreating culprit, would insure a general turnout in the vicinity, to stop the offender. If the thief had shrewdness, and was not too closely pursued, he often assumed a careless appearance, mingled unperceived with his pursuers, and joined in the "hue and cry." Woe to him who attracted suspicion by undue haste when such a cry was raised; for although his errand might be one of necessity or mercy, he was sure to be hurt before it was ascertained that he was not the offending person, and his only consolation was in the fact of his innocence, or the thought that his head, if some sorer, was wiser than before.

Scenes of violence were continually enacted in the prison. Murders that thrilled the blood with horror were at one time of frequent occurrence,—of which we shall speak more particularly in coming pages,—perpetrated by bands of desperadoes who jumped Uncle Sam's bounties before they were retained in the firm grasp of military vigilance, and, when fairly caught, rather than fight were taken prisoners voluntarily. Not an hour of the day passed without some terrible fight—often over trivial matters—taking place in the stockade. The reasons which provoked fights were not often plain; but one fact was ever apparent, viz., that hunger and privation did not sweeten sour tempers, or render the common disposition at all lamb-like. A piece of poor corn-bread, picked up in the dirt, a little Indian meal, or a meatless bone, which a dog or pig of New England extraction would turn up his nose at, would provoke violent discussions as to ownership, in which muscle, rather than equity, settled facts. Some of these personal encounters ended in a general fight, where all who were desirous of that kind of recreation took a part. It was quite a curious fact that when rations were scarcest in prison, fights were plentiest. In the absence of food, some took pleasure in beating each other. "I've not had anything to eat to-day, and would like to lick some varmint as has," said Kentucky Joe, a gaunt, half-starved, but never desponding fellow. "I'm your man," said Pat B., and at it they went, till Kentucky was beaten to his satisfaction, and acknowledged that "a 'varmint' who had eaten corn-dodger for breakfast was 'too much' for one 'as hadn't.'" The writer, seeing no fun in a muss, kept out of them, foreseeing misery enough, without a broken head to nurse. The great mass could ill afford to expend strength in such encounters, and it was usually easy to keep out of them without sneaking.

I have often, however, seen men who were weak with disease, and weak to such a degree that they could scarcely stand, engage in pugilistic encounters piteous to contemplate. I call to memory two almost skeleton men, whom I once saw engaged in fighting for the possession of a few pine knots! Bareheaded, in a broiling sun, barefooted, their clothes in tatters, they bit and scratched, and rolled in the dirt together. I left them, their hands clutched in each other's hair,—with barely remaining strength to rally a kick,—gazing into each other's eyes with the leaden, lustreless glare of famine stamped there—a look which I cannot describe, but which some comrade of misery will recognize.

The strong often tyrannized over the weak, and as we see it in all gatherings of men, the strong in physical health and in possessions kept their strength, while the many weak grew weaker and weaker, until they were crowded out of life into the small space grudgingly allowed them for graves. Each man stood or fell on merits different from those which had been valued by friends at home. He found himself measured by different standards of merit from those used in any of his previous walks of life. Rough native force or talent showed itself by ingenious devices for making the most of little. He who could make Indian meal and water into the most palatable form was "looked up to." He who could cook with little wood, and invent from the mud a fireplace in which to save fuel, was a genius! The producer of comforts from the squalid, crude material of life was respected as much as hunger would allow us to respect anything. He it was who got a start in the prison world, and managed to live.

It was desirable on the part of prisoners to follow some trade or occupation which should give to the individual means to purchase the few desirable luxuries which could be obtained of those who came into prison from among the rebels with permission to trade. By this method there were hopes of life, even if existence was misery. Yankee ingenuity was consequently taxed to the utmost to invent "from the rough" some kind of business that would pay—an onion, a potato, or an extra allowance of Indian meal per week. Under the fruitful maxim that "necessity is the mother of invention," it was surprising how trades and business started into life. Had these men been placed in a forest where raw material could readily be got at, I believe they would have produced every "item" of a city's wants, so well were we represented in the trades. The strivings for life were piteous, but often comical in their developments. Some traded their hats and boots, or a slyly-kept watch, for beans or flour, and with this elementary start began "sutlers' business." Another genius developed a process for converting Indian meal into beer, by souring it in water. And "sour beer," as it was termed, speedily became one of the institutions. This beer was vended around the camp by others, who pronounced it a cure for scurvy, colds, fever, gangrene, and all other ills the stockade was heir too, and they were many. You would at one part of the stockade hear a voice loudly proclaiming a cure for scurvy; you approach, and find him vending "sour beer;"—another proclaiming loudly a cure for diarrhœa; he would be selling "sour beer;" and so through a long catalogue of evils would be proclaimed their remedies.

One day I was almost crushed in a crowd who were attracted by a fellow crying aloud, "Stewed beans, with vinegar *on to um!*" The vinegar turned out to be "sour beer." Stuck upon a shingle I observed a sign which read, "Old Brewery; Bier for Sail, by the glass or bucketful, *hole sail,* retail, or no tail at all." I remember one ingenious fellow, who, with a jackknife and file and a few bits of wire, was engaged in getting into ticking order "played-out" watches, that had refused to go unless they were carried; and the ingenuity he displayed in coaxing them to tick was surprising. In one instance the watch tinker mentioned made for a friend of mine an entire watch-spring of whalebone, which set the watch ticking in such a tremendous manner, for a few minutes after being wound up, as to call forth the admiring ejaculation from the Secesh purchaser, "Gosh, how she does go it!" The watch stopped—"*rund* down," as the amazed Johnny afterwards said, "quicker nor a flash." You will readily understand that prisoners cared but little about watches except so far as they were tradable for Indian meal, hog, or hominy.

Another occupation was cooking beans and selling them by the plateful to such hungry ones as could afford to trade for them. Various were the means of "raising the wind" to obtain a supply to carry on the trade. Often some article of clothing, or buttons off the jacket, were traded for them. But a more common method was to trade the buttons or clothing for tobacco, and then trade tobacco for beans; for those addicted to the use of the weed would frequently remark that it was easier to go without a portion of their food, however scanty, than without their tobacco. In prison one thus paid the penalties of bad habits previously formed. One accustomed to the habit of taking a dram of something stimulating each day, died in prison for want of it. Habits, like chickens, "come home to roost," and were often the millstones that sunk their possessors into the hopeless misery which went before death. Thus, when only about half a pint of beans, uncooked, per day were issued, sometimes with a little bacon, men would lay aside a few each day to trade for tobacco.

The modes of selling were various; but the most common way of finding purchasers by those who had but a small capital of a few pints of beans, was to proceed to the principal thoroughfare,—for even here we were compelled to have paths unoccupied by recumbent men and their "traps," through a general understanding, or we should have continually trod on one another. Broadway, as we termed it, was the scene of most of the trading done in camp. The venders, sitting with their legs under them, like tailors, proclaimed loudly the quantity and quality of beans or mush they could sell for a stated price. Some would exultantly state that theirs had pepper and salt "on to um;" and sometimes vinegar was cried out as one of the virtues possessed by the vender of beans, and then there would be a rush to see, if not to eat. Sometimes I have seen on Broadway from fifty to seventy venders of beans, who, together with small gamblers with sweat-boards, on which could be staked five cents, and hasty-pudding dealers and sour beer sellers, all of whom sat on the ground, looking anxious, dirty, and hungry enough to make the hardest part of their task a resisting of the temptation to eat up their stock in trade. I cannot refrain from narrating my own experience in that line, it was so characteristic of experience common to those who engaged in like speculations.

Clifton V. and myself possessed a joint capital of an old watch, mention of which has been made, and a surplus of one pair of army shoes,— for I went barefoot, disdaining to abridge the freedom of my feet when it interfered with business. We invested them in beans, which were, like those usually issued, possessed, previous to our possession, by grubs and worms. The terms of our copartnership were, that he, "Cliff," was to do the selling, while I and a companion named Damon cooked, bargained for wood, and transacted the general business of the "concern." Accordingly Cliff showed his anxious face and raised his treble voice shrilly in the market-place. The first day's sale brought us about one pint of extra beans. The next day Cliff's hunger got the better of his judgment and firm resolve to be prudent, and he ate up near half our stock in trade, which was vexatious; but I could not reprove him, seeing how cheerful it made him feel, and how sorry he said he really was. Besides, his full stomach gave him rose-colored views of the morrow's trade.

The morrow came, and Cliff made a "ten-strike," selling off all the beans I could cook, and was beside himself at the prospects of our having enough to eat "right straight along." The next morning I invested largely in beans, in all about three quarts, wet measure, and borrowed a kettle that would cook about half of them, and paid for the convenience in trade. That day proved the ruin of the bean trade. Cliff came back despondently, declaring beans didn't sell; and the mystery was soon solved by the fact that on the south side of the branch they were issuing cooked beans. Whereupon, ascertaining beyond a doubt the truth of this, Cliff and myself sat down and ate one good square meal, did the same at supper time, finished them for breakfast next morning, and lived at least one day with full stomachs—a circumstance that seldom happened before or afterwards in our prison experience. Thus ended the bean trade.

After rations were issued, there would be a general meeting of a densely packed crowd, all trying to trade for something more palatable, or for that which they had not got. Some would cry out, "Who will trade cooked beans for raw?" "Who will trade wood for beans?" "Who will trade salt for wood?" while some speculator would trade little bits of tobacco for any kind of rations. The issue of rations was often a moment of fearful excitement. A crowd of five or six thousand, like a hungry pack of wolves, would fill the space before the gateway, all scrambling to get a look at the rations, as though even the sight of food did them good. At one time, during such a scene, one of the detailed men, who acted as a teamster,—and those so employed were always men that were loudest in blaming our government and "old Abe," and were insolent and well fed,—when one of the pack of hungry wretches put his hand out to clutch a falling crumb from the cart, the teamster beat his brains out with one blow of a club. He was tried by our stockade court of justice, (?) and condemned—to cart no more bread; owing, doubtless, to the fact of his having a few greenbacks, made in selling our rations.

Among the occupations of the prison was that of baker. The ovens were made of clay, kneaded and formed into bricks. The foundation was laid with those bricks while they were in a damp condition, being allowed to dry in the sun for two or three days, and then were ready as a basis for the oven. Sand was first carefully heaped upon the centre of the foundation, in shape of the interior of it, when done; over this mould the bricks were laid, and dried until the sand making the mould would bear removal, which was carefully done by the use of sticks, at the opening which was left for a door. A fire was then built inside, after which it was ready for use. There were only a favored few who got wood enough to consummate and carry on such an undertaking. The ovens described baked very good johnny-cake, and sometimes wheat biscuit. It was a convenience to be able to get rations cooked for three or four at halves. Thus our scanty rations often had to be diminished by one half, or eaten raw. There were others who followed the trade of bucket-makers, and very fair wooden buckets were made with no other tools than twine and a jackknife. As all water, with exceptional cases of those who owned wells, had to be brought from the brook,—often quite a distance for weak men to travel in the sun,—these were very desirable. There were several kettle-makers, who found material, somehow, of sheet tin and iron from the top of rail-cars, smuggled into prison by the rebels, who were fond of Yankee greenbacks. These were also a convenience to those who formed a mess, and made a saving of wood by cooking together. These kettles were made with no other implements than a common railroad spike. They were made in the manner government camp-kettles are made, by ingeniously bending the iron together in seams, in this manner rendering them water-tight without solder. Thus Yankee ingenuity developed resources where, at first sight, there seemed nothing but barrenness and misery. I never saw a friction-match in the stockade; I doubt if there were any; yet there were always fires somewhere,—how procured I could never understand, except on the supposition that they never went out.

I have entered thus minutely upon a description of these trades and occupations in prison, from the fact that it explains many apparently conflicting statements made by prisoners. While those thus engaged often got the means of subsistence, they were the exceptions of one to a thousand of the great mass of prisoners, who were daily perishing for want of food and from exposure. There was quite a sum of money circulating in camp, in the aggregate; but eventually it got into the hands of the Secesh, who were rabid for the possession of greenbacks. The rebels were constantly coming into the prison to trade, having first obtained permission of Wirz, the commandant of the "interior of the prison," as he was termed. They were fond of buying Yankee boots, watches, and buttons. All superfluous things, such as good caps, boots, &c., were freely traded in exchange for anything eatable, or for wood. One fact was quite observable—that when the Johnnies came in to trade the second time, they were sharper than they were at their first visit. The process of cutting their teeth was rather gradual; but after a while they would become a match at driving a sharp bargain with the sharpest kind of "Yanks," and prided themselves on what they termed Yankee tricks. Buttons were in great demand by them, especially New York and staff buttons, for which large prices were paid, and eagerly traded for.

On one occasion a Johnny came in to trade, who was evidently as unsophisticated and green as the vegetables he had for sale. He traded in the first place for a pair of army shoes, laid them down beside him, and while busy seeing to his "fixings," one of the boys passed the shoes around to a companion, who straight-way appeared in front, and before the Johnny had time to think of anything else, challenged his attention for a trade. A trade was agreed upon, and the price paid, before the Johnny found out that though progressing in trade, he had but one pair of shoes. So, for safety of these precious decorations, he picked them up, and holding them in his arms, indignantly declared, "Durned if I can trade with yourn Yanks in that sort o' way, no how." We were, according to his exposition of the matter, "rather considerable right smart at picking up traps what wan't thar own." He was thus entertaining the boys with these original views, when one of our fellows, just to clinch what had been so aptly stated by the chivalrous representative stepped up behind him and cut off four staff buttons, which adorned the rear of a long, swallow-tailed, butternut-colored, short-waisted coat. After executing this rear movement, he appeared in the crowd at the front, and offered them for sale. The Johnny took the bait, and traded his last vegetables for his own buttons, and started off highly pleased; and so were the boys. On the way out of prison our Secesh friend met a comrade, whose attention he called to the buttons, "like *um* he had on the tail" of his coat, whereupon his comrade looked behind, and informed him that "thar was not a durned button thar," when our trading Johnny loudly declared, with a rich sprinkling of oaths, that "these yere durned Yanks had orter have their ears buttoned back and be swallowed."

An Ohio boy at one time set himself up in the provision business by altering a greenback of one dollar into one hundred. We considered it fair to take every advantage of them we could contrive, and it amused us to hear them gravely charge us with want of honesty. Says one of them one day to me, "I've hearn that yourn Yanks, down thar whar you live, make wooden pumpkin seeds, and I'll be dod rot if I don't believe I got some of um and planted, a year afore this war, for not a durned one cum'd up 'cept what the pesky hins scratched up."

26

Walt Whitman (1819–1892)

from *Specimen Days*

In 1865, Whitman was fired from a clerkship in the Department of the Interior because the Secretary had been shown a copy of his poems, *Leaves of Grass*, and decided it was an immoral book. In response, his friend William O'Connor wrote (with Whitman's direction) a short apologia, *The Good Gray Poet* (1866), which portrayed him as a stalwart democrat who had served quietly and heroically all through the Civil War comforting wounded soldiers.

With *The Good Gray Poet*, Whitman's public image began to change from the sensual, rowdy, egotistical "rough" of *Leaves of Grass* to the martyred democratic saint, an image which served him very well for the rest of his life. It comported better with his middle age and with the fact that in 1873 he suffered a paralytic stroke. For his convalescence, Whitman left Washington and moved near his brother George in Camden, New Jersey, where he was visited by a growing number of English and American admirers. In the late 1870s he recovered further from the stroke by spending many months at Timber Creek, outside Camden.

Specimen Days (1882) is the "good grey poet's" memoir. It preserves the memories and images for which he wanted to be known and omitted (by its "skips and jumps") the supposedly immoral and more cosmic, tormented Whitman. It also preserved his voice, for there is a striking correlation between the book's material and method and the narrator's persona. Thus, its artifices of carelessness, kindness, and healthy and loving impulsiveness reveal as well as conceal. Whitman's service in the hospitals was indeed heroic—and a socially acceptable expression of his male amativeness, as he called his homosexual love. *Specimen Days* is the work of someone who had survived war, paralysis, public attack, and the risks in his own nature, and had grown into an older, mellower, and even more complex and accomplished man. Whitman sketches the contents of *Specimen Days*, which vary considerably, in footnote 1, included here but adjusted (in brackets) to indicate contents by sections rather than pages.

The standard biography of Whitman is Gay Wilson Allen's *Solitary Singer* (New York: New York Univ. Press, 1967). A scholarly edition of *Specimen Days* was prepared by Floyd Stovall for *The Collected Writings of Walt Whitman* and published by New York University Press in 1963.

A Happy Hour's Command

Down in the Woods, July 2d, 1882.—If I do it at all I must delay no longer. Incongruous and full of skips and jumps as is that huddle of diary-jottings, war-memoranda of 1862–'65, Nature-notes of 1877–'81, with Western and Canadian observations afterwards, all bundled up and tied by a big string, the resolution and indeed mandate comes to me this day, this hour,—(and what a day! what an hour just passing! the luxury of riant grass and blowing breeze, with all the shows of sun and sky and perfect temperature, never before so filling me body and soul)—to go home, untie the bundle, reel out diary-scraps and memoranda, just as they are, large or small, one after another, into print-pages,[1] and let the melange's lacking and wants of connection take care of themselves. It will illustrate one phase of humanity anyhow; how few of life's days and hours (and they not by relative value or proportion, but by chance) are ever noted. Probably another point too, how we give long preparations for some object, planning and delving and fashioning, and then, when the actual hour for doing arrives, find ourselves still quite unprepared, and tumble the thing together, letting hurry and crudeness tell the story better

---

1. These first three sections are nearly verbatim an off-hand letter of mine in January, 1882, to an insisting friend. Following, I give some gloomy experiences. The war of attempted secession has, of course, been the distinguishing event of my time. I commenced at the close of 1862, and continued steadily through '63, '64, and '65, to visit the sick and wounded of the army, both on the field and in the hospitals in and around Washington city. From the first I kept little note-books for impromptu jottings in pencil to refresh my memory of names and circumstances, and what was specially wanted, &c. In these I brief'd cases, persons, sights, occurrences in camp, by the bedside, and not seldom by the corpses of the dead. Some were scratch'd down from narratives I heard and itemized while watching, or waiting, or tending somebody amid those scenes. I have dozens of such little note-books left, forming a special history of those years, for myself alone, full of associations never to be possibly said or sung. I wish I could convey to the reader the associations that attach to these soil'd and creas'd livraisons, each composed of a sheet or two of paper, folded small to carry in the pocket, and fasten'd with a pin. I leave them just as I threw them by after the war, blotch'd here and there with more than one blood-stain, hurriedly written, sometimes at the clinique, not seldom amid the excitement of uncertainty, or defeat, or of action, or getting ready for it, or a march. Most of the pages from "The Stupor Passes" to and including "Typical Sodiers" are verbatim copies of those lurid and blood-smutch'd little note-books.

Very different are most of the memoranda that follow. Some time after the war ended I had a paralytic stroke, which prostrated me for several years. In 1876 I began to get over the worst of it. From this date, portions of several seasons, especially summers, I spent at a secluded haunt down in Camden county, New Jersey—Timber creek, quite a little river (it enters from the great Delaware, twelve miles away)—with primitive solitudes, winding stream, recluse and woody banks, sweet-feeding springs, and all the charms that birds, grass, wild-flowers, rabbits and squirrels, old oaks, walnut trees, &c., can bring. Through these times, and on these spots, the diary from "The Oaks and I" . . . onward was mostly written.

I suppose I publish and leave the whole gathering, first, from that eternal tendency to perpetuate and preserve which is behind all Nature, authors included; second, to symbolize two or three specimen interiors, personal and other, out of the myriads of my time, the middle range of the Nineteenth century in the New World; a strange, unloosen'd, wondrous time. But the book is probably without any definite purpose that can be told in a statement.

than fine work. At any rate I obey my happy hour's command, which seems curiously imperative. May-be, if I don't do anything else, I shall send out the most wayward, spontaneous, fragmentary book ever printed.

Answer to an Insisting Friend

You ask for items, details of my early life—of genealogy and parentage, particularly of the women of my ancestry, and of its far back Netherlands stock on the maternal side—of the region where I was born and raised, and my father and mother before me, and theirs before them—with a word about Brooklyn and New York cities, the times I lived there as lad and young man. You say you want to get at these details mainly as the go-befores and embryons of "Leaves of Grass." Very good; you shall have at least some specimens of them all. I have often thought of the meaning of such things—that one can only encompass and complete matters of that kind by exploring behind, perhaps very far behind, themselves directly, and so into their genesis, antecedents, and cumulative stages. Then as luck would have it, I lately whiled away the tedium of a week's half-sickness and confinement, by collating these very items for another (yet unfulfill'd, probably abandon'd,) purpose; and if you will be satisfied with them, authentic in date-occurrence and fact simply, and told my own way, garrulous-like, here they are. I shall not hesitate to make extracts, for I catch at any thing to save labor; but those will be the best versions of what I want to convey.

My Passion for Ferries

Living in Brooklyn or New York city from this time forward, my life, then, and still more the following years, was curiously identified with Fulton ferry, already becoming the greatest of its sort in the world for general importance, volume, variety, rapidity, and picturesqueness. Almost daily, later, ('50 to '60,) I cross'd on the boats, often up in the pilot-houses where I could get a full sweep, absorbing shows, accompaniments, surroundings. What oceanic currents, eddies, underneath—the great tides of humanity also, with ever-shifting movements. Indeed, I have always had a passion for ferries; to me they afford inimitable, streaming, never-failing, living poems. The river and bay scenery, all about New York island, any time of a fine day—the hurrying, splashing sea-tides—the changing panorama of steamers, all sizes, often a string of big ones outward bound to distant ports—the myriads of white-sail'd schooners, sloops, skiffs, and the marvellously beautiful yachts—the majestic sound boats as they rounded the Battery and came along towards 5, afternoon, eastward bound—the prospect off toward Staten island, or down the Narrows, or the other way up the Hudson—what refreshment of spirit such sights and experiences gave me years ago (and many a time since.) My old pilot friends, the Balsirs, Johnny Cole, Ira Smith, William White, and my young ferry friend, Tom Gere—how well I remember them all.

The Stupor Passes—Something Else Begins

But the hour, the day, the night pass'd, and whatever returns, an hour, a day, a night like that can never again return. The President, recovering himself, begins that very night—sternly, rapidly sets about the task of reorganizing his forces, and placing himself in positions for future and surer work. If there were nothing else of Abraham Lincoln for history to stamp him with, it is enough to send him with his wreath to the memory of all future time, that he endured that hour, that day, bitterer than gall—indeed a crucifixion day— that it did not conquer him—that he unflinchingly stemm'd it, and resolv'd to lift himself and the Union out of it.

Then the great New York papers at once appear'd (commencing that evening, and following it up the next morning, and incessantly through many days afterwards,) with leaders that rang out over the land with the loudest, most reverberating ring of clearest bugles, full of encouragement, hope, inspiration, unfaltering defiance. Those magnificent editorials! they never flagg'd for a fortnight. The "Herald" commenced them—I remember the articles well. The "Tribune" was equally cogent and inspiriting—and the "Times," "Evening Post," and other principal papers, were not a whit behind. They came in good time, for they were needed. For in the humiliation of Bull Run, the popular feeling north, from its extreme of superciliousness, recoil'd to the depth of gloom and apprehension.

(Of all the days of the war, there are two especially I can never forget. Those were the day following the news, in New York and Brooklyn, of that first Bull Run defeat, and the day of Abraham Lincoln's death. I was home in Brooklyn on both occasions. The day of the murder we heard the news very early in the morning. Mother prepared breakfast—and other meals afterwards—as usual; but not a mouthful was eaten all day by either of us. We each drank half a cup of coffee; that was all. Little was said. We got every newspaper morning and evening, and the frequent extras of that period, and pass'd them silently to each other.)

Down at the Front

Falmouth, Va., opposite Fredericksburgh, December 21, 1862.—Begin my visits among the camp hospitals in the army of the Potomac. Spend a good part of the day in a large brick mansion on the banks of the Rappahannock, used as a hospital since the battle—seems to have receiv'd only the worst cases. Out doors, at the foot of a tree, within ten yards of the front of the house, I notice a heap of amputated feet, legs, arms, hands, &c., a full load for a one-horse cart. Several dead bodies lie near, each cover'd with its brown woolen blanket. In the door-yard, towards the river, are fresh graves, mostly of officers, their names on pieces of barrel-staves or broken boards, stuck in the dirt. (Most of these bodies were subsequently taken up and transported north to their friends.) The large mansion is quite crowded upstairs and down, everything impromptu, no system, all bad enough, but I have no doubt the best that can be done; all the wounds pretty bad, some frightful, the men in their old clothes, unclean and bloody. Some of the wounded are rebel soldiers and officers, prisoners. One, a Mississippian, a captain, hit badly in leg, I talk'd with some time; he ask'd me for papers, which I gave him. (I saw him three months afterward in Washington, with his leg amputated, doing well.) I went through the rooms, downstairs and up. Some of the men were dying. I had nothing to give at that visit, but wrote a few letters to folks home, mothers, &c. Also talk'd to three or four, who seem'd most susceptible to it, and needing it.

After First Fredericksburg

December 23 to 31.—The results of the late battle are exhibited everywhere about here in thousands of cases, (hundreds die every day,) in the camp, brigade, and division hospitals. These are merely tents, and sometimes very poor ones, the wounded lying on the ground, lucky, if their blankets are spread on layers of pine or hemlock twigs, or small leaves. No cots; seldom even a mattress. It is pretty cold. The ground is frozen hard, and there is occasional snow. I go around from one case to another. I do not see that I do much good to these wounded and dying; but I cannot leave them. Once in a while some youngster holds on to me convulsively, and I do what I can for him; at any rate, stop with him and sit near him for hours, if he wishes it.

Besides the hospitals, I also go occasionally on long tours through the camps, talking with the men, &c. Sometimes at night among the groups around the fires, in their shebang enclosures of bushes. These are curious shows, full of characters and groups. I soon get acquainted anywhere in camp, with officers or men, and am always well used. Sometimes I go down on picket with the regiment I know best. As to rations, the army here at present seems to be tolerably well supplied, and the men have enough, such as it is, mainly salt pork and hard tack. Most of the regiments lodge in the flimsy little sheltertents. A few have built themselves huts of logs and mud, with fire-places.

Patent-Office Hospital

February 23.—I must not let the great hospital at the Patent-office pass away without some mention. A few weeks ago the vast area of the second story of that noblest of Washington buildings was crowded close with rows of sick, badly wounded and dying soldiers. They were placed in three very large apartments. I went there many times. It was a strange, solemn, and, with all its features of suffering and death, a sort of fascinating sight. I go sometimes at night to soothe and relieve particular cases. Two of the immense apartments are fill'd with high and ponderous glass cases, crowded with models in miniature of every kind of utensil, machine or invention, it ever enter'd into the mind of man to conceive; and with curiosities and foreign presents. Between these cases are lateral openings, perhaps eight feet wide and quite deep, and in these were placed the sick, besides a great long double row of them up and down through the middle of the hall. Many of them were very bad cases, wounds and amputations. Then there was a gallery running above the hall in which there were beds also. It was, indeed, a curious scene, especially at night when lit up. The glass cases, the beds, the forms lying there, the gallery above, and the marble pavement under foot—the suffering, and the fortitude to bear it in various degrees—occasionally, from some, the groan that could not be repress'd—sometimes a poor fellow dying, with emaciated face and glassy eye, the nurse by his side, the doctor also there, but no friend, no relative—such were the sights but lately in the Patent-office. (The wounded have since been removed from there, and it is now vacant again.)

The White House by Moonlight

February 24th.—A spell of fine soft weather. I wander about a good deal, sometimes at night under the moon. To-night took a long look at the President's house. The white portico—the palace-like, tall, round columns, spotless as snow—the walls also—the tender and soft moonlight, flooding the pale marble, and making peculiar faint languishing shades, not shadows—everywhere a soft transparent hazy, thin, blue moon-lace, hanging in the air—the brilliant and extra-plentiful clusters of gas, on and around the façade, columns, portico, &c.—everything so white, so marbly pure and dazzling, yet soft—the White House of future poems, and of dreams and dramas, there in the soft and copious moon—the gorgeous front, in the trees, under the lustrous flooding moon, full of reality, full of illusion—the forms of the trees, leafless, silent, in trunk and myriad-angles of branches, under the stars and sky—the White House of the land, and of beauty and night—sentries at the gates, and by the portico, silent, pacing there in blue overcoats—stopping you not at all, but eyeing you with sharp eyes, whichever way you move.

An Army Hospital Ward

Let me specialize a visit I made to the collection of barrack-like one-story edifices, Campbell hospital, out on the flats, at the end of the then horse railway route, one Seventh street. There is a long building appropriated to each ward. Let us go into ward 6. It contains to-day, I should judge, eighty or a hundred patients, half sick, half wounded. The edifice is nothing but boards, well whitewash'd inside, and the usual slender-framed iron bedsteads, narrow and plain. You walk down the central passage, with a row on either side, their feet towards you, and their heads to the wall. There are fires in large stoves, and the prevailing white of the walls is reliev'd by some ornaments, stars, circles, &c., made of evergreens. The view of the whole edifice and occupants can be taken at once, for there is no partition. You may hear groans or other sounds of unendurable suffering from two or three of the cots, but in the main there is quiet—almost a painful absence of demonstration; but the pallid face, the dull'd eye, and the moisture on the lip, are demonstration enough. Most of these sick or hurt are evidently young fellows from the country, farmers' sons, and such like. Look at the fine large frames, the bright and broad countenances, and the many yet lingering proofs of strong constitution and physique. Look at the patient and mute manner of our American wounded as they lie in such a sad collection; representatives from all New England, and from New York, and New Jersey, and Pennsylvania—indeed from all the States and all the cities—largely from the west. Most of them are entirely without friends or acquaintances here—no familiar face, and hardly a word of judicious sympathy or cheer, through their sometimes long and tedious sickness, or the pangs of aggravated wounds.

A Glimpse of War's Hell-Scenes

In one of the late movements of our troops in the valley, (near Upperville, I think,) a strong force of Moseby's mounted guerillas attack'd a train of wounded, and the guard of cavalry convoying them. The ambulances contain'd about 60 wounded, quite a number of them officers of rank. The rebels were in strength, and the capture of the train and its partial guard after a short snap was effectually accomplish'd. No sooner had our men surrender'd, the rebels instantly commenced robbing the train and murdering their prisoners, even the wounded. Here is the scene or a sample of it, ten minutes after. Among the wounded officers in the ambulances were one, a lieutenant of regulars, and another of higher rank. These two were dragg'd out on the ground on their backs, and were now surrounded by the guerillas, a demoniac crowd, each member of which was stabbing them in different parts of their bodies. One of the officers had his feet pinn'd firmly to the ground by bayonets stuck through them and thrust into the ground. These two officers, as afterwards found on examination, had receiv'd about twenty such thrusts, some of them through the mouth, face, &c. The wounded had all been dragg'd (to give a better chance also for plunder,) out of their wagons; some had been effectually dispatch'd, and their bodies were lying there lifeless and bloody. Others, not yet dead, but horribly mutilated, were moaning

389

or groaning. Of our men who surrender'd, most had been thus maim'd or slaughter'd.

At this instant a force of our cavalry, who had been following the train at some interval, charged suddenly upon the secesh captors, who proceeded at once to make the best escape they could. Most of them got away, but we gobbled two officers and seventeen men, in the very acts just described. The sight was one which admitted of little discussion, as may be imagined. The seventeen captur'd men and two officers were put under guard for the night, but it was decided there and then that they should die. The next morning the two officers were taken in the town, separate places, but in the centre of the street, and shot. The seventeen men were taken to an open ground, a little one side. They were placed in a hollow square, half-encompass'd by two of our cavalry regiments, one of which regiments had three days before found the bloody corpses of three of their men hamstrung and hung up by the heels to limbs of trees by Moseby's guerillas, and the other had not long before had twelve men, after surrendering, shot and then hung by the neck to limbs of trees, and jeering inscriptions pinn'd to the breast of one of the corpses, who had been a sergeant. Those three, and those twelve, had been found, I say, by these environing regiments. Now, with revolvers, they form'd the grim cordon of the seventeen prisoners. The latter were placed in the midst of the hollow square, unfasten'd, and the ironical remark made to them that they were now to be given "a chance for themselves." A few ran for it. But what use? From every side the deadly pills came. In a few minutes the seventeen corpses strew'd the hollow square. I was curious to know whether some of the Union soldiers, some few, (some one or two at least of the youngsters,) did not abstain from shooting on the helpless men. Not one. There was no exultation, very little said, almost nothing, yet every man there contributed his shot.

Multiply the above by scores, aye hundreds—verify it in all the forms that different circumstances, individuals, places, could afford—light it with every lurid passion, the wolf's, the lion's lapping thirst for blood—the passionate, boiling volcanoes of human revenge for comrades, brothers slain—with the light of burning farms, and heaps of smutting, smouldering black embers— and in the human heart everywhere black, worse embers—and you have an inkling of this war.

Gifts—Money—Discrimination

As a very large proportion of the wounded came up from the front without a cent of money in their pockets, I soon discover'd that it was about the best thing I could do to raise their spirits, and show them that somebody cared for them, and practically felt a fatherly or brotherly interest in them, to give them small sums in such cases, using tact and discretion about it. I am regularly supplied with funds for this purpose by good women and men in Boston, Salem, Providence, Brooklyn, and New York. I provide myself with a quantity of bright new ten-cent and five-cent bills, and, when I think it incumbent, I give 25 or 30 cents, or perhaps 50 cents, and occasionally a still larger sum to some particular case. As I have started this subject, I take opportunity to ventilate the financial question. My supplies, altogether voluntary, mostly confidential, often seeming quite Providential, were numerous and varied. For instance, there were two distant and wealthy ladies, sisters, who sent regularly, for two years, quite heavy sums, enjoining that their names should be kept secret. The same delicacy was indeed a frequent condition. From several I had *carte blanche*. Many were entire strangers. From these sources, during from two to three years, in the manner described, in the hospitals, I bestowed, as almoner for others, many, many thousands of dollars. I learn'd one thing conclusively—that beneath all the ostensible greed and heartlessness of our times there is no end to the generous benevolence of men and women in the United States, when once sure of their object. Another thing became clear to me—while *cash* is not amiss to bring up the rear, tact and magnetic sympathy and unction are, and ever will be, soverign still.

Typical Soldiers

Even the typical soldiers I have been personally intimate with,—it seems to me if I were to make a list of them it would be like a city directory. Some few only have I mention'd in the foregoing pages—most are dead—a few yet living. There is Reuben Farwell, of Michigan, (little 'Mitch;') Benton H. Wilson, color-bearer, 185th New York; Wm. Stansberry; Manvill Winterstein, Ohio; Bethuel Smith; Capt. Simms, of 51st New York, (kill'd at Petersburgh mine explosion,) Capt. Sam. Pooley and Lieut. Fred. McReady, same reg't. Also, same reg't., my brother, George W. Whitman—in active service all through, four years, re-enlisting twice—was promoted, step by step, (several times immediately after battles,) lieutenant, captain, major and lieut. colonel—was in the actions at Roanoke, Newbern, 2d Bull Run, Chantilly, South Mountain, Antietam, Fredericksburgh, Vicksburgh, Jackson, the bloody conflicts of the Wilderness, and at Spottsylvania, Cold Harbor, and afterwards around Petersburgh; at one of these latter was taken prisoner, and pass'd four or five months in secesh military prisons, narrowly escaping with life, from a severe fever, from starvation and half-nakedness in the winter. (What a history that 51st New York had! Went out early—march'd, fought everywhere—was in storms at sea, nearly wreck'd—storm'd forts—tramp'd hither and yon in Virginia, night and day, summer of '62—afterwards Kentucky and Mississippi—re-enlisted—was in all the engagements and campaigns, as above.) I strengthen and comfort myself much with the certainty that the capacity for just such regiments, (hundreds, thousands of them) is inexhaustible in the

United States, and that there isn't a county nor a township in the republic—nor a street in any city—but could turn out, and, on occasion, would turn out, lots of just such typical soldiers, whenever wanted.

The Oaks and I

Sept. 5, '77.—I write this, 11 A.M., shelter'd under a dense oak by the bank, where I have taken refuge from a sudden rain. I came down here, (we had sulky drizzles all the morning, but an hour ago a lull,) for the before-mention'd daily and simple exercise I am fond of—to pull on that young hickory sapling out there—to sway and yield to its tough-limber upright stem—haply to get into my old sinews some of its elastic fibre and clear sap. I stand on the turf and take these health-pulls moderately and at intervals for nearly an hour, inhaling great draughts of fresh air. Wandering by the creek, I have three or four naturally favorable spots where I rest—besides a chair I lug with me and use for more deliberate occasions. At other spots convenient I have selected, besides the hickory just named, strong and limber boughs of beech or holly, in easy-reaching distance, for my natural gymnasia, for arms, chest, trunk-muscles. I can soon feel the sap and sinew rising through me, like mercury to heat. I hold on boughs or slender trees caressingly there in the sun and shade, wrestle with their innocent stalwartness—and *know* the virtue thereof passes from them into me. (Or may-be we interchange—may-be the trees are more aware of it all then I ever thought.)

But now pleasantly imprison'd here under the big oak—the rain dripping, and the sky cover'd with leaden clouds—nothing but the pond on one side, and the other a spread of grass, spotted with the milky blossoms of the wild carrot—the sound of an axe wielded at some distant wood-pile—yet in this dull scene, (as most folks would call it,) why am I so (almost) happy here and alone? Why would any intrusion, even from people I like, spoil the charm? But am I alone? Doubtless there comes a time—perhaps it has come to me—when one feels through his whole being, and pronouncedly the emotional part, that identity between himself subjectively and Nature objectively which Schelling and Fichte are so fond of pressing. How it is I know not, but I often realize a presence here—in clear moods I am certain of it, and neither chemistry nor reasoning nor aesthetics will give the least explanation. All the past two summers it has been strengthening and nourishing my sick body and soul, as never before. Thanks, invisible physician, for thy silent delicious medicine, the day and night, thy waters and thy airs, the banks, the grass, the trees, and e'en the weeds!

Nights on the Mississippi

Oct. 29th, 30th, and 31st.—Wonderfully fine, with the full harvest moon, dazzling and silvery. I have haunted the river every night lately, where I could get a look at the bridge by moonlight. It is indeed a structure of perfection and beauty unsurpassable, and I never tire of it. The river at present is very low; I noticed to-day it had much more of a blue-clear look than usual. I hear the slight ripples, the air is fresh and cool, and the view, up or down, wonderfully clear, in the moonlight. I am out pretty late: it is so fascinating, dreamy. The cool night-air, all the influences, the silence, with those far-off eternal stars, do me good. I have been quite ill of late. And so, well-near the centre of our national demesne, these night views of the Mississippi.

Upon Our Own Land

"Always, after supper, take a walk half a mile long," says an old proverb, dryly adding, "and if convenient let it be upon your own land." I wonder does any other nation but ours afford opportunity for such a jaunt as this? Indeed has any previous period afforded it? No one, I discover, begins to know the real geographic, democratic, indissoluble American Union in the present, or suspect it in the future, until he explores these Central States, and dwells awhile observantly on their prairies, or amid their busy towns, and the mighty father of waters. A ride of two or three thousand miles, "on one's own land," with hardly a disconnection, could certainly be had in no other place than the United States, and at no period before this. If you want to see what the railroad is, and how civilization and progress date from it—how it is the conqueror of crude nature, which it turns to man's use, both on small scales and on the largest—come hither to inland America.

I return'd home, east, Jan. 5, 1880, having travers'd, to and fro and across, 10,000 miles and more. I soon resumed my seclusions down in the woods, or by the creek, or gaddings about cities, and an occasional disquisition, as will be seen following.

27

Mary Boykin Chesnut (1823–1886)

from *Diary during the War*

The wife of James Chesnut, who was a U.S. senator from South Carolina and later an aide to Jefferson Davis and a brigadier general in the Confederate Army, Mary Boykin Chesnut was ideally situated to keep a diary of life among the leaders of the South. Moreover, she was well-educated, loved novels (especially Thackeray's *Vanity Fair*), loved society, and had a very independent mind.

She also liked to write, and she recognized the historical significance of her experience and its literary potential—traits which were, paradoxically, both advantages and disadvantages, both supportive and contradictory. As her modern editor C. Vann Woodward has shown, what earlier editors had assumed was a "diary" in the conventional sense of a notebook made up of daily, sequential entries was actually a much improved, literary revision of earlier diaries, with the rewriting having been done between 1881 and 1884. Yet the polished version still looked like a diary, in forty-eight copybooks covering the period from February, 1861, to July, 1865, except for a break from August, 1862, to October, 1863, with the whole comprising a total of over twenty-five hundred pages. The break was caused by her having destroyed the notes for that period because of a raid on Richmond in 1863, but the gap was filled in by a 200-page narrative, done from memory, which was presented as if done in October, 1863.

For a full discussion of this complex compositional history, readers should see Woodward's long introduction to *Mary Chesnut's Civil War*. Her diary/autobiography also deserves reading in its entirety, both for its record of the war and for its reflection of her alert and caustic personality. Fortunately, however, even short excerpts of her book are very rich and suggestive. Her stories are usually brief, her wit sharp. Good stories and well-turned phrases were the delight of society— they were what made life in Charleston or Richmond so much more pleasant than life on a plantation or in a small town, and they were also what made memories of 1861–65 so important to preserve and distill after defeat. Chesnut's husband's words at the end of the diary, "Camden for life," suggest what punishment it was for her to be away from society and its gossip.

Reprinted from *Mary Chesnut's Civil War*, ed. C. Vann Woodward (New Haven: Yale Univ. Press, 1981). Copyright 1981 C. Vann Woodward, Sally Bland Metts, Barbara G. Carpenter, Sally Bland Johnson, and Katherine W. Herbert. Reprinted by permission of Yale University Press.

For more on Chesnut's life, see Elizabeth Muhlenfeld, *Mary Boykin Chesnut: A Biography* (Baton Rouge: Louisiana State Univ. Press, 1981). The excerpts below are from daily entries as these are given in C. Vann Woodward, ed., *Mary Chesnut's Civil War* (New Haven: Yale Univ. Press, 1981). All footnotes and bracketed editorial material are from that edition.

February 19, 1861. I left the brand-new Confederacy making—or remodeling—its Constitution. Everybody wanted Mr. Davis to be general in chief or president.

Keitt and Boyce[1] and a party preferred Howell Cobb[2] for president. And the fire-eaters per se wanted Barnwell Rhett.

I am despondent once more. If I thought them in earnest because they put their best in front, *at first*—what now? We have to meet tremendous odds by pluck, activity, zeal, dash, endurance of the toughest, military instinct. We had to choose the born leaders of men, people who could attract love and trust. Everywhere political intrigue is as rife as in Washington.

• • •

I wonder if it be a sin to think slavery a curse to any land. Sumner said not one word of this hated institution which is not true. Men and women are punished when their masters and mistresses are brutes and not when they do wrong—and then we live surrounded by prostitutes. An abandoned woman is sent out of any decent house elsewhere. Who thinks any worse of a negro or mulatto woman for being a thing we can't name? God forgive us, but ours is a *monstrous* system and wrong and iniquity. Perhaps the rest of the world is as bad—this *only* I see. Like the patriarchs of old our men live all in one house with their wives and their concubines, and the mulattoes one sees in every family exactly resemble the white children—and every lady tells you who is the father of all the mulatto children in everybody's household, but those in her own she seems to think drop from the clouds, or pretends so to think. Good women we have, *but* they talk of all *nastiness*—tho' they never do wrong, they talk day and night of [*erasures illegible save for the words* "all unconsciousness"] my disgust sometimes is boiling over—but they are, I believe, in conduct the purest women God ever made. Thank God for my countrywomen—alas for the men! No worse than men everywhere, but the lower their mistresses, the more degraded they must be.

My mother-in-law told me when I was first married not to send my female servants in the street on errands. They were then tempted, led astray—and

1. Lawrence Massillon Keitt of Orangeburg and William Waters Boyce of Edgefield, S.C. Both men were former U.S. congressmen and delegates to the Montgomery convention.
2. Howell Cobb, a former congressman, governor of Ga., and secretary of the treasury in the Buchanan administration, was chairman of the Montgomery convention and president of the Provisional Confederate Congress.

then she said placidly, so they told *me* when I came here, and I was very particular, *but you see with what result.*

Mr. Harris said it was so patriarchal. So it is—flocks and herds and slaves—and wife Leah does not suffice. Rachel must be *added,* if not *married.*[3] And all the time they seem to think themselves patterns—models of husbands and fathers.

Mrs. Davis told me everybody described my husband's father as an odd character—"a millionaire who did nothing for his son whatever, left him to struggle with poverty, &c." I replied—"Mr. Chesnut Senior thinks himself the best of fathers—and his son thinks likewise. I have nothing to say—but it is true. He has no money but what he makes as a lawyer." And again I say, my countrywomen are as pure as angels, tho' surrounded by another race who are the social evil!

June 28, 1861. In Mrs. Davis's drawing room last night, the president took a seat beside me on the sofa where I sat. He talked for nearly an hour. He laughed at our faith in our own powers. We are like the British. We think every Southerner equal to three Yankees at least. We will have to be equivalent to a dozen now. After his experience of the fighting qualities of Southerners in Mexico, he believes that we will do all that can be done by pluck and muscle, endurance, and dogged courage—dash and red-hot patriotism, &c. And yet his tone was not sanguine. There was a sad refrain running through it all. For one thing, either way, he thinks it will be a long war. That floored me at once. It has been too long for me already. Then said: before the end came, we would have many a bitter experience. He said only fools doubted the courage of the Yankees or their willingness to fight when they saw fit. And now we have stung their pride—we have roused them till they will fight like devils.

He said Mr. Chesnut's going as A.D.C. to Beauregard was a mistake. He ought to raise a regiment of his own. (So he ought!)

July 7, 1861. Lincoln wants four hundred millions of money—and men in proportion.

Can he get them?

He will find us a heavy handful.

Midnight. I hear Maria's guns.

We are always picking up some good thing of the rough Illinoisian's saying.

Lincoln objects to some man.

"Oh, he is too *interruptious.*"

3. In Genesis 29–30, Jacob, unhappy with his wife Leah, also marries her sister Rachel. He has children by both women and by their handmaidens as well. M. B. C. apparently believed old Mr. Chesnut had children by a slave whom she calls "Rachel." She confesses no such suspicions of her husband.

That is a horrid style of man or woman. The "interruptious"—I know the thing but had no name for it before.

July 24, 1861. Dr. Gibbes says he was at a country house near Manassas when a Federal soldier who had lost his way came in, exhausted. He asked for brandy, which the lady of the house gave him. Upon second thought he declined it. She brought it to him so promptly, he said he thought it might be poisoned. His mind was.

She was enraged.

"Sir, I am a Virginia woman. Do you think I could be as base as that? Here—Bill, Tom, disarm this man. He is our prisoner." The negroes came running, and the man surrendered without more ado. Another Federal was drinking at the well. A negro girl said, "You go in and see Missis." The man went in, and she followed crying triumphantly, "Look here—Missis, I got a prisoner too!"

They were not ripe for John Brown, you see.

This lady sent in her two prisoners, and Beauregard complimented her on her pluck and patriotism and presence of mind.

These negroes were rewarded by their owners. Now if slavery is as disagreeable as we think it, why don't they all march over the border, where they would be received with open arms? It amazes me. I am always studying these creatures. They are to me inscrutable in their ways and past finding out.

Dr. Gibbes says the faces of the dead grow as black as charcoal on the battlefield, and they shine in the sun.

Now this horrible vision of the dead on the battlefield haunts me.

August 23, 1861. But oh, such a day! since I wrote this morning.

Have been with Mrs. Randolph to all the hospitals.

I can never again shut out of view the sights I saw of human misery. I sit thinking, shut my eyes, and see it all. Thinking—yes, and there is enough to think about now, God knows. Gillands was the worst. Long rows of ill men on cots. Ill of typhoid fever, of every human ailment—dinner tables, eating, drinking, wounds being dressed—all horrors, to be taken in at one glance. That long tobacco house!

At the almshouse, Dr. Gibson in charge. He married a Miss Ayer of Philadelphia. He is fine looking and has charming manners. The very beau idéal of a family physician—so suave and gentle and pleasant. The Sisters of Charity are his nurses. That makes all the difference in the world. The sisters! They told us Mrs. Ricketts was there. Mrs. Randolph did not ask for her. One elderly sister—withered and wrinkled and yet with the face of an angel—

spoke severely to a young surgeon. "Stop that skylarking," she said. And he answered, "Where have you sent that pretty sister you had here yesterday? We all fell in love with her."

The venerable Sister of Charity was ministering to a Yankee with his arm cut off.

Everything was so clean—and in perfect order.

Dr. Gibson approached this presiding genius and asked her some questions. I did not hear her answer, but he said: "No. No, I have no time now—but it will be all right. Tomorrow we two will lay our heads together and arrange a new plan."

"Stop, doctor. We can't wait until tomorrow. It must be done tonight."

"All right," laughed the doctor—and he gravely turned to us. We had the joke all to ourselves, however. She did not see it.

After a while she said, "Honi soit qui mal y pense."

I said, "We did not know you angels of mercy made merry sometimes over your work." The wounded soldiers enjoyed every word that was said.

Occasionally one looked sulky, for were we not the hated Southerners? But I think as a general rule all that was forgotten in the hospital.

Then we went to the St. Charles. Horrors upon horrors again—want of organization. Long rows of them dead, dying. Awful smells, awful sights.

A boy from home had sent for me. He was lying in a cot, ill of fever. Next him a man died in convulsions while we stood there.

I was making arrangements with a nurse, hiring him to take care of this lad. I do not remember any more, for I fainted. Next that I knew of, the doctor and Mrs. Randolph were having me, a limp rag, put into the carriage at the door of the hospital.

Fresh air, I daresay, brought me to. First of all we had given our provisions to our Carolinians at Miss Sally Tompkins's. There they were, nice and clean and merry as grigs.

August 26, 1861. Evidently I am in for fever. Such headaches—and I am so miserably nervous and depressed.

The handsome A.D.C. felt it necessary as a precautionary measure to say his wife and child were at Fort Hamilton when Doubleday[4] of Fort Sumter fame arrived there.

• • •

"Why do you write in your diary at all, if, as you say, you have to contradict every day what you wrote yesterday?"

4. The reputed inventor of baseball, Abner Doubleday was a captain stationed in Charleston Harbor in 1860–61.

"Because I tell the tale as it is told to me. I write current rumor. I do not vouch for anything."

September 2, 1861. No discouragement now felt at the North. They take our forts and are satisfied for a while.

Then the English are sturdily neutral. Like the woman who saw her husband fight the bear, "it was the first fight she ever saw that she did not care who whipped."

November 27, 1861. On one side Mrs. Stowe, Greeley, Thoreau, Emerson, Sumner, in nice New England homes—clean, clear, sweet-smelling—shut up in libraries, writing books which ease their hearts of their bitterness to us, or editing newspapers—all [of] which pays better than anything else in the world. Even the politician's hobbyhorse—antislavery is the beast to carry him highest.

What self-denial do they practice? It is the cheapest philanthropy trade in the world—easy. Easy as setting John Brown to come down here and cut our throats in Christ's name.

Now, what I have seen of my mother's life, my grandmother's, my mother-in-law's:

These people were educated at Northern schools mostly—read the same books as their Northern contemners, the same daily newspapers, the same Bible—have the same ideas of right and wrong—are highbred, lovely, good, pious—doing their duty as they conceive it. They live in negro villages. They do not preach and teach hate as a gospel and the sacred duty of murder and insurrection, but they strive to ameliorate the condition of these Africans in every particular. They set them the example of a perfect life—life of utter self-abnegation. Think of these holy New Englanders, forced to have a negro village walk through their houses whenever they saw fit—dirty, slatternly, idle, ill-smelling by nature (when otherwise, it is the exception). These women are more troubled by their duty to negroes, have less chance to live their own lives in peace than if they were African missionaries. They have a swarm of blacks about them as children under their care—not as Mrs. Stowe's fancy paints them, but the hard, unpleasant, unromantic, undeveloped savage Africans. And they hate slavery worse than Mrs. Stowe. Bookmaking which leads you to a round of visits among crowned heads is an easier way to be a saint than martyrdom down here, doing unpleasant duty among them— with no reward but John-Browning drawn over your head in this world and threats of what is to come to you from blacker devils in the next. They have the plaudits of crowned heads. We take our chance, doing our duty as best we may among the woolly heads. I do not do anything whatever but get out of their way. When I come home, I see the negroes themselves. They look as comfortable as possible and I hear all they have to say. Then I see the overseer and the Methodist parson. *None* of these complain of each other. And I am satisfied. My husband supported his plantation by his law practice. Now it is running him in debt. We are bad managers. Our people have never earned their own bread.

Take this estate. John C says he could rent it from his grandfather and give him fifty thousand a year—then make twice as much more for himself. What does it do, actually? It all goes back in some shape to what are called slaves here—operatives, tenants &c elsewhere, peasantry &c. I doubt if ten thousand in money ever comes to this old gentleman's hands. When Mrs. Chesnut married South, her husband was as wealthy as her brothers-in-law, Mr. Binney or Mr. Stevens. How is it now? Their money has accumulated for their children. This old man's goes to support a horde of idle dirty Africans—while he is abused and vilified as a cruel slave-owner. I wish his "Uncle Tom"— for he has one who has never tasted calamity in any shape and whose gray hairs are honored, though they frame a black face—could be seen or could be heard as he tells of "me & master"—&c&c&c. I say we are no better than our judges North—and *no worse*. We are human beings of the nineteenth century—and slavery has to go, of course. All that has been gained by it goes to the North and to negroes. The slave-owners, when they are good men and women, are the martyrs. And as far as I have seen, the people here are quite as good as anywhere else. I hate slavery. I even hate the harsh authority I see parents think it their duty to exercise *toward their children*.

There now!! What good does it do to write all that? I have before me a letter I wrote to Mr. C while he was on our plantation in Mississippi in 1842. It is the most fervid abolition document I have ever read. I came across it, burning letters the other day. That letter I did not burn.

December 13, 1861. Everybody reads my journal, but since I have been making sketches of character at Mulberry I keep it under lock and key. Yesterday I handed this book to my new little maid Ellen, who is a sort of apprentice under Betsey, trying to learn her trade. When I gave Ellen the book I pointed to an armoire. She mistook the direction of my finger and took it into Miss Sally Chesnut's room, where she laid it on the table.

Today I looked for it in the armoire. It was gone. "Ellen, where is the book I write in? I gave it to you." She flew into Miss S. C.'s room, which happened to be empty just then, and brought it. Words were useless. And in my plain speaking and candor, what have I not said—intending no eye save mine to rest upon this page.

March 24, 1862. J. C. has been so nice this winter, so reasonable and considerate—that is, for a man. The night I came from Mme Togno's, instead of making a row about the lateness of the hour, he said he was "so wide awake and so hungry." So I put on my dressing gown and scrambled some eggs

&c&c, there on our own fire. And with our feet on the fender and the small supper table between us, we enjoyed the supper and a glorious gossip. Rather a pleasant state of things, when one's own husband is in a good humor and cleverer than all the men outside.

April 27, 1862. War seems a game of chess—but we have an unequal number of pawns to begin with. We had knights, kings, queens, bishops, and castles enough. But our skillful generals—whenever they cannot arrange the board to suit them exactly, they burn up everything and march away. We want them to save the *country.* They seem to think their whole duty is to destroy ships and *save* the *army.*

June 3, 1862. Comfort. Free schools are not everything. See this spelling.

Yankee epistles found in camp show how illiterate they can be, with all their boasted schools. Fredericksburg is spelled "Fretrexbug," medicine, "met-son," "to my *sweat* brother," &c&c.

"Well," said Mem, "Lieutenant Chesnut's horse bolts with him, but right into the heart of the enemy. No excuse like that man in the Crimea to make excuses that his horse bolted and took him out of the fight. Remember the sneer, 'We will not do Colonel ———'s (I forgot whose) magnificent horsemanship the injustice to say we believe him.'"

Mem gave me this scrap—one of her Jews is in it.

Isabel says when there is a battle and her brothers come out all right, Mem takes up on her Hebrew Bible and sings that glorious hymn of her namesake Miriam: "Sing ye to the Lord, for He hath triumphed, &c&c&c."

Mem is proud of her high lineage. She tells some great stories. Some man was terribly angry with his son, who had a weakness for some beautiful Jewess, swore at all Jews, and used bad language freely. Being high church and all that, he read the service for them on Sunday.

Son: "I do not want to hear anything from Isaiah or Solomon or Moses and the prophets—or Matthew, Mark, Luke, or John."

"Silence, sir—with your ribaldry."

"But, my father—you know they are only 'damned old Jews' anyhow."

Now, for the first time in my life, no book can interest me. But life is so real, so utterly earnest—fiction is so flat, comparatively. Nothing but what is going on in this distracted world of ours can arrest my attention for ten minutes at a time.

[1862–63] General Lee, Mr. Davis, &c&c—soldiers everywhere—want them [slaves] to be put in the army. Mr. Chesnut and Mr. Venable discussed the subject one night. Would they fight on our side or desert to the enemy? They

don't go to them, because they are comfortable where they are and expect to be free anyway.

When we were children our nurses gave us our tea out in the open air, on little pine tables scrubbed white as milk pails.

As he passed us with his slow and consequential step, we called, "Do, Dick—come and wait on us."

"No, little missies, I never wait on pine tables. Wait till you get big enough to put your legs under your pa's mahogany."

I taught him to read as soon as I could read myself—perched on his knife board. He won't look at me now. He looks over my head—he scents freedom in the air. He was always very ambitious. I do not think he ever troubled books much. But then as my father said, Dick, standing in front of his sideboard, had heard all subjects of earth or heaven discussed—and by the best heads in our world.

He is proud, too, in his way. Hetty his wife complained the other menservants were so fine in their livery.

"Nonsense, old woman—a butler never demeans himself to wear livery. He is always in plain clothes." Somewhere he had picked up that.

He is the first negro that I have felt a change in. They go about in their black masks, not a ripple or an emotion showing—and yet on all other subjects except the war they are the most excitable of all races. Now, Dick might make a very respectable Egyptian sphinx, so inscrutably silent is he.

He did deign to inquire about Gen. Richard Anderson. "He was my young Marster once. I always will like him better than anybody else."

When Dick married Hetty, the Anderson house was next door. The two families agreed to sell either Dick or Hetty, whichever consented to be sold. Hetty refused outright, and the Andersons sold Dick, that he might be with his wife. Magnanimous on the Andersons' part, for Hetty was only a lady's maid, and Dick was a trained butler on whom Mrs. Anderson had spent no end of pains in his dining room education. And of course if they had refused to sell Dick, Hetty had to go to them. Mrs. Anderson was very much disgusted with Dick's ingratitude when she found he was willing to leave them. As a butler he is a treasure. He is overwhelmed with dignity, but that does not interfere with his work at all. My father had a body servant who could imitate his master's voice perfectly. And he would call out from the yard after my father had mounted his horse.

"Dick, bring me my overcoat. I see you there, sir—hurry up." And when Dick hastened out, overcoat in hand—and only Simon! Particularly after several obsequious "Yes, Marster—just as Marster pleases," my mother had always to step out and prevent a fight. And Dick never forgave her laughing.

Once in Sumter, when my father was very busy preparing a law case, the mob in the street annoyed him, and he grumbled about as Simon made up his fire. Then he said in all his life he had never laughed so heartily. Suddenly he heard the Hon. S. D. Miller—Lawyer Miller, as the gentleman announced himself in the dark—appeal to the gentlemen to go away and leave a lawyer in peace to prepare his case for the next day—&c&c. My father said he could have sworn to his own voice. The crowd dispersed, and some noisy negroes came along. Upon them Simon rushed with the sulky whip, slashing around in the dark, calling himself Lawyer-Miller-who-was-determined-to-have-peace.

September 20, 1863. At Kingsville I caught a glimpse of our army. Longstreet's corps going west.

God bless the gallant fellows. Not one man intoxicated—not one rude word did I hear. It was a strange sight—miles, *apparently,* of platform cars— soldiers rolled in their blankets, lying in rows, heads and all covered, fast asleep. In their gray blankets, packed in regular order, they looked like swathed mummies.

One man near where I sat was writing on his knee. He used his cap for a desk, and he was seated on a rail. I watched him, wondering to whom that letter was to go. Home, no doubt—sore hearts for him there!

A feeling of awful depression laid hold of me. All these fine fellows going to kill or be killed. Why? And a word got to beating about my head like an old song—"the unreturning brave."

When a knot of boyish, laughing young creatures passed me, a queer thrill of sympathy shook me. Ah, I know how your home folks feel, poor children.

December 4, 1863. J. C. bought yesterday at the commissary's 1 barrel flour, 1 bushel potatoes, 1 peck of rice, 5 lbs. of salt beef, 1 peck of salt. All for sixty dollars. In the street a barrel of flour sells for one hundred and fifteen dollars.

January 1, 1864. . . . "General Edward Johnson says he got Grant a place. Esprit de corps, you know, would not bear to see an old army man driving a wagon. That was when he found him out west. Put out of the army for habitual drunkenness."

"He is their man, a bullheaded Suwarrow. He don't care a snap if they fall like the leaves fall. He fights to win, that chap. He is not distracted by a thousand side issues. He does not see them. He is narrow and sure, sees only in a straight line."

"Like Louis Napoleon—from a bath in the gutters, he goes straight up."

"Yes, like Lincoln, they have ceased to carp at him because he is a rough clown, no gentleman, &c&c. You never hear now of his nasty fun—only of his wisdom. It don't take much soap and water to wash the hands that the rod of empire sways. They talked of Lincoln's drunkenness, too. Now, since Vicksburg they have not a word to say against Grant's habits."

"He has the disagreeable habit of not retreating before irresistible veterans—or it is reculer pour mieux sauter—&c&c. You need not be afraid of a little dirt on the hands which wield a field marshal's baton, either."

"General Lee and Albert Sidney Johnston, they show blood and breeding. They are of the Bayard, the Philip Sidney order of soldiers."

"Listen, if General Lee had Grant's resources, he would have bagged the last Yankee or had them all safe back, packed up in Massachusetts."

"You mean, if he had not the weight of the negro question on him?"

"No, I mean, if he had Grant's unlimited allowance of the powers of war—men, money, ammunition, arms—

March 3, 1864. Then we prepared a luncheon for him. C. C. remained with me. She told me her life's history—the Burton Harrison imbroglio, the entanglement of the hour—&c&c&c. As Annie says of Buck, "I believe she only cares for B. H.—let them quarrel as they may."

After they left I sat down to *Romola*—and I was absorbed in it. How hardened we grow "to war and war's alarms." The enemies' cannon or our own are thundering in my ears—and I was dreadfully afraid some infatuated and frightened friend would come in to cheer, to comfort, and interrupt me. Am I the same poor soul who fell on her knees and prayed and wept and fainted as the first guns boomed from Fort Sumter?

August 19, 1864. Began my regular attendance in the Wayside Hospital, which was gotten up and is carried on by that good woman Jane Coles Fisher.

Today we gave wounded men (as they stopped for an hour at the station) their breakfast. Those who are able to come to the table do so. The badly wounded remain in wards prepared for them, where their wounds are dressed by nurses and surgeons, and we take bread and butter, beef, ham, &c&c, hot coffee, to them there.

One man had hair as long as a woman's. A vow, he said. He has pledged himself not to cut his hair until war [was] declared [over] and our Southern country *free*.

Four of them had made this vow. All were dead but himself. One was killed in Missouri, one in Virginia, and he left one at Kennesaw Mountain. This poor creature had one arm taken off at the socket. When I remarked that he was utterly disabled and ought not to remain in the army, he answered quickly.

"I am First Texas. If old Hood can go with one foot, I can go with one arm. Eh?"

How they quarreled and wrangled among themselves! Alabama, Mississippi, all loud for Joe Johnston—save and except the long-haired one-armed hero, who cried at the top of his voice,

"Oh, you all want to be kept in trenches and to go on retrenching. Eh?"

"Oh, if we had had a leader such as Stonewall, this war would have been over long ago. What we want is a leader!" shouted a cripple.

They were awfully smashed up—objects of misery, wounded, maimed, diseased. I was really upset and came home ill. This kind of thing unnerves me quite.

As [soon as] I came into my room I stood on the bare floor and made Ellen undress me and take every thread I had on and throw them all into a washtub out of doors. She had a bath ready for me and a dressing gown.

Brave soldiers—but, you are not nice.

Letters from the army. Grant's dogged stay about Richmond very disgusting and depressing to the spirits.

Perriman DePass's letter says they hope to stop Sherman.

Wade Hampton put in command of Southern cavalry.

"Now the Hamptons will be satisfied. And if General Hampton is ordered to supersede Lee, the row against Jeff Davis will subside in this latitude."

Read Dr. Doran's *Queens of the House of Hanover*.

Pleasant ladies, truly.

August 29, 1864. I take my hospital duty in the morning. Most persons prefer afternoon, but I dislike to give up my pleasant evenings. So I get up at five o'clock and go down in my carriage all laden with provisions. Mrs. Fisher and Mr. Bryan generally go with me. The provisions are sent by people to Mrs. Fisher. I am so glad to be a hospital nurse once more. I had excuses enough, but at heart I felt a coward and a skulker. I think I know how men feel who hire a substitute and shirk the fight. There must be no dodging duty. It will not do now to send provisions and pay for nurses.

Something inside of me kept calling out, Go, you shabby creature. You can't bear to see what those fine fellows have to bear.

November 6, 1864. Buck and Tudy went down to the hospital with me today. There were several wounded men to be given breakfast after their wounds were attended to by the surgeons and nurses. We are only in the feeding department. At one time I was on duty, detailed to see to the breakfast of four men who could not chew at all—so *cat lap* was the word. Hominy, rice with gravy, &c&c, milk and bread. One was shot in the eye, but his whole jaw was paralyzed. Another—and the worse case—had his tongue cut away by a shot, and his teeth with it. Fortunately the father of this one had him in charge.

The father told me that he was a Southern author—had written a songbook. Madame Pelletier was there and harangued us in French.

We worked like galley slaves from five in the morning until half-past eight, when the train bore away the whole of them, and we waved our handkerchiefs to them joyfully and sat down—tired to death.

A handsome specimen from Young's cavalry brigade told stories of the war—called Hampton Mars Wade and General Lee Ole Mars Robert. There was a table where all the men with crutches were sent, and Tudy told Buck to go and wait on them, which she did—her blue eyes swimming in tears all the time. She was so shy, so lovely, so efficient. All the same, I cannot bear young girls to go to hospitals, wayside or otherwise. The comments those men made on Buck's angelic beauty!

Mrs. Fisher, the good genius of our Wayside Hospital—just as her house was hospitably thrown open to a host of Virginia refugees—had her fine cow stolen by one of her own servants and made into beef before the theft was discovered. "Virtue is not rewarded in this world," said Isabella solemnly, "or Jane Fisher would never have a trouble."

Madame Pelletier denounced Calline to us. Poor Calline's want of manners infuriates the French woman. She spoke fiercely and in a foreign language, but Calline eyed us askance, as if she suspected what it all was about. Calline is a sandhiller—and rough to the hungry, sick, and sore soldiers.

A thousand dollars has slipped through my fingers already this week. At the commissaries I spent five hundred today for sugar, candles, a lamp, &c. Tallow candles are bad enough, but of them there seems to be an end, too. Now we are restricted to smoky terebene lamps—terrabene is a preparation of turpentine. When the chimney of the lamp cracks, as crack it will, we plaster up the place with paper, thick letter paper, preferring the highly glazed kind. In that hunt queer old letters come to light.

No wonder Mr. Peterkin said our provisions could be carried in a portemonnaie, and our money to buy them required a market basket to hold it. If you could see the pitiful little bundles this five hundred dollars bought. . . .

Our cool Captain writes from Wilmington: there are no gnats there—but they call his fine horses "critters."

A letter from the western army signed Western Man—out and out for peace—peace at any price. I call this treason.

Sherman in Atlanta has left Thomas to take care of Hood. Hood has 30,000 men—Thomas 40,000 now—and as many more as he wants—he has only to ring the bell and call for more. Grant can get all that he wants, both for himself and for Thomas. All the world open to them. We shut up in a Bastille.

We are at sea. Our boat has sprung a leak.

April 22, 1865. It has been a wild three days. Aides galloping around with messages. Yankees hanging over us like the sword of Damocles. We have been in queer straits. We sat up at Mrs. Bedon's, dressed, without once going to bed for forty-eight hours. And we were aweary. Mariana in the grange does not know anything about it. No Yankees to spright her or fright her there.

Colonel Cad Jones came with a dispatch, a sealed secret dispatch. It was for General Chesnut. I opened it.

Lincoln—old Abe Lincoln—killed—murdered—Seward wounded!

Why? By whom? It is simply maddening, all this.

I sent off messenger after messenger for General Chesnut. I have not the faintest idea where he is, but I know this foul murder will bring down worse miseries on us.

Mary Darby says: "But they murdered him themselves. No Confederates in Washington."

"But if they see fit to accuse us of instigating it?"

"Who murdered him?"

"Who knows!"

"See if they don't take vengeance on us, now that we are ruined and cannot repel them any longer."

Met Mr. Heyward. He said: "Plebiscitum it is. See, our army are deserting Joe Johnston. That is the people's vote against a continuance of the war. And the death of Lincoln—I call that a warning to tyrants. He will not be the last president put to death in the capital, though he is the first."

"Joe Johnston's army that he has risked his reputation to save from the very first year of the war—*deserting*. Saving his army by retreats, and now they are deserting *him*."

"Yes, Stonewall's tactics were the best—hard knocks, blow after blow in rapid succession, quick marches, surprises, victories quand même. That would have saved us. Watch, wait, retreat, ruined us. Now look out for bands of marauders, black and white, lawless disbanded soldiery from both armies."

An armistice, they say, is agreed on.

Taking stock, as the shopkeepers say. Heavy debts for the support of negroes during the war—and before, as far as we are concerned. No home—our husbands shot or made prisoners.

"Stop, Mrs. C. At best, Camden for life—that is worse than the galleys for you."

April 23, 1865. And these negroes—unchanged. The shining black mask they wear does not show a ripple of change—sphinxes. Ellen has had my diamonds to keep for a week or so. When the danger was over she handed them back to me, with as little apparent interest in the matter as if they were garden peas.

• • •

"Yesterday these poor fellows were heroes. Today they are only rebels to be hung or shot, at the Yankees' pleasure."

"One year ago we left Richmond. The Confederacy has double-quicked

407

downhill since then. One year since I stood in that beautiful Hollywood by little Joe Davis's grave."

"Burned towns, deserted plantations, sacked villages."

"You seem resolute to look the worst in the face," said General Chesnut wearily.

"Yes, poverty—no future, no hope."

"But no slaves—thank God," cried Buck.

"We would be the scorn of the world if the world thought of us at all. You see, we are exiles and paupers."

"Pile on the agony."

"How does our famous captain, the Great Lee, bear the Yankee's galling chain?" I asked.

"He knows how to possess his soul in patience," answered my husband shortly. "If there was no such word as subjugation, no debts, no poverty, no negro mobs backed by Yankees, if all things were well—you would shiver and feel benumbed." He went on pointing at me in an oratorical attitude. "Your sentence is pronounced—*Camden for life*."

28

Ulysses S. Grant (1822–1885)

from *Personal Memoirs of Ulysses S. Grant*

Readers of *The Education of Henry Adams* know Adams's unflattering portrait of Grant: a "pre-intellectual, archaic" enigma who as president started the country on "a policy of drift," while also seemingly blind to enormous corruption in government.[1]

The *Personal Memoirs of Ulysses S. Grant,* which conclude with the end of the Civil War in 1865, show a very different kind of man, although to many readers still a puzzling one. The two volumes, totalling over 1200 pages, begin with his ancestry and childhood and then proceed rapidly through his time at West Point to his service in the Mexican War. By 1854 he has resigned from the army. But in 1861, living in Galena, Illinois, he helps organize Illinois volunteers, and is made a colonel. Then, as the war progresses, he moves from battle to battle, gaining larger commands, besieging Vicksburg, taking it on July 4, 1863, and becoming lieutenant-general in March, 1864, with command of all the armies of the United States. As a result of Grant's ever-widening role, the reader gets an ever-expanding view of the magnitude of the war, while the *Memoirs* press on, as inevitable as fate. Yet, throughout, Grant's language remains modest and firm and without the exaggerated heroic tones, contentiousness, and self-justifications that became almost standard features in other autobiographies of Civil War officers.

Alexander Stephens, the vice-president of the Confederacy, said of Grant, "He is one of the most remarkable men I have ever met. He does not seem to be aware of his powers."[2] The comment is suggestive, and it is borne out by the famous story of Grant's first expecting to publish the *Memoirs* with the Century Company, which had promised only a ten percent royalty and predicted sales of only five to ten thousand copies. Grant had been swindled by business partners, was sick and in debt, and believed this was a good offer. But Mark Twain offered to publish them by subscription, and they soon sold 300,000 copies, earning $450,000 for Grant's family. (Grant died of cancer of the throat on July 23, 1885, a week after finishing the manuscript.)

While home on vacation from West Point, Grant was teased for wearing a

1. Henry Adams, *The Education of Henry Adams* (Boston: Houghton Mifflin, 1918), pp. 265, 267.
2. Edmund Wilson, *Patriotic Gore* (New York: Oxford Univ. Press, 1962), p. 142.

fancy military uniform, and he came to prefer utilitarian dress, as at Appomattox. This plain dress, in turn, fits with his plain language and his objection to misty legends like the "story of the apple tree" and how he supposedly returned Lee's sword. Yet Grant is still the stuff of legend, and he is often made a symbol of Union determination, the democratic values of the Union soldier, and the North's mastery of industrial warfare. Aspects of all these qualities show up here. So does the archetype with which the United States entered many other wars: that the country was a Sleeping Giant, peaceful and complacent until aroused to a just and mighty fury. Can a man have tapped into so many of the strongest legends, the latent narrative structures, in his culture and still been unaware of his power?

For further reflection, Grant can be compared to other military autobiographers like Black Hawk and Ethan Allen, to other writers about war like Chesnut, Sarah Benjamin and Nathan B. Jennings, and to the pacifists Dorothy Day and Roderick Seidenberg.

The excerpt below, headed "Negotiations at Appomattox—Interview with Lee at McLean's House—The terms of surrender—Lee's surrender—Interview with Lee after the Surrender," is the whole of Chapter 67 of the first edition of *Personal Memoirs of U.S. Grant* (New York: Charles L. Webster and Co., 1885). This is still the authoritative text, but the Library of America provides a good, available reprint. Two excellent short studies of Grant and his *Memoirs* appear in Edmund Wilson's chapter "Northern Soldiers: Ulysses S. Grant," in *Patriotic Gore* (New York: Oxford Univ. Press, 1962), and James M. Cox's "U.S. Grant: The Man in the *Memoirs*," in his *Recovering Literature's Lost Ground* (Baton Rouge: Louisiana State Univ. Press, 1989).

On the 8th I had followed the Army of the Potomac in rear of Lee. I was suffering very severely with a sick headache, and stopped at a farmhouse on the road some distance in rear of the main body of the army. I spent the night in bathing my feet in hot water and mustard, and putting mustard plasters on my wrists and the back part of my neck, hoping to be cured by morning. During the night I received Lee's answer to my letter of the 8th, inviting an interview between the lines on the following morning. But it was for a different purpose from that of surrendering his army, and I answered him as follows:

HEADQUARTERS ARMIES OF THE U. S.,
April 9, 1865.

GENERAL R. E. LEE,
      Commanding C. S. A.

Your note of yesterday is received. As I have no authority to treat on the subject of peace, the meeting proposed for ten A.M. to-day could lead to no good. I will state, however, General, that I am equally anxious for peace with yourself, and the whole North entertains the same feeling. The terms upon which peace can be had are well understood. By the South laying down their arms they will hasten that most desirable event, save thousands of human lives, and hundreds of millions of property not yet destroyed. Sincerely hoping that all our difficulties may be settled without the loss of another life, I subscribe myself, etc.,

U. S. GRANT,
Lieutenant-General.

I proceeded at an early hour in the morning, still suffering with the headache, to get to the head of the column. I was not more than two or three miles from Appomattox Court House at the time, but to go direct I would have to pass through Lee's army, or a portion of it. I had therefore to move south in order to get upon a road coming up from another direction.

When the white flag was put out by Lee, as already described, I was in this way moving towards Appomattox Court House, and consequently could not be communicated with immediately, and be informed of what Lee had done. Lee, therefore, sent a flag to the rear to advise Meade and one to the front to Sheridan, saying that he had sent a message to me for the purpose of having a meeting to consult about the surrender of his army, and asked for a suspension of hostilities until I could be communicated with. As they had heard nothing of this until the fighting had got to be severe and all going against Lee, both of these commanders hesitated very considerably about suspending hostilities at all. They were afraid it was not in good faith, and we had the Army of Northern Virginia where it could not escape except by some deception. They, however, finally consented to a suspension of hostilities for two hours to give an opportunity of communicating with me in that time, if possible. It was found that, from the route I had taken, they would probably not be able to communicate with me and get an answer back within the time fixed unless the messenger should pass through the rebel lines.

Lee, therefore, sent an escort with the officer bearing this message through his lines to me.

April 9, 1865.

GENERAL:—I received your note of this morning on the picketline whither I had come to meet you and ascertain definitely what terms were embraced in your proposal of yesterday with reference to the surrender of this army. I now request an interview in accordance with the offer contained in your letter of yesterday for that purpose.

R. E. LEE, General.

LIEUTENANT-GENERAL U. S. GRANT,
Commanding U. S. Armies.

When the officer reached me I was still suffering with the sick headache; but the instant I saw the contents of the note I was cured. I wrote the following note in reply and hastened on:

April 9, 1865.

GENERAL R. E. LEE,
Commanding C. S. Armies.

Your note of this date is but this moment (11.50 A.M.) received, in consequence of my having passed from the Richmond and Lynchburg road to the Farmville and

Lynchburg road. I am at this writing about four miles west of Walker's Church and will push forward to the front for the purpose of meeting you. Notice sent to me on this road where you wish the interview to take place will meet me.

U. S. GRANT,
Lieutenant-General.

I was conducted at once to where Sheridan was located with his troops drawn up in line of battle facing the Confederate army near by. They were very much excited, and expressed their view that this was all a ruse employed to enable the Confederates to get away. They said they believed that Johnston was marching up from North Carolina now, and Lee was moving to join him; and they would whip the rebels where they now were in five minutes if I would only let them go in. But I had no doubt about the good faith of Lee, and pretty soon was conducted to where he was. I found him at the house of a Mr. McLean, at Appomattox Court House, with Colonel Marshall, one of his staff officers, awaiting my arrival. The head of his column was occupying a hill, on a portion of which was an apple orchard, beyond a little valley which separated it from that on the crest of which Sheridan's forces were drawn up in line of battle to the south.

Before stating what took place between General Lee and myself, I will give all there is of the story of the famous apple tree.

Wars produce many stories of fiction, some of which are told until they are believed to be true. The war of the rebellion was no exception to this rule, and the story of the apple tree is one of those fictions based on a slight foundation of fact. As I have said, there was an apple orchard on the side of the hill occupied by the Confederate forces. Running diagonally up the hill was a wagon road, which, at one point, ran very near one of the trees, so that the wheels of vehicles had, on that side, cut off the roots of this tree, leaving a little embankment. General Babcock, of my staff, reported to me that when he first met General Lee he was sitting upon this embankment with his feet in the road below and his back resting against the tree. The story had no other foundation than that. Like many other stories, it would be very good if it was only true.

I had known General Lee in the old army, and had served with him in the Mexican War; but did not suppose, owing to the difference in our age and rank, that he would remember me; while I would more naturally remember him distinctly, because he was the chief of staff of General Scott in the Mexican War.

When I had left camp that morning I had not expected so soon the result that was then taking place, and consequently was in rough garb. I was without a sword, as I usually was when on horseback on the field, and wore a soldier's blouse for a coat, with the shoulder straps of my rank to indicate to the army who I was. When I went into the house I found General Lee.

We greeted each other, and after shaking hands took our seats. I had my staff with me, a good portion of whom were in the room during the whole of the interview.

What General Lee's feelings were I do not know. As he was a man of much dignity, with an impassible face, it was impossible to say whether he felt inwardly glad that the end had finally come, or felt sad over the result, and was too manly to show it. Whatever his feelings, they were entirely concealed from my observation; but my own feelings, which had been quite jubilant on the receipt of his letter, were sad and depressed. I felt like anything rather than rejoicing at the downfall of a foe who had fought so long and valiantly, and had suffered so much for a cause, though that cause was, I believe, one of the worst for which a people ever fought, and one for which there was the least excuse. I do not question, however, the sincerity of the great mass of those who were opposed to us.

General Lee was dressed in a full uniform which was entirely new, and was wearing a sword of considerable value, very likely the sword which had been presented by the State of Virginia; at all events, it was an entirely different sword from the one that would ordinarily be worn in the field. In my rough traveling suit, the uniform of a private with the straps of a lieutenant-general, I must have contrasted very strangely with a man so handsomely dressed, six feet high and of faultless form. But this was not a matter that I thought of until afterwards.

We soon fell into a conversation about old army times. He remarked that he remembered me very well in the old army; and I told him that as a matter of course I remembered him perfectly, but from the difference in our rank and years (there being about sixteen years' difference in our ages), I had thought it very likely that I had not attracted his attention sufficiently to be remembered by him after such a long interval. Our conversation grew so pleasant that I almost forgot the object of our meeting. After the conversation had run on in this style for some time, General Lee called my attention to the object of our meeting, and said that he had asked for this interview for the purpose of getting from me the terms I proposed to give his army. I said that I meant merely that his army should lay down their arms, not to take them up again during the continuance of the war unless duly and properly exchanged. He said that he had so understood my letter.

Then we gradually fell off again into conversation about matters foreign to the subject which had brought us together. This continued for some little time, when General Lee again interrupted the course of the conversation by suggesting that the terms I proposed to give his army ought to be written out. I called to General Parker, secretary on my staff, for writing materials, and commenced writing out the following terms:

APPOMATTOX C. H., VA.,
Ap l9th, 1865.

GEN. R. E. LEE,
Comd'g C. S. A.
GEN: In accordance with the substance of my letter to you of the 8th inst., I propose to receive the surrender of the Army of N. Va. on the following terms, to wit: Rolls of all the officers and men to be made in duplicate. One copy to be given to an officer designated by me, the other to be retained by such officer or officers as you may designate. The officers to give their individual paroles not to take up arms against the Government of the United States until properly exchanged, and each company or regimental commander sign a like parole for the men of their commands. The arms, artillery and public property to be parked and stacked, and turned over to the officer appointed by me to receive them. This will not embrace the side-arms of the officers, nor their private horses or baggage. This done, each officer and man will be allowed to return to their homes, not to be disturbed by United States authority so long as they observe their paroles and the laws in force where they may reside.

Very respectfully,
U. S. GRANT,
Lt. Gen.

When I put my pen to the paper I did not know the first word that I should make use of in writing the terms. I only knew what was in my mind, and I wished to express it clearly, so that there could be no mistaking it. As I wrote on, the thought occurred to me that the officers had their own private horses and effects, which were important to them, but of no value to us; also that it would be an unnecessary humiliation to call upon them to deliver their side arms.

No conversation, not one word, passed between General Lee and myself, either about private property, side arms, or kindred subjects. He appeared to have no objections to the terms first proposed; or if he had a point to make against them he wished to wait until they were in writing to make it. When he read over that part of the terms about side arms, horses and private property of the officers, he remarked, with some feeling, I thought, that this would have a happy effect upon his army.

Then, after a little further conversation, General Lee remarked to me again that their army was organized a little differently from the army of the United States (still maintaining by implication that we were two countries); that in their army the cavalrymen and artillerists owned their own horses; and he asked if he was to understand that the men who so owned their horses were to be permitted to retain them. I told him that as the terms were written they would not; that only the officers were permitted to take their private property. He then, after reading over the terms a second time, remarked that that was clear.

I then said to him that I thought this would be about the last battle of the war—I sincerely hoped so; and I said further I took it that most of the

414

men in the ranks were small farmers. The whole country had been so raided by the two armies that it was doubtful whether they would be able to put in a crop to carry themselves and their families through the next winter without the aid of the horses they were then riding. The United States did not want them and I would, therefore, instruct the officers I left behind to receive the paroles of his troops to let every man of the Confederate army who claimed to own a horse or mule take the animal to his home. Lee remarked again that this would have a happy effect.

He then sat down and wrote out the following letter:

> HEADQUARTERS ARMY OF NORTHERN VIRGINIA,
> *April* 9, 1865.
>
> GENERAL:—I received your letter of this date containing the terms of the surrender of the Army of Northern Virginia as proposed by you. As they are substantially the same as those expressed in your letter of the 8th inst., they are accepted. I will proceed to designate the proper officers to carry the stipulations into effect.
>
> R. E. Lee, General.
>
> LIEUT.-GENERAL U. S. GRANT.

While duplicates of the two letters were being made, the Union generals present were severally presented to General Lee.

The much talked of surrendering of Lee's sword and my handing it back, this and much more that has been said about it is the purest romance. The word sword or side arms was not mentioned by either of us until I wrote it in the terms. There was no premeditation, and it did not occur to me until the moment I wrote it down. If I had happened to omit it, and General Lee had called my attention to it, I should have put it in the terms precisely as I acceded to the provision about the soldiers retaining their horses.

General Lee, after all was completed and before taking his leave, remarked that his army was in a very bad condition for want of food, and that they were without forage; that his men had been living for some days on parched corn exclusively, and that he would have to ask me for rations and forage. I told him "certainly," and asked for how many men he wanted rations. His answer was "about twenty-five thousand:" and I authorized him to send his own commissary and quartermaster to Appomattox Station, two or three miles away, where he could have, out of the trains we had stopped, all the provisions wanted. As for forage, we had ourselves depended almost entirely upon the country for that.

Generals Gibbon, Griffin and Merritt were designated by me to carry into effect the paroling of Lee's troops before they should start for their homes— General Lee leaving Generals Longstreet, Gordon and Pendleton for them to confer with in order to facilitate this work. Lee and I then separated as cordially as we had met, he returning to his own lines, and all went into bivouac for the night at Appomattox.

Soon after Lee's departure I telegraphed to Washington as follows:

HEADQUARTERS APPOMATTOX C. H., VA.,
April 9th, 1865, 4.30 P.M.

HON. E. M. STANTON, SECRETARY OF WAR,
Washington.

General Lee surrendered the Army of Northern Virginia this afternoon on terms proposed by myself. The accompanying additional correspondence will show the conditions fully.

U. S. GRANT,
Lieut.-General.

When news of the surrender first reached our lines our men commenced firing a salute of a hundred guns in honor of the victory. I at once sent word, however, to have it stopped. The Confederates were now our prisoners, and we did not want to exult over their downfall.

I determined to return to Washington at once, with a view to putting a stop to the purchase of supplies, and what I now deemed other useless outlay of money. Before leaving, however, I thought I would like to see General Lee again; so next morning I rode out beyond our lines towards his headquarters, preceded by a bugler and a staff-officer carrying a white flag.

Lee soon mounted his horse, seeing who it was, and met me. We had there between the lines, sitting on horseback, a very pleasant conversation of over half an hour, in the course of which Lee said to me that the South was a big country and that we might have to march over it three or four times before the war entirely ended, but that we would now be able to do it as they could no longer resist us. He expressed it as his earnest hope, however, that we would not be called upon to cause more loss and sacrifice of life; but he could not foretell the result. I then suggested to General Lee that there was not a man in the Confederacy whose influence with the soldiery and the whole people was as great as his, and that if he would now advise the surrender of all the armies I had no doubt his advice would be followed with alacrity. But Lee said, that he could not do that without consulting the President first. I knew there was no use to urge him to do anything against his ideas of what was right.

I was accompanied by my staff and other officers, some of whom seemed to have a great desire to go inside the Confederate lines. They finally asked permission of Lee to do so for the purpose of seeing some of their old army friends, and the permission was granted. They went over, had a very pleasant time with their old friends, and brought some of them back with them when they returned.

When Lee and I separated he went back to his lines and I returned to the house of Mr. McLean. Here the officers of both armies came in great numbers, and seemed to enjoy the meeting as much as though they had been friends separated for a long time while fighting battles under the same flag.

416

For the time being it looked very much as if all thought of the war had escaped their minds. After an hour pleasantly passed in this way I set out on horseback, accompanied by my staff and a small escort, for Burkesville Junction, up to which point the railroad had by this time been repaired.

29

Frederick Douglass (1817?–1895)

from *Life and Times of Frederick Douglass*

The *Life and Times of Frederick Douglass* (1881, rev. ed. 1892) is not nearly so well known as his first autobiography, *The Narrative* . . . (1845), or his second, *My Bondage and My Freedom* (1855). It is 752 pages long. Its descriptions of slavery are not so direct and powerful. And the descriptions of the later years are often rambling, interrupted by long excerpts from letters and earlier writings. "What we have," one critic has written, "is a verbose and somewhat hackneyed story of a life, written by a man of achievement."[1]

Such a judgment may be too harsh, however. For one thing, the *Life and Times* contains some details about Douglass's early life which he had to omit from his first two autobiographies. Most important is the story of his escape, which is given in the first of the two selections below. It may not be as long and as exciting as the escapes in some other slave autobiographies, but it is still tense, and it shows how easy it might have been for a fugitive slave to be stopped.

Harsh judgments of *Life and Times* also fail to acknowledge the nature of this kind of autobiography. It *was* written by "a man of achievement." Less famous men and women simply did not have the materials. Douglass had known John Brown and been one of the first to hear Brown's plans for starting a guerrilla liberation movement. He had known Harriet Beecher Stowe. He had recruited black troops for the Union Army. After the Civil War he had been the nation's symbolic black leader and a minister to Haiti. *Life and Times* is for these reasons an important historical record and a good example of this kind of autobiography. Finally, as the second selection here illustrates, Douglass was well aware of the ways he was being used by the American whites (or "Caucasiàns") at a time when race prejudice was once again growing and becoming, in some ways, more patronizing and demeaning. He himself had been attacked during the late years of his life for marrying a white woman. In this justification for the last edition of his autobiography, he puts himself on the witness stand and relentlessly catalogues the ignorance and the prying "curiosity of my countrymen." He also has things to say about autobiography which every serious reader of it needs to consider.

1. Houston Baker, *The Journey Back: Issues in Black Literature and Criticism* (Chicago: Univ. of Chicago Press, 1980), pp. 44–45.

The source of the present selection is the revised edition of 1892. William S. McFeely's *Frederick Douglass* (New York: Norton, 1991) is the definitive biography. A new edition of Douglass's works, *The Frederick Douglass Papers*, ed. John W. Blassingame et al., is being published by Yale University Press.

[Details of His Escape from Slavery]

In the first narrative of my experience in slavery, written nearly forty years ago, and in various writings since, I have given the public what I considered very good reasons for withholding the manner of my escape. In substance these reasons were, first, that such publication at any time during the existence of slavery might be used by the master against the slave, and prevent the future escape of any who might adopt the same means that I did. The second reason was, if possible, still more binding to silence—for publication of details would certainly have put in peril the persons and property of those who assisted. Murder itself was not more sternly and certainly punished in the State of Maryland than was the aiding and abetting the escape of a slave. Many colored men, for no other crime than that of giving aid to a fugitive slave, have, like Charles T. Torrey, perished in prison. The abolition of slavery in my native State and throughout the country, and the lapse of time, render the caution hitherto observed no longer necessary. But, even since the abolition of slavery, I have sometimes thought it well enough to baffle curiosity by saying that while slavery existed there were good reasons for not telling the manner of my escape, and since slavery had ceased to exist there was no reason for telling it. I shall now, however, cease to avail myself of this formula, and, as far as I can, endeavor to satisfy this very natural curiosity. I should perhaps have yielded to that feeling sooner, had there been anything very heroic or thrilling in the incidents connected with my escape, for I am sorry to say I have nothing of that sort to tell; and yet the courage that could risk betrayal and the bravery which was ready to encounter death if need be, in pursuit of freedom, were essential features in the undertaking. My success was due to address rather than to courage; to good luck rather than to bravery. My means of escape were provided for me by the very men who were making laws to hold and bind me more securely in slavery. It was the custom in the State of Maryland to require of the free colored people to have what were called free papers. This instrument they were required to renew very often, and by charging a fee for this writing, considerable sums from time to time were collected by the State. In these papers the name, age, color, height and form of the free man were described, together with any scars or other marks upon his person which could assist in his identification. This device of slave-holding ingenuity, like other devices of wickedness, in some measure defeated itself—since more than one man could be found to answer the same general description. Hence many slaves could escape by personating the owner of one set of papers; and this was often done as follows: A slave nearly or sufficiently answering the description set forth in the papers, would borrow or hire them till he could by their means escape to a free state, and then, by mail or otherwise, return them to the owner. The operation was a hazardous one for the lender as well as for the borrower. A failure on the part of the fugitive to send back the papers would imperil his benefactor, and the discovery of the papers in possession of the wrong man would imperil both the fugitive and his friend. It was therefore an act of supreme trust on the part of a freeman of color thus to put in jeopardy his own liberty that another might be free. It was, however, not unfrequently bravely done, and was seldom discovered. I was not so fortunate as to sufficiently resemble any of my free acquaintances as to answer the description of their papers. But I had one friend—a sailor—who owned a sailor's protection, which answered somewhat the purpose of free papers—describing his person and certifying to the fact that he was a free American sailor. The instrument had at its head the American eagle, which at once gave it the appearance of an authorized document. This protection did not, when in my hands, describe its bearer very accurately. Indeed, it called for a man much darker than myself, and close examination of it would have caused my arrest at the start. In order to avoid this fatal scrutiny on the part of the railroad official, I had arranged with Isaac Rolls, a hackman, to bring my baggage to the train just on the moment of starting, and jumped upon the car myself when the train was already in motion. Had I gone into the station and offered to purchase a ticket, I should have been instantly and carefully examined, and undoubtedly arrested. In choosing this plan upon which to act, I considered the jostle of the train, and the natural haste of the conductor in a train crowded with passengers, and relied upon my skill and address in playing the sailor as described in my protection, to do the rest. One element in my favor was the kind feeling which prevailed in Baltimore and other seaports at the time, towards "those who go down to the sea in ships." "Free trade and sailors' rights" expressed the sentiment of the country just then. In my clothing I was rigged out in sailor style. I had on a red shirt and a tarpaulin hat and black cravat, tied in sailor fashion, carelessly and loosely about my neck. My knowledge of ships and sailor's talk came much to my assistance, for I knew a ship from stem to stern, and from keelson to cross-trees, and could talk sailor like an "old salt." On sped the train, and I was well on the way to Havre de Grace before the conductor came into the negro car to collect tickets and examine the papers of his black passengers. This was a critical moment in the drama. My whole future depended upon the decision of this conductor. Agitated I was while this ceremony was proceeding, but still, externally at least, I was apparently calm and self-possessed. He went on with his duty—examining several colored passengers before reaching me. He was somewhat harsh in tone and peremptory in manner until he reached me, when, strangely enough, and to my surprise and relief, his whole manner changed. Seeing that I did not readily produce my free papers, as the other colored persons in the car had done, he said to me in a friendly contrast with that observed towards the others: "I suppose you have your free papers?" To which I answered: "No, sir; I never carry my free papers to sea with me." "But you have something to show that you are a free man, have you not?" "Yes, sir," I answered; "I have a paper with the American eagle on it, that will carry me round the world." With this I drew from my deep sailor's pocket my seaman's protection, as before described. The merest glance at the paper satisfied him, and he took my fare and went on about his business. This moment of time was one of the most anxious I ever experienced. Had the conductor looked closely at the paper, he could not have failed to discover that it called for a very different looking person from myself, and in that case it would have been his duty to arrest me on the instant and send me back to Baltimore from the first station. When he left me with the assurance that I was all right, though much relieved, I realized that I was still in great danger: I was still in Maryland, and subject to arrest at any moment. I saw on the train several persons who would have known me in any other clothes, and I feared they might recognize me, even in my sailor "rig," and report me to the conductor, who would then subject me to a closer examination, which I knew well would be fatal to me.

Though I was not a murderer fleeing from justice, I felt, perhaps, quite as miserable as such a criminal. The train was moving at a very high rate of speed for that time of railroad travel, but to my anxious mind, it was moving far too slowly. Minutes were hours, and hours were days during this part of my flight. After Maryland I was to pass through Delaware—another slave State, where slavecatchers generally awaited their prey, for it was not in the interior of the State, but on its borders, that these human hounds were most vigilant and active. The border lines between slavery and freedom were the dangerous ones, for the fugitives. The heart of no fox or deer, with hungry hounds on his trail, in full chase, could have beaten more anxiously or noisily than did mine from the time I left Baltimore till I reached Philadelphia. The passage of the Susquehanna river at Havre de Grace was at that time made by ferry-boat, on board of which I met a young colored man by the name of Nichols, who came very near betraying me. He was a "hand" on the boat, but instead of minding his business, he insisted upon knowing me, and asking me dangerous questions as to where I was going, and when I was coming back, etc. I got away from my old and inconvenient acquaintance as soon as I could decently do so, and went to another part of the boat. Once across the river I encountered a new danger. Only a few days before I had been at work on a revenue cutter, in Mr. Price's shipyard, under the care of Captain McGowan. On the meeting at this point of the two trains, the one going south stopped on the track just opposite to the one going north, and it so happened that this Captain McGowan sat at a window where he could see me very distinctly, and would certainly have recognized me had he looked at me but for a second.

Fortunately, in the hurry of the moment, he did not see me, and the trains soon passed each other on their respective ways. But this was not the only hair-breadth escape. A German blacksmith, whom I knew well, was on the train with me, and looked at me very intently, as if he thought he had seen me somewhere before in his travels. I really believe he knew me, but had no heart to betray me. At any rate he saw me escaping and held his peace.

The last point of imminent danger, and the one I dreaded most, was Wilmington. Here we left the train and took the steamboat for Philadelphia. In making the change I again apprehended arrest, but no one disturbed me, and I was soon on the broad and beautiful Delaware, speeding away to the Quaker City. On reaching Philadelphia in the afternoon I inquired of a colored man how I could get on to New York? He directed me to the Willow street depot, and thither I went, taking the train that night. I reached New York Tuesday morning, having completed the journey in less than twenty-four hours. Such is briefly the manner of my escape from slavery—and the end of my experience as a slave.

[A Rationale for the 1892 Edition]

Ten years ago when the preceding chapters of this book were written, having then reached in the journey of life the middle of the decade beginning at sixty and ending at seventy, and naturally reminded that I was no longer young, I laid aside my pen with some such sense of relief as might be felt by a weary and overburdened traveler when arrived at the desired end of a long journey, or as an honest debtor wishing to be square with all the world might feel when the last dollar of an old debt was paid off. Not that I wished to be discharged from labor and service in the cause to which I have devoted my life, but from this peculiar kind of labor and service. I hardly need say to those who know me, that writing for the public eye never came quite as easily to me as speaking to the public ear. It is a marvel to me that under the circumstances I learned to write at all. It has been a still greater marvel that in the brief working period in which they lived and wrought, such men as Dickens, Dumas, Carlyle and Sir Walter Scott could have produced the works ascribed to them. But many have been the impediments with which I have had to struggle. I have, too, been embarrassed by the thought of writing so much about myself when there was so much else of which to write. It is far easier to write about others than about one's self. I write freely of myself, not from choice, but because I have, by my cause, been morally forced into thus writing. Time and events have summoned me to stand forth both as a witness and an advocate for a people long dumb, not allowed to speak for themselves, yet much misunderstood and deeply wronged. In the earlier days of my freedom, I was called upon to expose the direful nature of the slave system, by telling my own experience while a slave, and to do what I could thereby to make slavery odious and thus to hasten the day of emancipation. It was no time to mince matters or to stand upon a delicate sense of propriety, in the presence of a crime so gigantic as our slavery was, and the duty to oppose it so imperative. I was called upon to expose even my stripes, and with many misgivings obeyed the summons and tried thus to do my whole duty in this my first public work and what I may say proved to be the best work of my life.

Fifty years have passed since I entered upon that work, and now that it is ended, I find myself summoned again by the popular voice and by what is called the negro problem, to come a second time upon the witness stand and give evidence upon disputed points concerning myself and my emancipated brothers and sisters who, though free, are yet oppressed and are in as much need of an advocate as before they were set free. Though this is not altogether as agreeable to me as was my first mission, it is one that comes with such commanding authority as to compel me to accept it as a present duty. In it I am pelted with all sorts of knotty questions, some of which might be difficult even for Humboldt, Cuvier or Darwin, were they alive, to answer. They are questions which range over the whole field of science, learning and philosophy, and some descend to the depths of impertinent, unmannerly and vulgar curiosity. To be able to answer the higher range of these questions I should be profoundly versed in psychology, anthropology, ethnology, sociology, theology, biology, and all the other ologies, philosophies and sciences. There is no disguising the fact that the American people are much interested and mystified about the mere matter of color as connected with manhood. It seems to them that color has some moral or immoral qualities and especially the latter. They do not feel quite reconciled to the idea that a man of different color from themselves should have all the human rights claimed by themselves. When an unknown man is spoken of in their presence, the first question that arises in the average American mind concerning him and which must be answered is, Of what color is he? and he rises or falls in estimation by the answer given. It is not whether he is a good man or a bad man. That does not seem of primary importance. Hence I have often been bluntly and sometimes very rudely asked, of what color my mother was, and of what color was my father? In what proportion does the blood of the various races mingle in my veins, especially how much white blood and how much black blood entered into my composition? Whether I was not part Indian as well as African and Caucasian? Whether I considered myself more African than Caucasian, or the reverse? Whether I derived my intelligence from my father, or from my mother, from my white, or from my black blood? Whether persons of mixed blood are as strong and healthy as persons of either of the races whose blood they inherit? Whether persons of mixed blood do permanently remain of the mixed complexion or finally take on the complexion of one or the other of the two or more races of which they may be composed? Whether they live as long and raise as large families as other people? Whether they inherit only evil from both parents and good from neither? Whether evil dispositions are more transmissible than good? Why did I marry a person of my father's complexion instead of marrying one of my mother's complexion? How is the race problem to be solved in this country? Will the negro go back to Africa or remain here? Under this shower of purely American questions, more or less personal, I have endeavored to possess my soul in patience and get as much good out of life as was possible with so much to occupy my time; and, though often perplexed, seldom losing my temper, or abating heart or hope for the future of my people. Though I cannot say I have satisfied the curiosity of my countrymen on all the questions raised by them, I have, like all honest men on the witness stand, answered to the best of my knowledge and belief, and I hope I have never answered in such wise as to increase the hardships of any human being of whatever race or color.

When the first part of this book was written, I was, as before intimated, already looking toward the sunset of human life and thinking that my children would probably finish the recital of my life, or that possibly some other persons outside of family ties to whom I am known might think it worth while to tell what he or she might know of the remainder of my story. I considered, as I have said, that my work was done. But friends and publishers concur in the opinion that the unity and completeness of the work require that it shall be finished by the hand by which it was begun.

Many things touched me and employed my thoughts and activities between the years 1881 and 1891. I am willing to speak of them. Like most men who give the world their autobiographies I wish my story to be told as favorably towards myself as it can be with a due regard to truth. I do not wish it to be imagined by any that I am insensible to the singularity of my career, or to the peculiar relation I sustain to the history of my time and country. I know and feel that it is something to have lived at all in this Republic during the latter part of this eventful century, but I know it is more to have had some small share in the great events which have distinguished it from the experience of all other centuries. No man liveth unto himself, or ought to live unto himself. My life has conformed to this Bible saying, for, more than most men, I have been the thin edge of the wedge to open for my people a way in many directions and places never before occupied by them. It has been mine, in some degree, to stand as their defense in moral battle against the shafts of detraction, calumny and persecution, and to labor in removing and overcoming those obstacles which, in the shape of erroneous ideas and customs, have blocked the way to their progress. I have found this to be no hardship, but the natural and congenial vocation of my life. I had hardly become a thinking being when I first learned to hate slavery, and hence I was no sooner free than I joined the noble band of Abolitionists in Massachusetts, headed by William Lloyd Garrison and Wendell Phillips. Afterward, by voice and pen, in season and out of season, it was mine to stand for the freedom of people of all colors, until in our land the last yoke was broken and the last bondsman was set free. In the war for the Union I persuaded the colored man to become a soldier. In the peace that followed, I asked the Government to make him a citizen. In the construction of the rebellious States I urged his enfranchisement.

Much has been written and published during the last ten years purporting to be a history of the anti-slavery movement and of the part taken by the men and women engaged in it, myself among the number. In some of these narrations I have received more consideration and higher estimation than I perhaps deserved. In others I have not escaped underdeserved disparagement, which I may leave to the reader and to the judgment of those who shall come after me to reply to and to set right.

30

Lucy Larcom (1824–1893)
Mountain Friends

"To many, the word 'autobiography' implies nothing but conceit and egotism," Larcom wrote in her preface to *A New England Girlhood* (1889). "But these are not necessarily its characteristics. . . . For does not the whole world, seen and unseen, go into the making up of every human being?"

Such a theory of autobiography perfectly suits the story Larcom tells, which centers on her experiences in the Lowell, Massachusetts, cotton mills.

The mills had been started in 1822 by Francis Cabot Lowell and some associates, harnessing the water power of the Merrimack River and hiring farm girls as their workers. They wished to make the mills into a model of profitable and enlightened Christian enterprise. And for twenty or twenty-five years, until competition forced them to lower wages, the mills were. Anthony Trollope, one of the many foreign visitors, called Lowell an "industrial Utopia."

For Larcom, her Lowell years, approximately 1833–43, were an illustration of communal self-help and self-education. The girls all wanted to improve themselves and did it together. They attended classes and lectures, took music lessons, wrote poetry, and edited magazines. They also enjoyed the mill work, because it was preferable to housework, to which Larcom briefly returned to help her sister and to get relief from the factory's cotton dust. The hours were long, but strictly designated, the workers earned money, and they had more independence, companionship, and stimulation. Housework was respectable and important to Larcom, but Lowell broadened her horizons—among other things, it gave her "Mountain Friends."

"Mountain Friends," the whole of which is given below, is the ninth of the twelve chapters of a *New England Girlhood*. The beginning of this book tells of her childhood in Beverly, Massachusetts. The end tells of her going to pioneer in Illinois with her sister and brother-in-law and then studying at Monticello Seminary, from which she returned to the East in 1852 to teach at Wheaton Seminary. She later became a very popular poet and essayist.

The book was very well received, and, according to Daniel Dulany Addison, her first biographer, she intended to write a sequel covering her years of teaching, writing, and editing, and also her religious ideas.[1] But it is doubtful that another

1. Daniel Dulany Addison, *Lucy Larcom: Life, Letters, and Diary* (Boston: Houghton Mifflin, 1895), p. iii.

book could have been so good. The experience at Lowell united her ideals of "the mutual bonds of universal womanhood" and her ideals of autobiography. A later book might have contained more of the piety and pollyannaish-ness that sometimes mars accounts of this kind, while at the same time lacking its sense of close female bonding.

The text below is from *A New England Girlhood* (Boston: Houghton Mifflin, 1889). Shirley Marchalonis's *The Worlds of Lucy Larcom, 1824–1893* (Athens: Univ. of Georgia Press, 1989) is a modern biography. For a stimulating critical article, see Carol Holly, "Nineteenth-Century Autobiographies of Affiliation," in Paul John Eakin, ed., *American Autobiography: Retrospect and Prospect* (Madison: Univ. of Wisconsin Press, 1991).

The pleasure we found in making new acquaintances among our workmates arose partly from their having come from great distances, regions unknown to us, as the northern districts of Maine and New Hampshire and Vermont were, in those days of stage-coach traveling, when railroads had as yet only connected the larger cities with one another.

It seemed wonderful to me to be talking with anybody who had really seen mountains and lived among them. One of the younger girls, who worked beside me during my very first days in the mill, had come from far up near the sources of the Merrimack, and she told me a great deal about her home, and about farm-life among the hills. I listened almost with awe when she said that she lived in a valley where the sun set at four o'clock, and where the great snow-storms drifted in so that sometimes they did not see a neighbor for weeks.

To have mountain-summits looking down upon one out of the clouds, summer and winter, by day and by night, seemed to me something both delightful and terrible. And yet here was this girl to whom it all appeared like the merest commonplace. What she felt about it was that it was "awful cold, sometimes; the days were so short! and it grew dark so early!" Then she told me about the spinning, and the husking, and the sugar-making, while we sat in a corner together, waiting to replace the full spools by empty ones,—the work usually given to the little girls.

I had a great admiration for this girl, because she had come from those wilderness-regions. The scent of pine-woods and checkerberry-leaves seemed to hang about her. I believe I liked her all the better because she said "daown" and "haow." It was part of the mountain-flavor.

I tried, on my part, to impress her with stories of the sea; but I did not succeed very well. Her principal comment was, "They don't think much of sailors up *aour* way." And I received the impression, from her and others, and from my own imagination, that rural life was far more delightful than the life of towns.

427

But there is something in the place where we were born that holds us always by the heartstrings. A town that still has a great deal of the country in it, one that is rich in beautiful scenery and ancestral associations, is almost like a living being, with a body and a soul. We speak of such a town, if our birthplace, as of a mother, and think of ourselves as her sons and daughters.

So we felt, my sisters and I, about our dear native town of Beverly. Its miles of sea-border, almost every sunny cove and rocky headland of which was a part of some near relative's homestead, were only half a day's journey distant; and the misty ocean-spaces beyond still widened out on our imagination from the green inland landscape around us. But the hills sometimes shut us in, body and soul. To those who have been reared by the sea a wide horizon is a necessity, both for the mind and for the eye.

We had many opportunities of escape towards our native shores, for the larger part of our large family still remained there, and there was a constant coming and going among us. The stage-driver looked upon us as his especial charge, and we had a sense of personal property in the Salem and Lowell stage-coach, which had once, like a fairy-godmother's coach, rumbled down into our own little lane, taken possession of us, and carried us off to a new home.

My married sisters had families growing up about them, and they liked to have us younger ones come and help take care of their babies. One of them sent for me just when the close air and long days' work were beginning to tell upon my health, and it was decided that I had better go. The salt wind soon restored my strength, and those months of quiet family life were very good for me.

Like most young girls, I had a motherly fondness for little children, and my two baby-nephews were my pride and delight. The older one had a delicate constitution, and there was a thoughtful, questioning look in his eyes, that seemed to gaze forward almost sadly, and foresee that he should never attain to manhood. The younger, a plump, vigorous urchin, three or four months old, did, without doubt, "feel his life in every limb." He was my especial charge, for his brother's clinging weakness gave him, the first-born, the place nearest his mother's heart. The baby bore the family name, mine and his mother's; "our little Lark," we sometimes called him, for his wide-awakeness and his merry-heartedness. (Alas! neither of those beautiful boys grew up to be men! One page of my home-memories is sadly written over with their elegy, the "Graves of a Household." Father, mother, and four sons, an entire family, long since passed away from earthly sight.)

The tie between my lovely baby-nephew and myself became very close. The first two years of a child's life are its most appealing years, and call out all the latent tenderness of the nature on which it leans for protection. I think I should have missed one of the best educating influences of my youth, if I had not had the care of that baby for a year or more, just as I entered my teens. I was never so happy as when I held him in my arms, sleeping or waking; and he, happy anywhere, was always contented when he was with me.

I was as fond as ever of reading, and somehow I managed to combine baby and book. Dickens's "Old Curiosity Shop" was just then coming out in a Philadelphia weekly paper, and I read it with the baby playing at my feet, or lying across my lap, in an unfinished room given up to sea-chests and coffee-bags and spicy foreign odors. (My cherub's papa was a sea-captain, usually away on his African voyages.) Little Nell and her grandfather became as real to me as my darling charge, and if a tear from his nurse's eyes sometimes dropped upon his cheek as he slept, he was not saddened by it. When he awoke he was irrepressible; clutching at my hair with his stout pink fists, and driving all dream-people effectually out of my head. Like all babies, he was something of a tyrant; but that brief, sweet despotism ends only too soon. I put him gratefully down, dimpled, chubby, and imperious, upon the list of my girlhood's teachers.

My sister had no domestic help besides mine, so I learned a good deal about general house-work. A girl's preparation for life was, in those days, considered quite imperfect, who had no practical knowledge of that kind. We were taught, indeed, how to do everything that a woman might be called upon to do under any circumstances, for herself or for the household she lived in. It was one of the advantages of the old simple way of living, that the young daughters of the house were, as a matter of course, instructed in all these things. They acquired the habit of being ready for emergencies, and the family that required no outside assistance was delightfully independent.

A young woman would have been considered a very inefficient being who could not make and mend and wash and iron her own clothing, and get three regular meals and clear them away every day, besides keeping the house tidy, and doing any other needed neighborly service, such as sitting all night by a sick-bed. To be "a good watcher" was considered one of the most important of womanly attainments. People who lived side by side exchanged such services without waiting to be asked, and they seemed to be happiest of whom such kindnesses were most expected.

Every kind of work brings its own compensations and attractions. I really began to like plain sewing; I enjoyed sitting down for a whole afternoon of it, fingers flying and thoughts flying faster still,—the motion of the hands seeming to set the mind astir. Such afternoons used to bring me throngs of poetic suggestions, particularly if I sat by an open window and could hear the wind blowing and a bird or two singing. Nature is often very generous in opening her heart to those who must keep their hands employed. Perhaps it is because she is always quietly at work herself, and so sympathizes with her busy human friends. And possibly there is no needful occupation which is wholly unbeautiful. The beauty of work depends upon the way we meet it— whether we arm ourselves each morning to attack it as an enemy that must be vanquished before night comes, or whether we open our eyes with the sunrise to welcome it as an approaching friend who will keep us delightful company all day, and who will make us feel, at evening, that the day was well worth its fatigues.

I found my practical experience of housekeeping and baby-tending very useful to me afterwards at the West, in my sister Emilie's family, when she was disabled by illness. I think, indeed, that every item of real knowledge I ever acquired has come into use somewhere or somehow in the course of the years. But these were not the things I had most wished to do. The whole world of thought lay unexplored before me,—a world of which I had already caught large and tempting glimpses, and I did not like to feel the horizon shutting me in, even to so pleasant a corner as this. And the worst of it was that I was getting too easy and contented, too indifferent to the higher realities which my work and my thoughtful companions had kept keenly clear before me. I felt myself slipping into an inward apathy from which it was hard to rouse myself. I could not let it go on so. I must be where my life could expand.

It was hard to leave the dear little fellow I had taught to walk and to talk, but I knew he would not be inconsolable. So I only said "I must go,"—and turned my back upon the sea, and my face to the banks of the Merrimack.

When I returned I found that I enjoyed even the familiar, unremitting clatter of the mill, because it indicated that something was going on. I liked to feel the people around me, even those whom I did not know, as a wave may like to feel the surrounding waves urging it forward, with or against its own will. I felt that I belonged to the world, that there was something for me to do in it, though I had not yet found out what. Something to do; it might be very little, but still it would be my own work. And then there was the better something which I had almost forgotten,—*to be!* Underneath my dull thoughts the old aspirations were smouldering, the old ideals rose and beckoned to me through the rekindling light.

It was always aspiration rather than ambition by which I felt myself stirred. I did not care to outstrip others, and become what is called "distinguished," were that a possibility, so much as I longed to answer the Voice that invited, ever receding, up to invisible heights, however unattainable they might seem. I was conscious of a desire that others should feel something coming to them out of my life like the breath of flowers, the whisper of the winds, the warmth of the sunshine, and the depth of the sky. That, I felt, did not require great gifts or a fine education. We might all be that to each other. And there was no opportunity for vanity or pride in receiving a beautiful influence, and giving it out again.

I do not suppose that I definitely thought all this, though I find that the verses I wrote for our two mill magazines at about this time often expressed these and similar longings. They were vague, and they were too likely to dissipate themselves in mere dreams. But our aspirations come to us from a source far beyond ourselves. Happy are they who are "not disobedient unto the heavenly vision"!

A girl of sixteen sees the world before her through rose-tinted mists, a blending of celestial colors and earthly exhalations, and she cannot separate their elements, if she would; they all belong to the landscape of her youth. It is the mystery of the meeting horizons,—the visible beauty seeking to lose and find itself in the Invisible.

In returning to my daily toil among workmates from the hill-country, the scenery to which they belonged became also a part of my life. They brought the mountains with them, a new background and a new hope. We shared an uneven path and homely occupations; but above us hung glorious summits never wholly out of sight. Every blossom and every dewdrop at our feet was touched with some tint of that far-off splendor, and every pebble by the wayside was a messenger from the peak that our feet would stand upon by and by.

The true climber knows the delight of trusting his path, of following it without seeing a step before him, or a glimpse of blue sky above him, sometimes only knowing that it is the right path because it is the only one, and because it leads upward. This our daily duty was to us. Though we did not always know it, the faithful plodder was sure to win the heights. Unconsciously we learned the lesson that only by humble Doing can any of us win the lofty possibilities of Being. For indeed, what we all want to find is not so much our place as our path. The path leads to the place, and the place, when we have found it, is only a clearing by the roadside, an opening into another path.

And no comrades are so dear as those who have broken with us a pioneer road which it will be safe and good for others to follow; which will furnish a plain clue for all bewildered travelers hereafter. There is no more exhilarating human experience than this, and perhaps it is the highest angelic one. It may be that some such mutual work is to link us forever with one another in the Infinite Life.

The girls who toiled together at Lowell were clearing away a few weeds from the overgrown track of independent labor for other women. They practically said, by numbering themselves among factory girls, that in our country no real odium could be attached to any honest toil that any self-respecting woman might undertake.

I regard it as one of the privileges of my youth that I was permitted to grow up among those active, interesting girls, whose lives were not mere echoes of other lives, but had principle and purpose distinctly their own. Their vigor of character was a natural development. The New Hampshire girls who came to Lowell were descendants of the sturdy backwoodsmen who settled that State scarcely a hundred years before. Their grandmothers had suffered the hardships of frontier life, had known the horrors of savage warfare when the beautiful valleys of the Connecticut and the Merrimack were threaded with Indian trails from Canada to the white settlements. Those young women did justice to their inheritance. They were earnest and capable; ready to undertake anything that was worth doing. My dreamy, indolent nature was shamed into activity among them. They gave me a larger, firmer ideal of womanhood.

Often during the many summers and autumns that of late years I have spent among the New Hampshire hills, sometimes far up the mountain sides, where I could listen to the first song of the little brooks setting out on their journey to join the very river that flowed at my feet when I was a working-girl on its banks,—the Merrimack,—I have felt as if I could also hear the early music of my workmates' lives, those who were born among these glorious summits. Pure, strong, crystalline natures, carrying down with them the light of blue skies and the freshness of free winds to their place of toil, broadening and strengthening as they went on, who can tell how they have refreshed the world, how beautifully they have blended their being with the great ocean of results? A brook's life is like the life of a maiden. The rivers receive their strength from the rock-born rills, from the unfailing purity of the mountain-streams.

A girl's place in the world is a very strong one: it is a pity that she does not always see it so. It is strongest through her natural impulse to steady herself by leaning upon the Eternal Life, the only Reality; and her weakness comes also from her inclination to lean against something,—upon an unworthy support, rather than none at all. She often lets her life get broken into fragments among the flimsy trellises of fashion and conventionality, when it might be a perfect thing in the upright beauty of its own consecrated freedom.

Yet girlhood seldom appreciates itself. We often hear a girl wishing that she were a boy. That seems so strange! God made no mistake in her creation. He sent her into the world full of power and will to be a *helper;* and only He knows how much his world needs help. She is here to make this great house of humanity a habitable and a beautiful place, without and within,—a true home for every one of his children. It matters not if she is poor, if she has to toil for her daily bread, or even if she is surrounded by coarseness and uncongeniality: nothing can deprive her of her natural instinct to help, of her birthright as a helper. These very hindrances may, with faith and patience, develop in her a nobler womanhood.

No; let girls be as thankful that they are girls as that they are human beings; for they also, according to his own loving plan for them, were created in the image of God. Their real power, the divine dowry of womanhood, is that of receiving and giving inspiration. In this a girl often surpasses her brother; and it is for her to hold firmly and faithfully to her holiest instincts, so that when he lets his standard droop, she may, through her spiritual strength, be a standard-bearer for him. Courage and self-reliance are now held to be virtues as womanly as they are manly; for the world has grown wise enough to see that nothing except a life can really help another life. It is strange that it should ever have held any other theory about woman.

That was a true use of the word "help" that grew up so naturally in the rendering and receiving of womanly service in the old-fashioned New England household. A girl came into a family as one of the home-group, to share its burdens, to feel that they were her own. The woman who employed her, if her nature was at all generous, could not feel that money alone was an equivalent for a heart's service; she added to it her friendship, her gratitude and esteem. The domestic problem can never be rightly settled until the old idea of mutual help is in some way restored. This is a question for girls of the present generation to consider, and she who can bring about a practical solution of it will win the world's gratitude.

We used sometimes to see it claimed, in public prints, that it would be better for all of us mill-girls to be working in families, at domestic service, than to be where we were.

Perhaps the difficulties of modern housekeepers did begin with the opening of the Lowell factories. Country girls were naturally independent, and the feeling that at this new work the few hours they had of every-day leisure were entirely their own was a satisfaction to them. They preferred it to going out as "hired help." It was like a young man's pleasure in entering upon business for himself. Girls had never tried that experiment before, and they liked it. It brought out in them a dormant strength of character which the world did not previously see, but now fully acknowledges. Of course they had a right to continue at that freer kind of work as long as they chose, although their doing so increased the perplexities of the housekeeping problem for themselves even, since many of them were to become, and did become, American house-mistresses.

It would be a step towards the settlement of this vexed and vexing question if girls would decline to classify each other by their occupations, which among us are usually only temporary, and are continually shifting from one pair of hands to another. Changes of fortune come so abruptly that the millionaire's daughter of to-day may be glad to earn her living by sewing or sweeping tomorrow.

It is the first duty of every woman to recognize the mutual bond of universal womanhood. Let her ask herself whether she would like to hear herself or her sister spoken of as a shop-girl, or a factory-girl, or a servant-girl, if necessity had compelled her for a time to be employed in either of the ways indicated. If she would shrink from it a little, then she is a little inhuman when she puts her unknown human sisters who are so occupied into a class by themselves, feeling herself to be somewhat their superior. She is really the superior person who has accepted her work and is doing it faithfully, whatever it is. This designating others by their casual employments prevents one from making real distinctions, from knowing persons as persons. A false standard is set up in the minds of those who classify and of those who are classified.

Perhaps it is chiefly the fault of ladies themselves that the word "lady" has nearly lost its original meaning (a noble one) indicating sympathy and service;—bread-giver to those who are in need. The idea that it means something external in dress or circumstances has been too generally adopted by rich and poor; and this, coupled with the sweeping notion that in our country one person is just as good as another, has led to ridiculous results, like that of saleswomen calling themselves "salesladies." I have even heard a chambermaid at a hotel introduce herself to guests as "the chamberlady."

I do not believe that any Lowell mill-girl was ever absurd enough to wish to be known as a "factory-lady," although most of them knew that "factory-girl" did not represent a high type of womanhood in the Old World. But they themselves belonged to the New World, not to the Old; and they were making their own traditions, to hand down to their Republican descendants,—one of which was and is that honest work has no need to assert itself or to humble itself in a nation like ours, but simply to take its place as one of the foundation-stones of the Republic.

The young women who worked at Lowell had the advantage of living in a community where character alone commanded respect. They never, at their work or away from it, heard themselves contemptuously spoken of on account of their occupation, except by the ignorant or weak-minded, whose comments they were of course too sensible to heed.

We may as well acknowledge that one of the unworthy tendencies of womankind is towards petty estimates of other women. This classifying habit illustrates the fact. If we must classify our sisters, let us broaden ourselves by making large classifications. We might all place ourselves in one of two ranks—the women who do something, and the women who do nothing; the first being of course the only creditable place to occupy. And if we would escape from our pettinesses, as we all may and should, the way to do it is to find the key to other lives, and live in their largeness, by sharing their outlook upon life. Even poorer people's windows will give us a new horizon, and often a far broader one than our own.

31

Andrew Carnegie (1835–1919)

How I Served My Apprenticeship

Among the millionaires of the late nineteenth century, Andrew Carnegie is almost alone in having liked to think of himself as a literary man. He cultivated the company of Mark Twain, Matthew Arnold, and Herbert Spencer. He wrote essays for the *North American Review* and other magazines, and in 1886 he published a book, *Triumphant Democracy,* expounding his economic and political ideas. He also liked celebrating himself and the business ethic he lived by. "Attract attention," he advised young men. So, where many of his contemporaries avoided the public eye, Carnegie liked to show off. It might even be argued that his later beneficences— endowing 2507 public libraries, financing the Carnegie Institute of Technology, the Carnegie Foundation for the Advancement of Teaching, and the Carnegie Endowment for International Peace—were not merely done out of his belief that great fortunes should be given away, his "gospel of wealth," but out of his love of attention.

In this piece, he gives his life the kind of legendary status that is so strong in autobiographies addressed to children, while also helping to justify his success to himself. For men may lie when they talk to children, but they prefer not to think they do. They tend rather to be all the more certain of what they have said.

Youth's Companion, where the piece appeared in April, 1896, was also a magazine read by adults, as well as by adults reading to their children. Founded in 1829 by Nathaniel Willis, father of Sara P. (Fanny Fern) Willis, it was bought in 1857 by Daniel Sharp Ford, who, by the 1890s, raised its circulation from 4000 to 500,000. Carnegie took the opportunity to proselytize widely and simply for the glory of capitalism, combating the populist and progressive sentiments that had been rising since the depression of 1893. For him, nostalgia about childhood was not enough. He made his childhood into an economics lesson.

For biography, see Joseph F. Wall, *Andrew Carnegie* (New York: Oxford Univ. Press, 1970; 2d ed., Univ. of Pittsburgh Press, 1989), as well as Carnegie's complete *Autobiography* (Boston and New York: Houghton Mifflin, 1920).

It is a great pleasure to tell how I served my apprenticeship as a business man. But there seems to be a question preceding this: Why did I become a business man? I am sure that I should never have selected a business career if I had been permitted to choose.

The eldest son of parents who were themselves poor, I had, fortunately, to begin to perform some useful work in the world while still very young in order to earn an honest livelihood, and was thus shown even in early boyhood that my duty was to assist my parents and, like them, become, as soon as possible, a bread-winner in the family. What I could get to do, not what I desired, was the question.

When I was born my father was a well-to-do master weaver in Dunfermline, Scotland. He owned no less than four damask-looms and employed apprentices. This was before the days of steam-factories for the manufacture of linen. A few large merchants took orders, and employed master weavers, such as my father, to weave the cloth, the merchants supplying the materials.

As the factory system developed hand-loom weaving naturally declined, and my father was one of the sufferers by the change. The first serious lesson of my life came to me one day when he had taken in the last of his work to the merchant, and returned to our little home greatly distressed because there was no more work for him to do. I was then just about ten years of age, but the lesson burned into my heart, and I resolved then that the wolf of poverty should be driven from our door some day, if I could do it.

The question of selling the old looms and starting for the United States came up in the family council, and I heard it discussed from day to day. It was finally resolved to take the plunge and join relatives already in Pittsburg. I well remember that neither father nor mother thought the change would be otherwise than a great sacrifice for them, but that "it would be better for the two boys."

In after life, if you can look back as I do and wonder at the complete surrender of their own desires which parents make for the good of their children, you must reverence their memories with feelings akin to worship.

On arriving in Allegheny City (there were four of us: father, mother, my younger brother, and myself), my father entered a cotton factory. I soon followed, and served as a "bobbin-boy," and this is how I began my preparation for subsequent apprenticeship as a business man. I received one dollar and twenty cents a week, and was then just about twelve years old.

I cannot tell you how proud I was when I received my first week's own earnings. One dollar and twenty cents made by myself and given to me because I had been of some use in the world! No longer entirely dependent upon my parents, but at last admitted to the family partnership as a contributing member and able to help them! I think this makes a man out of a boy sooner than almost anything else, and a real man, too, if there be any germ of true manhood in him. It is everything to feel that you are useful.

I have had to deal with great sums. Many millions of dollars have since passed through my hands. But the genuine satisfaction I had from that one dollar and twenty cents out-weighs any subsequent pleasure in money-getting. It was the direct reward of honest, manual labor; it represented a week of very hard work—so hard that, but for the aim and end which sanctified it, slavery might not be much too strong a term to describe it.

For a lad of twelve to rise and breakfast every morning, except the blessed Sunday morning, and go into the streets and find his way to the factory and begin to work while it was still dark outside, and not be released until after darkness came again in the evening, forty minutes' interval only being allowed at noon, was a terrible task.

But I was young and had my dreams, and something within always told me that this would not, could not, should not last—I should some day get into a better position. Besides this, I felt myself no longer a mere boy, but quite a little man, and this made me happy.

A change soon came, for a kind old Scotsman, who knew some of our relatives, made bobbins, and took me into his factory before I was thirteen. But here for a time it was even worse than in the cotton factory, because I was set to fire a boiler in the cellar, and actually to run the small steam-engine which drove the machinery. The firing of the boiler was all right, for fortunately we did not use coal, but the refuse wooden chips; and I always liked to work in wood. But the responsibility of keeping the water right and of running the engine, and the danger of my making a mistake and blowing the whole factory to pieces, caused too great a strain, and I often awoke and found myself sitting up in bed through the night, trying the steam-gauges. But I never told them at home that I was having a hard tussle. No, no! everything must be bright to them.

This was a point of honor, for every member of the family was working hard, except, of course, my little brother, who was then a child, and we were telling each other only all the bright things. Besides this, no man would whine and give up—he would die first.

There was no servant in our family, and several dollars per week were earned by the mother by binding shoes after her daily work was done! Father was also hard at work in the factory. And could I complain?

My kind employer, John Hay,—peace to his ashes!—soon relieved me of the undue strain, for he needed some one to make out bills and keep his accounts, and finding that I could write a plain school-boy hand and could "cipher," he made me his only clerk. But still I had to work hard upstairs in the factory, for the clerking took but little time.

You know how people moan about poverty as being a great evil, and it seems to be accepted that if people had only plenty of money and were rich, they would be happy and more useful, and get more out of life.

As a rule, there is more genuine satisfaction, a truer life, and more obtained from life in the humble cottages of the poor than in the palaces of the rich. I always pity the sons and daughters of rich men, who are attended by servants, and have governesses at a later age, but am glad to remember that they do not know what they have missed.

They have kind fathers and mothers, too, and think that they enjoy the sweetness of these blessings to the fullest: but this they cannot do; for the poor boy who has in his father his constant companion, tutor, and model, and in his mother—holy name!—his nurse, teacher, guardian angel, saint, all in one, has a richer, more precious fortune in life than any rich man's son who is not so favored can possibly know, and compared with which all other fortunes count for little.

It is because I know how sweet and happy and pure the home of honest poverty is, how free from perplexing care, from social envies and emulations, how loving and how united its members may be in the common interest of supporting the family, that I sympathize with the rich man's boy and congratulate the poor man's boy; and it is for these reasons that from the ranks of the poor so many strong, eminent, self-reliant men have always sprung and always must spring.

If you will read the list of the immortals who "were not born to die," you will find that most of them have been born to the precious heritage of poverty.

It seems, nowadays, a matter of universal desire that poverty should be abolished. We should be quite willing to abolish luxury, but to abolish honest, industrious, self-denying poverty would be to destroy the soil upon which mankind produces the virtues which enable our race to reach a still higher civilization than it now possesses.

I come now to the third step in my apprenticeship, for I had already taken two, as you see—the cotton factory and then the bobbin factory; and with the third—the third time is the chance, you know—deliverance came. I obtained a situation as messenger boy in the telegraph office of Pittsburg when I was fourteen. Here I entered a new world.

Amid books, newspapers, pencils, pens and ink and writing-pads, and a clean office, bright windows, and the literary atmosphere, I was the happiest boy alive.

My only dread was that I should some day be dismissed because I did not know the city; for it is necessary that a messenger boy should know all the firms and addresses of men who are in the habit of receiving telegrams. But I was a stranger in Pittsburg. However, I made up my mind that I would learn to repeat successively each business house in the principal streets, and was soon able to shut my eyes and begin at one side of Wood Street, and call every firm successively to the top, then pass to the other side and call every firm to the bottom. Before long I was able to do this with the business streets generally. My mind was then at rest upon that point.

Of course every messenger boy wants to become an operator, and before the operators arrive in the early mornings the boys slipped up to the instruments and practised. This I did, and was soon able to talk to the boys in the other offices along the line, who were also practising.

One morning I heard Philadelphia calling Pittsburg and giving the signal, "Death message." Great attention was then paid to "death messages," and I thought I ought to try to take this one. I answered and did so, and went off and delivered it before the operator came. After that the operators sometimes used to ask me to work for them.

Having a sensitive ear for sound, I soon learned to take messages by the ear, which was then very uncommon—I think only two persons in the United States could then do it. Now every operator takes by ear, so easy it is to follow and do what any other boy can—if you only have to. This brought me into notice, and finally I became an operator, and received the, to me, enormous recompense of twenty-five dollars per month—three hundred dollars a year!

This was a fortune—the very sum that I had fixed when I was a factory-worker as the fortune I wished to possess, because the family could live on three hundred dollars a year and be almost or quite independent. Here it was at last! But I was soon to be in receipt of extra compensation for extra work.

The six newspapers of Pittsburg received telegraphic news in common. Six copies of each despatch were made by a gentleman who received six dollars per week for the work, and he offered me a gold dollar every week if I would do it, of which I was very glad indeed, because I always liked to work with news and scribble for newspapers.

The reporters came to a room every evening for the news which I had prepared, and this brought me into most pleasant intercourse with these clever fellows, and besides, I got a dollar a week as pocket-money, for this was not considered family revenue by me.

I think this last step of doing something beyond one's task is fully entitled to be considered "business." The other revenue, you see, was just salary obtained for regular work; but here was a little business operation upon my own account, and I was very proud indeed of my gold dollar every week.

The Pennsylvania Railroad shortly after this was completed to Pittsburg, and that genius, Thomas A. Scott, was its superintendent. He often came to the telegraph office to talk to his chief, the general superintendent, at Altoona, and I became known to him in this way.

When that great railway system put up a wire of its own, he asked me to be his clerk and operator; so I left the telegraph office—in which there is great danger that a young man may be permanently buried, as it were—and became connected with the railways.

The new appointment was accompanied by what was, to me, a tremendous increase of salary. It jumped from twenty-five to thirty-five dollars per month. Mr. Scott was then receiving one hundred and twenty-five dollars per month, and I used to wonder what on earth he could do with so much money.

I remained for thirteen years in the service of the Pennsylvania Railroad Company, and was at last superintendent of the Pittsburg division of the road, successor to Mr. Scott, who had in the meantime risen to the office of vice-president of the company.

One day Mr. Scott, who was the kindest of men, and had taken a great fancy to me, asked if I had or could find five hundred dollars to invest.

Here the business instinct came into play. I felt that as the door was opened for a business investment with my chief, it would be wilful flying in the face of providence if I did not jump at it; so I answered promptly:

"Yes, sir; I think I can."

"Very well," he said, "get it; a man has just died who owns ten shares in the Adams Express Company which I want you to buy. It will cost you fifty dollars per share, and I can help you with a little balance if you cannot raise it all."

Here was a queer position. The available assets of the whole family were not five hundred dollars. But there was one member of the family whose ability, pluck, and resource never failed us, and I felt sure the money could be raised somehow or other by my mother.

Indeed, had Mr. Scott known our position he would have advanced it himself; but the last thing in the world the proud Scot will do is to reveal his poverty and rely upon others. The family had managed by this time to purchase a small house and pay for it in order to save rent. My recollection is that it was worth eight hundred dollars.

The matter was laid before the council of three that night, and the oracle spoke: "Must be done. Mortgage our house. I will take the steamer in the morning for Ohio, and see uncle, and ask him to arrange it. I am sure he can." This was done. Of course her visit was successful—where did she ever fail?

The money was procured, paid over; ten shares of Adams Express Company stock was mine; but no one knew our little home had been mortgaged "to give our boy a start."

Adams Express stock then paid monthly dividends of one per cent, and the first check for five dollars arrived. I can see it now, and I well remember the signature of "J. C. Babcock, Cashier," who wrote a big "John Hancock" hand.

The next day being Sunday, we boys—myself and my ever-constant companions—took our usual Sunday afternoon stroll in the country, and sitting down in the woods, I showed them this check, saying, "Eureka! We have found it."

Here was something new to all of us, for none of us had ever received anything but from toil. A return from capital was something strange and new.

How money could make money, how, without any attention from me, this mysterious golden visitor should come, led to much speculation upon the part of the young fellows, and I was for the first time hailed as a "capitalist."

You see, I was beginning to serve my apprenticeship as a business man in a satisfactory manner.

A very important incident in my life occurred when, one day in a train, a nice, farmer-looking gentleman approached me, saying that the conductor had told him I was connected with the Pennsylvania Railroad, and he would like to show me something. He pulled from a small green bag the model of the first sleeping-car. This was Mr. Woodruff, the inventor.

Its value struck me like a flash. I asked him to come to Altoona the following week, and he did so. Mr. Scott, with his usual quickness, grasped the idea. A contract was made with Mr. Woodruff to put two trial cars on the Pennsylvania Railroad. Before leaving Altoona Mr. Woodruff came and offered me an interest in the venture, which I promptly accepted. But how I was to make my payments rather troubled me, for the cars were to be paid for in monthly instalments after delivery, and my first monthly payment was to be two hundred and seventeen dollars and a half.

I had not the money, and I did not see any way of getting it. But I finally decided to visit the local banker and ask him for a loan, pledging myself to repay at the rate of fifteen dollars per month. He promptly granted it. Never shall I forget his putting his arm over my shoulder, saying, "Oh, yes, Andy; you are all right!"

I then and there signed my first note. Proud day this; and surely now no one will dispute that I was becoming a "business man." I had signed my first note, and, most important of all,—for any fellow can sign a note,—I had found a banker willing to take it as "good."

My subsequent payments were made by the receipts from the sleeping-cars, and I really made my first considerable sum from this investment in the Woodruff Sleeping-car Company, which was afterward absorbed by Mr. Pullman—a remarkable man whose name is now known over all the world.

Shortly after this I was appointed superintendent of the Pittsburg division, and returned to my dear old home, smoky Pittsburg. Wooden bridges were then used exclusively upon the railways, and the Pennsylvania Railroad was experimenting with a bridge built of cast-iron. I saw that wooden bridges would not do for the future, and organized a company in Pittsburg to build iron bridges.

Here again I had recourse to the bank, because my share of the capital was twelve hundred and fifty dollars, and I had not the money; but the bank lent it to me, and we began the Keystone Bridge Works, which proved a great success. This company built the first great bridge over the Ohio River, three hundred feet span, and has built many of the most important structures since.

This was my beginning in manufacturing; and from that start all our other works have grown, the profits of one building the other. My "apprenticeship" as a business man soon ended, for I resigned my position as an officer of the Pennsylvania Railroad Company to give exclusive attention to business.

I was no longer merely an official working for others upon a salary, but a full-fledged business man working upon my own account.

I never was quite reconciled to working for other people. At the most, the railway officer has to look forward to the enjoyment of a stated salary, and he has a great many people to please; even if he gets to be president, he has sometimes a board of directors who cannot know what is best to be done; and even if this board be satisfied, he has a board of stock-holders to criticize him, and as the property is not his own he cannot manage it as he pleases.

I always liked the idea of being my own master, of manufacturing something and giving employment to many men. There is only one thing to think of manufacturing if you are a Pittsburger, for Pittsburg even then had asserted her supremacy as the "Iron City," the leading iron-and-steel-manufacturing city in America.

So my indispensable and clever partners, who had been my boy companions, I am delighted to say,—some of the very boys who had met in the grove to wonder at the five-dollar check,—began business, and still continue extending it to meet the ever-growing and ever-changing wants of our most progressive country, year after year.

Always we are hoping that we need expand no farther; yet ever we are finding that to stop expanding would be to fall behind; and even to-day the successive improvements and inventions follow each other so rapidly that we see just as much yet to be done as ever.

When the manufacturer of steel ceases to grow he begins to decay, so we must keep on extending. The result of all these developments is that three pounds of finished steel are now bought in Pittsburg for two cents, which is cheaper than anywhere else on the earth, and that our country has become the greatest producer of iron in the world.

And so ends the story of my apprenticeship and graduation as a business man.

PART SIX

Lives in Progress, 1900–1935

In February, 1904, William Dean Howells devoted his popular "Editor's Easy Chair" column in *Harper's Monthly Magazine* to an essay on autobiography, a kind of writing which he thought had been appearing very frequently just then. In October, 1909, and April, 1911, he wrote two more columns on it, each time reflecting more deeply on what it was and what he liked in it. It was, he said, one of the most entertaining kinds of literature—of universal interest and the least likely to be boring. It was the "most democratic province in the republic of letters," because it was open to everyone and a great story was potentially present in everyone's life. It was also a very modern form and, he wrote, "supremely the Christian contribution to the forms of literature," and he mentioned, in particular, Jonathan Edwards's "Personal Narrative" and Franklin's *Autobiography* as the first important American examples. He added, however, that, "Autobiography is a strange world, and there are many sorts of people in it whom the socially or morally sensitive would not like to consort with if they were to meet them in the flesh,"[1] thus simultaneously recognizing its diversity and begrudging it a certain freedom from genteel morality. Howells liked autobiographies best when their authors concentrated on their own lives, instead of merely writing memoirs, and when they wrote most sincerely.

That autobiography should have received such attention from the most influential and most respected man of letters in America was a clear sign that it was now a fully recognized literary genre. Howells also wrote several volumes of autobiography himself, further acknowledging its value, as well as his opinion that one might write each time of different aspects of one's self. At almost the same time as he was writing these column pieces, his friends and contemporaries Henry James, Mark Twain, and Henry Adams were writing their great autobiographies, and, in 1909, Anna Robeson Burr published

---

1. William Dean Howells, "Editor's Easy Chair," *Harper's Monthly Magazine* 119 (1909): 796–98. Other Howells columns that discuss autobiography are in volumes 108 (1904), pp. 478–82, and 122 (1911), pp. 795–98.

the first book on the subject, *Autobiography, a Critical and Comparative Study*. In 1913, Theodore Roosevelt would publish his *Autobiography,* the first full-length autobiography by a president or ex-president since Thomas Jefferson's.

The period beginning in the late nineteenth century and extending up to the First World War, what historians call the "Age of Reform" or "Progressive Era," would add even more to the richness and significance of American autobiography. The experience of reform—of changing government and society and of changing and being changed oneself—was an inevitable subject for a new kind of confession and conversion narrative. The experience of immigration to America, followed by the learning of new customs and the difficulties of acculturation or assimilation, was another vast subject. Between 1890 and 1910, over thirteen million immigrants arrived in the United States, raising the population to nearly ninety-two million by 1910. All the new technologies of the twentieth century—a comprehensive railroad network, printing presses that now turned out hundreds of thousands of copies of newspapers and magazines in the time once needed to print just thousands, and inventions like the electric streetcar, bicycle, automobile, telephone, and electric light—now visibly demonstrated the progressively increasing power of industrial civilization. There was no going back. The nostalgic autobiographers of Howells's generation could look back in memory to times of frontier piety and simplicity, but the future seemed concerned only with civilization, technology, and progress. Thus, the men and women who came of age between 1895 and 1920 (and who wrote their autobiographies through the longer period of about 1900–1935) lived "lives in progress." They were lives in motion, lives in which the metaphors of progress and reform were far more important than they had ever been before, and lives which, to a great degree, they tried to live according to the modern virtues of education, science, and efficiency.

This is not to say that they were all alike. Looking just at the better known autobiographers of this generation, one sees an incredibly diverse group. Jane Addams, Chicago social worker and peace activist. Edith Wharton, well-born New Yorker who became a best-selling novelist. Teddy Roosevelt. Lincoln Steffens and Ida Tarbell, journalists and muckrakers. Frederic C. Howe, reformer and public administrator. S. S. McClure, the founder of one of the major organs of journalistic muckraking, *McClure's Magazine*. Louis Sullivan and Frank Lloyd Wright, Chicago architects. Emma Goldman and Alexander Berkman, anarchists. Clarence Darrow, trial lawyer. Helen Keller, educator and advocate of the rights of the blind. Hamlin Garland, prairie farmer and author. Charles Eastman, a Sioux who became a medical doctor and an advocate of Indian rights. Booker T. Washington, the founder of Tuskegee Institute. W. E. B. Du Bois, a founder of the National Association for the Advancement of Colored People. William Allen White, newspaper editor from Emporia, Kansas. Immigrants like Mary Antin, Edward Bok, Abraham

Cahan, and Jacob Riis. And Indians like Geronimo and Sam Blowsnake, who did not voluntarily write their own stories but whose stories were solicited— Sam Blowsnake's by the young anthropologist Paul Radin and Geronimo's by the journalist S. M. Barrett.

Despite this diversity, these autobiographies had significant common features. All of their protagonists played out the latter part of their lives in the new industrial civilization that they celebrated or criticized. They wrote for newspapers, travelled on Pullman trains and ocean liners, lectured, organized clubs and associations, founded or went to new kinds of social institutions like settlement houses and graduate schools, and vacationed in summer cottages and cabins (to "get away" from these same new institutions). In such activities they were promoting causes and pursuing careers and professions, some of which were brand new. Indeed, one of the features of the new civilization is that it had so many new careers, such as anthropology, sociology, social work, and public administration, while the older professions and businesses like medicine, law, journalism, engineering, teaching, and banking became much more specialized. At the same time, there were hundreds of new problems on which critics and reformers could work, like monopolies, immigration, labor organizing, strikes, juvenile delinquency, "frenzied finance," "the shame of the cities," modern marriage, women's rights, race problems and "the color line," and the conservation of natural resources. Once in such a "career," one was then expected to "progress," a career being by definition a field for consecutive achievement and advancement, as opposed to just a "job" or an "occupation." Equally important, the career or profession usually required special training and a new special emphasis on being scientific. For it was science and the scientific method that underlay the new promise of social progress. Even Geronimo and Sam Blowsnake, who were the victims rather than the beneficiaries of this new civilization, can be located within this picture. The Apache chief Geronimo served his editor S. M. Barrett as a sort of baseline against which to measure the "progress" of other Americans. Sam Blowsnake, as the unnamed author of the *Autobiography of a Winnebago,* served Paul Radin's anthropological study of the Winnebago tribe.

The selections given below illustrate these features of Progressive Era autobiography in a variety of ways. Jack London's "What Life Means to Me" was written in 1904, at a point when he was rededicating himself to socialism, after his early success as a writer and a period as a college student had given him a glimpse of bourgeois comfort and respectability. The experience of rising out of the working class and then associating with society women, capitalists, and professors has, he says, enabled him to survey civilization more thoroughly, so that he can now write as a disinterested investigator rather than an agitator or someone just jealous of the classes above him. This has also enabled him to see what all classes have in common: "I saw the naked simplicities of the complicated civilization in which I lived." All men and women must sell themselves "to get food and shelter," he says, claiming to expose the hypocrisy of the upperclass men and women who pretend that they do not buy and sell. His illusions are gone, and he wants to shatter other illusions as well; indeed, he wants to work "shoulder to shoulder" with other socialists to "topple" the old order. But he still "look[s] forward to a time when man shall progress upon something worthier and higher than his stomach . . ." and he retains a "belief in the nobility and excellence of the human."

London's testimony aimed at reporting on his life as if it were a kind of experiment. His language was not only impassioned but also, in its way, clinical, stripping away deceptions, and he meant to persuade by giving empirical evidence (at least, as he thought of it), rather than by an appeal to higher morals and sentiments. This is another trait of the progressive as autobiographer, and, indeed, Randolph Bourne, another writer of this period, wrote an essay called "The Experimental Life," in which he wrote: "Life is not a campaign of battle, but a laboratory where its possibilities for the enhancement of happiness and the realization of ideals are to be tested and observed."[2] It was in this spirit that Bourne wrote of his own experience as "The Handicapped," not seeking sympathy but recounting what he had learned as a consequence of growing up handicapped.

John Muir, though from the preceding generation, was also an experimenter, as he explains both in the chapter given here from *The Story of My Boyhood and Youth* and in numerous parts of his books about conservation and the Sierra Nevada. As a boy, he was so overworked on his father's Wisconsin farm that he had to arise at 1:00 A.M. in order to have any time to read; so to get himself up he invented the alarm clock and tilting bed that he took to the state fair at Madison, Wisconsin, just before starting his college education. Later he undertook every new climb in the Sierra as a challenge to discover more about himself and his beloved mountains. His scientific achievement was the discovery of the glacial origin of the mountain canyons and valleys. His progressive vision was his realization that without legal protection the Yosemite and other valleys would be destroyed by mining, logging, and other commercial interests. His writing, which was almost all autobiographical, was a means of identifying himself with the wilderness and so promoting conservation.

From Muir's Wisconsin and California to Mary Antin's Boston may seem like a long way, but it is important to note that Muir, too, was an immigrant and that his collected work, too, might be called *The Promised Land*. Thanks to education and to the eagerness with which they adopted American manners and aspirations, both became assimilated very quickly—though not exactly into the so-called "mainstream" of American society, because both

2. Randolph S. Bourne, *Youth and Life* (Boston and New York: Houghton Mifflin, 1913), pp. 232–33.

also preserved their distinct kinds of independence. Muir was the solitary mountaineer. Antin upheld a special Emersonian universalism. But in writing autobiographies, in adopting this increasingly popular way of telling their stories and advocating their causes—conservation in Muir's case, racial and religious tolerance in Antin's—they clearly showed that they had become fully active and articulate members of the new civilization.

Writers such as W. E. B. Du Bois, Charlotte Perkins Gilman, and Roderick Seidenberg remained nearer to the fringes of their America, but their lives and writing also show passionate commitment to the ideals of social reform and human progress.

In 1920, when he published *Darkwater,* Du Bois was in the minority of American black leaders, which placed him in the minority of a minority, so to speak. The ideas and programs of Booker T. Washington still dominated the genteel side of American race relations, and lynch mobs dominated the less genteel side. During the Civil War, black troops had been trained mostly as work battalions, and after the war hate groups grew powerful in the Midwest as well as the South. In such an atmosphere, Du Bois's tones of reason and irony and his assemblages of fact and personal testimony were not likely to get a large hearing, but he persisted anyway, just as he had once persisted in getting himself a college and graduate education and a fellowship for further study in Germany. His scholarly studies, *The Suppression of the African Slave Trade to the United States of America, 1638–1870* and *The Philadelphia Negro,* were ample evidence of his faith in reason. Autobiography and the autobiographical essay, furthermore, enabled him to reach beyond scholars to a middle-class audience of people of goodwill from both races. Indeed, American progressives and reformers were overwhelmingly middle-class, despite exceptions like Jack London, and the fact that all these men and women were writing their autobiographies was another sign that autobiography had now become solidly middle-class. But the Negro middle class and the sympathetic white middle class that Du Bois addressed were still small. Du Bois and his allies spoke of black Americans advancing behind the leadership of their "talented tenth," a term and a concept which were, in a way, to anticipate the reality. But for the idea to become reality, the people in it needed to become known, too, and autobiography was a means.

At the very moment in 1919 when Du Bois wrote his autobiographical introduction to *Darkwater,* Roderick Seidenberg was in an army prison, protesting not racial injustice but the war and the necessary agent of large-scale war, military conscription. His supporters and future audience were even smaller than Du Bois's. But pacifism had been another expression of the broad progressive temper in the early 1900s, as perhaps best illustrated by William James's lecture-essay calling for "A Moral Equivalent of War." Pre-war pacifists, ranging from Andrew Carnegie to Jane Addams, looked upon war as a barbaric anachronism and thought that reason and progress, as implemented through international agencies like the Hague Court, would eliminate it. The American imperialists like Theodore Roosevelt were more powerful, winning the intense controversy over annexation of the Philippines, but even in 1916, as demonstrated by Woodrow Wilson's election slogan, "He Kept Us Out of War," there was still strong anti-war sentiment.[3] In April, 1917, with American entry into the war, those sentiments were suddenly held by only a small remnant of intellectuals, dedicated socialists, and members of little-understood religious sects like the Amish, Mennonites, and Quakers.

Roderick Seidenberg explains how these diverse men came together and led a highly successful work-stoppage at the Army Disciplinary Barracks at Fort Leavenworth, Kansas. In smuggling out their letters, diaries, and newspaper articles protesting against their treatment, they had also begun using these different kinds of autobiographical writing as propaganda, just as earlier prisoners, slaves, and victims of oppression had done. Yet it was not until 1932 that Seidenberg published the story of his experience. By then, disillusionment with the war had begun to make pacifism socially and intellectually respectable again. The "War to End All Wars" had only produced inflation and economic depression in Europe, followed by depression in America— and disgust over stories of arms manufacturers who had sold weapons to both sides. So pacifists like Seidenberg could find people ready to listen to their experiences. Moreover, telling of the experiences was a way to reintegrate themselves into the larger American society, to break the veil of secrecy or shame or mystery that inevitably surrounded all those who had taken controversial or unpopular positions. No one else could really tell such experiences for them, either. Only prisoners could speak for prisoners, and, conscience being nothing if not individual, each Conscientious Objector had to speak for himself.

Even so, one of the remarkable features of Roderick Seidenberg's essay is the way he speaks for more men than just himself. He uses "we" as often as "I": "We were absolutists." "We were steeled to something beyond ourselves." "We had learned to become fighters, and to fight hard." He praises the variety of men "in our group," and the comradeship among them. Ironically, they are a little American melting pot, a group more diverse and egalitarian than the conscripted army they "refuse to serve." In this way, Seidenberg and his fellow COs continued to affirm higher American values, even though once accused of cowardice and disloyalty. From the fringe—what some people might even have called a lunatic fringe—he attempted to restore American traditions of freedom, equality, and individualism.

Charlotte Perkins Gilman, in the two chapters "Love and Marriage" and "The Breakdown," from *The Living of Charlotte Perkins Gilman,* tells a story

---

3. On ties between pacificism and progressivism, see Charles Chatfield, "World War I and the Liberal Pacifist in the United States," *American Historical Review* 75 (December 1970): 1920–37.

which at the time seemed to isolate her from other men and women just as decisively as Du Bois and Seidenberg were isolated. Shortly after her marriage to a tender, devoted husband, she became unaccountably depressed. He stayed home and nursed her, yet she became worse. She spent sleepless nights and was feverish, nervous, and hysterical. The birth of a daughter briefly raised her spirits, but then she was depressed again. Finally, after attempts to cure herself by travel and after treatment by Dr. S. W. Mitchell, "the greatest nerve specialist in the country" and the expert on neurasthenia, the disease she supposedly had, she decided on a more radical measure: she decided to get a divorce. This was an almost unimaginable choice at that time (1887), and yet it was the decision that saved Gilman's life. It was also the decision that empowered her to undertake her studies of economics and to take up a life of agitation for fundamental changes in ideas of gender and work. She sought to rationalize and modernize domestic economy, applying progressivist thought to the home. In her short story "The Yellow Wallpaper," she wrote about the same experience, but stopped short of the divorce and left her fictional character on the brink of madness. That was an effective ending for fiction, but the facts are actually more dramatic. Her decisive, positive, radical change "validated her own decision to write, validated women's intellectual labor in general, and helped, finally, to invalidate neurasthenia as a role option."[4]

"Neurasthenia" was the fashionable disease of the late nineteenth and early twentieth centuries, a disease that a great number of the cultural leaders of this period were diagnosed as having. It was, however, a disease with different, often contradictory symptoms—dyspepsia, depression, lack of energy, excitability, insomnia, skin rashes, asthma, and headaches, to name a few—and different cures. It was also attributed to many different forces in American society—industrialization, rapid social change, the influx of millions of immigrants, the decline of older values, urbanization, and the creation of new wealth and greater leisure. As Tom Lutz has shown in *American Nervousness,* it was therefore available to all its sufferers as a way of providing themselves with a crisis, an interlude, or a kind of psychic space in which "to reexplain the world to themselves" (23). It even provided a story, a line of discourse for "refashioning of one's relation to a changing world" (25). Autobiography, because of its traditional structures of conversion, of recording a person's progress from captivity to freedom, from sickness to health, from an old to a new self, was thus a favored form for representing the neurasthenic's experience. Indeed, the more internal and supposedly rare and private the experience, the more it needed the confessional format of autobiography in which to be described. But the socializing and historicizing functions of autobiography also helped the neurasthenic to publicize his or her experience

4. Tom Lutz, *American Nervousness, 1903: An Anecdotal History* (Ithaca: Cornell Univ. Press, 1991), p. 231. Further references are given in text.

and reconnect with the larger society. Autobiography, we can see, was the neurasthenic American's ideal literary form.

Whether the particular autobiographers of this period were or were not neurasthenic, their concepts of self were heavily influenced by ideas of change, progress, and reform. Words such as "genius," "talent," "virtue," "nature," and "character" were no longer so static, helping people to locate themselves within a finite world. Lives were in progress.

32

Jack London (1876–1916)
What Life Means to Me

London's conflicting ideals appear in vivid relief in this 1904 autobiographical essay—on one side a Nietzschean worship of individual strength as the agent of progress and on the other side a belief in progress through socialism and class struggle.

London grew up in and around Oakland, California, raiding oyster beds as an "oyster pirate" at age fifteen and in 1893 signing onto the sealer *Sophie Sutherland* as an able seamen and hunting seals in the Western Pacific. Returning to California later that year, he did some newspaper writing, including a prize-winning account of a typhoon off Japan. For a time he roamed the United States as a hobo, then attended a year of high school and one semester at the University of California at Berkeley. He left college to write professionally, but was unable to sell his work. In 1897, he joined the Klondike gold rush, until scurvy forced him to return home. In 1898 and 1899, he published stories about the Yukon in the *Overland Monthly*, then struck greater success in 1900 when the *Atlantic Monthly* published one of his stories and Houghton Mifflin brought out a collection, *The Son of the Wolf*. From then on, he produced writing of all kinds at an astonishing pace, in all some forty-three volumes.

In 1901, London ran for mayor of Oakland for the Socialist Labor party and began lecturing and propagandizing for socialism. This essay comes out of that effort. He celebrates the toughness of the working class and attacks the hypocrisy and corruption of the ruling class. He also tries to proclaim the oneness of all humanity, but more often in terms of its appetites and baseness than its virtue. Another problem with his approach is that his iconoclasm frequently leads to gross over-simplifications, as in the implicit feminizing of wealth and society and masculinizing of the poor and the workers. Even science and sociology, usually beacons of hope to members of his generation, get knocked down.

London's underlying problem may be that he is too dependent on his personal testimony, for he becomes entangled in the inconsistencies resulting from his celebration of the working class and his celebration, too, of his own rise out of it. Thus he must attack the poor, in giving his motives to become rich, and then emphasize his disillusionment with the rich, to preserve his bond with working men.

In later life, London was less conflicted. His writing provided him with a comfortable income, and in 1907 he set off in his forty-five-foot yacht the *Snark* to sail around the world. When the trip was cut short by illness, he returned to his magnificent California ranch.

For biographical studies of London, see Joan D. Hedrick, *Solitary Comrade: Jack London and His Work* (Chapel Hill: Univ. of North Carolina Press, 1982) and James Lundquist, *Jack London: Adventures, Ideas, and Fiction* (New York: Ungar, 1987).

I was born in the working-class. Early I discovered enthusiasm, ambition, and ideals; and to satisfy these became the problem of my child-life. My environment was crude and rough and raw. I had no outlook, but an uplook rather. My place in society was at the bottom. Here life offered nothing but sordidness and wretchedness, both of the flesh and the spirit; for here flesh and spirit were alike starved and tormented.

Above me towered the colossal edifice of society, and to my mind the only way out was up. Into this edifice I early resolved to climb. Up above, men wore black clothes and boiled shirts, and women dressed in beautiful gowns. Also, there were good things to eat, and there was plenty to eat. This much for the flesh. Then there were the things of the spirit. Up above me, I knew, were unselfishness of the spirit, clean and noble thinking, keen intellectual living. I knew all this because I read "Seaside Library" novels, in which, with the exception of the villians and adventuresses, all men and women thought beautiful thoughts, spoke a beautiful tongue, and performed glorious deeds. In short, as I accepted the rising of the sun, I accepted that up above me was all that was fine and noble and gracious, all that gave decency and dignity to life, all that made life worth living and that remunerated one for his travail and misery.

But it is not particularly easy for one to climb up out of the working-class—especially if he is handicapped by the possession of ideals and illusions. I lived on a ranch in California, and I was hard put to find the ladder whereby to climb. I early inquired the rate of interest on invested money, and worried my child's brain into an understanding of the virtues and excellencies of that remarkable invention of man, compound interest. Further, I ascertained the current rates of wages for workers of all ages, and the cost of living. From all this data I concluded that if I began immediately and worked and saved until I was fifty years of age, I could then stop working and enter into participation in a fair portion of the delights and goodnesses that would then be open to me higher up in society. Of course, I resolutely determined not to marry, while I quite forgot to consider at all that great rock of disaster in the working-class world—sickness.

But the life that was in me demanded more than a meagre existence of scraping and scrimping. Also, at ten years of age, I became a newsboy on the streets of a city, and found myself with a changed uplook. All about me were still the same sordidness and wretchedness, and up above me was still the same paradise waiting to be gained; but the ladder whereby to climb was a different one. It was now the ladder of business. Why save my earnings and invest in government bonds, when, by buying two newspapers for five cents, with a turn of the wrist I could sell them for ten cents and double my capital? The business ladder was the ladder for me, and I had a vision of myself becoming a baldheaded and successful merchant prince.

Alas for visions! When I was sixteen I had already earned the title of "prince." But this title was given me by a gang of cut-throats and thieves, by whom I was called "The Prince of the Oyster Pirates." And at that time I had climbed the first rung of the business ladder. I was a capitalist. I owned a boat and a complete oyster-pirating outfit. I had begun to exploit my fellow-creatures. I had a crew of one man. As captain and owner I took two-thirds of the spoils, and gave the crew one-third, though the crew worked just as hard as I did and risked just as much his life and liberty.

This one rung was the height I climbed up the business ladder. One night I went on a raid amongst the Chinese fishermen. Ropes and nets were worth dollars and cents. It was robbery, I grant, but it was precisely the spirit of capitalism. The capitalist takes away the possessions of his fellow-creatures by means of a rebate, or of a betrayal of trust, or by the purchase of senators and supreme-court judges. I was merely crude. That was the only difference. I used a gun.

But my crew that night was one of those inefficients against whom the capitalist is wont to fulminate, because, forsooth, such inefficients increase expenses and reduce dividends. My crew did both. What of his carelessness he set fire to the big mainsail and totally destroyed it. There weren't any dividends that night, and the Chinese fishermen were richer by the nets and ropes we did not get. I was bankrupt, unable just then to pay sixty-five dollars for a new mainsail. I left my boat at anchor and went off on a bay-pirate boat on a raid up the Sacramento River. While away on this trip, another gang of bay pirates raided my boat. They stole everything, even the anchors; and later on, when I recovered the drifting hulk, I sold it for twenty dollars. I had slipped back the one rung I had climbed, and never again did I attempt the business ladder.

From then on I was mercilessly exploited by other capitalists. I had the muscle, and they made money out of it while I made but a very indifferent living out of it. I was a sailor before the mast, a longshoreman, a roustabout; I worked in canneries, and factories, and laundries; I mowed lawns, and cleaned carpets, and washed windows. And I never got the full product of my toil. I looked at the daughter of the cannery owner, in her carriage, and knew that it was my muscle, in part, that helped drag along that carriage on its rubber tires. I looked at the son of the factory owner, going to college, and knew that it was my muscle that helped, in part, to pay for the wine and good fellowship he enjoyed.

But I did not resent this. It was all in the game. They were the strong. Very well, I was strong. I would carve my way to a place amongst them and make money out of the muscles of other men. I was not afraid of work. I loved hard work. I would pitch in and work harder than ever and eventually become a pillar of society.

And just then, as luck would have it, I found an employer that was of the same mind. I was willing to work, and he was more than willing that I should work. I thought I was learning a trade. In reality, I had displaced two men. I thought he was making an electrician out of me; as a matter of fact, he was making fifty dollars per month out of me. The two men I had displaced had received forty dollars each per month; I was doing the work of both for thirty dollars per month.

This employer worked me nearly to death. A man may love oysters, but too many oysters will disincline him toward that particular diet. And so with me. Too much work sickened me. I did not wish ever to see work again. I fled from work. I became a tramp, begging my way from door to door, wandering over the United States and sweating bloody sweats in slums and prisons.

I had been born in the working-class, and I was now, at the age of eighteen, beneath the point at which I had started. I was down in the cellar of society, down in the subterranean depths of misery about which it is neither nice nor proper to speak. I was in the pit, the abyss, the human cesspool, the shambles and charnel-house of our civilization. This is the part of the edifice of society that society chooses to ignore. Lack of space compels me here to ignore it, and I shall say only that the things I there saw gave me a terrible scare.

I was scared into thinking. I saw the naked simplicities of the complicated civilization in which I lived. Life was a matter of food and shelter. In order to get food and shelter men sold things. The merchant sold shoes, the politician sold his manhood, and the representative of the people, with exceptions, of course, sold his trust; while nearly all sold their honor. Women, too, whether on the street or in the holy bond of wedlock, were prone to sell their flesh. All things were commodities, all people bought and sold. The one commodity that labor had to sell was muscle. The honor of labor had no price in the market-place. Labor had muscle, and muscle alone, to sell.

But there was a difference, a vital difference. Shoes and trust and honor had a way of renewing themselves. They were imperishable stocks. Muscle, on the other hand, did not renew. As the shoe merchant sold shoes, he continued to replenish his stock. But there was no way of replenishing the laborer's stock of muscle. The more he sold of his muscle, the less of it remained to him. It was his one commodity, and each day his stock of it diminished. In the end, if he did not die before, he sold out and put up his shutters. He was a muscle bankrupt, and nothing remained to him but to go down into the cellar of society and perish miserably.

I learned, further, that brain was likewise a commodity. It, too, was different from muscle. A brain seller was only at his prime when he was fifty or sixty years old, and his wares were fetching higher prices than ever. But a laborer was worked out or broken down at forty-five or fifty. I had been in the cellar of society, and I did not like the place as a habitation. The pipes and drains were unsanitary, and the air was bad to breathe. If I could not live on the parlor floor of society, I could, at any rate, have a try at the attic. It was true, the diet there was slim, but the air at least was pure. So I resolved to sell no more muscle, and to become a vender of brains.

Then began a frantic pursuit of knowledge. I returned to California and opened the books. While thus equipping myself to become a brain merchant, it was inevitable that I should delve into sociology. There I found, in a certain class of books, scientifically formulated, the simple sociological concepts I had already worked out for myself. Other and greater minds, before I was born, had worked out all that I had thought and a vast deal more. I discovered that I was a socialist.

The socialists were revolutionists, inasmuch as they struggled to overthrow the society of the present, and out of the material to build the society of the future. I, too, was a socialist and a revolutionist. I joined the groups of working-class and intellectual revolutionists, and for the first time came into intellectual living. Here I found keen-flashing intellects and brilliant wits; for here I met strong and alert-brained, withal horny-handed, members of the working-class; unfrocked preachers too wide in their Christianity for any congregation of Mammon-worshippers; professors broken on the wheel of university subservience to the ruling class and flung out because they were quick with knowledge which they strove to apply to the affairs of mankind.

Here I found, also, warm faith in the human, glowing idealism, sweetnesses of unselfishness, renunciation, and martyrdom—all the splendid, stinging things of the spirit. Here life was clean, noble, and alive. Here life rehabilitated itself, became wonderful and glorious; and I was glad to be alive. I was in touch with great souls who exalted flesh and spirit over dollars and cents, and to whom the thin wail of the starved slum child meant more than all the pomp and circumstance of commercial expansion and world empire. All about me were nobleness of purpose and heroism of effort, and my days and nights were sunshine and starshine, all fire and dew, with before my eyes, ever burning and blazing, the Holy Grail, Christ's own Grail, the warm human, long-suffering and maltreated, but to be rescued and saved at the last.

And I, poor foolish I, deemed all this to be a mere foretaste of the delights of living I should find higher above me in society. I had lost many illusions since the day I read "Seaside Library" novels on the California ranch. I was destined to lose many of the illusions I still retained.

As a brain merchant I was a success. Society opened its portals to me. I entered right in on the parlor floor, and my disillusionment proceeded rapidly.

I sat down to dinner with the masters of society, and with the wives and daughters of the masters of society. The women were gowned beautifully, I admit; but to my naïve surprise I discovered that they were of the same clay as all the rest of the women I had known down below in the cellar. "The colonel's lady and Judy O'Grady were sisters under their skins"—and gowns.

It was not this, however, so much as their materialism, that shocked me. It is true, these beautifully gowned, beautiful women prattled sweet little ideals and dear little moralities; but in spite of their prattle the dominant key of the life they lived was materialistic. And they were so sentimentally self-ish! They assisted in all kinds of sweet little charities, and informed one of the fact, while all the time the food they ate and the beautiful clothes they wore were bought out of dividends stained with the blood of child labor, and sweated labor, and of prostitution itself. When I mentioned such facts, expecting in my innocence that these sisters of Judy O'Grady would at once strip off their blood-dyed silks and jewels, they became excited and angry, and read me preachments about the lack of thrift, the drink, and the innate depravity that caused all the misery in society's cellar. When I mentioned that I couldn't quite see that it was the lack of thrift, the intemperance, and the depravity of a half-starved child of six that made it work twelve hours every night in a Southern cotton mill, these sisters of Judy O'Grady attacked my private life and called me an "agitator"—as though that, forsooth, settled the argument.

Nor did I fare better with the masters themselves. I had expected to find men who were clean, noble, and alive, whose ideals were clean, noble, and alive. I went about amongst the men who sat in the high places—the preach-ers, the politicians, the business men, the professors, and the editors. I ate meat with them, drank wine with them, automobiled with them, and studied them. It is true, I found many that were clean and noble; but with rare excep-tions, they were not *alive*. I do verily believe I could count the exceptions on the fingers of my two hands. Where they were not alive with rottenness, quick with unclean life, they were merely the unburied dead—clean and noble, like well-preserved mummies, but not alive. In this connection I may especially mention the professors I met, the men who live up to that decadent university ideal, "the passionless pursuit of passionless intelligence."

I met men who invoked the name of the Prince of Peace in their diatribes against war, and who put rifles in the hands of Pinkertons with which to shoot down strikers in their own factories. I met men incoherent with in-dignation at the brutality of prize-fighting, and who, at the same time, were parties to the adulteration of food that killed each year more babies than even red-handed Herod had killed.

I talked in hotels and clubs and homes and Pullmans and steamer-chairs with captains of industry, and marvelled at how little travelled they were in the realm of intellect. On the other hand, I discovered that their intellect, in the business sense, was abnormally developed. Also, I discovered that their morality, where business was concerned, was nil.

This delicate, aristocratic-featured gentleman, was a dummy director and a tool of corporations that secretly robbed widows and orphans. This gentleman, who collected fine editions and was an especial patron of literature, paid blackmail to a heavy-jowled, black-browed boss of a municipal machine. This editor, who published patent medicine advertisements and did not dare print the truth in his paper about said patent medicines for fear of losing the advertising, called me a scoundrelly demagogue because I told him that his political economy was antiquated and that his biology was contemporaneous with Pliny.

This senator was the tool and the slave, the little puppet of a gross, uneducated machine boss; so was this governor and this supreme court judge; and all three rode on railroad passes. This man, talking soberly and earnestly about the beauties of idealism and the goodness of God, had just betrayed his comrades in a business deal. This man, a pillar of the church and heavy contributor to foreign missions, worked his shop girls ten hours a day on a starvation wage and thereby directly encouraged prostitution. This man, who endowed chairs in universities, perjured himself in courts of law over a matter of dollars and cents. And this railroad magnate broke his word as a gentleman and a Christian when he granted a secret rebate to one of two captains of industry locked together in a struggle to the death.

It was the same everywhere, crime and betrayal, betrayal and crime—men who were alive, but who were neither clean nor noble, men who were clean and noble but who were not alive. Then there was a great, hopeless mass, neither noble nor alive, but merely clean. It did not sin positively nor deliberately; but it did sin passively and ignorantly by acquiescing in the current immorality and profiting by it. Had it been noble and alive it would not have been ignorant, and it would have refused to share in the profits of betrayal and crime.

I discovered that I did not like to live on the parlor floor of society. Intellectually I was bored. Morally and spiritually I was sickened. I remembered my intellectuals and idealists, my unfrocked preachers, broken professors, and clean-minded, class-conscious workingmen. I remembered my days and nights of sunshine and starshine, where life was all a wild sweet wonder, a spiritual paradise of unselfish adventure and ethical romance. And I saw before me, ever blazing and burning, the Holy Grail.

So I went back to the working-class, in which I had been born and where I belonged. I care no longer to climb. The imposing edifice of society above my head holds no delights for me. It is the foundation of the edifice that interests me. There I am content to labor, crowbar in hand, shoulder to shoulder with intellectuals, idealists, and class-conscious workingmen, getting a solid pry now and again and setting the whole edifice rocking. Some day, when we get a few more hands and crowbars to work, we'll topple it over, along with all its rotten life and unburied dead, its monstrous selfishness and sodden materialism. Then we'll cleanse the cellar and build a new habitation for mankind, in which there will be no parlor floor, in which all the rooms will be bright and airy, and where the air that is breathed will be clean, noble, and alive.

Such is my outlook. I look forward to a time when man shall progress upon something worthier and higher than his stomach, when there will be a finer incentive to impel men to action than the incentive of to-day, which is the incentive of the stomach. I retain my belief in the nobility and excellence of the human. I believe that spiritual sweetness and unselfishness will conquer the gross gluttony of to-day. And last of all, my faith is in the working-class. As some Frenchman has said, "The stairway of time is ever echoing with the wooden shoe going up, the polished boot descending."

November, 1905

33

Randolph Bourne (1886–1918)

The Handicapped

"Life will have little meaning for me," Bourne writes, "except as I am able to contribute toward some . . . ideal of social betterment. . . ." So does he show his allegiance to the major intellectual and social movement of his time, Progressivism.

Yet Bourne is different from other progressives like Charlotte Perkins Gilman in having been handicapped. He had a hunchback which was the result of spinal tuberculosis when he was four, and a misshapen face and deformed left ear which were the result of a messy birth, as he called it. He could never participate in Theodore Roosevelt's "robust life" or assume a confident public role in reform movements, as Gilman and so many others did. He was also about a generation younger, and he died at only thirty-two, a victim of the 1918–19 flu epidemic.

In that short life he managed to write an amazing number of essays, letters, book reviews, and sociological studies—a large part of these from a very compelling autobiographical perspective. "Youth," an essay which appeared in the *Atlantic Monthly* in April, 1912, made him a spokesman for young intellectuals. After graduating from Columbia University in 1913, he spent a year in Europe on a travelling fellowship, then became a contributing editor of the *New Republic*. In 1917, he moved to the *Seven Arts,* for which he wrote a series of powerful essays opposing American participation in the war.

This very early essay was unsigned. It was simply entitled "The Handicapped—By One of Them." Bourne apparently wanted to direct attention away from himself as an individual and towards the common experience of all persons similarly "in the world, but not of the world." Yet the way he gave that experience psychic reality was by talking intimately about himself. He also, by daring to write it, fought against the lowered expectations and the silence which he says surround the handicapped. Also crucial is his emphasis on friends as the keys that help him unlock himself. Readers are tacitly invited to become friends, too, whereupon he becomes more intimate, talking about his childhood, his ideals, and finally to others "who are situated as I am."

In its daring and in its bursting of conventional genteel reticence, then, this essay does show a new kind of vigor and hope and a new concept of self. Moreover, in taking on the paradoxes of how the handicapped are both similar and

different from others, it looks forward to a lot of later American autobiography
that took on the paradoxes of race, religion, class, and gender.

The text is from *The Atlantic Monthly* 108 (September 1911): 320–29. Bruce
Clayton, in *Forgotten Prophet: The Life of Randolph Bourne* (Baton Rouge: Louisiana
Univ. Press, 1984), provides the definitive biography.

It would not perhaps be thought, ordinarily, that the man whom physical
disabilities have made so helpless that he is unable to move around among
his fellows can bear his lot more happily, even though he suffer pain, and
face life with a more cheerful and contented spirit, than can the man whose
deformities are merely enough to mark him out from the rest of his fellows
without preventing him from entering with them into most of their common affairs and experiences. But the fact is that the former's very helplessness
makes him content to rest and not to strive. I know a young man so helplessly
deformed that he has to be carried about, who is happy in reading a little,
playing chess, taking a course or two in college, and all with the sunniest
goodwill in the world, and a happiness that seems strange and unaccountable
to my restlessness. He does not cry for the moon.

When one, however, is in full possession of his faculties, and can move
about freely, bearing simply a crooked back and an unsightly face, he is per-
force drawn into all the currents of life. Particularly if he has his own way in
the world to make, his road is apt to be hard and rugged, and he will penetrate to an unusual depth in his interpretation both of the world's attitude
toward such misfortunes, and of the attitude toward the world which such
misfortunes tend to cultivate in men like him. For he has all the battles of a
stronger man to fight, and he is at a double disadvantage in fighting them.
He has constantly with him the sense of being obliged to make extra efforts
to overcome the bad impression of his physical defects, and he is haunted
with a constant feeling of weakness and low vitality which makes effort more
difficult and renders him easily fainthearted and discouraged by failure. He
is never confident of himself, because he has grown up in an atmosphere
where nobody has been very confident of him; and yet his environment and
circumstances call out all sorts of ambitions and energies in him which, from
the nature of his case, are bound to be immediately thwarted. This attitude is
likely to keep him at a generally low level of accomplishment unless he have
an unusually strong will, and a strong will is perhaps the last thing to develop
under such circumstances.

That vague sense of physical uncomfortableness which is with him nearly
every minute of his waking day serves, too, to make steady application for
hours to any particular kind of work much more irksome than it is even to the
lazy man. No one but the deformed man can realize just what the mere fact of
sitting a foot lower than the normal means in discomfort and annoyance. For
one cannot carry one's special chair everywhere, to theatre and library and

train and schoolroom. This sounds trivial, I know, but I mention it because it furnishes a real, even though usually dim, "background of consciousness" which one has to reckon with during all one's solid work or enjoyment. The things that the world deems hardest for the deformed man to bear are perhaps really the easiest of all. I can truthfully say, for instance, that I have never suffered so much as a pang from the interested comments on my personal appearance made by urchins in the street, nor from the curious looks of people in the street and public places. To ignore this vulgar curiosity is the simplest and easiest thing in the world. It does not worry me in the least to appear on a platform if I have anything to say and there is anybody to listen. What one does get sensitive to is rather the inevitable way that people, acquaintances and strangers alike, have of discounting in advance what one does or says.

The deformed man is always conscious that the world does not expect very much from him. And it takes him a long time to see in this a challenge instead of a firm pressing down to a low level of accomplishment. As a result, he does not expect very much of himself; he is timid in approaching people, and distrustful of his ability to persuade and convince. He becomes extraordinarily sensitive to other people's first impressions of him. Those who are to be his friends he knows instantly, and further acquaintance adds little to the intimacy and warm friendship that he at once feels for them. On the other hand, those who do not respond to him immediately cannot by any effort either on his part or theirs overcome that first alienation.

This sensitiveness has both its good and bad sides. It makes friendship the most precious thing in the world to him, and he finds that he arrives at a much richer and wider intimacy with his friends than do ordinary men with their light, surface friendships, based on good fellowship or the convenience of the moment. But on the other hand this sensitiveness absolutely unfits him for business and the practice of a profession, where one must be "all things to all men," and the professional manner is indispensable to success. For here, where he has to meet a constant stream of men of all sorts and conditions, his sensitiveness to these first impressions will make his case hopeless. Except with those few who by some secret sympathy will seem to respond, his deformity will stand like a huge barrier between his personality and other men's. The magical good fortune of attractive personal appearance makes its way almost without effort in the world, breaking down all sorts of walls of disapproval and lack of interest. Even the homely person can attract by personal charm. But deformity cannot even be charming.

The doors of the deformed man are always locked, and the key is on the outside. He may have treasures of charm inside, but they will never be revealed unless the person outside cooperates with him in unlocking the door. A friend becomes, to a much greater degree than with the ordinary man, the indispensable means of discovering one's own personality. One only exists, so to speak, with friends. It is easy to see how hopelessly such a sensitiveness

461

incapacitates a man for business, professional, or social life, where the hasty and superficial impression is everything, and disaster is the fate of the man who has not all the treasures of his personality in the front window, where they can be readily inspected and appraised.

It thus takes the deformed man a long time to get adjusted to his world. Childhood is perhaps the hardest time of all. As a child he is a strange creature in a strange land. It was my own fate to be just strong enough to play about with the other boys, and attempt all their games and "stunts," without being strong enough actually to succeed in any of them. It never used to occur to me that my failures and lack of skill were due to circumstances beyond my control, but I would always impute them, in consequence of my rigid Calvinistic bringing-up, I suppose, to some moral weakness of my own. I suffered tortures in trying to learn to skate, to climb trees, to play ball, to conform in general to the ways of the world. I never resigned myself to the inevitable, but overexerted myself constantly in a grim determination to succeed. I was good at my lessons, and through timidity rather than priggishness, I hope, a very well-behaved boy at school; I was devoted, too, to music, and learned to play the piano pretty well. But I despised my reputation for excellence in these things, and instead of adapting myself philosophically to the situation, I strove (and have been striving ever since) to do the things I could not.

As I look back now it seems perfectly natural that I should have followed the standards of the crowd, and loathed my high marks in lessons and deportment, and the concerts to which I was sent by my aunt, and the exhibitions of my musical skill that I had to give before admiring ladies. Whether or not such an experience is typical of handicapped children, there is tragedy there for those situated as I was. For had I been a little weaker physically, I should have been thrown back on reading omnivorously and cultivating my music, with some possible results; while if I had been a little stronger, I could have participated in the play on an equal footing with the rest. As it was, I simply tantalized myself, and grew up with a deepening sense of failure, and a lack of pride in what I really excelled at.

When the world became one of dances and parties and social evenings and boy-and-girl attachments—the world of youth—I was to find myself still less adapted to it. And this was the harder to bear because I was naturally sociable, and all these things appealed tremendously to me. This world of admiration and gayety and smiles and favors and quick interest and companionship, however, is only for the well-begotten and the debonair. It was not through any cruelty or dislike, I think, that I was refused admittance; indeed they were always very kind about inviting me. But it was more as if a ragged urchin had been asked to come and look through the window at the light and warmth of a glittering party; I was truly in the world, but not of the world. Indeed there were times when one would almost prefer conscious cruelty to this silent, unconscious, gentle oblivion. And this is the tragedy, I suppose, not only of the deformed, but of all the ill-favored and unattractive to a greater or less degree. The world of youth is a world of so many conventions, and the abnormal in any direction is so glaringly and hideously abnormal.

Although it took me a long time to understand this, and I continued to attribute my failure mostly to my own character, trying hard to compensate for my physical deficiencies by skill and cleverness, I suffered comparatively few pangs, and got much better adjusted to this world than to the other. For I was older, and I had acquired a lively interest in all the social politics; I would get so interested in watching how people behaved, and in sizing them up, that only at rare intervals would I remember that I was really having no hand in the game. This interest just in the ways people are human has become more and more a positive advantage in my life, and has kept sweet many a situation that might easily have cost me a pang. Not that a person with my disabilities should be a sort of detective, evil-mindedly using his social opportunities for spying out and analyzing his friends' foibles, but that, if he does acquire an interest in people quite apart from their relation to him, he may go into society with an easy conscience and a certainty that he will be entertained and possibly entertaining, even though he cuts a poor enough social figure. He must simply not expect too much.

Perhaps the bitterest struggles of the handicapped man come when he tackles the business world. If he has to go out for himself to look for work, without fortune, training, or influence, as I personally did, his way will indeed be rugged. His disability will work against him for any position where he must be much in the eyes of men, and his general insignificance has a subtle influence in convincing those to whom he applies that he is unfitted for any kind of work. As I have suggested, his keen sensitiveness to other people's impressions of him makes him more than unusually timid and unable to counteract that fatal first impression by any display of personal force and will. He cannot get his personality over across that barrier. The cards seem stacked against him from the start. With training and influence something might be done, but alone and unaided his case is almost hopeless. At least, this was my own experience. We were poor relations, and our prosperous relatives thought they had done quite enough for us without sending me through college, and I did not seem strong enough to work my way through (although I have since done it). I started out auspiciously enough, becoming a sort of apprentice to a musician who had invented a machine for turning out music-rolls. Here, with steady work, good pay, and the comfortable consciousness that I was "helping support the family," I got the first pleasurable sensation of self-respect, I think, that I ever had. But with the failure of this business I was precipitated against the real world.[1]

1. Bourne describes this experience in "What Is Exploitation?," *The New Republic* 9 (1916): 12–14.

It would be futile to recount the story of my struggles: how I besieged for nearly two years firm after firm, in search of a permanent position, trying everything in New York in which I thought I had the slightest chance of success, meanwhile making a precarious living by a few music lessons. The attitude toward me ranged from "You can't expect us to create a place for you," to, "How could it enter your head that we should find any use for a man like you?" My situation was doubtless unusual. Few men handicapped as I was would be likely to go so long without arousing some interest and support in relative or friend. But my experience serves to illustrate the peculiar difficulties that a handicapped man meets if he has his own way to make in the world. He is discounted at the start; it is not business to make allowances for anybody; and while people were not cruel or unkind, it was the hopeless finality of the thing that filled one's heart with despair.

The environment of a big city is perhaps the worst possible that a man in such a situation could have. For the thousands of seeming opportunities lead one restlessly on and on, and keep one's mind perpetually unsettled and depressed. There is a poignant mental torture that comes with such an experience—the urgent need, the repeated failure, or rather the repeated failure even to obtain a chance to fail, the realization that those at home can ill afford to have you idle, the growing dread of encountering people—all this is something that those who have never been through it can never realize. Personally I know of no particular way of escape. One can expect to do little by one's own unaided efforts. I solved my difficulties only by evading them, by throwing overboard some of my responsibility, and taking the desperate step of entering college on a scholarship. Desultory work is not nearly so humiliating when one is using one's time to some advantage, and college furnishes an ideal environment where the things at which a man handicapped like myself can succeed really count. One's self-respect can begin to grow like a weed.

For at the bottom of all the difficulties of a man like me is really the fact that his self-respect is so slow in growing up. Accustomed from childhood to being discounted, his self-respect is not naturally very strong, and it would require pretty constant success in a congenial line of work really to confirm it. If he could only more easily separate the factors that are due to his physical disability from those that are due to his weak will and character, he might more quickly attain self-respect, for he would realize what he is responsible for, and what he is not. But at the beginning he rarely makes allowances for himself; he is his own severest judge. He longs for a "strong will," and yet the experience of having his efforts promptly nipped off at the beginning is the last thing on earth to produce that will.

Life, particularly if he is brought into harsh and direct touch with the real world, is a much more complex thing to him than to the ordinary man. Many of his inherited platitudes vanish at the first touch. Life appears to him as a grim struggle, where ability does not necessarily mean opportunity and success, nor piety sympathy and where helplessness cannot count on assistance and kindly interest. Human affairs seem to be running on a wholly irrational plan, and success to be founded on chance as much as on anything. But if he can stand the first shock of disillusionment, he may find himself enormously interested in discovering how they actually do run, and he will want to burrow into the motives of men, and find the reasons for the crass inequalities and injustices of the world he sees around him. He has practically to construct anew a world of his own, and explain a great many things to himself that the ordinary person never dreams of finding unintelligible at all. He will be filled with a profound sympathy for all who are despised and ignored in the world. When he has been through the neglect and struggles of a handicapped and ill-favored man himself, he will begin to understand the feelings of all the horde of the unpresentable and the unemployable, the incompetent and the ugly, the queer and crotchety people who make up so large a proportion of human folk.

We are perhaps too prone to get our ideas and standards of worth from the successful, without reflecting that the interpretations of life which patriotic legend, copybook philosophy, and the sayings of the wealthy give us are pitifully inadequate for those who fall behind in the race. Surely there are enough people to whom the task of making a decent living and maintaining themselves and their families in their social class, or of winning and keeping the respect of their fellows, is a hard and bitter task, to make a philosophy gained through personal disability and failure as just and true a method of appraising the life around us as the cheap optimism of the ordinary professional man. And certainly a kindlier, for it has no shade of contempt or disparagement about it.

It irritates me as if I had been spoken of contemptuously myself, to hear people called "common" or "ordinary," or to see that deadly and delicate feeling for social gradations crop out, which so many of our upper-middle-class women seem to have. It makes me wince to hear a man spoken of as a failure, or to have it said of one that he "doesn't amount to much." Instantly I want to know why he has not succeeded, and what have been the forces that have been working against him. He is the truly interesting person, and yet how little our eager-pressing, onrushing world cares about such aspects of life, and how hideously though unconsciously cruel and heartless it usually is.

Often I had tried in arguments to show my friends how much of circumstance and chance go to the making of success; and when I reached the age of sober reading, a long series of the works of radical social philosophers, beginning with Henry George, provided me with the materials for a philosophy which explained why men were miserable and overworked, and why there was on the whole so little joy and gladness among us—and which fixed the blame. Here was suggested a goal, and a definite glorious future, toward which all good men might work. My own working hours became filled with visions of how men could be brought to see all that this meant, and how I in particular might work some great and wonderful thing for human betterment. In more recent years, the study of history and social psychology and ethics has made those crude outlines sounder and more normal, and brought them into a saner relation to other aspects of life and thought, but I have not lost the first glow of enthusiasm, nor my belief in social progress as the first right and permanent interest for every thinking and true-hearted man or woman.

I am ashamed that my experience has given me so little chance to count in any way toward either the spreading of such a philosophy or toward direct influence and action. Nor do I yet see clearly how I shall be able to count effectually toward this ideal. Of one thing I am sure, however: that life will have little meaning for me except as I am able to contribute toward some such ideal of social betterment, if not in deed, then in word. For this is the faith that I believe we need today, all of us—a truly religious belief in human progress, a thorough social consciousness, an eager delight in every sign and promise of social improvement, and best of all, a new spirit of courage that will dare. I want to give to the young men whom I see—who, with fine intellect and high principles, lack just that light of the future on their faces that would give them a purpose and meaning in life—to them I want to give some touch of this philosophy—that will energize their lives, and save them from the disheartening effects of that poisonous counsel of timidity and distrust of human ideals which pours out in steady stream from reactionary press and pulpit.

It is hard to tell just how much of this philosophy has been due to my handicaps. If it is solely to my physical misfortunes that I owe its existence, the price has not been a heavy one to pay. For it has given me something that I should not know how to be without. For, however gained, this radical philosophy has not only made the world intelligible and dynamic to me, but has furnished me with the strongest spiritual support. I know that many people, handicapped by physical weakness and failure, find consolation and satisfaction in a very different sort of faith—in an evangelical religion, and a feeling of close dependence on God and close communion with him. But my experience has made my ideal of character militant rather than long-suffering.

I very early experienced a revulsion against the rigid Presbyterianism in which I had been brought up—a purely intellectual revulsion, I believe, because my mind was occupied for a long time afterward with theological questions, and the only feeling that entered into it was a sort of disgust at the arrogance of damning so great a proportion of the human race. I read T. W. Higginson's *The Sympathy of Religions* with the greatest satisfaction, and attended the Unitarian Church whenever I could slip away. This faith, while it still appeals to me, seems at times a little too static and refined to satisfy me with completeness. For some time there was a considerable bitterness in my heart at the narrowness of the people who could still find comfort in the old faith. Reading Buckle[2] and Oliver Wendell Holmes gave me a new contempt for "conventionality," and my social philosophy still further tortured me by throwing the burden for the misery of the world on these same good neighbors. And all this, although I think I did not make a nuisance of myself, made me feel a spiritual and intellectual isolation in addition to my more or less effective physical isolation.

Happily these days are over. The world has righted itself, and I have been able to appreciate and realize how people count in a social and group capacity as well as in an individual and personal one, and to separate the two in my thinking. Really to believe in human nature while striving to know the thousand forces that warp it from its ideal development—to call for and expect much from men and women, and not to be disappointed and embittered if they fall short—to try to do good with people rather than to them—this is my religion on its human side. And if God exists, I think that He must be in the warm sun, in the kindly actions of the people we know and read of, in the beautiful things of art and nature, and in the closeness of friendships. He may also be in heaven, in life, in suffering, but it is only in these simple moments of happiness that I feel Him and know that He is there.

Death I do not understand at all. I have seen it in its cruelest, most irrational forms, where there has seemed no excuse, no palliation. I have only known that if we were more careful, and more relentless in fighting evil, if we knew more of medical science, such things would not be. I know that a sound body, intelligent care and training, prolong life, and that the death of a very old person is neither sad nor shocking, but sweet and fitting. I see in death a perpetual warning of how much there is to be known and done in the way of human progress and betterment. And equally, it seems to me, is this true of disease. So all the crises and deeper implications of life seem inevitably to lead back to that question of social improvement, and militant learning and doing.

This, then, is the goal of my religion—the bringing of fuller, richer life to more people on this earth. All institutions and all works that do not have this for their object are useless and pernicious. And this is not to be a mere philosophic precept which may well be buried under a host of more immediate matters, but a living faith, to permeate one's thought, and transfuse one's life. Prevention must be the method against evil. To remove temptation from men, and to apply the stimulus which shall call forth their highest endeavors—these seem to me the only right principles of ethical endeavor. Not to

2. Henry Thomas Buckle (1821–62) was an erudite British historian who wrote *The History of Civilization in England.*

keep waging the age-long battle with sin and poverty, but to make the air around men so pure that foul lungs cannot breathe it—this should be our noblest religious aim.

Education—knowledge and training—I have felt so keenly my lack of these things that I count them as the greatest of means toward making life noble and happy. The lack of stimulus has tended with me to dissipate the power which might otherwise have been concentrated in some one productive direction. Or perhaps it was the many weak stimuli that constantly incited me and thus kept me from following one particular bent. I look back on what seems a long waste of intellectual power, time frittered away in groping and moping, which might easily have been spent constructively. A defect in one of the physical senses often means a keener sensitiveness in the others, but it seems that unless the sphere of action that the handicapped man has is very much narrowed, his intellectual ability will not grow in compensation for his physical defects. He will always feel that, had he been strong or even successful, he would have been further advanced intellectually, and would have attained greater command over his powers. For his mind tends to be cultivated extensively, rather than intensively. He has so many problems to meet, so many things to explain to himself, that he acquires a wide rather than a profound knowledge. Perhaps eventually, by eliminating most of these interests as practicable fields, he may tie himself down to one line of work; but at first he is pretty apt to find his mind rebellious. If he is eager and active, he will get a smattering of too many things, and his imperfect, badly trained organism will make intense application very difficult.

Now that I have talked a little of my philosophy of life, particularly about what I want to put into it, there is something to be said also of its enjoyment, and what I may hope to get out of it. I have said that my ideal of character was militant rather than long-suffering. It is true that my world has been one of failure and deficit—I have accomplished practically nothing alone, and can count only two or three instances where I have received kindly counsel and suggestion; moreover it still seems a miracle to me that money can be spent for anything beyond the necessities without being first carefully weighed and pondered over—but it has not been a world of suffering and sacrifice, my health has been almost criminally perfect in the light of my actual achievement, and life has appeared to me, at least since my more pressing responsibilities were removed, as a challenge and an arena, rather than a vale of tears. I do not like the idea of helplessly suffering one's misfortunes, of passively bearing one's lot. The Stoics depress me. I do not want to look on my life as an eternal making the best of a bad bargain. Granting all the circumstances, admitting all my disabilities, I want too to "warm both hands before the fire of life." What satisfactions I have, and they are many and precious, I do not want to look on as compensations, but as positive goods.

The difference between what the strongest of the strong and the most winning of the attractive can get out of life, and what I can, is after all so slight. Our experiences and enjoyments, both his and mine, are so infinitesimal compared with the great mass of possibilities; and there must be a division of labor. If he takes the world of physical satisfactions and of material success, I at least can occupy the far richer kingdom of mental effort and artistic appreciation. And on the side of what we are to put into life, although I admit that achievement on my part will be harder relatively to encompass than on his, at least I may have the field of artistic creation and intellectual achievement for my own. Indeed, as one gets older, the fact of one's disabilities fades dimmer and dimmer away from consciousness. One's enemy is now one's own weak will, and the struggle is to attain the artistic ideal one has set.

But one must have grown up, to get this attitude. And that is the best thing the handicapped man can do. Growing up will have given him one of the greatest, and certainly the most durable satisfaction of his life. It will mean at least that he is out of the woods. Childhood has nothing to offer him; youth little more. They are things to be gotten through with as soon as possible. For he will not understand, and he will not be understood. He finds himself simply a bundle of chaotic impulses and emotions and ambitions, very few of which, from the nature of the case, can possibly be realized or satisfied. He is bound to be at cross-grains with the world, and he has to look sharp that he does not grow up with a bad temper and a hateful disposition, and become cynical and bitter against those who turn him away. But grown up, his horizon will broaden; he will get a better perspective, and will not take the world so seriously as he used to, nor will failure frighten him so much. He can look back and see how inevitable it all was, and understand how precarious and problematic even the best regulated of human affairs may be. And if he feels that there were times when he should have been able to count upon the help and kindly counsel of relatives and acquaintances who remained dumb and uninterested, he will not put their behavior down as proof of the depravity of human nature, but as due to an unfortunate blindness which it will be his work to avoid in himself by looking out for others when he has the power.

When he has grown up, he will find that people of his own age and experience are willing to make those large allowances for what is out of the ordinary which were impossible to his younger friends, and that grown-up people touch each other on planes other than the purely superficial. With a broadening of his own interests, he will find himself overlapping other people's personalities at new points, and will discover with rare delight that he is beginning to be understood and appreciated—at least to a greater degree than when he had to keep his real interests hid as something unusual. For he will begin to see in his friends, his music and books, and his interest in people and social betterment, his true life; many of his restless ambitions will fade gradually away, and he will come to recognize all the more clearly some true ambition of his life that is within the range of his capabilities.

He will have built up his world, and have sifted out the things that are not going to concern him, and participation in which will only serve to vex and harass him. He may well come to count his deformity even as a blessing, for it has made impossible to him at last many things in the pursuit of which he would only fritter away his time and dissipate his interest. He must not think of "resigning himself to his fate"; above all he must insist on his own personality. For once really grown up, he will find that he has acquired self-respect and personality. Grown-up-ness, I think, is not a mere question of age, but of being able to look back and understand and find satisfaction in one's experience, no matter how bitter it may have been.

So to all who are situated as I am, I would say—Grow up as fast as you can. Cultivate the widest interests you can, and cherish all your friends. Cultivate some artistic talent, for you will find it the most durable of satisfactions, and perhaps one of the surest means of livelihood as well. Achievement is, of course, on the knees of the gods; but you will at least have the thrill of trial, and, after all, not to try is to fail. Taking your disabilities for granted, and assuming constantly that they are being taken for granted, make your social intercourse as broad and as constant as possible. Do not take the world too seriously, nor let too many social conventions oppress you. Keep sweet your sense of humor, and above all do not let any morbid feelings of inferiority creep into your soul. You will find yourself sensitive enough to the sympathy of others, and if you do not find people who like you and are willing to meet you more than halfway, it will be because you have let your disability narrow your vision and shrink up your soul. It will be really your own fault, and not that of your circumstances. In a word, keep looking outward; look out eagerly for those things that interest you, for people who will interest you and be friends with you, for new interests and for opportunities to express yourself. You will find that your disability will come to have little meaning for you, that it will begin to fade quite completely out of your sight; you will wake up some fine morning and find yourself, after all the struggles that seemed so bitter to you, really and truly adjusted to the world.

I am perhaps not yet sufficiently out of the wilderness to utter all these brave words. For, I must confess, I find myself hopelessly dependent on my friends and my environment. My friends have come to mean more to me than almost anything else in the world. If it is far harder work for a man in my situation to make friendships quickly, at least friendships once made have a depth and intimacy quite beyond ordinary attachments. For a man such as I am has little prestige; people do not want to impress him. They are genuine and sincere, talk to him freely about themselves, and are generally far less reticent about revealing their real personality and history and aspirations. And particularly is this so in friendships with young women. I have found their friendships the most delightful and satisfying of all. For all that social convention that insists that every friendship between a young man and woman must be on a romantic basis is necessarily absent in our case. There is no fringe around us to make our acquaintance anything but a charming companionship. With all my friends, the same thing is true. The first barrier of strangeness broken down, our interest is really in each other, and not in what each is going to think of the other, how he is to be impressed, or whether we are going to fall in love with each other. When one of my friends moves away, I feel as if a great hole had been left in my life. There is a whole side of my personality that I cannot express without him. I shudder to think of any change that will deprive me of their constant companionship. Without friends I feel as if even my music and books and interests would turn stale on my hands. I confess that I am not grown up enough to get along without them.

But if I am not yet out of the wilderness, at least I think I see the way to happiness. With health and a modicum of achievement, I shall not see my lot as unenviable. And if misfortune comes, it will only be something flowing from the common lot of men, not from my own particular disability. Most of the difficulties that flow from that I flatter myself I have met by this time of my twenty-fifth year, have looked full in the face, have grappled with, and find in nowise so formidable as the world usually deems them; no bar to my real ambitions and ideals.

34

Mary Antin (1881–1949)
Initiation

The Promised Land, which was published in 1912, after being serialized in the *Atlantic Monthly* in 1911, tells the story of Maryashe Antin's emigration from Polotzk, Russia, to Boston, where she became an outstanding student and a promising American writer. The early chapters describe in detail the privations and injustices of the Pale or "Pale of Settlement" in eastern Russia where Jews were required to live. Men were subject to conscription into the czar's army. Merchants paid protection money to avoid raids by the police. Gentiles and Jews never trusted one another. Education was all but closed to Jewish children, except for the Hebrew lessons and training in the Law given to boys. "A girl was 'finished' when she could read her prayers in Hebrew, following the meaning by the aid of the Yiddish translation especially prepared for women. If she could sign her name in Russian, do a little figuring, and write a letter in Yiddish to the parents of her betrothed, she was called *wohl gelehrent*—well-educated" (111).

The middle part of the book describes her quiet but passionate rebellion against these restrictions and traditions, her family's emigration to America in her early teens, and her rapid and joyful casting off of her early identity as "Mashke" of Polotzk to become "Mary Antin" of Boston. "With our despised immigrant clothing we shed also our impossible Hebrew names," she says, speaking for her parents, brother, and two sisters (187), just before she started school. School, as this chapter explains, was the most welcome part of her conversion. She was such a good student that she went on to the prestigious Girls' Latin School, where she met the daughters of Boston's social and intellectual elite, and made plans to go to Radcliffe. Instead, she married a biologist she had met through the Natural History Club at the Hale Settlement House in Boston and went with him to New York, where she continued her education at Barnard.

The Promised Land is therefore a monument to the immigrant's successful assimilation, willing and welcomed, and it makes a fascinating comparison to other immigrant autobiographies. The story, some readers will think, is too happy to be true. They may also object to her smugness. Yet she was not ashamed of her past, and she even attached a Yiddish-English glossary to the end of the book so that American readers could better understand Jewish customs. In 1941, with Hitler invading Russia, she published an essay expressing both her universalism and her solidarity with "my people." "I can no more return to the Jewish fold than I can return to my mother's womb; neither can I in decency continue to enjoy my accidental personal immunity from the penalties of being a Jew in a time of virulent anti-Semitism."[1] She had become a kind of latter-day Transcendentalist, and saw the universalism of all great religions as having their political fulfillment in democracy.

The whole of "Initiation," Chapter 10 in *The Promised Land,* is given below. There is no biography of Mary Antin, but there is a brief biographical introduction by Oscar Handlin in a reprint of *The Promised Land* (Boston: Houghton Mifflin, 1969). *Studies in American Jewish Literature* 5 (1986): 29–53 has articles on Antin by Richard Tuerk, Steven J. Rubin, and Evelyn Avery.

It is not worth while to refer to voluminous school statistics to see just how many "green" pupils entered school last September, not knowing the days of the week in English, who next February will be declaiming patriotic verses in honor of George Washington and Abraham Lincoln, with a foreign accent, indeed, but with plenty of enthusiasm. It is enough to know that this hundred-fold miracle is common to the schools in every part of the United States where immigrants are received. And if I was one of Chelsea's hundred in 1894, it was only to be expected, since I was one of the older of the "green" children, and had had a start in my irregular schooling in Russia, and was carried along by a tremendous desire to learn, and had my family to cheer me on.

I was not a bit too large for my little chair and desk in the baby class, but my mind, of course, was too mature by six or seven years for the work. So as soon as I could understand what the teacher said in class, I was advanced to the second grade. This was within a week after Miss Nixon took me in hand. But I do not mean to give my dear teacher all the credit for my rapid progress, nor even half the credit. I shall divide it with her on behalf of my race and my family. I was Jew enough to have an aptitude for language in general, and to bend my mind earnestly to my task; I was Antin enough to read each lesson with my heart, which gave me an inkling of what was coming next, and so carried me along by leaps and bounds. As for the teacher, she could best explain what theory she followed in teaching us foreigners to read. I can only describe the method, which was so simple that I wish holiness could be taught in the same way.

There were about half a dozen of us beginners in English, in age from six to fifteen. Miss Nixon made a special class of us, and aided us so skilfully and earnestly in our endeavors to "see-a-cat," and "hear-a-dog-bark," and "look-at-the-hen," that we turned over page after page of the ravishing history, eager to find out how the common world looked, smelled, and tasted in the strange

1. "House of the One Father," *Common Ground* 1, no. 3 (Spring 1941): 41.

speech. The teacher knew just when to let us help each other out with a word in our own tongue,—it happened that we were all Jews,—and so, working all together, we actually covered more ground in a lesson than the native classes, composed entirely of the little tots.

But we stuck—stuck fast—at the definite article; and sometimes the lesson resolved itself into a species of lingual gymnastics, in which we all looked as if we meant to bite our tongues off. Miss Nixon was pretty, and she must have looked well with her white teeth showing in the act; but at the time I was too solemnly occupied to admire her looks. I did take great pleasure in her smile of approval, whenever I pronounced well; and her patience and perseverance in struggling with us over that thick little word are becoming to her even now, after fifteen years. It is not her fault if any of us to-day give a buzzing sound to the dreadful English *th*.

I shall never have a better opportunity to make public declaration of my love for the English language. I am glad that American history runs, chapter for chapter, the way it does; for thus America came to be the country I love so dearly. I am glad, most of all, that the Americans began by being Englishmen, for thus did I come to inherit this beautiful language in which I think. It seems to me that in any other language happiness is not so sweet, logic is not so clear. I am not sure that I could believe in my neighbors as I do if I thought about them in un-English words. I could almost say that my conviction of immortality is bound up with the English of its promise. And as I am attached to my prejudices, I must love the English language!

Whenever the teachers did anything special to help me over my private difficulties, my gratitude went out to them, silently. It meant so much to me that they halted the lesson to give me a lift, that I needs must love them for it. Dear Miss Carrol, of the second grade, would be amazed to hear what small things I remember, all because I was so impressed at the time with her readiness and sweetness in taking notice of my difficulties.

Says Miss Carrol, looking straight at me:—

"If Johnnie has three marbles, and Charlie has twice as many, how many marbles has Charlie?"

I raise my hand for permission to speak.

"Teacher, I don't know vhat is tvice."

Teacher beckons me to her, and whispers to me the meaning of the strange word, and I am able to write the sum correctly. It's all in the day's work with her; with me, it is a special act of kindness and efficiency.

She whom I found in the next grade became so dear a friend that I can hardly name her with the rest, though I mention none of them lightly. Her approval was always dear to me, first because she was "Teacher," and afterwards, as long as she lived, because she was my Miss Dillingham. Great was my grief, therefore, when, shortly after my admission to her class, I incurred discipline, the first, and next to the last, time in my school career.

The class was repeating in chorus the Lord's Prayer, heads bowed on desks. I was doing my best to keep up by the sound; my mind could not go beyond the word "hallowed," for which I had not found the meaning. In the middle of the prayer a Jewish boy across the aisle trod on my foot to get my attention. "You must not say that," he admonished in a solemn whisper; "it's Christian." I whispered back that it was n't, and went on to the "Amen." I did not know but what he was right, but the name of Christ was not in the prayer, and I was bound to do everything that the class did. If I had any Jewish scruples, they were lagging away behind my interest in school affairs. How American this was: two pupils side by side in the schoolroom, each holding to his own opinion, but both submitting to the common law; for the boy at least bowed his head as the teacher ordered.

But all Miss Dillingham knew of it was that two of her pupils whispered during morning prayer, and she must discipline them. So I was degraded from the honor row to the lowest row, and it was many a day before I forgave that young missionary; it was not enough for my vengeance that he suffered punishment with me. Teacher, of course, heard us both defend ourselves, but there was a time and a place for religious arguments, and she meant to help us remember that point.

I remember to this day what a struggle we had over the word "water," Miss Dillingham and I. It seemed as if I could not give the sound of *w;* I said "vater" every time. Patiently my teacher worked with me, inventing mouth exercises for me, to get my stubborn lips to produce that *w;* and when at last I could say "village" and "water" in rapid alternation, without misplacing the two initials, that memorable word was sweet on my lips. For we had conquered, and Teacher was pleased.

Getting a language in this way, word by word, has a charm that may be set against the disadvantages. It is like gathering a posy blossom by blossom. Bring the bouquet into your chamber, and these nasturtiums stand for the whole flaming carnival of them tumbling over the fence out there; these yellow pansies recall the velvet crescent of color glowing under the bay window; this spray of honeysuckle smells like the wind-tossed masses of it on the porch, ripe and bee-laden; the whole garden in a glass tumbler. So it is with one who gathers words, loving them. Particular words remain associated with important occasions in the learner's mind. I could thus write a history of my English vocabulary that should be at the same time an account of my comings and goings, my mistakes and my triumphs, during the years of my initiation.

If I was eager and diligent, my teachers did not sleep. As fast as my knowledge of English allowed, they advanced me from grade to grade, without reference to the usual schedule of promotions. My father was right, when he often said, in discussing my prospects, that ability would be promptly recognized in the public schools. Rapid as was my progress, on account of the advantages with which I started, some of the other "green" pupils were not far behind me; within a grade or two, by the end of the year. My brother, whose childhood had been one hideous nightmare, what with the stupid rebbe, the cruel whip, and the general repression of life in the Pale, surprised my father by the progress he made under intelligent, sympathetic guidance. Indeed, he soon had a reputation in the school that the American boys envied; and all through the school course he more than held his own with pupils of his age. So much for the right and wrong way of doing things.

There is a record of my early progress in English much better than my recollections, however accurate and definite these may be. I have several reasons for introducing it here. First, it shows what the Russian Jew can do with an adopted language; next, it proves that vigilance of our public-school teachers of which I spoke; and last, I am proud of it! That is an unnecessary confession, but I could not be satisfied to insert the record here, with my vanity unavowed.

This is the document, copied from an educational journal, a tattered copy of which lies in my lap as I write—treasured for fifteen years, you see, by my vanity.

EDITOR "PRIMARY EDUCATION":—
This is the uncorrected paper of a Russian child twelve years old, who had studied English only four months. She had never, until September, been to school even in her own country and has heard English spoken *only* at school. I shall be glad if the paper of my pupil and the above explanation may appear in your paper.

M. S. DILLINGHAM.
Chelsea, Mass.

SNOW

Snow is frozen moisture which comes from the clouds.

Now the snow is coming down in feather-flakes, which makes nice snow-balls. But there is still one kind of snow more. This kind of snow is called snow-crystals, for it comes down in little curly balls. These snow-crystals are n't quiet as good for snow-balls as feather-flakes, for they (the snow-crystals) are dry: so they can't keep together as feather-flakes do.

The snow is dear to some children for they like sleighing.

As I said at the top—the snow comes from the clouds.

Now the trees are bare, and no flowers are to see in the fields and gardens, (we all know why) and the whole world seems like asleep without the happy birds songs which left us till spring. But the snow which drove away all these pretty and happy things, try, (as I think) not to make us at all unhappy; they covered up the branches of the trees, the fields, the gardens and houses, and the whole world looks like dressed in a beautiful white—instead of green—dress, with the sky looking down on it with a pale face.

And so the people can find some joy in it, too, without the happy summer.

MARY ANTIN.

And now that it stands there, with *her* name over it, I am ashamed of my flippant talk about vanity. More to me than all the praise I could hope to win by the conquest of fifty languages is the association of this dear friend with my earliest efforts at writing; and it pleases me to remember that to her I owe my very first appearance in print. Vanity is the least part of it, when I remember how she called me to her desk, one day after school was out, and showed me my composition—my own words, that I had written out of my own head—printed out, clear black and white, with my name at the end! Nothing so wonderful had ever happened to me before. My whole consciousness was suddenly transformed. I suppose that was the moment when I became a writer. I always loved to write,—I wrote letters whenever I had an excuse,—yet it had never occurred to me to sit down and write my thoughts for no person in particular, merely to put the word on paper. But now, as I read my own words, in a delicious confusion, the idea was born. I stared at my name: MARY ANTIN. Was that really I? The printed characters composing it seemed strange to me all of a sudden. If that was my name, and those were the words out of my own head, what relation did it all have to *me*, who was alone there with Miss Dillingham, and the printed page between us? Why, it meant that I could write again, and see my writing printed for people to read! I could write many, many, many things: I could write a book! The idea was so huge, so bewildering, that my mind scarcely could accommodate it.

I do not know what my teacher said to me; probably very little. It was her way to say only a little, and look at me, and trust me to understand. Once she had occasion to lecture me about living a shut-up life; she wanted me to go outdoors. I had been repeatedly scolded and reproved on that score by other people, but I had only laughed, saying that I was too happy to change my ways. But when Miss Dillingham spoke to me, I saw that it was a serious matter; and yet she only said a few words, and looked at me with that smile of hers that was only half a smile, and the rest a meaning. Another time she had a great question to ask me, touching my life to the quick. She merely put her question, and was silent; but I knew what answer she expected, and not being able to give it then, I went away sad and reproved. Years later I had my triumphant answer, but she was no longer there to receive it; and so her eyes look at me, from the picture on the mantel there, with a reproach I no longer merit.

I ought to go back and strike out all that talk about vanity. What reason have I to be vain, when I reflect how at every step I was petted, nursed, and encouraged? I did not even discover my own talent. It was discovered first by my father in Russia, and next by my friend in America. What did I ever do but write when they told me to write? I suppose my grandfather who drove a spavined horse through lonely country lanes sat in the shade of crisp-leaved oaks to refresh himself with a bit of black bread; and an acorn falling beside him, in the immense stillness, shook his heart with the echo, and left him wondering. I suppose my father stole away from the synagogue one long festival day, and stretched himself out in the sun-warmed grass, and lost himself in dreams that made the world of men unreal when he returned to them. And so what is there left for me to do, who do not have to drive a horse nor interpret ancient lore, but put my grandfather's question into words and set to music my father's dream? The tongue am I of those who lived before me, as those that are to come will be the voice of my unspoken thoughts. And so who shall be applauded if the song be sweet, if the prophecy be true?

I never heard of any one who was so watched and coaxed, so passed along from hand to helping hand, as was I. I always had friends. They sprang up everywhere, as if they had stood waiting for me to come. So here was my teacher, the moment she saw that I could give a good paraphrase of her talk on "Snow," bent on finding out what more I could do. One day she asked me if I had ever written poetry. I had not, but I went home and tried. I believe it was more snow, and I know it was wretched. I wish I could produce a copy of that early effusion; it would prove that my judgment is not severe. Wretched it was,—worse, a great deal, than reams of poetry that is written by children about whom there is no fuss made. But Miss Dillingham was not discouraged. She saw that I had no idea of metre, so she proceeded to teach me. We repeated miles of poetry together, smooth lines that sang themselves, mostly out of Longfellow. Then I would go home and write—oh, about the snow in our back yard!—but when Miss Dillingham came to read my verses, they limped and they lagged and they dragged, and there was no tune that would fit them.

At last came the moment of illumination: I saw where my trouble lay. I had supposed that my lines matched when they had an equal number of syllables, taking no account of accent. Now I knew better; now I could write poetry! The everlasting snow melted at last, and the mud puddles dried in the spring sun, and the grass on the common was green, and still I wrote poetry! Again I wish I had some example of my springtime rhapsodies, the veriest rubbish of the sort that ever a child perpetrated. Lizzie McDee, who had red hair and freckles, and a Sunday-school manner on weekdays, and was below me in the class, did a great deal better. We used to compare verses; and while I do not remember that I ever had the grace to own that she was the better poet, I do know that I secretly wondered why the teachers did not invite her to stay after school and study poetry, while they took so much pains with me. But so it was always with me: somebody did something for me all the time.

Making fair allowance for my youth, retarded education, and strangeness to the language, it must still be admitted that I never wrote good verse. But I loved to read it. My half-hours with Miss Dillingham were full of delight for me, quite apart from my new-born ambition to become a writer. What, then, was my joy, when Miss Dillingham, just before locking up her desk one evening, presented me with a volume of Longfellow's poems! It was a thin volume of selections, but to me it was a bottomless treasure. I had never owned a book before. The sense of possession alone was a source of bliss, and this book I already knew and loved. And so Miss Dillingham, who was my first American friend, and who first put my name in print, was also the one to start my library. Deep is my regret when I consider that she was gone before I had given much of an account of all her gifts of love and service to me.

About the middle of the year I was promoted to the grammar school. Then it was that I walked on air. For I said to myself that I was a *student* now, in earnest, not merely a school-girl learning to spell and cipher. I was going to learn out-of-the-way things, things that had nothing to do with ordinary life—things to *know*. When I walked home afternoons, with the great big geography book under my arm, it seemed to me that the earth was conscious of my step. Sometimes I carried home half the books in my desk, not because I should need them, but because I loved to hold them; and also because I loved to be seen carrying books. It was a badge of scholarship, and I was proud of it. I remembered the days in Vitebsk when I used to watch my cousin Hirshel start for school in the morning, every thread of his student's uniform, every worn copybook in his satchel, glorified in my envious eyes. And now I was myself as he: aye, greater than he; for I knew English, and I could write poetry.

If my head was not turned at this time it was because I was so busy from morning till night. My father did his best to make me vain and silly. He made much of me to every chance caller, boasting of my progress at school, and of my exalted friends, the teachers. For a school-teacher was no ordinary mortal in his eyes; she was a superior being, set above the common run of men by her erudition and devotion to higher things. That a school-teacher could be shallow or petty, or greedy for pay, was a thing that he could not have been brought to believe, at this time. And he was right, if he could only have stuck to it in later years, when a new-born pessimism, fathered by his perception that in America, too, some things needed mending, threw him to the opposite extreme of opinion, crying that nothing in the American scheme of society or government was worth tinkering.

He surely was right in his first appraisal of the teacher. The mean sort of teachers are not teachers at all; they are self-seekers who take up teaching as a business, to support themselves and keep their hands white. These same persons, did they keep store or drive a milk wagon or wash babies for a living, would be respectable. As trespassers on a noble profession, they are worth no more than the books and slates and desks over which they preside; so much furniture, to be had by the gross. They do not love their work. They contribute nothing to the higher development of their pupils. They busy themselves, not with research into the science of teaching, but with organizing political demonstrations to advance the cause of selfish candidates for public office, who promise them rewards. The true teachers are of another strain. Apostles all of an ideal, they go to their work in a spirit of love and inquiry, seeking not comfort, not position, not old-age pensions, but truth that is the soul of wisdom, the joy of big-eyed children, the food of hungry youth.

They were true teachers who used to come to me on Arlington Street, so my father had reason to boast of the distinction brought upon his house. For the schoolteacher in her trim, unostentatious dress was an uncommon visitor in our neighborhood; and the talk that passed in the bare little "parlor" over the grocery store would not have been entirely comprehensible to our next-door neighbor.

In the grammar school I had as good teaching as I had had in the primary. It seems to me in retrospect that it was as good, on the whole, as the public school ideals of the time made possible. When I recall how I was taught geography, I see, indeed, that there was room for improvement occasionally both in the substance and in the method of instruction. But I know of at least one teacher of Chelsea who realized this; for I met her, eight years later, at a great metropolitan university that holds a summer session for the benefit of school-teachers who want to keep up with the advance in their science. Very likely they no longer teach geography entirely within doors, and by rote, as I was taught. Fifteen years is plenty of time for progress.

When I joined the first grammar grade, the class had had a half-year's start of me, but it was not long before I found my place near the head. In all branches except geography it was genuine progress. I overtook the youngsters in their study of numbers, spelling, reading, and composition. In geography I merely made a bluff, but I did not know it. Neither did my teacher. I came up to such tests as she put me.

The lesson was on Chelsea, which was right: geography, like charity, should begin at home. Our text ran on for a paragraph or so on the location, boundaries, natural features, and industries of the town, with a bit of local history thrown in. We were to learn all these interesting facts, and be prepared to write them out from memory the next day. I went home and learned—learned every word of the text, every comma, every footnote. When the teacher had read my paper she marked it "EE." "E" was for "excellent," but my paper was absolutely perfect, and must be put in a class by itself. The teacher exhibited my paper before the class, with some remarks about the diligence that could overtake in a week pupils who had had half a year's start. I took it all as modestly as I could, never doubting that I was indeed a very bright little girl, and getting to be very learned to boot. I was "perfect" in geography, a most erudite subject.

But what was the truth? The words that I repeated so accurately on my paper had about as much meaning to me as the words of the Psalms I used to chant in Hebrew. I got an idea that the city of Chelsea, and the world in general, was laid out flat, like the common, and shaved off at the ends, to allow the north, south, east, and west to snuggle up close, like the frame around a picture. If I looked at the map, I was utterly bewildered; I could find no correspondence between the picture and the verbal explanations. With words I was safe; I could learn any number of words by heart, and sometime or other they would pop out of the medley, clothed with meaning. Chelsea, I read, was bounded on all sides—"bounded" appealed to my imagination— by various things that I had never identified, much as I had roamed about the town. I immediately pictured these remote boundaries as a six-foot fence in a good state of preservation, with the Mystic River, the towns of Everett and Revere, and East Boston Creek, rejoicing, on the south, west, north, and east of it, respectively, that they had got inside; while the rest of the world peeped in enviously through a knot hole. In the middle of this cherished area piano factories—or was it shoe factories?—proudly reared their chimneys, while the population promenaded on a *rope walk,* saluted at every turn by the benevolent inmates of the Soldiers' Home on the top of Powderhorn Hill.

Perhaps the fault was partly mine, because I always would reduce everything to a picture. Partly it may have been because I had not had time to digest the general definitions and explanations at the beginning of the book. Still, I can take but little of the blame, when I consider how I fared through my geography, right to the end of the grammar-school course. I did in time disentangle the symbolism of the orange revolving on a knitting-needle from the astronomical facts in the case, but it took years of training under a master of the subject to rid me of my distrust of the map as a representation of the earth. To this day I sometimes blunder back to my early impression that any given portion of the earth's surface is constructed upon a skeleton consisting of two crossed bars, terminating in arrowheads which pin the cardinal points into place; and if I want to find any desired point of the compass, I am inclined to throw myself flat on my nose, my head due north, and my outstretched arms seeking the east and west respectively.

For in the schoolroom, as far as the study of the map went, we began with the symbol and stuck to the symbol. No teacher of geography I ever had, except the master I referred to, took the pains to ascertain whether I had any sense of the facts for which the symbols stood. Outside the study of maps, geography consisted of statistics: tables of population, imports and exports, manufactures, and degrees of temperature; dimensions of rivers, mountains, and political states; with lists of minerals, plants, and plagues native to any given part of the globe. The only part of the whole subject that meant anything to me was the description of the aspect of foreign lands, and the manners and customs of their peoples. The relation of physiography to human history— what might be called the moral of geography—was not taught at all, or was touched upon in an unimpressive manner. The prevalence of this defect in the teaching of school geography is borne out by the surprise of the college freshman, who remarked to the professor of geology that it was curious to

moves on, though without a diploma, from the University of Wisconsin to "the University of the Wilderness."

The selection here is from Muir's *The Story of My Boyhood and Youth* (Boston: Houghton Mifflin, 1916; reprint, Madison: Univ. of Wisconsin Press, 1965). There have been several biographies of Muir, beginning with W. F. Badè, *The Life and Letters of John Muir* (1925).

When I told father that I was about to leave home, and inquired whether, if I should happen to be in need of money, he would send me a little, he said, "No; depend entirely on yourself." Good advice, I suppose, but surely needlessly severe for a bashful, home-loving boy who had worked so hard. I had the gold sovereign that my grandfather had given me when I left Scotland, and a few dollars, perhaps ten, that I had made by raising a few bushels of grain on a little patch of sandy abandoned ground. So when I left home to try the world I had only about fifteen dollars in my pocket.

Strange to say, father carefully taught us to consider ourselves very poor worms of the dust, conceived in sin, etc., and devoutly believed that quenching every spark of pride and self-confidence was a sacred duty, without realizing that in so doing he might at the same time be quenching everything else. Praise he considered most venomous, and tried to assure me that when I was fairly out in the wicked world making my own way I would soon learn that although I might have thought him a hard taskmaster at times, strangers were far harder. On the contrary, I found no lack of kindness and sympathy. All the baggage I carried was a package made up of the two clocks and a small thermometer made of a piece of old washboard, all three tied together, with no covering or case of any sort, the whole looking like one very complicated machine.

The aching parting from mother and my sisters was, of course, hard to bear. Father let David drive me down to Pardeeville, a place I had never before seen, though it was only nine miles south of the Hickory Hill home. When we arrived at the village tavern, it seemed deserted. Not a single person was in sight. I set my clock baggage on the rickety platform. David said goodbye and started for home, leaving me alone in the world. The grinding noise made by the wagon in turning short brought out the landlord, and the first thing that caught his eye was my strange bundle. Then he looked at me and said, "Hello, young man, what's this?"

"Machines," I said, "for keeping time and getting up in the morning, and so forth."

"Well! Well! That's a mighty queer get-up. You must be a Down-East Yankee. Where did you get the pattern for such a thing?"

"In my head," I said.

Some one down the street happened to notice the landlord looking intently at something and came up to see what it was. Three or four people in that little village formed an attractive crowd, and in fifteen or twenty min-utes the greater part of the population of Pardeeville stood gazing in a circle around my strange hickory belongings. I kept outside of the circle to avoid being seen, and had the advantage of hearing the remarks without being em-barrassed. Almost every one as he came up would say, "What's that? What's it for? Who made it?" The landlord would answer them all alike, "Why, a young man that lives out in the country somewhere made it, and he says it's a thing for keeping time, getting up in the morning, and something that I did n't understand. I don't know what he meant." "Oh, no!" one of the crowd would say, "that can't be. It's for something else—something mysterious. Mark my words, you'll see all about it in the newspapers some of these days." A curious little fellow came running up the street, joined the crowd, stood on tiptoe to get sight of the wonder, quickly made up his mind, and shouted in crisp, con-fident, cock-crowing style, "I know what that contraption's for. It's a machine for taking the bones out of fish."

This was in the time of the great popular phrenology craze, when the fences and barns along the roads throughout the country were plastered with big skull-bump posters, headed, "Know Thyself," and advising everybody to attend schoolhouse lectures to have their heads explained and be told what they were good for and whom they ought to marry. My mechanical bundle seemed to bring a good deal of this phrenology to mind, for many of the onlookers would say, "I wish I could see that boy's head,—he must have a tremendous bump of invention." Others complimented me by saying, "I wish I had that fellow's head. I'd rather have it than the best farm in the State."

I stayed overnight at this little tavern, waiting for a train. In the morning I went to the station, and set my bundle on the platform. Along came the thundering train, a glorious sight, the first train I had ever waited for. When the conductor saw my queer baggage, he cried, "Hello! What have we here?"

"Inventions for keeping time, early rising, and so forth. May I take them into the car with me?"

"You can take them where you like," he replied, "but you had better give them to the baggage-master. If you take them into the car they will draw a crowd and might get broken."

So I gave them to the baggage-master and made haste to ask the con-ductor whether I might ride on the engine. He good-naturedly said: "Yes, it's the right place for you. Run ahead, and tell the engineer what I say." But the engineer bluntly refused to let me on, saying: "It don't matter what the conductor told you. *I* say you can't ride on my engine."

By this time the conductor, standing ready to start his train, was watch-ing to see what luck I had, and when he saw me returning came ahead to meet me.

"The engineer won't let me on," I reported.

"Won't he?" said the kind conductor. "Oh! I guess he will. You come

485

down with me." And so he actually took the time and patience to walk the length of that long train to get me on to the engine.

"Charlie," said he, addressing the engineer, "don't you ever take a passenger?"

"Very seldom," he replied.

"Anyhow, I wish you would take this young man on. He has the strangest machines in the baggage-car I ever saw in my life. I believe he could make a locomotive. He wants to see the engine running. Let him on." Then in a low whisper he told me to jump on, which I did gladly, the engineer offering neither encouragement nor objection.

As soon as the train was started, the engineer asked what the "strange thing" the conductor spoke of really was.

"Only inventions for keeping time, getting folk up in the morning, and so forth," I hastily replied, and before he could ask any more questions I asked permission to go outside of the cab to see the machinery. This he kindly granted, adding, "Be careful not to fall off, and when you hear me whistling for a station you come back, because if it is reported against me to the superintendent that I allow boys to run all over my engine I might lose my job."

Assuring him that I would come back promptly, I went out and walked along the foot-board on the side of the boiler, watching the magnificent machine rushing through the landscapes as if glorying in its strength like a living creature. While seated on the cow-catcher platform, I seemed to be fairly flying, and the wonderful display of power and motion was enchanting. This was the first time I had ever been on a train, much less a locomotive, since I had left Scotland. When I got to Madison, I thanked the kind conductor and engineer for my glorious ride, inquired the way to the Fair, shouldered my inventions, and walked to the Fair Ground.

When I applied for an admission ticket at a window by the gate I told the agent that I had something to exhibit.

"What is it?" he inquired.

"Well, here it is. Look at it."

When he craned his neck through the window and got a glimpse of my bundle, he cried excitedly, "Oh! *you* don't need a ticket—come right in."

When I inquired of the agent where such things as mine should be exhibited, he said, "You see that building up on the hill with a big flag on it? That's the Fine Arts Hall, and it's just the place for your wonderful invention."

So I went up to the Fine Arts Hall and looked in, wondering if they would allow wooden things in so fine a place.

I was met at the door by a dignified gentleman, who greeted me kindly and said, "Young man, what have we got here?"

"Two clocks and a thermometer," I replied.

"Did you make these? They look wonderfully beautiful and novel and must, I think, prove the most interesting feature of the fair."

"Where shall I place them?" I inquired.

"Just look around, young man, and choose the place you like best, whether it is occupied or not. You can have your pick of all the building, and a carpenter to make the necessary shelving and assist you every way possible!"

So I quickly had a shelf made large enough for all of them, went out on the hill and picked up some glacial boulders of the right size for weights, and in fifteen or twenty minutes the clocks were running. They seemed to attract more attention than anything else in the hall. I got lots of praise from the crowd and the newspaper reporters. The local press reports were copied into the Eastern papers. It was considered wonderful that a boy on a farm had been able to invent and make such things, and almost every spectator foretold good fortune. But I had been so lectured by my father above all things to avoid praise that I was afraid to read those kind newspaper notices, and never clipped out or preserved any of them, just glanced at them and turned away my eyes from beholding vanity. They gave me a prize of ten or fifteen dollars and a diploma for wonderful things not down in the list of exhibits.

Many years later, after I had written articles and books, I received a letter from the gentleman who had charge of the Fine Arts Hall. He proved to be the Professor of English Literature in the University of Wisconsin at this Fair time, and long afterward he sent me clippings of reports of his lectures. He had a lecture on me, discussing style, etcetera, and telling how well he remembered my arrival at the Hall in my shirt-sleeves with those mechanical wonders on my shoulder, and so forth, and so forth. These inventions, though of little importance, opened all doors for me and made marks that have lasted many years, simply, I suppose, because they were original and promising.

I was looking around in the mean time to find out where I should go to seek my fortune. An inventor at the Fair, by the name of Wiard, was exhibiting an iceboat he had invented to run on the upper Mississippi from Prairie du Chien to St. Paul during the winter months, explaining how useful it would be thus to make a highway of the river while it was closed to ordinary navigation by ice. After he saw my inventions he offered me a place in his foundry and machine-shop in Prairie du Chien and promised to assist me all he could. So I made up my mind to accept his offer and rode with him to Prairie du Chien in his iceboat, which was mounted on a flat car. I soon found, however, that he was seldom at home and that I was not likely to learn much at his small shop. I found a place where I could work for my board and devote my spare hours to mechanical drawing, geometry, and physics, making but little headway, however, although the Pelton family, for whom I worked, were very kind. I made up my mind after a few months' stay in

Prairie du Chien to return to Madison, hoping that in some way I might be able to gain an education.

At Madison I raised a few dollars by making and selling a few of those bedsteads that set the sleepers on their feet in the morning,—inserting in the footboard the works of an ordinary clock that could be bought for a dollar. I also made a few dollars addressing circulars in an insurance office, while at the same time I was paying my board by taking care of a pair of horses and going errands. This is of no great interest except that I was thus winning my bread while hoping that something would turn up that might enable me to make money enough to enter the State University. This was my ambition, and it never wavered no matter what I was doing. No University, it seemed to me, could be more admirably situated, and as I sauntered about it, charmed with its fine lawns and trees and beautiful lakes, and saw the students going and coming with their books, and occasionally practicing with a theodolite in measuring distances, I thought that if I could only join them it would be the greatest joy of life. I was desperately hungry and thirsty for knowledge and willing to endure anything to get it.

One day I chanced to meet a student who had noticed my inventions at the Fair and now recognized me. And when I said, "You are fortunate fellows to be allowed to study in this beautiful place. I wish I could join you." "Well, why don't you?" he asked. "I have n't money enough," I said. "Oh, as to money," he reassuringly explained, "very little is required. I presume you're able to enter the Freshman class, and you can board yourself as quite a number of us do at a cost of about a dollar a week. The baker and milkman come every day. You can live on bread and milk." Well, I thought, maybe I have money enough for at least one beginning term. Anyhow I could n't help trying.

With fear and trembling, overladen with ignorance, I called on Professor Stirling, the Dean of the Faculty, who was then Acting President, presented my case, and told him how far I had got on with my studies at home, and that I had n't been to school since leaving Scotland at the age of eleven years, excepting one short term of a couple of months at a district school, because I could not be spared from the farm work. After hearing my story, the kind professor welcomed me to the glorious University—next, it seemed to me, to the Kingdom of Heaven. After a few weeks in the preparatory department I entered the Freshman class. In Latin I found that one of the books in use I had already studied in Scotland. So, after an interruption of a dozen years, I began my Latin over again where I had left off; and, strange to say, most of it came back to me, especially the grammar which I had committed to memory at the Dunbar Grammar School.

During the four years that I was in the University, I earned enough in the harvest-fields during the long summer vacations to carry me through the balance of each year, working very hard, cutting with a cradle four acres of wheat a day, and helping to put it in the shock. But, having to buy books and paying, I think, thirty-two dollars a year for instruction, and occasionally buying acids and retorts, glass tubing, bell-glasses, flasks, etc., I had to cut down expenses for board now and then to half a dollar a week.

One winter I taught school ten miles north of Madison, earning much-needed money at the rate of twenty dollars a month, "boarding round," and keeping up my University work by studying at night. As I was not then well enough off to own a watch, I used one of my hickory clocks, not only for keeping time, but for starting the school fire in the cold mornings, and regulating class-times. I carried it out on my shoulder to the old log schoolhouse, and set it to work on a little shelf nailed to one of the knotty, bulging logs. The winter was very cold, and I had to go to the schoolhouse and start the fire about eight o'clock to warm it before the arrival of the scholars. This was a rather trying job, and one that my clock might easily be made to do. Therefore, after supper one evening I told the head of the family with whom I was boarding that if he would give me a candle I would go back to the schoolhouse and make arrangements for lighting the fire at eight o'clock, without my having to be present until time to open the school at nine. He said, "Oh, young man, you have some curious things in the school-room, but I don't think you can do that." I said, "Oh, yes! It's easy," and in hardly more than an hour the simple job was completed. I had only to place a teaspoonful of powdered chlorate of potash and sugar on the stove-hearth near a few shavings and kindling, and at the required time make the clock, through a simple arrangement, touch the inflammable mixture with a drop of sulphuric acid. Every evening after school was dismissed, I shoveled out what was left of the fire into the snow, put in a little kindling, filled up the big box stove with heavy oak wood, placed the lighting arrangement on the hearth, and set the clock to drop the acid at the hour of eight; all this requiring only a few minutes.

The first morning after I had made this simple arrangement I invited the doubting farmer to watch the old squat schoolhouse from a window that overlooked it, to see if a good smoke did not rise from the stovepipe. Sure enough, on the minute, he saw a tall column curling gracefully up through the frosty air, but instead of congratulating me on my success he solemnly shook his head and said in a hollow, lugubrious voice, "Young man, you will be setting fire to the schoolhouse." All winter long that faithful clock fire never failed, and by the time I got to the schoolhouse the stove was usually red-hot.

At the beginning of the long summer vacations I returned to the Hickory Hill farm to earn the means in the harvest-fields to continue my University course, walking all the way to save railroad fares. And although I cradled four acres of wheat a day, I made the long, hard, sweaty day's work still longer and harder by keeping up my study of plants. At the noon hour I collected a large handful, put them in water to keep them fresh, and after supper got to work on them and sat up till after midnight, analyzing and classifying, thus leaving only four hours for sleep; and by the end of the first year, after taking up botany, I knew the principal flowering plants of the region.

I received my first lesson in botany from a student by the name of Griswold, who is now County Judge of the County of Waukesha, Wisconsin. In the University he was often laughed at on account of his anxiety to instruct others, and his frequently saying with fine emphasis, "Imparting instruction is my greatest enjoyment." One memorable day in June, when I was standing on the stone steps of the north dormitory, Mr. Griswold joined me and at once began to teach. He reached up, plucked a flower from an overspreading branch of a locust tree, and, handing it to me, said, "Muir, do you know what family this tree belongs to?"

"No," I said, "I don't know anything about botany."

"Well, no matter," said he, "what is it like?"

"It's like a pea flower," I replied.

"That's right. You're right," he said, "it belongs to the Pea Family."

"But how can that be," I objected, "when the pea is a weak, clinging, straggling herb, and the locust a big, thorny hardwood tree?"

"Yes, that is true," he replied, "as to the difference in size, but it is also true that in all their essential characters they are alike, and therefore they must belong to one and the same family. Just look at the peculiar form of the locust flower; you see that the upper petal, called the banner, is broad and erect, and so is the upper petal of the pea flower; the two lower petals, called the wings, are outspread and wing-shaped; so are those of the pea; and the two petals below the wings are united on their edges, curve upward, and form what is called the keel, and so you see are the corresponding petals of the pea flower. And now look at the stamens and pistils. You see that nine of the ten stamens have their filaments united into a sheath around the pistil, but the tenth stamen has its filament free. These are very marked characters, are they not? And, strange to say, you will find them the same in the tree and in the vine. Now look at the ovules or seeds of the locust, and you will see that they are arranged in a pod or legume like those of the pea. And look at the leaves. You see the leaf of the locust is made up of several leaflets, and so also is the leaf of the pea. Now taste the locust leaf."

I did so and found that it tasted like the leaf of the pea. Nature has used the same seasoning for both, though one is a straggling vine, the other a big tree.

"Now, surely you cannot imagine that all these similar characters are mere coincidences. Do they not rather go to show that the Creator in making the pea vine and locust tree had the same idea in mind, and that plants are not classified arbitrarily? Man has nothing to do with their classification. Nature has attended to all that, giving essential unity with boundless variety, so that the botanist has only to examine plants to learn the harmony of their relations."

This fine lesson charmed me and sent me flying to the woods and meadows in wild enthusiasm. Like everybody else I was always fond of flowers, attracted by their external beauty and purity. Now my eyes were opened to their inner beauty, all alike revealing glorious traces of the thoughts of God, and leading on and on into the infinite cosmos. I wandered away at every opportunity, making long excursions round the lakes, gathering specimens and keeping them fresh in a bucket in my room to study at night after my regular class tasks were learned; for my eyes never closed on the plant glory I had seen.

Nevertheless, I still indulged my love of mechanical inventions. I invented a desk in which the books I had to study were arranged in order at the beginning of each term. I also made a bed which set me on my feet every morning at the hour determined on, and in dark winter mornings just as the bed set me on the floor it lighted a lamp. Then, after the minutes allowed for dressing had elapsed, a click was heard and the first book to be studied was pushed up from a rack below the top of the desk, thrown open, and allowed to remain there the number of minutes required. Then the machinery closed the book and allowed it to drop back into its stall, then moved the rack forward and threw up the next in order, and so on, all the day being divided according to the times of recitation, and time required and allotted to each study. Besides this, I thought it would be a fine thing in the summer-time when the sun rose early, to dispense with the clock-controlled bed machinery, and make use of sunbeams instead. This I did simply by taking a lens out of my small spy-glass, fixing it on a frame on the sill of my bedroom window, and pointing it to the sunrise; the sunbeams focused on a thread burned it through, allowing the bed machinery to put me on my feet. When I wished to arise at any given time after sunrise, I had only to turn the pivoted frame that held the lens the requisite number of degrees or minutes. Thus I took Emerson's advice and hitched my dumping-wagon bed to a star.

I also invented a machine to make visible the growth of plants and the action of the sunlight, a very delicate contrivance, enclosed in glass. Besides this I invented a barometer and a lot of novel scientific apparatus. My room was regarded as a sort of show place by the professors, who oftentimes brought visitors to it on Saturdays and holidays. And when, some eighteen years after I had left the University, I was sauntering over the campus in time of vacation, and spoke to a man who seemed to be taking some charge of the grounds, he informed me that he was the janitor; and when I inquired what had become of Pat, the janitor in my time, and a favorite with the students, he replied that Pat was still alive and well, but now too old to do much work. And when I pointed to the dormitory room that I long ago occupied, he said:

"Oh! then I know who you are," and mentioned my name. "How comes it that you know my name?" I inquired. He explained that "Pat always pointed out that room to newcomers and told long stories about the wonders that used to be in it." So long had the memory of my little inventions survived.

Although I was four years at the University, I did not take the regular course of studies, but instead picked out what I thought would be most useful to me, particularly chemistry, which opened a new world, and mathematics and physics, a little Greek and Latin, botany and geology. I was far from satisfied with what I had learned, and should have stayed longer. Anyhow I wandered away on a glorious botanical and geological excursion, which has lasted nearly fifty years and is not yet completed, always happy and free, poor and rich, without thought of a diploma or of making a name, urged on and on through endless, inspiring, Godful beauty.

From the top of a hill on the north side of Lake Mendota I gained a last wistful, lingering view of the beautiful University grounds and buildings where I had spent so many hungry and happy and hopeful days. There with streaming eyes I bade my blessed Alma Mater farewell. But I was only leaving one University for another, the Wisconsin University for the University of the Wilderness.

36

W. E. B. Du Bois (1868–1963)

The Shadow of Years

W. E. B. Du Bois was a master at writing fierce, tough-minded, and yet visionary essays with an autobiographical perspective, a form of literature perfectly suited to his training as a sociologist and to his later work as editor of *The Crisis*, the journal of the National Association for the Advancement of Colored People. He helped to found the NAACP in 1909, so as to oppose Booker T. Washington's program of acceptance of menial labor and segregation, and he needed to write articles for *The Crisis* (and other journals) that combined sociological and historical data with the shocking and illustrative material of personal testimony. In that way he could both inform his biracial audiences and also give his readers a perspective they never got from white writers.

Darkwater (1920), subtitled *Voices from Within the Veil*, has many such essays, like "The Servant in the House," where he begins an attack on job discrimination by recalling his own refusal to accept service jobs, except for one summer at a hotel in Minnesota, and "Of Beauty and Death," where he gives his own experience of Jim Crow waiting rooms and railroad cars, as part of a build-up to attacking discrimination in the army in 1917–19. His anger, irony, and shifts of frame and context anticipate the essays of James Baldwin, Ralph Ellison, and other writers.

"The Shadow of Years," which is the introduction to *Darkwater*, is the most autobiographical of these essays, being about his family, childhood, and education—and the least polemical. But he still jabs at his white readers and shares laughs with his black ones. Through the entire account, he remains both disgusted by America and hopeful, telling of "Days of Disillusion" and ages of "Miracles." His progressivism shows up in the facts that the miracles outnumber the disillusions, that he used his comparative good fortune in life in order to help others, and that he worked as a scientist and writer, not an evangelical preacher.

Du Bois published two more autobiographies, *Dusk of Dawn* (1940) and *The Autobiography: A Soliloquy on Viewing My Life from the Last Decade of Its First Century* (1968). *Critical Essays on W. E. B. Du Bois*, ed. William L. Andrews (Boston: G. K. Hall, 1985), contains analyses of Du Bois and his work.

Reprinted from *Darkwater: Voices from Within the Veil* (New York: Harcourt, Brace and Howe, 1920) by permission of David G. Du Bois.

I was born by a golden river and in the shadow of two great hills, five years after the Emancipation Proclamation. The house was quaint, with clapboards running up and down, neatly trimmed, and there were five rooms, a tiny porch, a rosy front yard, and unbelievably delicious strawberries in the rear. A South Carolinian, lately come to the Berkshire Hills, owned all this—tall, thin, and black, with golden earrings, and given to religious trances. We were his transient tenants for the time.

My own people were part of a great clan. Fully two hundred years before, Tom Burghardt had come through the western pass from the Hudson with his Dutch captor, "Coenraet Burghardt," sullen in his slavery and achieving his freedom by volunteering for the Revolution at a time of sudden alarm. His wife was a little, black, Bantu woman, who never became reconciled to this strange land; she clasped her knees and rocked and crooned:

> Do bana coba—gene me, gene me!
> Ben d'nuli, ben d'le—

Tom died about 1787, but of him came many sons, and one, Jack, who helped in the War of 1812. Of Jack and his wife, Violet, was born a mighty family, splendidly named: Harlow and Ira, Cloë, Lucinda, Maria, and Othello! I dimly remember my grandfather, Othello,—or "Uncle Tallow,"—a brown man, strong-voiced and redolent with tobacco, who sat stiffly in a great high chair because his hip was broken. He was probably a bit lazy and given to wassail. At any rate, grandmother had a shrewish tongue and often berated him. This grandmother was Sarah—"Aunt Sally"—a stern, tall, Dutch-African woman, beak-nosed, but beautiful-eyed and golden-skinned. Ten or more children were theirs, of whom the youngest was Mary, my mother.

Mother was dark shining bronze, with a tiny ripple in her black hair, black-eyed, with a heavy, kind face. She gave one the impression of infinite patience, but a curious determination was concealed in her softness. The family were small farmers on Egremont Plain, between Great Barrington and Sheffield, Massachusetts. The bits of land were too small to support the great families born on them and we were always poor. I never remember being cold or hungry, but I do remember that shoes and coal, and sometimes flour, caused mother moments of anxious thought in winter, and a new suit was an event!

At about the time of my birth economic pressure was transmuting the family generally from farmers to "hired" help. Some revolted and migrated westward, others went cityward as cooks and barbers. Mother worked for some years at house service in Great Barrington, and after a disappointed love episode with a cousin, who went to California, she met and married Alfred Du Bois and went to town to live by the golden river where I was born.

Alfred, my father, must have seemed a splendid vision in that little valley under the shelter of those mighty hills. He was small and beautiful of face and feature, just tinted with the sun, his curly hair chiefly revealing his kinship to Africa. In nature he was a dreamer,—romantic, indolent, kind, unreliable. He had in him the making of a poet, an adventurer, or a Beloved Vagabond, according to the life that closed round him; and that life gave him all too little. His father, Alexander Du Bois, cloaked under a stern, austere demeanor a passionate revolt against the world. He, too, was small, but squarish. I remember him as I saw him first, in his home in New Bedford,—white hair close-cropped; a seamed, hard face, but high in tone, with a gray eye that could twinkle or glare.

Long years before him Louis XIV drove two Huguenots, Jacques and Louis Du Bois, into wild Ulster County, New York. One of them in the third or fourth generation had a descendant, Dr. James Du Bois, a gay, rich bachelor, who made his money in the Bahamas, where he and the Gilberts had plantations. There he took a beautiful little mulatto slave as his mistress, and two sons were born: Alexander in 1803 and John, later. They were fine, straight, clear-eyed boys, white enough to "pass." He brought them to America and put Alexander in the celebrated Cheshire School, in Connecticut. Here he often visited him, but one last time, fell dead. He left no will, and his relations made short shrift of these sons. They gathered in the property, apprenticed grandfather to a shoemaker; then dropped him.

Grandfather took his bitter dose like a thoroughbred. Wild as was his inner revolt against this treatment, he uttered no word against the thieves and made no plea. He tried his fortunes here and in Haiti, where, during his short, restless sojourn, my own father was born. Eventually, grandfather became chief steward on the passenger boat between New York and New Haven; later he was a small merchant in Springfield; and finally he retired and ended his days at New Bedford. Always he held his head high, took no insults, made few friends. He was not a "Negro"; he was a man! Yet the current was too strong even for him. Then even more than now a colored man had colored friends or none at all, lived in a colored world or lived alone. A few fine, strong, black men gained the heart of this silent, bitter man in New York and New Haven. If he had scant sympathy with their social clannishness, he was with them in fighting discrimination. So, when the white Episcopalians of Trinity Parish, New Haven, showed plainly that they no longer wanted black folk as fellow Christians, he led the revolt which resulted in St. Luke's Parish, and was for years its senior warden. He lies dead in the Grove Street Cemetery, beside Jehudi Ashmun.

Beneath his sternness was a very human man. Slyly he wrote poetry,—stilted, pleading things from a soul astray. He loved women in his masterful way, marrying three beautiful wives in succession and clinging to each with a certain desperate, even if unsympathetic, affection. As a father he was, naturally, a failure,—hard, domineering, unyielding. His four children reacted characteristically: one was until past middle life a thin spinster, the mental

495

image of her father; one died; one passed over into the white world and her children's children are now white, with no knowledge of their Negro blood; the fourth, my father, bent before grandfather, but did not break—better if he had. He yielded and flared back, asked forgiveness and forgot why, became the harshly-held favorite, who ran away and rioted and roamed and loved and married my brown mother.

So with some circumstance having finally gotten myself born, with a flood of Negro blood, a strain of French, a bit of Dutch, but, thank God! no "Anglo-Saxon," I come to the days of my childhood.

They were very happy. Early we moved back to Grandfather Burghardt's home,—I barely remember its stone fireplace, big kitchen, and delightful woodshed. Then this house passed to other branches of the clan and we moved to rented quarters in town,—to one delectable place "upstairs," with a wide yard full of shrubbery, and a brook; to another house abutting a rail-road, with infinite interests and astonishing playmates; and finally back to the quiet street on which I was born,—down a long lane and in a homely, cozy cottage, with a living-room, a tiny sitting-room, a pantry, and two attic bed-rooms. Here mother and I lived until she died, in 1884, for father early began his restless wanderings. I last remember urgent letters for us to come to New Milford, where he had started a barber shop. Later he became a preacher. But mother no longer trusted his dreams, and he soon faded out of our lives into silence.

From the age of five until I was sixteen I went to school on the same grounds,—down a lane, into a widened yard, with a big choke-cherry tree and two buildings, wood and brick. Here I got acquainted with my world, and soon had my criterions of judgment.

Wealth had no particular lure. On the other hand, the shadow of wealth was about us. That river of my birth was golden because of the woolen and paper waste that soiled it. The gold was theirs, not ours; but the gleam and glint was for all. To me it was all in order and I took it philosophically. I cordially despised the poor Irish and South Germans, who slaved in the mills, and annexed the rich and well-to-do as my natural companions. Of such is the kingdom of snobs!

Most of our townfolk were, naturally, the well-to-do, shading downward, but seldom reaching poverty. As playmate of the children I saw the homes of nearly every one, except a few immigrant New Yorkers, of whom none of us approved. The homes I saw impressed me, but did not overwhelm me. Many were bigger than mine, with newer and shinier things, but they did not seem to differ in kind. I think I probably surprised my hosts more than they me, for I was easily at home and perfectly happy and they looked to me just like ordinary people, while my brown face and frizzled hair must have seemed strange to them.

Yet I was very much one of them. I was a center and sometimes the leader of the town gang of boys. We were noisy, but never very bad,—and, indeed, my mother's quiet influence came in here, as I realize now. She did not try to make me perfect. To her I was already perfect. She simply warned me of a few things, especially saloons. In my town the saloon was the open door to hell. The best families had their drunkards and the worst had little else.

Very gradually,—I cannot now distinguish the steps, though here and there I remember a jump or a jolt—but very gradually I found myself assuming quite placidly that I was different from other children. At first I think I connected the difference with a manifest ability to get my lessons rather better than most and to recite with a certain happy, almost taunting, glibness, which brought frowns here and there. Then, slowly, I realized that some folks, a few, even several, actually considered my brown skin a misfortune; once or twice I became painfully aware that some human beings even thought it a crime. I was not for a moment daunted,—although, of course, there were some days of secret tears—rather I was spurred to tireless effort. If they beat me at anything, I was grimly determined to make them sweat for it! Once I remember challenging a great, hard farmer-boy to battle, when I knew he could whip me; and he did. But ever after, he was polite.

As time flew I felt not so much disowned and rejected as rather drawn up into higher spaces and made part of a mightier mission. At times I almost pitied my pale companions, who were not of the Lord's anointed and who saw in their dreams no splendid quests of golden fleeces.

Even in the matter of girls my peculiar phantasy asserted itself. Naturally, it was in our town voted bad form for boys of twelve and fourteen to show any evident weakness for girls. We tolerated them loftily, and now and then they played in our games, when I joined in quite as naturally as the rest. It was when strangers came, or summer boarders, or when the oldest girls grew up that my sharp senses noted little hesitancies in public and searchings for possible public opinion. Then I flamed! I lifted my chin and strode off to the mountains, where I viewed the world at my feet and strained my eyes across the shadow of the hills.

I was graduated from high school at sixteen, and I talked of "Wendell Phillips." This was my first sweet taste of the world's applause. There were flowers and upturned faces, music and marching, and there was my mother's smile. She was lame, then, and a bit drawn, but very happy. It was her great day and that very year she lay down with a sigh of content and has not yet awakened. I felt a certain gladness to see her, at last, at peace, for she had worried all her life. Of my own loss I had then little realization. That came only with the after-years. Now it was the choking gladness and solemn feel of wings! At last, I was going beyond the hills and into the world that beckoned steadily.

There came a little pause,—a singular pause. I was given to understand that I was almost too young for the world. Harvard was the goal of my dreams, but my white friends hesitated and my colored friends were silent. Harvard was a mighty conjure-word in that hill town, and even the mill owners' sons had aimed lower. Finally it was tactfully explained that the place for me was in the South among my people. A scholarship had been already arranged at Fisk, and my summer earnings would pay the fare. My relatives grumbled, but after a twinge I felt a strange delight! I forgot, or did not thoroughly realize, the curious irony by which I was not looked upon as a real citizen of my birth-town, with a future and a career, and instead was being sent to a far land among strangers who were regarded as (and in truth were) "mine own people."

Ah! the wonder of that journey, with its faint spice of adventure, as I entered the land of slaves; the never-to-be-forgotten marvel of that first supper at Fisk with the world "colored" and opposite two of the most beautiful beings God ever revealed to the eyes of seventeen. I promptly lost my appetite, but I was deliriously happy!

As I peer back through the shadow of my years, seeing not too clearly, but through the thickening veil of wish and after-thought, I seem to view my life divided into four distinct parts: the Age of Miracles, the Days of Disillusion, the Discipline of Work and Play, and the Second Miracle Age.

The Age of Miracles began with Fisk and ended with Germany. I was bursting with the joy of living. I seemed to ride in conquering might. I was captain of my soul and master of fate! I *willed* to do! It was done. I *wished!* The wish came true.

Now and then out of the void flashed the great sword of hate to remind me of the battle. I remember once, in Nashville, brushing by accident against a white woman on the street. Politely and eagerly I raised my hat to apologize. That was thirty-five years ago. From that day to this I have never knowingly raised my hat to a Southern white woman.

I suspect that beneath all of my seeming triumphs there were many failures and disappointments, but the realities loomed so large that they swept away even the memory of other dreams and wishes. Consider, for a moment, how miraculous it all was to a boy of seventeen, just escaped from a narrow valley: I willed and lo! my people came dancing about me,—riotous in color, gay in laughter, full of sympathy, need, and pleading; darkly delicious girls— "colored" girls—sat beside me and actually talked to me while I gazed in tongue-tied silence or babbled in boastful dreams. Boys with my own experiences and out of my own world, who knew and understood, wrought out with me great remedies. I studied eagerly under teachers who bent in subtle sympathy, feeling themselves some shadow of the Veil and lifting it gently that we darker souls might peer through to other worlds.

I willed and lo! I was walking beneath the elms of Harvard,—the name of allurement, the college of my youngest, wildest visions! I needed money; scholarships and prizes fell into my lap,—not all I wanted or strove for, but all I needed to keep in school. Commencement came and standing before governor, president, and grave, gowned men, I told them certain astonishing truths, waving my arms and breathing fast! They applauded with what now seems to me uncalled-for fervor, but then! I walked home on pink clouds of glory! I asked for a fellowship and got it. I announced my plan of studying in Germany, but Harvard had no more fellowships for me. A friend, however, told me of the Slater Fund and how the Board was looking for colored men worth educating. No thought of modest hesitation occurred to me. I rushed at the chance.

The trustees of the Slater Fund excused themselves politely. They acknowledged that they had in the past looked for colored boys of ability to educate, but, being unsuccessful, they had stopped searching. I went at them hammer and tongs! I plied them with testimonials and mid-year and final marks. I intimated plainly, impudently, that they were "stalling"! In vain did the chairman, Ex-President Hayes, explain and excuse. I took no excuses and brushed explanations aside. I wonder now that he did not brush me aside, too, as a conceited meddler, but instead he smiled and surrendered.

I crossed the ocean in a trance. Always I seemed to be saying, "It is not real; I must be dreaming!" I can live it again—the little, Dutch ship—the blue waters—the smell of new-mown hay—Holland and the Rhine. I saw the Wartburg and Berlin; I made the Harzreise and climbed the Brocken; I saw the Hansa towns and the cities and dorfs of South Germany; I saw the Alps at Berne, the Cathedral at Milan, Florence, Rome, Venice, Vienna, and Pesth; I looked on the boundaries of Russia; and I sat in Paris and London.

On mountain and valley, in home and school, I met men and women as I had never met them before. Slowly they became, not white folks, but folks. The unity beneath all life clutched me. I was not less fanatically a Negro, but "Negro" meant a greater, broader sense of humanity and world-fellowship. I felt myself standing, not against the world, but simply against American narrowness and color prejudice, with the greater, finer world at my back urging me on.

I builded great castles in Spain and lived therein. I dreamed and loved and wandered and sang; then, after two long years, I dropped suddenly back into "nigger"-hating America!

My Days of Disillusion were not disappointing enough to discourage me. I was still upheld by that fund of infinite faith, although dimly about me I saw the shadow of disaster. I began to realize how much of what I had called Will and Ability was sheer Luck! *Suppose* my good mother had preferred a steady income from my child labor rather than bank on the precarious dividend of my higher training? *Suppose* that pompous old village judge, whose dignity we often ruffled and whose apples we stole, had had his way and sent me while a child to a "reform" school to learn a "trade"? *Suppose* Principal Hosmer had been born with no faith in "darkies," and instead of giving me

Greek and Latin had taught me carpentry and the making of tin pans? *Suppose* I had missed a Harvard scholarship? *Suppose* the Slater Board had then, as now, distinct ideas as to where the education of Negroes should stop? Suppose *and* suppose! As I sat down calmly on flat earth and looked at my life a certain great fear seized me. Was I the masterful captain or the pawn of laughing sprites? Who was I to fight a world of color prejudice? I raise my hat to myself when I remember that, even with these thoughts, I did not hesitate or waver; but just went doggedly to work, and therein lay whatever salvation I have achieved.

First came the task of earning a living. I was not nice or hard to please. I just got down on my knees and begged for work, anything and anywhere. I wrote to Hampton, Tuskegee, and a dozen other places. They politely declined, with many regrets. The trustees of a backwoods Tennessee town considered me, but were eventually afraid. Then, suddenly, Wilberforce offered to let me teach Latin and Greek at $750 a year. I was overjoyed!

I did not know anything about Latin and Greek, but I did know of Wilberforce. The breath of that great name had swept the water and dropped into southern Ohio, where Southerners had taken their cure at Tawawa Springs and where white Methodists had planted a school; then came the little bishop, Daniel Payne, who made it a school of the African Methodists. This was the school that called me, and when re-considered offers from Tuskegee and Jefferson City followed, I refused; I was so thankful for that first offer.

I went to Wilberforce with high ideals. I wanted to help to build a great university. I was willing to work night as well as day. I taught Latin, Greek, English, and German. I helped in the discipline, took part in the social life, begged to be allowed to lecture on sociology, and began to write books. But I found myself against a stone wall. Nothing stirred before my impatient pounding! Or if it stirred, it soon slept again.

Of course, I was too impatient! The snarl of years was not to be undone in days. I set at solving the problem before I knew it. Wilberforce was a colored church-school. In it were mingled the problems of poorly-prepared pupils, an inadequately-equipped plant, the natural politics of bishoprics, and the provincial reactions of a country town loaded with traditions. It was my first introduction to a Negro world, and I was at once marvelously inspired and deeply depressed. I was inspired with the children,—had I not rubbed against the children of the world and did I not find here the same eagerness, the same joy of life, the same brains as in New England, France, and Germany? But, on the other hand, the ropes and myths and knots and hindrances; the thundering waves of the white world beyond beating us back; the scalding breakers of this inner world,—its currents and back eddies—its meanness and smallness—its sorrow and tragedy—its screaming farce!

In all this I was as one bound hand and foot. Struggle, work, fight as I

500

would, I seemed to get nowhere and accomplish nothing. I had all the wild intolerance of youth, and no experience in human tangles. For the first time in my life I realized that there were limits to my will to do. The Day of Miracles was past, and a long, gray road of dogged work lay ahead.

I had, naturally, my triumphs here and there. I defied the bishops in the matter of public extemporaneous prayer and they yielded. I bearded the poor, hunted president in his den, and yet was re-elected to my position. I was slowly winning a way, but quickly losing faith in the value of the way won. Was this the place to begin my life work? Was this the work which I was best fitted to do? What business had I, anyhow, to teach Greek when I had studied men? I grew sure that I had made a mistake. So I determined to leave Wilberforce and try elsewhere. Thus, the third period of my life began.

First, in 1896, I married—a slip of a girl, beautifully dark-eyed and thorough and good as a German housewife. Then I accepted a job to make a study of Negroes in Philadelphia for the University of Pennsylvania,—one year at six hundred dollars. How did I dare these two things? I do not know. Yet they spelled salvation. To remain at Wilberforce without doing my ideals meant spiritual death. Both my wife and I were homeless. I dared a home and a temporary job. But it was a different daring from the days of my first youth. I was ready to admit that the best of men might fail. I meant still to be captain of my soul, but I realized that even captains are not omnipotent in uncharted and angry seas.

I essayed a thorough piece of work in Philadelphia. I labored morning, noon, and night. Nobody ever reads that fat volume on "The Philadelphia Negro," but they treat it with respect, and that consoles me. The colored people of Philadelphia received me with no open arms. They had a natural dislike to being studied like a strange species. I met again and in different guise those curious cross-currents and inner social whirlings of my own people. They set me to groping. I concluded that I did not know so much as I might about my own people, and when President Bumstead invited me to Atlanta University the next year to teach sociology and study the American Negro, I accepted gladly, at a salary of twelve hundred dollars.

My real life work was done at Atlanta for thirteen years, from my twenty-ninth to my forty-second birthday. They were years of great spiritual upturning, of the making and unmaking of ideals, of hard work and hard play. Here I found myself. I lost most of my mannerisms. I grew more broadly human, made my closest and most holy friendships, and studied human beings. I became widely-acquainted with the real condition of my people. I realized the terrific odds which faced them. At Wilberforce I was their captious critic. In Philadelphia I was their cold and scientific investigator, with microscope and probe. It took but a few years of Atlanta to bring me to hot and indignant defense. I saw the race-hatred of the whites as I had never dreamed of it before,—naked and unashamed! The faint discrimination of my hopes and intangible dislikes paled into nothing before this great, red monster of cruel oppression. I held back with more difficulty each day my mounting indignation against injustice and misrepresentation.

With all this came the strengthening and hardening of my own character. The billows of birth, love, and death swept over me. I saw life through all its paradox and contradiction of streaming eyes and mad merriment. I emerged into full manhood, with the ruins of some ideals about me, but with others planted above the stars; scarred and a bit grim, but hugging to my soul the divine gift of laughter and withal determined, even unto stubbornness, to fight the good fight.

At last, forbear and waver as I would, I faced the great Decision. My life's last and greatest door stood ajar. What with all my dreaming, studying, and teaching was I going to *do* in this fierce fight? Despite all my youthful conceit and bumptiousness, I found developed beneath it all a reticence and new fear of forwardness, which sprang from searching criticisms of motive and high ideals of efficiency; but contrary to my dream of racial solidarity and notwithstanding my deep desire to serve and follow and think, rather than to lead and inspire and decide, I found myself suddenly the leader of a great wing of people fighting against another and greater wing.

Nor could any effort of mine keep this fight from sinking to the personal plane. Heaven knows I tried. That first meeting of a knot of enthusiasts, at Niagara Falls, had all the earnestness of self-devotion. At the second meeting, at Harper's Ferry, it arose to the solemnity of a holy crusade and yet without and to the cold, hard stare of the world it seemed merely the envy of fools against a great man, Booker Washington.

Of the movement I was willy-nilly leader. I hated the rôle. For the first time I faced criticism and *cared*. Every ideal and habit of my life was cruelly misjudged. I who had always overstriven to give credit for good work, who had never consciously stooped to envy was accused by honest colored people of every sort of small and petty jealousy, while white people said I was ashamed of my race and wanted to be white! And this of me, whose one life fanaticism had been belief in my Negro blood!

Away back in the little years of my boyhood I had sold the Springfield *Republican* and written for Mr. Fortune's *Globe*. I dreamed of being an editor myself some day. I am an editor. In the great, slashing days of college life I dreamed of a strong organization to fight the battles of the Negro race. The National Association for the Advancement of Colored People is such a body, and it grows daily. In the dark days at Wilberforce I planned a time when I could speak freely to my people and of them, interpreting between two worlds. I am speaking now. In the study at Atlanta I grew to fear lest my radical beliefs should so hurt the college that either my silence or the institution's ruin would result. Powers and principalities have not yet curbed my tongue and Atlanta still lives.

It all came—this new Age of Miracles—because a few persons in 1909 determined to celebrate Lincoln's Birthday properly by calling for the final emancipation of the American Negro. I came at their call. My salary even for a year was not assured, but it was the "Voice without reply." The result has been the National Association for the Advancement of Colored People and *The Crisis* and this book, which I am finishing on my Fiftieth Birthday.

Last year I looked death in the face and found its lineaments not unkind. But it was not my time. Yet in nature some time soon and in the fullness of days I shall die, quietly, I trust, with my face turned South and eastward; and, dreaming or dreamless, I shall, I am sure, enjoy death as I have enjoyed life.

37

Roderick Seidenberg (1890?–1973)
I Refuse to Serve

"I Refuse to Serve" (1932) is a personal testimony against military conscription by a World War I conscientious objector. It was published in H. L. Mencken's and George Jean Nathan's *American Mercury* at just the moment in the 1930s when deepening economic depression was creating widespread belief that the war had not "made the world safe for democracy" but mainly enriched arms makers. Pacifists, therefore, who had once been labeled traitors and been imprisoned and tortured, were now considered prophets. Meanwhile, Gandhi's massive demonstrations in India, such as the "Salt Satyagraha" of 1930, gave hopes that what William James had called "a moral equivalent of war" might indeed be found.

In 1917, the draft law required all men to register and be inducted into the army, after which they were to be given noncombatant service in the medical or supply corps, if their objections to war were considered sincere and based upon membership in recognized pacifist churches. But some, such as Roderick Seidenberg, who had been a friend of Randolph Bourne's at Columbia University, were political and philosophic objectors and also would not accept any form of noncombatant or alternative service. They, along with some religious objectors, became so-called "absolutists" and were all sent eventually to Fort Leavenworth. There, as Seidenberg describes, they pitted their wills against the army's, going on hunger strikes and refusing to work, organizing other prisoners, and secretly sending out reports on prison conditions. By January, 1919, outside journalists were also criticizing the army for continuing to enforce harsh wartime sentences. The result was that when the conscientious objectors turned a prison riot into a nonviolent work stoppage, the army negotiated. This was a major victory for the COs and their methods, and it anticipated in some ways the nonviolent tactics of both the 1930s labor movement and the 1960s civil rights movement.

A sense of pride and a sense of comradeship thus qualify and even overpower Seidenberg's bitterness. He and his fellow COs amply proved that they were not cowards and slackers. As autobiographer, he also wants to advertise the COs' discipline, solidarity, and success in attracting support from the other prisoners. Methods that persuaded both them and the army might persuade readers, too. At the same time he does not want to make pacifists into saints.

After the war, Seidenberg became an architect, and in the 1930s he wrote the segments on architecture for the State Guides series that had been underwritten by Roosevelt's Work Projects Administration (W.P.A.). He also wrote books on social theory, *Posthistoric Man, an Inquiry* (1950) and *Anatomy of the Future* (1961).

The text of "I Refuse to Serve" is taken from *The American Mercury* 25 (January 1932): 91–99. For a more extensive history of conscientious objectors in World War I, see Norman Thomas, *The Conscientious Objector in America* (New York: B. Huebsch, 1923), which was republished as *Is Conscience a Crime?* (New York: Vanguard, 1927). On CO autobiography, see Robert F. Sayre, "Rhetorical Defenses: the Autobiographies of World War I Conscientious Objectors," *Auto/ Biography Studies* 7 (Spring 1992): 62–81. There is no biography of Roderick Seidenberg. Some additional information can be found in his obituary in the *New York Times*, August 28, 1973, p. 38.

I

The Disciplinary Barracks of the Army are at Fort Leavenworth—not more than a stone's throw from the monument which marks the exact geographic center of the United States. Nothing, in those days of war, could have seemed to me more appropriate than a military prison at the very heart of America. I was a war resister, serving a life sentence at hard labor.

At Leavenworth, I soon learned, one helped the war even while resisting it. The Barracks constituted a kind of power station sending forth currents of fear, a prison with unseen dynamos that created tension and dread throughout the Army. If men had failed to respond willingly, they now labored in silence to maintain these ceaseless currents. The logic of the situation was at once bitter and peremptory. Like the militarists whose arguments demand always more force, the pacifist needed to answer with more resistance. I refused to work. Thus I quickly learned that prison has its prison; on the second day of my term I found myself in solitary confinement. The heretic was at last alone. Not alone, however, in what he had done. Thirty-five of us had refused to do anything whatsoever. We were absolutists.

To steal, rape or murder, to slap an officer's face and call him a son of a bitch—these are the standard peace-time entrance requirements to the Disciplinary Barracks. But in time of war too firm a belief in the words of Christ, too ardent a faith in the brotherhood of man, is even more acceptable. But prisons are democratic institutions, and no matter how one entered, one's number was stencilled on one's trousers and the back of one's shirt in white to mark a new beginning. One might rise and receive a white star as a trusty, but it was just as likely that one would sink, first into the red-numbered lock-step gang, and finally into solitary, where the digits in yellow marked the lowest depths of the vast military hierarchy. We sank to the yellow bottom, for our offense was the gravest one can commit—in prison. Even the murder gang, who had trampled to death an unfortunate "rat", enjoyed the comparative freedom of wandering about in a basement cell-block when they were not exercising in the sunlight of the yard. Our case was different; we had offended military pride. We must be broken.

The first to arrive at Leavenworth who refused to work were six stalwart Molokans, true Christians if ever there were any. They went cheerfully into the "hole," each one in a pitch-dark cell on bread and water, manacled standing to the bars of their cells for nine hours every day—to sleep, exhausted on the bare cement floor. Others followed. Evan Thomas, who had at first accepted work, hearing their fate, joined them in heroic protest. That is like him—a fiery spirit beneath his unflinching calm.

Leavenworth was taken by surprise. There were not enough dark cells. The officers had never before encountered a like demonstration. Each morning the executive officer inquired of our health and smilingly offered us the rock pile. Each morning we declined. Two weeks passed, and the executive officer no longer smiled. We had broken not only the rules of the institution, but its traditions as well. No one had ever stood this treatment for more than a few days. The commandant, Colonel Sedgewig Rice, paid us a visit. What were these men like? Who were they? What did they want?

One day, Prisoner 15122 was unshackled and led to the executive office. In the morning's mail the prison censor had found a bronze medal with appropriate testimonials from the Carnegie Hero Commission, inscribed to Howard Moore for bravery in risking his life to rescue a drowning girl. A hero medal for a yellow slacker! Would he care to tell the story to the assembled officers? Howard Moore had a disarming smile. He excused himself; there was nothing to tell. At the moment it was more important to be shackled.

Two weeks and a new trial! Reeling like drunkards, we returned from the executive office to our solitary cells. This time we were to have food, then another trial and two more weeks without food. But manacled we must be, nine hours every day. It was the end of December, 1919; the war had been over since the eleventh of November. The Molokans, refusing, because of their strange religious scruples, everything but a little milk, even when permitted food on the alternate fortnights, had stood the treatment for fifty-five days without a sign of weakening.

I was in the middle of my third term when word came from the Secretary of War that henceforth prisoners of the Army were no longer to be manacled. The Secretary, his feet planted on his desk, had listened coldly to the venerable Mrs. Fanny Villard, standing before him pleading. He would do nothing. Yet later he reversed his decision. We were placed in a stockade outside the prison walls—all but the two Hofer brothers, who had died.

II

Always there was a touch of comedy, a moment of ironic absurdity in a world that seemed altogether mad and phantasmal. For long the prison had been overcrowded. In the corridor of one solitary cell-block the authorities had placed the murder gang; in another, where I had been locked up, they housed the insane—a sad rabble of idiots, maniacs, degenerates and dissemblers—misfits even in jail. One of them hobbled about on a deformed foot, his face contorted by morbid vengeance. A cripple, he had thought to escape the draft. But he had been inducted—what a joke! Insubordination and impatience had brought him to Leavenworth. Now the officers delighted in assuring him, day after day, that he was to be discharged.

Another raged up and down in front of our cells like a hyena. He had contrived to escape in a packing box. The authorities got wind of it; they rode him around the grounds and deposited him at the railroad station. A few hours later they gathered him in, as softly as they had taken him out. His packing case was opened—in the executive office! Each man, in one sense or another, represented a triumph for the authorities.

These desperate wretches spent their days surging past our cells, up and down the long corridor, like furies, incoherent save in their obscenity. Their mumblings were an idiotic chorus to our thoughts. Was not the whole world mad? A young colored fellow rose to a kind of dubious leadership over this horde. He was powerful and nimble, and blessed with a golden tongue. In a moment of aberration—or was it delight—he had turned a machinegun on his company. If his mind was diseased, it was touched by genius. He affected a grand air of sobriety and a convenient deafness. Orders he treated with mock deliberation. Would he work, he was asked. What were the wages? He had a mother to support and brothers and sisters. Mothers were his especial concern and the chaplain his pet target.

"These here men, Chaplain," he once explained, pointing to some religious objectors, "they won't fight because Christ said not to fight."

"I came not to bring peace, but a sword," the chaplain quoted. The words had to be repeated. "A sword? What wars did He fight in, Chaplain?"

His most charming moments came at night, when the great prison was dark and silent. For a time the mob of demented prisoners would run about, some with sheets over their heads to frighten the newcomers, others still shouting the same foul obscenities they had roared all day. The hub-bub would rise to a mad bedlam of shrieks, jeers, cat-calls, a ghoulish dragging about of struggling bodies in the dark. Shouts and curses from the guards.

At last the cell-block would quiet. A half hour passed. In the stillness, suddenly, the melodious voice of the Negro mocked the ringing of a telephone bell. Ah, it was a friend, a relative, a sweetheart—Grace, Madge, Rosabelle. What delicious phantasies he unwound, what a gallery of people he portrayed!

One heard their voices, one knew what they said. He spoke to his rabbit, his dog. It was magnificent, touching, hilarious. "Good-bye, honey!" The words were long-drawn out and mournful. Then his voice rose in prayer:

O Lord, if it please Thee in Thy great mercy, visit the poor sinners in Leavenworth, and deliver us of our burdens. O Lord, let us see the big city, all electric lit up. And have the cooks give us jam and chocolate cake. For the chaplain says Thou art merciful, O Lord, and inscrutable and all-powerful. And O Lord, come down, come down to-night, in Thy mighty aeroplane and straighten out the chaplain's bow legs and set him on the straight and narrow path to virtue. Amen. . . . O Lord!

III

In the stockade beyond the prison wall we played, we read books, we received and wrote letters once more, and we ate, with relish, the indescribable food of Leavenworth. Half our number were religious objectors: Hutterites, Dunkards, Seventh Day Adventists, an orthodox Jew, and the six Molokans. The rest of us were so-called political objectors: Socialists, humanitarians, individualists. We talked. It was good to talk again. Acquaintance grew into friendship; we were held together by a common experience, whatever our individual points of view.

But the diversion of the day was the visit of Major Adler—chief psychiatrist of the Disciplinary Barracks, or should I say, the Vocational Training School, as he preferred to call it? The first time I saw him walking down our corridor beside the tall, elegantly-booted Colonel Rice, a short, frail, unmilitary man, his myopic, intelligent eyes peering from behind thick glasses, I asked myself how did he get into the Army—and a major at that! A moment later he was at my cell, shaking my shackled hand. Major Adler was a person behind his science, his psychiatry, and his labored militarism.

We were now subjected to the delicate mental probings of this kindly Harvard professor. He was not a man who believed in brute force—except perhaps on a national scale. Certainly he was above using force—after it had failed. If we could not be overwhelmed, perhaps we could be undermined. Psychiatry was brought into action as a form of depth-bombery. With infinite tact and a judicious show of esteem, we were invited to realize that our position as political objectors was altogether untenable. We were not a bad lot, but we were sadly misguided. It appeared, indeed, that we were intelligent. This was not to be inferred from our actions; it had simply been established by the Army intelligence tests. But if we were intelligent, we were all the more guilty of a deplorable lack of judgment.

This lack of judgment was due, not to our attitude toward war, but to our method of expressing it. We had, obviously, not stopped the war. We were not merely in the minority; we were ludicrously alone. It appeared that the acknowledged leader of the American intelligentsia, Professor John Dewey, had analyzed our attitude, and found us wanting. We were the victims of moral futility, of an ego-centric lack of judgment that was close to being culpable. Our conscience was largely self-conceit. If Professor Dewey's participation in the war enterprise had no other effect, it at least allayed the last doubts of the more liberal-minded officials about condemning us. His utterances were retailed with unction, and we were reminded of the high source whence they came.

Having staked all upon a war to end war, the liberal people were not above trick questions, false appeals and spurious arguments. Under the impact of such tactics the simplicity of our position gave way; we were forced to make elaborate efforts to define our principles, and to draw, with ever minuter distinctions, the nature of our stand. Our sincerity, it is true, was no longer in question. That had been officially conceded months ago, though no one knew, upon examining the question, precisely what sincerity might mean. Our lapses from rectitude, it was apparent, were of a subtler order; they arose from defections that only psychiatry could reveal.

We had refused to participate in organized slaughter; we were considered insensitive and unfeeling toward the higher causes of humanity. We had thought to stand aloof from the madness of war; we were anti-social and doctrinaire. We had taken what appeared to us the one direct and positive and unarguable position for peace; we were negative obstructionists. We had refrained from any propaganda, we believed in freedom of conscience; we were ego-centric heretics. We thought ourselves tolerably sane; we were psychopathic.

"All these things might be passed over," Major Adler announced with pontifical finality, "if only you people had the faith of your convictions." He looked about the barracks. "But I don't see any Christs or Savonarolas. You fellows are rationalizing; other people are acting. You're negative." Thus it appeared that the exponent of intelligence believed in nothing so much as action. He had acted; others had acted. If the human race had come to the brink of a precipice, what right had we to stop? He had hit the nail too hard. . . . "Did you men get your mail? How is the food? I'll see the executive officer about it." He was gone.

The major was to submit a report to Washington. Contrary to all regulations, impulsively, he read the report to us. It was not flattering. Yet, somehow, we came to the surface despite his psychiatric dissections. He recommended that we be discharged. . . . We wished him well. But it was without hope that we waited for the answer from Washington; we had taken the measure of the military. Two weeks later he returned, a strangely aloof man. He had brought back his own discharge!

IV

Life in a barracks is dreary at best. Twenty-four hours of the same company would be trying if that company were of one's own choosing. But here we were, thrown together through no will of our own, a strange lot—half of us praying, the other half arguing, all of us suffering from the sheer inanity of our position.

I tried to write. With meagre spirit I made some sketches. A drawing, poorly done, picturing a prisoner in solitary, reached New York, via underground channels, where it was printed as a marker. A copy of it found its way back to Leavenworth. The censor pasted it over his desk, little knowing that it had made a long trip home. Sending a kite over the wall was one of the prison entertainments. A kite is an underground letter. Smuggled from prisoner to prisoner, our mail would at last be added to that of the executive office. From here it went forth uncensored and unnoticed. At other times our letters were intrusted to a friendly guard or a sympathetic sergeant. Even in solitary we managed to remain in contact with the outside world. But that was not so simple.

The scheme by which it was accomplished was the work of Clark Getts, an objector who had access to every part of the prison. He was supposed to gather statistics; actually he contrived to do most everything else. Thus he would happen to be in the basement at the moment when we were having our fortnightly scrub. The basement was a huge place, dimly lighted. The shower-baths were at one end. Our clothes off, we gathered in a crowd under the taps like a herd of cattle. Getts, standing in the shadow of a column, would snatch off his clothes and join us. Naked, our numbers gone, it was impossible to tell one man from another. We let the water run like a deluge while we splashed. And Getts circled about, getting the address of a relative, bringing us the latest rumors, the news of the prison, the outlook at Washington, and the happenings at Versailles. It was all done in a cloud of steam and Getts was gone before we knew it. He was never detected, but he finally succeeded in reaching solitary himself for attempting to kite a letter.

We had been at the stockade a month now. Some more objectors stopped working and after a few days in solitary they were sent to our barracks. The effect of seeing us at play beyond the prison walls was not lost upon those who remained to toil and labor under harsh discipline. Friendly as the general prisoners were to the objectors, this could not fail to arouse a sense of injustice, and to add to the unrest of the prison. That unrest flared into a strike.

V

On Christmas Eve there had been a riot in the dining-hall. Fifteen hundred men went on a rampage. We were still in solitary, and I ventured to predict that we would be held responsible. We were. On Christmas Day we were lined up in front of our cells and lectured. It was our example that had caused the unrest among the men.

Actually the whole prison smoldered with a sense of injustice. The food was beyond description, a steamed and slimy flow of garbage. An objector, Ben Salmon, working in the commissary department, had called attention to the fact that hundreds of dollars were going astray.

He was immediately thrown into solitary. The men were bullied when they were not being spied upon by "rats," mostly depraved room-orderlies. But worst of all they smarted under the terrific sentences which were the common fate. Fifteen, twenty, forty years—it was all one to the poor wretches who were to spend the rest of their lives in that hell. Every day the huge lock-step gang wound its way like a great serpent to the rock quarries, full of resentment at the brutalities of the guards and the merciless work they were forced to do. One or two guards were killed. A race riot broke out. Rival gangs, for even prison has its gang life, its intrigues and its politics, were stealthily revenging themselves upon one another. The place was overcrowded and demoralized.

By the end of January things had come to such a pass that one day the first gang suddenly refused to work. That night the quartermaster's warehouse burned to the ground. The following morning, after having been called to work, the men were sent back to their cells. At noon they were all assembled once more in the prison yard, and called to their gangs. "First gang, second gang, third gang. . . ." No one moved. It must have been a terrifying moment.

Outside the walls the 49th Infantry awaited orders. Colonel Rice expostulated; again he asked the men to work. A few went; the rest stood with arms folded, which is the prescribed posture before prison officials. They were led back to their cells.

Now the men acted with quiet deliberation. Was it the work of the conscientious objectors, who were scattered throughout the prison on the work gangs and in the offices, and housed in all the seven wings? At the beginning of the strike they had organized themselves. Under the leadership of H. Austin Simons, the son of a judge, Carl Haesler, a Rhodes scholar from Oxford and instructor in philosophy at the University of Wisconsin, and others, the entire prison had been mobilized to stand firm with arms folded. There must be no violence! From the rail of the second tier, Simons made an impassioned speech to the men of his cell-block. His words carried the day. In each wing a committee drew up resolutions.

Colonel Rice was equally brave. He acknowledged that the prisoners had grievances, and wisely he consented to arbitrate. It was a momentous decision and a triumph for the prisoners. Colonel Rice listened to their demands: that men in solitary for complicity in the disturbance be immediately restored to regular status, that a telegram be sent to the Secretary of War petitioning for amnesty, that the commandant recognize a permanent grievance committee. Colonel Rice proposed to go to Washington himself to present the resolutions. The men were accorded a grant of time in order that the prison might vote upon the proposal. Unanimously they voted to resume work in the morning.

A general reduction of sentences followed the colonel's return; men were released, and a grievance committee became an established institution. But not for long. . . . Six months later the conscientious objectors who still remained were suddenly transferred to Fort Douglas in Utah, and six days later a second strike broke out.

It was crushed with bullets, and Leavenworth returned once more to the peaceful days of iron discipline.

VI

One morning, not long after the first strike, we were ordered to pack our belongings. Rumors flew about. Where were we going? Prisoners, like soldiers, are forever unreeling the future, galloping to some possible end with the speed of a cinema. We were taken to the guardhouse. No one knew why.

A new executive officer of the Disciplinary Barracks paid us a visit. He was exceptionally short—a little fellow with the rank of major. Gruffly he ordered the guardhouse sergeant to open our cell. He marched in, accompanied by two captains and two lieutenants. It was very impressive. He asked us to gather about him. Silence. Raising his head slightly, he announced that he was not afraid of any of us. There was an involuntary titter, followed by an embarrassing silence. "I'm not afraid of any of you or all of you!" he repeated sharply. "Well, Major," Howard Moore spoke up in that charming soft manner of his, "we're not afraid of you either." The major was thrown completely off his stride; the ice was broken. He smiled. "You fellows aren't so hardboiled as I thought. We'll get along all right. There're some damn regulations against it, or I'd have you shot, of course. Meantime, what are you going to do with yourselves? I could have some knitting sent down." Everybody laughed. We were friends.

The younger officers were more apt to be hostile. Few lieutenants could resist the temptation to distinguish themselves at our expense. One night we were treated to a drenching with a high pressure fire-hose. We had been talking after the lights were out. For this we spent the night barely above water, with our clothes, our shoes and all our belongings floating about us. An investigation followed. The lieutenant was duly exonerated, and the Third Assistant Secretary of War himself, the Hon. Frederick D. Keppel, explained that the officer's somewhat unusual measures had been justified, since he was faced with a mutiny. But we received no further punishment.

These little episodes served to break up the long monotony of our days and to remind us, if ever we should forget it, that we were in the hands of the military. But was not the whole world in the hands of the military? We, at least, had a measure of consolation in feeling that we had made a choice agreeable to ourselves, whatever the consequences. Perhaps, indeed, this was the secret of our strength—in a certain sense, we were aloof to what might happen to us. We were steeled to something beyond ourselves. We were obdurate with an ease that surprised us as much as it did the military, and if our resistance was calm, aloof, even indifferent, it was not without an explosive effect upon those whose business it was to break it down. "If those damn bastards only had a change of heart, I wouldn't mind having them in my outfit!" said a major. We had learned to become fighters, and to fight hard.

VII

New men were constantly added to our group, men who had stopped working. Our cells were badly overcrowded and once more we were shifted back to the Disciplinary Barracks. The first tier of cells in the sixth wing was to be our home, we were informed, until released. When would that be—in ten, in twenty years? Many of us still had life sentences. We did not take them seriously.

In time they were all reduced, now one, then another. They were reduced to three years, to five years or perhaps to one year. I received a sentence of a year and a half. The days moved slowly, to be checked off, one at a time, on a little calendar. The days turned into weeks and the weeks into months. Meanwhile the gates were open to us. Like the Christians in Shaw's "Androcles and the Lion," we had only to throw a pinch of incense on the altar of militarism to gain our freedom. Colonel Rice was surprised to find us adamant against accepting our "good time." Actually we had long ago lost this allowance, which he now offered to us under military parole. We might, moreover, have received immediate release, if only we had consented to do some work. The major in charge of construction asked me if I would assist in designing an officer's club-house. I declined—with regrets.

We now numbered close to a hundred men. We enjoyed such freedom as the cell-block permitted, but it was a dreary freedom at best. We were never permitted outside, even for exercise, and the months passed without our ever seeing the sunshine except through the barred windows. Some grew beards, others shaved their heads. What was there to do? Occasionally a man was discharged. We would celebrate, as best we could, his "butt"—his last day before release. Then the old routine once more.

Always we talked of the future—what we hoped to see, to experience, to feel; what we would eat, where we would go, what we would do. Caught by the enthusiasm of Jacob Wortsman, we planned an elaborate trip in a motor boat around the Panama Canal up along the wild, wooded shore of Canada to Alaska. We managed to get some chalk, and on the cement floor of the corridor we drew in full size the plans of our boat, its cabin, its engine, its decks, fore and aft, the scullery, the berths, in every detail. We were pleasantly mad.

I began to lose something of my New York provincialism and to learn of this America. Here were men from all quarters and from all walks of life: religious farmers from the Middle West who alone seemed capable of community living; I.W.W.'s from the Far West; Socialists from the East Side of New York; men from Chicago, from the South; men who had been sailors, carpenters, college students, tailors. One was a statistician, one a prize-fighter from Philadelphia, one a music teacher. . . . I missed a few of the older friends who were no longer with us—Evan Thomas, with whom I could talk of philosophy and a *Weltanschauung;* Maurice Hess, a Dunkard, now a college professor, a man of exceptional erudition and amazing courage behind the mildest exterior.

But most of all, in a way, I missed my friend Sam Solnitski. His racy, ironic humor helped many an hour along. In the guardhouse at Fort Riley, while we awaited trial, he would pace up and down with me, telling of his life in Poland, of his escape to America to avoid military service, of his days in this country as a skilled worker on the uppers of women's shoes—the very finest—for prostitutes! Best of all, however, he had read, it seemed to me, all of literature—in Yiddish. Now he told the grand stories of Maupassant, of Balzac, of Anatole France, in a mixture, half-English, half-Yiddish, which made these tales of elegant ladies and Parisian life more real than ever. Solnitski had distinguished himself at his court-martial. In his own way he had attempted to explain to the twelve precise majors of the court the reasons for his opposition to military service—but in vain. He broke off in despair, "Ow, shucks, what's the use!" The court stenographer immortalized the words.

There were other men no longer with us—Harold Gray, son of the Detroit multimillionaire; Harry Lee, the witty organizer of waiters, who had served "pimps and prostitutes, priests and politicians, but never a captain!"; Dunham, a Philadelphia Quaker, and a number of others I had come to know well. And always there were new men; Morris Kammon, a journalist; Gurgots, a heavy-set, intolerant labor agitator; Wilson, an I.W.W.—each with his own story—endless flashes of life, until one became wearied and confused.

Six months passed in this fashion. At four o'clock one sharp, cold morning we were ordered to pack our belongings; once more we were to be moved. Our prison clothes with their yellow numbers were left behind, we were given our old civilian suits. The prison yard lights glared into the oncoming light of day. The morning promised to be chilly and sombre. At the great outer gate we were shackled in pairs, then, under heavy guard, we left Leavenworth. Two by two, in a long column, we were marched to the railroad station.

Two days later, weary, exhausted, anxious, we arrived at Fort Douglas above Salt Lake City.

38

Charlotte Perkins Gilman (1860–1935)

Love and Marriage and The Breakdown

Rediscovered in the 1970s and '80s by the women's movement, Charlotte Perkins Gilman is now widely known, especially for the autobiographical short story "The Yellow Wallpaper" and the utopian novel *Herland*. But from the mid-1890s to World War I she was famous as a feminist and socialist, a popular lecturer, and the author of *Women and Economics* (1898) and many other books. After World War I, however, her progressive economic and political views went out of fashion, and she turned to writing her autobiography, completing all but the last chapter of it by 1925.

"Love and Marriage" and "The Breakdown" are chapters 7 and 8 of *The Living of Charlotte Perkins Gilman: An Autobiography*. They appear near the end of the first third and constitute the crisis of the book . . . and of the life, as here told.

In the opening of *The Living*, Gilman proudly tells of her New England ancestors (including Lyman Beecher, father of Harriet Beecher Stowe, who was her father's grandfather) and their traditions of self-discipline, intellectual achievement, and service to others. Less enviable is the story of how, when her father learned that her mother could bear no more children, he left her and went to California. Mrs. Perkins, Charlotte, and an older brother Thomas were so poor they had to move nineteen times in eighteen years, mostly living with relatives. Stung by her husband's rejection, Mrs. Perkins determined to harden her daughter against a similar fate and so gave Charlotte no expressions of affection. From these combined inspirations and deprivations, the adolescent daughter became a paragon of self-denial, hard work, physical health, and dedication to service. She also studied at the Rhode Island School for Design, and in May, 1884, married another artist, the handsome Charles Walter Stetson.

The experiences described below were first described in "The Yellow Wallpaper" (1892), and the two accounts make a fascinating comparison between "fiction" and the "factual fiction" that is autobiography. For additional interest, they can be compared to Gilman's "Why I Wrote 'The Yellow Wallpaper'" (1913).

Neither the "fictional" version nor the account of its writing mention her divorce from Stetson, which was the solution chosen in "The Breakdown." For where "The Yellow Wallpaper" is a story of descent into insanity, of a woman driven mad by perverse kindness, "The Breakdown" is the story of her clinging to her sanity and independence and bravely disobeying her doctor (the famous S. Weir Mitchell). The reasons for these different versions—and the different kinds of truth they possess—could be discussed at length. Clearly, Charlotte Stetson in 1891–92 and Charlotte Gilman in the 1920s were very different women, who conceived of themselves in very different ways. Another factor behind the different versions involves attitudes towards divorce, for fictional characters rarely had recourse to it. But a divorce like the Stetsons', with "no quarrel, no blame . . . , never an unkind word between us, unbroken mutual affection," would have been unthinkable in both art and life. This rationally chosen, unconventional, and humane choice in a way epitomizes the progressive temper.

In April, 1894, the divorce was finally granted. (It was difficult to obtain because there were no acceptable grounds for divorce as it was legally defined.) Within a year, Mr. Stetson married Grace Channing, Charlotte's life-long friend, and the three remained close friends, raising their daughter (Grace's stepdaughter) Katherine Beecher Stetson together. In 1900, Charlotte married George Houghton Gilman, her first cousin, and the close relationship continued, with the two couples sometimes living in adjoining houses or apartments.

The brief final chapter of *The Living* tells that in 1932 Mrs. Gilman learned that she had breast cancer. But, not wanting to suffer a long period of mortal pain, uselessness to society, and trouble and expense to friends and family, she prepared to take her own life, which she did, an editorial note explains, on August 17, 1935. Rationalist and progressive, independent crusader against debilitating social conventions, she had thus come as close as any autobiographer can come to including in her story her own death.

This selection is taken from *The Living of Charlotte Perkins Gilman: An Autobiography* (New York: Appleton-Century Co., 1935; reprint, Madison: Univ. of Wisconsin Press, 1990). For additional reading, see Ann J. Lane, *To Herland and Beyond: The Life and Work of Charlotte Perkins Gilman* (New York: Pantheon Books, 1990). For background on neurasthenia, see Tom Lutz, *American Nervousness, 1903: An Anecdotal History* (Ithaca: Cornell Univ. Press, 1991).

Love and Marriage

Looking back on my uncuddled childhood it seems to me a sad mistake of my heroic mother to withhold from me the petting I so craved, the sufficing comfort of maternal caresses. Denied that natural expression, my first memory of loving any one—not to mention the Polite Boy—was the pale and pious child in Hartford; the next was Hattie White, the next, and immeasurably the dearest, was Martha. Martha stayed. We were closely together, increasingly happy together, for four of those long years of girlhood. She was nearer and dearer than any one up to that time. This was love, but not sex.

That experience was in the Frog Prince affair, intense though remote, and never coming to anything at all. But while it lasted there was an unforgettable thrill in the mere sight of the "beloved object." Sex but not love.

With Martha I knew perfect happiness. We used to say to each other that we should never have to reproach ourselves with not realizing this joy while we had it; we did, thoroughly. We were not only extremely fond of each other, but we had fun together, deliciously. One summer while she was away we agreed to write letters describing not only things that happened, but things which didn't—and see if we could discriminate. Those were amazing letters. We wrote nonsense verses together in alternate lines, long ballads of adventure. I have one yet, written on a roll of three-inch ribbon paper.

Our best-loved sport was The One Word Game. This is not only such a delicious amusement, but such an unfailing rest and restorative for a weary and worried mind, that it is worth describing. The whole procedure is for each in turn to contribute one word (only one, save for proper names which may be given in full), to an unfolding story which no one composes, but which is most astonishingly produced by the successive additions. Any word which follows in grammatical sequence will do, no matter how sharply it disagrees with what the previous speaker had in mind.

The game was taught me with no rules whatever, but I have made these three, from experience. First, you must not try to make the story go your way, with, "Now you must say" this, or "Why didn't you say" that; it must be allowed to unfold from the successive words, the whole charm is in the total unexpectedness. Second, it must be about persons. "Once there was a pig," or the like, does not interest. Third, it should be a simple descriptive tale, like a child's fairy story, about persons and what they wore, said and did. As a sample—

"Mr. Aminadab Hugus—entered—his—uncle's—church—for—fish." (A player may put a period to the sentence if he chooses and if his word ends it.) "Unfortunately—Mrs. Hugus—did—Now here the person who said 'did' had in mind 'did not like fish,'" but the next player says "washing." (period)

For hilarious young persons this is simply a means of amusement, but for a lifetime I have found it an unfailing source of relaxation, a complete and refreshing change of mind. It touches combinations impossible to any single thought-process, it is like massage to the brain, it is a "sure fire laugh" that does not cost three dollars a seat. Never could any individual mind conceive of the exquisite absurdities which occur from the interplay. Two intimate minds are best, but any number who can similarly relax will do.

Four years of satisfying happiness with Martha, then she married and moved away. In our perfect concord there was no Freudian taint, but peace of mind, understanding, comfort, deep affection—and I had no one else.

My Mother and her half-sister, with whom I lived, were unutterably re-mote—alien—and out of hearing. So were the other people I knew. "Why she's still your friend, isn't she?" they said. Of course she was—but she was

517

gone. It was the keenest, the hardest, the most lasting pain I had yet known. There was no appreciation or sympathy anywhere.

I strove with it. "I wrote it out"—always a relief. I wrote "Grief is an emotion, it may be used as a spur to action—like anger, or love."

Also this, one of those I used to keep stuck in the edge of my looking-glass to see every day and gather strength from:

For Loneliness and Grief

If I live, (as live I do,) for others—if all my high desires for self-improvement are solely with a view to the elevation of the race—if my mission is to lead a self-sacrificing life and "give to him that asketh" as I go—to teach and guide, to love, protect and care for—then it behooves me to crush all personal sorrow and drop the whole ground of self-interest forever. Neither is this Quixotic or impossible. If I keep every physical law as far as I know, feed the mental life as I learn to more and more, and love every one as far as I can reach—why, it stands to reason that such a one will be cared for and made happy by mere reaction. It is and must be so. I thoroughly believe it. Strength will come, courage will come, yes, and peace and joy will follow, inevitably. Though my heart swell mountain-high it is only so much the higher thing to stand on. Strength! and Courage!

So I pushed on, working every minute of the day except for meals, and three hours in the evening mostly, and carrying this, to me so grievous pain, as best I could, finishing that year's diary thus:

A year of steady work. A quiet year and a hard one. A year of surprising growth. A year internally dedicated to discoveries and improvements. A year in which I knew the sweetness of a perfect friendship and have lost it forever. A year of marked advance in many ways, and with nothing conspicuous to regret. I am stronger, wiser and better than last year, and am fairly satisfied with the year's work. I have learned much of self-control and consideration for others; often think before I speak and can keep still on occasions. My memory begins to show the training it has had, I can get back what I want when I want it, pretty generally. Most of all I have learned what pain is, have learned the need of human sympathy by the unfilled want of it, and have gained the power to *give* it, which is worth while. This year I attained my majority—may I never lose it.

As to men: That unattainable Prince had lasted me for two years or so. Then I was very fond of the cousin who was so devotedly polite to me at first, and so rude afterward, so suddenly and unaccountably rude that I always felt he had been reasoned with by his family and sought to choke off my young affection by this sharp method. As I had not been in the least "in love" with him as with my tall actor, but was generally fond of him, this was something of a blow, though nothing compared to losing Martha later.

Meanwhile there were various youths in Providence who came and went harmlessly, only one being conspicuously attentive—and he was far from bright! Those I met in Cambridge were vastly more attractive, yet left small impression, and in my "home town" I am puzzled by the diary's frequent mention of young men. "Most devoted," "Walks home with me," and so on—and by my utter forgetfulness of any of them.

Then, in January, 1882, I met Charles Walter Stetson, the painter.

He was quite the greatest man, near my own age, that I had ever known. He stood alone, true to his art, in that prosaic mercantile town, handicapped with poverty, indifference and misunderstanding. His genius was marked; although largely self-taught, his work was already so remarkable for its jeweled color that a dishonest dealer tried to suborn him to paint Diazes for him—in vain.

In a very minor way I had been painting, drawing and teaching the same for years, and was able in some small degree to appreciate his splendid work, and wholly to sympathize with his gallant determination. In courage, in aspiration, in ideals, in bitter loneliness, we were enough alike to be drawn together.

Very promptly he asked me to marry him. Very promptly I declined. Then, reviewing the occurrence with that cold philosophy of mine, I asked myself, "Is it right so lightly to refuse what after all may be the right thing to do?" This is a vivid commentary on my strenuous youth. Between deprivation and denial from outside, and intensive self-denial from within, there was no natural response of inclination or desire, no question of, "Do I love him?" only, "Is it right?"

So I took up the matter again, said that I had no present wish to marry him, but that it was possible that I might in time, and that if he so desired he might come to see me for a year and we would find out—which he was very willing to do.

Followed a time of what earlier novelists used to call "conflicting emotions." There was the pleasure of association with a noble soul, with one who read and studied and cared for real things, of sharing high thought and purpose, of sympathy in many common deprivations and endurances. There was the natural force of sex-attraction between two lonely young people, the influence of propinquity.

Then, on my part, periods of bitter revulsion, of desperate efforts to regain the dispassionate poise, the balanced judgment I was used to. My mind was not fully clear as to whether I should or should not marry. On the one hand I knew it was normal and right in general, and held that a woman should be able to have marriage and motherhood, and do her work in the world also. On the other, I felt strongly that for me it was not right, that the nature of the life before me forbade it, that I ought to forego the more intimate personal happiness for complete devotion to my work.

Having lived so long on clear convictions, on definite well-reasoned decisions, there was something ignominious in feeling myself slip and waver in uncertainty. Once I demanded a year's complete separation, to recover clear judgment, but could not secure it. It was a terrible two years for me, and must have been wearing for him, but he held on. Then, at one time when he had met a keen personal disappointment, I agreed to marry him. After that, in spite of reactions and misgivings, I kept my word, but the period of courtship was by no means a happy one.

There are poems of this time which show deep affection, and high hopes, also doubt and uncertainty.

On the opening of the year of my wedding appears this cheerful inscription:

1883—1884. Midnight—Morning. With no pride, with little hope, with uncertain occasional happiness, with no glad energy and living power, with no faith or nearly none, but still, thank God! with firm belief in what is right and wrong, I begin the new year. Let me recognize fully that I do not look forward to happiness, that I have no decided hope of success. So long must I live. One does not die young who so desires it. Perhaps it was not meant for me to work as I intended. Perhaps I am not to be of use to others. I am weak. I anticipate a future of failure and suffering. Children sick and unhappy. Husband miserable because of my distress, and I—

I think sometimes that it may be the other way, bright and happy—but this comes oftenest, holds longest. But this life is marked for me. I will not withdraw, and let me at least learn to be uncomplaining and unselfish. Let me do my work and not fling my pain on others. Let me keep at least this ambition, to be good and a pleasure to *some* one, to some others, no matter what I feel myself.

More of this, and then:

And let me not forget to be grateful for what I have, some strength, some purpose, some design, some progress, some esteem, respect and affection. And some Love. Which I can neither see, feel nor believe in when the darkness comes. I mean this year to try hard for somewhat of my former force and courage. As I remember it was got by practice.

This was evidently a very black hour. Succeeding days show more cheer and vigor, as March 24th, "Then gym. enjoying it *intensely* and doing more than usual. Carried a girl on *one arm* and hip—easily!"

We were married in May, 1884. . . .

Mr. Stetson's father, a Baptist minister, married us, in the house on the corner of Manning and Ives Streets, and then, with some last things to carry, we walked down to Wayland Avenue, where our three rooms awaited us. We had the whole second floor, big corner rooms every one, and the young artist had made it beautiful.

"Do it just as you choose," I told him. "I have no tastes and no desires. I shall like whatever you do."

The house stood on a high bank, looking southward over the chimneys of a few small buildings below to the broad basin of the Seekonk, ringed at night with golden lights. White ducks drifted like magnolia petals along the still margins. Opposite us was a grove of tall pines—a pleasant place to walk and sit.

The housework for two in this tiny place was nothing to me, then some time I definitely devoted to deliberately breaking the regular habits of doing things on set days and hours in which I had been trained, repudiating the rigid New England schedule. Orderly habits of working are good, and later I established my own, but the immutable submission of the dutiful house-wives I know, bred rebellion in me.

I determined to learn to cook. "I won't have a cook-book in the house," quoth I. "I'm going to learn how." Knowing already the ordinary needful dishes, I began to alter the relative amount of ingredients, in small degree, and note the results, as of a little more sugar or less flour. Soon I learned the reaction of the different materials, and then was able to compose. The common method of merely following recipes is like studying music by learning a collection of tunes.

One of the most pleasing compliments of later years was that of a New York club man who told me I could command a high salary as chef in his club. During the period of experimentation no harm was done, I had enough practical knowledge to keep things edible, they merely varied from time to time, as indeed "home-cooking" frequently does.

Two instances were funny, however. Our first pair of chickens were in the oven. Walter went out to see how they were getting along. He sat down on the floor in front of the stove and laughed loud and long. I presently joined him in the position and the laughter. There lay the poor dears, their legs sticking out at casual angles, simply wreathed in stiff ringlets of slowly exuding stuffing, crisping as it oozed. I had made that stuffing too soft, the stitches wherewith it was sewed in too wide, the oven was too slow, and I had not tied their legs. But they tasted just as good.

The other experiment we gave to the neighbor's children; it was harmless but peculiar. Mother used to make a plain cake flavored with almond, of which I was fond. I made one, and in the course of my researches I put in more flour than was usual. The result was a meritorious cake, a solid cake of sterling character, a cake which would have gone well among lumbermen in winter, or lost in the woods with no other food. It lingered, that cake, growing no softer.

Then said I, "I will make 'trifle' of this cake." One might as well have undertaken to make a ballet dancer of a Swedish servant girl. "First it must be soaked in wine," I mused. I had no wine, and was a total abstainer at that. "Wine is a fruit juice," quoth I, and having no fruit at hand but apples and lemons, I made a thin apple-sauce, seasoned as usual with nutmeg, and vivified with a little lemon juice. In this I soaked the slices of cake, and up to that time the dish was good. I ate a piece and enjoyed it. Then came the soft custard, and never did I make a smoother one, flavoring it as I liked best, with cinnamon.

This in a tall glass dish, the piled slices of softened and enriched cake, the perfect custard flowing over all. My husband gazed upon it with a happy smile, and put some of the almond-apple-lemon-nutmeg-cinnamon mixture into his mouth. As many expressions chased across his countenance as were the tastes encountered, and with amazing discernment he unraveled the combination and named them all. It was a noble confection, but too composite, and served as a wholly sufficient lesson in the art of flavoring.

We were really very happy together. There was nothing to prevent it but that increasing depression of mine. My diary is full of thankfulness for happiness and prayers for deserving it, full of Walter's constant kindness and helpfulness in the work when I was not well—the not-wellness coming oftener and oftener.

The record dwells on delectable meals in full enumeration, as if I was a school-boy. As a note on current prices this: "Dinner vilely expensive, chops, six little chops, .50 cts.!" "Walter home about five. Brings me flowers. Dear boy!" "Walter gets most of the breakfast." "Amuse ourselves in the evenings with funny drawings." These were works of art of an unusual nature, a head and body to the waist being drawn by one of us and the paper folded back at the waist-line leaving the sides indicated; and then the other finished the legs, not knowing in the least what the other part was like. The results are surprising.

I think Walter was happy. A most successful exhibition in Boston had established him more favorably and enabled him to meet domestic expenses; and an order for a set of large etchings was added.

A lover more tender, a husband more devoted, woman could not ask. He helped in the housework more and more as my strength began to fail, for something was going wrong from the first. The steady cheerfulness, the strong, tireless spirit sank away. A sort of gray fog drifted across my mind, a cloud that grew and darkened.

"Feel sick and remain so all day." "Walter stays home and does everything for me." "Walter gets breakfast." October 10th: "I have coffee in bed mornings while Walter briskly makes fires and gets breakfast." "O dear! That I should come to this!" By October 13th the diary stops altogether, until January 1, 1885. "My journal has been long neglected by reason of ill-health. This day has not been a successful one as I was sicker than for some weeks. Walter also was not very well, and stayed at home, principally on my account. He has worked for me and for us both, waited on me in every tenderest way, played to me, read to me, done all for me as he always does. God be thanked for my husband."

February 16th: "A well-nigh sleepless night. Hot, cold, hot, restless, nervous, hysterical. Walter is love and patience personified, gets up over and over, gets me warm wintergreen, bromide, hot foot-bath, more bromide—all to no purpose."

Then, with impressive inscription: "March 23rd, 1885. This day, at about five minutes to nine in the morning, was born my child, Katharine."

> Brief ecstasy. Long pain.
> Then years of joy again.

Motherhood means giving. . . .

We had attributed all my increasing weakness and depression to pregnancy, and looked forward to prompt recovery now. All was normal and ordinary enough, but I was already plunged into an extreme of nervous exhaustion which no one observed or understood in the least. Of all angelic babies that darling was the best, a heavenly baby. My nurse, Maria Pease of Boston, was a joy while she lasted, and remained a lifelong friend. But after her month was up and I was left alone with the child I broke so fast that we sent for my mother, who had been visiting Thomas in Utah, and that baby-worshiping grandmother came to take care of the darling, I being incapable of doing that—or anything else, a mental wreck.

Presently we moved to a better house, on Humboldt Avenue near by, and a German servant girl of unparalleled virtues was installed. Here was a charming home; a loving and devoted husband; an exquisite baby, healthy, intelligent and good; a highly competent mother to run things; a wholly satisfactory servant—and I lay all day on the lounge and cried.

The Breakdown

In those days a new disease had dawned on the medical horizon. It was called "nervous prostration." No one knew much about it, and there were many who openly scoffed, saying it was only a new name for laziness. To be recognizably ill one must be confined to one's bed, and preferably in pain.

That a heretofore markedly vigorous young woman, with every comfort about her, should collapse in this lamentable manner was inexplicable. "You should use your will," said earnest friends. I had used it, hard and long, perhaps too hard and too long; at any rate it wouldn't work now.

"Force some happiness into your life," said one sympathizer. "Take an agreeable book to bed with you, occupy your mind with pleasant things." She did not realize that I was unable to read, and that my mind was exclusively occupied with unpleasant things. This disorder involved a growing melancholia, and that, as those know who have tasted it, consists of every painful mental sensation, shame, fear, remorse, a blind oppressive confusion, utter weakness, a steady brain-ache that fills the conscious mind with crowding images of distress.

The misery is doubtless as physical as a toothache, but a brain, of its own nature, gropes for reasons for its misery. Feeling the sensation fear, the mind suggests every possible calamity; the sensation shame—remorse—and one remembers every mistake and misdeeds of a lifetime, and grovels to the earth in abasement.

"If you would get up and do something you would feel better," said my mother. I rose drearily, and essayed to brush up the floor a little, with a dust-pan and small whiskbroom, but soon dropped those implements exhausted, and wept again in helpless shame.

I, the ceaselessly industrious, could do no work of any kind. I was so weak that the knife and fork sank from my hands—too tired to eat. I could not read nor write nor paint nor sew nor talk nor listen to talking, nor anything. I lay on that lounge and wept all day. The tears ran down into my ears on either side. I went to bed crying, woke in the night crying, sat on the edge of the bed in the morning and cried—from sheer continuous pain. Not physical, the doctors examined me and found nothing the matter.

The only physical pain I ever knew, besides dentistry and one sore finger, was having the baby, and I would rather have had a baby every week than suffer as I suffered in my mind. A constant dragging weariness miles below zero. Absolute incapacity. Absolute misery. To the spirit it was as if one were an armless, legless, eyeless, voiceless cripple. Prominent among the tumbling suggestions of a suffering brain was the thought, "You did it yourself! You did it yourself! You had health and strength and hope and glorious work before you—and you threw it all away. You were called to serve humanity, and you cannot serve yourself. No good as a wife, no good as a mother, no good at anything. And you did it yourself!" . . .

The baby? I nursed her for five months. I would hold her close—that lovely child!—and instead of love and happiness, feel only pain. The tears ran down on my breast. . . . Nothing was more utterly bitter than this, that even motherhood brought no joy.

The doctor said I must wean her, and go away, for a change. So she was duly weaned and throve finely on Mellins' Food, drinking eagerly from the cup—no bottle needed. With mother there and the excellent maid I was free to go.

Those always kind friends, the Channings, had gone to Pasadena to live, and invited me to spend the winter with them. Feeble and hopeless I set forth, armed with tonics and sedatives, to cross the continent. From the moment the wheels began to turn, the train to move, I felt better. A visit to my brother in Utah broke the journey.

He had gone west as a boy of nineteen, working as a surveyor in Nevada, and later, finding Utah quite a heaven after Nevada, had settled in Ogden and married there. At one time he was City Engineer. His wife knew of my coming, but it was to be a surprise to my brother, and succeeded.

He came to the door in his shirt-sleeves, as was the local custom, holding a lamp in his hand. There stood the sister he had not seen in eight years, calmly smiling.

"Good evening," said I with equanimity. This he repeated, nodding his head fatuously, "Good evening! Good evening! Good evening!" It was a complete success.

As I still bore a grudge for the teasing which had embittered my childish years, I enjoyed this little joke, already feeling so much better that I could enjoy. There was another little joke, too. He took me to ride in that vast, shining, mile-high valley, and pointing to some sharply defined little hills which looked about five or ten miles away, asked me how far I thought they were. But I had read stories of that dry, deceiving air, and solemnly replied, "Three hundred miles." They were forty, but that didn't sound like much.

Society in Ogden at that time was not exacting; the leading lady, I was told, was the wife of a railroad conductor. We went to a species of ball in a hotel. The bedrooms were all occupied by sleeping babies, as described in *The Virginian*. Among the dancers there was pointed out to me a man who had killed somebody—no one seemed to hold it against him; and another who had been scalped three times—the white patches were visible among the hair. I had thought scalping a more exhaustive process. At that rate a disingenuous savage could make three triumphant exhibits from one victim. As I did not dance we had a game of whist, and I was somewhat less than pleased to see each of the gentlemen playing bring a large cuspidor and set it by his side. They needed them.

From Utah to San Francisco—on which trip I first met the San Francisco flea. Long since he has been largely overcome, but then was what the newspapers call "a force to be reckoned with"—not California newspapers, of course.

My father was then at the head of the San Francisco Public Library. He met me on the Oakland side, and took me across to a room he had engaged for me for a day or two. Here he solemnly called on me, as would any acquaintance, and went with me across the ferry again when I started south.

"If you ever come to Providence again I hope you will come to see me," said I politely, as we parted, to which he courteously replied, "Thank you. I will bear your invitation in mind."

So down the great inland plain of California, over the Mojave Desert, and to heaven.

Pasadena was then but little changed from the sheep-ranch it used to be. The Channings had bought a beautiful place by the little reservoir at the corner of Walnut Street and Orange Avenue. Already their year-old trees were shooting up unbelievably, their flowers a glory.

The Arroyo Seco was then wild and clean, its steep banks a tangle of loveliness. About opposite us a point ran out where stood a huge twin live oak, still to be seen, but not to be reached by strangers. There was no house by them then, callas bloomed by the hydrant, and sweet alyssum ran wild in the grass.

Never before had my passion for beauty been satisfied. This place did not seem like earth, it was paradise. Kind and cogenial friends, pleasant society, amusement, out-door sports, the blessed mountains, the long, unbroken sweep of the valley, with snow-peaks at the far eastern end—with such surroundings I recovered so fast, to outward appearance at least, that I was taken for a vigorous young girl. Hope came back, love came back, I was eager to get home to husband and child, life was bright again.

The return trip was made a little sooner than I had intended because of a railroad war of unparalleled violence which drove prices down unbelievably. It seemed foolish not to take advantage of it, and I bought my ticket from Los Angeles to Chicago, standard, for $5.00. If I had waited for a few days more it could have been bought for $1. The eastern end was unchanged, twenty dollars from Chicago to Boston, but that cut-throat competition was all over the western roads, the sleepers had every berth filled, often two in each. So many traveled that it was said the roads made quite as much money as usual.

Leaving California in March, in the warm rush of its rich spring, I found snow in Denver, and from then on hardly saw the sun for a fortnight. I reached home with a heavy bronchial cold, which hung on long, the dark fog rose again in my mind, the miserable weakness—within a month I was as low as before leaving. . . .

This was a worse horror than before, for now I saw the stark fact—that I was well while away and sick while at home—a heartening prospect! Soon ensued the same utter prostration, the unbearable inner misery, the ceaseless tears. A new tonic had been invented, Essence of Oats, which was given me, and did some good for a time. I pulled up enough to do a little painting that fall, but soon slipped down again and stayed down. An old friend of my mother's, dear Mrs. Diman, was so grieved at this condition that she gave me a hundred dollars and urged me to go away somewhere and get cured.

At that time the greatest nerve specialist in the country was Dr. S. W. Mitchell of Philadelphia. Through the kindness of a friend of Mr. Stetson's living in that city, I went to him and took "the rest cure"; went with the utmost confidence, prefacing the visit with a long letter giving "the history of the case" in a way a modern psychologist would have appreciated. Dr. Mitchell only thought it proved self-conceit. He had a prejudice against the Beechers. "I've had two women of your blood here already," he told me scornfully. This eminent physician was well versed in two kinds of nervous prostration; that of the business man exhausted from too much work, and the society woman exhausted from too much play. The kind I had was evidently beyond him.

But he did reassure me on one point—there was no dementia, he said, only hysteria.

I was put to bed and kept there. I was fed, bathed, rubbed, and responded with the vigorous body of twenty-six. As far as he could see there was nothing the matter with me, so after a month of this agreeable treatment he sent me home, with this prescription:

"Live as domestic a life as possible. Have your child with you all the time." (Be it remarked that if I did but dress the baby it left me shaking and crying—certainly far from a healthy companionship for her, to say nothing of the effect on me.) "Lie down an hour after each meal. Have but two hours' intellectual life a day. And never touch pen, brush or pencil as long as you live."

I went home, followed those directions rigidly for months, and came perilously near to losing my mind. The mental agony grew so unbearable that I would sit blankly moving my head from side to side—to get out from under the pain. Not physical pain, not the least "headache" even, just mental torment, and so heavy in its nightmare gloom that it seemed real enough to dodge.

I made a rag baby, hung it on a doorknob and played with it. I would crawl into remote closets and under beds—to hide from the grinding pressure of that profound distress. . . .

Finally, in the fall of '87, in a moment of clear vision, we agreed to separate, to get a divorce. There was no quarrel, no blame for either one, never an unkind word between us, unbroken mutual affection—but it seemed plain that if I went crazy it would do my husband no good, and be a deadly injury to my child.

What this meant to the young artist, the devoted husband, the loving father, was so bitter a grief and loss that nothing would have justified breaking the marriage save this worse loss which threatened. It was not a choice between going and staying, but between going, sane, and staying, insane. If I had been of the slightest use to him or to the child, I would have "stuck it," as the English say. But this progressive weakening of the mind made a horror unnecessary to face; better for that dear child to have separated parents than a lunatic mother.

We had been married four years and more. This miserable condition of mind, this darkness, feebleness and gloom, had begun in those difficult years of courtship, had grown rapidly worse after marriage, and was now threatening utter loss; whereas I had repeated proof that the moment I left home I began to recover. It seemed right to give up a mistaken marriage.

Our mistake was mutual. If I had been stronger and wiser I should never have been persuaded into it. Our suffering was mutual too, his unbroken devotion, his manifold cares and labors in tending a sick wife, his adoring pride in the best of babies, all coming to naught, ending in utter failure—we sympathized with each other but faced a bitter necessity. The separation must come as soon as possible, the divorce must wait for conditions.

If this decision could have been reached sooner it would have been much better for me, the lasting mental injury would have been less. Such recovery as I have made in forty years, and the work accomplished, seem to show that the fear of insanity was not fulfilled, but the effects of nerve bankruptcy remain to this day. So much of my many failures, of misplay and misunderstanding and "queerness" is due to this lasting weakness, and kind friends so unfailingly refuse to allow for it, to believe it, that I am now going to some length in stating the case.

That part of the ruin was due to the conditions of childhood I do not doubt, and part to the rigid stoicism and constant effort in character-building of my youth; I was "over-trained," had wasted my substance in riotous— virtues. But that the immediate and continuing cause was mismarriage is proved by the instant rebound when I left home and as instant relapse on returning.

After I was finally free, in 1890, wreck though I was, there was a surprising output of work, some of my best. I think that if I could have had a period of care and rest then, I might have made full recovery. But the ensuing four years in California were the hardest of my life. The result has been a lasting loss of power, total in some directions, partial in others; the necessity for a laboriously acquired laziness foreign to both temperament and conviction, a crippled life.

But since my public activities do not show weakness, nor my writings, and since brain and nerve disorder is not visible, short of lunacy or literal "prostration," this lifetime of limitation and wretchedness, when I mention it, is flatly disbelieved. When I am forced to refuse invitations, to back out of work that seems easy, to own that I cannot read a heavy book, apologetically alleging this weakness of mind, friends gibber amiably, "I wish I had your mind!" I wish they had, for a while, as a punishment for doubting my word. What confuses them is the visible work I have been able to accomplish. They see activity, achievement, they do not see blank months of idleness; nor can they see what the work would have been if the powerful mind I had to begin with had not broken at twenty-four.

A brain may lose some faculties and keep others; it may be potent for a little while and impotent the rest of the time. Moreover, the work I have done has never been "work" in the sense of consciously applied effort. To write was always as easy to me as to talk. Even my verse, such as it is, flows as smoothly as a letter, is easier in fact. Perhaps the difficulty of answering letters will serve as an illustration of the weakness of mind so jocosely denied by would-be complimenters.

Here are a handful of letters—I dread to read them, especially if they are long—I pass them over to my husband—ask him to give me only those I must answer personally. These pile up and accumulate while I wait for a day when I feel able to attack them. A secretary does not help in the least, it is not the manual labor of writing which exhausts me, it is the effort to understand the letter, and make intelligent reply. I answer one, two, the next is harder, three—increasingly foggy, four—it's no use, I read it in vain, *I don't know what it says.* Literally, I can no longer understand what I read, and have to stop, with my mind like a piece of boiled spinach.

Reading is a simple art, common to most of us. As a child I read eagerly, greedily; as a girl I read steadily, with warm interest, in connected scientific study. No book seemed difficult. One of my Harvard boy friends told me no girl could read Clifford and understand him. Of course I got Clifford at once—and found him clear and easy enough.

After the débâcle I could read nothing—instant exhaustion preventing. As years passed there was some gain in this line; if a story was short and interesting and I was feeling pretty well I could read a little while. Once when well over forty I made a test, taking a simple book on a subject I was interested in—Lucy Salmon on the servant question. I read for half an hour with ease; the next half-hour was harder, but I kept on. At the end of the third I could not understand a word of it.

That surely is a plain instance of what I mean when I say my mind is weak. It is precisely that, weak. It cannot hold attention, cannot study, cannot listen long to anything, is always backing out of things because it is tired. A library, which was once to me as a confectioner's shop to a child, became an appalling weariness just to look at.

This does not involve loss of clear perception, lack of logic, failure to think straight when able to think at all. The natural faculties are there, as my books and lectures show. But there remains this humiliating weakness, and if I try to drive, to compel effort, the resulting exhaustion is pitiful.

To step so suddenly from proud strength to contemptible feebleness, from cheerful stoicism to a whimpering avoidance of any strain or irritation for fear of the collapse ensuing, is not pleasant, at twenty-four. To spend forty years and more in the patient effort of learning how to carry such infirmity so as to accomplish something in spite of it is a wearing process, full of mortification and deprivation. To lose books out of one's life, certainly more than ninety per cent of one's normal reading capacity, is no light misfortune.

"But you write books!" Yes, I have written enough to make a set of twenty-five, including volumes of stories, plays, verse, and miscellany; besides no end of stuff not good enough to keep. But this was all the natural expression of thought, except in the stories, which called for composition and were more difficult—especially the novels, which are poor. The power of expression remained, fortunately for me, and the faculty of inner perception, of seeing the relation of facts and their consequences.

I am not skilled in mental disorders, and cannot say what it was which paralyzed previous capacities so extensively, while leaving some in working order. Perhaps another instance will be indicative. For nearly all these broken years I could not look down an index. To do this one must form the matrix of a thought or word and look down the list until it fits. I could not hold that matrix at all, could not remember what I was looking for. To this day I'd rather turn the pages than look at the index.

Worst of all was the rapid collapse of my so laboriously built-up hand-made character. Eight years of honest conscientious nobly-purposed effort lost, with the will power that made it. The bitterness of that shame will not bear reviving even now.

All progress in definite study stopped completely. Even so light a subject as a language I have tried in vain—and I meant to learn so many! Lucky for me that the foundation laid in those years of selected study was broad and sound; and lucky again that with such a background, what I have been able to gather since has fitted in reliably.

In periods of special exhaustion, and those first years which should have meant recovery were such as to involve endless exhaustion, this feeble-mindedness often meant an almost infantile irresponsibility in what I said. At one of those times, in 1891, when I was so far below zero that I should have been in a sanitarium, but instead was obliged to meet people, there bustled up a brisk young woman to greet me. She told me her name, and added, perhaps noticing my empty eyes, "You don't remember me, do you!"

I looked at her and groped slowly about in that flaccid vacant brain of mine for some association. One memory arose, one picture of where I had seen her and with whom, but no saving grace of politeness, of common decency, of any consideration for her feelings. I spoke like a four-year-old child, because I thought of it and thought of nothing else—"Why yes, I remember you. I don't like your mother." It was true enough, but never in the world would I have said such a thing if I had been "all there."

There have been other offenses. My forgetfulness of people, so cruel a return for kindness; an absent-mindedness often working harm; many a broken engagement; unanswered letters and neglected invitations; much, very much of repeated failure of many kinds is due wholly to that continuing weakness of mind.

The word "exhaustion" is a loose term, carrying to most minds merely the idea of being tired, of which we all know something. There is a physical weariness when it "feels good to sit down"; the first two weeks of gymnasium work used to bring that lovely feeling.

Exhaustion of wilted nerves is quite another matter. There is no "appetite" in the mind, no interest in anything. To see, to hear, to think, to remember, to do anything, is incredible effort, as if trying to rise and walk under a prostrate circus tent, or wade in glue. It brings a heavy darkness, every idea presenting itself as a misfortune; an irritable unease which finds no rest, and an incapacity of decision which is fairly laughable.

For all the years in which I have had to pack a suit-case and start on a trip, that packing is dreaded; and often finds me at midnight, after several hours' attempt, holding up some article and looking at it in despair, utterly unable to make up my mind whether to take it or not. In one of the worst times, in 1896, I stood on a street corner for fifteen minutes, trying in vain to decide whether or not to take the car home.

As to the work accomplished in spite of all this. The lecturing is a perfectly natural expression of as natural clear thinking. It never has been felt as an effort, save when the audience was dull or combative. Yet at that I can only do so much of it; in regular Chautauqua work, for instance, I'm a failure.

The writing similarly is easy and swift expression, running at the rate of about a thousand words an hour for three hours—then it stops, no use trying to squeeze out any more. Any attempt at forced work stops everything for days. At that ordinary output the work I have accomplished would have required far less time, had I kept the natural power of my mind. All the writing, in easy five-day weeks, between four and five years; all the lectures, a thousand or more, with necessary traveling, another five years. All other work, as organizing, helping in club-work, every possible activity I can remember, including dressmaking and cooking and gardening, might be stretched to fill another five. There are fifteen years accounted for, out of, to date, forty-two.

That leaves twenty-seven years, a little lifetime in itself, taken out, between twenty-four and sixty-six, which I have lost. Twenty-seven adult years, in which, with my original strength of mind, the output of work could have been almost trebled. Moreover, this lifetime lost has not been spent in resting. It was always a time of extreme distress, shame, discouragement, misery.

Is a loss like this, suffering like this, to be met with light laughter and compliments? To be waved aside as if I were imagining it? It is true that the persistence of a well-trained physique is confusing to the average observer. A sympathetic lady once remarked, "Yes, it is a sad thing to see a strong mind in a weak body." Whereat I promptly picked her up and carried her around the room. "Please understand," said I, "that what ails me is a weak mind in a strong body." But she didn't understand, they never do. Only those near enough to watch the long, blank months of idleness, the endless hours of driveling solitaire, the black empty days and staring nights, know.

An orthodox visible disease that sends one to bed, as scarlet fever or mumps, is met by prompt sympathy. A broken arm, a sprained ankle, any physical mutilation, is a recognized misfortune. But the humiliating loss of a large part of one's brain power, of more than half one's working life, accompanied with deep misery and anguish of mind—this when complained of is met with amiable laughter and flat disbelief.

What is the psychology of it? Do these friends think it is more polite to doubt my word than to admit any discredit to my brain? Do they think I have been under some delusion as to all those years of weakness and suffering, or that I am pretending something in order to elicit undeserved commiseration? Or do they not think at all?

I try to describe this long limitation, hoping that with such power as is now mine, and such use of language as is within that power, this will convince any one who cares about it that this "Living" of mine had been done under a heavy handicap. . . .

That summer of 1887 was so dreadful, as I have said, that it drove me to the final decision that our marriage must end. Once the decision was made I breathed a little easier, there was a remote glimmer of hope. But we must wait till arrangements could be made, proper provision for the child, and so on.

All that winter Grace Channing kept my spirits up with her letters, with talk and plans for work, and in the summer of '88 she came east, and we spent some months together in Bristol, Rhode Island. There we wrote a play, in collaboration, and there gathered background for later work; and I revived with such companionship and interest. We came back to the city September 1st. She was to return to Pasadena on October 8th, and I planned to go with her.

For possible assets, there was my quarter interest in the old place in Hartford, still undivided, and half of which must be returned to my brother, who had earlier borrowed on his quarter for family use. With this for my one resource and a month to work in I promptly engaged carpenters to make the crates and boxes for such furniture as I meant to take.

"How can you engage them when you have no money?" asked Walter.

"I shall get the money by selling my property."

"How do you know you can?"

"I shall have to, to pay the carpenters."

And I did. Good Rowland Hazard II bought it for two thousand dollars, and I'm sure he got fully that when the place was sold, later. There were debts to pay, clothes to be made, the men to pay—all the work of breaking up housekeeping and packing for the journey.

Our pretty little home was dismantled. Mother was to go back to my brother in Utah. Mr. Stetson went to live in his studio. There was an elderly dressmaker well known to us, who had a desire to see California. She undertook to go with me, help with little Katharine and otherwise, and pay her own way back, if I furnished her fare going.

So I set forth on October 8th, with Katharine, Grace, this inadequate dressmaker, a large lunch-basket, my tickets, and all my remaining money in my pocket—ten dollars.

"What will you do when you get there?" asked anxious friends.

"I shall earn my own living."

"How do you know you can?"

"I shall have to when I get there."

PART SEVEN

Experimental Lives, 1920–1960

"One generation abandons the enterprises of another like stranded vessels."[1]

These words of Henry David Thoreau aptly express the way in which the generation of Americans that came of age during and after the First World War quickly gave up, at least for a time, their predecessors' work and faith and the concepts of self related to these. The millions of dead, the bungling and arrogance of the military, and the nightmare-world of muddy trenches and devastated no-man's lands made such "enterprises" as progress, reform, and social betterment seem like jokes. As Paul Fussell wrote in *The Great War and Modern Memory,* a study both of the literature of that war and its impact on the twentieth-century mind, World War I "was a hideous embarrassment to the prevailing Meliorist myth which had dominated the public consciousness for a century."[2] The heroism and romance, the sense of purpose, and the accompanying sense of a self in progress were swept away in the withering winds of irony and despair.

Fittingly, therefore, the most esteemed autobiography of the immediate post-war era was not another officer's memoir or a prisoner's story expressing faith and determination. It was *The Education of Henry Adams.* Adams had died in March, 1918, at the age of eighty. The *Education* was published in September, from a corrected copy of the private printing of 1907, and it shortly became a best-seller. It was also eagerly read and admired by Ezra Pound, T. S. Eliot, Sherwood Anderson, and many other writers and intellectuals of the new generation. Adams's corrosive ironies, his cosmic despair, and his sense of personal and cultural failure were all appropriate to the moods of what was to become known as "the lost generation."

"You are all a lost generation." Hemingway used these words as one of the epigraphs to *The Sun Also Rises* (1926), attributing them to Gertrude Stein. In *The Autobiography of Alice B. Toklas* (1933), she in turn attributed the

---

1. Henry D. Thoreau, *Walden,* ed. J. Lyndon Shanley (Princeton: Princeton Univ. Press, 1971), p. 11.
2. Paul Fussell, *The Great War and Modern Memory* (New York: Oxford Univ. Press, 1975), p. 8.

term to a French automobile mechanic, who had been talking of his poorly trained apprentices. But the term caught on, in any case, because it seemed to express the hedonistic (and also slightly romanticized) despair of post-war youth. It also spread with the success of Hemingway's autobiographical novel, which described the prematurely world-weary American expatriates Hemingway had known in Europe. Five or six years before, in 1920, F. Scott Fitzgerald's autobiographical first novel, *This Side of Paradise,* had been an equal sensation. Joyce's *Portrait of the Artist as a Young Man* (1916), Lawrence's *Sons and Lovers* (1913), and Proust's multi-volume *Remembrance of Things Past* also came to be known to Americans of the 1920s as models of autobiographical fiction. Indeed, autobiographical fiction became the favored form of the "lost generation," and many of its practitioners strove for such a level of achievement in it that most of them strongly resented having their work thought of as autobiography. Even Thomas Wolfe, whose long novels, beginning with *Look Homeward, Angel* (1929), became notorious for their subjectivity and self-absorption, resented being called an autobiographical writer.

The autobiographical novel, for this generation, was a work of art rather than referential history. Names were changed (usually) and characters were meant to be representatives of types of individuals rather than being the specific individuals they were modeled on. Incidents could be changed and invented, to be made more illustrative or dramatic. Dialogue could also be paraphrased or invented, and all language was expected to be more poetic and creative. It was heightened, polished, and made more economical, as had been done by Flaubert and Conrad, two admired predecessors. But perhaps the greatest difference between autobiography and the autobiographical novel was simply that the protagonist of the novel was more likely to be a young, unrecognized, non-heroic figure, such as Hemingway's Jake Barnes, than an older person who was famous and had played a recognized and active part in the world. The fictional protagonist was primarily a spectator, looking upon the world ironically and critically, like the artist. He even looked at himself that way, striving to be objective and without self-pity. Thus, though Jake Barnes once had been a soldier, he was now a wounded veteran who did not talk about the war or his wounds. Self-pity, sentimentality, and heroism were out. And even if the protagonist wanted to be the supreme artist, like Joyce's Stephen Daedalus, his ultimate goal was to stand outside his creation, "like the God of the creation, invisible, refined out of existence, indifferent, paring his finger nails."[3]

"Autobiography," therefore, came to be regarded as a pathetically inferior kind of writing. On the one hand, it was childish, something "anyone can write," as Gertrude Stein said, and likely to be boring, self-indulgent, and

3. James Joyce, *A Portrait of the Artist as a Young Man* (New York: Viking, 1968), p. 215.

formless. On the other hand, it was identified with older, famous people— ex-presidents' wives like Mrs. Taft and Mrs. Wilson (who published their auto- biographies in 1914 and 1939), retired preachers and missionaries, avuncular old Benjamin Franklin (who was mercilessly ridiculed by D. H. Lawrence in *Studies in Classic American Literature,* 1923, and William Carlos Williams in *In the American Grain,* 1925). It was also identified with the very reformers and progressives the new generation had abandoned. Calling a book an auto- biography or autobiographical was almost to patronize it, and, conversely, all good writing, even autobiographies, had to be exempted from the category. For example, when Ezra Pound wrote an essay on Henry James and wished to praise *A Small Boy and Others,* he said it was not really autobiography.[4]

These attitudes of the young American modernists were not necessarily the attitudes of the public. In 1921, Hamlin Garland received the Pulitzer Prize for *A Daughter of the Middle Border,* the sequel to his popular *A Son of the Middle Border* (1917). In 1926, he published a children's edition of his earlier "novel" *Boy Life on the Prairie* (1899), now calling it an autobiography. *The Autobiography of Benjamin Franklin* was a regular title on school reading lists. College literature courses included Victorian classics like *The Autobiog- raphy of John Stuart Mill* and began to include "new" American classics like *Walden.* Lesser-known, earlier autobiographies continued to have their many readers, including really loyal readers who regarded the authors as true heroes and notable writers. Joshua Slocum, the first solitary circumnavigator and author of *Sailing Alone Around the World* (1900), remained a patron saint of sailing writers, and his name was eventually taken by the Slocum Society, the association of single-handed ocean sailors. Thoreau had dozens of imita- tors, including Henry Beston in *The Outermost House* (1949). But the young modernists' scorn for autobiography meant that little original or experimental work would be done in it, or done in it and bear the name.

As we have been suggesting, however, the autobiographical novel must be seen historically as the genre of personal narrative in which the young mod- ernists primarily chose to work. The very fact that they were young and were not famous prior to their writing made the writing of "fiction" more feasible and acceptable. It was less egotistical (at least on the surface). It was more representational, being about "typical" and "realistic" and "universal" experi- ences like growing up, going to war, or being in love, and so more intimate. The novel was a realistic genre. For this reason, some autobiographical novels and short stories definitely belong in any broad history of autobiography and concepts of self.

Moreover, the very fact that so many young modernists experimented in life as well as in fiction, doing unorthodox, independent, or rebellious things,

---

4. Ezra Pound, "Henry James," in *The Literary Essays of Ezra Pound,* ed. T. S. Eliot (New York: New Directions, 1954), p. 328.

insured that some of them would, sooner or later, turn to more explicit kinds of autobiography in order to tell new stories, and that they would, thus, alter the form itself. One early example was e. e. cummings, who, like a number of other Americans, had been a volunteer ambulance driver with the French army. His *The Enormous Room* (1922) tells the story of his and a friend's arrest and their confinement in filthy French prisons for supposedly writing treasonous letters. Refusing to pity himself, while also satirizing French and American officials, cummings treats the experience as a modern Pilgrim's Progress. His fellow prisoners are "Delectable Mountains," a heterogeneous and rebellious group who all refuse to submit to prison discipline and so represent the causes of freedom and individuality against the authoritarian state. Although few of his contemporaries were as anarchistic as cummings, *The Enormous Room* does illustrate their general questioning not only of the state but of civilization itself. In "the enormous room," one day is no different from another, and time stands still, a proposition that thoroughly undercuts the old Victorian possibilities of progress and progressivism, which must take place in time. The prisoners, even if all very different from each other, are alike in their basic human needs and their capacity to bore or inspire or amuse. This undercuts ideas of the superior man's duties regarding his inferiors and dependents, another important self-concept among the Progressives. Finally, in cummings's prison, the comforts of life are no longer the gratifications of work and the luxuries of ocean liners and Pullman trains but the minimal pleasures of food, warmth, and a bath.

Another example of the explicitly autobiographical modernist was Anaïs Nin, who began writing her diaries at the age of eleven, and who continued because of her modernist awareness that "memory interfered and intercepted and distorted experience" and because she wanted to see her experience "in terms of a continuous evolution, observing all its transformations." The diary also "helped me to make the separation between my real self and the role-playing a woman is called upon to do." The diary "kept my other self alive." Another discovery she made was that the diary became "an incentive" to keep her life more interesting, opening herself to new friendships and encouraging her and her friends' growth. When she moved back to America at the time of the Second World War, the diary helped her to stay in touch with her earlier self. In all these ways, then, the diary both grew out of her sense of her life as an experiment, as something new and different and to be minutely observed, and became an essential instrument and aid to it. She kept a diary because she experimented, and experimented more boldly because she kept a diary.[5]

5. Anaïs Nin, "The Personal Life Deeply Lived," in *A Woman Speaks. The Lectures, Seminars, and Interviews of Anaïs Nin,* ed. Evelyn J. Hinz (Chicago: Swallow, 1975), pp. 153–62. Reprinted in *The American Autobiography,* ed. Albert E. Stone (Englewood Cliffs, NJ: Prentice-Hall, 1981), pp. 157–65.

Gertrude Stein also brought an extraordinary modern sensibility and modern experience to autobiography. As a student at Radcliffe in the 1890s, she had studied with William James and shared his interest in the processes of consciousness. Early experiments with narrative and point of view made her see autobiography as a literary and psychological and social issue, not simply a historical one. She also liked reading autobiographies, especially those of military and colonial leaders, Grant's *Memoirs* being one of her favorites. Meanwhile, her unusual life as lesbian, art collector, and leader of a Paris salon that included many of the American expatriates as well as new European painters like Picasso and Matisse, gave her unique material. One result was *The Autobiography of Alice B. Toklas* (1933), in which she described her own life as if written by her close companion and secretary, Alice B. Toklas. The book was such a success that she went on a lecture tour in the United States, and later wrote *Everybody's Autobiography* (1937) partially as an account of that tour. Wishing, as she said, "to tell what each one is without telling stories," she experimented with doing autobiographies as "portraits" rather than narratives, and wished to go beyond the comparatively traditional techniques she used in *The Autobiography of Alice B. Toklas*.

A rebel of a very different kind was Dorothy Day, author of *The Long Loneliness*. As she tells in its early chapters, her first ambition had been to become a novelist, and for a period in the 1920s she lived in Manhattan and on Staten Island with other young literary bohemians: Allen Tate, Kenneth Burke, Peggy and Malcolm Cowley, John Dos Passos, and an English biologist named Forster Batterham, who became, in effect, her common-law husband. Her first book was an autobiographical novel, *The Eleventh Virgin* (1924). She was also a political radical, having demonstrated for women's rights, and worked for *The Masses*. But as she grew happier in her independence, her love, and her enjoyment of the physical world, she also felt a need to express and share this happiness, which led, to her friends' amazement, to her joining the Catholic Church and to her founding, with the help of her new friend Peter Maurin, the Catholic Worker movement. Beginning with "hospitality houses" for the homeless and unemployed, and then launching the *Catholic Worker* newspaper (an ally and opposite of the Communist *Daily Worker*), the CW movement became a leader in nontraditional American Catholicism. Her second volume of autobiography, *From Union Square to Rome* (1938), describes this conversion.[6] Day and the Catholic Worker attracted other young Catholic intellectuals like Thomas Merton, and later inspired World War II pacifists and objectors to the Vietnam War. *The Long Loneliness* (1952) was a more traditional autobiography in the sense of being about her politics, her religious

6. June O'Connor, in "Dorothy Day as Autobiographer," *Religion* 20 (1990): 275–95, compares *The Eleventh Virgin, From Union Square to Rome, The Long Loneliness,* and Day's memoir of the Catholic Worker movement, *Loaves and Fishes* (1963).

conversion, and her social activism. Indeed, it is in some respects very similar to Jane Addams's *Twenty Years at Hull House*. But the life—the greater independence, the Catholic radicalism, and her having and raising a baby "out of wedlock," as people of her generation said—was more experimental than Addams's. Day and *The Long Loneliness* are of the "lost" generation, not the era of progress and optimism.

The most celebrated autobiographer of the Jazz Age (as he called it) was F. Scott Fitzgerald, whose series of three short confessional essays in *Esquire* in 1936 about his "Crack-Up" was a sobering conclusion to the high-life and extravagance of his life in the 1920s. Fitzgerald, who was also a Catholic, though a lapsed one, turned to the familiar conventions of the conversion narrative in order to tell a secular story with an underlying religious theme. The three essays, "Crack-Up," "Pasting It Together," and "Handle with Care," use slangy phrases but describe a classic three-stage journey from sin and despair, to conversion, to renewed faith. Adding to the religious nature of the story is the fact that Fitzgerald was trying to speak not just for himself but for his friends, his generation, and for the whole country. As he had previously been the hero of the Jazz Age, drinking bootleg cocktails and spending lavishly, he now sought to make himself at least a representative, if not the hero, of a sadder, wiser, more conscience-stricken era. "My recent experience parallels the wave of despair that swept the nation when the Boom was over," he says, still maintaing himself as spokesman for the nation. Such a spokesman serves the underlying religious purpose of uniting people, pulling them back together in a period of doubt. Though hardly as proud and boastful as Ethan Allen, he was also fabricating for himself a new identity, a national identity composed by his expression of national feelings.

The readiness with which many of Fitzgerald's friends both condemned and yet believed his "Crack-Up" essays is further evidence of the low opinion his generation had of autobiography—and of their innocence in reading it. If it was autobiography, then it had to be inferior to the novel, but if it was autobiography, it also must be true. They failed to see his artfulness—his achievement in adapting religious autobiography to his own purposes, and how he was in some ways hiding behind the persona of the reformed, confessing prodigal.

Yet, as the generation matured and its members continued with their unofficial, shared concepts of themselves as pioneers of modernism, experimenting in every art form and experimenting in styles of life, politics, and technology, their autobiographical experimentation continued, too. This is particularly true of the lives and autobiographies of black Americans and other Americans living on the fringes of supposedly "normal" middle-class, white society. As we have alredy seen, autobiography had long appealed to these Americans because their lives *were* different, and because they wished to express their protest and dissent or seek a way of integrating themselves within the rest of American society. These traditions, or conflicting traditions, continued during this long period from the 1920s through the 1950s.

The great new experience and experiment for black Americans, as for many other Americans in this period, was the move from small towns and farms to the city. In 1900, approximately sixty percent of the American population was still rural, a proportion that did not change very much until the First World War. But by 1960, seventy percent of the total American population and seventy-two percent of black Americans lived in cities. The city that attracted the largest numbers of black Americans was New York, with the result that in the 1920s Harlem became predominantly a black neighborhood and the site of a cultural renaissance. Writers had also come to Harlem—James Weldon Johnson and Zora Neal Hurston from Florida, Claude McKay from the Island of Jamaica, Langston Hughes from Missouri and Pennsylvania—and they joined with musicians and other artists in making it as exciting as other centers of modernism like Paris and Greenwich Village. Beginning in the 1930s, these four writers (and others) also wrote autobiographies of their experiences, adding a new dimension to the traditions of the slave narrative. The emphasis now was less on the oppressions of rural life and more on the excitement (and new oppressions) of urban life, including the experience of migration and transition.

A writer who was somewhat younger than these leaders of the Harlem Renaissance and who did not immediately go to New York but to Chicago was Richard Wright. His well-known autobiography *Black Boy* (1945) tells the frightening and courageous story of his childhood in Jackson, Mississippi, his youth in Memphis, Tennessee, and his departure for Chicago. With this emphasis on southern oppression and escape to the North, *Black Boy* recalls the contents and structure of a slave narrative. It is also like some slave-narratives in the occasional exaggeration and borrowing from other men's experiences in order for the author to make his experience seem more dramatic and universal. In this way it also resembles the autobiographical novels of the writers of this generation.[7] A work of Richard Wright which is not so well known is *American Hunger* (1977), which tells the further story of his experiences in Chicago after leaving the South, including his membership in the Communist Party. Reading *American Hunger,* one realizes how Wright continued to try new political and artistic experiments—and became disillusioned by them and by America in general.

It should be added that Wright's adventures with the Communist Party were not at all unusual. Many writers, artists, actors, film makers, and other Americans of the 1930s and early 1940s also were drawn to it. Lincoln Steffens, who had been one of the first to observe the results of the Commu-

7. For discussion of *Black Boy* and the problem of truth-telling in slave narratives, see Timothy Dow Adams, *Telling Lies in Modern American Autobiography* (Chapel Hill: Univ. of North Carolina Press, 1990), pp. 69–83.

nist Revolution, returned from the Soviet Union in 1919 with the exciting report, "I have seen the future and it works!" But with the Moscow trials and Hitler-Stalin pact of the late 1930s, communism became a fallen idol, and accounts of people's disillusionment with it became a prominent subgenre of autobiography, not only in America but in Europe as well. Parts of Lillian Hellman's autobiographies, such as *Pentimento* and *An Unfinished Woman*, offer late examples of the genre. The confessions of the ex-communist, some of which, like Whitaker Chambers's *Witness* (1952), were sensational and contributed to (or stemmed from) the furious anti-communism of the 1950s, were a fairly traditional autobiographical genre with a new content.

A radical, experimental, angry autobiographer who did not turn to communism was James Agee, author of *Let Us Now Praise Famous Men* (1941) and the autobiographical novels *The Morning Watch* (1951) and *A Death in the Family* (1957). Agee, a year younger than Richard Wright, was also from the South, and his description of the poor white tenant farmers of Alabama in *Let Us Now Praise Famous Men* complements Wright's description of black life in Mississippi. Wright wrote about his own life; Agee tried to record other lives more effectively and authentically by probing himself and purging himself of condescension. He and his collaborator, the photographer Walker Evans, tried to preserve the dignity of the families they lived with. They did not want them debased into trite, expendable ammunition for political protest, as Agee felt the communists would do. For these reasons—Agee's lyricism, his angry subjectivity, and his collaboration with Walker Evans—*Let Us Now Praise Famous Men* is one of the most experimental instances of autobiographical writing in this (or any other) period. It set a standard in personal journalism that the so-called "new journalists" of the 1960s aspired to.

Even *Black Elk Speaks,* the story of a supposedly very traditional Sioux medicine man, shows some effects of the modernist passion for experiment with new concepts of self. John G. Neihardt, who received and edited Black Elk's story in 1931, was actively looking for a traditional Indian—a figure most earlier friends of Indians had scorned and wanted to change. The ideal Indian of the Progressive Era had been Charles Eastman, who had become a medical doctor and the husband of the child-poet and missionary, Elaine Goodale. Black Elk's story appealed to the intellectual reaction against ideas of progress and to an interest in what was supposedly more authentic and primitive. Ironically, Black Elk himself, by the time he interviewed Neihardt, had already become a convert to Catholicism and served for many years as a leader among Indian Catholic laymen.[8] Black Elk, it might be said, had been leading an experimental life, too, both in the modernist sense of wanting to reject the past and in a still more profound sense of looking at all life as in

8. Raymond DeMallie, *The Sixth Grandfather: Black Elk's Teachings Given to John G. Neihardt* (Lincoln: Univ. of Nebraska Press, 1984), pp. 12–26.

some way tentative and changeable. In his conversations with Neihardt, he did not disclose much about his Catholicism, and, it appears, by the 1930s he was again more attracted to his earlier Sioux visions and the recovery and preservation of traditional Sioux ceremonies. Also, very few people in the 1930s and '40s read *Black Elk Speaks*. It was known mainly to anthropologists and to other, modernist defenders of Indian tradition like John Collier.

What the selections below all have in common, then, is their demonstration of how modernism and manifold forms of experiment, in life and in writing, changed concepts of self and definitions of autobiography.

39

F. Scott Fitzgerald (1896–1940)
The Crack-Up

When "The Crack-Up" first appeared in *Esquire* in February, 1936, many of F. Scott Fitzgerald's friends and fellow novelists were disgusted. The Great Depression had put millions of Americans in far more desperate straits than he was in, and he seemed to be whining. Such private confessions also seemed beneath the dignity of a novelist. To make matters worse, he was appearing in an expensive, upperclass men's magazine. "Christ, man, how do you find time in the middle of the general conflagration to worry about all that stuff?" John Dos Passos wrote him. "We're living in one of the damnedest tragic moments in history—if you want to go to pieces I think it's absolutely O.K. but I think you ought to write a first rate novel about it . . . instead of spilling it in little pieces for Arnold Gingrich [the *Esquire* publisher]." [1]

In the years since, however, beginning with the book of Fitzgerald's uncollected writings which Edmund Wilson edited and entitled *The Crack-Up* (1945), the version of his life which Fitzgerald gives here has become a basic part of his legend. Its simple, affecting pieces—early dreams, despair, and resolute stoicism—are classic, recalling hundreds of religious and secular conversion stories. Yet its language is fresh, lean, impudent, and colorful. Many phrases have become almost as familiar as passages in *The Great Gatsby*.

The assumption behind most readings of these three confessional essays, however—both the favorable and the critical—is the same: in them Fitzgerald was being unusually candid, artless, and personal. He was letting go with "self-revelation." He was writing from deep in "a real dark night of the soul." Liking it or rejecting it thus depends, supposedly, on how one feels about public confessions. "There are always those to whom all self-revelation is contemptible," says the author. But he brashly offends them in order to say what he has to say and reach other people who care.

A more cautious reading of these essays might begin by noting what they leave

1. John Dos Passos, "A Letter from John Dos Passos," in *The Crack-Up,* ed. Edmund Wilson, p. 311.

out. We know now from Fitzgerald biographers that at the point when he began them, in November, 1935, his wife Zelda had had several nervous breakdowns and been in a sequence of mental hospitals. His alcoholism was severe, despite his saying that he had "not tasted so much as a glass of beer for six months." And his debts were very high. Yet none of these things is mentioned. Nor does he write about his delays in finishing *Tender Is the Night* (1934) or complain about his fallen literary popularity. He could, in other words, have written more "self-revelation" than he did.

Instead, with his talk of "not being big enough to play football in college," and "not getting overseas during the war," he seems to be confessing "regrets" and broken dreams that many other men of his age and class may have had. This is true also of the "grave sentence" his doctor gave him. Even the metaphors, like the cracked plate, his "mortgaging" himself and "over-drawing at his bank," tend to touch many other people's experience and so universalize or disguise his own.

We might therefore ask whose autobiography this really is: his, his generation's, or the nation's? We might also ask, as we study the differences between "fiction" and "autobiography," whether Fitzgerald was more self-revelatory here or in a short story like "Babylon Revisited," which was written at about the same time.

The source of the text below is *The Crack-Up*, edited by Edmund Wilson, and all ellipses are from that edition. There are numerous good Fitzgerald biographies. The fullest is Matthew J. Bruccoli, *Some Sort of Epic Grandeur: The Life of F. Scott Fitzgerald* (New York: Harcourt Brace Jovanovich, 1981).

I

February, 1936

Of course all life is a process of breaking down, but the blows that do the dramatic side of the work—the big sudden blows that come, or seem to come, from outside—the ones you remember and blame things on and, in moments of weakness, tell your friends about, don't show their effect all at once. There is another sort of blow that comes from within—that you don't feel until it's too late to do anything about it, until you realize with finality that in some regard you will never be as good a man again. The first sort of breakage seems to happen quick—the second kind happens almost without your knowing it but is realized suddenly indeed.

Before I go on with this short history, let me make a general observation—the test of a first-rate intelligence is the ability to hold two opposed ideas in the mind at the same time, and still retain the ability to function. One should, for example, be able to see that things are hopeless and yet be determined to make them otherwise. This philosophy fitted on to my early adult life, when I saw the improbable, the implausible, often the "impossible," come true. Life was something you dominated if you were any good. Life yielded easily to intelligence and effort, or to what proportion could be mus-

tered of both. It seemed a romantic business to be a successful literary man—
you were not ever going to be as famous as a movie star but what note you
had was probably longer-lived—you were never going to have the power of a
man of strong political or religious convictions but you were certainly more
independent. Of course within the practice of your trade you were forever
unsatisfied—but I, for one, would not have chosen any other.

As the twenties passed, with my own twenties marching a little ahead of
them, my two juvenile regrets—at not being big enough (or good enough) to
play football in college, and at not getting overseas during the war—resolved
themselves into childish waking dreams of imaginary heroism that were good
enough to go to sleep on in restless nights. The big problems of life seemed
to solve themselves, and if the business of fixing them was difficult, it made
one too tired to think of more general problems.

Life, ten years ago, was largely a personal matter. I must hold in balance
the sense of the futility of effort and the sense of the necessity to struggle;
the conviction of the inevitability of failure and still the determination to
"succeed"—and, more than these, the contradiction between the dead hand
of the past and the high intentions of the future. If I could do this through
the common ills—domestic, professional and personal—then the ego would
continue as an arrow shot from nothingness to nothingness with such force
that only gravity would bring it to earth at last.

For seventeen years, with a year of deliberate loafing and resting out in
the center—things went on like that, with a new chore only a nice prospect
for the next day. I was living hard, too, but: "Up to forty-nine it'll be all
right," I said. "I can count on that. For a man who's lived as I have, that's all
you could ask."

—And then, ten years this side of forty-nine, I suddenly realized that I
had prematurely cracked.

II

Now a man can crack in many ways—can crack in the head—in which case
the power of decision is taken from you by others! or in the body, when one
can but submit to the white hospital world; or in the nerves. William Seabrook in an unsympathetic book tells, with some pride and a movie ending
of how he became a public charge. What led to his alcoholism or was bound
up with it, was a collapse of his nervous system. Though the present writer
was not so entangled—having at the time not tasted so much as a glass of
beer for six months—it was his nervous reflexes that were giving way—too
much anger and too many tears.

Moreover, to go back to my thesis that life has a varying offensive, the
realization of having cracked was not simultaneous with a blow, but with a
reprieve.

Not long before, I had sat in the office of a great doctor and listened to a grave sentence. With what, in retrospect, seems some equanimity, I had gone on about my affairs in the city where I was then living, not caring much, not thinking how much had been left undone, or what would become of this and that responsibility, like people do in books; I was well insured and anyhow I had been only a mediocre caretaker of most of the things left in my hands, even of my talent.

But I had a strong sudden instinct that I must be alone. I didn't want to see any people at all. I had seen so many people all my life—I was an average mixer, but more than average in a tendency to identify myself, my ideas, my destiny, with those of all classes that I came in contact with. I was always saving or being saved—in a single morning I would go through the emotions ascribable to Wellington at Waterloo. I lived in a world of inscrutable hostiles and inalienable friends and supporters.

But now I wanted to be absolutely alone and so arranged a certain insulation from ordinary cares.

It was not an unhappy time. I went away and there were fewer people. I found I was good-and-tired. I could lie around and was glad to, sleeping or dozing sometimes twenty hours a day and in the intervals trying resolutely not to think—instead I made lists—made lists and tore them up, hundreds of lists: of cavalry leaders and football players and cities, and popular tunes and pitchers, and happy times, and hobbies and houses lived in and how many suits since I left the army and how many pairs of shoes (I didn't count the suit I bought in Sorrento that shrunk, nor the pumps and dress shirt and collar that I carried around for years and never wore, because the pumps got damp and grainy and the shirt and collar got yellow and starch-rotted). And lists of women I'd liked, and of the times I had let myself be snubbed by people who had not been my betters in character or ability.

—And then suddenly, surprisingly, I got better.

—And cracked like an old plate as soon as I heard the news.

That is the real end of this story. What was to be done about it will have to rest in what used to be called the "womb of time." Suffice it to say that after about an hour of solitary pillow-hugging, I began to realize that for two years my life had been a drawing on resources that I did not possess, that I had been mortgaging myself physically and spiritually up to the hilt. What was the small gift of life given back in comparison to that?—when there had once been a pride of direction and a confidence in enduring independence.

I realized that in those two years, in order to preserve something—an inner hushmaybe, maybe not—I had weaned myself from all the things I used to love—that every act of life from the morning tooth-brush to the friend at dinner had become an effort. I saw that for a long time I had not liked people and things, but only followed the rickety old pretense of liking. I saw that even my love for those closest to me was become only an attempt to love, that my casual relations—with an editor, a tobacco seller, the child of a friend, were only what I remembered I *should* do, from other days. All in the same month I became bitter about such things as the sound of the radio, the advertisements in the magazines, the screech of tracks, the dead silence of the country—contemptuous at human softness, immediately (if secretly) quarrelsome toward hardness—hating the night when I couldn't sleep and hating the day because it went toward night. I slept on the heart side now because I knew that the sooner I could tire that out, even a little, the sooner would come that blessed hour of nightmare which, like a catharsis, would enable me to better meet the new day.

There were certain spots, certain faces I could look at. Like most Middle Westerners, I have never had any but the vaguest race prejudices—I always had a secret yen for the lovely Scandinavian blondes who sat on porches in St. Paul but hadn't emerged enough economically to be part of what was then society. They were too nice to be "chickens" and too quickly off the farmlands to seize a place in the sun, but I remember going round blocks to catch a single glimpse of shining hair—the bright shock of a girl I'd never know. This is urban, unpopular talk. It strays afield from the fact that in these latter days I couldn't stand the sight of Celts, English, Politicians, Strangers, Virginians, Negroes (light or dark), Hunting People, or retail clerks, and middlemen in general, all writers (I avoided writers very carefully because they can perpetuate trouble as no one else can)—and all the classes as classes and most of them as members of their class . . .

Trying to cling to something, I liked doctors and girl children up to the age of about thirteen and well-brought-up boy children from about eight years old on. I could have peace and happiness with these few categories of people. I forgot to add that I liked old men—men over seventy, sometimes over sixty if their faces looked seasoned. I liked Katharine Hepburn's face on the screen, no matter what was said about her pretentiousness, and Miriam Hopkins' face, and old friends if I only saw them once a year and could remember their ghosts.

All rather inhuman and undernourished, isn't it? Well, that, children, is the true sign of cracking up.

It is not a pretty picture. Inevitably it was carted here and there within its frame and exposed to various critics. One of them can only be described as a person whose life makes other people's lives seem like death—even this time when she was cast in the usually unappealing role of Job's comforter. In spite of the fact that this story is over, let me append our conversation as a sort of postscript:

"Instead of being so sorry for yourself, listen—" she said. (She always says "Listen," because she thinks while she talks—*really* thinks.) So she said: "Listen. Suppose this wasn't a crack in you—suppose it was a crack in the Grand Canyon."

"The crack's in me," I said heroically.

"Listen! The world only exists in your eyes—your conception of it. You can make it as big or as small as you want to. And you're trying to be a little puny individual. By God, if I ever cracked, I'd try to make the world crack with me. Listen! The world only exists through your apprehension of it, and so it's much better to say that it's not you that's cracked—it's the Grand Canyon."

"Baby et up all her Spinoza?"

"I don't know anything about Spinoza. I know—" She spoke, then, of old woes of her own, that seemed, in the telling, to have been more dolorous than mine, and how she had met them, over-ridden them, beaten them.

I felt a certain reaction to what she said, but I am a slow-thinking man, and it occurred to me simultaneously that of all natural forces, vitality is the incommunicable one. In days when juice came into one as an article without duty, one tried to distribute it—but always without success; to further mix metaphors, vitality never "takes." You have it or you haven't it, like health or brown eyes or honor or a baritone voice. I might have asked some of it from her, neatly wrapped and ready for home cooking and digestion, but I could never have got it—not if I'd waited around for a thousand hours with the tin cup of self-pity. I could walk from her door, holding myself very carefully like cracked crockery, and go away in the world of bitterness, where I was making a home with such materials as are found there—and quote to myself after I left her door:

"Ye are the salt of the earth. But if the salt hath lost its savour, wherewith shall it be salted?"
Matthew 5–13.

Pasting It Together

March, 1936

In a previous article this writer told about his realization that what he had before him was not the dish that he had ordered for his forties. In fact— since he and the dish were one, he described himself as a cracked plate, the kind that one wonders whether it is worth preserving. Your editor thought that the article suggested too many aspects without regarding them closely, and probably many readers felt the same way—and there are always those to whom all self-revelation is contemptible, unless it ends with a noble thanks to the gods for the Unconquerable Soul.

But I had been thanking the gods too long, and thanking them for nothing. I wanted to put a lament into my record, without even the background of the Euganean Hills to give it color. There weren't any Euganean hills that I could see.

Sometimes, though, the cracked plate has to be retained in the pantry, has to be kept in service as a household necessity. It can never again be warmed on the stove nor shuffled with the other plates in the dishpan; it will not be brought out for company, but it will do to hold crackers late at night or to go into the ice box under left-overs . . .

Hence this sequel—a cracked plate's further history.

Now the standard cure for one who is sunk is to consider those in actual destitution or physical suffering—this is an all-weather beatitude for gloom in general and fairly salutory day-time advice for everyone. But at three o'clock in the morning, a forgotten package has the same tragic importance as a death sentence, and the cure doesn't work—and in a real dark night of the soul it is always three o'clock in the morning, day after day. At that hour the tendency is to refuse to face things as long as possible by retiring into an infantile dream—but one is continually startled out of this by various contacts with the world. One meets these occasions as quickly and carelessly as possible and retires once more back into the dream, hoping that things will adjust themselves by some great material or spiritual bonanza. But as the withdrawal persists there is less and less chance of the bonanza—one is not waiting for the fade-out of a single sorrow, but rather being an unwilling witness of an execution, the disintegration of one's own personality . . .

Unless madness or drugs or drink come into it, this phase comes to a dead-end, eventually, and is succeeded by a vacuous quiet. In this you can try to estimate what has been sheared away and what is left. Only when this quiet came to me, did I realize that I had gone through two parallel experiences.

The first time was twenty years ago, when I left Princeton in junior year with a complaint diagnosed as malaria. It transpired, through an X-ray taken a dozen years later, that it had been tuberculosis—a mild case, and after a few months of rest I went back to college. But I had lost certain offices, the chief one was the presidency of the Triangle Club, a musical comedy idea, and also I dropped back a class. To me college would never be the same. There were to be no badges of pride, no medals, after all. It seemed on one March afternoon that I had lost every single thing I wanted—and that night was the first time that I hunted down the spectre of womanhood that, for a little while, makes everything else seem unimportant.

Years later I realized that my failure as a big shot in college was all right—instead of serving on committees, I took a beating on English poetry; when I got the idea of what it was all about, I set about learning how to write. On Shaw's principle that "If you don't get what you like, you better like what you get," it was a lucky break—at the moment it was a harsh and bitter business to know that my career as a leader of men was over.

Since that day I have not been able to fire a bad servant, and I am astonished and impressed by people who can. Some old desire for personal dominance was broken and gone. Life around me was a solemn dream, and I lived on the letters I wrote to a girl in another city. A man does not recover from such jolts—he becomes a different person and, eventually, the new person finds new things to care about.

The other episode parallel to my current situation took place after the war, when I had again over-extended my flank. It was one of those tragic loves doomed for lack of money, and one day the girl closed it out on the basis of common sense. During a long summer of despair I wrote a novel instead of letters, so it came out all right, but it came out all right for a different person. The man with the jingle of money in his pocket who married the girl a year later would always cherish an abiding distrust, an animosity, toward the leisure class—not the conviction of a revolutionist but the smouldering hatred of a peasant. In the years since then I have never been able to stop wondering where my friends' money came from, nor to stop thinking that at one time a sort of *droit de seigneur* might have been exercised to give one of them my girl.

For sixteen years I lived pretty much as this latter person, distrusting the rich, yet working for money with which to share their mobility and the grace that some of them brought into their lives. During this time I had plenty of the usual horses shot from under me—I remember some of their names—*Punctured Pride, Thwarted Expectation, Faithless, Show-off, Hard Hit, Never Again*. And after awhile I wasn't twenty-five, then not even thirty-five, and nothing was quite as good. But in all these years I don't remember a moment of discouragement. I saw honest men through moods of suicidal gloom—some of them gave up and died; others adjusted themselves and went on to a larger success than mine; but my morale never sank below the level of self-disgust when I had put on some unsightly personal show. Trouble has no necessary connection with discouragement—discouragement has a germ of its own, as different from trouble as arthritis is different from a stiff joint.

When a new sky cut off the sun last spring, I didn't at first relate it to what had happened fifteen or twenty years ago. Only gradually did a certain family resemblance come through—an over-extension of the flank, a burning of the candle at both ends; a call upon physical resources that I did not command, like a man over-drawing at his bank. In its impact this blow was more violent than the other two but it was the same in kind—a feeling that I was standing at twilight on a deserted range, with an empty rifle in my hands and the targets down. No problem set—simply a silence with only the sound of my own breathing.

In this silence there was a vast irresponsibility toward every obligation, a deflation of all my values. A passionate belief in order, a disregard of motives or consequences in favor of guess work and prophecy, a feeling that craft and industry would have a place in any world—one by one, these and other convictions were swept away. I saw that the novel, which at my maturity was the strongest and supplest medium for conveying thought and emotion from one human being to another, was becoming subordinated to a mechanical and communal art that, whether in the hands of Hollywood merchants or Russian idealists, was capable of reflecting only the tritest thought, the most obvious emotion. It was an art in which words were subordinate to images, where personality was worn down to the inevitable low gear of collaboration. As long past as 1930, I had a hunch that the talkies would make even the best selling novelist as archaic as silent pictures. People still read, if only Professor Canby's book of the month—curious children nosed at the slime of Mr. Tiffany Thayer in the drugstore libraries—but there was a rankling indignity, that to me had become almost an obsession, in seeing the power of the written word subordinated to another power, a more glittering, a grosser power . . .

I set that down as an example of what haunted me during the long night—this was something I could neither accept nor struggle against, something which tended to make my efforts obsolescent, as the chain stores have crippled the small merchant, an exterior force, unbeatable—

(I have the sense of lecturing now, looking at a watch on the desk before me and seeing how many more minutes—).

Well, when I had reached this period of silence, I was forced into a measure that no one ever adopts voluntarily: I was impelled to think. God, was it difficult! The moving about of great secret trunks. In the first exhausted halt, I wondered whether I had ever thought. After a long time I came to these conclusions, just as I write them here:

(1) That I had done very little thinking, save within the problems of my craft. For twenty years a certain man had been my intellectual conscience. That was Edmund Wilson.

(2) That another man represented my sense of the "good life," though I saw him once in a decade, and since then he might have been hung. He is in the fur business in the Northwest and wouldn't like his name set down here. But in difficult situations I had tried to think what *he* would have thought, how *he* would have acted.

(3) That a third contemporary had been an artistic conscience to me—I had not imitated his infectious style, because my own style, such as it is, was formed before he published anything, but there was an awful pull toward him when I was on a spot.

(4) That a fourth man had come to dictate my relations with other people when these relations were successful: how to do, what to say. How to make people at least momentarily happy (in opposition to Mrs. Post's theories of how to make everyone thoroughly uncomfortable with a sort of systematized vulgarity). This always confused me and made me want to go out and get drunk, but this man had seen the game, analyzed it and beaten it, and his word was good enough for me.

(5) That my political conscience had scarcely existed for ten years save as an element of irony in my stuff. When I became again concerned with the

system I should function under, it was a man much younger than myself who brought it to me, with a mixture of passion and fresh air.

So there was not an "I" any more—not a basis on which I could organize my self-respect—save my limitless capacity for toil that it seemed I possessed no more. It was strange to have no self—to be like a little boy left alone in a big house, who knew that now he could do anything he wanted to do, but found that there was nothing that he wanted to do—

(The watch is past the hour and I have barely reached my thesis. I have some doubts as to whether this is of general interest, but if anyone wants more, there is plenty left, and your editor will tell me. If you've had enough, say so—but not too loud, because I have the feeling that someone, I'm not sure who, is sound asleep—someone who could have helped me to keep my shop open. It wasn't Lenin, and it wasn't God.)

Handle with Care

April, 1936

I have spoken in these pages of how an exceptionally optimistic young man experienced a crack-up of all values, a crack-up that he scarcely knew of until long after it occurred. I told of the succeeding period of desolation and of the necessity of going on, but without benefit of Henley's familiar heroics, "my head is bloody but unbowed." For a check-up of my spiritual liabilities indicated that I had no particular head to be bowed or unbowed. Once I had had a heart but that was about all I was sure of.

This was at least a starting place out of the morass in which I floundered: "I felt—therefore I was." At one time or another there had been many people who had leaned on me, come to me in difficulties or written me from afar, believed implicitly in my advice and my attitude toward life. The dullest platitude monger or the most unscrupulous Rasputin who can influence the destinies of many people must have some individuality, so the question became one of finding why and where I had changed, where was the leak through which, unknown to myself, my enthusiasm and my vitality had been steadily and prematurely trickling away.

One harassed and despairing night I packed a brief case and went off a thousand miles to think it over. I took a dollar room in a drab little town where I knew no one and sunk all the money I had with me in a stock of potted meat, crackers and apples. But don't let me suggest that the change from a rather overstuffed world to a comparative asceticism was any Research Magnificent—I only wanted absolute quiet to think out why I had developed a sad attitude toward sadness, a melancholy attitude toward melancholy and a tragic attitude toward tragedy—*why I had become identified with the objects of my horror or compassion.*

Does this seem a fine distinction? It isn't: identification such as this spells the death of accomplishment. It is something like this that keeps insane people from working. Lenin did not willingly endure the sufferings of his proletariat, nor Washington of his troops, nor Dickens of his London poor. And when Tolstoy tried some such merging of himself with the objects of his attention, it was a fake and a failure. I mention these because they are the men best known to us all.

It was dangerous mist. When Wordsworth decided that "there had passed away a glory from the earth," he felt no compulsion to pass away with it, and the Fiery Particle Keats never ceased his struggle against t. b. nor in his last moments relinquished his hope of being among the English poets.

My self-immolation was something sodden-dark. It was very distinctly not modern—yet I saw it in others, saw it in a dozen men of honor and industry since the war. (I heard you, but that's too easy—there were Marxians among these men.) I had stood by while one famous contemporary of mine played with the idea of the Big Out for half a year; I had watched when another, equally eminent, spent months in an asylum unable to endure any contact with his fellow men. And of those who had given up and passed on I could list a score.

This led me to the idea that the ones who had survived had made some sort of clean break. This is a big word and is no parallel to a jail-break when one is probably headed for a new jail or will be forced back to the old one. The famous "Escape" or "run away from it all" is an excursion in a trap even if the trap includes the south seas, which are only for those who want to paint them or sail them. A clean break is something you cannot come back from; that is irretrievable because it makes the past cease to exist. So, since I could no longer fulfill the obligations that life had set for me or that I had set for myself, why not slay the empty shell who had been posturing at it for four years? I must continue to be a writer because that was my only way of life, but I would cease any attempts to be a person—to be kind, just or generous. There were plenty of counterfeit coins around that would pass instead of these and I knew where I could get them at a nickel on the dollar. In thirty-nine years an observant eye has learned to detect where the milk is watered and the sugar is sanded, the rhinestone passed for diamond and the stucco for stone. There was to be no more giving of myself—all giving was to be outlawed henceforth under a new name, and that name was Waste.

The decision made me rather exuberant, like anything that is both real and new. As a sort of beginning there was a whole shaft of letters to be tipped into the waste basket when I went home, letters that wanted something for nothing—to read this man's manuscript, market this man's poem, speak free on the radio, indite notes of introduction, give this interview, help with the plot of this play, with this domestic situation, perform this act of thoughtfulness or charity.

The conjuror's hat was empty. To draw things out of it had long been a sort of sleight of hand, and now, to change the metaphor, I was off the dispensing end of the relief roll forever.

The heady villainous feeling continued.

I felt like the beady-eyed men I used to see on the commuting train from Great Neck fifteen years back—men who didn't care whether the world tumbled into chaos tomorrow if it spared their houses. I was one with them now, one with the smooth articles who said:

"I'm sorry but business is business." Or:

"You ought to have thought of that before you got into this trouble." Or:

"I'm not the person to see about that."

And a smile—ah, I would get me a smile. I'm still working on that smile. It is to combine the best qualities of a hotel manager, an experienced old social weasel, a headmaster on visitors' day, a colored elevator man, a pansy pulling a profile, a producer getting stuff at half its market value, a trained nurse coming on a new job, a body-vender in her first rotogravure, a hopeful extra swept near the camera, a ballet dancer with an infected toe, and of course the great beam of loving kindness common to all those from Washington to Beverly Hills who must exist by virtue of the contorted pan.

The voice too—I am working with a teacher on the voice. When I have perfected it the larynx will show no ring of conviction except the conviction of the person I am talking to. Since it will be largely called upon for the elicitation of the word "Yes," my teacher (a lawyer) and I are concentrating on that, but in extra hours. I am learning to bring into it that polite acerbity that makes people feel that far from being welcome they are not even tolerated and are under continual and scathing analysis at every moment. These times will of course not coincide with the smile. This will be reserved exclusively for those from whom I have nothing to gain, old worn-out people or young struggling people. They won't mind—what the hell, they get it most of the time anyhow.

But enough. It is not a matter of levity. If you are young and you should write asking to see me and learn how to be a sombre literary man writing pieces upon the state of emotional exhaustion that often overtakes writers in their prime—if you should be so young and so fatuous as to do this, I would not do so much as acknowledge your letter, unless you were related to someone very rich and important indeed. And if you were dying of starvation outside my window, I would go out quickly and give you the smile and the voice (if no longer the hand) and stick around till somebody raised a nickel to phone for the ambulance, that is if I thought there would be any copy in it for me.

I have now at last become a writer only. The man I had persistently tried to be became such a burden that I have "cut him loose" with as little compunction as a Negro lady cuts loose a rival on Saturday night. Let the good people function as such—let the overworked doctors die in harness, with one week's "vacation" a year that they can devote to straightening out their family affairs, and let the underworked doctors scramble for cases at one dollar a throw; let the soldiers be killed and enter immediately into the Valhalla of their profession. That is their contract with the gods. A writer need have no such ideals unless he makes them for himself, and this one has quit. The old dream of being an entire man in the Goethe-Byron-Shaw tradition, with an opulent American touch, a sort of combination of J. P. Morgan, Topham Beauclerk and St. Francis of Assisi, has been relegated to the junk heap of the shoulder pads worn for one day on the Princeton freshman football field and the overseas cap never worn overseas.

So what? This is what I think now: that the natural state of the sentient adult is a qualified unhappiness. I think also that in an adult the desire to be finer in grain than you are, "a constant striving" (as those people say who gain their bread by saying it) only adds to this unhappiness in the end—that end that comes to our youth and hope. My own happiness in the past often approached such an ecstasy that I could not share it even with the person dearest to me but had to walk it away in quiet streets and lanes with only fragments of it to distil into little lines in books—and I think that my happiness, or talent for self-delusion or what you will, was an exception. It was not the natural thing but the unnatural—unnatural as the Boom; and my recent experience parallels the wave of despair that swept the nation when the Boom was over.

I shall manage to live with the new dispensation, though it has taken some months to be certain of the fact. And just as the laughing stoicism which has enabled the American Negro to endure the intolerable conditions of his existence has cost him his sense of the truth—so in my case there is a price to pay. I do not any longer like the postman, nor the grocer, nor the editor, nor the cousin's husband, and he in turn will come to dislike me, so that life will never be very pleasant again, and the sign *Cave Canem* is hung permanently just above my door. I will try to be a correct animal though, and if you throw me a bone with enough meat on it I may even lick your hand.

40

Gertrude Stein (1874–1946)

from *The Gradual Making*
of "The Making of Americans"

The Making of Americans (1925) is Gertrude Stein's least read and most ambitious book, a 925-page novel based in part on the experiences of her and her family in evolving from immigrants into "Americans." It is repetitious, plotless, and cha-otic—the consequence of some of Stein's conflicting or unperfected theories of modern fiction. It was written between 1902 and 1911, but waited many years to be published.

Yet Stein thought so highly of the book as one of the ground-breaking ex-periments in modern fiction that she lectured about it on her trip to America in 1934–35. Hence this autobiographical lecture-essay about the writing of the book and what she was trying to do in it.

Simply stated, her theory was that all human character is essentially ex-pressible in a range of psychological types, types which are basically changeless except as the language in which they are "composed" changes. This language, "the composition in which we live," as she called it in another lecture,[1] comes out most forcibly in the unconscious patterns of ordinary speech—of repetitions, with shifting emphases and meanings, and without description and sequential narrative.

What she does in this essay, therefore, is express her character through her own patterns of speech: her way of asserting something and then repeating it with slight changes of words, word order, and emphasis. She tells how she arrived at her theory and how she attempted to use it, quoting passages from the book to illustrate it.

Such repetitions have made Stein seem like an oracle or a jokester, or just made readers ignore her. But when one approaches her style in the right spirit and takes it at the right pace, it becomes subtle and insightful. The sentence in the middle of this selection, "Slowly every one in continuous repeating, to their minutest variation, comes to be clearer to some one," applies to how the style works. The ensuing sentences about how people understand one another, about

Reprinted from *Lectures in America,* by Gertrude Stein. Copyright 1935 and renewed 1963 by Alice B. Toklas. Reprinted by permission of Random House, Inc., and the Estate of Gertrude Stein.
1. Stein, "Portraits and Repetition," in *Lectures in America,* p. 165.

history, and about resemblances and differences and how people feel about them are brilliant. They could be seen as representing Stein's theory of autobiography.

The selection below is taken from *Lectures in America* (New York: Random House, 1935). Stein's source citations of *The Making of Americans* within the text have been retained as given there. The indispensable book on Stein is Richard Bridgman, *Gertrude Stein in Pieces* (New York: Oxford Univ. Press, 1970).

I am going to read what I have written to read, because in a general way it is easier even if it is not better and in a general way it is better even if it is not easier to read what has been written than to say what has not been written. Any way that is one way to feel about it.

And I want to tell you about the gradual way of making The Making of Americans. I made it gradually and it took me almost three years to make it, but that is not what I mean by gradual. What I mean by gradual is the way the preparation was made inside of me. Although as I tell it it will sound historical, it really is not historical as I still very much remember it. I do remember it. That is I can remember it. And if you can remember, it may be history but it is not historical.

To begin with, I seem always to be doing the talking when I am anywhere but in spite of that I do listen. I always listen. I always have listened. I always have listened to the way everybody has to tell what they have to say. In other words I always have listened in my way of listening until they have told me and told me until I really know it, that is know what they are.

I always as I admit seem to be talking but talking can be a way of listening that is if one has the profound need of hearing and seeing what every one is telling.

And I began very early in life to talk all the time and to listen all the time. At least that is the way I feel about it.

I cannot remember not talking all the time and all the same feeling that while I was talking while I was seeing that I was not only hearing but seeing while I was talking and that at the same time the relation between myself knowing I was talking and those to whom I was talking and incidentally to whom I was listening were coming to tell me and tell me in their way everything that made them.

Those of you who have read The Making of Americans I think will very certainly understand.

When I was young and I am talking of a period even before I went to college part of this talking consisted in a desire not only to hear what each one was saying in every way everybody has of saying it but also then of helping to change them and to help them change themselves.

I was very full of convictions in those days and I at that time thought that the passion I had for finding out by talking and listening just how everybody was always telling everything that was inside them that made them that one, that this passion for knowing the basis of existence in each one was in me to help them change themselves to become what they should become. The changing should of course be dependent upon my ideas and theirs theirs as much as mine at that time.

And so in those early days I wanted to know what was inside each one which made them that one and I was deeply convinced that I needed this to help them change something.

Then I went to college and there for a little while I was tremendously occupied with finding out what was inside myself to make me what I was. I think that does happen to one at that time. It had been happening before going to college but going to college made it more lively. And being so occupied with what made me myself inside me, made me perhaps not stop talking but for awhile it made me stop listening.

At any rate that is the way it seems to me now looking back at it.

While I was at college and doing philosophy and psychology I became more and more interested in my own mental and physical processes and less in that of others and all I then was learning of what made people what they were came to me by experience and not by talking and listening.

Then as I say I became more interested in psychology, and one of the things I did was testing reactions of the average college student in a state of normal activity and in the state of fatigue induced by their examinations. I was supposed to be interested in their reactions but soon I found that I was not but instead that I was enormously interested in the types of their characters that is what I even then thought of as the bottom nature of them, and when in May 1898 I wrote my half of the report of these experiments I expressed these results as follows:

In these descriptions it will be readily observed that habits of attention are reflexes of the complete character of the individual.

Then that was over and I went to the medical school where I was bored and where once more myself and my experiences were more actively interesting me than the life inside of others.

But then after that once more I began to listen, I had left the medical school and I had for the moment nothing to do but talk and look and listen, and I did this tremendously.

I then began again to think about the bottom nature in people, I began to get enormously interested in hearing how everybody said the same thing over and over again with infinite variations but over and over again until finally if you listened with great intensity you could hear it rise and fall and tell all that that there was inside them, not so much by the actual words they said or the thoughts they had but the movement of their thoughts and words endlessly the same and endlessly different.

Many things then come out in the repeating that make a history of each one for any one who always listens to them. Many things come out of each one and as one listens to them listens to all the repeating in them, always this comes to be clear about them, the history of them of the bottom nature in them, the nature or natures mixed up in them to make the whole of them in anyway it mixes up in them. Sometime then there will be a history of every one.

When you come to feel the whole of anyone from the beginning to the ending, all the kind of repeating there is in them, the different ways at different times repeating comes out of them, all the kinds of things and mixtures in each one, anyone can see then by looking hard at any one living near them that a history of everyone must be a long one. A history of any one must be a long one, slowly it comes out from them from their beginning to their ending, slowly you can see it in them the nature and the mixtures in them, slowly everything comes out from each one in the kind of repeating each one does in the different parts and kinds of living they have in them, slowly then the history of them comes out from them, slowly then any one who looks well at any one will have the history of the whole of that one. Slowly the history of each one comes out of each one. Sometime then there will be a history of every one. Mostly every history will be a long one. Slowly it comes out of each one, slowly any one who looks at them gets the history of each part of the living of any one in the history of the whole of each one that sometime there will be of every one.

The Making of Americans (Harcourt, Brace & Co.), Page 128.

Repeating then is in every one, in every one their being and their feeling and their way of realizing everything and every one comes out of them in repeating. More and more then everyone comes to be clear to some one.

Slowly every one in continuous repeating, to their minutest variation, comes to be clearer to some one. Every one who ever was or is or will be living sometimes will be clearly realized by some one. Sometime there will be an ordered history of every one. Slowly every kind of one comes into ordered recognition. More and more then it is wonderful in living the subtle variations coming clear into ordered recognition, coming to make every one a part of some kind of them, some kind of men and women. Repeating then is in every one, every one then comes sometime to be clearer to some one, sometime there will be then an orderly history of every one who ever was or is or will be living.

The Making of Americans.

Then I became very interested in resemblances, in resemblances and slight differences between people. I began to make charts of all the people I had ever known or seen, or met or remembered.

Every one is always busy with it, no one of them then ever want to know it that every one looks like some one else and they see it mostly every one dislikes to hear it. It is very important to me to always know it, to always see it which one looks like others and to tell it.—The Making of Americans, page 211. I write for myself and strangers, I do this for my own sake and for the sake of those who know I know it that they look like other ones, that they are separate and yet always repeated. There are some who like it that I know they are like many others and repeat it, there are many who never can really like it.

Every one is one inside them, every one reminds some one of some other one who is or was or will be living. Every one has it to say of each one he is like such a one I see it in him, every one has it to say of each one she is like some one else I can tell by remembering. So it goes on always in living, every one is always remembering some one who is resembling to the one at whom they are then looking. So they go on repeating, every one is themselves inside them and every one is resembling to others and that is always interesting.

The Making of Americans, Page 212.

I began to see that as I saw when I saw so many students at college that all this was gradually taking form. I began to get very excited about it. I began to be sure that if I could only go on long enough and talk and hear and look and see and feel enough and long enough I could finally describe really describe every kind of human being that ever was or is or would be living.

I got very wrapped up in all this. And I began writing The Making of Americans.

Let me read you some passages to show you how passionately and how desperately I felt about all this.

I am altogether a discouraged one. I am just now altogether a discouraged one. I am going on describing men and women.

The Making of Americans, Page 308.

I have been very glad to have been wrong. It is sometimes a very hard thing to win myself to having been wrong about something. I do a great deal of suffering.

The Making of Americans, Page 310.

I was sure that in a kind of a way the enigma of the universe could in this way be solved. That after all description is explanation, and if I went on and on and on enough I could describe every individual human being that could possibly exist. I did proceed to do as much as I could.

Some time then there will be every kind of a history of every one who ever can or is or was or will be living. Some time then there will be a history of every one from their beginning to their ending. Sometime then there will be a history of all of them, of every kind of them, of every one, of every bit of living they ever have in them, of them when there is never more than a beginning to them, of every kind of them, of every one when there is very little beginning and then there is an ending, there will then sometime be a history of every one there will be a history of everything that ever was or is or will be them, of everything that was or is or will be all of any one or all of all of them. Sometime then there will be a history of every one, of everything or anything that is all them or any part of them and sometime then there will be a history of how anything or everything comes out from every one, comes out from every one or any one from the beginning to the ending of the being in them. Sometime then there must be a history of every one who ever was or is or will be living. As one sees every one in their living, in their loving, sitting, eating, drinking, sleeping, walking, working, thinking, laughing, as any one sees all of them from their beginning to their ending, sees them when they are little babies or children or young grown men and women or growing older men and women or old men and women then one knows it in them that sometime there will be a history of all of them, that sometime all of them will have the last touch of being, a history of them can give to them, sometime then there will be a history of each one, of all the kinds of them, of all the ways any one can know them, of all the ways each one is inside her or inside him, of all the ways anything of them comes out from them. Sometime then there will be a history of every one and so then every one will have in them the last touch of being a history of any one can give to them.

The Making of Americans, Page 124.

This is then a beginning of the way of knowing everything in every one, of knowing the complete history of each one who ever is or was or will be living. This is then a little description of the winning of so much wisdom.

The Making of Americans, Page 217.

41

James Agee (1909–1955)

from *Let Us Now Praise Famous Men*

James Agee was born in Knoxville, Tennessee, the son of middle-class parents. When his father died in an automobile accident when Agee was six, his mother, who had artistic interests, took over his education, sending him at age ten to St. Andrew's, a boarding school near Sewanee, Tennessee, but moving to Sewanee to be near him. He later went to Phillips Exeter and Harvard College.

On graduating in 1932, during the depression, Agee got a job writing for *Fortune* magazine, the prosperous new business magazine which pioneered in documentary journalism. Two articles Agee did on the Tennessee Valley Authority, the government's experiment in land reclamation, hydroelectric power, and flood control, won praise from Henry Luce, *Fortune*'s owner. In 1936, Agee and a documentary photographer, Walker Evans, were assigned to do a piece on southern tenant farmers, focusing on the daily life of a supposedly typical farmer and his family.

But Agee found it "curious, not to say obscene and thoroughly terrifying" that a magazine should "pry intimately into the lives of an undefended and appallingly damaged group of human beings," with profit its ultimate motive and neither its editors nor its readers equally exposed or at risk.[1] The article Agee wrote was ten times longer than assigned and was also "too personal" and "too violent."[2] Agee then got a contract with Harper and Brothers to develop the article into a book to be titled *Cotton Tenants: Three Families*. But when this manuscript was submitted in 1939, it too was rejected. Agee said he would not make "certain required changes through which it might be less unpalatable to the general reader."[3] Finally, in September, 1941, it was published by Houghton Mifflin, with only the removal of "anglo-saxon monosyllables" that were "illegal in Massachusetts."[4]

1. Agee, *Let Us Now Praise Famous Men*, p. 7.
2. William Stott, *Documentary Expression and Thirties America* (Chicago: Univ. of Chicago Press, 1986), p. 262.
3. Stott, *Documentary Expression*, p. 263.
4. Agee, *Let Us Now Praise Famous Men*, pp. 456, xiv.

What Agee had done was to break the rules of documentary journalism, which held that the author must be a rigorously objective spectator. He had introduced his own feelings—his anger, tenderness, and, as he called it, the full "individual, anti-authoritative human consciousness."[5] In so doing, he exposed himself and his life just as daringly as he exposed the lives of the three families he wrote about. At one point, thinking of himself alone in the Gudger house, he even recalled how as a boy left alone in his grandfather's house he had pryed into forbidden drawers and closets and masturbated on other people's beds. Such self-exposure some critics called distracting, egotistical, and motivated from guilt. But Agee's defense was that uncovering the vulnerable reality of other lives necessitated recognizing his own. He wrote to shock, but also with great respect for human dignity. Significantly, the title of the book is from the forty-fourth chapter of Ecclesiasticus, in a song praising the heroes of Israel's past.

The short selection here, entitled "A Country Letter," does not go deeply into Agee's own past, but it describes the setting of the Gudger house with Agee himself as an on-site, introspective observer. He also, towards the end, imagines himself losing his own "shape and weight and self" and becoming each person in the house, a kind of universal, Whitmanian auto/biographer of every one.

For additional biographical information on Agee, see Victor A. Kramer, *James Agee* (Boston: Twayne, 1975). The selection here is from *Let Us Now Praise Famous Men* (Boston: Houghton Mifflin, 1941).

It is late in a summer night, in a room of a house set deep and solitary in the country; all in this house save myself are sleeping; I sit at a table, facing a partition wall; and I am looking at a lighted coal-oil lamp which stands on the table close to the wall, and just beyond the sleeping of my relaxed left hand; with my right hand I am from time to time writing, with a soft pencil, into a school-child's composition book; but just now, I am entirely focused on the lamp, and light.

It is of glass, light metal colored gold, and cloth of heavy thread.

The glass was poured into a mold, I guess, that made the base and bowl, which are in one piece; the glass is thick and clean, with icy lights in it. The base is a simply fluted, hollow skirt; stands on the table; is solidified in a narrowing, a round inch of pure thick glass, then hollows again, a globe about half flattened, the globe-glass thick, too; and this holds oil, whose silver line I see, a little less than half down the globe, its level a very little—for the base is not quite true—tilted against the axis of the base.

This 'oil' is not at all oleaginous, but thin, brittle, rusty feeling, and sharp; taken and rubbed between forefinger and thumb, it so cleanses their grain that it sharpens their mutual touch to a new coin edge, or the russet nipple of a breast erected in cold; and the odor is clean, cheerful and humble, less

---

5. Agee, *Let Us Now Praise Famous Men*, p. xiv.

alive by far than that of gasoline, even a shade watery: and a subtle sweating of this oil is on the upward surface of the globe, as if it stood through the glass, and as if the glass were a pitcher of cool water in a hot room. I do not understand nor try to deduce this, but I like it; I run my thumb upon it and smell of my thumb, and smooth away its streaked print on the glass; and I wipe my thumb and forefinger dry against my pants, and keep on looking.

In this globe, and in this oil that is clear and light as water, and reminding me of creatures and things once alive which I have seen suspended in jars in a frightening smell of alcohol—serpents, tapeworms, toads, embryons, all drained one tan pallor of absolute death; and also of the serene, scarved flowers in untroubled wombs (and pale-tanned too, flaccid, and in the stench of exhibited death, those children of fury, patience and love which stand in the dishonors of accepted fame, and of the murdering of museum staring); in this globe like a thought, a dream, the future, slumbers the stout-weft strap of wick, and up this wick is drawn the oil, toward heat; through a tight, flat tube of tin, and through a little slotted smile of golden tin, and there ends fledged with flame, in the flue; the flame, a clean, fanged fan:

I:

The light in this room is of a lamp. Its flame in the glass is of the dry, silent and famished delicateness of the latest lateness of the night, and of such ultimate, such holiness of silence and peace that all on earth and within extremest remembrance seems suspended upon it in perfection as upon reflective water: and I feel that if I can by utter quietness succeed in not disturbing this silence, in not so much as touching this plain of water, I can tell you anything within realm of God, whatsoever it may be, that I wish to tell you, and that what so ever it may be, you will not be able to help but understand it.

It is the middle and pure height and whole of summer and a summer night, the held breath, of a planet's year; high shored sleeps the crested tide: what day of the month I do not know, which day of the week I am not sure, far less what hour of the night. The dollar watch I bought a few days ago, as also from time to time I buy a ten cent automatic pencil, and use it little before I lose all track of it, ran out at seventeen minutes past ten the day before yesterday morning, and time by machine measure was over for me at that hour, and is a monument. I know of the lateness and full height by the quietly starved brightness of my senses, which some while ago made the transition past any need for sleep without taking much notice of it, as, in the late darkness, the long accustomed liner loses the last black headland, and quietly commends her forehead upon the long open home of the sea: and by a quality in the night itself not truly apparent to any one of the senses, yet, by some indirection, to every sense in one, of a most complete and universally shared withdrawal to source, like that brief paralysis which enchants a city while wreaths are laid to a cenotaph, and, muted, a bugle's inscription shines, in the tightening just before the relaxation of this swarmed, still, silence, till, hats-on, gears grow and smooth, the lifted foot arrested in the stopshot completes its step, once more the white mane of the drayhorse flurrs in the sunny air: now vibrates all that vast stone hive: into resumption, reassumption, of casual living.

And it is in these terms I would tell you, at all leisure, and in all detail, whatever there is to tell: of where I am; of what I perceive.

Lamplight here, and lone, late: the odor is of pine that has stood shut on itself through the heat of a hot day: the odor of an attic at white noon: and all of the walls save that surface within immediate touch of the lamp, where like water slept in lantern light the grain is so sharply discerned in its retirement beyond the sleep of the standing shape of pines, and the pastings and pinnings of sad ornaments, are a most dim scarce-color of grayed silver breathed in yellow red which is the hue and haze in the room; and above me, black: where, beyond bones of rafters underlighted, a stomach sucked against the spine in fear, the roof draws up its peak: and this is a frightening dark, which has again to do with an attic: for it is the darkness that stands just up the stairs, sucking itself out of sight of the light, from an attic door left ajar, noticed on your way to bed, and remembered after you are there: so that I muse what not quite creatures and what not quite forms are suspended like bats above and behind my bent head; and how far down in their clustered weight they are stealing while my eyes are on this writing; and how skillfully swiftly they suck themselves back upward into the dark when I turn my head: and above all, why they should be so coy, who, with one slather of cold membranes drooping, could slap out light and have me: and who own me since all time's beginning. Yet this mere fact of thinking holds them at distance, as crucifixes demons, so lightly and well that I am almost persuaded of being merely fanciful; in which exercise I would be theirs most profoundly beyond rescue, not knowing, and not fearing, I am theirs.

Above that shell and carapace, more frail against heaven than fragilest membrane of glass, nothing, straight to the terrific stars: whereof all heaven is chalky; and of whom the nearest is so wild a reach my substance wilts to think on: and we, this Arctic flower snow-rooted, last matchflame guarded on a windy plain, are seated among these stars alone: none to turn to, none to make us known; a little country settlement so deep, so lost in shelve and shade of dew, no one so much as laughs at us. Small wonder how pitiably we love our home, cling in her skirts at night, rejoice in her wide star-seducing smile, when every star strikes us sick with the fright: do we really exist at all?

> This world is not my home, I'm, only passing through,
> My treasures and my hopes, are, all, beyond the sky,

I've many, friends, and kindreds, that's gone, along before,
And I can't, feel, at home, in this world, any, more.

And thus, too, these families, not otherwise than with every family in the earth, how each, apart, how inconceivably lonely, sorrowful, and remote! Not one other on earth, nor in any dream, that can care so much what comes to them, so that even as they sit at the lamp and eat their supper, the joke they are laughing at could not be so funny to anyone else; and the littlest child who stands on the bench solemnly, with food glittering all over his cheeks in the lamplight, this littlest child I speak of is not there, he is of another family, and it is a different woman who wipes the food from his cheeks and takes his weight upon her thighs and against her body and who feeds him, and lets his weight slacken against her in his heavying sleep; and the man who puts another soaked cloth to the skin cancer on his shoulder; it is his wife who is looking on, and his child who lies sunken along the floor with his soft mouth broad open and his nakedness up like a rolling dog, asleep: and the people next up the road cannot care in the same way, not for any of it: for they are absorbed upon themselves: and the negroes down beyond the spring have drawn their shutters tight, the lamplight pulses like wounded honey through the seams into the soft night, and there is laughter: but nobody else cares. All over the whole round earth and in the settlements, the towns, and the great iron stones of cities, people are drawn inward within their little shells of rooms, and are to be seen in their wondrous and pitiful actions through the surfaces of their lighted windows by thousands, by millions, little golden aquariums, in chairs, reading, setting tables, sewing, playing cards, not talking, talking, laughing inaudibly, mixing drinks, at radio dials, eating, in shirt-sleeves, carefully dressed, courting, teasing, loving, seducing, undressing, leaving the room empty in its empty light, alone and writing a letter urgently, in couples married, in separate chairs, in family parties, in gay parties, preparing for bed, preparing for sleep: and none can care, beyond that room; and none can be cared for, by any beyond that room: and it is small wonder they are drawn together so cowardly close, and small wonder in what dry agony of despair a mother may fasten her talons and her vampire mouth upon the soul of her struggling son and drain him empty, light as a locust shell: and wonder only that an age that has borne its children and must lose and has lost them, and lost life, can bear further living; but so it is:

A man and a woman are drawn together upon a bed and there is a child and there are children:

First they are mouths, then they become auxiliary instruments of labor: later they are drawn away, and become the fathers and mothers of children, who shall become the fathers and mothers of children:

Their father and their mother before them were, in their time, the children each of different parents, who in their time were each children of parents:

This has been happening for a long while: its beginning was before stars: It will continue for a long while: no one knows where it will end:

While they are still drawn together within one shelter around the center of their parents, these children and their parents together compose a family:

This family must take care of itself; it has no mother or father: there is no other shelter, nor resource, nor any love, interest, sustaining strength or comfort, so near, nor can anything happy or sorrowful that comes to anyone in this family possibly mean to those outside it what it means to those within it: but it is, as I have told, inconceivably lonely, drawn upon itself as tramps are drawn round a fire in the cruelest weather; and thus and in such loneliness it exists among other families, each of which is no less lonely, nor any less without help or comfort, and is likewise drawn in upon itself:

Such a family lasts, for a while: the children are held to a magnetic center:

Then in time the magnetism weakens, both of itself in its tiredness of aging and sorrow, and against the strength of the growth of each child, and against the strength of pulls from outside, and one by one the children are drawn away:

Of those that are drawn away, each is drawn elsewhere toward another: once more a man and a woman, in a loneliness they are not liable at that time to notice, are tightened together upon a bed: and another family has begun:

Moreover, these flexions are taking place every where, like a simultaneous motion of all the waves of the water of the world: and these are the classic patterns, and this is the weaving, of human living: of whose fabric each individual is a part: and of all parts of this fabric let this be borne in mind:

Each is intimately connected with the bottom and the extremest reach of time:

Each is composed of substances identical with the substance of all that surrounds him, both the common objects of his disregard, and the hot centers of stars:

All that each person is, and experiences, and shall never experience, in body and in mind, all these things are differing expressions of himself and of one root, and are identical: and not one of these things nor one of these persons is ever quite to be duplicated, nor replaced, nor has it ever quite had precedent: but each is a new and incommunicably tender life, wounded in every breath, and almost as hardly killed as easily wounded: sustaining, for a while, without defense, the enormous assaults of the universe:

So that how it can be that a stone, a plant, a star, can take on the burden of being; and how it is that a child can take on the burden of breathing; and how through so long a continuation and cumulation of the burden of each moment one on another, does any creature bear to exist, and not break utterly to fragments of nothing: these are matters too dreadful and fortitudes too gigantic to meditate long and not forever to worship:

Just a half-inch beyond the surface of this wall I face is another surface, one of the four walls which square and collaborate against the air another room, and there lie sleeping, on two iron beds and on pallets on the floor, a man and his wife and her sister, and four children, a girl, and three harmed boys. Their lamp is out, their light is done this long while, and not in a long while has any one of them made a sound. Not even straining, can I hear their breathing: rather, I have a not quite sensuous knowledge of a sort of suspiration, less breathing than that indiscernible drawing-in of heaven by which plants live, and thus I know they rest and the profundity of their tiredness, as if I were in each one of these seven bodies whose sleeping I can almost touch through this wall, and which in the darkness I so clearly see, with the whole touch and weight of my body: George's red body, already a little squat with the burden of thirty years, knotted like oakwood, in its clean white cotton summer union suit that it sleeps in; and his wife's beside him, Annie Mae's, slender, and sharpened through with bone, that ten years past must have had such beauty, and now is veined at the breast, and the skin of the breast translucent, delicately shriveled, and blue, and she and her sister Emma are in plain cotton shifts; and the body of Emma, her sister, strong, thick and wide, tall, the breasts set wide and high, shallow and round, not yet those of a full woman, the legs long thick and strong; and Louise's green lovely body, the dim breasts faintly blown between wide shoulders, the thighs long, clean and light in their line from hip to knee, the head back steep and silent to the floor, the chin highest, and the white shift up to her divided thighs; and the tough little body of Junior, hardskinned and gritty, the feet crusted with sores; and the milky and strengthless littler body of Burt whose veins are so bright in his temples; and the shriveled and hopeless, most pitiful body of Squinchy, which will not grow:

But it is not only their bodies but their postures that I know, and their weight on the bed or on the floor, so that I lie down inside each one as if exhausted in a bed, and I become not my own shape and weight and self, but that of each of them, the whole of it, sunken in sleep like stones; so that I know almost the dreams they will not remember, and the soul and body of each of these seven, and of all of them together in this room in sleep, as if they were music I were hearing, each voice in relation to all the others, and all audible, singly, and as one organism, and a music that cannot be communicated: and thus they lie in this silence, and rest.

42

Richard Wright (1908–1960)
from *The God That Failed*

Richard Wright's most famous autobiography, *Black Boy* (1945), gives a tense and inspiring account of his early life, and yet it is incomplete and misleading in several ways. On one hand, it exaggerates some of the horrors of his southern childhood; on the other, it omits references to some white people who befriended him, to his own stature among groups of black youth, and to the educational advantages he had from people he knew and members of his own family who were school teachers.[1] Moreover, by ending as it does with his departure for the North (and being published just five years after his great literary success *Native Son*, in 1940), *Black Boy* conveys the over-simple message that once he had left the South he was less oppressed and his genius bloomed.[2]

A fuller picture of his life and sense of his range as an autobiographer comes from reading his accounts of the rest of his early years which were originally written for a volume called *The Horror and the Glory*, which was to be published with *Black Boy*, the two together to be entitled *American Hunger* or *Black Hunger*. When *Black Boy* was published separately, Wright went ahead and published many portions of *The Horror and the Glory* in magazines and other places.

The first three chapters, parts of which appeared in *Mademoiselle*, dealt with the early experiences in Chicago. His first job was in a delicatessen where he could not believe that the owner would trust him and that white waitresses would be friendly. Yet when he worked as a janitor in a hospital, the doctors refused to recognize his intelligence. The last three chapters describe his experiences with the Communist Party. These were first told in the August, 1944, *Atlantic Monthly* ("I Tried to Be a Communist"); then retold in a collection of essays by Wright and five other European and American ex-communists, *The God That Failed*, edited by Richard Crossman and published by Harper and Row (Wright's publisher) in 1949.

1. For a summary of the exaggerations and omissions in *Black Boy*, see David L. Dudley, *My Father's Shadow: Intergenerational Conflict in African American Men's Autobiography* (Philadelphia: Univ. of Pennsylvania Press, 1991), pp. 113–14.
2. Michel Fabre, "Afterword," to Richard Wright, *American Hunger* (New York: Harper and Row, 1977), pp. 139–40.

Today *The God That Failed* is almost forgotten, but in its time it was a cornerstone in the building of an anti-communist, intellectual left. Other contributors were Arthur Koestler, Ignazio Silone, André Gide, Louis Fischer, and Stephen Spender—men who were not turncoats or heroes of the right like Whitaker Chambers. The book was assigned in many college courses and promoted Wright as an intellectual as well as a novelist.

The selection here is the last quarter of Wright's essay in *The God That Failed.* He has already bristled under doctrinaire Party orders and had the humiliating experience of going to New York for a Party writers' conference but not being given a hotel reservation because he was a Negro. So he has announced his resignation, but he continues to be harassed, as represented here. His experience makes an interesting comparison with the chapters on "the Brotherhood" in Ralph Ellison's *Invisible Man.*

Yet disillusionment with the Communist Party is not the only message in *American Hunger.* One may also sense Wright's despair with all America. Because of its fear, the nation, too, fails to recognize someone who wants to help it.

In 1947, Wright established permanent residence in Paris and went on to become a leader in organizations of Third World, anti-colonial intellectuals, such as the Bandung, Indonesia, Conference of 1955. He died of a heart attack in Paris in 1960.

The selection below is taken from *The God That Failed,* ed. Richard Crossman (New York: Harper and Row, 1947). The two major biographies of Wright are Constance Webb, *Richard Wright* (New York: G. P. Putnam, 1968), and Michel Fabre, *The Unfinished Quest of Richard Wright* (New York: William Morrow, 1973).

I was transferred by the relief authorities from the South Side Boys' Club to the Federal Negro Theater to work as a publicity agent. There were days when I was acutely hungry for the incessant analyses that went on among the comrades,[3] but whenever I heard news of the Party's inner life, it was of charges and countercharges, reprisals and counter-reprisals.

The Federal Negro Theater, for which I was doing publicity, had run a series of ordinary plays, all of which had been revamped to "Negro style," with jungle scenes, spirituals, and all. For example, the skinny white woman who directed it, an elderly missionary type, would take a play whose characters were white, whose theme dealt with the Middle Ages, and recast it in terms of Southern Negro life with overtones of African backgrounds. Contemporary plays dealing realistically with Negro life were spurned as being controversial. There were about forty Negro actors and actresses in the theater, lolling about, yearning, disgruntled.

What a waste of talent, I thought. Here was an opportunity for the production of a worth-while Negro drama and no one was aware of it. I studied the situation, then laid the matter before white friends of mine who

---

3. "Comrades": Communist Party members. [R. F. S.]

held influential positions in the Works Progress Administration. I asked them to replace the white woman—including her quaint aesthetic notions—with someone who knew the Negro and the theater. They promised me that they would act.

Within a month the white woman director had been transferred. We moved from the South Side to the Loop and were housed in a first-rate theater. I successfully recommended Charles DeSheim, a talented Jew, as director. DeSheim and I held long talks during which I outlined what I thought could be accomplished. I urged that our first offering should be a bill of three one-act plays, including Paul Green's *Hymn to the Rising Sun,* a grim, poetical, powerful one-acter dealing with chain-gang conditions in the South.

I was happy. At last I was in a position to make suggestions and have them acted upon. I was convinced that we had a rare chance to build a genuine Negro theater. I convoked a meeting and introduced DeSheim to the Negro company, telling them that he was a man who knew the theater, who would lead them toward serious dramatics. DeSheim made a speech wherein he said that he was not at the theater to direct it, but to help the Negroes to direct it. He spoke so simply and eloquently that they rose and applauded him.

I then proudly passed out copies of Paul Green's *Hymn to the Rising Sun* to all members of the company. DeSheim assigned reading parts. I sat down to enjoy adult Negro dramatics. But something went wrong. The Negroes stammered and faltered in their lines. Finally they stopped reading altogether. DeSheim looked frightened. One of the Negro actors rose.

"Mr. DeSheim," he began, "we think this play is indecent. We don't want to act in a play like this before the American public. I don't think any such conditions exist in the South. I lived in the South and I never saw any chain gangs. Mr. DeSheim, we want a play that will make the public love us."

"What kind of play do you want?" DeSheim asked them.

They did not know. I went to the office and looked up their records and found that most of them had spent their lives playing cheap vaudeville because the legitimate theater was barred to them, and now it turned out they wanted none of the legitimate theater, that they were scared spitless at the prospects of appearing in a play that the public might not like, even though they did not understand that public and had no way of determining its likes or dislikes.

I felt—but only temporarily—that perhaps the whites were right, that Negroes were children and would never grow up. DeSheim informed the company that he would produce any play they liked, and they sat like frightened mice, possessing no words to make known their vague desires.

When I arrived at the theater a few mornings later, I was horrified to find that the company had drawn up a petition demanding the ousting of DeSheim. I was asked to sign the petition and I refused.

"Don't you know your friends?" I asked them.

They glared at me. I called DeSheim to the theater and we went into a frantic conference.

"What must I do?" he asked.

"Take them into your confidence," I said. "Let them know that it is their right to petition for a redress of their grievances."

DeSheim thought my advice sound and, accordingly, he assembled the company and told them that they had a right to petition against him if they wanted to, but that he thought any misunderstandings that existed could be settled smoothly.

"Who told you that we were getting up a petition?" a black man demanded.

DeSheim looked at me and stammered wordlessly.

"There's an Uncle Tom in the theater!" a black girl yelled.

After the meeting a delegation of Negro men came to my office and took out their pocketknives and flashed them in my face.

"You get the hell off this job before we cut your bellybutton out!" they said.

I telephoned my white friends in the Works Progress Administration: "Transfer me at once to another job, or I'll be murdered."

Within twenty-four hours DeSheim and I were given our papers. We shook hands and went our separate ways.

I was transferred to a white experimental theatrical company as a publicity agent and I resolved to keep my ideas to myself, or, better, to write them down and not attempt to translate them into reality.

★

One evening a group of Negro Communists called at my home and asked to speak to me in strict secrecy. I took them into my room and locked the door.

"Dick," they began abruptly, "the Party wants you to attend a meeting Sunday."

"Why?" I asked. "I'm no longer a member."

"That's all right. They want you to be present," they said.

"Communists don't speak to me on the street," I said. "Now, why do you want me at a meeting?"

They hedged. They did not want to tell me.

"If you can't tell me, then I can't come," I said.

They whispered among themselves and finally decided to take me into their confidence.

"Dick, Ross is going to be tried," they said.

"For what?"

They recited a long list of political offenses of which they alleged that he was guilty.

"But what has that got to do with me?"

"If you come, you'll find out," they said.

"I'm not that naïve," I said. I was suspicious now. Were they trying to lure me to a trial and expel me? "This trial might turn out to be mine."

They swore that they had no intention of placing me on trial, that the Party merely wanted me to observe Ross's trial so that I might learn what happened to "enemies of the working class."

As they talked, my old love of witnessing something new came over me. I wanted to see this trial, but I did not want to risk being placed on trial myself.

"Listen," I told them. "I'm not guilty of Nealson's charges. If I showed up at this trial, it would seem that I am."

"No, it won't. Please come."

"All right. But, listen. If I'm tricked, I'll fight. You hear? I don't trust Nealson. I'm not a politician and I cannot anticipate all the funny moves of a man who spends his waking hours plotting."

Ross's trial took place that following Sunday afternoon. Comrades stood inconspicuously on guard about the meeting hall, at the doors, down the street, and along the hallways. When I appeared, I was ushered in quickly. I was tense. It was a rule that once you had entered a meeting of this kind you could not leave until the meeting was over; it was feared that you might go to the police and denounce them all.

Ross, the accused, sat alone at a table in the front of the hall, his face distraught. I felt sorry for him; yet I could not escape feeling that he enjoyed this. For him, this was perhaps the highlight of an otherwise bleak existence.

In trying to grasp why Communists hated intellectuals, my mind was led back again to the accounts I had read of the Russian Revolution. There had existed in Old Russia millions of poor, ignorant people who were exploited by a few educated, arrogant noblemen, and it became natural for the Russian Communists to associate betrayal with intellectualism. But there existed in the Western world an element that baffled and frightened the Communist Party: the prevalence of self-achieved literacy. Even a Negro, entrapped by ignorance and exploitation—as I had been—could, if he had the will and the love for it, learn to read and understand the world in which he lived. And it was these people that the Communists could not understand.

The trial began in a quiet, informal manner. The comrades acted like a group of neighbors sitting in judgment upon one of their kind who had stolen a chicken. Anybody could ask and get the floor. There was absolute freedom of speech. Yet the meeting had an amazingly formal structure of its own, a structure that went as deep as the desire of men to live together.

A member of the Central Committee of the Communist Party rose and gave a description of the world situation. He spoke without emotion and piled up hard facts. He painted a horrible but masterful picture of Fascism's aggression in Germany, Italy, and Japan.

I accepted the reason why the trial began in this manner. It was imperative that here be postulated against what or whom Ross's crimes had been committed. Therefore there had to be established in the minds of all present a vivid picture of mankind under oppression. And it was a true picture. Perhaps no organization on earth, save the Communist Party, possesses so detailed a knowledge of how workers lived, for its sources of information stemmed directly from the workers themselves.

The next speaker discussed the role of the Soviet Union as the world's lone workers' state—how the Soviet Union was hemmed in by enemies, how the Soviet Union was trying to industrialize itself, what sacrifices it was making to help workers of the world to steer a path toward peace through the idea of collective security.

The facts presented so far were as true as any facts could be in this uncertain world. Yet not one word had been said of the accused, who sat listening like any other member. The time had not yet come to include him and his crimes in this picture of global struggle. An absolute had first to be established in the minds of the comrades so that they could measure the success or failure of their deeds by it.

Finally a speaker came forward and spoke of Chicago's South Side, its Negro population, their suffering and handicaps, linking all that also to the world struggle. Then still another speaker followed and described the tasks of the Communist Party of the South Side. At last, the world, the national, and the local pictures had been fused into one overwhelming drama of moral struggle in which everybody in the hall was participating. This presentation had lasted for more than three hours, but it had enthroned a new sense of reality in the hearts of those present, a sense of man on earth. With the exception of the church and its myths and legends, there was no agency in the world so capable of making men feel the earth and the people upon it as the Communist Party.

Toward evening the direct charges against Ross were made, not by the leaders of the Party, but by Ross's friends, those who knew him best! It was crushing. Ross wilted. His emotions could not withstand the weight of the moral pressure. No one was terrorized into giving information against him. They gave it willingly, citing dates, conversations, scenes. The black mass of Ross's wrongdoing emerged slowly and irrefutably.

The moment came for Ross to defend himself. I had been told that he had arranged for friends to testify in his behalf, but he called upon no one. He stood, trembling; he tried to talk and his words would not come. The hall was as still as death. Guilt was written in every pore of his black skin. His hands shook. He held on to the edge of the table to keep on his feet. His personality, his sense of himself, had been obliterated. Yet he could not have been so humbled unless he had shared and accepted the vision that had crushed him, the common vision that bound us all together.

"Comrades," he said in a low, charged voice, "I'm guilty of all the charges, all of them."

His voice broke in a sob. No one prodded him. No one tortured him. No one threatened him. He was free to go out of the hall and never see another Communist. But he did not want to. He could not. The vision of a communal world had sunk down into his soul and it would never leave him until life left him. He talked on, outlining how he had erred, how he would reform.

I knew, as I sat there, that there were many people who thought they knew life who had been skeptical of the Moscow trials. But they could not have been skeptical had they witnessed this astonishing trial. Ross had not been doped; he had been awakened. It was not a fear of the Communist Party that had made him confess, but a fear of the punishment that he would exact of himself that made him tell of his wrongdoings. The Communists had talked to him until they had given him new eyes with which to see his own crime. And then they sat back and listened to him tell how he had erred. He was one with all the members there, regardless of race or color; his heart was theirs and their hearts were his; and when a man reaches that state of kinship with others, that degree of oneness, or when a trial has made him kin after he has been sundered from them by wrongdoing, then he must rise and say, out of a sense of the deepest morality in the world: "I'm guilty. Forgive me."

This, to me, was a spectacle of glory; and yet, because it had condemned me, because it was blind and ignorant, I felt that it was a spectacle of horror. The blindness of their limited lives—lives truncated and impoverished by the oppression they had suffered long before they had ever heard of Communism—made them think that I was with their enemies. American life had so corrupted their consciousness that they were unable to recognize their friends when they saw them. I knew that if they had held state power I should have been declared guilty of treason and my execution would have followed. And I knew that they felt, with all the strength of their black blindness, that they were right.

I could not stay until the end. I was anxious to get out of the hall and into the streets and shake free from the gigantic tension that had hold of me. I rose and went to the door; a comrade shook his head, warning me that I could not leave until the trial had ended.

"You can't leave now," he said.

"I'm going out of here," I said, my anger making my voice louder than I intended.

We glared at each other. Another comrade came running up. I stepped forward. The comrade who had rushed up gave the signal for me to be allowed to leave. They did not want violence, and neither did I. They stepped aside.

I went into the dark Chicago streets and walked home through the cold, filled with a sense of sadness. Once again I told myself that I must learn to stand alone. I did not feel so wounded by their rejection of me that I wanted to spend my days bleating about what they had done. Perhaps what I had already learned to feel in my childhood saved me from that futile path. I lay in bed that night and said to myself: "I'll be for them, even though they are not for me."

★

From the Federal Experimental Theater I was transferred to the Federal Writers' Project, and I tried to earn my bread by writing guidebooks. Many of the writers on the project were members of the Communist Party and they kept their revolutionary vows that restrained them from speaking to "traitors of the working class." I sat beside them in the office, ate next to them in restaurants, and rode up and down in the elevators with them, but they always looked straight ahead, wordlessly.

After working on the project for a few months, I was made acting supervisor of essays and straightway I ran into political difficulties. One morning the administrator of the project called me into his office.

"Wright, who are your friends on this project?" he asked.

"I don't know," I said. "Why?"

"Well, you ought to find out soon," he said.

"What do you mean?"

"Some people are asking for your removal on the ground that you are incompetent," he said.

"Who are they?"

He named several of my erstwhile comrades. Yes, it had come to that. They were trying to take the bread out of my mouth.

"What do you propose to do about their complaints?" I asked.

"Nothing," he said, laughing. "I think I understand what's happening here. I'm not going to let them drive you off this job."

I thanked him and rose to go to the door. Something in his words had not sounded right. I turned and faced him.

"*This* job?" I repeated. "What do you mean?"

"You mean to say that you don't know?" he asked.

"Know what? What are you talking about?"

"Why did you leave the Federal Negro Theater?"

"I had trouble there. They drove me off the job, the Negroes did."

"And you don't think that they had any encouragement?" he asked me ironically.

I sat again. This was deadly. I gaped at him.

"You needn't fear here," he said. "You work, write."

"It's hard to believe that," I murmured.

"Forget it," he said.

But the worst was yet to come. One day at noon I closed my desk and went down in the elevator. When I reached the first floor of the building, I saw a picket line moving to and fro in the streets. Many of the men and women carrying placards were old friends of mine, and they were chanting for higher wages for Works Progress Administration artists and writers. It was not the kind of picket line that one was not supposed to cross, and as I started away from the door I heard my name shouted:

"There's Wright, that goddamn Trotskyite!"

"We know you, you—!"

"Wright's a traitor!"

For a moment it seemed that I ceased to live. I had now reached that point where I was cursed aloud in the busy streets of America's second-largest city. It shook me as nothing else had.

Days passed. I continued on my job, where I functioned as the shop chairman of the union which I had helped to organize, though my election as shop chairman had been bitterly opposed by the Party. In their efforts to nullify my influence in the union, my old comrades were willing to kill the union itself.

As May Day of 1936 approached, it was voted by the union membership that we should march in the public procession. On the morning of May Day I received printed instructions as to the time and place where our union contingent would assemble to join the parade. At noon, I hurried to the spot and found that the parade was already in progress. In vain I searched for the banners of my union local. Where were they? I went up and down the streets, asking for the location of my local.

"Oh, that local's gone fifteen minutes ago," a Negro told me. "If you're going to march, you'd better fall in somewhere."

I thanked him and walked through the milling crowds. Suddenly I heard my name called. I turned. To my left was the Communist Party's South Side section, lined up and ready to march.

"Come here!" an old Party friend called to me.

I walked over to him.

"Aren't you marching today?" he asked me.

"I missed my union local," I told him.

"What the hell," he said. "March with us."

"I don't know," I said, remembering my last visit to the headquarters of the Party, and my status as an "enemy."

"This is May Day," he said. "Get into the ranks."

"You know the trouble I've had," I said.

"That's nothing," he said. "Everybody's marching today."

"I don't think I'd better," I said, shaking my head.

"Are you scared?" he asked. "This is *May Day*."

He caught my right arm and pulled me into line beside him. I stood talking to him, asking about his work, about common friends.

"Get out of our ranks!" a voice barked.

I turned. A white Communist, a leader of the district of the Communist Party, Cy Perry, a slender, close-cropped fellow, stood glaring at me.

"I—It's May Day and I want to march," I said.

"Get out!" he shouted.

"I was invited here," I said.

I turned to the Negro Communist who had invited me into the ranks. I did not want public violence. I looked at my friend. He turned his eyes away. He was afraid. I did not know what to do.

"You asked me to march here," I said to him.

He did not answer.

"Tell him that you did invite me," I said, pulling his sleeve.

"I'm asking you for the last time to get out of our ranks!" Cy Perry shouted.

I did not move. I had intended to, but I was beset by so many impulses that I could not act. Another white Communist came to assist Perry. Perry caught hold of my collar and pulled at me. I resisted. They held me fast. I struggled to free myself.

"Turn me loose!" I said.

Hands lifted me bodily from the sidewalk; I felt myself being pitched headlong through the air. I saved myself from landing on my head by cluthing a curbstone with my hands. Slowly I rose and stood. Perry and his assistant were glaring at me. The rows of white and black Communists were looking at me with cold eyes of nonrecognition. I could not quite believe what had happened, even though my hands were smarting and bleeding. I had suffered a public, physical assault by two white Communists with black Communists looking on. I could not move from the spot. I was empty of any idea about what to do. But I did not feel belligerent. I had outgrown my childhood.

Suddenly, the vast ranks of the Communist Party began to move. Scarlet banners with the hammer and sickle emblem of world revolution were lifted, and they fluttered in the May breeze. Drums beat. Voices were chanting. The tramp of many feet shook the earth. A long line of set-faced men and women, white and black, flowed past me.

I followed the procession to the Loop and went into Grant Park Plaza and sat upon a bench. I was not thinking; I could not think. But an objectivity of vision was being born within me. A surging sweep of many odds and ends came together and formed an attitude, a perspective. "They're blind," I said to myself. "Their enemies have blinded them with too much oppression." I lit a cigarette and I heard a song floating over the sunlit air:

Arise, you pris'ners of starvation!

I remembered the stories I had written, the stories in which I had assigned a role of honor and glory to the Communist Party, and I was glad that they were down in black and white, were finished. For I knew in my heart that I should never be able to write that way again, should never be able to feel with that simple sharpness about life, should never again express such passionate hope, should never again make so total a commitment of faith.

A better world's in birth. . . .

The procession still passed. Banners still floated. Voices of hope still chanted.

I headed toward home alone, really alone now, telling myself that in all the sprawling immensity of our mighty continent the least-known factor of living was the human heart, the least-sought goal of being was a way to live a human life. Perhaps, I thought, out of my tortured feelings I could fling a spark into this darkness. I would try, not because I wanted to, but because I felt that I had to if I were to live at all.

I would hurl words into this darkness and wait for an echo; and if an echo sounded, no matter how faintly, I would send other words to tell, to march, to fight, to create a sense of the hunger for life that gnaws in us all, to keep alive in our hearts a sense of the inexpressibly human.

43

Dorothy Day (1897–1980)
Having a Baby and *Love Overflows*

Although she has not been canonized by the Church, Dorothy Day has been called a saint by many of her admirers; and as with saints, her behavior was often puzzling to her friends. As the following two chapters from *The Long Loneliness* (1952) illustrate, her behavior was also not the kind traditional hagiographers celebrated for imitation by the young. Yet, as Day tells it, it has a profound consistency.

The early chapters of *The Long Loneliness* tell of her childhood in Berkeley and Oakland, California (her father was a sports editor of a San Francisco paper), ending with the great earthquake of 1905 and her memories of the compassion among the victims. After the quake the family moved to Chicago, where Day showed early promise as a writer. She worked her way through the University of Illinois at Champaign-Urbana, and then wrote for socialist papers in New York. She supported numerous radical causes and was arrested in a women's rights demonstration in Washington, D.C. In the 1920s, she divided her time between Greenwich Village and a beach house on Staten Island which she shared with Forster Batterham, a British biologist and anarchist who was her common-law husband. She was extremely happy, sexually fulfilled, and artistically productive.

Unlike many religious conversions, therefore, hers did not come about from misery and dissatisfaction. Nor did it lead to a rejection of her political past. She remained an anarchist, pacifist, and advocate of the homeless and oppressed. In fact, the Catholic Worker Houses of Hospitality which she founded in the 1930s with her new friend Peter Maurin (Forster Batterham left her when she joined the Church) and which she wrote about in her last volume of autobiography, *Loaves and Fishes* (1963), became famous examples of direct action.

All these changes and continuities in her life seem epitomized in these two chapters, which tell of her overwhelming joy in the birth of her daughter, her decision to have her baptized a Catholic, and her own baptism a year later (in the summer of 1928). Her autobiography is a unique combination of tradition and change, social commitment and religious piety.

Our source is *The Long Loneliness* (New York: Harper and Row, 1981). The definitive biography of Day is by William Miller, *Dorothy Day: A Biography* (San Francisco: Harper and Row, 1982). An excellent study of *The Long Loneliness* and her other autobiographies is by June O'Connor, "Dorothy Day as Autobiographer," *Religion* 20 (1990): 275–95.

Having a Baby

I was surprised that I found myself beginning to pray daily. I could not get down on my knees, but I could pray while I was walking. If I got down on my knees I thought, "Do I really believe? Whom am I praying to?" A terrible doubt came over me, and a sense of shame, and I wondered if I was praying because I was lonely, because I was unhappy.

But when I walked to the village for the mail, I found myself praying again, holding in my pocket the rosary that Mary Gordon gave me in New Orleans some years before. Maybe I did not say it correctly but I kept on saying it because it made me happy.

Then I thought suddenly, scornfully, "Here you are in a stupor of content. You are biological. Like a cow. Prayer with you is like the opiate of the people." And over and over again in my mind that phrase was repeated jeeringly, "Religion is the opiate of the people."

"But," I reasoned with myself, "I am praying because I am happy, not because I am unhappy. I did not turn to God in unhappiness, in grief, in despair—to get consolation, to get something from Him."

And encouraged that I was praying because I wanted to thank Him, I went on praying. No matter how dull the day, how long the walk seemed, if I felt sluggish at the beginning of the walk, the words I had been saying insinuated themselves into my heart before I had finished, so that on the trip back I neither prayed nor thought but was filled with exultation.

Along the beach I found it appropriate to say the *Te Deum*. When I worked about the house, I found myself addressing the Blessed Virgin and turning toward her statue.

It is so hard to say how this delight in prayer grew on me. The year before, I was saying as I planted seeds in the garden, "I *must* believe in these seeds, that they fall into the earth and grow into flowers and radishes and beans. It is a miracle to me because I do not understand it. Neither do naturalists understand it. The very fact that they use glib technical phrases does not make it any less of a miracle, and a miracle we all accept. Then why not accept God's mysteries?"

I began to go to Mass regularly on Sunday mornings.

When Freda went into town, I was alone. Forster was in the city all week, only coming out week ends. I finished the writing I was doing and felt at loose ends, thinking enviously of my friends going gaily about the city, about their work, with plenty of companionship.

The fact that I felt restless was a very good reason to stay on the beach and content myself with my life as a sybaritic anchorite. For how could I be a true anchorite with such luxuries as the morning paper, groceries delivered to the door, a beach to walk on, and the water to feast my eyes on? And then the fresh fish and clams, mushrooms, Jerusalem artichokes, such delicacies right at hand. I invited Lefty to supper and discussed with him the painting of the house. I read Dickens every evening.

In spite of my desire for a sociable week in town, in spite of a desire to pick up and flee from my solitude, I took joy in thinking of the idiocy of the pleasures I would indulge in if I were there. Cocktail parties, with prohibition drinks, dinners, the conversation or lack of it, dancing in a smoky crowded room when one might be walking on the beach, the dull, restless cogitations which come after dissipating one's energies—things which struck me with renewed force every time I spent days in the city. My virtuous resolutions to indulge in such pleasure no more were succeeded by a hideous depression when neither my new-found sense of religion, my family life, my work nor my surroundings were sufficient to console me. I thought of death and was overwhelmed by the terror and the blackness of both life and death. And I longed for a church near at hand where I could go and lift up my soul.

It was pleasant rowing about in the calm bay with Forster. The oyster boats were all out, and far on the horizon, off Sandy Hook, there was a four-masted vessel. I had the curious delusion that several huge holes had been stove in her side, through which you could see the blue sky. The other vessels seemed sailing in the air, quite indifferent to the horizon on which they should properly have been resting. Forster tried to explain to me scientific facts about mirages and atmospheric conditions, and, on the other hand, I pointed out to him how our senses lie to us.

But it was impossible to talk about religion or faith to him. A wall immediately separated us. The very love of nature, and the study of her secrets which was bringing me to faith, cut Forster off from religion.

I had known Forster a long time before we contracted our common-law relationship, and I have always felt that it was life with him that brought me natural happiness, that brought me to God.

His ardent love of creation brought me to the Creator of all things. But when I cried out to him, "How can there be no God, when there are all these beautiful things," he turned from me uneasily and complained that I was never satisfied. We loved each other so strongly that he wanted to remain in the love of the moment; he wanted me to rest in that love. He cried out against my attitude that there would be nothing left of that love without a faith.

I remembered the love story in Romain Rolland's *Jean Christophe*, the story of his friend and his engrossing marriage, and how those young people exhausted themselves in the intensity of their emotions.

I could not see that love between man and woman was incompatible with love of God. God is the Creator, and the very fact that we were begetting a child made me have a sense that we were made in the image and likeness of God, co-creators with him. I could not protest with Sasha about "that initial agony of having to live." Because I was grateful for love, I was grateful for life, and living with Forster made me appreciate it and even reverence it still more. He had introduced me to so much that was beautiful and good that I felt I owed to him too this renewed interest in the things of the spirit.

He had all the love of the English for the outdoors in all weather. He used to insist on walks no matter how cold or rainy the day, and this dragging me away from my books, from my lethargy, into the open, into the country, made me begin to breathe. If breath is life, then I was beginning to be full of it because of him. I was filling my lungs with it, walking on the beach, resting on the pier beside him while he fished, rowing with him in the calm bay, walking through fields and woods—a new experience entirely for me, one which brought me to life, and filled me with joy.

I had been passing through some years of fret and strife, beauty and ugliness—even some weeks of sadness and despair. There had been periods of intense joy but seldom had there been the quiet beauty and happiness I had now. I had thought all those years that I had freedom, but now I felt that I had never known real freedom nor even had knowledge of what freedom meant.

Now, just as in my childhood, I was enchained, tied to one spot, unable to pick up and travel from one part of the country to another, from one job to another. I was tied down because I was going to have a baby. No matter how much I might sometimes wish to flee from my quiet existence, I could not, nor would I be able to for several years. I had to accept my quiet and stillness, and accepting it, I rejoiced in it.

For a long time I had thought I could not bear a child, and the longing in my heart for a baby had been growing. My home, I felt, was not a home without one. The simple joys of the kitchen and garden and beach brought sadness with them because I felt myself unfruitful, barren. No matter how much one was loved or one loved, that love was lonely without a child. It was incomplete.

I will never forget my blissful joy when I was first sure that I was pregnant—I had wanted a baby all the first year we were together. When I was finally sure, it was a beautiful June day and we were going on a picnic to Tottenville to see a circus, Malcolm and Peggy, Forster and I. It was a circus in a tent, and it was Peggy who insisted on going. We brought dandelion wine and pickled eels and good home-made bread and butter. A fantastic lunch, but I remember enjoying the root beer and popcorn later, and feeling so much in love, so settled, so secure that now I had found what I was looking for.

It did not last all through my pregnancy, that happiness. There were conflicts because Forster did not believe in bringing children into such a world as we lived in. He still was obsessed by the war. His fear of responsibility, his dislike of having the control of others, his extreme individualism made him feel that he of all men should not be a father.

Our child was born in March at the end of a harsh winter. In December I had come in from the country and taken an apartment in town. My sister came to stay with me, to help me over the last hard months. It was good to be there, close to friends, close to a church where I could pray. I read the *Imitation of Christ* a great deal during those months. I knew that I was going to have my child baptized, cost what it may. I knew that I was not going to have her floundering through many years as I had done, doubting and hesitating, undisciplined and amoral. I felt it was the greatest thing I could do for my child. For myself, I prayed for the gift of faith. I was sure, yet not sure. I postponed the day of decision.

A woman does not want to be alone at such a time. Even the most hardened, the most irreverent, is awed by the stupendous fact of creation. Becoming a Catholic would mean facing life alone and I clung to family life. It was hard to contemplate giving up a mate in order that my child and I could become members of the Church. Forster would have nothing to do with religion or with me if I embraced it. So I waited.

Those last months of waiting I was too happy to know the unrest of indecision. The days were slow in passing, but week by week the time came nearer. I spent some time in writing, but for the most part I felt a great stillness. I was incapable of going to meetings, of seeing many people, of taking up the threads of my past life.

When the little one was born, my joy was so great that I sat up in bed in the hospital and wrote an article for the *New Masses* about my child, wanting to share my joy with the world. I was glad to write this joy for a workers' magazine because it was a joy all women knew, no matter what their grief at poverty, unemployment and class war. The article so appealed to my Marxist friends that the account was reprinted all over the world in workers' papers. Diego Rivera, when I met him some four years afterward in Mexico, greeted me as the author of it. And Mike Gold, who was at that time editor of the *New Masses,* said it had been printed in many Soviet newspapers and that I had rubles awaiting me in Moscow.

When Tamar Teresa—for that is what I named her—was six weeks old, we went back to the beach. It was April and, though it was still cold, it was definitely spring.

Every morning while she napped on the sunny porch, well swathed in soft woolen blankets, I went down to the beach and with the help of Lefty brought up driftwood, enough to last until next morning. Forster was home only week ends and then he chopped enough wood to last a few days. But when the wind was high and piercing it penetrated the house so that much wood was needed, and it was a pleasure to tramp up and down the beach in the bright sun and collect wood which smelled of seaweed, brine and tar. It was warmer outside than it was in the house, and on the porch Teresa was nicely sheltered. Sometimes in the afternoon I put her in her carriage and went out along the woods, watching, almost feeling the buds bursting through their warm coats. Song sparrows, woodpeckers, hawks, crows, robins, nuthatches and of course laughing gulls made the air gay with their clamor. Starlings chattered in the branches of the old pine in front of the porch. We collected azalea buds, dogwood, sassafras and apple-tree branches to decorate the room. Best of all there were skunk cabbages, gleaming mottled-green, dark red, and yellow, small enough to make a most decorative centerpiece, propped up with stones. They were never so colorful as they were that year, and spring after spring since I have watched for them thrusting up vigorously in marshy places. Skunk cabbages and the spring peepers—these tiny frogs— mean that the winter is over and gone.

There was arbutus still buried under the leaves so that one had to look carefully for it like buried treasure. There were spring beauties and adder's-tongue and dandelion greens. The year before I had been planting radishes on March first but this year gardening gave way to more delightful tasks.

Supper always was early and the baby comfortably tucked away before it was dark. Then, tired with all the activities that so rejoiced and filled my days, I sat in the dusk in a stupor of contentment.

Yet always those deep moments of happiness gave way to a feeling of struggle, of a long silent fight still to be gone through. There had been the physical struggle, the mortal combat almost, of giving birth to a child, and now there was coming the struggle for my own soul. Tamar would be baptized, and I knew the rending it would cause in human relations around me. I was to be torn and agonized again, and I was all for putting off the hard day.

Love Overflows

"Thou shalt love the Lord thy God with thy whole heart and with thy whole soul and with thy whole mind." This is the first Commandment.

The problem is, how to love God? We are only too conscious of the hardness of our hearts, and in spite of all that religious writers tell us about *feeling* not being necessary, we do want to feel and so know that we love God.

"Thou wouldst not seek Him if thou hadst not already found Him," Pascal says, and it is true too that you love God if you want to love Him. One of the disconcerting facts about the spiritual life is that God takes you at your word. Sooner or later one is given a chance to prove his love. The very word "diligo," the Latin word used for "love," means "I prefer." It was all very well to love God in His works, in the beauty of His creation which was crowned for me by the birth of my child. Forster had made the physical world come alive for me and had awakened in my heart a flood of gratitude. The final object of this love and gratitude was God. No human creature could receive or contain so vast a flood of love and joy as I often felt after the birth of my child. With this came the need to worship, to adore. I had heard many say that they wanted to worship God in their own way and did not need a Church in which to praise Him, nor a body of people with whom to associate themselves. But I did not agree to this. My very experience as a radical, my whole make-up, led me to want to associate myself with others, with the masses, in loving and praising God. Without even looking into the claims of the Catholic Church, I was willing to admit that for me she was the one true Church. She had come down through the centuries since the time of Peter, and far from being dead, she claimed and held the allegiance of the masses of people in all the cities where I had lived. They poured in and out of her doors on Sundays and holy days, for novenas and missions. What if they were compelled to come in by the law of the Church, which said they were guilty of mortal sin if they did not go to Mass every Sunday? They obeyed that law. They were given a chance to show their preference. They accepted the Church. It may have been an unthinking, unquestioning faith, and yet the chance certainly came, again and again, "Do I prefer the Church to my own will," even if it was only the small matter of sitting at home on a Sunday morning with the papers? And the choice was the Church.

There was the legislation of the Church in regard to marriage, a stumbling block to many. That was where I began to be troubled, to be afraid. To become a Catholic meant for me to give up a mate with whom I was much in love. It got to the point where it was the simple question of whether I chose God or man. I had known enough of love to know that a good healthy family life was as near to heaven as one could get in this life. There was another sample of heaven, of the enjoyment of God. The very sexual act itself was used again and again in Scripture as a figure of the beatific vision. It was not because I was tired of sex, satiated, disillusioned, that I turned to God. Radical friends used to insinuate this. It was because through a whole love, both physical and spiritual, I came to know God.

From the time Tamar Teresa was born I was intent on having her baptized. There had been that young Catholic girl in the bed next to me at the hospital who gave me a medal of St. Thérèse of Lisieux.

"I don't believe in these things," I told her, and it was another example of people saying what they do not mean.

"If you love someone you like to have something around which reminds you of them," she told me.

It was so obvious a truth that I was shamed. Reading William James' *Varieties of Religious Experience* had acquainted me with the saints, and I had read the life of St. Teresa of Avila and fallen in love with her. She was a mystic and a practical woman, a recluse and a traveler, a cloistered nun and yet most active. She liked to read novels when she was a young girl, and she wore a bright red dress when she entered the convent. Once when she was traveling from one part of Spain to another with some other nuns and a priest to start a convent, and their way took them over a stream, she was thrown from her donkey. The story goes that our Lord said to her, "That is how I treat my friends." And she replied, "And that is why You have so few of them." She called life a "night spent at an uncomfortable inn." Once when she was trying to avoid that recreation hour which is set aside in convents for nuns to be together, the others insisted on her joining them, and she took castanets and danced. When some older nuns professed themselves shocked, she retorted, "One must do things sometimes to make life more bearable." After she was a superior she gave directions when the nuns became melancholy, "to feed them steak," and there were other delightful little touches to the story of her life which made me love her and feel close to her. I have since heard a priest friend of ours remark gloomily that one could go to hell imitating the imperfections of the saints, but these little incidents brought out in her biography made her delightfully near to me. So I decided to name my daughter after her. That is why my neighbor offered me a medal of St. Thérèse of Lisieux, who is called the little Teresa.

Her other name came from Sasha's sister Liza. She had named her daughter Tamar, which in Hebrew means "little palm tree," and knowing nothing of the unhappy story of the two Tamars in the Old Testament, I named my child Tamar also. Tamar is one of the forebears of our Lord, listed in the first chapter of Matthew, and not only Jews and Russians, but also New Englanders used the name.

What a driving power joy is! When I was unhappy and repentant in the past I turned to God, but it was my joy at having given birth to a child that made me do something definite. I wanted Tamar to have a way of life and instruction. We all crave order, and in the Book of Job, hell is described as a place where no order is. I felt that "belonging" to a Church would bring that order into her life which I felt my own had lacked. If I could have felt that communism was the answer to my desire for a cause, a motive, a way to walk in, I would have remained as I was. But I felt that only faith in Christ could give the answer. The Sermon on the Mount answered all the questions as to how to love God and one's brother. I knew little about the Sacraments, and yet here I was believing, knowing that without them Tamar would not be a Catholic.

I did not know any Catholics to speak to. The grocer, the hardware storekeeper, my neighbors down the road were Catholics, yet I could not bring myself to speak to them about religion. I was full of the reserves I noted in my own family. But I could speak to a nun. So when I saw a nun walking down the road near St. Joseph's-by-the-Sea, I went up to her breathlessly and asked her how I could have my child baptized. She was not at all reticent about asking questions and not at all surprised at my desires. She was a simple old sister who had taught grade school all her life. She was now taking care of babies in a huge home on the bay which had belonged to Charles Schwab, who had given it to the Sisters of Charity. They used it for summer retreats for the Sisters and to take care of orphans and unmarried mothers and their babies.

Sister Aloysia had had none of the university summer courses that most Sisters must take nowadays. She never talked to me about the social encyclicals of the Popes. She gave me a catechism and brought me old copies of the *Messenger of the Sacred Heart*, a magazine which, along with the Kathleen Norris type of success story, had some good solid articles about the teachings of the Church. I read them all; I studied my catechism; I learned to say the Rosary; I went to Mass in the chapel by the sea; I walked the beach and I prayed; I read the *Imitation of Christ*, and St. Augustine, and the New Testament. Dostoevski, Huysmans (what different men!) had given me desire and background. Huysmans had made me at home in the Church.

"How can your daughter be brought up a Catholic unless you become one yourself?" Sister Aloysia kept saying to me. But she went resolutely ahead in making arrangements for the baptism of Tamar Teresa.

"You must be a Catholic yourself," she kept telling me. She had no reticence. She speculated rather volubly at times on the various reasons why she thought I was holding back. She brought me pious literature to read, saccharine stories of virtue, emasculated lives of saints young and old, back numbers of pious magazines. William James, agnostic as he was, was more help. He had introduced me to St. Teresa of Avila and St. John of the Cross.

Isolated as I was in the country, knowing no Catholics except my neighbors, who seldom read anything except newspapers and secular magazines, there was not much chance of being introduced to the good Catholic literature of the present day. I was in a state of dull content—not in a state to be mentally stimulated. I was too happy with my child. What faith I had I held on to stubbornly. The need for patience emphasized in the writings of the saints consoled me on the slow road I was traveling. I would put all my affairs in the hands of God and wait.

Three times a week Sister Aloysia came to give me a catechism lesson, which I dutifully tried to learn. But she insisted that I recite word for word, with the repetition of the question that was in the book. If I had not learned my lesson, she rebuked me, "And you think you are intelligent!" she would say witheringly. "What is the definition of grace—actual grace and sanctifying grace? My fourth-grade pupils know more than you do!"

I hadn't a doubt but that they did. I struggled on day by day, learning without question. I was in an agreeable and lethargic, almost bovine state of mind, filled with an animal content, not wishing to inquire into or question the dogmas I was learning. I made up my mind to accept what I did not understand, trusting light to come, as it sometimes did, in a blinding flash of exultation and realization.

She criticized my housekeeping. "Here you sit at your typewriter at ten o'clock and none of your dishes done yet. Supper and breakfast dishes besides. . . . And why don't you calcimine your ceiling? It's all dirty from wood smoke."

She brought me vegetables from the garden of the home, and I gave her fish and clams. Once I gave her stamps and a dollar to send a present to a little niece and she was touchingly grateful. It made me suddenly realize that, in spite of Charlie Schwab and his estate, the Sisters lived in complete poverty, owning nothing, holding all things in common.

I had to have godparents for Tamar, and I thought of Aunt Jenny, my mother's sister, the only member of our family I knew who had become a Catholic. She had married a Catholic and had one living child, Grace. I did not see them very often but I looked them up now and asked Grace and her husband if they would be godparents to my baby. Tamar was baptized in July. We went down to Tottenville, the little town at the south end of the island; there in the Church of Our Lady, Help of Christians, the seed of life was implanted in her and she was made a child of God.

We came back to the beach house to a delightful lunch of boiled lobsters and salad. Forster had caught the lobsters in his traps for the feast and then did not remain to partake of it. He left, not returning for several days. It was his protest against my yearnings toward the life of the spirit, which he considered a morbid escapism. He exulted in his materialism. He well knew the dignity of man. Heathen philosophers, says Matthias Scheeben, a great modern theologian, have called man a miracle, the marrow and the heart of the world, the most beautiful being, the king of all creatures. Forster saw man in the light of reason and not in the light of faith. He had thought of the baptism only as a mumbo jumbo, the fuss and flurry peculiar to woman. At first he had been indulgent and had brought in the lobsters for the feast. And then he had become angry with some sense of the end to which all this portended. Jealousy set in and he left me.

As a matter of fact, he left me quite a number of times that coming winter and following summer, as he felt my increasing absorption in religion. The tension between us was terrible. Teresa had become a member of the Mystical Body of Christ. I didn't know anything of the Mystical Body or I might have felt disturbed at being separated from her.

But I clutched her close to me and all the time I nursed her and bent over that tiny round face at my breast, I was filled with a deep happiness that nothing could spoil. But the obstacles to my becoming a Catholic were there, shadows in the background of my life.

I had become convinced that I would become a Catholic; yet I felt I was betraying the class to which I belonged, the workers, the poor of the world, with whom Christ spent His life. I wrote a few articles for the *New Masses* but did no other work at that time. My life was crowded in summer because friends came and stayed with me, and some of them left their children. Two little boys, four and eight years old, joined the family for a few months and my days were full, caring for three children and cooking meals for a half-dozen persons three times a day.

Sometimes when I could leave the baby in trusted hands I could get to the village for Mass on Sunday. But usually the gloom that descended on the household, the scarcely voiced opposition, kept me from Mass. There were some feast days when I could slip off during the week and go to the little chapel on the Sisters' grounds. There were "visits" I could make, unknown to others. I was committed, by the advice of a priest I consulted, to the plan of waiting, and trying to hold together the family. But I felt all along that when I took the irrevocable step it would mean that Tamar and I would be alone, and I did not want to be alone. I did not want to give up human love when it was dearest and tenderest.

During the month of August many of my friends, including my sister, went to Boston to picket in protest against the execution of Sacco and Vanzetti, which was drawing near. They were all arrested again and again.

Throughout the nation and the world the papers featured the struggle for the lives of these two men. Radicals from all over the country gathered in Boston, and articles describing those last days were published, poems were written. It was an epic struggle, a tragedy. One felt a sense of impending doom. These men were Catholics, inasmuch as they were Italians. Catholics by tradition, but they had rejected the Church.

Nicola Sacco and Bartolomeo Vanzetti were two anarchists, a shoemaker and a fish peddler who were arrested in 1920 in connection with a payroll robbery at East Braintree, Massachusetts, in which two guards were killed. Nobody paid much attention to the case at first, but as the I.W.W. and the Communists took up the case it became a *cause célèbre*. In August, 1927, they were executed. Many books have been written about the case, and Vanzetti's prison letters are collected in one volume. He learned to write English in prison, and his prose, bare and simple, is noble in its earnestness.

While I enjoyed the fresh breeze, the feel of salt water against the flesh, the keen delight of living, the knowledge that these men were soon to pass from this physical earth, were soon to become dust, without consciousness, struck me like a physical blow. They were here now; in a few days they would be no more. They had become figures beloved by the workers. Their letters, the warm moving story of their lives, had been told. Everyone knew Dante, Sacco's young son. Everyone suffered with the young wife who clung with bitter passion to her husband. And Vanzetti with his large view, his sense of peace at his fate, was even closer to us all.

He wrote a last letter to a friend which has moved many hearts as great poetry does:

I have talked a great deal of myself [he wrote]. But I even forget to name Sacco. Sacco too is a worker, from his boyhood a skilled worker, lover of work, with a good job and pay, a bank account, a good and lovely wife, two beautiful children and a neat little home, at the verge of a wood near a brook.

Sacco is a heart of faith, a lover of nature and man.

A man who gave all, who sacrificed all for mankind, his own wife, his children, himself and his own life.

Sacco has never dreamed to steal, never to assassinate.

He and I never brought a morsel of bread to our mouths, from our childhood to today which has not been gained by the sweat of our brows. Never.

O yes, I may be more witful, as some have put it, I am a better blabber than he is, but many many times in hearing his heartful voice ringing a faith sublime, in considering his supreme sacrifice, remembering his heroism, I felt small at the presence of his greatness and found myself compelled to fight back from my eyes the tears, and quanch my heart, trobling to my throat to not weep before him,—this man called thief, assassin and doomed. . . .

If it had not been for these things I might have lived out my life talking at street corners to scorning men. I might have died, unmarked, unknown, a failure. This is our career and our triumph.

Never in our full life could we hope to do such work
for tolerance, for justice,
for man's understanding of man,
as we now do by accident.

Our words, our lives, our pains—nothing!

The taking of our lives,—lives of a good shoe maker
and a poor fish peddler—all!

That last moment belongs to us
—that agony is our triumph.

The day they died, the papers had headlines as large as those which proclaimed the outbreak of war. All the nation mourned. All the nation, I mean, that is made up of the poor, the worker, the trade unionist—those who felt most keenly the sense of solidarity—that very sense of solidarity which made me gradually understand the doctrine of the Mystical Body of Christ whereby we are the members one of another.

Forster was stricken over the tragedy. He had always been more an anarchist than anything else in his philosophy, and so was closer to these two men than to Communist friends. He did not eat for days. He sat around the house in a stupor of misery, sickened by the cruelty of life and men. He had always taken refuge in nature as being more kindly, more beautiful and peaceful than the world of men. Now he could not even escape through nature, as he tried to escape so many problems in life.

During the time he was home he spent days and even nights out in his boat fishing, so that for weeks I saw little of him. He stupefied himself in his passion for the water, sitting out on the bay in his boat. When he began to recover he submerged himself in maritime biology, collecting, reading only scientific books, and paying no attention to what went on around him. Only the baby interested him. She was his delight. Which made it, of course, the harder to contemplate the cruel blow I was going to strike him when I became a Catholic. We both suffered in body as well as in soul and mind. He would not talk about the faith and relapsed into a complete silence if I tried to bring up the subject. The point of my bringing it up was that I could not become a Catholic and continue living with him, because he was averse to any ceremony before officials of either Church or state. He was an anarchist and an atheist, and he did not intend to be a liar or a hypocrite. He was a creature of utter sincerity, and however illogical and bad-tempered about it all, I loved him. It was killing me to think of leaving him.

Fall nights we read a great deal. Sometimes he went out to dig bait if there were a low tide and the moon was up. He stayed out late on the pier fishing, and came in smelling of seaweed and salt air; getting into bed, cold with the chill November air, he held me close to him in silence. I loved him in every way, as a wife, as a mother even. I loved him for all he knew and pitied him for all he didn't know. I loved him for the odds and ends I had to fish out of his sweater pockets and for the sand and shells he brought in with his fishing. I loved his lean cold body as he got into bed smelling of the sea, and I loved his integrity and stubborn pride.

It ended by my being ill the next summer. I became so oppressed I could not breathe and I awoke in the night choking. I was weak and listless and one doctor told me my trouble was probably thyroid. I went to the Cornell clinic for a metabolism test and they said my condition was a nervous one. By winter the tension had become so great that an explosion occurred and we separated again. When he returned, as he always had, I would not let him in the house; my heart was breaking with my own determination to make an end, once and for all, to the torture we were undergoing.

The next day I went to Tottenville alone, leaving Tamar with my sister, and there with Sister Aloysia as my godparent, I too was baptized conditionally, since I had already been baptized in the Episcopal Church. I made my first confession right afterward, and looked forward the next morning to receiving communion.

I had no particular joy in partaking of these three sacraments, Baptism,

Penance and Holy Eucharist. I proceeded about my own active participation in them grimly, coldly, making acts of faith, and certainly with no consolation whatever. One part of my mind stood at one side and kept saying, "What are you doing? Are you sure of yourself? What kind of an affectation is this? What act is this you are going through? Are you trying to induce emotion, induce faith, partake of an opiate, the opiate of the people?" I felt like a hypocrite if I got down on my knees, and shuddered at the thought of anyone seeing me.

At my first communion I went up to the communion rail at the *Sanctus* bell instead of at the *Domine, non sum dignus,* and had to kneel there all alone through the consecration, through the *Pater Noster,* through the *Agnus Dei*— and I had thought I knew the Mass so well! But I felt it fitting that I be humiliated by this ignorance, by this precipitance.

I speak of the misery of leaving one love. But there was another love too, the life I had led in the radical movement. That very winter I was writing a series of articles, interviews with the workers, with the unemployed. I was working with the Anti-Imperialist League, a Communist affiliate, that was bringing aid and comfort to the enemy, General Sandino's forces in Nicaragua. I was just as much against capitalism and imperialism as ever, and here I was going over to the opposition, because of course the Church was lined up with property, with the wealthy, with the state, with capitalism, with all the forces of reaction. This I had been taught to think and this I still think to a great extent. "Too often," Cardinal Mundelein said, "has the Church lined up on the wrong side." "Christianity," Bakunin said, "is precisely the religion par excellence, because it exhibits, and manifests, to the fullest extent, the very nature and essence of every religious system, which is the impoverishment, enslavement, and annihilation of humanity for the benefit of divinity."

I certainly believed this, but I wanted to be poor, chaste and obedient. I wanted to die in order to live, to put off the old man and put on Christ. I loved, in other words, and like all women in love, I wanted to be united to my love. Why should not Forster be jealous? Any man who did not participate in this love would, of course, realize my infidelity, my adultery. In the eyes of God, any turning toward creatures to the exclusion of Him is adultery and so it is termed over and over again in Scripture.

I loved the Church for Christ made visible. Not for itself, because it was so often a scandal to me. Romano Guardini said the Church is the Cross on which Christ was crucified; one could not separate Christ from His Cross, and one must live in a state of permanent dissatisfaction with the Church.

The scandal of businesslike priests, of collective wealth, the lack of a sense of responsibility for the poor, the worker, the Negro, the Mexican, the Filipino, and even the oppression of these, and the consenting to the oppression of them by our industrialist-capitalist order—these made me feel often that priests were more like Cain than Abel. "Am I my brother's keeper?" they seemed to say in respect to the social order. There was plenty of charity but too little justice. And yet the priests were the dispensers of the Sacraments, bringing Christ to men, all enabling us to put on Christ and to achieve more nearly in the world a sense of peace and unity. "The worst enemies would be those of our own household," Christ had warned us.

We could not root out the tares without rooting out the wheat also. With all the knowledge I have gained these twenty-one years I have been a Catholic, I could write many a story of priests who were poor, chaste and obedient, who gave their lives daily for their fellows, but I am writing of how I felt at the time of my baptism.

Not long afterward a priest wanted me to write a story of my conversion, telling how the social teaching of the Church had led me to embrace Catholicism. But I knew nothing of the social teaching of the Church at that time. I had never heard of the encyclicals. I felt that the Church was the Church of the poor, that St. Patrick's had been built from the pennies of servant girls, that it cared for the emigrant, it established hospitals, orphanages, day nurseries, houses of the Good Shepherd, homes for the aged, but at the same time, I felt that it did not set its face against a social order which made so much charity in the present sense of the word necessary. I felt that charity was a word to choke over. Who wanted charity? And it was not just human pride but a strong sense of man's dignity and worth, and what was due to him in justice, that made me resent, rather than feel proud of so mighty a sum total of Catholic institutions. Besides, more and more they were taking help from the state, and in taking from the state, they had to render to the state. They came under the head of Community Chest and discriminatory charity, centralizing and departmentalizing, involving themselves with bureaus, building, red tape, legislation, at the expense of human values. By "they," I suppose one always means the bishops, but as Harry Bridges once pointed out to me, "they" also are victims of the system.

It was an age-old battle, the war of the classes, that stirred in me when I thought of the Sacco-Vanzetti case in Boston. Where were the Catholic voices crying out for these men? How I longed to make a synthesis reconciling body and soul, this world and the next, the teachings of Prince Peter Kropotkin and Prince Demetrius Gallitzin, who had become a missionary priest in rural Pennsylvania.

Where had been the priests to go out to such men as Francisco Ferrer in Spain, pursuing them as the Good Shepherd did His lost sheep, leaving the ninety and nine of their good parishioners, to seek out that which was lost, bind up that which was bruised. No wonder there was such a strong conflict going on in my mind and heart.

44

Anaïs Nin (1903–1977)
from *The Diary of Anaïs Nin*

Anaïs Nin (pronounced "anna-ees neen") began her diary in 1914 on a ship from Barcelona to New York. Her mother was a classical singer of aristocratic French and Danish parentage; her father was a Spanish composer and musician. But he was frequently unfaithful and had sent his wife, Anaïs, and two sons to New York, saying he would join them later. Anaïs began the diary as a letter to her absent father, whom she loved and admired but feared. It was years before she would see him again.

The diary continued for the rest of her life, finally filling over two hundred manuscript notebooks. It covered her schooling in New York, where her mother turned to giving singing lessons. It chronicled her years in Paris after the First World War, where her husband Hugh Guiler was a banker; her break from him and friendship with Henry Miller; her other friendships and acquaintances with a great number of artists, writers, psychoanalysts, and film-makers; her travels; and her numerous other writings and difficulties in publishing them. For Nin clearly wished fame and success as a novelist and critic (her first book was *D. H. Lawrence: An Unprofessional Study*), and once turned to writing erotica in order to support herself and raise money to give to friends. She also had conflicting impulses about the diary, which some friends urged her at times to quit. She wrote of it as being like an appeal to her father, a mirror, a window, a drug addiction, an obsession, and a form of dream and revelation of the unconscious. During the Second World War, simply keeping it safe was a serious problem.

Finally, in 1966, she published the first volume of *The Diary of Anaïs Nin, 1931–1934*, based on the manuscript volumes 30 to 40. But it was not a word-for-word transcription. Working with an editor, Gunther Stuhlmann, who, she said later, helped her "with the balance" and "structure" of the narrative, so she did not "get lost in the detailed work," [1] she had cut out approximately half of the material. She

Excerpts from *The Diary of Anaïs Nin, Volume Two: 1934–1939*, copyright © 1967 by Anaïs Nin, reprinted by permission of Harcourt Brace and Company. Excerpts from *The Diary of Anaïs Nin, Volume Three, 1939–1944*, copyright © 1969 by Anaïs Nin, reprinted by permission of Harcourt Brace and Company. Excerpts from *The Diary of Anaïs Nin, Volume Five, 1947–1955*, copyright © 1974 by Anaïs Nin, reprinted by permission of Harcourt Brace and Company. All excerpts are also reprinted from *The Diaries of Anaïs Nin*, by permission of Peter Owen Publishers, London.
1. Duane Schneider, *An Interview with Anaïs Nin* (Athens, OH: Duane Schneider, 1970), p. 10;

also occasionally moved pieces out of the original order of composition, which itself had sometimes been sporadic, revised more or less heavily, and even wrote things anew. The original material also included letters to her, excerpts from fiction, excerpts from friends' diaries, and copies of book reviews; and these she selected, edited, and moved around as well. The result blurs simple distinctions between diary, autobiography, and fiction. Two critics call it "a journal-novel."[2] Another prefers to treat it as really an autobiography.[3]

Volumes 2–6, taking her from 1934 to 1966, appeared over the next ten years (1967–76), and they were edited along the same lines. Volume 7 (1966–74) appeared in 1980, after Nin's death from cancer in 1977. Between 1978 and 1985, *The Early Diary of Anaïs Nin* (1914–31), not edited by Nin, was published in four volumes, "essentially in the form in which it was written."[4] It makes a useful contrast with *The Diary*, a basic difference being that most entries in it are dated, whereas in the *Diary* specific dates are dropped and entries are loosely identified only by month and year. Still another version of the diary is in *Henry and June: From the Unexpurgated Diary of Anaïs Nin* (San Diego: Harcourt Brace Jovanovich, 1986).

Representing such a massive work in just a few pages of excerpts is practically impossible. But the following passages give an idea of Nin's passions for experiment and variety, for studying herself as a woman, and for friendships and social intercourse. The description of her costume for the masquerade "to which we would come dressed as our madness" is also stunning. It is a surrealist image of herself and her diary.

The excerpts below are from volumes 2, 3, and 5 of the six-volume *Diary of Anaïs Nin* (Harcourt, Brace, and World, 1967–74). Two useful studies of Nin and the diaries are Benjamin Franklin V and Duane Schneider, *Anaïs Nin: An Introduction* (Athens: Ohio Univ. Press, 1979), and Nancy Scholar, *Anaïs Nin* (Boston: Twayne, 1984). Claudia Roth Pierpont's "Sex, Lies, and Thirty-Five Thousand Pages" (*The New Yorker* 69 [March 1, 1993]: 74–90), is a thoughtful attack on her work.

from April, 1936

A trip to Morocco. A short but vivid one. I fell in love with Fez. Peace. Dignity. Humility. I have just left the balcony where I stood listening to the evening prayer rising over the white city. A religious emotion roused by the Arabs' lives, by the simplicity of it, the fundamental beauty. Stepping into the labyrinth of their streets, streets like intestines, two yards wide, into the

---

quoted in Benjamin Franklin V and Duane Schneider, *Anaïs Nin: An Introduction* (Athens: Ohio Univ. Press, 1979), p. 170.

2. Franklin and Schneider, *Anaïs Nin,* p. 176.

3. Nancy Scholar, *Anaïs Nin* (Boston: Twayne, 1984), p. 15ff.

4. John Ferrone, "Editor's Note," in *Linotte: The Early Diary of Anaïs Nin, 1914–1920* (New York: Harcourt Brace Jovanovich, 1978), p. ix.

abyss of their dark eyes, into peace. The rhythm affects one first of all. The slowness. Many people on the streets. You touch elbows. They breathe into your face, but with a silence, a gravity, a dreaminess. Only the children cry and laugh and run. The Arabs are silent. The little square room open on the street in which they sit on the ground, on the mud, with their merchandise around them. They are weaving, they are sewing, baking bread, chiseling jewels, repairing knives, making guns for the Berbers in the mountains. They are dying wool in vast cauldrons, big cauldrons full of dye in which they dip their bunches of silk and wool. Their hands are emerald green, violet, Orient blue. They are making sienna earth pottery, weaving rugs, shaving, shampooing and writing legal documents right there, under your eyes. One Arab is asleep over his bag of saffron. Another is praying with his beads while selling herbs. Further, a big tintamarre, the street of copperwork. Little boys are beating copper trays with small hammers, beating a design into them, beating copper lamps, Aladdin's lamps. Little boys and old men do the work. They hold the tray between their legs. The younger men walk down the street in their burnouses, going I know not where, some so beautiful one thinks they are women. The women are veiled. They are going to the mosque, probably. At a certain hour all selling, all work ceases and they all go to the mosque. But first of all they wash their faces, their feet, their sore eyes, their leprous noses, their pockmarked skins at the fountain. They shed their sandals. Some of the old men and old women never leave the mosque. They squat there forever until death overtakes them. Women have their own entrance. They kiss the wall of the mosque as they pass. To make way for a donkey loaded with kindling wood, I step into a dark doorway. A choking stench overwhelms me. This stench is everywhere. It takes a day to get used to it. It makes you feel nauseated at first. It is the smell of excrement, saffron, leather being cured, sandalwood, olive oil being used for frying, nut oil on the bodies, incense, muskrat, so strong that at first you cannot swallow food. There is mud on the white burnous, on the Arab legs. Children's heads shaved, with one tuft of hair left. The women with faces uncovered and tattooed are the primitive Berbers from the mountains, wives of warriors, not civilized. I saw the wives of one Arab, five of them sitting on a divan, like mountains of flesh, enormous, with several chins and several stomachs, and diamonds set in their foreheads.

The streets and houses are inextricably woven, intricately interwoven, by bridges from one house to another, passageways covered with lattice, creating shadows on the ground. They seem to be crossing within a house, you never know when you are out in a street or in a patio, or a passageway, as half of the houses are open on the street, you get lost immediately. Mosques run into a merchant's home, shops into mosques, now you are under a trellised roof covered with rose vines, now walking in utter darkness through a tunnel, behind a donkey raw and bleeding from being beaten, and now you are on a bridge built by the Portuguese. Now admire lacy trelliswork done by the

Andalusians, and now look at the square next to the mosque where the poor are allowed to sleep on mats.

Everywhere the Arab squats and waits. Anywhere. An old Arab is teaching a young one a religious chant. Another is defecating carefully, conscientiously. Another is begging, showing all his open sores, standing near the baker baking bread in ovens built in the earth.

The atmosphere is so clear, so white and blue, you feel you can see the whole world as clearly as you see Fez. The birds do not chatter as they do in Paris, they chant, trill with operatic and tropical fervor. The poor are dressed in sackcloths, the semi-poor in sheets and bathtowels, the well-to-do women in silks and muslins. The Jews wear a black burnous. In the streets and in the houses of the poor the floor is of stamped earth. Houses are built of sienna-red earth, sometimes whitewashed. The olive oil is pressed out in the street too, under large wooden wheels.

I had letters of introduction. First I visited Si Boubekertazi. He sat in his patio, on pillows. A beautiful Negro woman, a concubine, brought a copper tray full of delicacies. And tea served in tiny cups without handles.

At the house of Driss Mokri Montasseb I was allowed to visit the harem. Seven wives of various ages, but all of them fat, sat around a low table eating candy and dates. We discussed nail polish. They wanted some of mine, which was pearly. They told me how they made up their eyes. They bought kohl dust at the market, filled their eyes with it. The eyes smart and cry, and so the black kohl marks the edges and gives that heavily accented effect.

Pasha El Glaoui de Marrakesh offered me a military escort to visit the city. He said it was absolutely necessary. He signaled to a soldier standing at his door, who never left me from then on except when I went to my hotel room to sleep.

De Sidi Hassan Benanai received me under the fine spun-gold colonnades. But he had just begun a forty-day fast and prayer, so he sat in silence, counting his beads, and tea was served in silence, and he continued to pray, occasionally smiling at me, and bowing his head, until I left.

From outside, the houses are uniformly plain, with high walls covered with flowers. One cannot tell when one is entering a luxurious abode. The door may be of beautiful ironwork. There may be two, or four, or six guards at the door. But inside, the walls are all mosaics, or painted, and the stucco worked like lace, the ceilings painted in gold. The pillows are of silk. The Negro women are simply dressed but always beautiful. One does not see the children or the wives.

The white burnous is called a *jelabba*.

Mystery and labyrinth. Complex streets. Anonymous walls. Secret luxury. Secrecy of these houses without windows on the streets. The windows and door open on the patio. The patio has a fountain and lovely plants. There is a labyrinth design in the arrangement of the gardens. Bushes are placed to form a puzzle so you might get lost. They love the feeling of being lost. It has been interpreted as a desire to reproduce the infinite.

Fez. One always, sooner or later, comes upon a city which is an image of one's inner cities. Fez is an image of my inner self. This may explain my fascination for it. Wearing a veil, full and inexhaustible, labyrinthian, so rich and variable I myself get lost. Passion for mystery, the unknown, and for the infinite, the uncharted.

. . .

On the way back, landing at Cádiz, I saw the same meager palm trees I had carefully observed when I was eleven years old, on my way to America. I saw the cathedral I had described minutely in my child-diary. I saw the city in which women did not go out very much, the city, I said, where I would never live because I liked independence.

When I landed in Cádiz I found the palm trees, the cathedral, but not the child I was. The last vestiges of my past were lost in the ancient city of Fez, which was built so much like my own life, with its tortuous streets, its silences, secrecies, its labyrinths and its covered faces. In the city of Fez I became aware that the little demon which had devoured me for twenty years, the little demon of depression which I had fought for twenty years, had ceased eating me. I was at peace, walking through the streets of Fez, absorbed in a world outside of myself, a past which was not my past, by sickness one could touch and name, leprosy and syphilis.

I walked with the Arabs, sang and prayed with them to a god who ordained acceptance. With the Arabs I crouched in stillness. Streets without issues, such as the streets of my desires. Forget the issue and lie under the mud-colored walls, listen to the copper being beaten, watch the dyers dipping their silks in orange buckets. Through the streets of my own labyrinth, I walked in peace at last, with an acceptance of myself, of my strength, of my weakness. The blunders I made lay like garbage in the doorsteps and nourished the flies. The places I did not reach were forgotten because the Arab on his donkey, or on his mule, or on his naked feet, walked forever between the walls of Fez. The failures were the inscriptions on the walls half effaced, and those books eaten by the mice, the childhood was rotting away in the museums, the crazy men were tied in chains and I walked free because I let the ashes fall, the old flesh die, I let death efface, I let the inscriptions crumble, I let the cypresses watch the tombs. I did not fight for completeness, against the fragments devoured by the past or today's detritus under my feet. What the river did not carry away nourished the flies. I could go with the Arabs to the cemetery with colored rugs and bird cages for a little feast of talk, so little did death matter, or disease, or tomorrow. Night watchman sleeping on the stone steps, or mud, in soiled burnous, I too can sleep anywhere. There were in Fez, as in my life, streets which led nowhere, impasses which remained a mystery. There must also be walls. The tips of minarets can only rise as high because of the walls.

It was in Cádiz that I lay down in a hotel room and fell into a dolorous, obsessional reverie, a continuous secret melody of jealousy, fear, doubt, and it was in Cádiz that I stood up and broke the evil curse, as if by a magical act of will, I broke the net, the evil curse of obsession. I learned how to break it. It was symbolized by my going into the street. From that day on, suffering became intermittent, subject to interruptions, distractions, not a perpetual condition. I was able to distract myself. I could live for hours without the malady of doubt. There were silences in my head, periods of peace and enjoyment. I could abandon myself completely to the pleasure of multiple relationships, to the beauty of the day, to the joys of the day. It was as if the cancer in me had ceased gnawing me. The cancer of introspection.

It seemed to have happened suddenly, like a miracle, but it was the result of years of struggle, of analysis, of passionate living. Introspection is a devouring monster. You have to feed it with much material, much experience, many people, many places, many loves, many creations, and then it ceases feeding on you.

From that moment on, what I experienced were emotional dramas which passed like storms, and left peace behind them.

from **August, 1937**

. . . Man today is like a tree that is withering at the roots. And most women painted and wrote nothing but imitations of phalluses. The world was filled with phalluses, like totem poles, and no womb anywhere. I must go the opposite way from Proust who found eternal moments in creation. I must find them in life. My work must be the closest to the life flow. I must install myself inside of the seed, growth, mysteries. I must prove the possibility of instantaneous, immediate, spontaneous art. My art must be like a miracle. Before it goes through the conduits of the brain and becomes an abstraction, a fiction, a lie. It must be for woman, more like a personified ancient ritual, where every spiritual thought was made visible, enacted, represented.

A sense of the infinite in the present, as the child has.

Woman's role in creation should be parallel to her role in life. I don't mean the good earth. I mean the bad earth too, the demon, the instincts, the storms of nature. Tragedies, conflicts, mysteries are personal. Man fabricated a detachment which became fatal. Woman must not fabricate. She must descend into the real womb and expose its secrets and its labyrinths. She must describe it as the city of Fez, with its Arabian Nights gentleness, tranquility and mystery. She must describe the voracious moods, the desires, the worlds contained in each cell of it. For the womb has dreams. It is not as simple as the good earth. I believe at times that man created art out of fear of exploring woman. I believe woman stuttered about herself out of fear of what she had to say. She covered herself with taboos and veils. Man invented a woman to suit his needs. He disposed of her by identifying her with nature and then paraded his contemptuous domination of nature. But woman is not nature only.

She is the mermaid with her fish-tail dipped in the unconscious. Her creation will be to make articulate this obscure world which dominates man, which he denies being dominated by, but which asserts its domination in destructive proofs of its presence, madness.

from October, 1937

. . . The entire mystery of pleasure in a woman's body lies in the intensity of the pulsation just before the orgasm. Sometimes it is slow, one-two-three, three palpitations which then project a fiery and icy liqueur through the body. If the palpitation is feeble, muted, the pleasure is like a gentler wave. The pocket seed of ecstasy bursts with more or less energy, when it is richest it touches every portion of the body, vibrating through every nerve and cell. If the palpitation is intense, the rhythm and beat of it is slower and the pleasure more lasting. Electric flesh-arrows, a second wave of pleasure falls over the first, a third which touches every nerve end, and now the third like an electric current traversing the body. A rainbow of color strikes the eyelids. A foam of music falls over the ears. It is the gong of the orgasm. There are times when a woman feels her body but lightly played on. Others when it reaches such a climax it seems it can never surpass. So many climaxes. Some caused by tenderness, some by desire, some by a word or an image seen during the day. There are times when the day itself demands a climax, days of cumulative sensations and unexploded feelings. There are days which do not end in a climax, when the body is asleep or dreaming other dreams. There are days when the climax is not pleasure but pain, jealousy, terror, anxiety. And there are days when the climax takes place in creation, a white climax. Revolution is another climax. Sainthood another.

from October, 1937

. . . Hélène is changing the curtains of her bedroom. Gonzalo is working for the revolution in Peru, underground. Helba is sitting like an inmate in an asylum doing nothing for hours, or sewing and resewing rags. Henry is writing *Tropic of Capricorn,* and as Larry said: "a new dimension without emotion." Henry's creation at times resembles insanity, because it is experience disconnected from feeling—like an anesthetized soul injected with ether. I ask myself: those who get disconnected from a human world of feeling, for whatever reason, who live in a world of their own, wasn't their human core weak to begin with? Where are the deep sources of feeling in my father and in Henry which life succeeded in atrophying? Why is it that I never get cut off from pity, sympathy, participation, in spite of the fact that I am living out my own dream, my interior vision, my fantasies without any interruptions. I dream, I kiss, I have orgasms, I get exalted, I leave the world, I float, I cook, I sew, have nightmares, write in my head, compose, decompose, improvise, invent, I listen to all, I hear all that is said, I feel Spain, I am aware, I am everywhere, I am open to wounds, open to love, I am rooted to my devotions, I *am never separate,* never cut off, never blind, deaf, absent. I hold on to the dream which makes life possible, to the creation which transfigures, to the God who sustains, to the crimes which give life, to the illusions which make the marvelous possible. I hold on to the poetry and the human simplicities. I write about the labyrinth, the womb, Fez, and I carry electric bulbs to Gonzalo's home. Larry is sitting crosslegged on the floor like a soft blond Hindu, with a catlike suppleness and writing with a branding iron.

from Winter, 1939

I left a Paris lit in a muted way like the inside of a cathedral, full of shadowy niches, black corners, twinkling oil lamps. In the half mist hanging over it, violet, blue, and green lights looked like stained-glass windows all wet and alive with candlelight. I could not have recognized the faces of those I was leaving. My bags were carried by a soldier whose shoes were too big for him. I suffered deeply from the wrench of separation. I felt every cell and cord which tied me to France snapping in me, the parting from a pattern of life I loved, from an atmosphere rich, creative and human, from intimacy with a people and a city. I was parting from a rhythm rooted very deeply in me, from mysterious, enveloped nights, from an obsession with war which gave a bitter and vivid taste to all our living, from the sound of anti-aircraft guns, of airplanes passing, of sirens lamenting like foghorns on stormy nights at sea.

I could not believe that there could be, anywhere in the world, space and air where the nightmare of war did not exist.

On the train to Irún. On the way to take the hydroplane from Portugal. It seems as if I will never tear myself away from France. Each mile of the journey, each landscape, each little station, each face, causes a painful separation. I carry with me only two briefcases filled with recent diaries. At the last moment, when I had taken all the volumes out of the vault in the Paris bank and packed them in two suitcases, I found that the cost of excess weight far exceeded the money I had. So the bulk of the diaries went back into the vault. And now, in the train, I feel despondent, ashamed to be saved from catastrophe, to abandon my friends to an unknown fate.

For the second time in my life, America looms as a refuge. My mind is journeying backwards in time. I think of the Maginot Line, which crossed near Louveciennes, in the Forest of Marly. We stumbled upon it one day on a hike. A young soldier took us through part of it. He was very proud. A cement labyrinth with apertures only for gun barrels. He showed us a vast empty pool, which he explained would be filled with acid to dissolve the bodies of the dead. I think of my concierge, who lost her husband in the First World War and might lose her son in the Second. I think of the Pierre Chareaus in danger because they are Jews, and those who escaped from Germany and are now once more afraid for their lives.

from September, 1940

While I was away *Life* magazine came to photograph the place. A piano was hauled up with pulleys to the top of an ancient tree. Levitation must be encouraged. Dali was at his easel.*

While I was away there were other happenings. Caresse was divorcing her Southern gentleman husband. He had heard that Caresse had filled her house with artists. He arrived one night, opened all the doors and turned on all the lights. Alas, there was no orgy! He found Mr. and Mrs. Dali asleep in one room, Caresse asleep in another room, Henry alone in another room, John and Flo Dudley asleep in another room. He ordered everyone to leave, but as no one paid any attention to him, he rushed down the stairs, shouting that he would destroy all of Dali's paintings. At this the Dalis became alarmed, they dressed, ran downstairs, packed all the paintings and drove away.

The general obsession with observing only historical or sociological movements, and not a particular human being (which is considered with such righteousness here) is as mistaken as a doctor who does not take an interest in a particular case. Every particular case is an experience that can be valuable to the understanding of the illness.

There is an opacity in individual relationships, and an insistence that the writer make the relation of the particular to the whole which makes for a kind of farsightedness. I believe in just the opposite. Every individual is representative of the whole, a symptom, and should be intimately understood, and this would give a far greater understanding of mass movements and sociology.

Also, this indifference to the individual, total lack of interest in intimate knowledge of the isolated, unique human being, atrophies human reactions and humanism. Too much social consciousness, and not a bit of insight into human beings.

*The photograph appeared in *Life*, April 7, 1941. [Stuhlmann's note.]

• • •

What I like in John Dudley is his rhythm. Rhythm is what I most like about America. The language of jazz musicians has savor, color, vibrancy. The reflectiveness, reverie, of Europe is not possible because of the tempo. This tempo prevents experience from seeping in, sinking in, penetrating.

I respond to intensity, but I also like reflection to follow action, for then understanding is born, and understanding prepares me for the next day's acts.

My social consciousness is different from that of the Americans. It is not expressed in group work, in collective activity. It consists in giving help to the exceptional person who is struggling to educate himself, who is gifted but has no opportunities, no guidance.

My lack of faith in the men who lead us is that they do not recognize the irrational in men, they have no insight, and whoever does not recognize the personal, individual drama of man cannot lead them.

Psychology has ceased to be for me a mere therapy for neurotic moments. It is not only the neurotic who lives by irrational impulses rooted deeply in his experience, but everyone. This may be more or less masked by outward conventionalities. This individual irrational should be isolated and understood before it becomes an aggregate. The masses are merely an accumulation of such blind impulses. Nations, leaders, history, could be analyzed and understood as nonrational behavior can be.

In fact, most of the time the leaders have been those who symbolized nonrational emotions for the masses and therefore their negative, or destructive tendencies.

from December, 1940

A CABLE FROM PARIS. THE BOX OF DIARIES WAS TRACED AND FOUND LYING IN ONE OF THE SMALL FRENCH RAILROAD STATIONS. THE WAR HAD PASSED IT BY. IT WAS SHIPPED BACK TO THE BANK AND REPLACED IN THE VAULT.

from April, 1941

Caresse Crosby came. Canada Lee is starring in *Native Son*. We went to the play together. Then to Harlem, where Canada Lee runs a night club. We talked. Drank. Listened to jazz. Some jazz flamboyant, some creating tensions not by increased loudness but by the subtlety of its gradations. Some jazz is like velvet, some like silk, some like electric shocks, some like seduction, some like a drug.

How could one not love the people who created such a music, in which the rhythm of the heart and of the body is so human and the voice so warm, emotions so deep. Charlie Parker, Fats Waller, Duke Ellington, Benny Goodman, Cootie Williams, Benny Carter, Teddy Hill, Chick Webb, Mary Lou Williams, Count Basie, Lionel Hampton.

And Canada Lee with his eye injured in boxing, the only profession besides music in which the Negro can shine, is allowed to shine, as the poor boys of Spain were allowed only the possibility of demonstrating valor and quality in bullfights. Canada Lee, with his warm, orange-toned voice, his one unclouded eye glowing with tenderness and joy, his stance loose-limbed, natural; in life relaxed, in music and acting tense, alert, swift, and as accurate as a hunter.

The place is a cloud of smoke, the faces very near, the hypnosis of jazz all-enveloping and, even at its most screaming moments, dissolving the heart and throbbing with life.

Caresse and Canada have been friends for a long time.

Caresse is one of those who are concerned about our lives becoming less meaningful than in Europe, less vital, less sparkling and warm. We talked about this with Canada. The only authentic life of emotion and warmth seemed to be right there, at that moment, with the jazz, and the soft voices and the constant sense of touch between them. We feel more restrictions, less freedom, less tolerance, less intimacy with other human beings. Except here in Harlem.

from Fall, 1953

. . . Paul and Renate thought of a masquerade to which we would come dressed as our madness.

I wore a skin-colored leotard, leopard-fur earrings glued to the tips of my naked breasts, and a leopard-fur belt around my waist. Gil Henderson painted on my bare back a vivid jungle scene. I wore eyelashes two inches long. My hair was dusted with gold powder. My head was inside of a birdcage. From within the cage, through the open gate, I pulled out an endless roll of paper on which I had written lines from my books. The ticker tape of the unconscious. I unwound this and handed everyone a strip with a message.

When we arrived the entire house was softly lighted with candles.

Renate met us at the door. She was wearing a merry-widow hat, a waist cincher, and a black leotard. An iridescent scarf enveloped her. She carried two death masks on sticks. As she removed one mask, a second, identical mask was revealed. Her costume was inspired by José Guadalupe Posada's portrayal of voluptuous females with skulls for heads. Her madness was a conflict between sensuality and death. Her madness was: she *is* what she pretends to be.

Paul's madness was to escape his angel blondness. He died his hair black and wore a black mustache. He appeared half pirate, half Spanish Don Juan.

My escort was in a black leotard covered with plastic eyes. He carried two eyes on the tip of a wire projecting from his forehead. He had two eyes pinned on his genital region. He was all eyes, the spectator, the shy spectator.

PART EIGHT

Quests for Identity, 1960–

All autobiography involves a quest for identity: a re-seeing of the past, a reconstruction of the paths that led to the present, a definition of the self, or an attempt to defend the self. Each of these efforts entails, to some degree, a search for the self, in order to present a version of this self to an audience of one's self and others.

Only in the last generation, however, have autobiographers and their readers seemed to become truly aware of how autobiography creates the self. In the 1920s, in his attack on Benjamin Franklin's *Autobiography*, D. H. Lawrence never considered that the *Autobiography* might have been a means Franklin used to examine or create a self. Instead, Lawrence took Franklin's character as something already complete when Franklin wrote. Yet, it is now quite common to regard the *Autobiography* as a means by which Franklin remade and even invented himself: his text is not just a statement of self, but a process of finding and inventing it.

That we have come to see autobiographies this way is reflected in the parallel development and popularization of the word *identity*. According to the *Oxford English Dictionary* the word is derived from *idem*, the Latin for *same*, and in early usage it meant sameness or likeness. It signified the opposite of diversity. In the seventeenth century, it also came to be applied to persons and to the "continuity of personality," "the sameness of a person at all times or in all circumstances." In this sense, it commonly referred to internal and essential qualities, and to consciousness, rather than to external features.

During the Second World War, a group of psychiatrists working at a veterans' clinic began to use the term "identity crisis" to describe patients who had "lost a sense of personal sameness and historical continuity." Soon Erik Erikson and his associates "recognized the same central disturbance in young people whose sense of confusion is due, rather, to a war within themselves, and in confused rebels and destructive delinquents who war on their society."[1] When Erikson went on to develop his very influential concept of

---

1. Erik Erikson, *Identity: Youth and Crisis* (New York: W. W. Norton, 1968), p. 17.

the life cycle, he focused on youth as the period of identity formation. The revolt of youth in the 1960s, Erikson speculated, was caused by changes within western society—changes in technology, culture, and human expectations— which had disrupted how youth (and other people) knew themselves and each other. The affinity between person and culture could be broken when one changed without the other.

Persons and cultures also need change, however; it is how they grow and learn to adapt. This seems particularly true in the United States of the 1960s, when it was finally waking up, or being awakened, to its long-festering racial injustice, its entrenched poverty, and the brutality of the war in Vietnam. In the summer of 1963, over 100,000 people took part in a "March on Washington" to demand the passage of a Civil Rights Act. From 1965 to 1967, there were massive riots in the black ghettos of cities across the country. Demonstrations and sit-ins against the Vietnam War and in favor of new programs like Black Studies occurred at nearly all the major universities. The publication of Rachel Carson's *Silent Spring,* in 1962, also began to make people aware of the dangers of DDT and other chemicals that had once been seen as benign and as scientific miracles. Meanwhile, television changed the way people learned about and experienced these changes in the world. In November, 1963, following the Kennedy assassination, the whole country watched television day and night and saw Jack Ruby, a previously unknown, small nightclub owner, shoot Lee Harvey Oswald, the once unknown assassin. In July, 1969, it watched men land and walk on the moon. Television could almost instantly gain the attention of the whole country, and possibly even the whole world, momentarily uniting it or alarming it. In the process, television made great heroes or villains out of people once as unknown as any of the millions of people in the audience. The age of the instant celebrity had begun.

Spinoffs of the creation of the instant celebrity were the invention of the commissioned autobiography, the publishing of more ghost-written autobiographies, and the "unauthorized biography"—books about such men and women who could capitalize on their quick electronic stardom. In the 1970s, for instance, there were autobiographies of the Watergate burglars and White House staff members who planned the burglary. By the 1980s, television (and radio) had also become a standard agency in the promotion of new books, including new, mass-market autobiographies. Authors routinely appeared on local and national talk-shows, morning, noon, and night, to give a quick résumé of their books and to recount the emblematic events in their lives that would explain the writing of the book and relate it to the audience's interest and experience.

There are other reasons for this surge in the writing, reading, and talking about autobiographies than just the new media and the related changes in book marketing, however. In a culture that is changing fast and struggling to deal with the conflicts of permanence and change, people are inevitably interested in how other people are handling these conflicts and opportunities, how they are "coping." For this, the writer did not have to have been a Watergate burglar, a hostage in Iran, or an astronaut to have a significant story. Quite the opposite. People were more likely to be interested in things that were also happening to them—divorce, a drug problem, a weight problem, teenage pregnancy, the loss of a job, a "midlife crisis," alcoholism, retirement, abortion, a change of religion, living with a serious disease, and so on. Autobiographies merged in such cases with self-help books (and were often read by groups of people discussing some common problem). They could also be inspirational and about success, two long-standing traditions in American autobiography. With the nation going through a "national identity crisis," as it was sometimes called, there was inevitable interest in individual identity crises and their endings, sad or happy.

The increasingly frequent use of the word *identity* also seems to have changed its meaning. For some people, the word no longer has its traditional association with sameness but connotes something which is the core or essence of a person's being. It is almost a synonym for self. It also seems, sometimes, to be nudging aside the traditional terms "character" and "personality." *Character* traditionally referred to someone's moral worth, or lack of it, and to virtue, although it obviously carried other meanings as well. *Personality* applied more to what is entertaining, or even flashy and distracting. One "turns on the personality," but one does not "turn on character." *Identity* seems more serious than personality, less pretentious and moralistic than character, but still related to one's basic *integrity*. Identity can change and can or must be searched for. It is also something which is usually shared with other people of the same race, culture, or background, as in "black identity," "feminine identity," or "middle-class identity." And this should remind us that identity, in being shared with others, does have to be more or less the same in all those people, something like a theme with many variations.[2]

These changes in the vocabulary of selfhood are vitally important to the American autobiographies of this current or most recent generation, the autobiographies written from approximately 1960 to 1990. Finding one's identity, in the sense of what is unique and also what is shared, what is permanent but also subject to change, and what is real and yet also in some ways an artifice (a product of culture and history), and then expressing, explaining, and interpreting it has been the great goal of the best recent autobiographers.

Nobody Knows My Name, the title of James Baldwin's book, virtually an-

2. For further discussion of the questions of culture, identity, and self in autobiography, see Sidonie Smith, *A Poetics of Women's Autobiography: Marginality and the Fictions of Self-Representation* (Bloomington: Indiana Univ. Press, 1987) and Paul John Eakin, *Touching the World: Reference in Autobiography* (Princeton: Princeton Univ. Press, 1992), particularly "Theories of the Self," pp. 74–77.

nounces his need to make his name, the designator of his identity, known—known to those who would miss it or misinterpret it or mistake him for someone else. They might miss it because, from arrogance, they had habitually paid no attention to "Negroes" (Baldwin's term). Or they might mistake him because when they looked at him they did not see *him* but one of the stereotypes of Negro character which they had acquired from the American past. The title of Ralph Ellison's great novel, *Invisible Man* (1952), announced almost exactly the same problem. The black man in America did not suffer from being "highly visible," as some experts said; he was invisible, operating always from behind a host of masks and shadows of himself. Thus one of the things the autobiographies and autobiographical essays of Baldwin, Ellison, and other black writers of the 1960s and '70s did was to analyze these masks and try to show the authors in more complexity and depth. They also, on occasion, attempted to defend themselves against the false accusations and misrepresentations which white Americans made about them. As a part of this whole difficult, painful but also liberating process, we might note that the word "Negro" itself gave way to "black" or "Black" and "Afro-American."

A careful reader of Baldwin's "Discovery of What It Means to Be American" will see that his exposure of these stereotypes and misrepresentations generates the intense emotional power of his essay. A "Negro" was somehow not expected to discover what it means to be an American. He was expected to be "only" a Negro, an inferior American. Thus Baldwin aroused his white readers' secret prejudices and fears and kept all his readers uncertain of what role he would play next—the expatriate, the man of letters, the responsible citizen, the angry prophet, or something else the reader had never seen before. As a man writing from Paris, he also appropriated some of the status, favorable and unfavorable, of the American expatriates of a generation before. He could talk in a worldly way of French waiters being better than American waiters. He could talk of his friends from different parts of the French capital.

Saying these things and, consequently, manipulating his readers' emotional expectations, Baldwin was indeed "discovering what it means to be an American." He was carving out a new identity for himself as American, black American, writer, and prophet. He was using the autobiographical essay to discover his powers and to create who he was.

The autobiographies of Jewish-Americans of this period make an interesting comparision with those of Afro-Americans like Baldwin. Jews, too, faced discrimination by the white Christian majority, but had made much faster progress in overcoming it, as measured by admissions to elite schools and colleges, access to the professions, good salaries, and houses in suburbs, though they were still barred from many private clubs. Jewish traditions, however, continued to hold great meaning to Jewish Americans. The irony of Abraham Cahan's autobiographical novel, *The Rise of David Levinsky* (1917), was that as the hero succeeded in American business and "rose" to become a millionaire, he "fell" as a Jew. At the end of the book he realizes sadly, "My past and present do not comport well"—a lament that has been called "the tragedy of Jewish irreconciliation with America."[3] Even Mary Antin's confident integration into American life, as described in *The Promised Land,* was later qualified by her writing just at the beginning of World War II that she had to remember her Jewish past and try to preserve solidarity with the Jews still in Russia and Europe. After the war, the horrifying revelations of the Holocaust and the establishment of Israel made Jews all the more aware of their Jewish identity.

Thus, in post-war Jewish-American autobiographies, the conflicts of culture are intense, and the quest for identity is complicated by the recognitions of different interpretations of both "Jewish" and "American." In *A Walker in the City* (1951), the first of Alfred Kazin's three volumes of autobiography, the young Kazin is just as eager to shed his immigrant past as Mary Antin was. In the next two volumes, *Starting Out in the Thirties* (1965) and *New York Jew* (1978), he is successful, like Levinsky. He also tries harder than Levinsky to make his past and present "comport well." *Starting Out in the Thirties* is full of the excitement of becoming a writer and teacher and working on *On Native Grounds,* his classic study of American literary realism. Kazin kept a certain Jewish sense of being an outsider to American culture, but by playing a leading role in the writing of American literary history, he was also discovering and possessing American culture, defining it for other Americans. This status as both the outsider and the authority seems confirmed in *New York Jew,* where Kazin seems almost to invite the antagonism of the old Gentile establishment. He is now proud of being what they detest. He also does not wish to drop his ancestral past into the great American melting pot. He wishes to hang on to his particularity just as tenaciously as any descendants of the *Mayflower* who once dreaded a "New York Jew's" entry into "their" colleges or clubs.

"One of the longest journeys in the world," Norman Podhoretz began, in his autobiography *Making It* (1967), "is the journey from Brooklyn to Manhattan—or at least from certain neighborhoods in Brooklyn to certain parts of Manhattan." He added that "I have made that journey." But because of his smugness and brazenness about it, many readers have never felt quite comfortable with him and his story. They further resent his absorption in the literary circles of Columbia University and *Commentary* magazine. Still, Podhoretz seems to speak for a lot of Brooklynites and ex-Brooklynites when he says that as a child he did not think of himself as an American. "I came

3. Alvin H. Rosenfeld, "Inventing the Jew: Notes on Jewish Autobiography," in *The American Autobiography,* ed. Albert E. Stone (Englewood Cliffs, NJ: Prentice-Hall, 1981), p. 139.

from Brooklyn, and in Brooklyn there were no Americans; there were Jews and Negroes and Italians and Poles and Irishmen. Americans lived in New England, in the South, in the Midwest: alien people in alien places."[4]

Where Kazin and Podhoretz clung to their ethnic heritage in order, finally, not to identify with those "alien people in alien places," Allen Ginsberg attempted both to celebrate his Jewish past and to universalize it as a piece of all human experience. It was a bold undertaking, but then "Kaddish" is an extraordinary autobiography. It is a poem, first of all, and therefore a better medium than prose for Ginsberg's extended and seemingly spontaneous lyrical flights. Its models are not other autobiographies but works like Shelley's "Adonais," the Jewish Kaddish, the Buddhist Book of Answers, and Ray Charles's singing.

Nevertheless, his "Kaddish" is full of the particulars of the early twentieth-century Jewish-American immigrant experience. Naomi Ginsberg grew up in Newark, New Jersey, and it was as far from the tenements of Newark to the fashionable streets of Manhattan as it was from Podhoretz's Brooklyn. She was a communist union organizer, who sang hymns and workers' songs, went to union summer camps, and was full of "mad idealism." In this sense, as Ginsberg tells it, her story could have been the story of thousands of people in the early American labor movement. The sad difference is that in 1919 Naomi began to have nervous breakdowns. Later, with the approach of World War II, she saw Hitler, Mussolini, Roosevelt, and the FBI spying on her. Allen, we gather, became her caretaker—the person she would still trust, the person who at just twelve had the responsibility of taking her to a rest home in southern New Jersey, and the person she sometimes seductively flirted with. It was, in turn, Allen who inherited her idealism, her visionary fears and ecstasy, and also her tendencies to madness, as the world defines it. This identification with his mother contributes to the profound autobiographical nature of the poem. Different as they are, the poet and his mother are also so much alike that their stories are fitted together like lock and key. Her message that "The key is in the sunlight at the window" is the eternal mother's message: to come home, to let himself in, to cease being the prodigal ("Get married Allen don't take drugs"), and to know himself by knowing her.

Black and Jewish Americans were not the only ones to seek their identities by reclaiming their racial and cultural heritages in the process defining their relation to the rest of America. One of the most unusual was N. Scott Momaday's quest for his Kiowa heritage, recreated in *The Way to Rainy Mountain* (1969) and *The Names* (1976). As he explains in the latter, his father was Kiowa, but he himself had been raised mainly at Jemez Pueblo in New Mexico, where for twenty-five years his parents taught school. Later he went to a military school and the University of New Mexico, then took a Ph.D. in

4. Norman Podhoretz, *Making It* (New York: Bantam, 1969), pp. 3, 62.

English at Stanford University in 1963. *The Way to Rainy Mountain* poetically records a journey from the northern Rocky Mountains out onto the Great Plains and then down to Rainy Mountain in Oklahoma, a journey which follows the historic path of the Kiowa in the eighteenth and nineteenth centuries. Along the way, as it were, Momaday juxtaposes Kiowa legends, as told by his father and his ancestors (and recovered from ethnographic works), with historical material and his own memories and observations. The combination is *original* autobiography in the fullest sense—a search for origins as well as a new and different kind of book. It also serves as a kind of abbreviated Kiowa tribal history and example of Plains Indian experience, thus giving the book an even greater historical interest than usual.

In *The Names,* Momaday told a more particular family history, including the story of his mother Natachee Scott, who was descended from white Tennesseeans. But her name, "Natachee," had come from a great-grandmother who was Cherokee, and this was the ancestor the teen-age girl chose to identify with. "She imagined who she was," wrote Momaday, adding that "this act of imagination was, I believe, among the most important events of my mother's early life, as later the same essential act was to be among the most important of my own."[5] Such a statement epitomizes the role of imagination in modern ethnic identity quests. Identity, to such an autobiographer, is not given, fixed, and changeless. It is an act of passion, will, and vision working upon the diverse materials of history. These materials of history, moreover, are also viewed as created things, being as they are the results of earlier acts of passion (like a sexual union), legal procedures (like marriage), and will or accident (like someone's saving the stories, records, or photographs with which the autobiographer works).

Maxine Hong Kingston's "No Name Woman," from *The Woman Warrior,* and Richard Rodriguez's account of his experience with skin color and his definition of machismo, from *Hunger of Memory,* provide further illustrations of modern ethnic identity quests. Kingston's makes a fascinating comparison to Momaday's, because in it, too, identity is a fusion of ancient myth or legend, various kinds of history (some of which are on the verge of legend), and personal memory. Rodriguez's book is a good contrast to Baldwin's, because it deals more with race as a social and economic issue in America and with the more immediate experiences of prejudice. But Rodriguez takes a much more conservative position than Baldwin did. In fact, before his book was even published, he had announced in various journalistic articles that he opposed bilingual education in schools because he thought it so important for children to be required to learn English as the "public" American language, the language which had enabled him to participate fully in American life. As a very well-educated Mexican-American, he had, in turn, won schol-

5. N. Scott Momaday, *The Names* (New York: Harper and Row, 1976), p. 25.

arships to prestigious universities and so did not consider himself as needing the assistance of affirmative action programs.

Rodriguez's articles against bilingual education and affirmative action made him widely sought as a conservative lecturer. His autobiography was, in turn, sought as a further statement and explanation of his views, and it became hotly controversial. As such, it is a perfect example of the interplay among media, public issues, and autobiography. Yet there are precedents for *Hunger of Memory* as an apologia. Rodriguez insisted that he had been misunderstood and his message oversimplified. He argued that he really opposed affirmative action because it gave unfair advantages to people who did not need help, such as the educated middle class, and deflected attention from the poor and uneducated who needed more special programs like Headstart. His book should, therefore, be read in full, along with the well-reasoned replies that it provoked from other Mexican-Americans.[6]

The Woman Warrior has also been attacked. Chinese-Americans have accused Kingston of misrepresenting Chinese-American experience, making her own life over into something exotically "oriental," and distorting Chinese legends. Frank Chin has raised the additional argument that *The Woman Warrior* is untrue to Chinese tradition because autobiography is a "peculiarly Christian literary weapon."[7] Indeed, the debate raises questions not only about Chinese-American autobiography but about autobiography in general.[8]

Many other autobiographies have come out of the political controversies of the sixties, seventies, and eighties. *The Autobiography of Malcolm X* (1965) was solicited by publishers after Alex Haley's widely read interview with Malcolm X in *Playboy*. The difficulty which Malcolm X and Black Muslims had in obtaining sympathetic reports from white journalists made a partnership with Haley very valuable, even though Malcolm X at first distrusted him. Ron Kovic's *Born on the Fourth of July* was the account of his service in Vietnam, his being wounded, and his conversion from a born patriot and believer in the war into an anti-war activist. Kate Millett's *Flying* (1974) was her account of her discovery of herself and her deeper sexuality in the process of becoming a feminist. In *Farewell to Manzanar* (1973), Jeanne Wakatsuki Houston told of her coming of age in an internment camp for Japanese-Americans during

---

6. See, for example, Tomas Rivera, "Richard Rodriguez' *Hunger of Memory* as Humanistic Antithesis," *MELUS* 11 (Winter 1984): 5–13, and Victor Villanueva, Jr., "Whose Voice Is It Anyway? Rodriguez' Speech in Retrospect," *English Journal* 76 (December 1987): 17–21. For a review of the controversies, see Raymond A. Paredes, "Autobiography and Ethnic Politics: Richard Rodriguez's *Hunger of Memory*," in *Multicultural Autobiography: American Lives,* ed. James Robert Payne (Knoxville: Univ. of Tennessee Press, 1992), pp. 280–96.
7. Frank Chin, "This Is Not An Autobiography," *Genre* 18 (Summer 1985): 109.
8. See Sau-ling Cynthia Wong, "Autobiography as Guided Chinatown Tour? Maxine Hong Kingston's *The Woman Warrior* and the Chinese-American Autobiographical Controversy," in *Multicultural Autobiography,* ed. Payne, pp. 248–79.

World War II. In her essay included here, "Beyond Manzanar," she describes her later conflicts between Japanese and American concepts of womanhood. Her conflicts will be understandable to many other women (and men) caught between cultures and between traditions.

At the same time, earlier American identity quests which had been ignored or forgotten were rediscovered. *Black Elk Speaks* is now recognized as a classic Native-American autobiography. Yet, between its initial publication in 1932 and the late 1960s, when it began to be read by a few anthropologists, hippies, and young Indians, it had been virtually forgotten. Suddenly, Black Elk's account of his visions and his later finding his role in Oglala Sioux society as a medicine man and healer had enormous appeal.[9]

Some other classic autobiographies rediscovered in this last generation are Harriet E. Wilson's *Our Nig; or, Sketches from the Life of a Free Black* (1859), Harriet Jacobs's *Incidents in the Life of a Slave Girl* (1861), Carlos Bulosan's *America Is in the Heart* (1943), and Zora Neale Hurston's *Dust Tracks on a Road* (1942). In the latter case, Alice Walker took the lead, having discovered Hurston in the course of trying to write a short story about voodoo. Until then, as she says in her autobiographical essay, "Looking for Zora,"[10] she had never heard of Hurston's work. Once found, her affinities with Hurston were so great that she identified with Hurston on many levels. Hurston became a role-model, a teacher, and an inspiration.

The universal need for such models is surely another reason for the continued and growing popularity of autobiography in the last generation. From its beginnings, autobiography has been written to be used as instruction. But the early religious autobiography was generally much narrower in focus and more inclined to leave out material that might show the subject's faults or have a detrimental effect on the reader. Such selectivity was even more pronounced in didactic, inspirational autobiographies like Lydia Sigourney's *Letters of Life* and Lucy Larcom's *A New England Girlhood*. A reader could turn to them for moral elevation, but not for much consolation or sympathy. Autobiographies such as Maya Angelou's *I Know Why the Caged Bird Sings* (1970) or Patricia Hampl's *A Romantic Education* (1981) represent more of the ups and downs, the disappointments and struggles, and the uncertainties of life. By telling their tales, Angelou and Hampl make the lives of other women in similar times and places easier to live and easier to tell about. Their identity quests help readers to find their own identities.

In the chapter from *Black Is a Woman's Color,* bell hooks goes a step further by telling a series of stories which are not just representative or illustrative

9. See Robert F. Sayre, "Vision and Experience in *Black Elk Speaks*," *College English* 32 (February 1971): 509–35.
10. In Alice Walker, *In Search of Our Mothers' Gardens: Womanist Prose* (New York: Harcourt Brace, 1983), pp. 93–116.

ones but ones which could be even more central to contemporary culture. The six stories in this provocative chapter have as their subjects the straigtening of hair, the discovering of jazz and poetry, memories of her father's attacks on her mother, her mother's leaving, and her own rebellion against her mother. The stories move from a relatively innocent initiation into black sisterhood to a very dangerous, passionate initiation into our society's conflicts of authority: the socially accepted but unjust authority of an abusive father, the inadequate authority of a submissive mother, and a daughter's unsure efforts to establish her own new authority. Clearly, this series of stories is more than just hooks's own "life" or *bios*. It is what another black woman autobiographer, Audre Lord, called "bio-mythography," an extension of autobiography into a personal-cultural mythology. Autobiography has long had a certain mythic function—think of Franklin's *Autobiography;* primarily, however, an autobiography is *one* person's story, where a myth is *everybody's* story, a story which has either happened to everybody or which everybody shares in. Hooks's stories qualify as myth in these senses. Without being a full cultural hero, someone, say, who in slaying a dragon has saved everyone in the village, she has made herself someone around whose story others can tell their stories and talk of their needs for liberation, and its pains and obstacles, thus helping these others to liberate or, as hooks says, "to recover" themselves.

Race and gender are not the only sources of modern identity, however. The true "guardian of identity," Erik Erikson thought, was "*ideology,*" and he italicized the term to give it the widest possible meaning, applying it to any social system that conveyed to its members a faith that "the best people will come to rule and rule will develop the best in people."[11] One of the reasons for identity confusion in modern America, therefore, may actually be that we have so many rival ideologies, yet such an oversimplified dominant public one. That is to say, the dominant modern American ideology of free enterprise, which represents the self-made man rising to "rule" simply by being "best," in the process showering himself and his family with consumer comforts, is one that nearly every American over the age of eighteen has at some time or another found to be a hollow lie or one offering goals that do not satisfy. "Sexist" and "racist" are only the latest epithets directed at it. Its older critics long ago found it selfish, deceitful, and spiritually lacking.

Thus we end this selection with two contemporary American autobiographies that represent yet two more American "ideologies." The first is Wendell Berry's story of his finding "all I need" in his "marginal farm" in Kentucky. It brings to mind Daniel Boone's autobiography, for the "great-great-great-grandfather" of Berry's who first settled there in 1803 would have been a contemporary of Boone's. But where Boone was interested in settlements and was as restless and violent as many other Americans of 1800, Berry is

11. Erikson, *Identity*, pp. 133–34.

interested in *re-settlement,* and there is an enormous difference. Berry tells in this essay (as in many of his other novels, poems, and essays) of the time, work, and thought he has given to correcting the abuses of the restless, violent exploiters of the land. No crops on hillsides, such as the early settlers tried to grow. A return to farming with horses, which the later farmers and developers had abandoned. And promotion of subsistence, "marginal" farming, even though acknowledging that he also depends on the income from his writing. But he does this not only because he is ecologically conscious, he does it because he truly loves his land. The land and proper husbanding of it are his ideology, the truest guardian of his identity that he can imagine. His first Kentucky ancestor may have been a contemporary of Boone's, but Berry's ideological ancestors are Jefferson and Thoreau.

Modern autobiographers who are close to Berry are other nature writers and ecologists, even though their own physical turf may be as far away as Anne LaBastille's cabin in the Adirondacks or Edward Abbey's house trailer in Arches National Monument, celebrated in *Desert Solitaire,* or Gary Snyder's homes in the "back country." They all identify with nature and a place, which in turn means that the more they know that place and the more eloquently they can describe and protect it, the better they can identify themselves.

Another person strongly identified with place is Annie Dillard, who in 1974 became famous almost overnight for *Pilgrim at Tinker Creek.* But unlike Berry, she has not chosen to stay in one place. In the years since *Tinker Creek,* she has lived in many other places, such as Middletown, Connecticut, and Bellingham, Washington. In *An American Childhood,* she celebrated Pittsburgh, a very unlikely place because it is so different from "Tinker Creek" in rural Virginia. But it was the town where she grew up, and it was, therefore, inextricably connected for her with all the awakenings, discoveries, and rebellions of childhood and youth. Her parents' and grandparents' houses, a friend's house in the mountains outside Pittsburgh, the Allegheny, the Monongahela, and the Ohio rivers, the Pittsburgh Pirates, and the outstanding local libraries and museums all contributed to making her who she was.

Something else that Dillard said about writing *An American Childhood* is also very important to the issue of autobiography and identity, however. In a talk that she gave at the New York Public Library shortly before the book was published, she said,

My advice to memoir writers is to embark upon a memoir for the same reason that you would embark on any other book: to fashion a text. Don't hope in a memoir to preserve your memories. If you prize your memories as they are, by all means avoid— eschew—writing a memoir. Because it is in a certain way to lose them. You can't put together a memoir without cannibalizing your own life for parts. The work battens on your memories. And it replaces them.[12]

12. Annie Dillard, "To Fashion a Text," in *Inventing the Truth: The Art and Craft of Memoir,* ed. William Zinsser (Boston: Houghton Mifflin, 1987), p. 70.

Not all writers of memoirs and autobiographies might agree with Dillard, but many critics and careful readers of autobiography today would. The text—the words on paper—are not the reality. They are a book, not a life. And they reshape the life—"cannibalizing" it, as Dillard says—until there may be very little of it left. The words on paper also have an independent force because of the echoes and shades of meaning which they carry from elsewhere, from other books and from other texts of all kinds. Furthermore, traditions of autobiography shape the kinds of texts the author chooses to write, as we have pointed out before.

So the modern identity quest in autobiography is a complex process. From one point of view, the words make the new life, even though the author chooses the words, being more or less conscious of what words he or she is using and exerting more or less freedom in choosing them. On the other hand, since autobiography is a referential art, the words must also refer to facts, and the facts, in turn, have to do with the deeds and events and places that the author-as-actor performed or experienced. And yet these deeds and events and places and the memories of them become cannibalized in the writing.

Adapting Dillard's metaphor of cannibalism, we might compare the whole process to a kind of food chain. Words eat memories, which have grown fat on experience. Experience happens to and is caused by persons. Persons seek their identities and start to write words, which again start eating up memories, changing the identities. The process is also like a food chain in that it is not necessarily a perfect circle. The creatures in it may cross over: new experiences may arise and eat up memories before the words even get to them. And all this takes place in a forest we might call Culture, which both sustains and destroys all the creatures—the words, memories, experiences, persons, and identities—as well as all the little micro-creatures within them. Moreover, the process never stops. We can imaginatively halt it and look at a part of it, but it is ever-moving, and all parts are necessary, all interdependent.

This, then, is the ecology of modern autobiography, in which Americans continue to seek their identities and express their latest concepts of self.

45

James Baldwin (1924–1990)

The Discovery of What It Means to Be an American

Born in New York, James Baldwin attended public schools in Harlem and gradu-ated from De Witt Clinton High School in 1942, where he co-edited the school newspaper with Richard Avedon, the future photographer. In his teens he was also a "boy preacher" for several years at the Fireside Pentecostal Assembly.

Moving to Greenwich Village in 1944, he was introduced to Richard Wright, who liked his writing and helped him to win two literary fellowships, and whom he followed, in 1948, to Paris. There he finished *Go Tell It on the Mountain* (1953), a novel based on the religious experiences of his boyhood, and began to publish a number of powerful personal essays about the race problem in America. *Notes of a Native Son* (1955) was his first collection of these, *Nobody Knows My Name* (1961) was his second, and a third, *The Fire Next Time* (1963), became a best-seller. The essay below was first published in the *New York Times Book Review* (January 25, 1959) and was later the opening essay in *Nobody Knows My Name*.

In his essays Baldwin spoke both intimately and analytically about his experi-ences as a black in America, while at the same time insisting on his right and responsibility to speak as any other American and to attack the prejudices that would make him "*merely* a Negro." He made his personal identity quest a public issue, breaking out of the racial stereotypes that had made him "nameless." Thus in this essay he speaks as both white and black. He identifies with Henry James and the traditions of American artist-exiles and is also "as American as any Texas G.I." Yet he listens to Bessie Smith "to dig back to the way I myself must have spoken when I was a pickaninny."

Baldwin was later attacked by white and black writers. In *Advertisements for Myself,* Norman Mailer called him too introspective, saying he would never be a great writer till he "smashed the perfumed dome of his ego." Eldridge Cleaver's *Soul on Ice* attacked him as a homosexual who lacked black pride and was not sufficiently militant. Cleaver and later black writers wished to discover not what it means to be an American but what it means to be black. Both Baldwin and Cleaver had become public figures, however, largely because of brilliant autobiographical essays.

The definitive biography is James Campbell, *Talking at the Gates: A Life of James Baldwin* (New York: Viking, 1991).

"It is a complex fate to be an American," Henry James observed, and the principal discovery an American writer makes in Europe is just how complex this fate is. America's history, her aspirations, her peculiar triumphs, her even more peculiar defeats, and her position in the world—yesterday and today— are all so profoundly and stubbornly unique that the very word "America" remains a new, almost completely undefined and extremely controversial proper noun. No one in the world seems to know exactly what it describes, not even we motley millions who call ourselves Americans.

I left America because I doubted my ability to survive the fury of the color problem here. (Sometimes I still do.) I wanted to prevent myself from becoming *merely* a Negro; or, even, merely a Negro writer. I wanted to find out in what way the *specialness* of my experience could be made to connect me with other people instead of dividing me from them. (I was as isolated from Negroes as I was from whites, which is what happens when a Negro begins, at bottom, to believe what white people say about him.)

In my necessity to find the terms on which my experience could be related to that of others, Negroes and whites, writers and non-writers, I proved, to my astonishment, to be as American as any Texas G.I. And I found my experience was shared by every American writer I knew in Paris. Like me, they had been divorced from their origins, and it turned out to make very little difference that the origins of white Americans were European and mine were African—they were no more at home in Europe than I was.

The fact that I was the son of a slave and they were the sons of free men meant less, by the time we confronted each other on European soil, than the fact that we were both searching for our separate identities. When we had found these, we seemed to be saying, why, then, we would no longer need to cling to the shame and bitterness which had divided us so long.

It became terribly clear in Europe, as it never had been here, that we knew more about each other than any European ever could. And it also became clear that, no matter where our fathers had been born, or what they had endured, the fact of Europe had formed us both, was part of our identity and part of our inheritance.

I had been in Paris a couple of years before any of this became clear to me. When it did, I, like many a writer before me upon the discovery that his props have all been knocked out from under him, suffered a species of breakdown and was carried off to the mountains of Switzerland. There, in that absolutely alabaster landscape, armed with two Bessie Smith records and a typewriter, I began to try to re-create the life that I had first known as a child and from which I had spent so many years in flight.

It was Bessie Smith, through her tone and her cadence, who helped me to dig back to the way I myself must have spoken when I was a pickaninny, and to remember the things I had heard and seen and felt. I had buried them very deep. I had never listened to Bessie Smith in America (in the same way that, for years, I would not touch watermelon), but in Europe she helped to reconcile me to being a "nigger."

I do not think that I could have made this reconciliation here. Once I was able to accept my role—as distinguished, I must say, from my "place"— in the extraordinary drama which is America, I was released from the illusion that I hated America.

The story of what can happen to an American Negro writer in Europe simply illustrates, in some relief, what can happen to any American writer there. It is not meant, of course, to imply that it happens to them all, for Europe can be very crippling, too; and, anyway, a writer, when he has made his first breakthrough, has simply won a crucial skirmish in a dangerous, un-ending and unpredictable battle. Still, the breakthrough is important, and the point is that an American writer, in order to achieve it, very often has to leave this country.

The American writer, in Europe, is released, first of all, from the necessity of apologizing for himself. It is not until he is released from the habit of flex-ing his muscles and proving that he is just a "regular guy" that he realizes how crippling this habit has been. It is not necessary for him, there, to pretend to be something he is not, for the artist does not encounter in Europe the same suspicion he encounters here. Whatever the Europeans may actually think of artists, they have killed enough of them off by now to know that they are as real—and as persistent—as rain, snow, taxes or businessmen.

Of course, the reason for Europe's comparative clarity concerning the different functions of men in society is that European society has always been divided into classes in a way that American society never has been. A Euro-pean writer considers himself to be part of an old and honorable tradition— of intellectual activity, of letters—and his choice of a vocation does not cause him any uneasy wonder as to whether or not it will cost him all his friends. But this tradition does not exist in America.

On the contrary, we have a very deep-seated distrust of real intellectual effort (probably because we suspect that it will destroy, as I hope it does, that myth of America to which we cling so desperately). An American writer fights his way to one of the lowest rungs on the American social ladder by means of pure bull-headedness and an indescribable series of odd jobs. He probably has been a "regular fellow" for much of his adult life, and it is not easy for him to step out of that lukewarm bath.

We must, however, consider a rather serious paradox: though American society is more mobile than Europe's, it is easier to cut across social and occupational lines there than it is here. This has something to do, I think, with the problem of status in American life. Where everyone has status, it is also perfectly possible, after all, that no one has. It seems inevitable, in any case, that a man may become uneasy as to just what his status is.

But Europeans have lived with the idea of status for a long time. A man can be as proud of being a good waiter as of being a good actor, and in neither case feel threatened. And this means that the actor and the waiter can have a freer and more genuinely friendly relationship in Europe than they are likely to have here. The waiter does not feel, with obscure resentment, that the actor has "made it," and the actor is not tormented by the fear that he may find himself, tomorrow, once again a waiter.

This lack of what may roughly be called social paranoia causes the American writer in Europe to feel—almost certainly for the first time in his life— that he can reach out to everyone, that he is accessible to everyone and open to everything. This is an extraordinary feeling. He feels, so to speak, his own weight, his own value.

It is as though he suddenly came out of a dark tunnel and found himself beneath the open sky. And, in fact, in Paris, I began to see the sky for what seemed to be the first time. It was borne in on me—and it did not make me feel melancholy—that this sky had been there before I was born and would be there when I was dead. And it was up to me, therefore, to make of my brief opportunity the most that could be made.

I was born in New York, but have lived only in pockets of it. In Paris, I lived in all parts of the city—on the Right Bank and the Left, among the bourgeoisie and among *les misérables,* and knew all kinds of people, from pimps and prostitutes in Pigalle to Egyptian bankers in Neuilly. This may sound extremely unprincipled or even obscurely immoral: I found it healthy. I love to talk to people, all kinds of people, and almost everyone, as I hope we still know, loves a man who loves to listen.

This perpetual dealing with people very different from myself caused a shattering in me of preconceptions I scarcely knew I held. The writer is meeting in Europe people who are not American, whose sense of reality is entirely different from his own. They may love or hate or admire or fear or envy this country—they see it, in any case, from another point of view, and this forces the writer to reconsider many things he had always taken for granted. This reassessment, which can be very painful, is also very valuable.

This freedom, like all freedom, has its dangers and its responsibilities. One day it begins to be borne in on the writer, and with great force, that he is living in Europe as an American. If he were living there as a European, he would be living on a different and far less attractive continent.

This crucial day may be the day on which an Algerian taxi-driver tells him how it feels to be an Algerian in Paris. It may be the day on which he passes a café terrace and catches a glimpse of the tense, intelligent and troubled face of Albert Camus. Or it may be the day on which someone asks him to explain Little Rock and he begins to feel that it would be simpler—and, corny as the words may sound, more honorable—to go to Little Rock than sit in Europe, on an American passport, trying to explain it.

This is a personal day, a terrible day, the day to which his entire sojourn has been tending. It is the day he realizes that there are no untroubled countries in this fearfully troubled world; that if he has been preparing himself for anything in Europe, he has been preparing himself—for America. In short, the freedom that the American writer finds in Europe brings him, full circle, back to himself, with the responsibility for his development where it always was: in his own hands.

Even the most incorrigible maverick has to be born somewhere. He may leave the group that produced him—he may be forced to—but nothing will efface his origins, the marks of which he carries with him everywhere. I think it is important to know this and even find it a matter for rejoicing, as the strongest people do, regardless of their station. On this acceptance, literally, the life of a writer depends.

The charge has often been made against American writers that they do not describe society, and have no interest in it. They only describe individuals in opposition to it, or isolated from it. Of course, what the American writer is describing is his own situation. But what is Anna Karenina describing if not the tragic fate of the isolated individual, at odds with her time and place?

The real difference is that Tolstoy was describing an old and dense society in which everything seemed—to the people in it, though not to Tolstoy—to be fixed forever. And the book is a masterpiece because Tolstoy was able to fathom, and make us see, the hidden laws which really governed this society and made Anna's doom inevitable.

American writers do not have a fixed society to describe. The only society they know is one in which nothing is fixed and in which the individual must fight for his identity. This is a rich confusion, indeed, and it creates for the American writer unprecedented opportunities.

That the tensions of American life, as well as the possibilities, are tremendous is certainly not even a question. But these are dealt with in contemporary literature mainly compulsively; that is, the book is more likely to be a symptom of our tension than an examination of it. The time has come, God knows, for us to examine ourselves, but we can only do this if we are willing to free ourselves of the myth of America and try to find out what is really happening here.

Every society is really governed by hidden laws, by unspoken but profound assumptions on the part of the people, and ours is no exception. It is up to the American writer to find out what these laws and assumptions are. In a society much given to smashing taboos without thereby managing to be liberated from them, it will be no easy matter.

It is no wonder, in the meantime, that the American writer keeps running off to Europe. He needs sustenance for his journey and the best models he can find. Europe has what we do not have yet, a sense of the mysterious and inexorable limits of life, a sense, in a word, of tragedy. And we have what they sorely need: a new sense of life's possibilities.

In this endeavor to wed the vision of the Old World with that of the New, it is the writer, not the statesman, who is our strongest arm. Though we do not wholly believe it yet, the interior life is a real life, and the intangible dreams of people have a tangible effect on the world.

46

Allen Ginsberg (1926–)
Kaddish

The Kaddish, which means "holy" in Aramaic, refers to any of five different prayers which have been recited in Jewish services for thousands of years. One of these, the Mourner's Kaddish, is a prayer for the bereaved to recite in honor of their loved ones. Two lines of it—"Yisborach, v'yistabach . . . b'rich hu"—are quoted in Section II of the poem and then translated in lines 1–2 of the "Hymmnn" section. Nevertheless, as this excerpt illustrates, the prayer does not speak of loss, mention the dead, or mention the feelings of the Mourner. It simply praises God as the supreme source of peace, the eternal power and eternal rest.

In the poem "Kaddish," Allen Ginsberg mixes this Jewish tradition with very intimate, painful memories of his mother Naomi Ginsberg's death after years of madness, suicide attempts, and confinements in mental hospitals. He also writes frankly and realistically and sometimes humorously about his own life—his homosexuality, his taking drugs, his rivalry with his brother, his restless travels, his visions, and his ambition to be a great visionary poet. It is possibly the most autobiographical poem Ginsberg has written, and all his work has been autobiographical, as a part of his aesthetic of spontaneity, expressiveness, and energy.

However, with the exception of Part II, which, as said in the poem, was written in twenty straight hours, after a night without sleep, the poem was not written quickly. According to Ginsberg's account in "How 'Kaddish' Happened," Part IV was written first; then a year later parts I and II; and still later Part V. (He does not mention Part III.)[1] He also waited a year before making a clean draft of the manuscript, fearful that the poem was too long, disorderly, and private— a rather startling thing for Ginsberg the supposedly wild man to admit. But it has since been recognized as a great poem: both ecstatic and controlled, funny and sad, personal and universal.

The text below is from *Collected Poems 1947–1980* (New York: Harper and Row, 1984). Barry Miles, *Ginsberg: A Biography* (New York: Viking, 1989), is the

"Kaddish for Naomi Ginsberg 1894–1956" from *Collected Poems 1947–1980* by Allen Ginsberg, copyright © 1959, 1984 by Allen Ginsberg, is reprinted by permission of HarperCollins Publishers, Inc., and Penguin Books Ltd.
1. In *The Poetics of the New American Poetry*, ed. Donald Allen and Warren Tallman (New York: Grove, 1973), pp. 345–47.

latest biography. Jane Kramer's *Allen Ginsberg in America* (New York: Random House, 1969) is an invaluable study of the man and the myth. *On the Poetry of Allen Ginsberg,* ed. Lewis Hyde (Ann Arbor: Univ. of Michigan Press, 1984), has a rich collection of reviews, essays, and documents.

For Naomi Ginsberg 1894–1956

I

Strange now to think of you, gone without corsets & eyes, while I walk on the sunny pavement of Greenwich Village.

downtown Manhattan, clear winter noon, and I've been up all night, talking, talking, reading the Kaddish aloud, listening to Ray Charles blues shout blind on the phonograph

the rhythm the rhythm—and your memory in my head three years after— And read Adonais' last triumphant stanzas aloud—wept, realizing how we suffer—

And how Death is that remedy all singers dream of, sing, remember, prophesy as in the Hebrew Anthem, or the Buddhist Book of Answers—and my own imagination of a withered leaf—at dawn—

Dreaming back thru life, Your time—and mine accelerating toward Apocalypse,

the final moment—the flower burning in the Day—and what comes after,

looking back on the mind itself that saw an American city

a flash away, and the great dream of Me or China, or you and a phantom Russia, or a crumpled bed that never existed—

like a poem in the dark—escaped back to Oblivion—

No more to say, and nothing to weep for but the Beings in the Dream, trapped in its disappearance,

sighing, screaming with it, buying and selling pieces of phantom, worshipping each other,

worshipping the God included in it all—longing or inevitability?—while it lasts, a Vision—anything more?

It leaps about me, as I go out and walk the street, look back over my shoulder, Seventh Avenue, the battlements of window office buildings shouldering each other high, under a cloud, tall as the sky an instant—and the sky above—an old blue place.

or down the Avenue to the South, to—as I walk toward the Lower East Side—where you walked 50 years ago, little girl—from Russia, eating the first poisonous tomatoes of America—frightened on the dock—

then struggling in the crowds of Orchard Street toward what?—toward Newark—

toward candy store, first home-made sodas of the century, handchurned ice
cream in backroom on musty brownfloor boards—
Toward education marriage nervous breakdown, operation, teaching school,
and learning to be mad, in a dream—what is this life?
Toward the Key in the window—and the great Key lays its head of light on
top of Manhattan, and over the floor, and lays down on the sidewalk—
in a single vast beam, moving, as I walk down First toward the Yiddish
Theater—and the place of poverty
you knew, and I know, but without caring now—Strange to have moved thru
Paterson, and the West, and Europe and here again,
with the cries of Spaniards now in the doorstoops doors and dark boys on
the street, fire escapes old as you
—Tho you're not old now, that's left here with me—
Myself, anyhow, maybe as old as the universe—and I guess that dies with
us—enough to cancel all that comes—What came is gone forever
every time—
That's good! That leaves it open for no regret—no fear radiators, lacklove,
torture even toothache in the end—
Though while it comes it is a lion that eats the soul—and the lamb, the soul,
in us, alas, offering itself in sacrifice to change's fierce hunger—hair
and teeth—and the roar of bonepaln, skull bare, break rib, rot-skin,
braintricked Implacability.
Ai! ai! we do worse! We are in a fix! And you're out, Death let you out, Death
had the Mercy, you're done with your century, done with God, done
with the path thru it—Done with yourself at last—Pure—Back to the
Babe dark before your Father, before us all—before the world—
There, rest. No more suffering for you. I know where you've gone, it's good.
No more flowers in the summer fields of New York, no joy now, no more fear
of Louis,
and no more of his sweetness and glasses, his high school decades, debts,
loves, frightened telephone call, conception beds, relatives, hands—
No more of sister Elanor,—she gone before you—we kept it secret—you
killed her—or she killed herself to bear with you—an arthritic heart—
But Death's killed you both—No matter—
Nor your memory of your mother, 1915 tears in silent movies weeks and
weeks—forgetting, agrieve watching Marie Dressler address humanity,
Chaplin dance in youth,
or Boris Godinov, Chaliapin's at the Met, halling his voice of a weeping
Czar—by standing room with Elanor & Max—watching also the Capitalists take seats in Orchestra, white furs, diamonds,
with the YPSL's hitch-hiking thru Pennsylvania, in black baggy gym skirts
pants, photograph of 4 girls holding each other round the waste, and
laughing eye, too coy, virginal solitude of 1920

all girls grown old, or dead, now, and that long hair in the grave—lucky to
have husbands later—

You made it—I came too—Eugene my brother before (still grieving now
and will gream on to his last stiff hand, as he goes thru his cancer—or
kill—later perhaps—soon he will think—)

And it's the last moment I remember, which I see them all, thru myself,
now—tho not you

I didn't foresee what you felt—what more hideous gape of bad mouth came
first—to you—and were you prepared?

To go where? In that Dark—that—in that God? a radiance? A Lord in
the Void? Like an eye in the black cloud in a dream? Adonoi at last,
with you?

Beyond my remembrance! Incapable to guess! Not merely the yellow skull in
the grave, or a box of worm dust, and a stained ribbon—Deathshead
with Halo? can you believe it?

Is it only the sun that shines once for the mind, only the flash of existence,
than none ever was?

Nothing beyond what we have—what you had—that so pitiful—yet Triumph,

to have been here, and changed, like a tree, broken, or flower—fed to the
ground—but mad, with its petals, colored, thinking Great Universe,
shaken, cut in the head, leaf stript, hid in an egg crate hospital, cloth
wrapped, sore—freaked in the moon brain, Naughtless.

No flower like that flower, which knew itself in the garden, and fought the
knife—lost

Cut down by an idiot Snowman's icy—even in the Spring—strange ghost
thought—some Death—Sharp icicle in his hand—crowned with old
roses—a dog for his eyes—cock of a sweatshop—heart of electric irons.

All the accumulations of life, that wear us out—clocks, bodies, consciousness, shoes, breasts—begotten sons—your Communism—'Paranoia'
into hospitals.

You once kicked Elanor in the leg, she died of heart failure later. You of stroke.
Asleep? within a year, the two of you, sisters in death. Is Elanor happy?

Max grieves alive in an office on Lower Broadway, lone large mustache
over midnight Accountings, not sure. His life passes—as he sees—
and what does he doubt now? Still dream of making money, or that
might have made money, hired nurse, had children, found even your
Immortality, Naomi?

I'll see him soon. Now I've got to cut through—to talk to you—as I didn't
when you had a mouth.

Forever. And we're bound for that, Forever—like Emily Dickinson's horses—
headed to the End.

They know the way—These Steeds—run faster than we think—it's our own
    life they cross—and take with them.

    Magnificent, mourned no more, marred of heart, mind behind, married dreamed, mortal changed—Ass and face done with murder.

    In the world, given, flower maddened, made no Utopia, shut under pine, almed in Earth, balmed in Lone, Jehovah, accept.

    Nameless, One Faced, Forever beyond me, beginningless, endless, Father in death. Tho I am not there for this Prophecy, I am unmarried, I'm hymnless, I'm Heavenless, headless in blisshood I would still adore

    Thee, Heaven, after Death, only One blessed in Nothing-ness, not light or darkness, Dayless Eternity—

    Take this, this Psalm, from me, burst from my hand in a day, some of my Time, now given to Nothing—to praise Thee—But Death

    This is the end, the redemption from Wilderness, way for the Wonderer, House sought for All, black handkerchief washed clean by weeping— page beyond Psalm—Last change of mine and Naomi—to God's perfect Darkness—Death, stay thy phantoms!

II

    Over and over—refrain—of the Hospitals—still haven't written your history—leave it abstract—a few images run thru the mind—like the saxaphone chorus of houses and years—remembrance of electrical shocks.

    By long nites as a child in Paterson apartment, watching over your nervousness—you were fat—your next move—

    By that afternoon I stayed home from school to take care of you— once and for all—when I vowed forever that once man disagreed with my opinion of the cosmos, I was lost—

    By my later burden—vow to illuminate mankind—this is release of particulars—(mad as you)—(sanity a trick of agreement)—

    But you stared out the window on the Broadway Church corner, and spied a mystical assassin from Newark,

    So phoned the Doctor—'OK go way for a rest'—so I put on my coat and walked you downstreet—On the way a grammarschool boy screamed, unaccountably—'Where you goin Lady to Death'? I shuddered—

    and you covered your nose with motheaten fur collar, gas mask against poison sneaked into downtown atmosphere, sprayed by Grandma—

    And was the driver of the cheesebox Public Service bus a member of the gang? You shuddered at his face, I could hardly get you on—to New York, very Times Square, to grab another Greyhound—

where we hung around 2 hours fighting invisible bugs and jewish sickness—breeze poisoned by Roosevelt—

out to get you—and me tagging along, hoping it would end in a quiet room in a victorian house by a lake.

Ride 3 hours thru tunnels past all American industry, Bayonne preparing for World War II, tanks, gas fields, soda factories, diners, locomotive roundhouse fortress—into piney woods New Jersey Indians—calm towns— long roads thru sandy tree fields—

Bridges by deerless creeks, old wampum loading the streambed— down there a tomahawk or Pocahantas bone—and a million old ladies voting for Roosevelt in brown small houses, roads off the Madness highway—

perhaps a hawk in a tree, or a hermit looking for an owl-filled branch—

All the time arguing—afraid of strangers in the forward double seat, snoring regardless—what busride they snore on now?

'Allen, you don't understand—it's—ever since those 3 big sticks up my back—they did something to me in Hospital, they poisoned me, they want to see me dead—3 big sticks, 3 big sticks—

'The Bitch! Old Grandma! Last week I saw her, dressed in pants like an old man, with a sack on her back, climbing up the brick side of the apartment

'On the fire escape, with poison germs, to throw on me—at night— maybe Louis is helping her—he's under her power—

'I'm your mother, take me to Lakewood' (near where Graf Zeppelin had crashed before, all Hitler in Explosion) 'where I can hide.'

We got there—Dr. Whatzis rest home—she hid behind a closet— demanded a blood transfusion.

We were kicked out—tramping with Valise to unknown shady lawn houses—dusk, pine trees after dark—long dead street filled with crickets and poison ivy—

I shut her up by now—big house REST HOME ROOMS—gave the landlady her money for the week—carried up the iron valise—sat on bed waiting to escape—

Neat room in attic with friendly bedcover—lace curtains—spinning wheel rug—Stained wallpaper old as Naomi. We were home.

I left on the next bus to New York—lay my head back in the last seat, depressed—the worst yet to come?—abandoning her, rode in torpor—I was only 12.

Would she hide in her room and come out cheerful for breakfast? Or lock her door and stare thru the window for side-street spies? Listen at keyholes for Hitlerian invisible gas? Dream in a chair—or mock me, by—in front of a mirror alone?

12 riding the bus at nite thru New Jersey, have left Naomi to Parcae in Lakewood's haunted house—left to my own fate bus—sunk in a seat—

all violins broken—my heart sore in my ribs—mind was empty—Would she were safe in her coffin—

Or back at Normal School in Newark, studying up on America in a black skirt—winter on the street without lunch—a penny a pickle—home at night to take care of Elanor in the bedroom—

First nervous breakdown was 1919—she stayed home from school and lay in a dark room for three weeks—something bad—never said what—every noise hurt—dreams of the creaks of Wall Street—

Before the grey Depression—went upstate New York—recovered—Lou took photo of her sitting crossleg on the grass—her long hair wound with flowers—smiling—playing lullabies on mandoline—poison ivy smoke in left-wing summer camps and me in infancy saw trees—

or back teaching school, laughing with idiots, the back-ward classes—her Russian speciality—morons with dreamy lips, great eyes, thin feet & sicky fingers, swaybacked, rachitic—

great heads pendulous over Alice in Wonderland, a blackboard full of CAT.

Naomi reading patiently, story out of a Communist fairy book—Tale of the Sudden Sweetness of The Dictator—Forgiveness of Warlocks—Armies Kissing—

Deathsheads Around the Green Table—The King & the Workers—Paterson Press printed them up in the 30's till she went mad, or they folded, both.

O Paterson! I got home late that nite. Louis was worried. How could I be so—didn't I think? I shouldn't have left her. Mad in Lakewood. Call the Doctor. Phone the home in the pines. Too late.

Went to bed exhausted, wanting to leave the world (probably that year newly in love with R—— my high school mind hero, jewish boy who came a doctor later—then silent neat kid—

I later laying down life for him, moved to Manhattan—followed him to college—Prayed on ferry to help mankind if admitted—vowed, the day I journeyed to Entrance Exam—

by being honest revolutionary labor lawyer—would train for that—inspired by Sacco Vanzetti, Norman Thomas, Debs, Altgeld, Sandburg, Poe—Little Blue Books. I wanted to be President, or Senator.

ignorant woe—later dreams of kneeling by R's shocked knees declaring my love of 1941—What sweetness he'd have shown me, tho, that I'd wished him & despaired—first love—a crush—

Later a mortal avalanche, whole mountains of homosexuality, Matterhorns of cock, Grand Canyons of asshole—weight on my melancholy head—

meanwhile I walked on Broadway imagining Infinity like a rubber ball without space beyond—what's outside?—coming home to Graham Avenue still melancholy passing the lone green hedges across the street, dreaming after the movies—)

The telephone rang at 2AM—Emergency—she'd gone mad—Naomi hiding under the bed screaming bugs of Mussolini—Help! Louis! Buba! Fascists! Death!—the landlady frightened—old fag attendant screaming back at her—

Terror, that woke the neighbors—old ladies on the second floor recovering from menopause—all those rags between thighs, clean sheets, sorry over lost babies—husbands ashen—children sneering at Yale, or putting oil in hair at CCNY—or trembling in Montclair State Teachers College like Eugene—

Her big leg crouched to her breast, hand outstretched Keep Away, wool dress on her thighs, fur coat dragged under the bed—she barricaded herself under bedspring with suitcases.

Louis in pyjamas listening to phone, frightened—do now?—Who could know?—my fault, delivering her to solitude?—sitting in the dark room on the sofa, trembling, to figure out—

He took the morning train to Lakewood, Naomi still under bed—thought he brought poison Cops—Naomi screaming—Louis what happened to your heart then? Have you been killed by Naomi's ecstasy?

Dragged her out, around the corner, a cab, forced her in with valise, but the driver left them off at drugstore. Bus stop, two hours' wait.

I lay in bed nervous in the 4-room apartment, the big bed in living room, next to Louis' desk—shaking—he came home that nite, late, told me what happened.

Naomi at the prescription counter defending herself from the enemy—racks of children's books, douche bags, aspirins, pots, blood—'Don't come near me—murderers! Keep away! Promise not to kill me!'

Louis in horror at the soda fountain—with Lakewood girlscouts—coke addicts—nurses—busmen hung on schedule—Police from country precinct, dumbed—and a priest dreaming of pigs on an ancient cliff?

Smelling the air—Louis pointing to emptiness?—Customers vomiting their cokes—or staring—Louis humiliated—Naomi triumphant—The Announcement of the Plot. Bus arrives, the drivers won't have them on trip to New York.

Phonecalls to Dr. Whatzis, 'She needs a rest,' The mental hospital—State Greystone Doctors—'Bring her here, Mr. Ginsberg.'

Naomi, Naomi—sweating, bulge-eyed, fat, the dress unbuttoned at one side—hair over brow, her stocking hanging evilly on her legs—screaming for a blood transfusion—one righteous hand upraised—a shoe in it—barefoot in the Pharmacy—

The enemies approach—what poisons? Tape recorders? FBI? Zhdanov hiding behind the counter? Trotsky mixing rat bacteria in the back of the store? Uncle Sam in Newark, plotting deathly perfumes in the Negro district? Uncle Ephraim, drunk with murder in the politician's bar, scheming of Hague? Aunt Rose passing water thru the needles of the Spanish Civil War?

till the hired $35 ambulance came from Red Bank——Grabbed her arms—strapped her on the stretcher—moaning, poisoned by imaginaries, vomiting chemicals thru Jersey, begging mercy from Essex County to Morristown—

And back to Greystone where she lay three years—that was the last breakthrough, delivered her to Madhouse again—

On what wards—I walked there later, oft—old catatonic ladies, grey as cloud or ash or walls—sit crooning over floorspace—Chairs—and the wrinkled hags acreep, accusing—begging my 13-year-old mercy—

'Take me home'—I went alone sometimes looking for the lost Naomi, taking Shock—and I'd say, 'No, you're crazy Mama,—Trust the Drs.'—

And Eugene, my brother, her elder son, away studying Law in a furnished room in Newark—

came Paterson-ward next day—and he sat on the broken-down couch in the living room—'We had to send her back to Greystone'—

—his face perplexed, so young, then eyes with tears—then crept weeping all over his face—'What for?' wail vibrating in his cheekbones, eyes closed up, high voice—Eugene's face of pain.

Him faraway, escaped to an Elevator in the Newark Library, his bottle daily milk on windowsill of $5 week furn room downtown at trolley tracks—

He worked 8 hrs. a day for $20/wk—thru Law School years—stayed by himself innocent near negro whorehouses.

Unlaid, poor virgin—writing poems about Ideals and politics letters to the editor Pat Eve News—(we both wrote, denouncing Senator Borah and Isolationists—and felt mysterious toward Paterson City Hall—

I sneaked inside it once—local Moloch tower with phallus spire & cap o' ornament, strange gothic Poetry that stood on Market Street—replica Lyons' Hotel de Ville—

wings, balcony & scrollwork portals, gateway to the giant city clock, secret map room full of Hawthorne—dark Debs in the Board of Tax—Rembrandt smoking in the gloom—

Silent polished desks in the great committee room—Aldermen? Bd of Finance? Mosca the hairdresser aplot—Crapp the gangster issuing orders from the john—The madmen struggling over Zone, Fire, Cops & Backroom Metaphysics—we're all dead—outside by the bus-stop Eugene stared thru childhood—

where the Evangelist preached madly for 3 decades, hard-haired, cracked & true to his mean Bible—chalked Prepare to Meet Thy God on civic pave—

or God is Love on the railroad overpass concrete—he raved like I
would rave, the lone Evangelist—Death on City Hall—)

But Gene, young,—been Montclair Teachers College 4 years—taught
half year & quit to go ahead in life—afraid of Discipline Problems—dark sex
Italian students, raw girls getting laid, no English, sonnets disregarded—and
he did not know much—just that he lost—

so broke his life in two and paid for Law—read huge blue books and
rode the ancient elevator 13 miles away in Newark & studied up hard for the
future

just found the Scream of Naomi on his failure doorstep, for the final
time, Naomi gone, us lonely—home—him sitting there—

Then have some chicken soup, Eugene. The Man of Evangel wails in
front of City Hall. And this year Lou has poetic loves of suburb middle-age—
in secret—music from his 1937 book—Sincere—he longs for beauty—

No love since Naomi screamed—since 1923?—now lost in Greystone
ward—new shock for her—Electricity, following the 40 Insulin.

And Metrasol had made her fat.

So that a few years later she came home again—we'd much advanced
and planned—I waited for that day—my Mother again to cook &—play the
piano—sing at mandoline—Lung Stew, & Stenka Razin, & the communist
line on the war with Finland—and Louis in debt—suspected to be poisoned
money—mysterious capitalisms

—& walked down the long front hall & looked at the furniture. She
never remembered it all. Some amnesia. Examined the doilies—and the dining room set was sold—

the Mahogany table—20 years love—gone to the junk man—we still
had the piano—and the book of Poe—and the Mandolin, tho needed some
string, dusty—

She went to the backroom to lay down in bed and ruminate, or nap,
hide—I went in with her, not leave her by herself—lay in bed next to her—
shades pulled, dusky, late afternoon—Louis in front room at desk, waiting—
perhaps boiling chicken for supper—

'Don't be afraid of me because I'm just coming back home from the
mental hospital—I'm your mother—'

Poor love, lost—a fear—I lay there—Said, 'I love you Naomi,'—stiff,
next to her arm. I would have cried, was this the comfortless lone union?—
Nervous, and she got up soon.

Was she ever satisfied? And—by herself sat on the new couch by
the front windows, uneasy—cheek leaning on her hand—narrowing eye—at
what fate that day—

Picking her tooth with her nail, lips formed an O, suspicion—

thought's old worn vagina—absent sideglance of eye—some evil debt written in the wall, unpaid—& the aged breasts of Newark come near—

May have heard radio gossip thru the wires in her head, controlled by 3 big sticks left in her back by gangsters in amnesia, thru the hospital—caused pain between her shoulders—

Into her head—Roosevelt should know her case, she told me—Afraid to kill her, now, that the government knew their names—traced back to Hitler—wanted to leave Louis' house forever.

One night, sudden attack—her noise in the bathroom—like croaking up her soul—convulsions and red vomit coming out of her mouth—diarrhea water exploding from her behind—on all fours in front of the toilet—urine running between her legs—left retching on the tile floor smeared with her black feces—unfainted—

At forty, varicosed, nude, fat, doomed, hiding outside the apartment door near the elevator calling Police, yelling for her girl-friend Rose to help—

Once locked herself in with razor or iodine—could hear her cough in tears at sink—Lou broke through glass green-painted door, we pulled her out to the bedroom.

Then quiet for months that winter—walks, alone, nearby on Broadway, read Daily Worker—Broke her arm, fell on icy street—

Began to scheme escape from cosmic financial murder plots—later she ran away to the Bronx to her sister Elanor. And there's another saga of late Naomi in New York.

Or thru Elanor or the Workman's Circle, where she worked, addressing envelopes, she made out—went shopping for Campbell's tomato soup—saved money Louis mailed her—

Later she found a boyfriend, and he was a doctor—Dr. Isaac worked for National Maritime Union—now Italian bald and pudgy old doll—who was himself an orphan—but they kicked him out—Old cruelties—

Sloppier, sat around on bed or chair, in corset dreaming to herself—'I'm hot—I'm getting fat—I used to have such a beautiful figure before I went to the hospital—You should have seen me in Woodbine—' This in a furnished room around the NMU hall, 1943.

Looking at naked baby pictures in the magazine—baby powder advertisements, strained lamb carrots—'I will think nothing but beautiful thoughts.'

Revolving her head round and round on her neck at window light in summertime, in hypnotize, in doven-dream recall—

'I touch his cheek, I touch his cheek, he touches my lips with his hand, I think beautiful thoughts, the baby has a beautiful hand.'—

Or a No-shake of her body, disgust—some thought of Buchenwald—

some insulin passes thru her head—a grimace nerve shudder at Involuntary (as shudder when I piss)—bad chemical in her cortex—'No don't think of that. He's a rat.'

Naomi: 'And when we die we become an onion, a cabbage, a carrot, or a squash, a vegetable.' I come downtown from Columbia and agree. She reads the Bible, thinks beautiful thoughts all day.

'Yesterday I saw God. What did he look like? Well, in the afternoon I climbed up a ladder—he has a cheap cabin in the country, like Monroe, NY the chicken farms in the wood. He was a lonely old man with a white beard.

'I cooked supper for him. I made him a nice supper—lentil soup, vegetables, bread & butter—miltz—he sat down at the table and ate, he was sad.

'I told him, Look at all those fightings and killings down there, What's the matter? Why don't you put a stop to it?

'I try, he said—That's all he could do, he looked tired. He's a bachelor so long, and he likes lentil soup.'

Serving me meanwhile, a plate of cold fish—chopped raw cabbage dript with tapwater—smelly tomatoes—week-old health food—grated beets & carrots with leaky juice, warm—more and more disconsolate food—I can't eat it for nausea sometimes—the Charity of her hands stinking with Manhattan, madness, desire to please me, cold undercooked fish—pale red near the bones. Her smells—and oft naked in the room, so that I stare ahead, or turn a book ignoring her.

One time I thought she was trying to make me come lay her—flirting to herself at sink—lay back on huge bed that filled most of the room, dress up round her hips, big slash of hair, scars of operations, pancreas, belly wounds, abortions, appendix, stitching of incisions pulling down in the fat like hideous thick zippers—ragged long lips between her legs—What, even, smell of asshole? I was cold—later revolted a little, not much—seemed perhaps a good idea to try—know the Monster of the Beginning Womb—Perhaps—that way. Would she care? She needs a lover.

Yisborach, v'yistabach, v'yispoar, v'yisroman, v'yisnaseh, v'yishador, v'yishalleh, v'yishallol, sh'meh d'kudsho, b'rich hu.

And Louis reestablishing himself in Paterson grimy apartment in negro district—living in dark rooms—but found himself a girl he later married, falling in love again—tho sere & shy—hurt with 20 years Naomi's mad idealism.

Once I came home, after longtime in N.Y., he's lonely—sitting in the bedroom, he at desk chair turned round to face me—weeps, tears in red eyes under his glasses—

That we'd left him—Gene gone strangely into army—she out on her own in NY, almost childish in her furnished room. So Louis walked downtown to postoffice to get mail, taught in highschool—stayed at poetry desk, forlorn—ate grief at Bickford's all these years—are gone.

Eugene got out of the Army, came home changed and lone—cut off his nose in jewish operation—for years stopped girls on Broadway for cups of coffee to get laid—Went to NYU, serious there, to finish Law.—

And Gene lived with her, ate naked fishcakes, cheap, while she got crazier—He got thin, or felt helpless, Naomi striking 1920 poses at the moon, half-naked in the next bed.

bit his nails and studied—was the weird nurse-son—Next year he moved to a room near Colombia—though she wanted to live with her children—

'Listen to your mother's plea, I beg you'—Louis still sending her checks—I was in bughouse that year 8 months—my own visions unmentioned in this here Lament—

But then went half mad—Hitler in her room, she saw his mustache in the sink—afraid of Dr. Isaac now, suspecting that he was in on the Newark plot—went up to Bronx to live near Elanor's Rheumatic Heart—

And Uncle Max never got up before noon, tho Naomi at 6 AM was listening to the radio for spies—or searching the windowsill,

for in the empty lot downstairs, an old man creeps with his bag stuffing packages of garbage in his hanging black overcoat.

Max's sister Edie works—17 years bookeeper at Gimbels—lived downstairs in apartment house, divorced—so Edie took in Naomi on Rochambeau Ave—

Woodlawn Cemetery across the street, vast dale of graves where Poe once—Last stop on Bronx subway—lots of communists in that area.

Who enrolled for painting classes at night in Bronx Adult High School—walked alone under Van Cortlandt Elevated line to class—paints Naomiisms—

Humans sitting on the grass in some Camp No-Worry summers yore—saints with droopy faces and long-ill-fitting pants, from hospital—

Brides in front of Lower East Side with short grooms—lost El trains running over the Babylonian apartment rooftops in the Bronx—

Sad paintings—but she expressed herself. Her mandolin gone, all strings broke in her head, she tried. Toward Beauty? or some old life Message?

But started kicking Elanor, and Elanor had heart trouble—came upstairs and asked her about Spydom for hours,—Elanor frazzled. Max away at office, accounting for cigar stores till at night.

'I am a great woman—am truly a beautiful soul—and because of that they (Hitler, Grandma, Hearst, the Capitalists, Franco, Daily News, the 20's, Mussolini, the living dead) want to shut me up—Buba's the head of a spider network—'

Kicking the girls, Edie & Elanor—Woke Edie at midnite to tell her she was a spy and Elanor a rat. Edie worked all day and couldn't take it—She was organizing the union.—And Elanor began dying, upstairs in bed.

The relatives call me up, she's getting worse—I was the only one left—Went on the subway with Eugene to see her, ate stale fish—

'My sister whispers in the radio—Louis must be in the apartment—his mother tells him what to say—LIARS!—I cooked for my two children—I played the mandolin—'

Last night the nightingale woke me/ Last night when all was still/ it sang in the golden moonlight/ from on the wintry hill. She did.

I pushed her against the door and shouted 'DON'T KICK ELANOR!' —she stared at me—Contempt—die—disbelief her sons are so naive, so dumb—'Elanor is the worst spy! She's taking orders!'

'—No wires in the room!'—I'm yelling at her—last ditch, Eugene listening on the bed—what can he do to escape that fatal Mama—'You've been away from Louis years already—Grandma's too old to walk—'

We're all alive at once then—even me & Gene & Naomi in one mythological Cousinesque room—screaming at each other in the Forever—I in Columbia jacket, she half undressed.

I banging against her head which saw Radios, Sticks, Hitlers—the gamut of Hallucinations—for real—her own universe—no road that goes elsewhere—to my own—No America, not even a world—

That you go as all men, as Van Gogh, as mad Hannah, all the same—to the last doom—Thunder, Spirits, Lightning!

I've seen your grave! O strange Naomi! My own—cracked grave! Shema Y'Israel—I am Svul Avrum—you—in death?

Your last night in the darkness of the Bronx—I phone-called—thru hospital to secret police.

That came, when you and I were alone, shrieking at Elanor in my ear—who breathed hard in her own bed, got thin—

Nor will forget, the doorknock, at your fright of spies,—Law advancing, on my honor—Eternity entering the room—you running to the bathroom undressed, hiding in protest from the last heroic fate—

staring at my eyes, betrayed—the final cops of madness rescuing me—from your foot against the broken heart of Elanor,

your voice at Edie weary of Gimbels coming home to broken radio—and Louis needing a poor divorce, he wants to get married soon—Eugene dreaming, hiding at 125 St., suing negros for money on crud furniture, defending black girls—

Protests from the bathroom—Said you were sane—dressing in a cotton robe, your shoes, then new, your purse and newspaper clippings—no—your honesty—

as you vainly made your lips more real with lipstick, looking in the mirror to see if the Insanity was Me or a carful of police.

or Grandma spying at 78—Your vision—Her climbing over the walls of the cemetery with political kidnapper's bag—or what you saw on the walls of the Bronx, in pink nightgown at midnight, staring out the window on the empty lot—

Ah Rochambeau Ave—Playground of Phantoms—last apartment in the Bronx for spies—last home for Elanor or Naomi, here these communist sisters lost their revolution—

'All right—put on your coat Mrs.—let's go—We have the wagon downstairs—you want to come with her to the station?'

The ride then—held Naomi's hand, and held her head to my breast, I'm taller—kissed her and said I did it for the best—Elanor sick—and Max with heart condition—Needs—

To me—'Why did you do this?'—'Yes Mrs., your son will have to leave you in an hour'—The Ambulance

came in a few hours—drove off at 4 AM to some Bellevue in the night downtown—gone to the hospital forever. I saw her led away—she waved, tears in her eyes.

Two years, after a trip to Mexico—bleak in the flat plain near Brentwood, scrub brush and grass around the unused RR train track to the crazyhouse—

new brick 20 story central building—lost on the vast lawns of madtown on Long Island—huge cities of the moon.

Asylum spreads out giant wings above the path to a minute black hole—the door—entrance thru crotch—

I went in—smelt funny—the halls again—up elevator—to a glass door on a Woman's Ward—to Naomi—Two nurses buxom white—They led her out, Naomi stared—and I gaspt—She'd had a stroke—

Too thin, shrunk on her bones—age come to Naomi—now broken into white hair—loose dress on her skeleton—face sunk, old! withered—cheek of crone—

One hand stiff—heaviness of forties & menopause reduced by one heart stroke, lame now—wrinkles—a scar on her head, the lobotomy—ruin, the hand dipping downwards to death—

O Russian faced, woman on the grass, your long black hair is crowned with flowers, the mandolin is on your knees—

Communist beauty, sit here married in the summer among daisies, promised happiness at hand—

holy mother, now you smile on your love, your world is born anew, children run naked in the field spotted with dandelions, they eat in the plum tree grove at the end of the meadow and find a cabin where a white-haired negro teaches the mystery of his rainbarrel—

blessed daughter come to America, I long to hear your voice again, remembering your mother's music, in the Song of the Natural Front—

O glorious muse that bore me from the womb, gave suck first mystic life & taught me talk and music, from whose pained head I first took Vision—

Tortured and beaten in the skull—What mad hallucinations of the damned that drive me out of my own skull to seek Eternity till I find Peace for Thee, O Poetry—and for all humankind call on the Origin

Death which is the mother of the universe!—Now wear your naked-ness forever, white flowers in your hair, your marriage sealed behind the sky—no revolution might destroy that maidenhood—

O beautiful Garbo of my Karma—all photographs from 1920 in Camp Nicht-Gedeiget here unchanged—with all the teachers from Newark—Nor Elanor be gone, nor Max await his specter—nor Louis retire from this High School—

Back! You! Naomi! Skull on you! Gaunt immortality and revolution come—small broken woman—the ashen indoor eyes of hospitals, ward grey-ness on skin—

'Are you a spy?' I sat at the sour table, eyes filling with tears—'Who are you? Did Louis send you?—The wires—'

in her hair, as she beat on her head—'I'm not a bad girl—don't murder me!—I hear the ceiling—I raised two children—'

Two years since I'd been there—I started to cry—She stared—nurse broke up the meeting a moment—I went into the bathroom to hide, against the toilet white walls

'The Horror' I weeping—to see her again—'The Horror'—as if she were dead thru funeral rot in—'The Horror!'

I came back she yelled more—they led her away—'You're not Allen—' I watched her face—but she passed by me, not looking—

Opened the door to the ward,—she went thru without a glance back, quiet suddenly—I stared out—she looked old—the verge of the grave—'All the Horror!'

Another year, I left NY—on West Coast in Berkeley cottage dreamed of her soul—that, thru life, in what form it stood in that body, ashen or manic, gone beyond joy—

near its death—with eyes—was my own love in its form, the Naomi, my mother on earth still—sent her long letter—& wrote hymns to the mad—Work of the merciful Lord of Poetry.

that causes the broken grass to be green, or the rock to break in grass—

642

or the Sun to be constant to earth—Sun of all sunflowers and days on bright
iron bridges—what shines on old hospitals—as on my yard—

Returning from San Francisco one night, Orlovsky in my room—
Whalen in his peaceful chair—a telegram from Gene, Naomi dead—

Outside I bent my head to the ground under the bushes near the
garage—knew she was better—

at last—not left to look on Earth alone—2 years of solitude—no
one, at age nearing 60—old woman of skulls—once long-tressed Naomi
of Bible—

or Ruth who wept in America—Rebecca aged in Newark—David
remembering his Harp, now lawyer at Yale

or Svul Avrum—Israel Abraham—myself—to sing in the wilderness
toward God—O Elohim!—so to the end—2 days after her death I got her
letter—

Strange Prophecies anew! She wrote—'The key is in the window, the
key is in the sunlight at the window—I have the key—Get married Allen
don't take drugs—the key is in the bars, in the sunlight in the window.

Love,

your mother'

which is Naomi—

Hymmnn

In the world which He has created according to his will Blessed Praised Mag-
nified Lauded Exalted the Name of the Holy One Blessed is He! In the
house in Newark Blessed is He! In the madhouse Blessed is He! In the
house of Death Blessed is He!

Blessed be He in homosexuality! Blessed be He in Paranoia! Blessed be He in
the city! Blessed be He in the Book!

Blessed be He who dwells in the shadow! Blessed be He! Blessed be He!

Blessed be you Naomi in tears! Blessed be you Naomi in fears! Blessed Blessed
Blessed in sickness!

Blessed be you Naomi in Hospitals! Blessed be you Naomi in solitude! Blest
be your triumph! Blest be your bars! Blest be your last years' loneliness!

Blest be your failure! Blest be your stroke! Blest be the close of your eye! Blest
be the gaunt of your cheek! Blest be your withered thighs!

Blessed be Thee Naomi in Death! Blessed be Death! Blessed be Death!

Blessed be He Who leads all sorrow to Heaven! Blessed be He in the end!

Blessed be He who builds Heaven in Darkness! Blessed Blessed Blessed be
He! Blessed be He! Blessed be Death on us All!

III

Only to have not forgotten the beginning in which she drank cheap sodas in
the morgues of Newark,
only to have seen her weeping on gray tables in long wards of her universe
only to have known the weird ideas of Hitler at the door, the wires in her
head, the three big sticks
rammed down her back, the voices in the ceiling shrieking out her ugly early
lays for 30 years,
only to have seen the time-jumps, memory lapse, the crash of wars, the roar
and silence of a vast electric shock,
only to have seen her painting crude pictures of Elevateds running over the
rooftops of the Bronx
her brothers dead in Riverside or Russia, her lone in Long Island writing a
last letter—and her image in the sunlight at the window
'The key is in the sunlight at the window in the bars the key is in the sunlight,'
only to have come to that dark night on iron bed by stroke when the sun
gone down on Long Island
and the vast Atlantic roars outside the great call of Being to its own
to come back out of the Nightmare—divided creation—with her head lain
on a pillow of the hospital to die
—in one last glimpse—all Earth one everlasting Light in the familiar black-
out—no tears for this vision—
But that the key should be left behind—at the window—the key in the
sunlight—to the living—that can take
that slice of light in hand—and turn the door—and look back see
Creation glistening backwards to the same grave, size of universe,
size of the tick of the hospital's clock on the archway over the white door—

IV

O mother
what have I left out
O mother
what have I forgotten
O mother
farewell
with a long black shoe
farewell
with Communist Party and a broken stocking
farewell
with six dark hairs on the wen of your breast
farewell

with your old dress and a long black beard around the vagina
farewell
with your sagging belly
with your fear of Hitler
with your mouth of bad short stories
with your fingers of rotten mandolins
with your arms of fat Paterson porches
with your belly of strikes and smokestacks
with your chin of Trotsky and the Spanish War
with your voice singing for the decaying overbroken workers
with your nose of bad lay with your nose of the smell of the pickles of Newark
with your eyes
with your eyes of Russia
with your eyes of no money
with your eyes of false China
with your eyes of Aunt Elanor
with your eyes of starving India
with your eyes pissing in the park
with your eyes of America taking a fall
with your eyes of your failure at the piano
with your eyes of your relatives in California
with your eyes of Ma Rainey dying in an ambulance
with your eyes of Czechoslovakia attacked by robots
with your eyes going to painting class at night in the Bronx
with your eyes of the killer Grandma you see on the horizon from the Fire-
    Escape
with your eyes running naked out of the apartment screaming into the hall
with your eyes being led away by policemen to an ambulance
with your eyes strapped down on the operating table
with your eyes with the pancreas removed
with your eyes of appendix operation
with your eyes of abortion
with your eyes of ovaries removed
with your eyes of shock
with your eyes of lobotomy
with your eyes of divorce
with your eyes of stroke
with your eyes alone
with your eyes
with your eyes
with your Death full of Flowers

V

Caw caw caw crows shriek in the white sun over grave stones in Long Island
Lord Lord Lord Naomi underneath this grass my halflife and my own as hers
caw caw my eye be buried in the same Ground where I stand in Angel
Lord Lord great Eye that stares on All and moves in a black cloud
caw caw strange cry of Beings flung up into sky over the waving trees
Lord Lord O Grinder of giant Beyonds my voice in a boundless field in Sheol
Caw caw the call of Time rent out of foot and wing an instant in the universe
Lord Lord an echo in the sky the wind through ragged leaves the roar of
      memory
caw caw all years my birth a dream caw caw New York the bus the broken
      shoe the vast highschool caw caw all Visions of the Lord
Lord Lord Lord caw caw caw Lord Lord Lord caw caw caw Lord

Paris, December 1957–New York, 1959

47

N. Scott Momaday (1934–)
from *The Way to Rainy Mountain*
and *The Names*

The Way to Rainy Mountain (1969) is a short book that poetically retraces the route of the Kiowa two hundred years ago from the northern Rocky Mountains onto the Great Plains and down to Oklahoma. It is in three parts, "The Setting Out," "The Going On," and "The Closing In," and is framed by a brief "Introduction" and "Epilogue." Within each of the parts the narrative proceeds through the representation of three different kinds of material: myth, history, and personal memory, distinguished by three different type faces. There are also ink drawings and designs by Al Momaday, Momaday's father.

Thus *The Way to Rainy Mountain* is in a sense collaborative autobiography, a tradition in Native American personal narrative. Coup stories and hunting stories were often told by several people, with one supporting or adding to what another said, and the tribal histories such as "Winter Counts" were kept by one person, but when they were told, they could be filled out by other people's memories. Momaday's collaborators are not only his father but also the old anonymous myth tellers and the other Kiowa he interviewed.

The selection below is the beginning of "Setting Out."

Momaday's *The Names* (1976) is more like a family scrapbook. It has old family portraits and snapshots with handwritten captions. The material is also more specific to Momaday himself and his family, especially his mother. Had Momaday not first published his novel *House Made of Dawn* (1968; Pulitzer Prize 1969), *The Way to Rainy Mountain,* and several other books, there probably would have been no occasion for publishing *The Names;* nevertheless, the comments on imagination and the reconstruction of his childhood definitions of "Indian" go well beyond the material of the celebrity autobiography.

The texts below are from *The Way to Rainy Mountain* (New York: Ballantine, 1969) and *The Names* (New York: Harper and Row, 1976). Matthias Schubnell, *N. Scott Momaday: The Cultural and Literary Background* (Norman: Univ. of Oklahoma Press, 1985), provides useful biographical information. *Ancestral Voices: Conversa-*

tions with N. Scott Momaday, by Charles L. Woodard (Lincoln: Univ. of Nebraska Press, 1989), provides further information.

from The Way to Rainy Mountain

I

You know, everything had to begin, and this is how it was: the Kiowas came one by one into the world through a hollow log. They were many more than now, but not all of them got out. There was a woman whose body was swollen up with child, and she got stuck in the log. After that, no one could get through, and that is why the Kiowas are a small tribe in number. They looked all around and saw the world. It made them glad to see so many things. They called themselves *Kwuda,* "coming out."

They called themselves Kwuda *and later* Tepda, *both of which mean "coming out." And later still they took the name* Gaigwu, *a name which can be taken to indicate something of which the two halves differ from each other in appearance. It was once a custom among Kiowa warriors that they cut their hair on the right side of the head only and on a line level with the lobe of the ear, while on the left they let the hair grow long and wore it in a thick braid wrapped in otter skin. "Kiowa" is indicated in sign language by holding the hand palm up and slightly cupped to the right side of the head and rotating it back and forth from the wrist. "Kiowa" is thought to derive from the softened Comanche form of* Gaigwu.

I remember coming out upon the northern Great Plains in the late spring. There were meadows of blue and yellow wildflowers on the slopes, and I could see the still, sunlit plain below, reaching away out of sight. At first there is no discrimination in the eye, nothing but the land itself, whole and impenetrable. But then smallest things begin to stand out of the depths—herds and rivers and groves—and each of these has perfect being in terms of distance and of silence and of age. Yes, I thought, now I see the earth as it really is; never again will I see things as I saw them yesterday or the day before.

from The Names

The Jefferson Davis Monument at Fairview was dedicated in 1929, one hundred and twenty-one years after Davis' birth. It is an impressive structure, a concrete obelisk which rises 351 feet above a twenty-acre park. It is a principal thing in the landscape. The construction was long and erratic. Natachee and this monument grew up together. In 1929 my mother was a Southern belle; she was about to embark upon an extraordinary life. It was about this time that she began to see herself as an Indian. That dim native heritage became a fascination and a cause for her, inasmuch, perhaps, as it enabled her to assume an attitude of defiance, an attitude which she assumed with particular style and satisfaction; it became her. She imagined who she was. This act of the imagination was, I believe, among the most important events of my mother's early life, as later the same essential act was to be among the most important of my own.

She was already a raving beauty. She had very black hair and very blue eyes; her skin was clear and taut, of an olive complexion, and her bones were fine and well shaped. She moved gracefully and directly, with certain confidence. Above all, she expected the world to be interesting; she would not stand to be bored. Her cousins, who were plain, called her the Queen of Sheba, which pleased her mightily. But she was more particularly Natachee, or "Little Moon," as she sometimes said, and she drew a blanket about her and placed a feather in her hair. And she went off to Haskell Institute, the Indian school at Lawrence, Kansas. Her roommate there was a Kiowa girl, Lela Ware. Destinies began to converge then, in 1929.

. . .

I invented history. In April's thin white light, in the white landscape of the Staked Plains, I looked for tracks among the tufts of coarse, brittle grass, amid the stones, beside the tangle of dusty hedges. When I look back upon those days—days of infinite promise and steady adventure and the certain sanctity of childhood—I see how much was there in the balance. The past and the future were simply the large contingencies of a given moment; they bore upon the present and gave it shape. One does not pass through time, but time enters upon him, in his place. As a child, I knew this surely, as a matter of fact; I am not wise to doubt it now. Notions of the past and future are essentially notions of the present. In the same way an idea of one's ancestry and posterity is really an idea of the self. About this time I was formulating an idea of myself.

Miss Johnson said Mayre not Mary why doesn't she talk the way she's supposed to and that Tommy the dirty rat I'll knock his block off and not care if he tells he tells everything and the time Billy Don and I got spanked because we were throwing snowballs and broke a window the one on the side not the driver's side and the lady was smiling until that happened driving slowly and smiling and the glass went crack it was only cracked and then she got mad not really mad but oh oh now we have to do something about that this and that you'll never know just how much I love you I didn't want to go to Mrs. Powell's because she has all those nice things in her house and you have to sit still and she watches you and one time she wouldn't even let me eat an orange in her car it smells she said and your fingers get sticky she said and I don't like her crummy cactus garden either well I like it but there are a lot of better cactuses over by Billy Don's dad's place I wonder who that girl was the soldier's girl on the library lawn and they were having their picture taken and the soldier was trying to touch her down there and she was giggling and I heard the twins laughing about it and I wanted to laugh too but the girl was pretty and I thought she should not have let him do that she's really good and decent probably maybe she was ashamed and didn't know what to do but laugh that's the way I am sometimes oh my gosh mom and dad heard me yesterday and I was singing You're in the army now you're not behind the plow you'll never get rich you son of a bitch and they heard me and weren't mad but said not to sing that even if all the other kids were singing it I think dad wasn't sure and said he said son of a bee didn't he and mom said yes he did and I did but I didn't know it I really didn't know it and one time in the arbor Lucius told me I said some bad words and Aunt Clara heard me and I didn't know I had said them how could I just forget like that Lucius and Marland and Justin Lee and Ponzi we used to play around the arbor and the outhouse and tell jokes and smoke why did Burt tell me he was smoking oak leaves and that was all right well he's a lot older but I bet that wasn't oak leaves maybe it was anyway John was in the shower and I was playing at the sink in the kitchen and I wasn't trying to make the water hot but he thought I was well what's today Wednesday or Thursday no Saturday Saturday at the show when the crook came out on the porch and he started to smoke a cigarette and everyone thought Bob had got killed I didn't though the crook fell then and we all yelled like crazy next time old Bob will get in trouble again and Hopalong Casidy is coming to the Reel Fred Jackson is a sergeant is he yes but he got busted someone said for fighting for hitting his commanding officer he's pretty okay to me why does he like those records Glenn Miller and Tommy Dorsey and Harry James Sleepy lagoon mom and dad too dad likes that music I think maybe at the Avalon When the lights go on again all over the world oh Billy Don and Burleigh those dumb guys this morning no yesterday no this morning I had to keep them quiet because mom was sleeping she loves to sleep late I don't like it though I like to get up but I had breakfast in bed I made it eggs and toast and jam and I took it to my bed and ate it in bed well I don't do it all the time I pledge allegiance to the flag indivisible My country 'tis of thee sweet land of liberty oh gosh Guadalcanal it isn't so bad to get shot I guess if it's a flesh wound get the medic but they strafe the beach John says the Zeros are more maneuverable but a lot slower than the P-39s and the Mustangs what do they call the P-38s they're so awful fast I'm in a Bell P-39 okay no a Flying Tiger okay sons of the rising sun this is for my kid brother ha gotcha oh oh there's a Zero on my tail eeeeeeooooooooooooow lost him in the clouds just dropped down and let him go over me and climbed up oh he can't believe it he's in may sights crosshairs there Tojo that's for the Sullivans well Chuck you can paint four more Zeros on old Sally here no I'm okay thanks honorable colonel we must stop

Momaday he comes from nowhere from the sun I tell you he's not human
they say he's an Indian that he wears an eagle feather has the eyes the heart
of an eagle he must be stopped there son of the rising sun that's for Major
Anderson eeeeeeeeeooooooooow what oh another medal oh it was nothing
sir it was for my kid brother sir he got his over Burma it was for the Sullivan
boys and Major Anderson what lead the eagle squadron yessir thank you sir
it's a great honor

I don't want to see Louise again not since I made that lemonade and she
was the only one who bought some shoot for a nickel it was and she came
across the street and said it was good and cold and thanked me I hate Henry
Aldridge too what was that really neat program The Monkey's Paw The Most
Dangerous Game The Mollé Mystery Theatre

I asked Billy Don if his mom and dad told him stories when he went to
bed and he laughed once upon a time there were three pigs Rootie and Tootie
and Pootie and Mickey Mouse and Minnie Mouse Scotty had a brand-new
red car and it was snowing outside Billy Don began to laugh he got so tickled
and we were all surprised because gosh it was right there in school what is it
Billy Don the teacher said and he said oh nothing you wouldn't understand I
was just thinking and we all laughed like heck it was so funny Ida was sent out
of the room and I felt funny about that that she was sent outside and knew
that we were all talking about her gee and Miss Marshall said you must not
be cruel some people do not have as much as you do and Ida can't help it her
clothes are old and dirty I found her crying in the bathroom and you must
not be cruel you must make her feel that you are all her friends and then we
all went out of our way to be friendly even Charles you're an Indian Charles
said and I said yes Indians are no good he said and I said you're a liar he can't
stand to be called that gosh anything but that and he's so tough so I took
it back

Grandma I miss you I fell sorry for you when I come to see you and see
you and go away I know you're lonely I like to see you I love to see you in the
arbor cooking and talking to us you goot boy you say Scotty you goot boy
and you used to carry me on your back in your shawl and hold me in your lap
and I came to sleep with you and you're so soft and warm and I like the smell
of you your hair is so thick and heavy it is so black except for the gray here
and there you buy me candy corn and candy orange slices jellybeans animal
crackers I like to watch you sew and make beadwork let's go to town grandma
to the store you have so much money always Uncle Jimmy has money sometimes he buys me something down by Lonewolf his land everyone says he's
going to give me some land someday oh yes Miss Marshall my dad's people
the Kiowas they have a lot of land in Oklahoma my uncle is going to give me
some land quite a lot of it someday no ma'am he's not a farmer but he owns
farmland yes ma'am it's very strange well yes ma'am I'm a Kiowa yes ma'am
I'm sure it's not Keeowa no ma'am I can't say the Lord's Prayer in Kiowa I

can't say much of anything really my dad can yes ma'am I *am* proud to be so American I know it ma'am Lay that pistol down babe

Oh I feel so dumb I can't answer all those questions I don't know how to be a Kiowa Indian my grandmother lives in a house it's like your house Miss Marshall or Billy Don's house only it doesn't have lights and light switches and the toilet is outside and you have to carry wood in from the woodpile and water from the well but that isn't what makes it Indian its my grandma the way she is the way she looks her hair in braids the clothes somehow yes the way she talks she doesn't speak English so well Scotty you goot boy she says wait I know why it's an Indian house because there are pictures of Indians on the walls photographs of people with long braids and buckskin clothes dresses and shirts and moccasins and necklaces and beadwork yes that's it and there is Indian stuff all around blankets and shawls bows and arrows everyone there acts like an Indian everyone even me and my dad when we're there we eat meat and everyone talks Kiowa and the old people wear Indian clothes well those dresses dark blue and braids and hats and there is laughing Indians laugh a lot and they sing oh yes they love to sing sometimes when an old man comes to visit he sits in the living room and pretty soon he just begins to sing loud with his eyes closed but really loud and his head nodding and in the arbor there are sometimes pretty often a lot of people and lots to eat and everyone sings and sometimes there are drums too and it goes on through the night *that*'s Indian my dad sets out poles on the river and we eat catfish *that*'s Indian and grandma goes to Rainy Mountain Baptist Church *that*'s Indian and my granddad Mammedaty is buried at Rainy Mountain and some of the stones there have peyote pictures on them and you can hear bobwhites there and see terrapins and scissortails and that's Indian too

I gave mom Evening in Paris perfume and a little handkerchief and she was thrilled said so Mother's Day but when I was just a kid last year two years ago I can't remember I went on an Easter egg hunt at school no the park and I got some Easter eggs but I ate them and brought home nothing and was ashamed forever

I'll have a sweetheart in the war and she will look like Faye Emerson when I was at grandma's I had a picture of Faye Emerson it was in a magazine I think and she was my sweetheart and I talked to her all the time I love you darling don't worry oh I know it's tough war is heck but though there's one motor gone we will still carry on Faye yes Faye Emerson Montclair New Jersey if anything happens to me Billy Don see that she gets this letter we were going to be married and live in a little bungalow out west hear that Billy Don that's it time to go thumbs up buddy old pal take care of things take care of that leg pal I'll miss you Oh don't sit under the apple tree with anyone else but me anyone else but me anyone else but me I'm gonna dance with the dolly with the hole in her stocking while her knees keep a knocking while her toes keep a rocking hi'ya Hitler here's one for Major Jordan okay Billy Don you take the ball see and lateral to me and then run out straight sure I can throw it that far can you run that far they won't know what hit them there's a game tonight isn't there oh I love the games the air is cold and full of music and shouting the field is so green under the lights and the stripes are so white so much excitement I heard one of the high-schoolers say the Cavemen were going to win that if they couldn't win on the field they were sure as heck going to beat them off the field everything depends on the game this game the Eagles and the Cavemen I got as close as I could I could see how hard they were playing playing so hard they were crying some of them their arms and legs bandaged and blood showing through cussing at each other I was kind of scared and the quarterback called the signals and the ball was in the air and the helmets and pads cracked together oh it was grand I love football nothing could be better than to be a great football player a back a quarterback or a fullback I told the Canons that I was a tailback but I don't know what that is

48

Maxine Hong Kingston (1940–)
No Name Woman

Maxine Hong was born in Stockton, California, and graduated from the University of California, Berkeley, in 1962. Her father, who had been a poet and calligrapher in China, had immigrated to New York in the 1920s and become part-owner of a laundry. He sent money back to his wife, who used some of it to study medicine and midwifery. In the late 1930s he sent for her and they were finally reunited, after twelve years.

The Woman Warrior (1976) goes way beyond such biographical data as this, however, for it fuses ancient Chinese legends, family history, and personal memory into a new kind of autobiography of consciousness. It fuses these materials as closely together as the growing daughter felt them, until the reader, too, cannot be sure where they meet.

The selection below, the first and shortest of the book's five chapters, is a good example. This chapter is entitled "No Name Woman": it is, as Kingston tells it, a story her mother, Brave Orchid, told about the author's father's sister, who has no name and must never be referred to because she had an illegitimate child. Both internal and external evidence, however, indicate that this is a proverbial story which Chinese mothers told to their daughters at puberty to warn them against having sex before or outside of marriage. So it isn't "true." Yet if the young Maxine thought it was true and believed it for so many years that it shaped her life, what are we to say?

The later chapters tell more combinations of myth and family memory, or "talk-stories," as the daughter heard them from her mother—stories of a legendary Chinese woman warrior, stories of Brave Orchid's encounters with ghosts while she was a medical student in China, stories of relatives, and stories of Maxine's childhood. In all, the over-arching theme is the power of speech itself—the power of the teller of the "talk-story" to create reality and so fashion an identity for herself.

Kingston's stories also make a fascinating comparison with other stories of first- and second-generation immigrants and all stories that question the nature of identity: whether identity is something immutable and transcendent, whether it is based on action and historical circumstance, or whether it is created in language, narrative, and "talk-story."

Kingston's second volume of autobiography, *China Men*, was published in 1980. For additional biographical information, see the entry in *Contemporary Authors: New Revision Series*, vol. 13 (1984), pp. 289–94. There is an excellent critical study of *The Woman Warrior* in Paul John Eakin's *Fictions in Autobiography* (Princeton: Princeton Univ. Press, 1985).

"You must not tell anyone," my mother said, "what I am about to tell you. In China your father had a sister who killed herself. She jumped into the family well. We say that your father has all brothers because it is as if she had never been born.

"In 1924 just a few days after our village celebrated seventeen hurry-up weddings—to make sure that every young man who went 'out on the road' would responsibly come home—your father and his brothers and your grandfather and his brothers and your aunt's new husband sailed for America, the Gold Mountain. It was your grandfather's last trip. Those lucky enough to get contracts waved goodbye from the decks. They fed and guarded the stowaways and helped them off in Cuba, New York, Bali, Hawaii. 'We'll meet in California next year,' they said. All of them sent money home.

"I remember looking at your aunt one day when she and I were dressing; I had not noticed before that she had such a protruding melon of a stomach. But I did not think, 'She's pregnant,' until she began to look like other pregnant women, her shirt pulling and the white tops of her black pants showing. She could not have been pregnant, you see, because her husband had been gone for years. No one said anything. We did not discuss it. In early summer she was ready to have the child, long after the time when it could have been possible.

"The village had also been counting. On the night the baby was to be born the villagers raided our house. Some were crying. Like a great saw, teeth strung with lights, files of people walked zigzag across our land, tearing the rice. Their lanterns doubled in the disturbed black water, which drained away through the broken bunds. As the villagers closed in, we could see that some of them, probably men and women we knew well, wore white masks. The people with long hair hung it over their faces. Women with short hair made it stand up on end. Some had tied white bands around their foreheads, arms, and legs.

"At first they threw mud and rocks at the house. Then they threw eggs and began slaughtering our stock. We could hear the animals scream their deaths—the roosters, the pigs, a last great roar from the ox. Familiar wild heads flared in our night windows; the villagers encircled us. Some of the faces stopped to peer at us, their eyes rushing like searchlights. The hands flattened against the panes, framed heads, and left red prints.

"The villagers broke in the front and the back doors at the same time, even though we had not locked the doors against them. Their knives dripped with the blood of our animals. They smeared blood on the doors and walls. One woman swung a chicken, whose throat she had slit, splattering blood in red arcs about her. We stood together in the middle of our house, in the family hall with the pictures and tables of the ancestors around us, and looked straight ahead.

"At that time the house had only two wings. When the men came back, we would build two more to enclose our courtyard and a third one to begin a second courtyard. The villagers pushed through both wings, even your grandparents' rooms, to find your aunt's, which was also mine until the men returned. From this room a new wing for one of the younger families would grow. They ripped up her clothes and shoes and broke her combs, grinding them underfoot. They tore her work from the loom. They scattered the cooking fire and rolled the new weaving in it. We could hear them in the kitchen breaking our bowls and banging the pots. They overturned the great waist-high earthenware jugs; duck eggs, pickled fruits, vegetables burst out and mixed in acrid torrents. The old woman from the next field swept a broom through the air and loosed the spirits-of-the-broom over our heads. 'Pig.' 'Ghost.' 'Pig,' they sobbed and scolded while they ruined our house.

"When they left, they took sugar and oranges to bless themselves. They cut pieces from the dead animals. Some of them took bowls that were not broken and clothes that were not torn. Afterward we swept up the rice and sewed it back up into sacks. But the smells from the spilled preserves lasted. Your aunt gave birth in the pigsty that night. The next morning when I went for the water, I found her and the baby plugging up the family well.

"Don't let your father know that I told you. He denies her. Now that you have started to menstruate, what happened to her could happen to you. Don't humiliate us. You wouldn't like to be forgotten as if you had never been born. The villagers are watchful."

Whenever she had to warn us about life, my mother told stories that ran like this one, a story to grow up on. She tested our strength to establish realities. Those in the emigrant generations who could not reassert brute survival died young and far from home. Those of us in the first American generations have had to figure out how the invisible world the emigrants built around our childhoods fits in solid America.

The emigrants confused the gods by diverting their curses, misleading them with crooked streets and false names. They must try to confuse their offspring as well, who, I suppose, threaten them in similar ways—always trying to get things straight, always trying to name the unspeakable. The Chinese I know hide their names; sojourners take new names when their lives change and guard their real names with silence.

Chinese-Americans, when you try to understand what things in you are

Chinese, how do you separate what is peculiar to childhood, to poverty, insanities, one family, your mother who marked your growing with stories, from what is Chinese? What is Chinese tradition and what is the movies?

If I want to learn what clothes my aunt wore, whether flashy or ordinary, I would have to begin, "Remember Father's drowned-in-the-well sister?" I cannot ask that. My mother has told me once and for all the useful parts. She will add nothing unless powered by Necessity, a riverbank that guides her life. She plants vegetable gardens rather than lawns; she carries the odd-shaped tomatoes home from the fields and eats food left for the gods.

Whenever we did frivolous things, we used up energy; we flew high kites. We children came up off the ground over the melting cones our parents brought home from work and the American movie on New Year's Day—*Oh, You Beautiful Doll* with Betty Grable one year, and *She Wore a Yellow Ribbon* with John Wayne another year. After the one carnival ride each, we paid in guilt; our tired father counted his change on the dark walk home.

Adultery is extravagance. Could people who hatch their own chicks and eat the embryos and the heads for delicacies and boil the feet in vinegar for party food, leaving only the gravel, eating even the gizzard lining—could such people engender a prodigal aunt? To be a woman, to have a daughter in starvation time was a waste enough. My aunt could not have been the lone romantic who gave up everything for sex. Women in the old China did not choose. Some man had commanded her to lie with him and be his secret evil. I wonder whether he masked himself when he joined the raid on her family.

Perhaps she had encountered him in the fields or on the mountain where the daughters-in-law collected fuel. Or perhaps he first noticed her in the marketplace. He was not a stranger because the village housed no strangers. She had to have dealings with him other than sex. Perhaps he worked an adjoining field, or he sold her the cloth for the dress she sewed and wore. His demand must have surprised, then terrified her. She obeyed him; she always did as she was told.

When the family found a young man in the next village to be her husband, she had stood tractably beside the best rooster, his proxy, and promised before they met that she would be his forever. She was lucky that he was her age and she would be the first wife, an advantage secure now. The night she first saw him, he had sex with her. Then he left for America. She had almost forgotten what he looked like. When she tried to envision him, she only saw the black and white face in the group photograph the men had had taken before leaving.

The other man was not, after all, much different from her husband. They both gave orders: she followed. "If you tell your family, I'll beat you. I'll kill you. Be here again next week." No one talked sex, ever. And she might have separated the rapes from the rest of living if only she did not have to buy her oil from him or gather wood in the same forest. I want her fear to have lasted just as long as rape lasted so that the fear could have been contained. No drawn-out fear. But women at sex hazarded birth and hence lifetimes. The fear did not stop but permeated everywhere. She told the man, "I think I'm pregnant." He organized the raid against her.

On nights when my mother and father talked about their life back home, sometimes they mentioned an "outcast table" whose business they still seemed to be settling, their voices tight. In a commensal tradition, where food is precious, the powerful older people made wrongdoers eat alone. Instead of letting them start separate new lives like the Japanese, who could become samurais and geishas, the Chinese family, faces averted but eyes glowering sideways, hung on to the offenders and fed them leftovers. My aunt must have lived in the same house as my parents and eaten at an outcast table. My mother spoke about the raid as if she had seen it, when she and my aunt, a daughter-in-law to a different household, should not have been living together at all. Daughters-in-law lived with their husbands' parents, not their own; a synonym for marriage in Chinese is "taking a daughter-in-law." Her husband's parents could have sold her, mortgaged her, stoned her. But they had sent her back to her own mother and father, a mysterious act hinting at disgraces not told me. Perhaps they had thrown her out to deflect the avengers.

She was the only daughter; her four brothers went with her father, husband, and uncles "out on the road" and for some years became western men. When the goods were divided among the family, three of the brothers took land, and the youngest, my father, chose an education. After my grandparents gave their daughter away to her husband's family, they had dispensed all the adventure and all the property. They expected her alone to keep the traditional ways, which her brothers, now among the barbarians, could fumble without detection. The heavy, deep-rooted women were to maintain the past against the flood, safe for returning. But the rare urge west had fixed upon our family, and so my aunt crossed boundaries not delineated in space.

The work of preservation demands that the feelings playing about in one's guts not be turned into action. Just watch their passing like cherry blossoms. But perhaps my aunt, my forerunner, caught in a slow life, let dreams grow and fade and after some months or years went toward what persisted. Fear at the enormities of the forbidden kept her desires delicate, wire and bone. She looked at a man because she liked the way the hair was tucked behind his ears, or she liked the question-mark line of a long torso curving at the shoulder and straight at the hip. For warm eyes or a soft voice or a slow walk—that's all—a few hairs, a line, a brightness, a sound, a pace, she gave up family. She offered us up for a charm that vanished with tiredness, a pigtail that didn't toss when the wind died. Why, the wrong lighting could erase the dearest thing about him.

It could very well have been, however, that my aunt did not take subtle enjoyment of her friend, but, a wild woman, kept rollicking company. Imagining her free with sex doesn't fit, though. I don't know any women like that, or men either. Unless I see her life branching into mine, she gives me no ancestral help.

To sustain her being in love, she often worked at herself in the mirror, guessing at the colors and shapes that would interest him, changing them frequently in order to hit on the right combination. She wanted him to look back.

On a farm near the sea, a woman who tended her appearance reaped a reputation for eccentricity. All the married women blunt-cut their hair in flaps about their ears or pulled it back in tight buns. No nonsense. Neither style blew easily into heart-catching tangles. And at their weddings they displayed themselves in their long hair for the last time. "It brushed the backs of my knees," my mother tells me. "It was braided, and even so, it brushed the backs of my knees."

At the mirror my aunt combed individuality into her bob. A bun could have been contrived to escape into black streamers blowing in the wind or in quiet wisps about her face, but only the older women in our picture album wear buns. She brushed her hair back from her forehead, tucking the flaps behind her ears. She looped a piece of thread, knotted into a circle between her index fingers and thumbs, and ran the double strand across her forehead. When she closed her fingers as if she were making a pair of shadow geese bite, the string twisted together catching the little hairs. Then she pulled the thread away from her skin, ripping the hairs out neatly, her eyes watering from the needles of pain. Opening her fingers, she cleaned the thread, then rolled it along her hairline and the tops of her eyebrows. My mother did the same to me and my sisters and herself. I used to believe that the expression "caught by the short hairs" meant a captive held with a depilatory string. It especially hurt at the temples, but my mother said we were lucky we didn't have to have our feet bound when we were seven. Sisters used to sit on their beds and cry together, she said, as their mothers or their slaves removed the bandages for a few minutes each night and let the blood gush back into their veins. I hope that the man my aunt loved appreciated a smooth brow, that he wasn't just a tits-and-ass man.

Once my aunt found a freckle on her chin, at a spot that the almanac said predestined her for unhappiness. She dug it out with a hot needle and washed the wound with peroxide.

More attention to her looks than these pullings of hairs and pickings at spots would have caused gossip among the villagers. They owned work clothes and good clothes, and they wore good clothes for feasting the new seasons. But since a woman combing her hair hexes beginnings, my aunt rarely found an occasion to look her best. Women looked like great sea snails—the corded wood, babies, and laundry they carried were the whorls on their backs. The Chinese did not admire a bent back; goddesses and warriors stood straight.

Still there must have been a marvelous freeing of beauty when a worker laid down her burden and stretched and arched.

Such commonplace loveliness, however, was not enough for my aunt. She dreamed of a lover for the fifteen days of New Year's, the time for families to exchange visits, money, and food. She plied her secret comb. And sure enough she cursed the year, the family, the village, and herself.

Even as her hair lured her imminent lover, many other men looked at her. Uncles, cousins, nephews, brothers would have looked, too, had they been home between journeys. Perhaps they had already been restraining their curiosity, and they left, fearful that their glances, like a field of nesting birds, might be startled and caught. Poverty hurt, and that was their first reason for leaving. But another, final reason for leaving the crowded house was the never-said.

She may have been unusually beloved, the precious only daughter, spoiled and mirror gazing because of the affection the family lavished on her. When her husband left, they welcomed the chance to take her back from the in-laws; she could live like the little daughter for just a while longer. There are stories that my grandfather was different from other people, "crazy ever since the little Jap bayoneted him in the head." He used to put his naked penis on the dinner table, laughing. And one day he brought home a baby girl, wrapped up inside his brown western-style greatcoat. He had traded one of his sons, probably my father, the youngest, for her. My grandmother made him trade back. When he finally got a daughter of his own, he doted on her. They must have all loved her, except perhaps my father, the only brother who never went back to China, having once been traded for a girl.

Brothers and sisters, newly men and women, had to efface their sexual color and present plain miens. Disturbing hair and eyes, a smile like no other, threatened the ideal of five generations living under one roof. To focus blurs, people shouted face to face and yelled from room to room. The immigrants I know have loud voices, unmodulated to American tones even after years away from the village where they called their friendships out across the fields. I have not been able to stop my mother's screams in public libraries or over telephones. Walking erect (knees straight, toes pointed forward, not pigeon-toed, which is Chinese-feminine) and speaking in an inaudible voice, I have tried to turn myself American-feminine. Chinese communication was loud, public. Only sick people had to whisper. But at the dinner table, where the family members came nearest one another, no one could talk, not the outcasts nor any eaters. Every word that falls from the mouth is a coin lost. Silently they gave and accepted food with both hands. A preoccupied child who took his bowl with one hand got a sideways glare. A complete moment of total attention is due everyone alike. Children and lovers have no singularity here, but my aunt used a secret voice, a separate attentiveness.

She kept the man's name to herself throughout her labor and dying; she did not accuse him that he be punished with her. To save her inseminator's name she gave silent birth.

He may have been somebody in her own household, but intercourse with a man outside the family would have been no less abhorrent. All the village were kinsmen, and the titles shouted in loud country voices never let kinship be forgotten. Any man within visiting distance would have been neutralized as a lover—"brother," "younger brother," "older brother"—one hundred and fifteen relationship titles. Parents researched birth charts probably not so much to assure good fortune as to circumvent incest in a population that has but one hundred surnames. Everybody has eight million relatives. How useless then sexual mannerisms, how dangerous.

As if it came from an atavism deeper than fear, I used to add "brother" silently to boys' names. It hexed the boys, who would or would not ask me to dance, and made them less scary and as familiar and deserving of benevolence as girls.

But, of course, I hexed myself also—no dates. I should have stood up, both arms waving, and shouted out across libraries, "Hey, you! Love me back." I had no idea, though, how to make attraction selective, how to control its direction and magnitude. If I made myself American-pretty so that the five or six Chinese boys in the class fell in love with me, everyone else— the Caucasian, Negro, and Japanese boys—would too. Sisterliness, dignified and honorable, made much more sense.

Attraction eludes control so stubbornly that whole societies designed to organize relationships among people cannot keep order, not even when they bind people to one another from childhood and raise them together. Among the very poor and the wealthy, brothers married their adopted sisters, like doves. Our family allowed some romance, paying adult brides' prices and providing dowries so that their sons and daughters could marry strangers. Marriage promises to turn strangers into friendly relatives—a nation of siblings.

In the village structure, spirits shimmered among the live creatures, balanced and held in equilibrium by time and land. But one human being flaring up into violence could open up a black hole, a maelstrom that pulled in the sky. The frightened villagers, who depended on one another to maintain the real, went to my aunt to show her a personal, physical representation of the break she had made in the "roundness." Misallying couples snapped off the future, which was to be embodied in true offspring. The villagers punished her for acting as if she could have a private life, secret and apart from them.

If my aunt had betrayed the family at a time of large grain yields and peace, when many boys were born, and wings were being built on many houses, perhaps she might have escaped such severe punishment. But the men—hungry, greedy, tired of planting in dry soil—had been forced to leave the village in order to send food-money home. There were ghost plagues, bandit plagues, wars with the Japanese, floods. My Chinese brother and sister had died of an unknown sickness. Adultery, perhaps only a mistake during good times, became a crime when the village needed food.

The round moon cakes and round doorways, the round tables of graduated sizes that fit one roundness inside another, round windows and rice bowls—these talismans had lost their power to warn this family of the law: a family must be whole, faithfully keeping the descent line by having sons to feed the old and the dead, who in turn look after the family. The villagers came to show my aunt and her lover-in-hiding a broken house. The villagers were speeding up the circling of events because she was too shortsighted to see that her infidelity had already harmed the village, that waves of consequences would return unpredictably, sometimes in disguise, as now, to hurt her. This roundness had to be made coin-sized so that she would see its circumference: punish her at the birth of her baby. Awaken her to the inexorable. People who refused fatalism because they could invent small resources insisted on culpability. Deny accidents and wrest fault from the stars.

After the villagers left, their lanterns now scattering in various directions toward home, the family broke their silence and cursed her. "Aiaa, we're going to die. Death is coming. Death is coming. Look what you've done. You've killed us. Ghost! Dead ghost! Ghost! You've never been born." She ran out into the fields, far enough from the house so that she could no longer hear their voices, and pressed herself against the earth, her own land no more. When she felt the birth coming, she thought that she had been hurt. Her body seized together. "They've hurt me too much," she thought. "This is gall, and it will kill me." With forehead and knees against the earth, her body convulsed and then relaxed. She turned on her back, lay on the ground. The black well of sky and stars went out and out and out forever; her body and her complexity seemed to disappear. She was one of the stars, a bright dot in blackness, without home, without a companion, in eternal cold and silence. An agoraphobia rose in her, speeding higher and higher, bigger and bigger; she would not be able to contain it; there would no end to fear.

Flayed, unprotected against space, she felt pain return, focusing her body. This pain chilled her—a cold, steady kind of surface pain. Inside, spasmodically, the other pain, the pain of the child, heated her. For hours she lay on the ground, alternately body and space. Sometimes a vision of normal comfort obliterated reality: she saw the family in the evening gambling at the dinner table, the young people massaging their elders' backs. She saw them congratulating one another, high joy on the mornings the rice shoots came up. When these pictures burst, the stars drew yet further apart. Black space opened.

She got to her feet to fight better and remembered that old-fashioned women gave birth in their pigsties to fool the jealous, pain-dealing gods, who do not snatch piglets. Before the next spasms could stop her, she ran to the pigsty, each step a rushing out into emptiness. She climbed over the fence and knelt in the dirt. It was good to have a fence enclosing her, a tribal person alone.

Laboring, this woman who had carried her child as a foreign growth that sickened her every day, expelled it at last. She reached down to touch the hot, wet, moving mass, surely smaller than anything human, and could feel that it was human after all—fingers, toes, nails, nose. She pulled it up on to her belly, and it lay curled there, butt in the air, feet precisely tucked one under the other. She opened her loose shirt and buttoned the child inside. After resting, it squirmed and thrashed and she pushed it up to her breast. It turned its head this way and that until it found her nipple. There, it made little snuffling noises. She clenched her teeth at its preciousness, lovely as a young calf, a piglet, a little dog.

She may have gone to the pigsty as a last act of responsibility: she would protect this child as she had protected its father. It would look after her soul, leaving supplies on her grave. But how would this tiny child without family find her grave when there would be no marker for her anywhere, neither in the earth nor the family hall? No one would give her a family hall name. She had taken the child with her into the wastes. At its birth the two of them had felt the same raw pain of separation, a wound that only the family pressing tight could close. A child with no descent line would not soften her life but only trail after her, ghost-like, begging her to give it purpose. At dawn the villagers on their way to the fields would stand around the fence and look.

Full of milk, the little ghost slept. When it awoke, she hardened her breasts against the milk that crying loosens. Toward morning she picked up the baby and walked to the well.

Carrying the baby to the well shows loving. Otherwise abandon it. Turn its face into the mud. Mothers who love their children take them along. It was probably a girl; there is some hope of forgiveness for boys.

"Don't tell anyone you had an aunt. Your father does not want to hear her name. She has never been born." I have believed that sex was unspeakable and words so strong and fathers so frail that "aunt" would do my father mysterious harm. I have thought that my family, having settled among immigrants who had also been their neighbors in the ancestral land, needed to clean their name, and a wrong word would incite the kinspeople even here. But there is more to this silence: they want me to participate in her punishment. And I have.

In the twenty years since I heard this story I have not asked for details nor said my aunt's name; I do not know it. People who can comfort the dead can also chase after them to hurt them further—a reverse ancestor worship. The real punishment was not the raid swiftly inflicted by the villagers, but the family's deliberately forgetting her. Her betrayal so maddened them, they saw to it that she would suffer forever, even after death. Always hungry, always needing, she would have to beg food from other ghosts, snatch and steal it from those whose living descendants give them gifts. She would have to fight the ghosts massed at crossroads for the buns a few thoughtful citizens leave to decoy her away from village and home so that the ancestral spirits could feast unharassed. At peace, they could act like gods, not ghosts, their descent lines providing them with paper suits and dresses, spirit money, paper houses, paper automobiles, chicken, meat, and rice into eternity—essences delivered up in smoke and flames, steam and incense rising from each rice bowl. In an attempt to make the Chinese care for people outside the family, Chairman Mao encourages us now to give our paper replicas to the spirits of outstanding soldiers and workers, no matter whose ancestors they may be. My aunt remains forever hungry. Goods are not distributed evenly among the dead.

My aunt haunts me—her ghost drawn to me because now, after fifty years of neglect, I alone devote pages of paper to her, though not origamied into houses and clothes. I do not think she always means me well. I am telling on her, and she was a spite suicide, drowning herself in the drinking water. The Chinese are always very frightened of the drowned one, whose weeping ghost, wet hair hanging and skin bloated, waits silently by the water to pull down a substitute.

49

Jeanne Wakatsuki Houston (1934–)

Beyond Manzanar

Manzanar, which means "apple orchard" in Spanish, was the name of a large internment camp which the U.S. government built for Japanese and Japanese Americans in World War II. It was in eastern California, in the Owens Valley, on the eastern side of the Sierras. Along with her mother, brothers, and sisters, Jeanne Wakatsuki was taken there in 1942, from their home in Long Beach. Her father, a commercial fisherman, had been arrested earlier and sent to a camp in North Dakota, having been falsely accused of communicating with Japanese submarines off the California coast. They were part of the 110,000 people of Japanese ancestry moved from homes on the West Coast by the War Relocation Authority.

In 1973, assisted by her husband, the writer James Houston, she published a powerful memoir of the experience, *Farewell to Manzanar.* It tells of the pain and humiliation of the internment, the consequences to her family, her father's shattered pride and heavy drinking, the makeshift arrangements people made, and the difficulties the family had in starting over again after the war. It also tells of ballet classes, baton twirling, picnics, and other more normal childhood activities. A movie based on the book has been broadcast on television.

This autobiographical essay, which was written in 1978, is both a sequel to the book and an independent exploration of the ambivalences in being an American woman of Japanese descent. On one side is the example of her mother, who, though independent enough to have married for love, fully accepted Japanese ideals of wifely and motherly behavior. On the other side are the ideals of personal fulfillment, not through sacrifice and cooperation, but through self-assertion and competition. The conflict is further complicated because the two sides are internalized and felt in different ways at different ages and in different moods. Friends, brothers, sisters, and children also give conflicting advice and evoke different impulses.

The essay is reprinted from *Beyond Manzanar: Views of Asian-American*

Womanhood (Santa Barbara: Capra Press, 1985), pp. 7–25. More information about Houston can be found both in *Farewell to Manzanar* and in the essay she wrote for the Gale *Contemporary Authors Autobiography Series,* vol. 16.

I

My mother married for love. This was rare among Japanese immigrants living in America during that time—1915. Most were men who had to send for wives from their provinces in Japan via the *Baishakunin* or matchmaker, who exchanged photographs for the prospective couple and made the arrangements. This is not to say that love did not develop or occur among these couples. What is significant about this "Picture Bride" phenomenon is that the reasons for marriage were not love and affection. Marriages were arranged to perpetuate the family.

My mother was eighteen and living in Spokane, Washington, when she met and fell in love with my father, a student ten years older than herself. She had been promised to someone else, a steady, hard-working farmer and friend of her family. In absolute defiance of her tradition and training to be dutifully obedient to the authority of parents, she ran away with my father. Thus, their marriage became the first step towards assimilation into American culture; romantic love had intertwined itself among the responsibilities which defined their roles as husband/father, wife/mother. Perhaps it was this love, unexhibited but pervasive, which softened the sharp facts of the inequities in their relationship, in her acquiescence to *his* needs and demands. In my immature years I could not understand how she could tolerate his volatile temperament, his arrogance and obsession with dignity, and his "kingly" presence in the home. I was in my teens then, not fully assimilated, but trying desperately to be as American as Doris Day. My parents did not behave like the parents of my Caucasian friends, and this was embarrassing for me.

Mama worked very hard. She would garden, cook, care for us when we were ill, and after the World War II internment of Japanese Americans she even went to work in a fish cannery to supplement the family income, which was minimal at the time. I remember one day in Santa Monica, before the war, when I was six years old watching her scrub clothes, my arms barely reaching over the bathtub's edge, and she on her knees, rubbing soapy shirts against a tin washboard. I watched her silent and sweatstreaked face, her hair greying wispily around her temples. I filled with terror as I envisioned her dying because she worked too hard. I started to cry.

When I told her my fears she only laughed and said, "I like to wash clothes. It gives me time to think of other things in my head." She tapped her forehead. "Besides, I'm not a washerwoman. This is just a chore. I'm your mother."

I did not then understand the weight of her explanation. Being mother was not only enough for her, it was a prized identity. It meant she had a family, and in her world—her peers and community almost exclusively of Japanese descent—the family was supreme. Thus, the chores and duties which she inherited as Japanese wife and mother were not her identity as such; they were just a means to accomplish the end, which was to keep her family intact, happy and well. She never confused her tasks with who she was.

This concept of the inner self, which I have begun only recently to understand as a result of my attempts to rediscover my Japanese "roots," allowed her to form her own image, distinct from the one in the exterior world. This ability to create a psychological privacy, inherited from a people who for centuries have had to create their own internal "space" in an overpopulated island, gave her the freedom, of which she was so deprived in her role as Japanese wife and mother. This was her way to survive . . . and to succeed. She did both with grace and with love. I think of the many people I know today (myself included) who have become so obsessed with freedom and independence. We resent our family, our jobs, our relationships . . . any responsibilities that seem to inhibit our mobility. I have so many more choices than my mother had, so much more external independence; yet, it was not until recently that I realized mobility and time do not mean freedom. The freedom is *within* me. I must *feel* free to be free.

I believe my mother was a fulfilled person. She had ten children who loved her devotedly. Even ten years after her passing, I can truthfully say not a day passes that I do not think of her, not with grief, but with love and gratitude. What Japanese mother could be a failure when even after death her children do not abandon her? This brings to mind a comment made to me by a Japanese-American friend commenting on American values and the family. "We abandon each other when we need each other the most," he said. "We abandon the young and the old. We send our young to nursery schools as early as we can get them in . . . just when they need our love and presence more than any time in their lives. We send our old and sickly to institutions to die alone. Where is our love responsibility? Where is that feeling of responsibility for each other that the family instills? Where is the family?"

There was a time when I would not declare my love for her. Not until I was in college did I realize my Caucasian peers seemed to have a different attitude from mine. Or, at least, they talked about their mothers differently. During my freshman year at San Jose State College I took the required General Psychology course and was exposed for the first time to Freud and Jung, as were most of my classmates. I was stunned to hear them discuss their mothers so impersonally and often with great hostility. It seemed everyone had something negative to say about a "domineering, materialistic, guilt-evoking, aggressive" mother. I did not understand then that this was merely a way of asserting independence, of striking out at the one authority in their lives that emotionally held them to the "nest." What was clear to me was that mother and motherhood were not "sacred" to them in the same way it was to me. They celebrated Mother's Day, which we never did, yet I heard such resentment surrounding that day, I used to wonder why it was celebrated.

Years later I was again keenly reminded of that period in my life. I was working as the Student Activities Coordinator at one of the colleges at the University of California in Santa Cruz. Among my duties was the responsibility for room assignments and changes. One day, a Chicano student came into my office requesting a room change. He was clearly agitated. I offered to act as mediator or counselor if there was a misunderstanding with his roommate. Reluctantly, he said, "I don't know about these Anglos. My roommate talks so badly about his mother. He calls her a bitch. This hurts me very much. I love my mother. I know she is sacrificing for me, crawling on her hands and knees in the strawberry fields of Delano so I can come to the University. I'm afraid I will hurt him if I have to keep rooming with him." I felt my throat tighten and my eyes fill with tears. I was touched by his love and loyalty, his willingness to overtly challenge an attitude so acceptable within the dominant culture and so unacceptable within his.

The word "sacrifice," spoken by my Caucasian friends in reference to their mothers, always carried connotations of guilt and manipulative martyrdom. It did not carry that taint for me or for the Mexican student. In fact, I have found that most of my friends from ethnic minority backgrounds will readily say, if it is so, that they knew their mothers sacrificed their own comforts, or worked so that they could go to school or have a graduation suit . . . no guilt implied, just a recognition and acceptance of it with gratitude.

I think Japanese women of my mother's generation who were mothers were fortunate because their role was highly valued by their society . . . their society being the community of other Japanese immigrants. The family and community prized her role, and when she fulfilled that role, she prized herself. She not only knew her worth, she *felt* her significance. There was no celebration of "Mother's Day," but there was no question that *Oka-san* was respected and loved by her culture.

Her role as wife to my father is not as clear-cut in my memory. Whereas her world in the home, in the immediate Japanese community, did not differ much from the society in which she and her mother were raised, my father's world was very different. He had to earn a living for his family in an environment both alien and hostile to him. My mother, already inherently prepared to subordinate herself in their relationship, knew this and zealously sought for ways to elevate his position in the family. He had to absorb the humiliations "out there": she would absorb them at home. After all, was he not doing this for his family, protecting her, acting as the buffer between herself and that alien *hakujin* world?

She served him, with grace and naturalness. I conjure up the image of her calm, smooth face, her alert brown eyes scanning his stockings for holes as she carefully laid them and his underwear out at the foot of their bed. She did this faithfully every morning I can remember when he was at home. He was always served first at meals. She cooked special things for him and sat next to him at the table, vigilantly aware of his needs, handing him the condiments and pouring his tea before he could ask. She drew his bath and massaged him and laid his clothes out when he dressed up. As I was growing up I accepted these rituals to be the natural expressions of a wife's love for her husband. There was no question in my mind that my mother loved my father; that is why she served him. This attitude, that to serve meant to love, became an integral part of my psychological make-up and a source for confusion when I later began to relate to men.

There was also no question in my mind that my father was absolute authority in their relationship and in his relationship to his children. During and after the Second World War, and our three years interned at Manzanar, when his dreams and economic situation had hit bottom, and he was too old to start over again as he had already done several times, he raged at his wife and family and drank. His frustration toward the society that rejected and humiliated him caused him to turn on his own and on himself. I never understood how she so patiently endured him during those times. But she never abandoned him, understanding, as I did not, the reasons for his anguish, for his sense of failure.

Even though respect for him diminished then, I always felt that he was very powerful and that he dominated her with this power. As they grew older and inevitable thoughts of their passing entered my mind, I worried that she would be lost if he died first. When that sad day arrived I learned what is meant by the Asian truism "softness is strength." I had taken my gravely ill father, along with my mother, to see his doctor. The doctor informed me privately that we should take him to the hospital where he would be comfortable, as he could not live more than ten days.

It was raining. Numbly I drove the car towards the hospital, straining to see through blurred windshields and my own tears. My mother was not crying. "Riku," he said, weakly. He never called her Riku . . . always "Mama." "Don't leave me. Stay with me at the hospital. They won't know how to cook for me . . . or how to care for me." She patted his hand. He said, "You've been a good wife. You've always been the strong one."

Not wanting him to tire, I tried to quiet him. He sat erect and roared like a lion. "Shut up!" I quaked at his forcefulness, but felt some comfort in knowing he could still "save face" and be the final authority to his children, even at death's door. My mother's quiet strength filled the car as she stroked his forehead. Without tears or panic she assured him she would stay with him until the end.

He died that afternoon a few hours after he entered the hospital. For the ten years that my mother survived him, she never once appeared lost or rudderless, as I feared she would be with him gone. Hadn't he been the center of her life? Hadn't the forms in their relationship, the rituals of their roles all affirmed his power over her? No. She had been the strong one. The structure had been created for him; but it was her essence that had sustained it.

II

The memories surrounding my awareness of being female fall into two categories: those of the period before World War II, when the family made up my life, and those after the war when I entered puberty, and my world expanded to include the ways and values of my Caucasian peers. I did not think about my Asian-ness and how it influenced my self-image as a female until I married.

In remembering myself as a small child, I find it hard to separate myself from the entity of the family. I was too young to be given "duties" according to my sex, and I was unaware that this was the organizational basis for operating the family. I took it for granted that everyone just did what had to be done to keep things running smoothly. My five older sisters helped my mother with domestic duties. My four older brothers helped my father in the fishing business. What I vaguely recall about the sensibility surrounding our sex differences was that my sisters and I all liked to please our brothers. Moreover, we tried to attract positive attention from Papa. A smile or affectionate pat from him was like a gift from heaven. Somehow, we never felt this way about Mama. We took her love for granted. But there was something special about Papa.

I never identified this as one of the blessings of maleness. After all, I played with my brother Kiyo, two years older than myself, and I never felt there was anything special about him. I could even make him cry. My older brothers were fun-loving, boisterous and very kind to me, especially when I made them laugh with my imitations of Carmen Miranda dancing, or Bonnie Baker singing "Oh, Johnny." But Papa was different. His specialness came not from being male, but from being the authority.

After the war, and the closing of the camps, my world drastically changed. The family had disintegrated, my father was no longer "Godlike" despite my mother's attempt to sustain that pre-war image of him. I was spending most of my time with my new Caucasian friends and learning new values that clashed with the values of my parents. It was also time that I assumed the duties girls were supposed to do—cooking, cleaning the house, washing and ironing clothes. I remember washing and ironing my brothers' shirts, careful to press the collars correctly, trying not to displease them. I cannot ever remember my brothers performing domestic chores while I lived at home. Yet, even though they may not have been working "out there," as the men were supposed to do, I did not resent it. It would have embarrassed me to see my brothers doing the dishes. Their reciprocation came in a different way. They were very protective of me and made me feel good and important for being a female. If my brother Ray had extra money, he would sometimes buy me a sexy sweater like my Caucasian friends wore, which Mama wouldn't buy for me. My brothers taught me to ride a bicycle, to drive a car, took me to my first dance, and proudly introduced me to their friends.

Although the family had changed, my identity as a female within it did not differ much from my older sisters' who grew up before the war. The males and females supported each other but for different reasons. No longer was the survival of the family as a group our primary objective; we cooperated to help each other survive "out there" in the complicated world that had weakened Papa.

We were living in Long Beach then. My brothers encouraged me to run for school office, to try out for majorette and song leader, and to run for Queen of various festivities. They were proud that I was breaking social barriers still closed to them. It was acceptable for an Oriental male to excel academically and in sports. But to gain recognition socially in a society that had been fed the stereotyped model of the Asian male as cook, houseboy or crazed *Kamikaze* pilot, was almost impossible. The more alluring myth of mystery and exotica that surrounds the Oriental female made it easier, though no less inwardly painful.

Whenever I succeeded in the *hakujin* world, my brothers were supportive, whereas Papa would be disdainful, undermined by my obvious capitulation to the ways of the West. I wanted to be like my Caucasian friends. Not only did I want to look like them, I wanted to act like them. I tried hard to be outgoing and socially aggressive, and to act confidently, like my girl friends. At home I was careful not to show these traits to my father. For him it was bad enough that I did not even look very Japanese; I was too big, and I walked too assertively. My breasts were large, and besides that I showed them off with those sweaters the *hakujin* girls wore! My behavior at home was never calm and serene, but around my father I still tried to be as Japanese as I could.

As I passed puberty and grew more interested in boys, I soon became aware that an Oriental female evoked a certain kind of interest from males. I was still too young to understand how or why an Oriental female fascinated Caucasian men, and of course, far too young to see then that it was a form of "not being seen." My brothers would warn me, "Don't trust the *hakujin* boys. They only want one thing. They'll treat you like a servant and expect you to wait on them hand and foot. They don't know how to be nice to you." My brothers never dated Caucasian girls. In fact, I never really dated Caucasian boys until I went to college. In high school, I used to sneak out to dances and parties where I would meet them. I wouldn't even dare to think what Papa would do if he knew.

What my brothers were saying was that I should not act towards Caucasian males as I did towards them. I must not "wait on them" or allow them to think I would, because they wouldn't understand. In other words, be a Japanese female around Japanese men and act *hakujin* around Caucasian men. This double identity within a "double standard" resulted not only in confusion of my role or roles as female, but also in who or what I was racially. With the admonitions of my brothers lurking deep in my consciousness, I would try to be aggressive, assertive and "come on strong" towards Caucasian men. I mustn't let them think I was submissive, passive and all-giving, like Madame Butterfly. With Asian males I would tone down my natural enthusiasm and settle into patterns instilled in me through the models of my mother and my sisters. I was not comfortable in either role.

I found I was more physically attracted to Caucasian men. Although T.V. and film were not nearly as pervasive as they are now, we still had an abundance of movie magazines and films from which to garner our idols for crushes and fantasy. For years I was madly in love with Lon McAllister and Alan Ladd. Bruce Lee and O.J. Simpson were absent from the idol-making media. Asian men became like "family" to me: they were my brothers. Of course, no one was like my father. He was so powerful. The only men who might possess some of that power were those whose control and dominance over his life diminished his. Those would be the men who interested me.

Although I was attracted to males who looked like someone in a Coca-Cola ad, I yearned for the expressions of their potency to be like that of Japanese men, like that of my father: unpredictable, dominant, and brilliant—yet sensitive and poetic. I wanted a blond Samurai.

When I met him during those college years in San Jose, I was surprised to see how readily my mother accepted the idea of our getting married. My father had passed away, but I was still concerned about her reaction. All of my married brothers and sisters had Japanese American mates. I would be the first to marry a Caucasian. "He's a strong man and will protect you. I'm all for it," she said. Her main concern for me was survival. Knowing that my world was the world of the *hakujin,* she wanted me to be protected, even if it meant marriage to one. It was 1957, and inter-racial couples were a rare sight to see. She felt that my husband-to-be was strong because he was acting against the norms of his culture, perhaps even against his parents' wishes. From her vantage point, where family and group opinion out-weighed the individual's, this willingness to oppose them was truly a show of strength.

When we first married I wondered if I should lay out his socks and underwear every morning like my mother used to do. But my brothers' warning would float up from the past: don't be subservient to Caucasian men or they will take advantage. So I compromised and laid them out whenever I thought to do it . . . which grew less and less often as the years passed. His first reaction to this wifely gesture was to be uncomfortably pleased. Then he was puzzled by its sporadic occurrence, which did not seem to be an act of apology, or a sign that I wanted something. On the days when I felt I should be a good Japanese wife, I did it. On other days, when I felt American and assertive, I did not.

When my mother visited us, as she often did, I had to be on good behavior, much to my husband's pleasure and surprise. I would jump up from the table to fill his empty water glass (if she hadn't beat me to it) or butter his roll. If I didn't notice that his plate needed refilling, she would kick me under the table and reprimand me with a disapproving look. Needless to say, we never had mother-in-law problems. He would often ask with hope in his voice "when is your mother coming to visit?"

Despite the fact that early in our marriage we had become aware of the "images" we had married and were trying to relate to each other as the real people we were, he still hoped deep in his heart that I was his exotic, mysterious but ever available *Cho-Cho san*. And I still saw him as my Anglo Samurai, wielding his sword of integrity, slaying the dragons that prevented my acceptance as an equal human being in his world, now mine.

My mother dutifully served my father throughout their marriage. I never felt she resented it. I served my brothers and father and did not resent it. I was made to feel not only important for performing duties of my role, but absolutely integral for the functioning of the family. I realized a very basic difference in attitude between Japanese and American culture towards serving another. In my family, to serve another could be uplifting, a gracious gesture that elevated oneself. For many white Americans it seems that serving another is degrading, an indication of dependency or weakness in character, or a low place in the social ladder. To be ardently considerate is to be "self-effacing" or apologetic.

My father used to say, "Serving humanity is the greatest virtue. Giving service of yourself is more worthy than selling the service or goods of another." He would prefer that we be maids in someone's home, serving someone well, than be salesgirls where our function would be to exchange someone else's goods, handling money. Perhaps it was his way to rationalize and give pride to the occupations open to us as Orientals. Nevertheless, his words have stayed with me, giving me spiritual sustenance at times when I perceived that my willingness to give was misconstrued as a need to be liked or an act of manipulation to get something.

I was talking about this subject with an Asian American woman friend, recently widowed, whose husband had also been Asian American. He had been a prominent surgeon, highly thought of in the community where we live. She is forty-two, third generation Chinese, born in San Francisco, articulate, intelligent and a professional therapist for educationally handicapped children. She "confessed" her reticence to let her Caucasian friends know she served her husband. "There is such a stereotyped view that is laid on us. They just don't understand *why* we do what we do!"

She told me of an incident when she remarked to a Caucasian friend that she polished her husband's shoes. Her friend turned on her in mock fury and said, "Don't you dare let my husband know you do that!" My friend said she felt ashamed, humiliated, that she had somehow betrayed this woman by seeming subordinate to her husband.

"I served him in many ways," she said. "Even though he was a graduate of Stanford and professionally successful, he drove himself to work harder and longer to compete because he felt he was handicapped by being Chinese. You know our Asian men, the ones raised with values from the old country are not equipped to compete like white American men. They are not conditioned to be outwardly aggressive and competitive. It was agony for my husband, and I knew he was out there doing it for us, so I tried to make it easier for him at home." As I looked at her I could see her compassion, and for a flickering moment I saw my mother. A generation had passed, but some things had not changed that much.

My husband and I often joke that the reason we have stayed married for so long is that we continually mystify each other with responses and attitudes that are plainly due to our different backgrounds. For years I frustrated him with unpredictable silences and accusative looks. I felt a great reluctance to tell him what I wanted or what needed to be done in the home. I was inwardly furious that I was being put into the position of having to *tell* him what to do. I felt my femaleness, in the Japanese sense, was being degraded. I did not want to be the authority. That would be humiliating for him and for me. He, on the other hand, considering the home to be under my dominion, in the American sense, did not dare to impose on me what he thought I wanted. He wanted me to tell him or make a list, like his parents.

Entertaining socially was also confusing. Up to recent times, I still hesitated to sit at one head of our rectangular dining table when my husband sat at the other end. It seemed right to be seated next to him, helping him serve the food. Sometimes I did it anyway, but only with our close friends who didn't misread my physical placement as psychological subservience.

At dinner parties I always served the men first, until I noticed the women glaring at me. I became self-conscious about it and would try to remember to serve the women first. Sometimes I would forget and automatically turn to a man. I would catch myself abruptly, dropping a bowl of soup all over him. Then I would have to serve him first anyway, as a gesture of apology. My unconscious Japanese instinct still managed to get what it wanted.

Now I just entertain according to how I feel that day. If my Japanese sensibility is stronger I act accordingly and feel comfortable. If I want to go all-American I can do that too, I have come to accept the cultural hybridness of my personality, to recognize it as a strength and not weakness. Because I am culturally neither pure Japanese nor pure American does not mean I am less of a person. It means I have been enriched with the heritage of both.

As I look back on my marriage and try to compare it to the marriage of my parents, it seems ludicrous to do so—like comparing a sailboat to a jet airliner. Both get you there, but one depends on the natural element of wind and the other on modern technology. What does emerge as a basic difference is directly related to the Japanese concept of cooperation for group survival and the American value of competition for the survival of the individual. My Japanese family cooperated to survive economically and spiritually. Although sibling rivalry was subtly present, it was never allowed the ferocity of expression we allow our children. I see our children compete with each other. I have felt my husband and I compete with each other—not always in obvious ways, such as professional recognition or in the comparison of role responsibilities, but in attitudes toward self-fulfillment. "I love you more than you love me," or "My doing nothing is more boring than your doing nothing."

Competition does provide some challenge and excitement in life. Yet carried to extremes in personal relationships it can become destructive. How can you fully trust someone you are in competition with? And when trust breaks down, isolation and alienation set in.

I find another basic difference between my mother and myself in how we relate to sons. I try very consciously not to indulge my son, as my mother indulged my brothers. My natural inclination is to do as she did. So I try to restrain it. In fact, I find myself being harder on him, afraid that my constrained Japanese training to please the male might surface, crippling instead of equipping him for future relationships with females who may not be of my background, hampering his emotional survival in the competitive and independent world he will face when he leaves the nest.

How my present attitudes will affect my children in later years remains to be seen. My world is radically different from mother's world, and all indications point to an even wider difference in our world from our children's. Whereas my family's struggle and part of my own was racially based, I do not foresee a similar struggle for our children. Their bi-racialness is, indeed, a factor in their identity and self-image, but I feel their struggle will be more to sustain human dignity in a world rapidly dehumanizing itself with mechanization and technology. My hope is they have inherited that essential trait ethnic minorities in this country have so sharply honed: a strong will to survive.

★

As a mother I have often found myself hearkening again to imagined words of advice from my parents. I hear my mother say, "Love yourself. Nurture your children and your family with love and emotional support. Accept change if it means protecting your loved ones."

I hear my father say, "We are all brothers. Brother must not be pitted against brother. Race must not be pitted against race. We do not raise ourselves at the expense of others. Through cooperation we advance together as human beings."

I see the yin and the yang of their sensibilities and acknowledge how the combination has formed my own, which I feel can be summed up in the following way: "In this game of life you are only as good as your partner, your partner being the other in a one-to-one personal relationship, or a race or ethnic group coexisting with a dominant culture. The best game is when partners are equal, in top form, sharing their diversities, and enriching their experience. Dominating a partner only weakens the game, unbalancing it, lessening its vigor and quality. It is my hope in these changing times that the rules for the game will improve, encouraging understanding and, thus, acceptance and respect for all partners."

50

Wendell Berry (1934–)

The Making of a Marginal Farm

As this autobiographical essay perfectly illustrates, Wendell Berry is both a farmer and a writer, and he seems to allow neither a permanent priority.

He was, as he explains, born in Henry County, Kentucky, and now lives there. In between, he went to the University of Kentucky (A.B., 1956; M.A., 1957) and the writing program at Stanford University. He also taught at Stanford, Georgetown, and New York University, and held a Guggenheim Fellowship in Italy and France. But unlike many distinguished contemporary writers and professors he no longer moves.

Berry is an eloquent advocate of the eighteenth-century Jeffersonian farmer. For him, the small, self-supporting yeoman is independent and the backbone of democracy. He thinks and acts for himself and resists demagoguery. He in turn supports democratic government because it represents and supports him. He is also the best husbandman to the land because he wants it to continue to sustain him and his family.

With these virtues under great pressure from all sides—corporations, universities, city-dwellers, and larger farmers—and meanwhile forgotten or turned into slogans and shibboleths, Berry has not only written about them but attempted to prove that a person can still live by them. He has also used the standard of the Jeffersonian farmer-intellectual to write harsh and prophetic judgments of modern industrial capitalism, such as *The Unsettling of America* (1977).

To Berry, therefore, "marginal farming," is not something to eliminate but the very opposite: the wise, just, instructive, environmentally right and socially and aesthetically beneficial way to live. What's more, as he says, in "settling on this place, I began to *live* in my subject." He "pass[ed] through the surface." The farm became the expression of himself, as he was the caretaker, keeper, defender, and voice of the farm. Yet Berry might also say that this formulation is too fancy, or too neat. He says it better himself: "our reclamation project has been, for me, less a matter of idealism or morality than a kind of self-preservation."

The source of "Making of a Marginal Farm" is *Recollected Essays, 1965–1980* (San Francisco: North Point Press, 1981). There is no biography of Berry. The article by Gary Tolliver in the *Dictionary of Literary Biography*, vol. 5 (1980), is authoritative, however, Tolliver also having written his Ph.D. dissertation on Berry (Ohio Univ., 1978). A good critical article is William Merrill Decker's "The Wild, the Divine, and the Human World: Rereading Wendell Berry," *North Dakota Quarterly* 59 (Spring 1991): 242–58.

One day in the summer of 1956, leaving home for school, I stopped on the side of the road directly above the house where I now live. From there you could see a mile or so across the Kentucky River Valley, and perhaps six miles along the length of it. The valley was a green trough full of sunlight, blue in its distances. I often stopped here in my comings and goings, just to look, for it was all familiar to me from before the time my memory began: woodlands and pastures on the hillsides; fields and croplands, wooded slew-edges and hollows in the bottoms; and through the midst of it the tree-lined river passing down from its headwaters near the Virginia line toward its mouth at Carrollton on the Ohio.

Standing there, I was looking at land where one of my great-great-great-grandfathers settled in 1803, and at the scene of some of the happiest times of my own life, where in my growing-up years I camped, hunted, fished, boated, swam, and wandered—where, in short, I did whatever escaping I felt called upon to do. It was a place where I had happily been, and where I always wanted to be. And I remember gesturing toward the valley that day and saying to the friend who was with me: "That's all I need."

I meant it. It was an honest enough response to my recognition of its beauty, the abundance of its lives and possibilities, and of my own love for it and interest in it. And in the sense that I continue to recognize all that, and feel that what I most need is here, I can still say the same thing.

And yet I am aware that I must necessarily mean differently—or at least a great deal more—when I say it now. Then I was speaking mostly from affection, and did not know, by half, what I was talking about. I was speaking of a place that in some ways I knew and in some ways cared for, but did not live in. The differences between knowing a place and living in it, between cherishing a place and living responsibly in it, had not begun to occur to me. But they are critical differences, and understanding them has been perhaps the chief necessity of my experience since then.

I married in the following summer, and in the next seven years lived in a number of distant places. But, largely because I continued to feel that what I needed was here, I could never bring myself to want to live in any other place. And so we returned to live in Kentucky in the summer of 1964, and that autumn bought the house whose roof my friend and I had looked down on eight years before, and with it "twelve acres more or less." Thus I began a profound change in my life. Before, I had lived according to expectation rooted in ambition. Now I began to live according to a kind of destiny rooted in my origins and in my life. One should not speak too confidently of one's "destiny;" I use the word to refer to causes that lie deeper in history and character than mere intention or desire. In buying the little place known as Lanes Landing, it seems to me, I began to obey the deeper causes.

We had returned so that I could take a job at the University of Kentucky in Lexington. And we expected to live pretty much the usual academic life: I would teach and write; my "subject matter" would be, as it had been, the few square miles in Henry County where I grew up. We bought the tiny farm at Lanes Landing, thinking that we would use it as a "summer place," and on that understanding I began, with the help of two carpenter friends, to make some necessary repairs on the house. I no longer remember exactly how it was decided, but that work had hardly begun when it became a full-scale overhaul.

By so little our minds had been changed: this was not going to be a house to visit, but a house to live in. It was as though, having put our hand to the plow, we not only did not look back, but could not. We renewed the old house, equipped it with plumbing, bathroom, and oil furnace, and moved in on July 4, 1965.

Once the house was whole again, we came under the influence of the "twelve acres more or less." This acreage included a steep hillside pasture, two small pastures by the river, and a "garden spot" of less than half an acre. We had, besides the house, a small barn in bad shape, a good large building that once had been a general store, and a small garage also in usable condition. This was hardly a farm by modern standards, but it was land that could be used, and it was unthinkable that we would not use it. The land was not good enough to afford the possibility of a cash income, but it would allow us to grow our food—or most of it. And that is what we set out to do.

In the early spring of 1965 I had planted a small orchard; the next spring we planted our first garden. Within the following six or seven years we reclaimed the pastures, converted the garage into a henhouse, rebuilt the barn, greatly improved the garden soil, planted berry bushes, acquired a milk cow—and were producing, except for hay and grain for our animals, nearly everything that we ate: fruit, vegetables, eggs, meat, milk, cream, and butter. We built an outbuilding with a meat room and a food-storage cellar. Because we did not want to pollute our land and water with sewage, and in the process waste nutrients that should be returned to the soil, we built a composting privy. And so we began to attempt a life that, in addition to whatever else it was, would be responsibly agricultural. We used no chemical fertilizers. Except for a little rotenone, we used no insecticides. As our land and our food became healthier, so did we. And our food was of better quality than any that we could have bought.

We were not, of course, living an idyll. What we had done could not have been accomplished without difficulty and a great deal of work. And we had made some mistakes and false starts. But there was great satisfaction, too, in restoring the neglected land, and in feeding ourselves from it.

Meanwhile, the forty-acre place adjoining ours on the downriver side had been sold to a "developer," who planned to divide it into lots for "second homes." This project was probably doomed by the steepness of the ground and the difficulty of access, but a lot of bulldozing—and a lot of damage— was done before it was given up. In the fall of 1972, the place was offered for sale and we were able to buy it.

We now began to deal with larger agricultural problems. Some of this new land was usable; some would have to be left in trees. There were perhaps fifteen acres of hillside that could be reclaimed for pasture, and about two and a half acres of excellent bottomland on which we would grow alfalfa for hay. But it was a mess, all of it badly neglected, and a considerable portion of it badly abused by the developer's bulldozers. The hillsides were covered with thicket growth; the bottom was shoulder high in weeds; the diversion ditches had to be restored; a bulldozed gash meant for "building sites" had to be mended; the barn needed a new foundation, and the cistern a new top; there were no fences. What we had bought was less a farm than a reclamation project—which has now, with a later purchase, grown to seventy-five acres.

While we had only the small place, I had got along very well with a Gravely "walking tractor" that I owned, and an old Farmall A that I occasionally borrowed from my Uncle Jimmy. But now that we had increased our acreage, it was clear that I could not continue to depend on a borrowed tractor. For a while I assumed that I would buy a tractor of my own. But because our land was steep, and there was already talk of a fuel shortage—and because I liked the idea—I finally decided to buy a team of horses instead. By the spring of 1973, after a lot of inquiring and looking, I had found and bought a team of five-year-old sorrel mares. And—again by the generosity of my Uncle Jimmy, who has never thrown any good thing away—I had enough equipment to make a start.

Though I had worked horses and mules during the time I was growing up, I had never worked over ground so steep and problematical as this, and it had been twenty years since I had worked a team over ground of any kind. Getting started again, I anticipated every new task with uneasiness, and sometimes with dread. But to my relief and delight, the team and I did all that needed to be done that year, getting better as we went along. And over the years since then, with that team and others, my son and I have carried on our farming the way it was carried on in my boyhood, doing everything with our horses except baling the hay. And we have done work in places and in weather in which a tractor would have been useless. Experience has shown us—or re-shown us—that horses are not only a satisfactory and economical means of power, especially on such small places as ours, but are probably *necessary* to the most conservative use of steep land. Our farm, in fact, is surrounded by potentially excellent hillsides that were maintained in pasture until tractors replaced the teams.

Another change in our economy (and our lives) was accomplished in the fall of 1973 with the purchase of our first wood-burning stove. Again the petroleum shortage was on our minds, but we also knew that from the pasture-clearing we had ahead of us we would have an abundance of wood that otherwise would go to waste—and when that was gone we would still have our permanent wood lots. We thus expanded our subsistence income to include heating fuel, and since then have used our furnace only as a "backup system" in the coldest weather and in our absences from home. The horses also contribute significantly to the work of fuel-gathering; they will go easily into difficult places and over soft ground or snow where a truck or a tractor could not move.

As we have continued to live on and from our place, we have slowly begun its restoration and healing. Most of the scars have now been mended and grassed over, most of the washes stopped, most of the buildings made sound; many loads of rocks have been hauled out of the fields and used to pave entrances or fill hollows; we have done perhaps half of the necessary fencing. A great deal of work is still left to do, and some of it—the rebuilding of fertility in the depleted hillsides—will take longer than we will live. But in doing these things we have begun a restoration and a healing in ourselves.

I should say plainly that this has not been a "paying proposition." As a reclamation project, it has been costly both in money and in effort. It seems at least possible that, in any other place, I might have had little interest in doing any such thing. The reason I have been interested in doing it here, I think, is that I have felt implicated in the history, the uses, and the attitudes that have depleted such places as ours and made them "marginal."

I had not worked long on our "twelve acres more or less" before I saw that such places were explained almost as much by their human history as by their nature. I saw that they were not "marginal" because they were unfit for human use, but because in both culture and character *we* had been unfit to use them. Originally, even such steep slopes as these along the lower Kentucky River Valley were deep-soiled and abundantly fertile; "jumper" plows and generations of carelessness impoverished them. Where yellow clay is at the surface now, five feet of good soil may be gone. I once wrote that on some of the nearby uplands one walks as if "knee-deep" in the absence of the original soil. On these steeper slopes, I now know, that absence is shoulder-deep.

That is a loss that is horrifying as soon as it is imagined. It happened easily, by ignorance, indifference, "a little folding of the hands to sleep." It cannot be remedied in human time; to build five feet of soil takes perhaps fifty or sixty thousand years. This loss, once imagined, is potent with despair. If a people in adding a hundred and fifty years to itself subtracts fifty thousand from its land, what is there to hope?

And so our reclamation project has been, for me, less a matter of idealism or morality than a kind of self-preservation. A destructive history, once it is understood as such, is a nearly insupportable burden. Understanding it is a disease of understanding, depleting the sense of efficacy and paralyzing effort, unless it finds healing work. For me that work has been partly of the mind, in what I have written, but that seems to have depended inescapably on work of the body and of the ground. In order to affirm the values most native and necessary to me—indeed, to affirm my own life as a thing decent in possibility—I needed to know in my own experience that this place did not have to be abused in the past, and that it can be kindly and conservingly used now.

With certain reservations that must be strictly borne in mind, our work here has begun to offer some of the needed proofs.

Bountiful as the vanished original soil of the hillsides may have been, what remains is good. It responds well—sometimes astonishingly well—to good treatment. It never should have been plowed (some of it never should have been cleared), and it never should be plowed again. But it can be put in pasture without plowing, and it will support an excellent grass sod that will in turn protect it from erosion, if properly managed and not overgrazed.

Land so steep as this cannot be preserved in row crop cultivation. To subject it to such an expectation is simply to ruin it, as its history shows. Our rule, generally, has been to plow no steep ground, to maintain in pasture only such slopes as can be safely mowed with a horse-drawn mower, and to leave the rest in trees. We have increased the numbers of livestock on our pastures gradually, and have carefully rotated the animals from field to field, in order to avoid overgrazing. Under this use and care, our hillsides have mended and they produce more and better pasturage every year.

As a child I always intended to be a farmer. As a young man, I gave up that intention, assuming that I could not farm and do the other things I wanted to do. And then I became a farmer almost unintentionally and by a kind of necessity. That wayward and necessary becoming—along with my marriage, which has been intimately a part of it—is the major event of my life. It has changed me profoundly from the man and the writer I would otherwise have been.

There was a time, after I had left home and before I came back, when this place was my "subject matter." I meant that too, I think, on the day in 1956 when I told my friend, "That's all I need." I was regarding it, in a way too easy for a writer, as a mirror in which I saw myself. There was obviously a sort of narcissism in that—and an inevitable superficiality, for only the surface can reflect.

In coming home and settling on this place, I began to *live* in my subject, and to learn that living in one's subject is not at all the same as "having" a subject. To live in the place that is one's subject is to pass through the surface. The simplifications of distance and mere observation are thus destroyed. The obsessively regarded reflection is broken and dissolved. One sees that the mirror was a blinder; one can now begin to see where one is. One's relation to one's subject ceases to be merely emotional or esthetical, or even merely critical, and becomes problematical, practical, and responsible as well. Because it must. It is like marrying your sweetheart.

Though our farm has not been an economic success, as such success is usually reckoned, it is nevertheless beginning to make a kind of economic sense that is consoling and hopeful. Now that the largest expenses of purchase and repair are behind us, our income from the place is beginning to run ahead of expenses. As income I am counting the value of shelter, subsistence, heating fuel, and money earned by the sale of livestock. As expenses I am counting maintenance, newly purchased equipment, extra livestock feed, newly purchased animals, reclamation work, fencing materials, taxes, and insurance.

If our land had been in better shape when we bought it, our expenses would obviously be much smaller. As it is, once we have completed its restoration, our farm will provide us a home, produce our subsistence, keep us warm in winter, and earn a modest cash income. The significance of this becomes apparent when one considers that most of this land is "unfarmable" by the standards of conventional agriculture, and that most of it was producing nothing at the time we bought it.

And so, contrary to some people's opinion, it *is* possible for a family to live on such "marginal" land, to take a bountiful subsistence and some cash income from it, and, in doing so, to improve both the land and themselves. (I believe, however, that, at least in the present economy, this should not be attempted without a source of income other than the farm. It is now extremely difficult to pay for the best of farmland by farming it, and even "marginal" land has become unreasonably expensive. To attempt to make a living from such land is to impose a severe strain on land and people alike.)

I said earlier that the success of our work here is subject to reservations. There are only two of these, but both are serious.

The first is that land like ours—and there are many acres of such land in this country—can be conserved in use only by competent knowledge, by a great deal more work than is required by leveler land, by a devotion more particular and disciplined than patriotism, and by ceaseless watchfulness and care. All these are cultural values and resources, never sufficiently abundant in this country, and now almost obliterated by the contrary values of the so-called "affluent society."

One of my own mistakes will suggest the difficulty. In 1974 I dug a small pond on a wooded hillside that I wanted to pasture occasionally. The excavation for that pond—as I should have anticipated, for I had better reason than I used—caused the hillside to slump both above and below. After six years the slope has not stabilized, and more expense and trouble will be required to stabilize it. A small hillside farm will not survive many mistakes of that order. Nor will a modest income.

The true remedy for mistakes is to keep from making them. It is not in the piecemeal technological solutions that our society now offers, but in a change of cultural (and economic) values that will encourage in the whole population the necessary respect, restraint, and care. Even more important, it is in the possibility of settled families and local communities, in which the knowledge of proper means and methods, proper moderations and restraints, can be handed down, and so accumulate in place and stay alive; the experience of one generation is not adequate to inform and control its actions. Such possibilities are not now in sight in this country.

The second reservation is that we live at the lower end of the Kentucky River watershed, which has long been intensively used, and is increasingly abused. Strip mining, logging, extractive farming, and the digging, draining, roofing, and paving that go with industrial and urban "development," all have seriously depleted the capacity of the watershed to retain water. This means not only that floods are higher and more frequent than they would be if the watershed were healthy, but that the floods subside too quickly, the watershed being far less a sponge, now, than it is a roof. The floodwater drops suddenly out of the river, leaving the steep banks soggy, heavy, and soft. As a result, great strips and blocks of land crack loose and slump, or they give way entirely and disappear into the river in what people here call "slips."

The flood of December 1978, which was unusually high, also went down extremely fast, falling from banktop almost to pool stage within a couple of days. In the aftermath of this rapid "drawdown," we lost a block of bottomland an acre square. This slip, which is still crumbling, severely damaged our place, and may eventually undermine two buildings. The same flood started a slip in another place, which threatens a third building. We have yet another building situated on a huge (but, so far, very gradual) slide that starts at the river and, aggravated by two state highway cuts, goes almost to the hilltop. And we have serious river bank erosion the whole length of our place.

What this means is that, no matter how successfully we may control erosion on our hillsides, our land remains susceptible to a more serious cause of erosion that we cannot control. Our river bank stands literally at the cutting edge of our nation's consumptive economy. This, I think, is true of many "marginal" places—it is true, in fact, of many places that are not marginal. In its consciousness, ours is an upland society; the ruin of watersheds, and what that involves and means, is little considered. And so the land is heavily taxed to subsidize an "affluence" that consists, in reality, of health and goods stolen from the unborn.

Living at the lower end of the Kentucky River watershed is what is now known as "an educational experience"—and not an easy one. A lot of information comes with it that is severely damaging to the reputation of our people and our time. From where I live and work, I never have to look far to see that the earth does indeed pass away. But however that is taught, and however bitterly learned, it is something that should be known, and there is a certain good strength in knowing it. To spend one's life farming a piece of the earth so passing is, as many would say, a hard lot. But it is, in an ancient sense, the human lot. What saves it is to love the farming.

51

Richard Rodriguez (1944–)

from *Complexion*

Published in 1982, *Hunger of Memory* has been a controversial book. Conservatives have liked it for its opposition to affirmative action and bilingual education; the left has objected that, as an exceptionally talented, well-educated young man, Rodriguez does not speak for all Mexican-Americans or members of minorities.

In the book, Rodriguez acknowledges his good fortune. His parents aspired to the middle class and sent him and his brother and sisters to good Catholic schools in Sacramento, California. They did not live in a barrio. When Richard's teachers suggested to his parents that he would learn English faster if English were spoken at home, the family obliged. Later, he felt very grateful because "What I needed to learn in school was that I had the right—and the obligation—to speak the public language of *los gringos*" (19). He became an outstanding student, won a scholarship to Stanford, and did graduate work in English literature at Columbia University, the Warburg Institute in London, and the University of California, Berkeley. At Berkeley in 1975, he then had his pick of jobs at prestigious colleges. Not feeling like a member of a "disadvantaged minority," however, and not approving of affirmative action, which gave "benefits for the relative few because of the absence of the many" (164), he turned them down. Then, he says, he retired to an apartment in San Francisco to write "this intellectual autobiography" (175).

As this selection from the chapter "Complexion" shows, Rodriguez was not spared insecurity about his skin color. With his Spanish and Mexican inheritance, he also held different values and different definitions of manhood. The latter part of this short selection is typical of his gentle insistence on explaining misunderstood cultural differences and establishing his individual relationships to them. As he says at the end of *Hunger of Memory*, reversing the stoicism and insularity of his parents, "I have come to think that there is a place for the deeply personal in public life" (185).

The selection is taken from *Hunger of Memory* (Boston: David R. Godine,

1982). For further biographical information about Richard Rodriguez, see *Contemporary American Authors,* vol. 110 (1984), pp. 429–30.

Complexion. My first conscious experience of sexual excitement concerns my complexion. One summer weekend, when I was around seven years old, I was at a public swimming pool with the whole family. I remember sitting on the damp pavement next to the pool and seeing my mother, in the spectators' bleachers, holding my younger sister on her lap. My mother, I noticed, was watching my father as he stood on a diving board, waving to her. I watched her wave back. Then saw her radiant, bashful, astonishing smile. In that second I sensed that my mother and father had a relationship I knew nothing about. A nervous excitement encircled my stomach as I saw my mother's eyes follow my father's figure curving into the water. A second or two later, he emerged. I heard him call out. Smiling, his voice sounded, buoyant, calling me to swim to him. But turning to see him, I caught my mother's eye. I heard her shout over to me. In Spanish she called through the crowd: "Put a towel on over your shoulders." In public, she didn't want to say why. I knew.

That incident anticipates the shame and sexual inferiority I was to feel in later years because of my dark complexion. I was to grow up an ugly child. Or one who thought himself ugly. (*Feo.*) One night when I was eleven or twelve years old, I locked myself in the bathroom and carefully regarded my reflection in the mirror over the sink. Without any pleasure I studied my skin. I turned on the faucet. (In my mind I heard the swirling voices of aunts, and even my mother's voice, whispering, whispering incessantly about lemon juice solutions and dark, *feo* children.) With a bar of soap, I fashioned a thick ball of lather. I began soaping my arms. I took my father's straight razor out of the medicine cabinet. Slowly, with steady deliberateness, I put the blade against my flesh, pressed it as close as I could without cutting, and moved it up and down across my skin to see if I could get out, somehow lessen, the dark. All I succeeded in doing, however, was in shaving my arms bare of their hair. For as I noted with disappointment, the dark would not come out. It remained. Trapped. Deep in the cells of my skin.

Throughout adolescence, I felt myself mysteriously marked. Nothing else about my appearance would concern me so much as the fact that my complexion was dark. My mother would say how sorry she was that there was not money enough to get braces to straighten my teeth. But I never bothered about my teeth. In three-way mirrors at department stores, I'd see my profile dramatically defined by a long nose, but it was really only the color of my skin that caught my attention.

I wasn't afraid that I would become a menial laborer because of my skin. Nor did my complexion make me feel especially vulnerable to racial abuse. (I didn't really consider my dark skin to be a racial characteristic. I would have been only too happy to look as Mexican as my light-skinned older brother.) Simply, I judged myself ugly. And, since the women in my family had been the ones who discussed it in such worried tones, I felt my dark skin made me unattractive to women.

Thirteen years old. Fourteen. In a grammar school art class, when the assignment was to draw a self-portrait, I tried and I tried but could not bring myself to shade in the face on the paper to anything like my actual tone. With disgust then I would come face to face with myself in mirrors. With disappointment I located myself in class photographs—my dark face undefined by the camera which had clearly described the white faces of classmates. Or I'd see my dark wrist against my long-sleeved white shirt.

I grew divorced from my body. Insecure, overweight, listless. On hot summer days when my rubber-soled shoes soaked up the heat from the sidewalk, I kept my head down. Or walked in the shade. My mother didn't need anymore to tell me to watch out for the sun. I denied myself a sensational life. The normal, extraordinary, animal excitement of feeling my body alive— riding shirtless on a bicycle in the warm wind created by furious self-propelled motion—the sensations that first had excited in me a sense of my maleness, I denied. I was too ashamed of my body. I wanted to forget that I had a body because I had a brown body. I was grateful that none of my classmates ever mentioned the fact.

I continued to see the *braceros,* those men I resembled in one way and, in another way, didn't resemble at all. On the watery horizon of a Valley afternoon, I'd see them. And though I feared looking like them, it was with silent envy that I regarded them still. I envied them their physical lives, their freedom to violate the taboo of the sun. Closer to home I would notice the shirtless construction workers, the roofers, the sweating men tarring the street in front of the house. And I'd see the Mexican gardeners. I was unwilling to admit the attraction of their lives. I tried to deny it by looking away. But what was denied became strongly desired.

In high school physical education classes, I withdrew, in the regular company of five or six classmates, to a distant corner of a football field where we smoked and talked. Our company was composed of bodies too short or too tall, all graceless and all—except mine—pale. Our conversation was usually witty. (In fact we were intelligent.) If we referred to the athletic contests around us, it was with sarcasm. With savage scorn I'd refer to the 'animals' playing football or baseball. It would have been important for me to have joined them. Or for me to have taken off my shirt, to have let the sun burn dark on my skin, and to have run barefoot on the warm wet grass. It would have been very important. Too important. It would have been too telling a gesture—to admit the desire for sensation, the body, my body.

Fifteen, sixteen. I was a teenager shy in the presence of girls. Never dated. Barely could talk to a girl without stammering. In high school I went to several dances, but I never managed to ask a girl to dance. So I stopped going. I cannot remember high school years now with the parade of typical images: bright drive-ins or gliding blue shadows of a Junior Prom. At home most weekend nights, I would pass evenings reading. Like those hidden, precocious adolescents who have no real-life sexual experiences, I read a great deal of romantic fiction. "You won't find it in your books," my brother would playfully taunt me as he prepared to go to a party by freezing the crest of the wave in his hair with sticky pomade. Through my reading, however, I developed a fabulous and sophisticated sexual imagination. At seventeen, I may not have known how to engage a girl in small talk, but I had read *Lady Chatterley's Lover*.

It annoyed me to hear my father's teasing: that I would never know what "real work" is; that my hands were so soft. I think I knew it was his way of admitting pleasure and pride in my academic success. But I didn't smile. My mother said she was glad her children were getting their educations and would not be pushed around like *los pobres*. I heard the remark ironically as a reminder of my separation from *los braceros*. At such times I suspected that education was making me effeminate. The odd thing, however, was that I did not judge my classmates so harshly. Nor did I consider my male teachers in high school effeminate. It was only myself I judged against some shadowy, mythical Mexican laborer—dark like me, yet very different.

Language was crucial. I knew that I had violated the ideal of the *macho* by becoming such a dedicated student of language and literature. *Machismo* was a word never exactly defined by the persons who used it. (It was best described in the 'proper' behavior of men.) Women at home, nevertheless, would repeat the old Mexican dictum that a man should be *feo, fuerte, y formal*. "The three *F*'s," my mother called them, smiling slyly. *Feo* I took to mean not literally ugly so much as ruggedly handsome. (When my mother and her sisters spent a loud, laughing afternoon determining ideal male good looks, they finally settled on the actor Gilbert Roland, who was neither too pretty nor ugly but had looks "like a man.") *Fuerte*, "strong," seemed to mean not physical strength as much as inner strength, character. A dependable man is *fuerte*. *Fuerte* for that reason was a characteristic subsumed by the last of the three qualities, and the one I most often considered—*formal*. To be *formal* is to be steady. A man of responsibility, a good provider. Someone *formal* is also constant. A person to be relied upon in adversity. A sober man, a man of high seriousness.

I learned a great deal about being *formal* just by listening to the way my father and other male relatives of his generation spoke. A man was not silent necessarily. Nor was he limited in the tones he could sound. For example, he could tell a long, involved, humorous story and laugh at his own humor with high-pitched giggling. But a man was not talkative the way a woman could be. It was permitted a woman to be gossipy and chatty. (When one heard many voices in a room, it was usually women who were talking.) Men spoke much less rapidly. And often men spoke in monologues. (When one voice sounded in a crowded room, it was most often a man's voice one heard.) More important than any of this was the fact that a man never verbally revealed his emotions. Men did not speak about their unease in moments of crisis or danger. It was the woman who worried aloud when her husband got laid off from work. At times of illness or death in the family, a man was usually quiet, even silent. Women spoke up to voice prayers. In distress, women always sounded quick ejaculations to God or the Virgin; women prayed in clearly audible voices at a wake held in a funeral parlor. And on the subject of love, a woman was verbally expansive. She spoke of her yearning and delight. A married man, if he spoke publicly about love, usually did so with playful, mischievous irony. Younger, unmarried men more often were quiet. (The *macho* is a silent suitor. *Formal*.)

At home I was quiet, so perhaps I seemed *formal* to my relations and other Spanish-speaking visitors to the house. But outside the house—my God!—I talked. Particularly in class or alone with my teachers, I chattered. (Talking seemed to make teachers think I was bright.) I often was proud of my way with words. Though, on other occasions, for example, when I would hear my mother busily speaking to women, it would occur to me that my attachment to words made me like her. Her son. Not *formal* like my father. At such times I even suspected that my nostalgia for sounds—the noisy, intimate Spanish sounds of my past—was nothing more than effeminate yearning.

High school English teachers encouraged me to describe very personal feelings in words. Poems and short stories I wrote, expressing sorrow and loneliness, were awarded high grades. In my bedroom were books by poets and novelists—books that I loved—in which male writers published feelings the men in my family never revealed or acknowledged in words. And it seemed to me that there was something unmanly about my attachment to literature. Even today, when so much about the myth of the *macho* no longer concerns me, I cannot altogether evade such notions. Writing these pages, admitting my embarrassment or my guilt, admitting my sexual anxieties and my physical insecurity, I have not been able to forget that I am not being *formal*.

So be it.

52

Annie Dillard (1945–)

from *An American Childhood*

Annie Dillard's *Pilgrim at Tinker Creek* (1974) was a book of nature essays and personal meditations based on a year's residence, in 1972, in the Roanoke valley of rural Virginia. It won the Pulitzer Prize and was often compared to Thoreau's *Walden*.

More extensively autobiographical than *Tinker Creek* is her *An American Childhood* (1987), which is about her childhood and adolescence in upper-middle-class Pittsburgh in the prosperous, confident 1950s and early '60s. It is a story of her dawn of memory and consciousness, running on into a very privileged education and self-education. She collects butterflies and classifies rocks and minerals, studies drawing, practices the piano, reads omnivorously, and spends comfortable vacations with her wealthy paternal grandparents on Lake Erie and in Florida. She also rebels against her family's respectable Presbyterian church and the class traditions enshrined in country clubs and private schools. Like other young artists from other cities, she dreams of someday escaping. But Annie Dillard (Dillard was the name of her first husband) also seems grateful for the advantages she had as Annie Doak, eldest daughter of Pam and Frank Doak and big sister to Amy and Molly.

The following untitled chapter balances these joys and frustrations of being brilliant and spontaneous, and troubled and troublesome, in a town which is stuffy but also comforting and nurturing. It is also humorous. But was the humor felt at the time or only seen later?

The escape which Annie Doak did make was to Hollins College in Roanoke, Virginia, where she majored in English and graduated Phi Beta Kappa in 1967.

The selection below is from *An American Childhood* (New York: Harper and Row, 1988). There is no biography of Dillard. The sketch in the *Dictionary of Literary Biography, Yearbook* (1980) is informative, however, and the sketch in *Contemporary Authors* (New Revision Series, vol. 3) has a lengthy survey of reviews of her work.

Now it was May. Daylight Saving Time had begun; the colored light of the long evenings fairly split me with joy. White trillium had bloomed and gone on the forested slopes in Fox Chapel. The cliffside and riverside patches of woods all over town showed translucent ovals of yellow or ashy greens; the neighborhood trees on Glen Arden Drive had blossomed in white and red.

Baseball season had begun, a season which recalled but could never match last year's National League pennant and seventh-game World Series victory over the Yankees, when we at school had been so frenzied for so many weeks they finally and wisely opened the doors and let us go. I had walked home from school one day during that series and seen Pittsburgh's Fifth Avenue emptied of cars, as if the world were over.

A year of wild feelings had passed, and more were coming. Without my noticing, the drummer had upped the tempo. Someone must have slipped him a signal when I wasn't looking; he'd speeded things up. The key was higher, too. I had a driver's license. When I drove around in Mother's old Dodge convertible, the whole town smelled good. And I did drive around the whole town. I cruised along the blue rivers and across them on steel bridges, and steered up and down the scented hills. I drove winding into and out of the steep neighborhoods across the Allegheny River, neighborhoods where I tried in vain to determine in what languages the signs on storefronts were written. I drove onto boulevards, highways, beltways, freeways, and the turnpike. I could drive to Guatemala, drive to Alaska. Why, I asked myself, did I drive to—of all spots on earth—our garage? Why home, why school?

Throughout the long, deadly school afternoons, we junior and senior girls took our places in study hall. We sat at desks in a roomful of desks, whether or not we had something to do, until four o'clock.

Now this May afternoon a teacher propped open the study hall's back door. The door gave onto our hockey field and, behind it, Pittsburgh's Nabisco plant, whence, O Lordy, issued the smell of shortbread today; they were baking Lorna Doones. Around me sat forty or fifty girls in green cotton jumpers and spring-uniform white bucks. They rested their chins on the heels of both hands and leaned their cheeks on curled fingers; their propped heads faced the opened pages of *L'Étranger, Hamlet, Vanity Fair*. Some girls leaned back and filed their nails. Some twisted stiff pieces of their hair, to stay not so much awake as alive. Sometimes in health class, when we were younger, we had all been so bored we hooked our armpits over our chairs' backs so we cut off all circulation to one arm, in an effort to kill that arm for something to do, or cause a heart attack, whichever came first. We were, in fact, getting a dandy education. But sometimes we were restless. Weren't there some wars being fought somewhere that I, for one, could join?

I wrote a name on a notebook. I looked at the study-hall ceiling and tried to see that boy's familiar face—light and dark, bold-eyed, full of feeling—on the inside of my eyelids. Failing that, I searched for his image down the long speckled tunnel or corridor I saw with my eyes closed. As if visual memory were a Marx brothers comedy, I glimpsed swift fragments—a wry corner of his lip, a pointy knuckle, a cupped temple—which crossed the corridor so fast I recognized them only as soon as they vanished. I opened my eyes and wrote his name. His depth and complexity were apparently infinite. From the tip of his lively line of patter to the bottom of his heartbroken, hopeful soul was the longest route I knew, and the best.

The heavy, edible scent of shortbread maddened me in my seat, made me so helpless with longing my wrists gave out; I couldn't hold a pen. I looked around constantly to catch someone's eye, anyone's eye.

It was a provocative fact, which I seemed to have discovered, that we students outnumbered our teachers. Must we then huddle here like sheep? By what right, exactly, did these few women keep us sitting here in this clean, bare room to no purpose? Lately I had been trying to enflame my friends with the implications of our greater numbers. We could pull off a riot. We could bang on the desks and shout till they let us out. Then we could go home and wait for dinner. Or we could bear our teachers off on our shoulders, and— what? Throw them into the Lorna Doone batter? I got no takers.

I had finished my work long ago. "Works only on what interests her," the accusation ran—as if, I reflected, obedience outranked passion, as if sensible people didn't care what they stuck in their minds. Today as usual no one around me was ready for action. I took a fresh sheet of paper and copied on it random lines in French:

> *Ô saisons, ô châteaux!*
> Is it through these endless nights that you sleep
>   in exile
> Ô million golden birds, ô future vigor?
> Oh, that my keel would split! Oh, that I would
>   go down in the sea!

I had struck upon the French Symbolists, like a canyon of sharp crystals underground, like a long and winding corridor lined with treasure. These poets popped into my ken in an odd way: I found them in a book I had rented from a drugstore. Carnegie and school libraries filled me in. I read Enid Starkie's Rimbaud biography. I saved my allowance for months and bought two paperbound poetry books, the Penguin *Rimbaud*, and a Symbolist anthology in which Paul Valéry declaimed, "*Azure! c'est moi.* . . ." I admired Gérard de Nerval. This mad writer kept a lobster as a pet. He walked it on a leash along the sidewalks of Paris, saying, "It doesn't bark, and knows the secrets of the deep."

I loved Rimbaud, who ran away, loved his skinny, furious face with the wild hair and snaky, unseeing eyes pointing in two directions, and his poems' confusion and vagueness, their overwritten longing, their hatred, their sky-shot lyricism, and their oracular fragmentation, which I enhanced for myself by reading and retaining his stuff in crazed bits, mostly from *Le Bateau Ivre,* The Drunken Boat. (The drunken boat tells its own story, a downhill, downstream epic unusually full of words.)

Now in study hall I saw that I had drawn all over this page; I got out another piece of paper. Rimbaud was damned. He said so himself. Where could I meet someone like that? I wrote down another part:

> There is a cathedral that goes down and a lake
>   that goes up.
> There is a troupe of strolling players in costume,
>   glimpsed on the road through the edge of
>   the trees.

I looked up from the new page I had already started to draw all over. Except for my boyfriend, the boys I knew best were out of town. They were older, prep-school and college boys whose boldness, wit, breadth of knowledge, and absence of scruples fascinated me. They cruised the deb party circuit all over Pennsylvania, holding ever-younger girls up to the light like chocolates, to determine how rich their centers might be. I smiled to recall one of these boys: he was so accustomed to the glitter of society, and so sardonic and graceful, that he carried with him at all times, in his jacket pocket, a canister of dance wax. Ordinary boys carried pocket knives for those occasions which occur unexpectedly, and this big, dark-haired boy carried dance wax for the same reason. When the impulse rose, he could simply sprinkle dance wax on any hall or dining-room floor, take a girl in his arms, and whirl her away. I had known these witty, handsome boys for years, and only recently understood that when they were alone, they read books. In public, they were lounge lizards; they drank; they played word games, filling in the blanks desultorily; they cracked wise. These boys would be back in town soon, and my boyfriend and I would join them.

Whose eye could I catch? Everyone in the room was bent over her desk. Ellin Hahn was usually ready to laugh, but now she was working on something. She would call me as soon as we got home. Every day on the phone, I unwittingly asked Ellin some blunt question about the social world around us, and at every question she sighed and said to me, "You still don't get it"— or often, as if addressing a jury of our incredulous peers, "She still doesn't get it!"

Looking at the study-hall ceiling, I dosed myself almost fatally with the oxygen-eating lines of Verlaine's "The long sobs / of the violins / of autumn / wound my heart / with a languor / monotone."

This unsatisfying bit of verse I repeated to myself for ten or fifteen minutes, by the big clock, over and over, clobbering myself with it, the way Molly, when she had been a baby, banged the top of her head on her crib.

> Ô world, ô college, ô dinner . . .
> Ô unthinkable task . . .

Funny how badly I'd turned out. Now I was always in trouble. It felt as if I was doing just as I'd always done—I explored the neighborhood, turning over rocks. The latest rocks were difficult. I'd been in a drag race, of all things, the previous September, and in the subsequent collision, and in the hospital; my parents saw my name in the newspapers, and their own names in the newspapers. Some boys I barely knew had cruised by that hot night and said to a clump of us girls on the sidewalk, "Anybody want to come along for a drag race?" I did, absolutely. I loved fast driving.

It was then, in the days after the drag race, that I noticed the ground spinning beneath me, all bearings lost, and recognized as well that I had been loose like this—detached from all I saw and knowing nothing else— for months, maybe years. I whirled through the air like a bull-roarer spun by a lunatic who'd found his rhythm. The pressure almost split my skin. What else can you risk with all your might but your life? Only a moment ago I was climbing my swing set, holding one cold metal leg between my two legs tight, and feeling a piercing oddness run the length of my gut—the same sensation that plucked me when my tongue touched tarnish on a silver spoon. Only a moment ago I was gluing squares of paper to rocks; I leaned over the bedroom desk. I was drawing my baseball mitt in the attic, under the plaster-stain ship; a pencil study took all Saturday morning. I was capturing the flag, turning the double play, chasing butterflies by the country-club pool. Throughout these many years of childhood, a transparent sphere of time-lessness contained all my running and spinning as a glass paperweight holds flying snow. The sphere of this idyll broke; time unrolled before me in a line. I woke up and found myself in juvenile court. I was hanging from crutches; for a few weeks after the drag race, neither knee worked. (No one else got hurt.) In juvenile court, a policeman wet all ten of my fingertips on an ink pad and pressed them, one by one, using his own fingertips, on a form for the files.

Turning to the French is a form of suicide for the American who loves literature—or, as the joke might go, it is at least a cry for help. Now, when I was sixteen, I had turned to the French. I flung myself into poetry as into Niagara Falls. Beauty took away my breath. I twined away; I flew off with my eyes rolled up; I dove down and succumbed. I bought myself a plot in Valéry's marine cemetery, and moved in: cool dirt on my eyes, my brain smooth as a cannonball. It grieves me to report that I tried to see myself as a sobbing fountain, apparently serene, tall and thin among the chill marble monuments of the dead. Rimbaud wrote a lyric that gently described a man sleeping out in the grass; the sleeper made a peaceful picture, until, in the poem's last line, we discover in his right side two red holes. This, and many another literary false note, appealed to me.

I'd been suspended from school for smoking cigarettes. That was a month earlier, in early spring. Both my parents wept. Amy saw them weeping; horrified, she began to cry herself. Molly cried. She was six, missing her front teeth. Like Mother and me, she had pale skin that turned turgid and red when she cried; she looked as if she were dying of wounds. I didn't cry, because, actually, I was an intercontinental ballistic missile, with an atomic warhead; they don't cry.

Why didn't I settle down, straighten out, shape up? I wondered, too. I thought that joy was a childish condition that had forever departed; I had no glimpse then of its return the minute I got to college. I couldn't foresee the pleasure—or the possibility—of shedding sophistication, walking away from rage, and renouncing French poets.

While I was suspended from school, my parents grounded me. During that time, Amy began to visit me in my room.

When she was thirteen, Amy's beauty had grown inconspicuous; she seemed merely pleasant-looking and tidy. Her green uniform jumper fit her neatly; her thick hair was smoothly turned under; her white McMullen collars looked sweet. She had a good eye for the right things; people respected her for it. I think that only we at home knew how spirited she could get. "Oh, no!" she cried when she laughed hard. "Oh, no!" Amy adored our father, rather as we all did, from afar. She liked boys whose eyebrows met over their noses. She liked boys, emphatically; she followed boys with her big eyes, awed.

In my room, Amy listened to me rant; she reported her grade's daily gossip, laughed at my jokes, cried, "Oh, no!" and told me about the book she was reading, Wilkie Collins, *The Woman in White*. I liked people to tell me about the books they were reading. Next year, Amy was going to boarding school in Philadelphia; Mother had no intention of subjecting the family to two adolescent maelstroms whirling at once in the same house.

Late one night, my parents and I sat at the kitchen table; there was a truce. We were all helpless, and tired of fighting. Amy and Molly were asleep.
"What are we going to do with you?"
Mother raised the question. Her voice trembled and rose with emotion. She couldn't sit still; she kept getting up and roaming around the kitchen. Father stuck out his chin and rubbed it with his big hands. I covered my eyes. Mother squeezed white lotion into her hands, over and over. We all smoked; the ashtray was full. Mother walked over to the sink, poured herself some

ginger ale, ran both hands through her short blond hair to keep it back, and shook her head.

She sighed and said again, looking up and out of the night-black window, "Dear God, what are we going to do with you?" My heart went out to them. We all seemed to have exhausted our options. They asked me for fresh ideas, but I had none. I racked my brain, but couldn't come up with anything. The U.S. Marines didn't take sixteen-year-old girls.

Outside the study hall that May, a cardinal sang his round-noted song, and a robin sang his burbling song, and I slumped at my desk with my heart pounding, too harried by restlessness to breathe. I collected poems and learned them. I found the British war poets—World War I: Rupert Brooke, Edmund Blunden, Siegfried Sassoon, and especially Wilfred Owen, who wrote bitterly without descending to sarcasm. I found Asian and Middle Eastern poetry in translation—whole heaps of lyrics fierce or limp—which I ripped to fragments for my collection. I wanted beauty bare of import; I liked language in strips like pennants.

Under the spell of Rimbaud I wrote a poem that began with a line from *Une Saison en Enfer,* "Once, if I remember well," and continued, "My flesh did lie confined in hell." It ended, slantingly, to my own admiration, "And in my filth did I lie still." I wrote other poems, luscious ones, in the manner of the Song of Songs. One teacher, Miss Hickman, gave her lunch hour to meet with us about our poems.

It galled me that adults, as a class, approved the writing and memorization of poetry. Wasn't poetry secret and subversive? One sort of poetry was full of beauty and longing; it exhaled, enervated and helpless, like Li Po. Other poems were threats and vows. They inhaled; they poured into me a power I could not spend. The best of these, a mounted Arabic battle cry, I recited to myself by the hour, hoping to trammel the teachers' drone with hoofbeats.

I dosed myself with pure lyricism; I lived drugged on sensation, as I had lived alert on sensation as a little child. I wanted to raise armies, make love to armies, conquer armies. I wanted to swim in the stream of beautiful syllables until I tired. I wanted to bust up the Ellis School with my fists.

One afternoon at Judy Schoyer's house, I saw a white paperback book on a living-room chair: Lucretius, *On the Nature of Things.* Lucretius, said the book's back cover, had flourished in the first century B.C. This book was a prose translation of a long poem in Latin hexameters, the content of which was ancient physics mixed with philosophy. Why was this book in print? Why would anyone read wrong science, the babblings of a poet in a toga—why but from disinterested intellectual curiosity? I regarded the white paperback book as if it had been a meteorite smoldering on the chair's silk upholstery.

It was Judy's father's book. Mr. Schoyer loaned me the book when he was finished with it, and I read it; it was deadly dull. Nevertheless, I admired Judy's lawyer father boundlessly. I could believe in him for months at a time. His recreation proceeded from book to book, and had done so all his life. He had, I recalled, majored in classical history and literature. He wanted to learn the nature of things. He read and memorized poetry. He quizzed us about current events—what is your opinion of our new Supreme Court justice? On the other hand, his mother's family were Holyokes, and he hadn't raised a hand to rescue Judy from having to come out in Salem, Massachusetts. She had already done so, and would not talk about it.

Judy was tall now, high-waisted, graceful, messy still; she smiled forgivingly, smiled ironically, behind her thick glasses. Her limbs were thin as stalks, and her head was round. She spoke softly. She laughed at anything chaotic. Her family took me to the ballet, to the Pittsburgh Symphony, to the Three Rivers Arts Festival; they took me ice skating on a frozen lake in Highland Park, and swimming in Ohiopyle, south of town where the Youghiogheny River widens over flat rock outcrops.

After school, we piled in Judy's jeep. Out of the jeep's open back I liked to poke the long barrel of a popgun, slowly, and aim it at the drivers of the cars behind us, and shoot the cork, which then swung from its string. The drivers put up their hands in mock alarm, or slumped obligingly over their wheels. Pittsburghers were wonderful sports.

All spring long I crawled on my pin. I was reading *General Semantics*—Alfred Korzybski's early stab at linguistics; I'd hit on it by accident, in books with the word "language" in their titles. I read Freud's standard works, which interested me at first, but they denied reason. Denying reason had gotten Rimbaud nowhere. I read without snobbery, excited and alone, wholly free in the indifference of society. I read with the pure, exhilarating greed of readers sixteen, seventeen years old; I felt I was exhuming lost continents and plundering their stores. I knocked open everything in sight—Henry Miller, Helen Keller, Hardy, Updike, and the French. The war novels kept coming out, and so did John O'Hara's. I read popular social criticism with Judy and Ellin—*The Ugly American, The Hidden Persuaders, The Status Seekers*. I thought social and political criticism were interesting, but not nearly so interesting as almost everything else.

Ralph Waldo Emerson, for example, excited me enormously. Emerson was my first crack at Platonism, Platonism as it had come bumping and skidding down the centuries and across the ocean to Concord, Massachusetts. Emerson was a thinker, full time, as Pasteur and Salk were full-time biologists. I wrote a paper on Emerson's notion of the soul—the oversoul, which, if I could banish from my mind the thought of galoshes (one big galosh, in which we have our being), was grand stuff. It was metaphysics at last, poetry with import, philosophy minus the Bible. And Emerson incited to riot, flouting every authority, and requiring each native to cobble up an original relation with the universe. Since rioting seemed to be my specialty, if only by default, Emerson gave me heart.

Enervated, fanatic, filled long past bursting with oxygen I couldn't use, I hunched skinny in the school's green uniform, etiolated, broken, bellicose, starved, over the back-breaking desk. I sighed and sighed but never emptied my lungs. I said to myself, "O breeze of spring, since I dare not know you, / Why part the silk curtains by my bed?" I stuffed my skull with poems' invisible syllables. If unauthorized persons looked at me, I hoped they'd see blank eyes.

On one of these May mornings, the school's headmistress called me in and read aloud my teachers' confidential appraisals. Madame Owens wrote an odd thing. Madame Owens was a sturdy, affectionate, and humorous woman who had lived through two world wars in Paris by eating rats. She had curly black hair, rouged cheeks, and long, sharp teeth. She swathed her enormous body in thin black fabrics; she sat at her desk with her tiny ankles crossed. She chatted with us; she reminisced.

Madame Owens's kind word on my behalf made no sense. The headmistress read it to me in her office. The statement began, unforgettably, "Here, alas, is a child of the twentieth century." The headmistress, Marion Hamilton, was a brilliant and strong woman whom I liked and respected; the school's small-minded trustees would soon run her out of town on a rail. Her black hair flared from her high forehead. She looked up at me significantly, raising an eyebrow, and repeated it: "Here, alas, is a child of the twentieth century."

I didn't know what to make of it. I didn't know what to do about it. You got a lot of individual attention at a private school.

My idea was to stay barely alive, pumping blood and exchanging gases just enough to sustain life—but certainly not enough so that anyone suspected me of sentience, certainly not enough so that I woke up and remembered anything—until the time came when I could go.

> *C'est elle, la petite morte, derrière les rosiers* . . .
> It is she, the little dead girl, behind the rose bushes . . .
> the child left on the jetty washed out to sea,
> the little farm child following the lane
> whose forehead touches the sky.

bell hooks (c. 1953–)
from *Black Is a Woman's Color*

Ain't I A Woman (1981), bell hooks's first book, was a pioneering contribution to black feminism, and it launched her on a prominent career as teacher, author, and lecturer. But in it she said very little about herself, preferring, as she said later, to keep the narrative impersonal and not emphasize her own experiences. The name "bell hooks" (uncapitalized) was a pseudonym.

Since then, however, she has revealed more about herself and her reasons for writing. Her full name is Gloria Jean Watkins. She was born in rural Kentucky and attended segregated schools until her sophomore year of high school. She went to Stanford University, worked with other black women at the Berkeley Telephone Office in 1973–74, and then went to graduate school in English at the University of Wisconsin and the University of Southern California, finishing her work at the University of California, Santa Cruz. She has taught English, African American Studies, and Women's Studies at Oberlin, Yale, and the City College of New York.

Her later work has also become more autobiographical. As a means of overcoming the effects of oppression of black women, she has worked privately and with other women on what she calls "self-recovery," a significant term which simultaneously suggests personal history and personal therapy. A thoughtful reader can see how the chapter below is an example of such an effort. Here, too, however, she writes not only as "I," but also as "we" and "she" and one of the daughters—all ways of generalizing her experiences. These experiences convey much of cultural portent, beginning with her account of hair-straightening, which invites comparisons with the "conk" story in *The Autobiography of Malcolm X*.

In a short essay called "Writing Autobiography," she has also written about the experience of writing. "I began to think of the work I was doing as both fiction and autobiography," she says, like what "Audre Lorde, in her autobiographically-based work *Zami,* calls bio-mythography."[1] Another revealing comment is that the telling of these stories brought "both a sense of reunion [with the past]

Reprinted from "Black Is a Woman's Color," *Callaloo* 12 (1989) by permission of Johns Hopkins University Press.

1. bell hooks, *Talking Back: Thinking Feminist, Thinking Black* (Boston: South End Press, 1989), pp. 157–58.

and a sense of release." In another essay, "To Gloria, Who Is She: On Using a Pseudonym," she tells of choosing the name "bell hooks" both to honor a great-grandmother on her mother's side and because it evoked a "much that I am not" and had "a strong sound . . . of a strong woman." [2] We can therefore ask to what degree "Black Is a Woman's Color" brings "release," and whether it is by bell or Gloria.

The selection here is the excerpt from "Black Is a Woman's Color" published in *Callaloo* 12 (1989): 382–88.

Good hair—that's the expression. We all know it, begin to hear it when we are small children. When we are sitting between the legs of mothers and sisters getting our hair combed. Good hair is hair that is not kinky, hair that does not feel like balls of steel wool, hair that does not take hours to comb, hair that does not need tons of grease to untangle, hair that is long. Real good hair is straight hair, hair like white folks' hair. Yet no one says so. No one says your hair is so nice, so beautiful because it is like white folks' hair. We pretend that the standards we measure our beauty by are our own invention—that it is questions of time and money that lead us to make distinctions between good hair and bad hair. I know from birth that I am lucky, lucky to have hair at all for I was bald for two years, then lucky finally to have thin almost straight hair, hair that does not need to be hot combed.

We are six girls who live in a house together. We have different textures of hair, short, long, thin, thick. We do not appreciate these differences. We do not celebrate the variety that is ourselves. We do not run our fingers through each other's dry hair after it is washed. We sit in the kitchen and wait our turn for the hot comb, wait to sit in the chair by the stove smelling grease, feeling the heat warm our scalp like a sticky hot summer sun.

For each of us, getting our hair pressed is an important ritual. It is not a sign of our longing to white. It is not a sign of our quest to be beautiful. We are girls. It is a sign of our desire to be women. It is a gesture that says we are approaching womanhood. It is a rite of passage. Before we reach the appropriate age we wear braids and plaits that are symbols of our innocence, our youth, our childhood. Then we are comforted by the parting hands that comb and braid, comforted by the intimacy and bliss. There is a deeper intimacy in the kitchen on Saturday when hair is pressed, when fish is fried, when sodas are passed around, when soul music drifts over the talk. We are women together. This is our ritual and our time. It is a time without men. It is a time when we work to meet each other's needs, to make each other beautiful in whatever way we can. It is a time of laughter and mellow talk. Sometimes it is an occasion for tears and sorrow. Mama is angry, sick of it all, pulling the hair too tight, using too much grease, burning one ear and then the next.

2. hooks, *Talking Back*, pp. 160–61.

At first I cannot participate in the ritual. I have good hair that does not need pressing. Without the hot comb I remain a child, one of the uninitiated. I plead, I beg, I cry for my turn. They tell me once you start you will be sorry. You will wish you had never straightened your hair. They do not understand that it is not the straightening I seek but the chance to belong, to be one in this world of women. It is finally my turn. I am happy. Happy even though my thin hair straightened looks like black thread, has no body, stands in the air like ends of barbed wire; happy even though the sweet smell of unpressed hair is gone forever. Secretly I had hoped that the hot comb would transform me, turn the thin good hair into thick nappy hair, the kind of hair I like and long for, the kind you can do anything with, wear in all kinds of styles. I am bitterly disappointed in the new look.

A senior in high school, I want to wear a natural, an afro. I want never to get my hair pressed again. It is no longer a rite of passage, a chance to be intimate in the world of women. The intimacy masks betrayal. Together we change ourselves. The closeness, an embrace before parting, a gesture of farewell to love and one another.

★

Jazz, she learns from her father, is the black man's music, the working man, the poor man, the man on the street. Different from the blues because it does not simply lament, moan, express sorrow; it expresses everything. She listens to a record he is playing, to a record that is being played on the radio. It is the music of John Coltrane. Her father says this is a musician who understands all the black man is longing for, that he takes this longing and blows it out of his saxophone. Like the alchemist, he turns lead into gold. To listen, her father tells her, is to feel understood. She listens, wanting this jazz not to be beyond her, wanting it to address the melancholy parts of her soul. To her, black people make the most passionate music. She knows that there is no such thing as natural rhythm. She knows it is the intensity of feeling, the constant knowing that death is real and a possibility that makes the music what it is. She knows that it is the transformation of suffering and sorrow into sound that bears witness to the black past. In her dreams she has seen the alchemist turning lead into gold.

On communion Sundays they sing without musical accompaniment. They keep alive the old ways, the call and response. They sing slow and hold each note as if it is caught in the trap of time and struggling to be free. Like the bread and the wine, they do it this way so as not to forget what the past has been. She listens to the strength in the voices of elderly women as they call out. She sings in the choir. She loves the singing. She looks forward to choir practice on Wednesday night. It is the only weekday night that they are away from home. They sit in the basement of the church singing. They sing "hush children, hush children, somebody's calling my name, oh my lord, oh my lordy, what shall I do."

At home her mama listens to music. On Friday nights she sits in her corner on the couch, smoking one cigarette, drinking one can of beer, playing records, staring sadly into the smoke as Brooke Benton sings "you don't miss you water till your well runs dry." Saturday morning they clean house and listen to music. They listen to the soul music on the radio. It is the only time they can hear a whole program with black music. Every other day is country and western or rock 'n roll. In between vacuuming, dusting, and sweeping they listen to the latest songs and show each other the latest dances. She likes to dance, but they make fun of her. She cannot slow dance. She does not know how to follow the lead. She gives up dancing, spends her time listening to the music.

She likes to hear the music of Louis Armstrong. She likes to see the pleasure he brings to her father's face. They watch him on the Ed Sullivan show, making funny faces, singing in his deep voice. It is the trumpet sound that they are waiting for. When he pulls the handkerchief from his pocket to wipe away the dripping sweat she is reminded of the right-hand men of God weeping into thin squares of cotton. She imagines tears mingled with Satchmo's sweat, that they are tears of gratitude, that he too is giving thanks for finding in his horn yet another sweet stretching sound he did not know was there.

She wants to express herself—to speak her mind. To them it is just talking back. Each time she opens her mouth she risks punishment. They punish her so often she begins to feel they are persecuting her. When she learns the word *scapegoat* in vocabulary lesson, she is sure it accurately describes her lot in life. Her wilderness, unlike the one the goat is led into, is a wilderness of spirit. They abandon her there to get on with the fun things of life. She lies in her bed upstairs after being punished yet again. She can hear the sound of their laughter, their talk. No one hears her crying. Even though she is young, she comes to understand the meaning of exile and loss. They say that she is really not a young girl but an old woman born again into a young girl's body. They do not know how to speak the old woman's language so they are afraid of her. She might be a witch. They have given her a large thick paperback of original fairy tales. On page after page, an old woman is eating children, thinking some wicked deed, performing evil magic. She is not surprised that they fear the old woman inside her. She understands that the old woman in the fairy tales do evil because they are misunderstood. She is a lover of old women. She does not mind at all when they look at her and say she must be ninety, look at the way she walks. No! They say she must be at least a hundred. Only a hundred-year-old woman could walk so slow.

Their world is the only world there is. To be exiled from it is to be without life. She cries because she is in mourning. They will not let her wear the color black. It is not a color for girls. To them she already looks too old. She would just look like a damn fool in a black dress. Black is a woman's color.

She finds another world in books. Escaping into the world of novels is one way she learns to enjoy life. However, novels only ease the pain momentarily as she holds the book in hand, as she reads. It is poetry that changes everything. When she discovers the Romantics it is like losing a part of herself and recovering it. She reads them night and day, all the time. She memorizes poems. She recites them while ironing or washing dishes. Reading Emily Dickinson she senses that the spirit can grow in the solitary life. She reads Edna St. Vincent Millay's "Renascence," and she feels with the lines the suppression of spirit, the spiritual death, and the longing to live again. She reads Whitman, Wordsworth, Coleridge. Whitman shows her that language, like the human spirit, need not be trapped in conventional form or traditions. For school she recites "O Captain, My Captain." She would rather recite from *Song of Myself,* but they do not read it in school. They do not read it because it would be hard to understand. She cannot understand why everyone hates to read poetry. She cannot understand their moans and groans. She wishes they did not have to recite poems in school. She cannot bear to hear the frightened voices stumbling through lines as if they are a wilderness and a trap. At home she has an audience. They will turn off the television set and listen to her latest favorite.

She writes her own poetry in secret. She does not want to explain. Her poems are about love and never about death. She is always thinking about death and never about love. She knows that they will think it better to discover secret poems about love. She knows they never speak of death. The punishments continue. She eases her pain in poetry, using it to make the poems live, using the poems to keep on living.

★

They have never heard their mama and daddy fussing or fighting. They have heard him be harsh, complain that the house should be cleaner, that he should not have to come home from work to a house that is not cleaned just right. They know he gets mad. When he gets mad about the house he begins to clean it himself to show that he can do better. Although he never cooks, he knows how. He would not be able to judge her cooking if he did not cook himself. They are afraid of him when he is mad. They go upstairs to get out of his way. He does not come upstairs. Taking care of children is not a man's work. It does not concern him. He is not even interested—that is, unless something goes wrong. Then he can show her that she is not very good at parenting. They know she is a good mama, "the best." Even though they fear him they are not moved by his opinions. She tries to remember a time when she felt loved by him. She remembers it as being the time when she was a baby girl, a small girl. She remembers him taking her places, taking her to the world inhabited by black men, the barber shop, the pool hall. He took his affections away from her abruptly. She never understood why, only that they went and did not come back. She remembered trying to do whatever she could to bring them back, only they never came. Growing up she stopped trying. He mainly ignored her. She mainly tried to stay out of his way. In her own way she grew to hate wanting his love and not being able to get it. She hated that part of herself that kept wanting his love or even just his approval long after she could see that he was never, never going to give it.

Out of nowhere he comes home from work angry. He reaches the porch yelling and screaming at the woman inside. Yelling that she is his wife and that he can do with her what he wants. They do not understand what is happening. He is pushing, hitting, telling her to shut up. She is pleading, crying. He does not want to hear, to listen. They catch his angry words in their hands like lightning bugs. They store them in a jar to sort them out later. Words about other men, about phone calls, about how he had told her. They do not know what he has told her. They have never heard them in an angry discussion, an argument.

She thinks of all the nights she lies awake in her bed hearing the woman's voice, her mother's voice, hearing his voice. She wonders if it is then that he is telling her the messages he refers to now. Yelling, screaming, hitting, they stare at the red blood that trickles through the crying mouth. They cannot believe that this pleading, crying woman, this woman who does not fight back, is the same person they know. The person they know is strong, gets things done, is a woman of ways and means, a woman of action. They do not know her still, paralyzed, waiting for the next blow, pleading. They do not know her afraid. Even if she does not hit back they want her to run, to run and to not stop running. She wants her to hit him with the table light, the ash tray near her hand. She does not want to see her like this, not fighting back. He notices them long enough to tell them to get out, go upstairs. She refuses to move. She cannot move. She cannot leave her alone. When he says "What are you staring at, do you want some too," she is afraid enough to move, but she does not take her orders from him. She asks the woman if it is right to leave her alone. The woman nods her head yes. She still stands still. It is his movement in her direction that sends her up the stairs. She cannot believe they are not taking a stand, that they go to sleep. She cannot bear their betrayal. When he is not looking she creeps down the steps. She wants the woman to know that she is not alone. She wants to bear witness.

★

All that she does not understand about marriage, about men and women, is explained to her one night. In her dark place on the stairs she is seeing over and over again the still body of the woman pleading, crying, the moving body of the man angry, yelling. She sees that the man has a gun. She hears him tell the woman that he will kill her. She sits in her place on the stair and demands to know of herself if she is able to come to the rescue, if she is willing to fight, if she is ready to die. Her body shakes with the answers. She is fighting back the tears. When he leaves the room she comes to ask the woman if she is all right, if there is anything she can do. The woman's voice is full of tenderness and hurt. She is now in her role as mother. She tells her daughter to go upstairs and go to sleep, that everything will be all right. The daughter does not believe her. Her eyes are pleading. She does not want to be told to go. She hovers in the shadows. When he returns he tells her that he has told her to get her ass upstairs. She does not look at him. He turns to the woman, tells her to leave, tells her to take the daughter with her.

The woman does not protest. She moves like a robot, hurriedly throwing things into suitcases, boxes. She says nothing to the man. He is still screaming, muttering. When she tried to say to him he was wrong, so wrong, he is more angry, threatening. All the neat drawers are emptied out on the bed, all the precious belongings that can be carried, stuffed, are to be taken. There is sorrow in every gesture, sorrow and pain. It is so thick she feels that she could gather it up in her hands. It is like a dust collecting on everything. She is seeing that the man owns everything, that the woman has only her clothes, her shoes, and other personal belongings. She is seeing that the woman can be told to go, can be sent away in the silent, long hours of the night. She is hearing in her head the man's threats to kill. She can feel the cool metal against her cheek. She can hear the click, the blast. She can see her body falling. No, it is not her body, it is the body of love. It is the death of love she is witnessing. If love were alive she believes it would stop everything. It would steady the man's voice, it would calm his rage. It would take the woman's hand, caress her cheek and with a clean handkerchief wipe her eyes. The gun is pointed at love. He lays it on the table. He wants her to finish her packing and go.

She is again in her role as mother. She tells the daughter that she does not have to flee in the middle of the night, that it is not her fight. The daughter is silent. She is staring into the woman's eyes. She is looking for the bright lights, the care and adoration she has shown the man. The eyes are dark with grief, swollen. She feels that a fire inside the woman is dying out, that she is cold. She is sure the woman will freeze to death if she goes out into the night alone. She takes her hand. She wants to go with her. Yet she hopes there will be no going. She hopes that when the mother's brother comes he will be strong enough to take love's body, and give it mouth to mouth the life it has lost. She hopes he will talk to the man, guide him. She cannot believe the calm way he lifts suitcase, box, sack, carries it to the car without question. She cannot bear the silent agreement that the man is right, that he has done what men are able to do. She cannot take the bits and pieces of her mother's heart and put them together again.

I am always fighting with mama. Everything has come between us. She no longer stands between me and all that would hurt me. She is hurting me. This is my dream of her—that she will stand between me and all that hurts me, that she will protect me at all cost. It is only a dream. In some way I understand that it has to do with marriage, that to be the wife to the husband she must be willing to sacrifice even her daughters for his good. For the mother it is not simple. She is always torn. She works hard to fulfill his needs, our needs. When they are not the same she must maneuver, manipulate, choose. She has chosen. She has decided in his favor. She is a religious woman. She has been told that a man should obey God, that a woman should obey man, that children should obey their fathers and mothers, particularly their mothers. I will not obey.

She says that she punishes me for my own good. I do not know what it is I have done this time. I know that she is ready with her switches, that I am to stand still while she lashes out again and again. In my mind there is the memory of a woman sitting still while she is being hit, punished. In my mind I am remembering how much I want that woman to fight back. Before I can think clearly, my hands reach out, grab the switches, are raised as if to hit her back. For a moment she is stunned, unbelieving. She is shocked. She tells me that I must never ever as long as I live raise my hand against my mother. I tell her I do not have a mother. She is even more shocked; she is enraged. She lashes out again. This time I am still. This time I cry. I see the hurt in her eyes when I say "I do not have a mother." I am ready to be punished because I did not want to hurt. I am ashamed. I am torn. I do not want to stand still and be punished but I do not want to hurt her. It is better to hurt than to cause her pain. She warns me that she will tell him when he comes home, that I may be punished again. I cannot understand her acts of betrayal. I cannot understand that she must be against me to be for him. He and I are strangers. Deep in the night we parted from one another, knowing that nothing would ever be the same. He did not say goodbye. I did not look him in the face. Now we avoid one another. He speaks to me through her.

Although they act as if everything between them is the same, that life is as it was, it is only a game. They are only pretending. There is no pain in the pretense. All pain is hidden. Secrets find a way out in sleep. They say to the mother she cries in her sleep, calls out. In her sleep is the place of remembering. It is the place where there is no pretense. She is dreaming always the same dream. A movie is showing. It is a tragic story of jealousy and lost love. It is called "A Crime of Passion." In the movie a man has killed his wife and daughter. He has killed his wife because he believes she has lovers. He has killed the daughter because she witnesses the death of the wife. At his job he is calm and quiet, a hardworking man, a family man. Neighbors come to testify that the dead woman was young and restless, that the daughter was wild and rebellious. Everyone sympathizes with the man. His story is so sad that they begin to weep. All their handkerchiefs are clean and white. They are like flags waving. They are a signal of peace, of surrender. They are a gesture to the man that he can go on with life.

Bibliographies
Index

A READING LIST OF OTHER
AMERICAN AUTOBIOGRAPHIES

The autobiographies listed here would be excellent to read in conjunction with the selections in this anthology. For easy correlation, the items of this bibliography are arranged chronologically and listed under the same categories used in the main part of the text. Dictated autobiographies are listed under the name of the speaker-subject, with the editor's name given after the title. The dates given are the dates of first publication. Where publication dates were various or long after the fact, dates of composition are given in parentheses.

1. Explorers, Governors, Pilgrims, and Captives (1607–1700)

Bradford, William. *Of Plymouth Plantation.* (1620–50).

De Vaca, Cabeza. *Adventures in the Unknown Interior of America.* 1542.

Shepard, Thomas. *The Autobiography of Thomas Shepard, the Celebrated Minister of Cambridge, N. E.* 1832.

Winthrop, John. *Journal "History of New England."* (1630–49).

2. Great Awakenings, New Individuals (1700–1775)

Byrd, William. *History of the Dividing Line, Progress to the Mines, Journey to the Land of Eden.* (1728–36).

de Crevecoeur, Hector St. John. *Letters from an American Farmer.* 1782.

Franklin, Benjamin. *The Autobiography of Benjamin Franklin.* (1771–90).

Paine, Thomas. "Autobiographical Sketch." 1779.

Pinckney, Eliza(beth) Lucas. *Journal & Letters.* (1739–62).

Woolman, John. *The Journal of John Woolman, and a Plea for the Poor.* 1774.

3. National Identities (1776–1837)

Apess, William. *A Son of the Forest.* 1831.

Crockett, David. *The Autobiography of D. Crockett.* 1834.

Equiano, Olaudah. *The Interesting Narrative of the Life of Olaudah Equiano, or Gustavus Vassa, the African.* 1789.

Grant, Anne MacVicar. *Memoirs of an American Lady.* 1808.

Hunter, John Dunn. *Memoirs of a Captivity among the Indians of North America.* 1824.

Irving, Washington. *The Sketch-Book of Jeffrey Crayon.* 1819.

Irving, Washington. *A Tour on the Prairies.* 1835.

Jefferson, Thomas. *Autobiography.* 1821.

Jemison, Mary. *A Narrative of the Life of Mrs. Mary Jemison,* ed. James Everett Seaver. 1824.

Pattie, James O. *The Personal Narrative of James O. Pattie.* 1831.

Royall, Anne Newport. *Letters from Alabama, 1817–22.* 1830.

Rush, Benjamin. *The Autobiography of Benjamin Rush.* (1789–1813).

Trist, Elizabeth House. *The Travel Diary of Elizabeth House Trist: Philadelphia to Natchez, 1783–84.*

4. Self-Liberators (1836–1865)

Cartwright, Peter. *The Autobiography of Peter Cartwright.* 1857.

Craft, William. *Running a Thousand Miles for Freedom; or the Escape of William and Ellen Craft from Slavery.* 1860.

Dana, Richard Henry. *Two Years Before the Mast.* 1840.

Douglass, Frederick. *Narrative of the Life of Frederick Douglass.* 1845.

Douglass, Frederick. *My Bondage and My Freedom.* 1855.

Henson, Josiah. *The Life of Josiah Henson, Formerly a Slave. . . .* 1849.

Henson, Josiah. *Truth Stranger Than Fiction: Father Henson's Story of His Own Life.* 1858.

Henson, Josiah. *An Autobiography of the Reverend . . . , From 1789 to 1881.* 1881.

Jacobs, Harriet A. *Incidents in the Life of a Slave Girl.* 1861.

Parkman, Francis. *The Oregon Trail.* 1849.

Thoreau, Henry David. *Walden.* 1854.

Whitman, Walt. *Leaves of Grass.* 1855.

5. Survivors and Self-Teachers (1865–1915)

Adams, Henry. *The Education of Henry Adams.* 1918.

Eastman, Charles. *An Indian Boyhood.* 1902.

Eastman, Charles. *From the Deep Woods to Civilization.* 1916.

James, Henry. *A Small Boy and Others.* 1913.

James, Henry. *Notes of a Son and Brother.* 1914.

James, Henry. *The Middle Years.* 1917.

Hale, Edward Everett. *A New England Boyhood.* 1909.

Howells, William Dean. *My Year in a Log Cabin.* 1893.

Howells, William Dean. *My Literary Passions.* 1895.

Howells, William Dean. *Literary Friends and Acquaintance.* 1902.

Howells, William Dean. *Boys Town.* 1904.

Howells, William Dean. *Years of My Youth.* 1916.

Riis, Jacob. *The Making of an American.* 1902.

Sedgwick, Catharine M. *Life and Letters of Catharine M. Sedgwick.* 1871.

Sherman, John. *Sherman's Recollections of Forty Years in the House, Senate, and Cabinet.* 1895.

Sherman, William Tecumseh. *Memoirs of General William T. Sherman.* 1876.

Slocum, Joshua. *Sailing Alone Around the World.* 1900.

Twain, Mark. *Mark Twain's Autobiography.* 1924.

Wallace, Lew. *An Autobiography.* 1906.

6. Lives in Progress (1900–1935)

Addams, Jane. *Twenty Years at Hull House.* 1910.

Berkman, Alexander. *Prison Memoirs of an Anarchist.* 1912.

Black Elk. *Black Elk Speaks,* ed. John G. Neihardt. 1932.

[Blowsnake, Sam.] *The Autobiography of a Winnebago,* ed. Paul Radin. 1920.

Bok, Edward. *The Americanization of Edward Bok.* 1920.

Darrow, Clarence. *The Story of My Life.* 1932.

Dreiser, Theodore. *A Book About Myself.* 1922. (Republished as *Newspaper Days,* 1931.)

Dreiser, Theodore. *Dawn.* 1931.

Du Bois, W. E. B. *The Souls of Black Folk.* 1903.

Du Bois, W. E. B. *Dusk of Dawn: An Essay Toward an Autobiography of a Race Concept.* 1940.

Du Bois, W. E. B. *The Autobiography of W. E. B. Du Bois: A Soliloquy on Viewing My Life from the Last Decade of Its First Century.* 1968.

Garland, Hamlin. *Boy Life on the Prairie.* 1899.

Garland, Hamlin. *A Son of the Middle Border.* 1917.

Geronimo. *Geronimo's Story of His Life,* ed. S. M. Barrett. 1906.

Goldman, Emma. *Living My Life.* 1931.

Keller, Helen. *The Story of My Life.* 1905.

Muir, John. *My First Summer in the Sierra.* 1911.

Sinclair, Upton. *American Outpost.* 1932.

Sinclair, Upton. *Autobiography.* 1962.

Steffens, Lincoln. *The Autobiography of Lincoln Steffens.* 1931.

Sullivan, Louis. *The Autobiography of an Idea.* 1924.

Tarbell, Ida M. *All in a Day's Work.* 1939.

Washington, Booker T. *Up From Slavery.* 1901.

Wharton, Edith. *A Backward Glance.* 1934.

Wright, Frank Lloyd. *An Autobiography.* 1932.

7. Experimental Lives (1920–1960)

Agee, James. *A Death in the Family.* 1957.

Aiken, Conrad. *Ushant.* 1952.

Anderson, Sherwood. *A Story Teller's Story.* 1924.

Beston, Henry. *The Outermost House.* 1949.

Chambers, Whitaker. *Witness.* 1952.

Cowley, Malcolm. *Exiles Return.* 1934.

Cowley, Malcolm. *The Dream of the Golden Mountains.* 1980.

cummings, e. e. *The Enormous Room.* 1922.

Dahlberg, Edward. *Because I Was Flesh.* 1963.

Glasgow, Ellen. *The Woman Within.* 1954.

Guthrie, Woody. *Bound for Glory.* 1943.

Hellman, Lillian. *An Unfinished Woman.* 1969.

Hellman, Lillian. *Pentimento.* 1973.

Hellman, Lillian. *Scoundrel Time.* 1976.

Hemingway, Ernest. *A Moveable Feast.* 1964.

Hughes, Langston. *The Big Sea.* 1940.

Hughes, Langston. *I Wonder as I Wander.* 1956.

Hurston, Zora Neal. *Dust Tracks on a Road.* 1942.

Kazin, Alfred. *A Walker in the City.* 1951.

Kazin, Alfred. *Starting out in the Thirties.* 1965.

Kazin, Alfred. *New York Jew.* 1978.

Kerouac, Jack. *On the Road.* 1957.

Laird, Carobeth. *Encounter with an Angry God.* 1975.
Leopold, Aldo. *A Sand County Almanac.* 1949.
Lindberg, Charles A. *The Spirit of St. Louis.* 1953.
McCarthy, Mary. *Memories of a Catholic Girlhood.* 1957.
Merton, Thomas. *The Seven Storey Mountain.* 1948.
Mountain Wolf Woman. *Mountain Wolf Woman,* ed. Nancy Lurie. 1961.
Nabokov, Vladimir. *Speak, Memory.* 1951.
Nearing, Helen, and Scott Nearing. *Living the Good Life: How to Live Sanely and Simply in a Troubled World.* 1954.
Percy, William Alexander. *Lanterns on the Levee.* 1941.
Sone, Monica. *Nisei Daughter.* 1953.
Stein, Gertrude. *The Autobiography of Alice B. Toklas.* 1935.
Williams, William Carlos. *The Autobiography of William Carlos Williams.* 1951.
Wilson, Edmund. *A Piece of My Mind: Reflections at Sixty.* 1956.
Wolfe, Thomas. *The Story of a Novel.* 1936.
Wong, Jade Snow. *Fifth Chinese Daughter.* 1945.

8. Quests for Identity (1960–)

Abbey, Edward. *Desert Solitaire.* 1968.
Abbott, Shirley. *The Bookmaker's Daughter.* 1991.
Angelou, Maya. *I Know Why the Caged Bird Sings.* 1970.
Auster, Paul. *The Invention of Solitude.* 1982.
Bauer, Douglas. *Prairie City, Iowa: Three Seasons at Home.* 1979.
Conroy, Frank. *Stop-Time.* 1967.
Ellison, Ralph. *Shadow and Act.* 1964.
Exley, Fred. *A Fan's Notes.* 1968.
Haley, Alex. *Roots: The Saga of an American Family.* 1976.
Hampl, Patricia. *A Romantic Education.* 1980.
Howard, Jane. *A Different Woman.* 1973.
Howard, Maureen. *Facts of Life.* 1978.
John Fire Lame Deer. *Lame Deer, Seeker of Visions.* 1972.
Kovic, Ron. *Born on the Fourth of July.* 1976.
LaBastille, Anne. *Woodswoman.* 1976.
Lowell, Robert. *Life Studies.* 1959.
Mailer, Norman. *Advertisements for Myself.* 1959.
Mailer, Norman. *Armies of the Night.* 1968.
Malcolm X. *The Autobiography of Malcolm X.* 1966.
Millett, Kate. *Flying.* 1974.
Morris, Willie. *North Towards Home.* 1967.
Price, Reynolds. *Clear Pictures: First Loves, First Guides.* 1989.
Simon, Kate. *Bronx Primitive: Portraits in a Childhood.* 1982.
Suleri, Sara. *Meatless Days.* 1989.
Walker, Alice. *In Search of Our Mothers' Gardens.* 1983.
Welty, Eudora. *One Writer's Beginnings.* 1984.
Wolff, Geoffrey. *The Duke of Deception.* 1979.
Wolff, Tobias. *This Boy's Life.* 1989.

Adams, Timothy Dow. *Telling Lies in Modern American Autobiography*. Chapel Hill: University of North Carolina Press, 1990.

Adams, Timothy Dow, and Rebecca Hogan, eds. *Studies in Women's Autobiography*. *Auto/Biography Studies* 4 (1988), special issue.

Addis, Patricia K. *Through a Woman's I: An Annotated Bibliography of American Women's Autobiographical Writings, 1946–1976*. Metuchen, NJ: Scarecrow Press, 1983.

Anderson, Linda. *Women and Autobiography*. New York: St. Martin's Press, 1990.

Andrews, William L. "Forgotten Voices of Afro-American Autobiography, 1865–1930." *Auto/Biography Studies* 2 (1986–87): 21–27.

Andrews, William L. *To Tell a Free Story: The First Century of Afro-American Autobiography, 1760–1865*. Champaign-Urbana: University of Illinois Press, 1986.

Andrews, William L., ed. *African American Autobiography: A Collection of Critical Essays*. Englewood Cliffs, NJ: Prentice-Hall, 1993.

Andrews, William L., and Nellie Y. McKay, eds. *Twentieth-Century Autobiography*. *Black American Literature Forum* 24 (Summer 1990), special issue.

Arksey, Laura, Nancy Pries, and Marcia Reed, comps. *American Diaries: An Annotated Bibliography of Published American Diaries*. Vol. 1, *Diaries Written from 1492 to 1844*. Detroit: Gale Research Co., 1983.

Baker, Houston A. *Blues, Ideology, and Afro-American Literature*. Chicago: University of Chicago Press, 1984.

Baker, Houston A. *The Journey Back*. Chicago: University of Chicago Press, 1980.

Barton, Rebecca Chalmers. *Witnesses for Freedom: Negro Americans in Autobiography*. New York: Harper, 1948. Reprint, Oakdale, NY: Dowling College Press, 1976.

Bataille, Gretchen M., and Kathleen Mullen Sands. *American Indian Women: Telling their Lives*. Lincoln: University of Nebraska Press, 1984.

Bayliss, John F. *Black Slave Narratives*. New York: Macmillan, 1970.

Benstock, Shari, ed. *The Private Self: Theory and Practice of Women's Autobiographical Writings*. Chapel Hill: University of North Carolina Press, 1988.

Bercovitch, Sacvan. *The Puritan Origins of the American Self*. New Haven: Yale University Press, 1975.

Bercovitch, Sacvan. "The Ritual of American Autobiography: Edwards, Franklin, Thoreau." *Revue Française d'Études Américaines* 14 (1982): 139–50.

Blasing, Mutlu Konuk. *The Art of Life: Studies in American Autobiographical Literature*. Austin: University of Texas Press, 1977.

Boelhower, William. *Immigrant Autobiography in the United States*. Verona, Italy: Essedue, 1982.

Boelhower, William. *Through a Glass Darkly: Ethnic Semiosis in American Literature*. New York: Oxford University Press, 1987.

Braxton, Joanne M. *Black Women Writing Autobiography: A Tradition within a Tradition*. Philadelphia: Temple University Press, 1989.

Brereton, Virginia Lieson. *From Sin to Salvation: Stories of Women's Conversions, 1800 to the Present*. Indiana University Press, 1991.

Brignano, Russell C., comp. *Black Americans in Autobiography: An Annotated Bibliography of Autobiographies and Autobiographical Books Written since the Civil War*. Durham, NC: Duke University Press, 1974.

Briscoe, Mary Louise, Barbara Tobias, and Lynn Z. Bloom, comps. *American Autobiography, 1945–1980: A Bibliography*. Madison: University of Wisconsin Press, 1982.

Brodzki, Bella, and Celeste Schenck, eds. *Life/Lines: Theorizing Women's Autobiography*. Ithaca: Cornell University Press, 1989.

Brumble, H. David, III. *American Indian Autobiography*. Berkeley: University of California Press, 1988.

Brumble, H. David, III, comp. *An Annotated Bibliography of American Indian and Eskimo Autobiographies*. Lincoln: University of Nebraska Press, 1981.

Brumble, H. David III, comp. "A Supplement to *An Annotated Bibliography of American Indian and Eskimo Autobiographies*." *Western American Literature* 17 (1982): 242–60.

Bruss, Elizabeth W. *Autobiographical Acts: The Changing Situation of a Literary Genre*. Baltimore: Johns Hopkins University Press, 1976.

Buckley, Jerome Hamilton. *The Turning Key: Autobiography and the Subjective Impulse since 1800*. Cambridge: Harvard University Press, 1984.

Buell, Lawrence. "Transcendentalist Self-Examination and Autobiographical Tradition." In *Literary Transcendentalism: Style and Vision in the American Renaissance*, 265–83. Ithaca: Cornell University Press, 1973.

Burgher, Mary. "Images of Self and Race in Autobiographies of Black Women." In *Sturdy Black Bridges: Visions of Black Women in Literature*, ed. Roseann P. Bell, Bettye J. Parker, and Beverly Guy-Sheftall, 107–22. Garden City, NY: Anchor, 1979.

Burr, Anna Robeson. *The Autobiography: A Critical and Comparative Study*. Boston: Houghton Mifflin, 1909.

Butterfield, Stephen. *Black Autobiography in America*. Amherst: University of Massachusetts Press, 1974.

Cooke, Michael G. "Modern Black Autobiography in the Tradition." In *Romanticism*, ed. David Thorburn and Geoffrey Hartman, 255–80. Ithaca: Cornell University Press, 1973.

Cooley, Thomas. *Educated Lives: The Rise of Modern Autobiography in America*. Columbus: Ohio State University Press, 1976.

Costanzo, Angelo. *Surprising Narrative: Olaudah Equiano and the Beginnings of Black Autobiography*. Westport, CT: Greenwood, 1987.

Cott, Nancy F. *The Bonds of Womanhood: "Woman's Sphere" in New England, 1780–1835*. New Haven: Yale University Press, 1977.

Couser, G. Thomas. *Altered Egos: Authority in American Autobiography*. New York: Oxford University Press, 1989.

Couser, G. Thomas. *American Autobiography: The Prophetic Mode*. Amherst: University of Massachusetts Press, 1979.

Cox, James M. *Recovering Literature's Lost Ground: Essays in American Autobiography*. Baton Rouge: Louisiana State University Press, 1989.

Culley, Margo, ed. *A Day at a Time: The Diary Literature of American Women: From 1764 to the Present*. New York: Feminist Press, 1986.

Culley, Margo, ed. *American Women's Autobiography: Fea(s)ts of Memory*. Madison: University of Wisconsin Press, 1992.

Davis, Charles T., and Henry Louis Gates, Jr., eds. *The Slave's Narrative*. New York: Oxford University Press, 1985.

deMan, Paul. "Autobiography as De-facement." *Modern Language Notes* 94 (1979): 919–30.

Dodd, Philip, ed. *Modern Selves: Essays on Modern British and American Autobiography*. London: Frank Cass, 1986.

Dodd, Philip, and Simon Dentith. "The Uses of Autobiography." *Literature and History* 14 (1988): 4–22.

Dudley, David L. *My Father's Shadow: Intergenerational Conflict in African American Men's Autobiography*. Philadelphia: University of Pennsylvania Press, 1992.

Eakin, Paul John. *Fictions in Autobiography: Studies in the Art of Self-Invention*. Princeton: Princeton University Press, 1985.

Eakin, Paul John. *Touching the World: Reference in Autobiography*. Princeton: Princeton University Press, 1992.

Eakin, Paul John, ed. *American Autobiography: Retrospect and Prospect*. Madison: University of Wisconsin Press, 1991.

Egan, Susanna. *Patterns of Experience in Autobiography*. Chapel Hill: University of North Carolina Press, 1984.

Elbaz, Robert. *The Changing Nature of the Self: A Critical Study of the Autobiographic Discourse*. Iowa City: University of Iowa Press, 1987.

Erikson, Erik H. *Childhood and Society*. New York: W. W. Norton, 1950.

Fichtelberg, Joseph. *The Complex Image: Faith and Method in American Autobiography*. Philadelphia: University of Pennsylvania Press, 1989.

Fleishman, Avrom. *Figures of Autobiography: The Language of Self-Writing in Victorian and Modern England*. Berkeley and Los Angeles: University of California Press, 1983.

Forbes, Harriette M. *New England Diaries: 1602–1800: A Descriptive Catalogue of Diaries, Orderly Books, and Sea Journals*. New York: Russell and Russell, 1967.

Foster, Frances Smith. "Adding Color and Contour to Early American Self-Portraitures: Autobiographical Writings of Afro-American Women." In *Conjuring: Black Women, Fiction, and Literary Tradition*, ed. Marjorie Pryse and Hortense J. Spillers, 25–30. Bloomington: Indiana University Press, 1985.

Foster, Frances Smith. *Witnessing Slavery: The Development of Ante-bellum Slave Narratives*. 2d. ed. Madison: University of Wisconsin Press, 1994.

Fothergill, Robert A. *Private Chronicles: A Study of English Diaries*. London: Oxford University Press, 1974.

Fox-Genovese, Elizabeth. "To Write Myself: The Autobiographies of Afro-American

Women." In *Feminist Issues in Literary Scholarship*, ed. Shari Benstock, 161–80. Bloomington: Indiana University Press, 1987.

Franklin, H. Bruce. *The Victim as Criminal and Artist*. New York: Oxford University Press, 1978.

Franklin, Wayne. *Discoverers, Explorers, Settlers: The Diligent Writers of Early America*. Chicago: University of Chicago Press, 1979.

Gates, Henry Louis. *The Signifying Monkey: A Theory of Afro-American Literary Criticism*. New York: Oxford University Press, 1988.

Gates, Henry Louis, general ed. *The Schomburg Library of Nineteenth-Century Black Women Writers*. 30 vols. New York: Oxford University Press, 1988.

Gunn, Janet Varner. *Autobiography: Toward a Poetics of Experience*. Philadelphia: University of Pennsylvania Press, 1982.

Hart, Frances R. "Notes for an Anatomy of Modern Autobiography." *New Literary History* 1 (1970): 485–511.

Hart, Frances R. "History Talking to Itself: Public Personality in Recent Memoir." *New Literary History* 11 (1979): 193–210.

Hoffmann, Leonore, and Margo Culley, eds. *Women's Personal Narratives: Essays in Criticism and Pedagogy*. New York: Modern Language Association, 1985.

Holte, James Craig. *The Ethnic I: A Sourcebook for Ethnic American Autobiography*. New York: Greenwood, 1988.

Holte, James Craig. "The Representative Voice: Autobiography and the Ethnic Experience." *MELUS* 9 (1982): 25–46.

Hornung, Alfred, ed. *Autobiography and Democracy in America,* special issue of *Amerikastudien* 35, no.3, 1990.

Howarth, William L. "Some Principles of Autobiography." *New Literary History* 5 (1974): 363–81.

Jacobson, Joanne. *Authority and Alliance in the Letters of Henry Adams*. Madison: University of Wisconsin Press, 1992.

Jacobson, Marcia. "The Mask of Fiction: William Dean Howells's Experiments in Autobiography." *Biography* 10 (1987): 55–67.

Jay, Paul. *Being in the Text*. Ithaca: Cornell University Press, 1984.

Jelinek, Estelle C. "Disguise Autobiographies: Women Masquerading as Men." *Women's Studies International Forum* (1986), special issue on women's autobiographies.

Jelinek, Estelle C. *The Tradition of Women's Autobiography: From Antiquity to the Present*. Boston: Twayne, 1986.

Jelinek, Estelle C., ed. *Women's Autobiography: Essays in Criticism*. Bloomington: Indiana University Press, 1980.

Kaplan, Louis, comp. *A Bibliography of American Autobiographies*. Madison: University of Wisconsin Press, 1961.

Kazin, Alfred. "Autobiography as Narrative." *Michigan Quarterly Review* 3 (1964): 210–16.

Klotman, Phyliss R. "The Slave Narrative and the Western: Popular Literature of the Nineteenth Century." *North Dakota Quarterly* 41 (1973): 40–54.

Kolodny, Annette. "The Lady's Not for Spurning: Kate Millett and the Critics." *Contemporary Literature* 17 (1976): 541–62.

Kolodny, Annette. *The Land Before Her*. Chapel Hill: University of North Carolina Press, 1984.

Krupat, Arnold. "American Autobiography: The Western Tradition." *Georgia Review* 35 (1981): 307–17.

Krupat, Arnold. *For Those Who Come After: A Study of Native American Autobiography*. Berkeley and Los Angeles: University of California Press, 1985.

Krupat, Arnold. *The Voice in the Margin: Native American Literature and the Canon*. Berkeley and Los Angeles: University of California Press, 1989.

Leibowitz, Herbert. *Fabricating Lives: Explorations in American Autobiography*. New York: Alfred A. Knopf, 1989.

Lejeune, Philippe. *L'Autobiographie en France*. Paris: Armand Colin, 1971.

Lejeune, Philippe. *Le pacte autobiographique*. Paris: Editions du Seuil, 1975.

Lejeune, Philippe. *On Autobiography*. Ed. Paul John Eakin. Minneapolis: University of Minnesota Press, 1989.

Lillard, Richard G. *American Life in Autobiography: A Descriptive Guide*. Stanford: Stanford University Press, 1956.

Lionnet, Francoise. *Autobiographical Voices: Race, Gender, Self-Portraiture*. Ithaca: Cornell University Press, 1989.

Mandel, Barrett John. "The Autobiographer's Art." *Journal of Aesthetics and Art Criticism* 27 (1968): 215–26.

Mandel, Barrett John. "The Didactic Achievement of Malcolm X's Autobiography." *Afro-American Studies* 2 (1972): 269–74.

Margolies, Edward. "Ante-bellum Slave Narratives: Their Place in American Literary History." *Studies in Black Literature* 4 (1973): 1–8.

Matthews, William. "Seventeenth-Century Autobiography." In *Autobiography, Biography, and the Novel*. 3–28. Berkeley: University of California Press, 1973.

Matthews, William, comp. *American Diaries: An Annotated Bibliography of American Diaries Written Prior to the Year 1861*. Berkeley: University of California Press, 1945.

Mazlish, Bruce. "Autobiography and Psycho-Analysis: Between Truth and Self-Deception." *Encounter* 35 (1970): 28–37.

Misch, Georg. *A History of Autobiography in Antiquity*. Translated by E. W. Dickes. 2 vols. 1907. Reprint, London: Routledge and Kegan Paul, 1950.

Narratives of Captivity among the Indians of North America: A List of Books and Manuscripts on This Subject in the Edward E. Ayer Collection of the Newberry Library. Chicago: Newberry Library, 1961.

O'Brien, Lynn Woods. *Plains Indian Autobiographies*. Boise, ID: Boise State College Press, 1973.

Olney, James. *Metaphors of Self: The Meaning of Autobiography*. Princeton: Princeton University Press, 1972.

Olney, James. "The Value of Autobiography for Comparative Studies: African vs. Western Autobiography." *Comparative Civilizations Review* 2 (1979): 52–64.

Olney, James, ed. *Autobiography: Essays Theoretical and Critical*. Princeton: Princeton University Press, 1980.

Olney, James, ed. *Studies in Autobiography*. New York: Oxford University Press, 1988.

Osofsky, Gilbert, ed. *Puttin' On Ole Massa*. New York: Harper and Row, 1969.

Padilla, Genaro M. *My History, Not Yours: The Formation of Mexican American Autobiography*. Madison: University of Wisconsin Press, 1993.

Padilla, Genaro M. "The Recovery of Chicano Nineteenth-Century Autobiography." *American Quarterly* 40 (September 1988): 286–306.

Padilla, Genaro M., ed. *Chicano Autobiographies: An Anthology.* Albuquerque: University of New Mexico Press, 1989.

Pascal, Roy. *Design and Truth in Autobiography.* Cambridge: Harvard University Press, 1960.

Payne, James Robert. *Multicultural Autobiography: American Lives.* Knoxville: University of Tennessee Press, 1992.

Pilling, John. *Autobiography and Imagination: Studies in Self-Scrutiny.* London: Routledge and Kegan Paul, 1981.

Rawick, George P. *The American Slave: A Composite Autobiography.* 19 vols. Westport, CT: Greenwood, 1972.

Reagon, Bernice Johnson. "My Black Mothers and Sisters, or On Beginning a Cultural Autobiography." *Feminist Studies* 8 (Spring 1982): 81–95.

Renza, Louis. "The Veto of the Imagination: A Theory of Autobiography." *New Literary History* 9 (1977): 1–26.

Rhodes, Carolyn H. *First Person Female American: A Selected and Annotated Bibliography of the Autobiographies of American Women Living after 1950.* Troy, NY: Whitston, 1980.

Ruoff, A. LaVonne Brown. "George Copway: Nineteenth-Century American Indian Autobiographer." *Auto/Biography Studies* 3 (1987): 6–17.

Sayre, Robert F. *The Examined Self: Benjamin Franklin, Henry Adams, Henry James.* Princeton: Princeton University Press, 1964. Reprint, Madison: University of Wisconsin Press, 1988.

Sayre, Robert F. "The Proper Study: Autobiographies in American Studies." *American Quarterly* 29 (1977): 241–62.

Sayre, Robert F. "Religious Autobiography." In the *Encyclopedia of the American Religious Experience,* ed. C. H. Lippy and P. W. Williams, vol. 2, 1223–36. New York: Charles Scribner's Sons, 1988.

Schmidt, Jan Zlotnik. "The Other: A Study of the Persona in Several Contemporary Women's Autobiographies." *CEA Critic* 43 (1980): 24–31.

Schultz, Elizabeth. "To Be Black and Blue: The Blues Genre in Black American Autobiography." *Kansas Quarterly* 7.3 (1975): 81–96.

Sekora, John, and Darwin T. Turner, eds. *The Art of Slave Narrative.* Macomb, IL: Western Illinois University, 1982.

Seeley, John. *Prophetic Waters: The River in Early American Life and Literature.* New York: Oxford University Press, 1977.

Shapiro, Stephen A. "The Dark Continent of Literature: Autobiography." *Contemporary Literature Studies* 5 (1968): 421–52.

Shea, Daniel B., Jr. *Spiritual Autobiography in Early America.* Princeton: Princeton University Press, 1968. Reprint, Madison: University of Wisconsin Press, 1988.

Smith, Sidonie. *A Poetics of Women's Autobiography: Marginality and the Fictions of Self-Representation.* Bloomington: Indiana University Press, 1987.

Smith, Sidonie. "The Impact of Critical Theory on the Study of Autobiography: Marginality, Gender, and Autobiographical Practice." *Auto/Biography Studies* 3 (1987): 1–12.

Smith, Sidonie. *Where I'm Bound: Patterns of Slavery and Freedom in Black American Autobiography.* Westport, CT: Greenwood Press, 1974.

Smith, Sidonie, and Julia Watson, eds. *De/Colonizing the Subject: The Poetics of Gender in Women's Autobiography.* Minneapolis: University of Minnesota Press, 1992.

Smith, Valerie. *Self-Discovery and Authority in Afro-American Narrative*. Cambridge: Harvard University Press, 1987.

Sollers, Werner. *Beyond Ethnicity: Consent and Descent in American Culture*. New York: Oxford University Press, 1986.

Spacks, Patricia Ann Meyer. *Imagining a Self: Autobiography and Novel in Eighteenth-Century England*. Cambridge: Harvard University Press, 1976.

Spacks, Patricia Ann Meyer. "Women's Stories, Women's Selves." *Hudson Review* 30 (1977): 29–46.

Spender, Dale, ed. *Personal Chronicles: Women's Autobiographical Writings. Women's Studies International Forum* 10 (1987), special issue.

Spengemann, William C. *The Forms of Autobiography: Episodes in the History of a Literary Genre*. New Haven: Yale University Press, 1980.

Spengemann, William, and L. R. Lundquist. "Autobiography and the American Myth." *American Quarterly* 17 (1965): 501–19.

Starobinski, Jean. "The Style of Autobiography." In *Literary Style: A Symposium*, ed. Seymour Chatman, 285–94. New York: Oxford University Press, 1971.

Stepto, Robert B. *From Behind the Veil: A Study of Afro-American Narrative*. Champaign-Urbana: University of Illinois Press, 1979.

Stone, Albert E. "The Sea and the Self: Travel as Experience and Metaphor in Early American Autobiography." *Genre* 7 (1974): 279–304.

Stone, Albert E. *Autobiographical Occasions and Original Acts: Versions of American Identity from Henry Adams to Nate Shaw*. Philadelphia: University of Pennsylvania Press, 1982.

Stone, Albert E., ed. *The American Autobiography: A Collection of Critical Essays*. Englewood Cliffs, NJ: Prentice-Hall, 1981.

Swann, Brian, and Arnold Krupat, eds. *I Tell You Now: Autobiographical Essays by Native American Writers*. Lincoln: University of Nebraska Press, 1987.

Taylor, Gordon O. *Chapters of Experience: Studies in 20th Century American Autobiography*. New York: St. Martin's, 1983.

Tuerk, Richard. "Assimilation in Jewish-American Autobiography: Mary Antin and Ludwig Lewisohn." *Auto/Biography Studies* 3 (Summer 1987): 26–33.

Weintraub, Karl J. "Autobiography and Historical Consciousness." *Critical Inquiry* 1 (1975): 821–48.

Weintraub, Karl J. *The Value of the Individual: Self and Circumstance in Autobiography*. Chicago: University of Chicago Press, 1978.

Wong, Hertha Dawn. *Sending My Heart Back Across the Years: Tradition and Innovation in Native American Autobiography*. Oxford: Oxford University Press, 1992.

Znaniecki, Florian, and William Thomas. *The Polish Peasant in Europe and America*. Chicago: University of Chicago Press, 1918–20.

This index incorporates subject headings for the Introduction, section introductions, and headnotes with information on authors and selections. Italicized page numbers after an author or title indicate the text of that selection.

Wisconsin Studies in American Autobiography
WILLIAM L. ANDREWS
General Editor

Robert F. Sayre
The Examined Self: Benjamin Franklin, Henry Adams, Henry James

Daniel B. Shea
Spiritual Autobiography in Early America

Lois Mark Stalvey
The Education of a WASP

Margaret Sams
Forbidden Family: A Wartime Memoir of the Philippines, 1941–1945
Edited, with an introduction, by Lynn Z. Bloom

Journeys in New Worlds: Early American Women's Narratives
Edited by William L. Andrews

Mark Twain
Mark Twain's Own Autobiography:
The Chapters from the North American Review
Edited, with an introduction, by Michael J. Kiskis

American Autobiography: Retrospect and Prospect
Edited by Paul John Eakin

Charlotte Perkins Gilman
The Living of Charlotte Perkins Gilman: An Autobiography
Introduction by Ann J. Lane

Caroline Seabury
The Diary of Caroline Seabury: 1854–1863
Edited, with an introduction, by Suzanne L. Bunkers

Cornelia Peake McDonald
A Woman's Civil War: A Diary with Reminiscenes of the War,
from March 1862
Edited, with an introduction, by Minrose G. Gwin

Marian Anderson
My Lord, What a Morning
Introduction by Nellie Y. McKay

American Women's Autobiography: Fea(s)ts of Memory
Edited, with an introduction, by Margo Culley

Frank Marshall Davis
Livin' the Blues: Memoirs of a Black Journalist and Poet
Edited, with an introduction, by John Edgar Tidwell

Joanne Jacobson
Authority and Alliance in the Letters of Henry Adams

Kamau Brathwaite
The Zea Mexican Diary
Foreword by Sandra Pouchet Paquet

Genaro M. Padilla
My History, Not Yours:
The Formation of Mexican American Autobiography

Frances Smith Foster
Witnessing Slavery: The Development
of Ante-bellum Slave Narratives

Native American Autobiography: An Anthology
Edited, with an introduction, by Arnold Krupat

American Lives: An Anthology of Autobiographical Writing
Edited, with an introduction, by Robert F. Sayre